TULANE

TULANE

The Emergence of a
Modern University, 1945–1980

Clarence L. Mohr and Joseph E. Gordon

LOUISIANA STATE UNIVERSITY PRESS Baton Rouge

Designer: Glynnis Weston
Typeface: Bodoni
Typesetter: Crane Composition, Inc.
Printer and binder: Thomson-Shore, Inc.

Library of Congress Cataloging-in-Publication Data
Mohr, Clarence L.
   Tulane : the emergence of a modern university, 1945–1980 / Clarence L. Mohr and Joseph E.
Gordon.
      p. cm.
   Includes bibliographical references and index.
   ISBN 0-8071-2553-9 (cloth : alk. paper)
   1. Tulane University—History—20th century. I.Gordon, Joseph E. II. Title.
   LD5438.8 .M65 2000
   378.763'35—dc21

                                           00-010540

To the memory of

RUFUS CARROLLTON HARRIS

Dean of the Tulane University School of Law, 1927–1937
President of Tulane University, 1937–1960

CONTENTS

Contents

ILLUSTRATIONS

all courtesy of Tulane University

Illustrations

PREFACE AND ACKNOWLEDGMENTS

In 1990 Tulane president Eamon M. Kelly expressed a desire to see the university's formal history extended beyond the period covered in John P. Dyer's 1965 study, *Tulane: The Biography of a University*. After consultation with various members of the Tulane community, Kelly asked Joseph E. Gordon, dean emeritus of the College of Arts and Sciences, to take on the project. Gordon agreed, with the stipulation that a professional historian be appointed to coauthor the work. Clarence L. Mohr, associate professor of history at Tulane, was subsequently invited to join the project, which began in the 1990–91 academic year. As the work progressed, tasks and responsibilities were divided between the authors as expedience and practicality dictated. Both authors engaged in archival research, conducted oral interviews, and prepared reference material in a variety of forms. Actual writing and organization of the text fell primarily to Professor Mohr. The final product, however, represents a collaborative effort for which each author assumes joint responsibility.

It was understood from the outset that the new study would be undertaken in the spirit of full and free inquiry which Tulane University has exemplified throughout its 150-year history. Toward that end, the authors entered into a written memorandum of understanding with President Kelly and Tulane Board of Administrators chairman Robert Boh, in which unrestricted access to university records was guaranteed and control of the book's content was placed exclusively in the hands of the authors. Both the letter and spirit of the agreement have been scrupulously observed by all parties, and no question concerning the intellectual integrity of the project has ever arisen. The university administration has assisted the project through grants of released time to conduct research and writing.

Wishing to benefit as fully as possible from the knowledge and insight of colleagues in Tulane's several schools and colleges, the authors requested President Kelly to appoint a faculty oversight committee whose members would make themselves available from time to time to receive reports on the book's progress and to offer advice on a wide range of matters. A total of six individuals served on the committee, including: Professor Louis E. Barrilleaux, dean of University College; Professor Donald Pizer, Department of English; Professor emerita Jessie Poesch, Newcomb Department of Art History; Professor Lawrence Powell, Department of History; and the late Professor Clifford Newman, School of Medicine, who was succeeded by Professor John Salvaggio, School of Medicine. The group held its initial meeting during the project's first year and convened at regular intervals thereafter to read and discuss draft chapters and offer timely and valuable suggestions on a host of matters. The authors deeply appreciate the committee's many contributions, even as we absolve its members from responsibility for whatever defects or shortcomings the published work may possess.

Many other people within and outside the university placed the authors in their debt. President Kelly and his two immediate predecessors, F. Sheldon Hackney and Herbert E. Longenecker, were more than generous in making themselves available for taped interviews and candid dialogue. Their insights were often acute and their cooperation was invaluable. Although the project began several years after the death of Rufus Carrollton Harris, his personality and academic vision emerged with stunning clarity from the extensive documentary record of his twenty-three-year tenure in Gibson Hall. Several interviews with Kathryn Davis, secretary to all Tulane presidents from Rufus Harris through Sheldon Hackney, filled in many blanks concerning people and events over a span of four decades. In the Department of History, the late Professor Charles Davis shared numerous irreverent recollections of university life from the 1950s onward.

Most of the research for this volume was carried out in the Tulane University Archives, located in the Special Collections division of the Howard-Tilton Memorial Library. While it is impractical to name all those who assisted in archival matters, special appreciation is extended to staff members Ann Case and Courtney Page, to Special

Collections head Wilbur Meneray, and to university archivist Robert Scherer. Wynona Burmaster, secretary to the Board of Administrators, deserves special thanks for assistance with Board material. During the summer of 1996, Jeffrey R. Turner, a history doctoral candidate at Tulane, spent several weeks as a full-time archival researcher for the project. His diligence and resourcefulness in pursuing difficult tasks added depth to the narrative and speeded the book to completion.

PROLOGUE

More than thirty years have elapsed since the appearance of John P. Dyer's *Tulane: The Biography of a University, 1834–1965*. As the first published history of Tulane, Dyer's book presented a comprehensive portrait of the university's past, devoting thirteen of sixteen chapters to the decades prior to 1940 and confining discussion of more recent events to the book's last sixty pages. The result was a useful, if selective, overview of developments in the years after World War II— partly academic history and partly a firsthand account of Tulane's postwar metamorphosis as viewed by one who understood the warp and woof of campus decision making. At times Dyer's account revealed as much by its silences as by its explicit conclusions. Disputes over academic freedom and athletics received delicate handling, and the vast and controversial subject of desegregation was dispatched in a scant three pages.

Building upon Dyer's work, *Tulane: The Emergence of a Modern University, 1945–1980* seeks to explore the university's recent past in greater depth and from a somewhat different intellectual vantage point than the one available to scholars in the late 1950s and early 1960s. Like Dyer, the authors of the present volume believe that institutional history ultimately revolves around people rather than bureaucratic structures or social science abstractions. Without resorting to a "great man" or "great woman" approach to historical explanation, we have attempted to identify many of the individuals—administrators, professors, and students—whose actions have exerted a shaping influence on the university during periods of both calm and crisis. Of course, we have also been concerned with the larger environment surrounding individual actors as they made choices in response to the pressures of both internal and external forces.

Like most institutional histories, this one has several interrelated objectives. First and foremost the book seeks to present an account of Tulane in which the postwar generation will be able to recognize itself. In pursuit of this goal we have relied heavily upon archival sources, quoting liberally from original documents to convey the temper of the times and to establish the concrete details of many important episodes. Because our aim is to depict the university as a whole, Tulane's individual schools and colleges appear in the text only when they illuminate some larger institutional trajectory or provide insight into the themes and events under discussion. There has been no effort to provide equal time for all branches of the university. Each of Tulane's modern academic components deserves much fuller treatment than is possible in a work of this kind. We hope that our efforts may encourage those interested in Newcomb and Tulane Colleges—as well as the Schools of Law, Social Work, and Engineering—to provide the kind of detailed investigations already available for University College and the Schools of Medicine, Business Administration, and Architecture.

For all its unique aspects, Tulane's history during the last half century has been intimately bound up with changes taking place at the regional and national level. A number of overarching developments frame the Tulane experience after 1945 and help define its central themes. Like other American universities, Tulane was profoundly influenced by the postwar growth of federal and private support for academic research and by the high qualitative standards which accompanied external funding. The university also responded to the powerful forces of educational supply and demand set in motion by the GI Bill and sustained by rising birth rates. If purists object to the claim that the history of postwar higher education is the history of the baby boom writ large, perhaps most will agree that in New Orleans, as elsewhere, a strong gravitational pull linked the destiny of higher learning to the rise of a new generation. Both Tulane and its students were coming of age during the postwar era, and neither phenomenon can be adequately described without reference to the other.

Demography, of course, is not destiny—except perhaps for those who would seek to reduce human experience to the positivist categories of a narrow social science. As the following pages seek to make clear, those associated with the university helped make their own future through decisions taken on a number of key issues facing the world of higher education in the postwar decades. It is thus in the study of choices, in the tracing out of paths followed and in the recognition of roads not taken, that the story of modern Tulane assumes its full meaning as a chapter in the ongoing drama of America's perennial love/hate relationship with the world of higher learning. Tulane's sense of itself and of its mission to society was given new shape and direction after 1945 by the cold war, the civil rights struggle, and the clash between liberal and utilitarian values that occurred as universities took on multiple roles as avenues to professional or white-collar employment, platforms for social criticism, and "instruments of national purpose."[1]

Readers familiar with the larger history of McCarthyism and academic freedom in American universities will find much in Tulane's experience that fits readily into the explanatory framework developed by leading historians over the past half century. Perhaps, as some have argued, a portion of the blame for constraints imposed upon the spirit of free inquiry at the height of America's anti-Communist frenzy can be laid at the doorstep of liberal academics who placed institutional loyalty and professional self-interest ahead of concern for the rights of embattled colleagues. At best, however, such an explanation is incomplete, ignoring as it does the many tactical compromises forced upon southern academic leaders who sought to seize the research opportunities that the cold war offered while holding at bay the forces of racial extremism and right-wing zealotry. For Tulane president Rufus Harris, the risks inherent in linking pure research to military sponsorship were apparent from the beginning. But the benefits (political as well as economic) were equally apparent, and the alternatives were few and unappealing. Far from experiencing a "collective failure of nerve" in the face of cold war pressures, Harris and other academic liberals maneuvered skillfully, and quite often successfully, to minimize the impact of reactionary tendencies upon the university and to affirm the school's commitment to the core values of serious intellectual life.[2]

1. The phrase "instruments of national purpose" received wide dissemination in Clark Kerr's influential essay, *The Uses of the University* (Cambridge: Harvard University Press, 1963).

2. See, for example, Richard Hofstadter and Walter P. Metzger, *The Development of Academic Freedom in the United States* (New York: Columbia University Press, 1955); Robert M. MacIver, *Academic Freedom in Our Time* (New York: Columbia University Press, 1955); Ellen Schrecker, *No Ivory Tower: McCarthyism and the Universities* (New York: Oxford University Press, 1986; quotation on p. 309).

Such efforts mark the late 1940s and early 1950s at Tulane as a period of courage and optimism, but they ultimately beg the question of whether intellectual freedom in any full sense of the word could be established within a segregated society. To comprehend the cold war at Tulane—or indeed at any college in the Deep South—is to confront head-on the festering issue of race. It was segregation above all else that made Tulane a southern school, and it was the university's inability to break swiftly and cleanly with its racialist past that cast a shadow of impending tragedy over an otherwise promising future.

As a southern institution striving for recognition on a national stage, Tulane faced the challenge of transcending its past without repudiating what was of lasting value in its rich and distinctive educational heritage. The problem was most sharply delineated in the matters having to do with racial integration, but Tulanians also grappled with the burden of southern history when disputes arose over athletics, censorship, and the legitimacy of ROTC. Besides placing the university temporarily at odds with many alumni and local residents, the controversy aroused by the issues of the mid- and late 1960s helped illuminate the internal dynamics of a struggle for generational identity that was being played out in various forms on campuses throughout the United States. Occurring at a moment when college attendance was becoming the normative path to adulthood for a majority of middle-class youth, Tulane's brief but intense encounter with civil rights activism, antiwar dissent, and student power highlights the role of youth subcultures in challenging reigning orthodoxies and in initiating long-term shifts in political and social behavior. The passage of three decades leaves little doubt that events at Tulane in the late 1960s comprised a small segment in a larger cultural fault line that would eventually bisect postwar America, distinguishing baby boom children from their parents, whose generational reference points were located in the economic catastrophe of the 1930s and the dislocations of World War II rather than in the experiences of college life.[3]

At a minimum, the story of Tulane in the 1960s should remind those who study or teach in American universities that their own institutions have in a very real sense "made history." On the threshold of a new millennium, the university's recent past remains highly relevant to all

3. Helen Lefkowitz Horowitz, *Campus Life, Undergraduate Cultures from the End of the Eighteenth Century to the Present* (Chicago: University of Chicago Press, 1987) provides a penetrating and highly useful analysis of student groups and their connection to larger social forces.

those who would engage the challenges inherent in advanced technology and economic globalism. Although rarely discussed today in the categories advanced by the student Left, such issues permeate the world of contemporary higher learning. And it should come as no surprise that during the presidency of Eamon Kelly (1980–98), Tulane has had occasion to revisit many of the issues left unresolved by the compromises and accommodations of earlier decades. Several of the more important threads linking the contemporary university with the period covered in this book are highlighted in the epilogue to the present volume. Believing that intelligent engagement with the past can and should inform decisions about the present while giving shape to visions of the future, the authors will regard themselves as amply repaid if their labors afford an element of perspective for those destined to continue the ongoing dialogue over Tulane's raison d'être.

INTRODUCTION

The history of Tulane in the decades since 1945 comprises the most recent chapter in a story that began in the middle years of the nineteenth century. Tracing its origins to the Medical College of Louisiana, which was founded by seven young New Orleans physicians in 1834, Tulane University came into being some fifty years later, in 1884, when the Louisiana Legislature turned over the assets of the defunct University of Louisiana in New Orleans to the seventeen Administrators of a fund established by New Orleans merchant Paul Tulane "for the promotion and encouragement of intellectual, moral, and industrial education" among local residents. The property thus transferred included the Medical College, Law Department, and male undergraduate Collegiate Department (the present-day Paul Tulane College), which had comprised the publicly supported University of Louisiana in antebellum days. The Tulane gift of something less than $2 million became the new university's endowment. In 1887, Josephine Le Monnier Newcomb donated a sum larger than that received from Paul Tulane to establish a coordinate women's college within the university. Named for Newcomb's daughter, Harriet Sophie, the H. Sophie Newcomb College remained physically apart from the St. Charles Avenue campus of Tulane until the time of World War I.[1]

Readers with a firsthand knowledge of Tulane in recent times will detect in the circumstances described above the faint but indelible out-

1. Unless otherwise stated, factual information about Tulane in the following paragraphs is taken from John P. Dyer, *Tulane: The Biography of a University, 1834–1965* (New York: Harper and Row, 1966).

lines of the university's contemporary character. From the beginning, medical education and other fields of professional training, such as law, engineering, and architecture—all of which were offered during the 1880s—have loomed large in Tulane's history. An initial concern with women's education that was quite advanced for its time and place has proven remarkably resilient in the face of twentieth-century challenges to the coordinate college model. Finally, the university's initial contract or legal relationship with the State of Louisiana contained the germ of an ongoing ambiguity concerning the school's nonpublic but not exclusively private status.

At a somewhat deeper level, the early history of Tulane also points up the fallacy of attempting to understand educational institutions apart from the underlying historical forces at work in any given era. If the story of post-1945 Tulane reflects the larger impact of the baby boom, the cold war, and the civil rights struggle, the university's founding and early development were at least equally bound up with the growth of southern cities in the Gilded Age, the rising influence of an urban middle class, and the advent of compulsory racial segregation in the generation after Reconstruction. At the beginning of the twentieth century Tulane's charismatic and visionary president, Edwin A. Alderman, sought to link the university with an agenda of regional modernization that included support for public schooling and a new utilitarian (Alderman would have said "democratic") conception of higher learning's basic mission. With the classical curriculum in retreat, Tulane professors increasingly assumed the role of trained experts in the solution of economic and social problems.

These tendencies accelerated in the decades surrounding World War I, as Tulane added a College of Commerce in 1914 (now the A. B. Freeman School of Business) and a School of Social Work in 1921. Headed by Elizabeth Wisner, Tulane's first female academic dean, the new School of Social Work gave the university a commanding position in the single most important area of emerging professional opportunity for career-minded southern women. Part-time study for teachers had been available at Tulane since 1907, and in 1914 the new College of Commerce also established a night division. During the late 1930s, evening colleges became a standard component of the typical urban university, and in 1942, amid the pressures of war mobilization, Tulane consolidated its night classes into a permanent administrative unit called University College.[2]

These developments were harbingers of greater changes still to come. Perhaps the most significant factor distinguishing post-1945 Tulane from the university of the interwar decades was an increased emphasis upon research and original scholarship in all academic divisions from the late 1940s onward. Although master's-level work had been available in selected fields since the late nineteenth century, Tulane focused on undergraduate and professional education throughout the 1920s and 1930s, when private philanthropy was transforming Ivy League schools into a national network of research universities. With the notable exception of Tulane's School of Medicine, which adopted standardized admissions tests in 1930 after being singled out by educational critic Abraham Flexner as one of the very few southern medical programs showing genuine promise, national academic distinction seemed little more than a distant dream for most units of the university. Among many Tulane faculty members and administrators, however, pressure was building for a reordering of institutional priorities in the interests of research and greater academic rigor.[3]

The reshaping of academic culture is, of necessity, an incremental process. Preliminary manifestations of the university's postwar emphasis may be glimpsed during the 1930s in special "double subject" (i.e., interdisciplinary) undergraduate classes that were team-taught by English professor Roger P. McCutcheon and political scientist Herman C. Nixon. High academic prerequisites kept enrollments in the experimental courses below fifteen students, and "with no worship of numbers," those admitted did "heavy work excessively well" in the combined field of nineteenth-century history and literature. As Professor Nixon explained, there were "no exemptions and no [special] honors, the attraction being the experience of able students working together with the stimulating clash of minds and ideas. The meetings

2. John P. Dyer, *Ivory Towers in the Marketplace: The Evening College in American Education* (Indianapolis: Bobbs-Merrill, 1956), 37–9; Robert G. Sherer, *University College: A History of Access to Opportunity, 1942–1992* (New Orleans: Tulane University Office of University Relations, 1992).

3. Roger L. Geiger, *To Advance Knowledge: The Growth of American Research Universities, 1900–1940* (New York: Oxford University Press, 1986), chap. 5; John Duffy, *The Tulane University Medical Center: One Hundred and Fifty Years of Medical Education* (Baton Rouge: Louisiana State University Press, 1984), 119, 155.

frequently run over the time limit, with conferences and group sessions outside of the schedule. The results . . . inspire the wish that such ventures may increase." Increase they would during the 1950s and 1960s, as a permanent scholars and honors program evolved in tandem with a vastly expanded commitment to graduate study.[4]

Academic enhancement after 1945 went hand in hand with changes in the makeup of the student body and the architectural configuration of the campus. From the 1950s onward undergraduates came less often from New Orleans and Louisiana, lived on campus in greater numbers, and were selected with greater academic rigor. In order to appreciate the magnitude of Tulane's physical and demographic transformation during the 1950s and 1960s, it may be useful to present a snapshot of the university in 1940–41, the last prewar academic year. Catalogs and admissions literature of the period describe Tulane as a private, coeducational, residential, and commuter university. Future television journalist Howard K. Smith (A&S, '36) was more explicit, characterizing the St. Charles Avenue campus as "strictly an urban place for learning," with no women in Arts and Sciences classes, "no dormitories, no student center except for the steps of Gibson Hall, not much of an auditorium," and classrooms furnished with "antique desks," badly defaced by generations of hard use. The commuter aspect of student life tended to predominate since, with the exception of three Newcomb College dormitories (Josephine Louise House, known fondly as "J. L.," Warren House, and Doris Hall), on-campus housing was scarce. Athletes were the principal occupants of other residential spaces, such as the building now named Fortier Hall. Most male and many female students commuted by automobile or streetcar from family residences, or walked to class from neighborhood homes whose owners rented out rooms to gain supplementary income. In February 1941, a total of 4,130 students registered for classes, approximately one-third of whom received small amounts of financial aid in the form of jobs or scholarships.[5]

In the athletic realm football was the dominant sport, with a considerably larger base of fan support than would be the case a generation later. Under coach Red Dawson, a team of high promise ended the

4. H. Clarence Nixon, "Colleges and Universities," in *Culture in the South*, ed. W. T. Couch (Chapel Hill: University of North Carolina Press, 1933), 239–47 (all quotations on p. 246).
5. Howard K. Smith, *Events Leading up to My Death: The Life of a Twentieth Century Reporter* (New York: St. Martin's Press, 1996), 23–5 (all quotations on p. 23).

1940–41 season with a lackluster five and five record, including a typical loss to archrival Louisiana State University. Social life among students centered heavily in fraternities and sororities, differing little from the pattern prevailing at most universities in the region, if Mardi Gras and other New Orleans distractions are left aside. In 1940, however, the dedication of a student center, financed largely through alumni donations, provided a long-needed focal point for student activities on campus. Among the university's officially sanctioned extracurricular pursuits, college journalism occupied a more serious and elevated status than would later be the case, with law and other professional students taking an active role in the editing and publication of the *Hullabaloo*. The paper's columnists in 1940–41 included William R. "Bill" Monroe, destined for postwar fame as a radio and television journalist affiliated with NBC News and its influential program *Meet the Press*. Only four years earlier, in 1936, future network newsman Howard K. Smith had graduated from the College of Arts and Sciences. In 1940–41 Hale Boggs, a Law School graduate and another former *Hullabaloo* staffer, had just resigned as Tulane's alumni secretary to campaign successfully for a seat in the U.S. House of Representatives.

Domestic issues preoccupied Tulanians throughout the Great Depression, and opinion about the war in Europe was still divided in the presidential election of 1940, when a small poll of Tulane students gave a slight advantage to Republican Wendell Willkie. Although the academic year ended with the United States at peace, the era of isolationism was rapidly drawing to a close. Tulane president Rufus Harris, who had taken office in 1937, openly supported a more active U.S. role in Europe, including aid for Great Britain. A few months later, Pearl Harbor would plunge the nation and the university into world affairs in a manner that would admit of no postwar retreat from global responsibility. In 1942, Harris began the curricular and personnel adjustments necessary to place the university on a war footing, a subject discussed more fully in chapters one and two of this book. Before the end of hostilities, some 147 Tulane professors and administrative personnel entered military service, in company with some 4,000 alumni. Neither Harris nor anyone else could have fully anticipated the magnitude of the changes that the war would set in motion. And, in truth, the years from 1942 to 1945 offered little opportunity for reflection. But by the time Japanese representatives signed instruments of surrender in the aftermath of Hiroshima and Nagasaki—episodes of nuclear devastation made possible through an unprecedented mobilization of American academic science—there could be little doubt that a new era had dawned for the United States, for American higher education, and, not least, for Tulane.

TULANE

SETTING THE AGENDA
Research, Selectivity, and Coordination

Writing in 1946, as returning veterans and their families flooded onto a campus only recently vacated by U.S. Navy trainees, Tulane president Rufus Carrollton Harris predicted that the university's transition from war to peace would constitute the most complex episode in the school's 112-year history.[1] Events of the next decade not only proved Harris correct, but established the importance of World War II as a demarcation line separating two great epochs in Tulane's development. At the time of Pearl Harbor, Tulane remained firmly within the bounds of an academic mission that had changed little during the preceding generation. Serving a constituency that was predominantly local, the university maintained what was essentially an open admissions policy for white undergraduates, only a tiny proportion of whom actually lived on the campus. Collective identity among students and alumni found expression through the ritualized ceremonies of college football, replete with All-American players, Southeastern Conference Championships, and postseason appearances in the Rose Bowl and Sugar Bowl. The Sugar Bowl had even begun in Tulane's stadium, with the Green Wave's 1935 victory over Temple University. Communities based upon shared professional concerns could be found in the Schools of Engineering, Commerce, Social Work, Law, and Medicine, with each division possessing considerable autonomy under a somewhat tenuous scheme of central administration that also encompassed the College of Arts and Sciences for male undergraduates and the H. Sophie New-

1. "Report of the President of Tulane University, Session 1945–1946," *Bulletin, The Tulane University of Louisiana*, series 48, no. 3 (March 1947): 4–5 (hereafter cited as *Tulane Bulletin*). Annual presidential reports will be cited as separate publications beginning in the year 1950.

comb College for women. With graduate education still confined largely to master's-level work, research and publication remained at best a secondary priority for most faculty members. Having emerged from the depression with its modest $13 million endowment intact, Tulane seemed wedded to a defensive, pay-as-you-go fiscal strategy that left no room for bold initiatives requiring new assets. Always mindful of the need for support from the local community, university officials placed more emphasis upon cultivating good town-gown relations than upon reshaping public opinion.[2]

Apart from the School of Medicine, where grants from the Rockefeller Foundation had begun to quicken the pulse of scientific investigation, Tulane had precious little in common with the major research universities that shouldered the bulk of federally financed research and training during World War II.[3] Like other tuition-dependent schools, Tulane escaped fiscal disaster during the war largely through altering its curriculum to serve military needs. The resulting emphasis upon training in engineering and technical fields to the detriment of liberal arts seemed a small price to pay for student deferments and military tuition revenues secured through various phases of the Army Specialized Training Program and the all-important navy V-12 program that paid tuition and living costs for the 1,000 or so student-sailors housed on Tulane's campus each semester after mid-1943. By the war's last months, revenue from the navy totaled nearly $800,000 and com-

2. John P. Dyer, *Tulane: The Biography of a University 1834–1965* (New York: Harper and Row, 1966), 202–38, 247. Tulane's relationship with the local community during the 1930s and 1940s is discussed in chap. 2 of the present work.

3. Dyer, *Tulane*, 252; John Duffy, *The Tulane University Medical Center: One Hundred and Fifty Years of Medical Education* (Baton Rouge: Louisiana State University Press, 1984), 160–1, 163–4. Prior to World War II major foundation grants to Tulane's medical school provided operating expenses and increased endowment to support programs in tropical medicine, preventative medicine, and psychiatry. By the early 1940s, however, the medical faculty had secured four modest research grants from the Rockefeller Foundation. Tulane University, *Annual Report of the Treasurer for the Fiscal Year Ending August 31, 1942* (n.p., n.d.), table 4, Tulane University Archives. Roger L. Geiger, *To Advance Knowledge: The Growth of American Research Universities, 1900–1940* (New York: Oxford University Press, 1986), chap. 6 and passim depicts the network of privately funded research universities on the eve of World War II. A comprehensive outline of the role of public and private research universities in the war effort may be derived from the multivolume series Science in World War II, which describes the work of all divisions of the Office of Scientific Research and Development and the National Defense Research Committee. For an assessment of OSRD's postwar significance, see Adam Yarmolinsky, *The Military Establishment: Its Impacts on American Society* (New York: Harper and Row, 1971), 289–95.

Central Building. Dormitory for navy V-12 program, 1943.

prised some 16 percent of the educational budget. Momentarily, at least, federal payments allowed Tulane to show a small operating surplus despite the heavy initial expenditures required to provide housing for navy students.[4]

If the war experience proved that significant benefits could flow from a government-university partnership, academic mobilization also provided clear evidence of the problems inherent in federal patronage. Given the narrow aims of military education, distortions and inequities were inevitable. Tulane's strengths in engineering and medicine had been crucial factors in the navy's decision to grant the university a V-12 contract. Not surprisingly, the Schools of Engineering and Medicine fared considerably better than other academic divisions after 1943. While humanities instruction languished in the College of

4. John M. Blum, *V Was for Victory: Politics and American Culture during World War II* (New York: Harcourt, Brace, Jovanovich, 1976), 141–3, 352; Arthur G. Nurah, "History of Tulane University," unpublished manuscript, Tulane University Library, 1910–17. See also the 1943–44 annual reports of the president, dean of arts and sciences, and dean of engineering in *Tulane Bulletin*, series 46, no. 2 (February 1945): 6–13, 20–5. On the impact of navy revenues, see Tulane University, *Annual Report of the Treasurer for the Year Ended June 30, 1945* (New Orleans, 1945), 5 (Charts of Sources and Disposition), 11 (Statement of Current Income), 33; "Report of the President . . . 1945–1946," 6.

Arts and Sciences, the medical school actually strengthened its advanced offerings in war-related specialties. The war's impact on research at Tulane was even more one-sided. In 1943, Graduate Dean Roger P. McCutcheon reported that a smaller and weary faculty produced little scholarship and seemed indifferent to professional advancement. Lacking a separate endowment and bereft of tuition revenue when enrollments dipped below forty students, the Graduate School found itself in a state of "suspended animation." Much of the blame could be placed upon the navy's insistence upon paying only for undergraduate instruction of a "very elementary grade." Under the terms of Tulane's navy contract, any graduate courses taught by university faculty had the effect of reducing the amount of federal compensation. In the medical school, however, "research suffered surprisingly little," as six separate federal contracts from the Office of Scientific Research and Development provided the impetus for "a good deal of worthwhile experimental endeavor" by seven different faculty members.[5]

Wartime changes in research funding, curricular emphasis, and patterns of institutional finance were harbingers of a new reality that would engulf American colleges once peace was restored. Movement toward greater interdependence between government and higher learning was apparent across the entire spectrum of postsecondary education after 1945, as federal revenue supported both mass undergraduate education for veterans and a burgeoning program of peacetime defense research that fueled the expansion of academic science. Unfolding simultaneously during the late 1940s, the two undertakings represented opposing tendencies within a national education policy that sought to promote democratic aspirations for upward mobility

5. "Report of the Dean of the Graduate School . . . 1943–1944," *Tulane Bulletin*, series 46, no. 2 (February 1945): 39–40 (first quotation); Roger P. McCutcheon to Howard Munford Jones, 3 August 1943, box 39, Rufus C. Harris Papers, Tulane University Library (hereafter cited as RCH Papers) (second quotation); "Report of the Dean, School of Medicine, Session 1942–1943," *Tulane Bulletin*, series 45, no. 8 (1 July 1944): 39 (third quotation); "Report of the Dean, School of Medicine, Session 1944–1945," *Tulane Bulletin*, series 47, no. 8, p. 33 (fourth quotation); E. C. Andrus et al., eds., *Advances in Military Medicine, Made by American Investigators Working under the Sponsorship of the Committee on Medical Research*, vol. 2, Science in World War II (Boston: Little, Brown, 1948), 836, 838, 842, 846, 851, 876. At Tulane, as elsewhere, OSRD projects addressed specific medical problems of immediate wartime relevance, e.g., syphilis, malaria and other fevers, and infected wounds and fractures. Cf. Timothy C. Jacobson, *Making Medical Doctors: Science and Medicine at Vanderbilt since Flexner* (Tuscaloosa: University of Alabama Press, 1987), 245–9.

through college training while also fulfilling the necessarily elitist requirements of advanced research.[6]

For Tulane administrators, decisions about how to respond to the unprecedented challenges of the postwar era were shaped by basic economic considerations. Where state universities might look to per capita legislative appropriations to absorb the cost of educating more students, Tulane, as a private institution, necessarily employed a different economic calculus. Throughout the 1950s student tuition and fees consistently represented the largest single component of annual operating revenues (roughly 28–36 percent). But tuition alone could not begin to cover instructional costs, much less compensate for a small endowment that even after more than doubling its value between 1950 and 1959 actually produced a considerably smaller percentage of operating expenses at the end of the decade than at the beginning. Calculated on a per student basis, Tulane's endowment represented only a fraction of the assets available to peer institutions like Vanderbilt or Duke, and supplied no more than 10–16 percent of the annual budget.[7]

From the beginning, the university's most pressing annual need was for additional operating revenue, over and above the amount secured from tuition and the endowment. As a practical matter, the quest for economic stability meant increased emphasis upon fundraising to offset projected deficits that grew from $90,000 in 1950–51 to well over $1 million by the 1960–61 academic year. With enrollments temporarily slumping in response to demographic pressures and the departure of the veterans during the early 1950s, both President Harris and the Board of Administrators linked academic modernization to an ambitious development program embracing alumni, business corporations, private foundations, and government agencies. Beginning with

6. Blum, *V Was for Victory*, 141 (quotation); Yarmolinsky, *Military Establishment*, 291–323; Dael Wolfe, *The Home of Science: The Role of the University* (New York: McGraw-Hill, 1972), 113–6. The impact of federal research funding at Tulane receives detailed consideration in chap. 3 of the present study. The best point of departure for examining the tensions between elitist and democratic impulses in postwar education is *Higher Education for American Democracy: A Report of the President's Commission on Higher Education*, 6 vols. (Washington, D.C.: GPO, 1947). On the links between the cold war, meritocratic educational ideology, and new patterns of institutional hierarchy, see Steven Brint and Jerome Karabel, *The Diverted Dream: Community Colleges and the Promise of Educational Opportunity in America, 1900–1985* (New York: Oxford University Press, 1989), 79–92 and passim.

7. Tulane University, *Report of the Comptroller . . . June 30, 1952*, 6; Tulane University, *Financial Report*, 1957–58, p. 6; ibid., 1960–61, p. 4; Dyer, *Tulane*, 241–2.

a goal of $30 million, the campaign soon acquired a full-time director and staff and elevated its sights to the target figure of $96 million.[8]

Private foundations would play an especially important role in Tulane's postwar development. After 1945 the Rockefeller-financed General Education Board, long a patron of struggling southern schools, shifted its focus to the development of graduate education at a few key research universities in the region. GEB grants to Tulane totaling $1.7 million helped launch new Ph.D. programs in political science, sociology, and economics. By the end of the decade an equal amount had been spent on Tulane's graduate school by the GEB and the Carnegie Foundation, leaving no doubt as to the priorities of major philanthropies.[9] As the scope of foundation giving expanded during the 1950s to include not only new Rockefeller programs for third world development but also a wide array of domestic educational grants from the socially conscious Ford Foundation (whose assets dwarfed even the Rockefeller millions), superior academic performance remained a crucial prerequisite for either private or federal research support. In order to secure its share of the available wealth, Tulane was compelled to measure itself by the same yardstick applied to wealthier and more prestigious institutions. National stature, in other words, had now become a prerequisite for pursuing the university's traditional goal of regional excellence.[10]

8. Dyer, *Tulane*, 245–7; Minutes of the Board of Administrators of the Tulane Educational Fund, 13 June 1950 (Finance Committee Report), 14 June 1954, 9 April 1958, 3 June 1959, 20 April 1960, Tulane University Library (hereafter cited as BOA Minutes). Because the Board minutes are preserved in several different formats in the Tulane library, only the date of a particular meeting will be cited. On the upward revision of long-range goals for increasing the endowment, see Tulane University, *Report of the President: 1950–51*, p. 3; *1957–58*, 4–5; *1958–59*, p. 33 (hereafter cited as *President's Report*). All in Tulane University Archives.

9. George B. Tindall, *The Emergence of the New South, 1913–1945* (Baton Rouge: Louisiana State University Press, 1967), 499–500. Support for graduate education from the General Education Board included a 1951 grant of $1.2 million to be matched by $1 million from Tulane (plus an additional $500,000 if the university's 1951 fundraising goal was reached) and a further grant of $1 million in 1959. Graduate support from the Carnegie Foundation for the Advancement of Teaching included $300,000 in 1951, $250,000 in 1957, and $150,000 in 1960. Numerous additional grants supported specific programs or research projects. Robert D. Calkins to Rufus C. Harris, 5 April 1951, BOA Papers, July 1948–June 1951; *President's Report*, 1950–51, p. 3; BOA Minutes, 11 December 1951, 10 February 1954, 8 May 1957, 11 March 1959, 15 June 1960.

10. Robert H. Bremer, *American Philanthropy* (Chicago: University of Chicago Press, 1960), 177–83; Dean Rusk as told to Richard Rusk, *As I Saw It* (New York: W. W. Norton,

Even without the economic incentive provided by merit-based philanthropy and federal research contracts, Harris probably would have needed little urging to launch a postwar drive for academic excellence. His desire to stress quality over quantity had been clear when he assumed Tulane's presidency in 1937, and it was reaffirmed in 1943 when he served on the Roosevelt administration's Committee on Post-War Educational Opportunities for Service Personnel, a group chaired by General William H. Osborne. Fearful that open-ended federal subsidies would attract weak students and tempt colleges to lower academic standards, Harris joined other members of the Osborne committee in proposing a limited aid program that would, in effect, have restored the pre-1942 educational status quo.[11] But once Congress enacted a far more liberal package of veterans' benefits, Harris was quick to realize that neither the GI Bill nor the dramatic enrollment expansion of the postwar era posed a serious threat to the maintenance of qualitative distinctions in the structure of higher learning. Instead of radical leveling tendencies, the cold war produced an increased emphasis upon research universities as sources of weapons technology and social or economic policy initiatives in the fight against Communism. In the domestic realm, higher education of all kinds was widely seen as a route to upward social mobility. Echoing many of the themes contained in the report of President Truman's 1948 Commission on Higher Education, Harris agreed with Harvard president James B.

1990), chap. 10, esp. 182–6. Roger L. Geiger, "American Foundations and Academic Social Science, 1945–1960," *Minerva* 26 (autumn 1988): 315–41, concludes that southern universities, including Tulane, received some grants on the basis of geographical proximity to Latin America. Most Carnegie, Rockefeller, and Ford grants went to nonsouthern schools, however, and the "totals received by the private universities corresponded closely with their rankings" in a 1957 survey. The National Science Foundation's commitment to a "best science" criterion that excluded most southern institutions is documented in J. Merton England, *A Patron for Pure Science: The National Science Foundation's Formative Years, 1945–57* (Washington, D.C.: GPO, 1982), chap. 12 and passim.

11. Dyer, *Tulane*, 208–9, 240–1; House of Representatives, *Preliminary Report of the Armed Forces Committee on Post-War Educational Opportunities for Service Personnel, October 27, 1943*, 78th Cong., 1st sess., 1943, H. Doc. 344, esp. 6, 9. On fears of "cheap education" by Harris and other southern educators, see BOA Minutes, 8 October 1952; H. Claude Horack to Rufus C. Harris, 12 November 1943; Harris to Horack, 18 November 1943; Goodrich C. White to Francis J. Brown, 22 July 1943. All correspondence in box 64, RCH Papers. On the role of leading higher education organizations in shaping the GI Bill, see Hugh Hawkins, *Banding Together: The Rise of National Associations in American Higher Education, 1887–1950* (Baltimore: Johns Hopkins University Press, 1992), 152–6.

Rufus Carrollton Harris, President, 1937–60.

Conant that the ideals of access and excellence could be accommodated through a growing educational system in which schools were distinguished by degrees of selectivity and differing levels of emphasis upon teaching and research. Under Harris's leadership, Tulane would seek to establish its position in higher education's upper echelon, among research universities devoted to the discovery of new knowledge and to the preparation of academically talented undergraduates.[12]

Reduced to its essentials, Harris's program for Tulane involved a greatly increased emphasis upon graduate training and advanced research, together with a sustained effort to enhance quality in matters

12. The fullest and most carefully elaborated statements of Harris's educational philosophy appear in his annual presidential reports for the decade of the 1950s. See esp. *President's Report:* 1950–51, pp. 16–9; 1952–53, pp. 4–7; 1955–56, pp. 4–7; and 1958–59 for a retrospective summary. Cf. James B. Conant, "Education for a Classless Society," *Atlantic Monthly* 165 (May 1940): 593–602; idem, *Education in a Divided World* (Cambridge: Harvard University Press, 1948); idem, *Education and Liberty* (Cambridge: Harvard University Press, 1953); idem, *Citadel of Learning* (New Haven: Yale University Press, 1976). See also Conant to Harris, 9 January 1952, box 29, RCH Papers.

ranging from faculty recruitment to undergraduate admissions. Pursuing these goals would require organizational changes in the interest of efficiency, as well as significant modifications in Tulane's institutional culture. At the administrative level, closer coordination between individual schools and colleges would help lay the foundation for an expanded program of graduate study. Enrichment in undergraduate education would depend, in part, upon the creation of a campus-based residential community during an eventful half decade in which the university managed to shed forever its image as an urban streetcar institution, while acquiring many attributes of a decidedly un-southern cosmopolitanism. As a new research and living environment took shape, the task of reconciling Tulane's intellectual priorities with the competing cultural claims and fiscal demands of a major athletic program loomed increasingly large. For both symbolic and substantive reasons, attempts to curb the excesses of intercollegiate football touched off an extended controversy involving alumni, board members, the president, and the faculty. The resulting power struggle over institutional identity would help set the stage for Harris's premature retirement in 1959, while sowing the seeds of further conflict during the 1960s over the issues left unresolved at Harris's departure. In the aggregate, changes during the 1950s represented, if not a coming of age, at least the beginning of a dramatic metamorphosis that would mark Tulane's emergence onto the national scene.

II

From the beginning, graduate education set the pace for Tulane's broad institutional changes. Viewed in raw quantitative terms, the expansion of graduate programs during the 1950s was little short of spectacular. Throughout the two decades immediately preceding the end of World War II, Tulane conferred only twenty-eight Ph.D.'s, all in medical specialties. Most of the traditional academic disciplines offered graduate work, but only at the master's level. In 1944, with the launching of a doctoral program in chemistry, the picture began to change. By 1950, Ph.D. work was offered in seven medical fields and nine other disciplines, including history, English, mathematics, French, German, Spanish, psychology, and zoology. Despite temporary setbacks in particular fields, this expansion continued throughout the next decade. By 1960, Tulane had a total of twenty-eight doctoral programs, with eight additional fields in the planning stage.[13]

Although previous historians have chronicled in considerable detail Tulane's accomplishments in the graduate field through the early 1960s, the essential elements of that complex story stand out with greater clarity after the passage of an additional three decades. At the risk of some oversimplification, the pattern of development may be summarized as follows. Beginning in 1944, Tulane managed in the space of some fifteen years to expand its existing base in medical research and to replicate the broad range of Ph.D. level training available at older, more affluent research institutions in other regions. The change was reflected in soaring Graduate School enrollments, which nearly doubled between 1951 and 1960, growing from less than 400 to more than 750, while professional school numbers held steady at the level of 1,200–1,300 students per year. Despite the time lag required to produce tangible results from newly initiated doctoral programs, Tulane's annual Ph.D. production kept pace with expanding enrollments. The twenty-three Ph.D.'s conferred in 1960 equaled the southern average for 1950–62 and represented a 100-percent increase over the eleven doctorates Tulane had awarded a decade earlier. The addition of new doctoral programs depended heavily upon the willingness of the Rockefeller, Carnegie, Ford, and other foundations to contribute endowment capital, sometimes on a dollar-for-dollar matching basis, while also providing direct cash support for graduate stipends, reduced teaching loads, faculty research leaves, and selective salary supplements. Throughout the expansionary cycle (which continued into the late 1960s), expenses and expectations ran consistently ahead of available assets, a condition that contributed to the already strong pressure for deficit spending.[14]

13. Dyer, *Tulane*, 252–62. Annual reports from the dean of the Graduate School reveal the following development of Ph.D. programs at Tulane through 1960–61: prior to 1944, anatomy, biochemistry, parasitology, pharmacology, physiology; 1944–45, chemistry, microbiology; 1947–48, English, French, German, history, mathematics, psychology, Spanish; 1950–51, zoology; 1952–53, economics, political science, sociology; 1954–55, philosophy; 1958–59, anthropology; 1959–60, physics, psychodynamics; 1960–61, chemical engineering, geology, Italian, mechanical engineering, theater.

14. The above figures represent fall semester totals included in Tulane University Financial

For Tulane, as for many other universities, the expansion of graduate education provided enhanced institutional stature and access to new revenues, even as it ushered in a growing dependence upon governmental research funds to cover faculty salaries and other instructional costs. A few statistics will suffice to indicate the economic impact of advanced research. During the academic year 1946–47, Tulane's research expenditures totaled less than $213,000. By 1949–50, the figure had climbed to nearly $750,000, a sum that would double within the next five years. But the nearly $1.6 million received for sponsored research in 1954–55 would itself seem small when compared to the 1959–60 expenditure of almost $4 million. Throughout the 1950s, Tulane's research budget consisted primarily of federal grants. Medical school faculty received the lion's share of government funding for projects sponsored by the National Institutes of Health and the research divisions of various armed services, particularly the Office of Naval Research and the Army Research Office. Elsewhere in the university, federal science funding came mostly through military channels until increased revenue from the National Science Foundation and the U.S. Public Health Service helped redress the imbalance toward the end of the decade.[15]

Although Tulane during the 1950s could scarcely have been described as a federally subsidized university in the sense of Harvard or MIT, the rapid growth of government-sponsored research provided

and Statistical Profile, schedules 1–9, pp. 29–30, RCH Papers. This document was one of several prepared for submission to the Ford Foundation. Professional school enrollments include undergraduate components in architecture, business, and engineering. The aggregate statistics conceal sharp enrollment declines in the two latter fields by the end of the decade. James Francis Fouche, "The Tulane Graduate School of Business Administration: An Oral-Institutional History" (Ph.D. diss., University of Florida, 1978), 142; Tulane University School of Engineering Annual Report, 1959–60, p. 2, box 32, RCH Papers; Allan M. Cartter, "Qualitative Aspects of Southern University Education," *Southern Economic Journal* 32 (July 1965 [supplement]): 39–69, esp. table 2. See also Tulane University Non-Statistical Profile schedule 10, section 3, for a summary of the Ford Foundation grants from 1950 to 1960. Eleven separate grants totaling $5,358,714 supported a wide array of programs in the Schools of Law, Medicine, and Business Administration as well as the Graduate School, the College of Arts and Sciences, and University College.

15. *Annual Report of the Treasurer . . . June 30, 1948*, 7; *Report of the President . . . 1954–55*, 18; Tulane Financial and Statistical Profile, schedules 1–9, p. 1. The shifting origins of external funding are most reliably set forth in the detailed "Statement of Restricted Current Funds for Research" contained in Tulane's annual *Financial Report*. The subject of externally funded research receives extended treatment in the following chapter.

much of the impetus behind the expansion of graduate education. As early as 1951, President Harris informed the Board of Administrators that Tulane "would be in a bad way" without the research funding provided by the Office of Naval Research, the Public Health Service, and the Veterans Administration. "The way that most of the federal grants aid us," Harris explained, was by "allowing some of the funds to go for overhead and by allowing the investigators to spend a substantial portion of their time teaching." Several years later Tulane's comptroller, Clarence Scheps, was considerably more emphatic when he advised the Board that the university's operation was dependent "to a very large degree" upon grants from the federal government and private foundations. This was particularly true of the medical school, where external grants covered a "large portion of instructional salaries, as well as equipment." In 1955, Tulane was already receiving well over $100,000 per year in overhead reimbursement from research grants. By the 1959–60 academic year, the portion of Tulane's budget derived from sponsored research was twice as large as that provided by endowment income.[16]

Led by medicine and the natural sciences, Tulane's push into graduate education had a profound effect upon all parts of the university. Within the space of a single decade, graduate training and research would become the connecting thread linking the various colleges and professional schools to a larger agenda of qualitative improvement. Throughout the late 1940s and early 1950s, Dean McCutcheon had worked effectively to lay the foundations for a university-wide consensus on graduate expansion, often intervening personally to quicken the pulse of lethargic departments. But it was only after English professor Robert M. Lumiansky succeeded McCutcheon as graduate dean in 1954 that graduate education moved indisputably onto center stage. By virtually any standards Lumiansky deserves to be called an imposing figure. An athletic 200-pounder with a heroic war record, he had chaired Tulane's English department since 1949, while gaining national recognition for his translations and critical studies of Chaucer. Throughout the decade preceding his appointment as graduate dean, Lumiansky had spoken eloquently on behalf of the humanities as a

16. BOA Minutes, 13 November 1951 (first–third quotations), 8 June 1955 (fourth–fifth quotations); Tulane University, *Financial Report, 1960–61*, 3.

necessary foundation for training in scientific or technical fields.[17] Although the resources available for graduate study varied widely according to field, Lumiansky sought to advance the cause of humanistic scholarship by placing doctoral study in philosophy, history, literature, drama, musicology, and ancient or modern languages on an equal footing with programs in the natural and social sciences. His agenda had broad internal support, and the force of Lumiansky's personality became a key factor in sustaining the Graduate School's momentum. Nearly thirty years after Lumiansky's departure from New Orleans, elder statesmen of the Arts and Sciences faculty still spoke with undisguised enthusiasm about the spirit of optimism and expanding horizons that had inspired Tulanians to improvise in pursuit of excellence during the mid- and late 1950s.[18] Lumiansky himself captured the essence of the situation when he reported in 1957 that the graduate faculty seemed "steadily involved in a sort of three-ring circus of meetings, discussions, surveys, proposals, and reappraisals." If a "seemingly permanent state of confusion" surrounded efforts to raise Tulane's graduate school "as quickly as possible to the level of the very best in the country," the inconvenience was a small price to pay for securing broad faculty concern with the "really vital issues involved in top flight graduate work."[19]

In practice, of course, acclaim for Lumiansky's program was never universal, even among those who stood to benefit most directly from enhanced support for research and graduate teaching. To the extent that Tulane's new priorities threatened to disrupt the existing balance of power within disciplines and faculties, or among schools and colleges, some degree of controversy was necessarily associated with any departure from the status quo. Issues ranging from the qualifications

17. Dyer, *Tulane*, 252–7. For a characteristically forthright statement of McCutcheon's philosophy, see Roger P. McCutcheon, "Significant Problems in the Improvement of Instruction at the Graduate Level," *Southern Association Quarterly* 11 (May 1947): 363–6. On Lumiansky, see "Profile of an Educator," *New Orleans Item*, 13 December 1953, p. 15.

18. Informal conversations between the authors and the late Charles Till Davis, who joined Tulane's history faculty near the beginning of Lumiansky's deanship, and who provided recollections that were especially vivid. For good summaries of Lumiansky's priorities in graduate education, see his synopsis, "A Plan for Identifying and Recruiting Outstanding Students for College Teaching," in *Southern University Conference 1958* (no. 2687), 21–5, and his "Encouragement," *Graduate Journal* 4 (fall 1961): 246–8.

19. Report of the Dean of the Graduate School, 1956–57, box 32, RCH Papers, 7 (hereafter Graduate School Dean's Report).

Robert M. Lumiansky,
Professor of English. Dean of the Graduate
School, 1954–63; Provost, 1960–63.

for membership in the graduate faculty to the proper role of graduate teaching assistants in departmental instruction often provoked extended discussion. Certain matters, such as Lumiansky's obliquely worded proposal to "discontinue our present practice of expecting the same individual to play a key role in both the undergraduate and graduate programs," touched a particularly sensitive faculty nerve, causing the dean to disavow any presumed scheme to create a "'master race' of graduate professors."[20]

Tensions over these and other Graduate School issues were exacerbated on the uptown campus by the division of departmental faculties between the College of Arts and Sciences and Newcomb College. From the beginning, Tulane's Board of Administrators had controlled the Newcomb endowment (valued at over $3.5 million in 1923), and since

20. Graduate School Dean's Report, 1954–55, box 32, RCH Papers, 3–4, 8; Report of the Needs of the Graduate School for the Three Years Beginning with the 1955–56 Fiscal Year, box 30, RCH Papers, 8–9 (all quotations). Dean McCutcheon had been concerned with the role of teaching assistants since the late 1940s and it was upon his suggestion that Lumiansky studied the matter during his first year.

1918 the college had occupied a Broadway location contiguous to the rest of Tulane's campus. The 1918 move occurred at a time when Tulane was making the first serious efforts to exert centralized administrative control over the university's semi-independent professional schools, a fact that gave rise to a corresponding fear of diminished autonomy on the part of the Newcomb faculty. Dr. Brandt V. B. Dixon, Newcomb's chief administrative officer and self-designated president from 1887–1919, tended to regard closer identification with Tulane as a dangerous development that might weaken his own authority. His attitude helped foster a tradition of chronic anxiety over the college's future.[21]

From the vantage point of the early 1950s, Harris saw Newcomb's persistent "spirit of separation" as an historical anachronism that stood in the way of necessary change.[22] Over time the geographic boundaries between Newcomb and the larger university had grown indistinct. But a deeply ingrained tradition of concern for collegiate prerogatives was alive and well in the postwar decades, sustained by the administrative jurisdiction of separate deans, the existence of a separate alumni office for Newcomb, and the practice of housing the A&S and Newcomb components of each department in separate buildings or occasionally on different floors of the same building. Both the physical and the bureaucratic aspects of this collegiate division posed problems for a central administration intent on mobilizing Tulane's limited resources for maximum effect at the graduate level. In 1954, after previously obtaining Board approval to redesignate Newcomb's art and music programs as departments rather than schools (a term that time had rendered outmoded), Harris began to consolidate lines of authority through the appointment of special department heads called "University chairs," who assumed responsibility for matters involving the graduate program of each academic discipline. In effect the University chairs exercised joint authority over both the Arts and Sciences and the Newcomb components of their departments.[23]

21. Dyer, *Tulane*, 52 (quotation)–56, 180–1, 250–1; [Logan Wilson], *Some Plain Facts About Newcomb College Finances*, printed leaflet, 1950, box 32, RCH Papers, 3.

22. Rufus C. Harris to Joseph M. Jones, 24 July 1953, box 23, F. Sheldon Hackney Papers, Tulane University Archives (hereafter cited FSH Papers). This document contains a detailed summary of what Harris regarded as the salient points in the modern history of Newcomb's relationship to the larger university.

23. Dyer, *Tulane*, 250–2; BOA Minutes, 14 January 1952. In 1944–45 a wide-ranging survey of opinion among Newcomb faculty, students, and alumnae reaffirmed the college's traditional aims and objectives. Some six years later Dean Logan Wilson affirmed both the "autonomous"

III

Described at the time as an effort at *"coordination, not integration or unification,"* the plan was in reality an important first step toward the eventual merging of the Arts and Sciences and Newcomb faculties into a single entity. Requiring nearly four decades to complete, the unification process was attended by controversy at its inception as well as in its final stages during the 1980s. From start to finish, the arguments had less to do with substantive curricular or procedural matters than with unresolved (and often unacknowledged) contradictions surrounding women's education during an era when the principles of individual merit often were compromised by tacit concessions to traditional views concerning male prerogative and feminine domesticity.[24] On the face of it, Newcomb had much to gain from identifying its mission with the larger university goals of research, qualitative rigor, and graduate or professional preparation. While searching for a candidate to fill Newcomb deanship during the early 1950s, President Harris visited the South's leading private women's colleges and concluded that "in the total picture," Newcomb substantially excelled its regional counterparts. When compared to "small, isolated boarding schools" like Hollins, Sweet Briar, Randolph Macon, and Agnes Scott, Newcomb could claim many advantages, including the resources of a major research library and the "inspiration of graduate teaching" that Harris deemed essential for recruiting a strong faculty and fostering a rigorous intellectual environment. With proper alumnae support, the president believed, Newcomb "should be the outstanding college for women in the South." Harris's reaffirmation of Newcomb's regional mission in female education pointed unmistakably toward a reformulation of basic assumptions. Almost without realizing it, those who accepted the seemingly artless line of reasoning would come to identify

status of Newcomb and the need for "increased coordination with related divisions of the University" in his part of the February 1951 Committee on University Planning and Development Progress Report, box 30, RCH Papers, 31. The specific measures to achieve this result were embodied in a Proposal to Further Coordination between Departments in Newcomb College and the College of Arts and Sciences, box 30, RCH Papers, transmitted to deans and selected faculty on 9 November 1954.

24. Proposal to Further Coordination between Departments in Newcomb College and the College of Arts and Sciences, 1 (quotation); Barbara M. Solomon, *In the Company of Educated Women* (New Haven: Yale University Press, 1985), chap. 12.

Newcomb's stature among women's colleges as a function of its inclusion in the university's larger graduate-level agenda.[25]

The subtleties of Harris's argument were not lost upon John R. Hubbard, the young historian who assumed the post of Newcomb dean during the 1953–54 academic year, just in time to help inaugurate the new system of coordination through University department chairs. In his first annual report, Hubbard echoed the basic sentiments expressed two years earlier by a special Committee on University Planning and Development, chaired by Vice President Fred C. Cole, himself a departmental colleague of Hubbard. In an otherwise upbeat assessment of Tulane's future, the committee had cited three historic impediments to overall progress: inadequate fundraising, a "preoccupation with local loyalty," and the fact that each individual college had "worked primarily to further its own program" while paying little attention to the "development of the University as a whole." Dean Hubbard agreed that relations between Newcomb and other colleges should be governed by the "primary aim of building a university of the first rank." Tulane's limited resources made "two separate and distinct ventures in the liberal arts manifestly indefensible" and led inexorably to the conclusion that "integration must supplant competition" in all future relations between Newcomb and the College of Arts and Sciences.[26]

For the remainder of the decade, Hubbard worked tirelessly to achieve curricular uniformity and departmental symmetry between Newcomb and the College of Arts and Sciences. After "spirited" discussions, Newcomb's biology department was split into the separate Departments of Botany and Zoology. More lengthy negotiations resulted in the approval of the Bachelor of Fine Arts degree for men, and, somewhat later, of the Bachelor of Sciences for women. The issue of excessive localism was addressed to a limited extent through Newcomb's adoption of a Junior Year Abroad program in 1954–55, and more fully by Hubbard's successful campaign to broaden the geographical base of female undergraduate admissions.[27]

25. BOA Minutes, 18 February 1952.

26. Committee on University Planning and Development, Progress Report, box 30, RCH Papers, 11 (first–fourth quotations); Report of the Dean of the H. Sophie Newcomb Memorial College, Session 1953–1954, box 32, RCH Papers, 26 (hereafter cited as Newcomb Dean's Report; fifth–sixth quotations).

27. Newcomb Dean's Report, 1953–54, box 52, RCH Papers, 4, 5 (quotation); Newcomb

Although Hubbard had the temerity to go on record with blunt assertions that Newcomb should abandon regional complacency and recognize its unfavorable competitive position when compared to the elite women's colleges of the Northeast and Far West, he took pains to approach the elusive goal of intra-university cooperation with due regard for faculty and alumnae concerns over the possible loss of collegiate identity. Upon launching the coordination effort in 1954, Hubbard felt compelled to couple his announcement with a Churchillian declaration that he had not become dean of the college "to preside over the liquidation of its institutional integrity." But if Newcomb's survival as a separate college was never in doubt, the precise meaning of its new relationship to the College of Arts and Sciences remained unclear. When the first list of University department chairs was drawn up in 1955, only six out of twenty such posts went to Newcomb faculty, and that number later shrank to five when theater and speech professor Monroe Lippman went on leave and was replaced by an Arts and Sciences colleague. In some departments, moreover, the designation of University chairs became a source of contention between Newcomb and Arts and Sciences factions rather than a step toward disciplinary unity. The Department of Sociology and Anthropology furnished the most truculent display of intercollege antagonism when Arts and Sciences professor Forrest E. LaViolette denounced the "Machiavellian" appointment of a Newcomb professor to be University chair. Construing the action as an "administrative insult," LaViolette went on to develop a series of unflattering comparisons between the Newcomb and Arts and Sciences components of his department. What distinguished the A&S faculty, it seemed, was a combination of "greater teaching strength," vastly superior "actual and potential research and publishing strength," a deeper "sensitivity to contemporary currents of thought," and even a "greater feeling of interpersonal stimulation." As the true "locus of power" in departmental affairs, the A&S faculty would "set the conditions" for graduate work and all related matters, administrative appointments to the contrary notwithstanding. "[O]ur

---

Dean's Report, 1955–56, p. 10; "The Bachelor of Fine Arts Degree for Men" and "The Bachelor of Science Degree for Women," extracts from a 2 December 1957 letter of Arts and Sciences dean William W. Peery, in Senate Committee on University Educational Policy Minutes, 8 January 1958, box 30, RCH Papers. On the origins of the Junior Year Abroad, see Newcomb Dean's Report, 1953–54, pp. 9–13. On the quest for geographic diversity, see Newcomb Dean's Report, 1956–57, box 32, RCH Papers, 1–8.

educational aims are clearer and less confused because we are not on the staff of a young woman's college," LaViolette observed with a concluding flourish.[28]

In retrospect, the latter comment takes on a significance above and beyond its offhandedly sexist dismissal of female higher learning. By raising the issue of educational aims, LaViolette had inadvertently exposed the basis for substantive opposition to the entire scheme of collegiate restructuring under Graduate School auspices. As previously mentioned, the postwar era was one of renewed debate over the relative importance in the curriculum of college women of career and professional training versus marital and domestic abilities. In 1953, Newcomb itself had helped clarify the underlying issues by hosting a symposium on "Trends in Liberal Arts Education for Women." Among the nationally prominent figures who participated in the two-day event were advocates of sharply contradictory philosophies, as well as various middle-ground positions. Easily the most flamboyant speaker was Mills College president Lynn White, whose rather self-serving brand of "feminine education" included a deemphasis on graduate training and assertions that women would profit from instruction in "the theory and preparation of a Basque Paella, or a well-marinated shish kabob."[29] In New Orleans, however, White downplayed the culinary theme when arguing that women's colleges, with "women scholars of the first quality," provided the "chief means by which a girl may discover self-respect and explore her potentialities." Probably the most trenchant and nuanced presentation of the Newcomb symposium came from Dean Nancy Lewis of Brown University's Pembroke College. Turning contemporary masculine wisdom on its head, Lewis opened her talk with a half-serious critique of higher education for failing to prepare the typical male "to function adequately in his role as a family member." After developing her remarks into a full-blown parody of fashionable Freudian claims about female anxieties, Lewis turned her attention to women, stressing their gross underrepresentation at the Ph.D. level and calling for an undergraduate curriculum that would

28. Newcomb Dean's Report, 1953–54, p. 27 (first quotation); University Chairmen, 1955–56 session, 1956–57 session, box 39, RCH Papers; Forrest E. LaViolette to Rufus C. Harris, 10 February 1955, box 39, RCH Papers (all subsequent quotations).

29. Lynn White, *Educating Our Daughters* (New York: Harpers, 1950), 78; Solomon, *In the Company of Educated Women*, 191–200 (quotations on 191, 192); BOA Minutes, 12 May 1952, 14 October 1953.

foster the "fullest possible development" of the female student's "intellectual and spiritual powers." Lewis was the only speaker whose remarks were not reported in the local press.[30]

By linking Newcomb's future to the development of graduate education, Tulane appeared to emphasize the primacy of intellect in undergraduate women. But not everyone was persuaded that the new relationship would operate in the manner that President Harris envisioned. In 1955 the University mathematics chairman, William L. Duren Jr., himself an Arts and Sciences professor, challenged Harris directly on the new orthodoxy. For Duren, the most important issues in any collaborative arrangement with Newcomb concerned undergraduate teaching rather than graduate work, and in this area Newcomb's mission within the larger university seemed unclear. "I think we ought to understand how we are proposing to educate young women and not presume that the education of young women at Newcomb will be well served as an adjunct to the big graduate school," Duren admonished the president.[31]

The basis of Duren's concern apparently had less to do with the career versus domesticity curricular debate than with a perception that the Newcomb's faculty's "former isolationism" had been replaced by a "sharp demand for equality in the graduate program." The resulting struggle to divide the "graduate pie" seemed to offer an unpromising framework within which to formulate undergraduate educational strategies. Many of Duren's concerns were echoed by Dean Hubbard as he struggled to reconcile the priorities of a small female liberal arts college with the demands of graduate research. Having promised in 1954 to effect change without compromising Newcomb's "unique character," Hubbard insisted that steadily rising enrollments would involve "no serious deviation" from the tradition of keeping classes small enough to promote a sense of "genuine rapport between teacher and student." By 1957, concern had shifted from the problem of class size to the more thorny issue of graduate versus undergraduate teaching. While acknowledging that a balance between the two commitments was difficult to maintain, Hubbard worried that the rapid expansion of graduate offerings had created a false sense of priorities in some de-

30. *Trends in Liberal Arts Education for Women* (New Orleans, 1954), 107, 114, 123 (all quotations); *New Orleans States*, 5 November 1953; *New Orleans Item*, 6 November 1953; BOA Minutes, 11 November 1953.

31. William L. Duren Jr. to Rufus C. Harris, 7 February 1955, box 39, RCH Papers.

partments. To any professors who might be tempted to think that their energies should be reserved "exclusively for the graduate school," the dean issued a cautionary reminder. Providing the "finest undergraduate program in this region" was Newcomb's raison d'être, and all faculty thus shared a "fundamental responsibility" for undergraduate teaching. Newcomb students, in turn, had a right to expect the "best talents" the faculty could provide. What Hubbard did not say, but what most Newcomb faculty undoubtedly realized, was that undergraduate teaching pursued in isolation from original scholarship would be tantamount to professional suicide. The message was conveyed in a variety of ways, but nowhere more convincingly than in decisions on promotion and tenure. During 1956, for example, a total of thirty-three Arts and Sciences faculty sought promotion but only five received favorable consideration at the college level. According to Dean William Peery, the principal reason for denying promotion to the remaining twenty-eight applicants was lack of scholarly productivity. Or, as Peery preferred to say, those rejected were faculty who had "not accepted their responsibility as university professors to contribute to as well as to dispense knowledge." Such pronouncements left little doubt that the old order was changing.[32]

Tensions between research, graduate work, and undergraduate teaching manifested themselves in all of Tulane's academic divisions, but at Newcomb the issues were complicated by contradictory attitudes toward women both within and outside the academic world. Theoretically women of the 1950s were free to pursue advanced study and to enter professions on the same basis as men. Some actually did so. In 1957, for example, Tulane enrolled a total of 218 full-time women students in divisions other than Newcomb College. Most were registered in the School of Social Work (71) and the Graduate School (60), but an additional 51 single women had established beachheads in such traditionally male professions as business administration (26), medicine (12), architecture (6), engineering (4), and law (3).[33] Outside social work, the female percentage of Tulane's graduate and profes-

32. Ibid. (first–second quotations); Newcomb Dean's Report, 1953–54, p. 26; Report on the Needs of Newcomb College for the Three Years Beginning with the Fiscal Year 1955–56, box 30, RCH Papers, 3 (third–fourth quotations); Newcomb Dean's Report, 1956–57, p. 11 (fifth–eighth quotations); College of Arts and Sciences, Annual Report of the Dean, 1955–56, box 7, RCH Papers, 12 (hereafter cited as A&S Dean's Report), ninth quotation.

33. F[lorence] W. Tappino to Clarence Scheps, 16 September 1957; Scheps to Rufus C. Harris, 10 October 1957, box 24, RCH Papers.

sional enrollment remained small or minuscule during the 1950s, but by comparison with earlier eras it seemed impressive. When Rose Mary Decker and Lutee Wheat enrolled as freshmen engineering students in 1954, they entered a college that had graduated only seven female engineers in the previous thirty-two years. Both women received considerable "kidding" from their male peers and seem to have been regarded as academic oddities when registering for classes in other divisions of Tulane. "Everybody thinks we've mixed up our schedules because we're the only girls," they explained. Three years later, Decker became the only female engineering graduate in a class of sixty-five and only the second woman ever to specialize in electrical engineering at Tulane. When interviewed before leaving New Orleans for a job in California's booming defense industry, Decker was asked to assess the difficulty of entering a male profession. The words in her brief reply seem carefully chosen. "At first there is generally some difficulty," she said without elaborating. "However, a woman can go forward if she has the desire, and does a good job." The sentiments were appropriate for the occasion and the audience, including presumably a new male employer. Equally revealing, perhaps, was the qualifier that followed. "Of course, I've always been lucky."[34]

As the decade wore on, a significant minority of Tulane's female undergraduates elected to pursue advanced studies. A poll of 1961 Arts and Sciences graduates—virtually all male—revealed that some 81 percent planned to attend graduate or professional school. During the same period, Dean Hubbard estimated that 25 percent of Newcomb graduates, including 40 percent of those who had participated in the Junior Year Abroad program, would seek higher degrees. The experiences of Tulane's graduate and professional women during the 1950s—together with the example of Newcomb graduates like Diane Fournet Davis, who received the Ph.D. in physics from MIT in 1957—lent a certain credence to the gender-neutral, individualist rationale for subsuming women's education into a larger, research-oriented academic mission.[35] Followed to its logical conclusion, the meritocratic definition of educational equality that flourished in the cold war era left little

34. *New Orleans Times-Picayune*, 10 January 1954, in Tulane clipping scrapbooks (first–second quotations); *New Orleans Item*, 20 June 1957, in Tulane clipping scrapbooks (third–fifth quotations).

35. Herbert E. Longenecker to Nils Y. Wessel, 26 June 1962, box 24, RCH Papers; *New Orleans Times-Picayune*, 26 June 1957, in Tulane clipping scrapbooks.

room for anything other than a strict coeducational view of higher learning. No one dared to put the matter so bluntly at Tulane during the 1950s, but in various ways President Harris expressed impatience with the principal arguments used to justify single-sex institutions. Proponents of women's colleges frequently pointed out that their schools offered female faculty and administrators more opportunities for leadership than were available in coeducational settings. Lynn White had expounded this very theme at considerable length during the 1953 Newcomb symposium. Yet Harris took virtually the opposite stance, stressing the competitive advantages arising from Newcomb's overwhelmingly male faculty and administration. At several southern women's colleges, Harris believed, female presidents had proved "unable or unwilling to get strong men on the faculty." In the absence of male professors, the schools allegedly lost "vitality" and became "too much of a convent." Even when speaking more favorably of Newcomb's regional competitors, Harris sometimes gave vent to sentiments on female education that were tinged with sexual condescension. In a particularly candid moment, he praised Georgia's Agnes Scott College as "quite good" because it possessed the kind of "snob appeal" that was "good up to a point for a women's college."[36]

During the 1950s and for sometime thereafter, Tulane had few women faculty in its upper ranks and no female deans or senior administrators. If anything, the era saw a retreat from the modest advances of the World War II years, when Professor Clara de Milt had served as temporary chair of Newcomb's chemistry department and physicist Rose Mooney of the Newcomb faculty became one of the highest-ranking female scientists on the Manhattan Project, serving as associate chief of the x-ray structure section of the Manhattan District's Metallurgical Laboratory in Chicago.[37] Although the wives of men in authority undoubtedly exerted informal influence over some matters, their public role during the 1950s was largely ornamental in nature. Here again Harris minced no words about women's proper

36. BOA Minutes, 18 February 1952.

37. Margaret W. Rossiter, *Women Scientists in America before Affirmative Action, 1940–1972* (Baltimore: Johns Hopkins University Press, 1995), 5, 9. According to Dyer, *Tulane,* appendix 7, only thirteen of Newcomb's thirty-six full professors between 1948 and 1965 were female. No studies comparing research accomplishment, faculty rank, and compensation for men and women were undertaken during the 1950s. Strictly speaking, Newcomb College did have one female dean, Anna Many, the longtime Counselor to Women whose title was changed from "acting dean" to "dean" the year before her retirement in 1953.

sphere. When discussing the difficulty of identifying and retaining suitable deans (a term that was presumptively masculine at Tulane), Harris explained that few individuals possessed the full range of attributes demanded by the New Orleans environment. In addition to scholarly credentials, administrative ability, and a pleasing personality, the well-qualified applicant for a Tulane deanship also needed a "charming wife," or more precisely, the kind of woman who "may be a social asset . . . with the faculty of the college as well as in the city." Several years later, when naming a new dean for the College of Arts and Sciences, Harris was quick to note that the successful candidate had "an able and attractive wife." Although the matrimonial expectations established for Tulane deans and the social demands placed upon their wives were less unique than Harris tried to claim, his comments effectively underscored the marginal position of women—whether wives, students, or female faculty—on most southern campuses. An awareness of this larger social reality formed the backdrop for all discussions of Newcomb College, subtly overriding the asexual logic of liberal individualism.[38]

Despite the unequal treatment of women at Tulane during the 1950s, resistance to the merging of Newcomb College with its male counterpart probably had little if anything to do with incipient feminism on the part of female faculty members. The college's separatist spirit can more accurately be seen as a culturally conditioned defensiveness rooted in the school's history and perpetuated by male and female professors who found themselves linked to the feminine component of a predominantly male enterprise. An attentive listener to Harris's comments on the importance of male faculty and the subordinate role of academic wives would have detected clear echoes of the gender anxiety expressed by college modernizers during the late nineteenth and early twentieth centuries, when America's first modern universities took shape.[39] Like the educational spokesman of an earlier era, Harris seemed bent upon eradicating all effete or effeminate connotations from the image of Tulane as a research university. Although

38. BOA Minutes, 17 April 1952, item 4 of president's monthly report (first–second quotations); ibid., 18 May 1955 (third quotation).

39. Geraldine Joncich Clifford, "'Shaking Dangerous Questions from the Crease': Gender and American Higher Education," *Feminist Issues* 3 (fall 1983): 3–62, esp. 48–53, brings the issue into clear focus for the late nineteenth and early twentieth centuries.

President Harris and Deans, 1950. Standing: Paul Brosman (Law), James M. Robert (Engineering), Harris, Logan Wilson (Newcomb), Maxwell Lapham (Medicine), Fred C. Cole (Arts and Sciences). Seated: Roger P. McCutcheon (Graduate School), Forrest U. Lake (Admissions), Elizabeth Wisner (Social Work).

women would have a place in the new Tulane, women's education of the traditional separate type would not. The position was inherently ambiguous, and in the circumstances it is hardly surprising that the Newcomb–Arts and Sciences coordination scheme evoked contradictory responses from faculty in both colleges. Depending upon a professor's individual outlook, the new relationship represented either a threat to the sequestered tranquillity of the feminine liberal arts ideal or a promise to bring women's education into the academic mainstream.

Dean Hubbard, needless to say, took the latter view. He was quick to emphasize those areas in which Newcomb's practices reinforced larger university aims. On the critically important subject of undergraduate admissions, Newcomb provided a model that the College of Arts and Sciences would eventually emulate. At Tulane, as at the older research universities of the Northeast, the shift to selective or merit-based admissions began at the postgraduate and professional level in the years after World War I. Tulane's medical school led the way, with standardized admissions testing during the 1930s, but financial considerations precluded undergraduate selectivity for roughly a decade. The Graduate School first administered the Graduate Record Exam in 1945 and began requiring it the next year. Arguably Tulane's first real encounter with restricted admissions in the College of Arts and Sciences came between 1946 and 1949, when the flood of applications for admission under the GI Bill prompted university officials to establish a list of criteria for determining admissions priority. As set forth in official publications during 1946, Tulane's policy gave preference to current or formerly enrolled students, followed by wartime high school graduates who had entered military service immediately upon graduation, and finally civilian high school graduates of the postwar era. Within each category of new applicants, superior academic performance was either an admissions requirement or a basis for ranking those seeking admission. Actual admissions procedures were at once more specific and more flexible than the published rules would suggest. New applicants ranking in the upper half of their high school class, and transfer students possessing above a C average, received preferential consideration. At the same time, however, students deemed ineligible under the above criteria could gain admission by making adequate scores on special tests administered by the university.[40]

In most fundamental respects, Tulane's admissions standards bore a close resemblance to those of peer institutions like Rice, Emory, and Vanderbilt, where special testing options also existed. Initially (in 1946) Tulane had a stated policy of giving preference to Louisiana residents "when all other considerations are equal." Apparently the university did not go so far as to read applications from alumni children before considering other applicants, a practice common to many private institutions, including Vanderbilt.[41]

40. Roger L. Geiger, *To Advance Knowledge*, 129–39, 221; Duffy, *Tulane Medical Center*, 155; "Report of the Dean of the Graduate School, Session 1945–1946," in *Tulane Bulletin*, series 48, no. 3 (March 1947): 40; Preamble and Resolutions of the Senate Committee on University Educational Policy, 7 January 1946, box 30, RCH Papers; "Report of the Dean of Admissions, Session 1946–1947," in *Tulane Bulletin*, series 48, no. 13 (November 1947): 54–6.

41. Cliff W. Wing Jr., interview by Joseph Gordon, 12 June 1992 (audiotape in the author's possession). Between 1947 and 1953 Tulane personnel conducted six different investigations of admissions requirements and practices at peer institutions within and outside the South. For the Rice, Emory, and Vanderbilt comparisons, see BOA Minutes, 11 November 1953. Also see Paul K. Conkin, *Gone with the Ivy: A Biography of Vanderbilt University* (Knoxville: University of Tennessee Press, 1985), 470; Marcia Graham Synnott, *The Half-Opened Door: Discrimination*

Most of the late 1940s' modifications in Tulane's admissions policies were simply temporary measures grafted onto a substructure of conventional and not very rigorous entrance requirements. But if policies designed to cope with GI Bill applications set few long-term precedents, quite the opposite was true of Newcomb's decision to adopt the College Entrance Examination Board's Scholastic Aptitude Test as a requirement for all applicants beginning with the 1948–49 academic year. When endorsing the change in March 1947, the University Senate's Committee on Educational Policy also recommended that Tulane's other undergraduate divisions follow Newcomb's lead. Fully a decade would elapse before the suggestion was implemented, and in the intervening years, Newcomb's experiment with selective admissions would come to embody many of the key goals and strategic assumptions that Harris sought to establish for Tulane as a whole.[42]

Under Dean Logan Wilson and his successor John Hubbard, Newcomb employed SAT requirements as part of a long-range effort to increase the size, quality, and geographical diversity of the college's applicant pool. Particularly under Hubbard, pursuing these interrelated goals implied a basic recasting of institutional identity within a national as opposed to a local or regional frame of reference. Initially Newcomb's declining enrollments precluded any serious attempt to turn away students with low test scores.[43] By the mid-1950s, however, applications were again increasing and for the rest of the decade Hubbard hammered away relentlessly at the danger of academic parochialism. Had the intellectual caliber of Newcomb students improved over time? Perhaps, but average SAT scores of 954 were "nothing to brag about." Were Newcomb's enrollments once again approaching the all-time high of 910 established in 1946–47? Yes, but attrition rates were unacceptably high. Worse still, the college's annual pool of applicants remained considerably smaller than that of the fourteen

and Admissions at Harvard, Yale, and Princeton, 1900–1970 (Westport, Conn.: Greenwood Press, 1979), 152, 154, 157, 206–8.

42. Report of the Senate Committee on Educational Policy, 1946–47 (summary of meeting on 5 March 1947), box 30, RCH Papers, 2.

43. Upon reviewing admissions policy in 1954, Hubbard described the preceding eight years as "a period of declining enrollment wherein only minimal entrance requirements were enforced and the selective process had to give way to the pressure of financial exigency." Newcomb Dean's Report, 1953–54, p. 3. Wilson had voiced similar sentiments in his 1948–49 report, which noted that Newcomb depended upon tuition for roughly 65 percent of its annual budget.

women's colleges "with which we like to compare ourselves," a list that included all of the elite Seven Sisters of the Northeast but only three southern institutions. Judged against this national yardstick, Newcomb was in an "exceedingly poor competitive situation" and simply could "not measure up academically" to its rivals. Newcomb's traditional claim to stature among southern women's colleges seemed suddenly overshadowed by the chilling realization that "we have been too provincial for too long."[44]

When the preceding statements were written in 1958, the age of selective admissions was rapidly dawning on the remainder of Tulane's undergraduate landscape. Beginning with the 1957–58 academic year, both the College of Arts and Sciences and University College, as well as the Schools of Architecture, Engineering, and Business Administration, joined Newcomb in requiring SAT scores of new applicants. The new policy, however, contained a loophole allowing exceptions on an individual or group basis "under some circumstances." A cynic might look back on the piecemeal progress toward tougher entrance standards and conclude that undergraduate women faced the earliest and most rigorous exposure to academic winnowing, while promising football players remained largely immune from serious preadmission scrutiny. In reality, a number of considerations—including anxiety over athletic recruitment and uncertainty about future enrollment prospects—helped delay the extension of SAT requirements to all undergraduate divisions. Among members of the Board of Administrators, deep-seated concern over football and the all-important matter of annual tuition revenue went hand in hand with a reluctance to act in ways that might alienate Tulane from its local and regional bases of support. The Board's understandable, if somewhat contradictory, desire to enhance the university's stature as a research institution while clinging to a traditional conception of its undergraduate mission complicated a number of policy decisions throughout the decade of the 1950s. In the push for selective admissions, a persistent tension between local and cosmopolitan values shaped the ongoing dialogue over Tulane's institutional identity.[45]

44. Newcomb Dean's Report, 1957–58, box 32, RCH Papers, 3–4.
45. BOA Minutes, 14 December 1955 (quotation). The evolution of a policy on university-wide selective admissions may be followed in: First Report of the Special Committee on Admissions and Standards to the Committee on Educational Policy of the University Senate, 4 February 1954, box 30, RCH Papers; University Senate Minutes, 8 March 1954, box 30, RCH

IV

From the beginning, President Harris linked proposed changes in admissions policy to the larger goal of securing Tulane's place in the evolving educational hierarchy of postwar America. Harris's wartime experience with the planning phase of veterans' education had involved careful assessment of the human and institutional implications of enrollment growth. As the nation embarked upon an era of dramatically expanded educational access, it seemed inevitable that some colleges would be more accessible than others. The lesson that Harris drew for Tulane was one of quality over quantity. "I do not think we wish to try to compete with the state institutions in providing mass education," Harris advised the Board of Administrators in 1953. Enlarging upon the theme a few months later, he argued that pressures to "water down" initial college instruction to the equivalent of "13th and 14th grades" offered Tulane the opportunity to distinguish its own program on the basis of "quality" and "selectivity." Within this context, the need for stricter admissions requirements was "assumed to be evident."[46]

Even as Harris voiced these confident words, he was fully aware that Board members Lester J. Lautenschlaeger, Darwin S. Fenner, and Joseph Jones—among others—harbored serious misgivings about the impact of higher standards upon sports, enrollments, and local alumni support. Up to a point, the concerns could be alleviated through reassuring statistics about rising application pressure and open-ended athletic escape clauses. But in the long run, the fate of selective admissions as a university-wide policy would hinge upon the Board's willingness to accept and endorse the strategy's underlying rationale. As a matter of practical necessity, the case for extending SAT requirements beyond Newcomb College became inextricably bound up with other aspects of Tulane's metamorphosis into a national research university.

During the five-year period between Harris's initial discussion of selective admissions in 1953 and the actual implementation of the policy in 1958, the connection between SAT requirements and other dimensions of institutional change became abundantly clear. Throughout

---

Papers; BOA Minutes, 21 April 1954; University Senate Minutes, 3 October 1955; BOA Minutes, 12 October 1955.

46. BOA Minutes: 13 May 1953 (first quotation); 14 October 1953 (second–fifth quotations); 11 November 1953 (last quotation).

University commencement, ca. 1953.

those years, Tulane was engaged in an ambitious construction program that by 1960 would result in the expenditure of some $8,296,000 for seven new student residence halls, plus additions to two existing structures. Financed primarily through low-interest federal loans, the new dormitories were a visible sign of the university's shift from state and local to regional and national patterns of undergraduate recruiting.[47] Another step toward undergraduate diversity took place in 1956, when Tulane psychology professor Cliff W. Wing Jr. was named director of admissions. For the next six years Wing, a testing and quantitative expert, together with Joseph E. Gordon, who became associate director of admissions in 1957, took on the challenging task of devising admissions policies that would "reflect as accurately as possible the ed-

47. Tulane University Non-Statistical Profile, schedule 10, sections 1–3 (16 January 1961), p. 27 isolates the $8,296,000 from a larger total of $23,500,060 spent on new construction between 1950 and 1960. Specific projects are enumerated on pp. 28–31. Totals appearing in Tulane's annual *Financial Report* reflect work in progress and are less comprehensive. On the importance of low-interest federal loans, see also BOA Minutes, 14 January 1952; University Senate Minutes, 17 January 1952, box 65, RCH Papers.

ucational standards of the University."[48] In addition to establishing the relative importance of standardized tests in predicting academic success, the admissions office sought to identify and attract talented high school seniors for Tulane's freshman class. The effort involved an expanded use of informational techniques—targeted mailings, high school visits, and on-campus conferences for secondary school counselors—that would become routine aspects of what a later generation would unapologetically describe as "academic marketing."[49] To a certain extent higher entrance requirements could, in themselves, enhance Tulane's appeal to bright applicants, particularly if the university's rigorous standards were accompanied by appropriate economic incentives. In fields like medicine and law, where the number of applicants traditionally exceeded the available places in a given year's entering class, it had long been customary for students to apply simultaneously to a number of different schools in anticipation of a high rejection rate. By the mid-1950s, a similar competitive anxiety had overtaken many high school seniors in the face of demographic studies predicting increases of 124–250 percent in the college age population in various southern states by 1970. With Tulane's application pool growing between eight and twelve percent a year during the second half of the 1950s, well-qualified students responded by applying to several schools and, when possible, weighing institutional prestige against cost before making a final decision on where to enroll. Financial aid thus became a vital component in Tulane's attempt to claim a larger share of the best and brightest high school prospects.[50]

Throughout the 1950s Tulane undergraduates had access, in some degree, to the more common varieties of college financial assistance—scholarships or tuition waivers based upon need and academic merit, loans, and campus employment. The number of freshman scholarships rose modestly from 174 in 1953–54 to over 200 by the end of the

48. Dyer, *Tulane*, 326; BOA Minutes, 13 March 1957 (quotation). At the time of his appointment Wing was one of the very few, if not the only, U.S. college admissions directors with Ph.D. training as a psychological testing and measurements specialist. Wing would later undertake research and advisory assignments for the Educational Testing Service and the College Scholarship Service.

49. Cliff W. Wing Jr., "Admissions Research at Tulane University," in *Institutional Research on College Students, Papers Presented at Swannanoa Conference, Warren Wilson College . . . August 14–18, 1961*, ed. Kenneth M. Wilson (n.p., 1962), 162–8; BOA Minutes, 13 November 1957 (see esp. item 5 of president's monthly report); Wing interview, 12 June 1992.

50. BOA Minutes, 13 October 1954, 13 March 1957.

decade. After 1955, the university also derived some benefit from the new nationwide program for National Merit Scholarships supported by the Ford Foundation. Although recipients of the one thousand highly coveted annual awards tended to gravitate toward prominent Ivy League schools or elite liberal arts colleges, Tulane managed to enroll five National Merit scholars during the program's second year. An even more important result of the 1957 competition grew out of the admission office's decision to send personal letters to all National Merit finalists who had *not* received awards. The effort yielded 438 replies that led to applications from 116 students, nearly half of whom (55) enrolled in the 1957 freshman class.[51]

The most dramatic expansion of undergraduate financial aid involved loans rather than scholarships. In 1957 the Board of Administrators established funds to provide long-term loans for both graduate and undergraduate students. Financed entirely from university resources, the program marked a significant departure from traditional policies of very limited financial assistance. Students responded to the loan option in larger numbers than initially anticipated, causing the university's total investment in student lending to grow from roughly $15,000 in 1956 to nearly $400,000 by December 31, 1959. A new chapter in the history of student aid began in 1958 with Congressional passage of the National Defense Education Act, providing fellowships for graduate study and low-interest undergraduate loans. Tulane participated in the program from its inception, and by the spring of 1960 the university had received $276,000 in federal loan funds, matched by a 10 percent institutional contribution. To put the matter somewhat differently, the total value of student loans at Tulane was nearly 47 times larger in 1960 than it had been in 1956.[52]

Without the stimulus of increased student aid, the job of implementing selective admissions would have been vastly more difficult. Even with financial support, the new policies took hold only gradually. Initially the degree of actual selectivity accompanying the shift to SAT requirements was comparatively slight. In 1957, for example, Tulane's various daytime undergraduate schools and colleges received approximately 2,100 completed applications. Only 150 applicants were re-

51. Ibid., 9 October 1957.
52. Ibid., 13 February 1957; 21 January 1960, esp. appendix 3 of president's monthly report; 11 May 1960, esp. item 6 of president's monthly report.

jected, some 7 percent of the total. The rejected applicants comprised the bottom 18 percent of their high school graduating class and scored in the lowest 5.5 percent of those taking the SAT nationally. Developments the next year followed a similar pattern. By May 31, 1958, Tulane had rejected only 44 out of 906 complete applications, a refusal rate of 5 percent. The characteristics of the 1958 entering class showed correspondingly little evidence of intellectual elitism. Some 23 percent of the freshmen were not expected to earn a C average, while 9 percent were "clearly not college prospects" despite their classification "a notch above those rejected." Transfer students did nothing to change the overall picture, since 30 percent had less than a C average when accepted, including 13 percent with a GPA of 1.5 (D) or below. After reviewing the data for Harris early in 1959, admissions director Wing betrayed a note of exasperation with critics of the new standards. "I do not see how this possibly could be misconstrued to mean that Tulane is difficult to enter, or that only those students who might apply to Eastern schools would be qualified for admission," Wing protested. All in all it seems most accurate to conclude that Tulane had considerable success in attracting highly qualified students during the late 1950s while continuing to accept a substantial number of applicants with weak academic credentials.[53]

Whatever the statistics may have indicated, not all university officials were satisfied with the drift of events. Although the degree of actual selectivity remained low, any move to restrict access during an era of rising applications had the inevitable effect of excluding local applicants who would otherwise have gained admission. Aware that a "serious public relations problem" might arise if Tulane's policy was not adequately explained to local supporters, Harris could scarcely have been encouraged by the initial reactions of his own Board of Administrators. When discussing the new admissions guidelines with the Board in March 1957, Harris acknowledged that the university would be compelled to turn away more local applicants than in previous years. "We must give our places to the best of the applicants," he declared in remarks that also affirmed Tulane's "obligation" to deny admission to students who stood "little or no chance" of academic success. The implications of Harris's argument rankled Board members

53. Ibid., 13 November 1957, item 3 of president's monthly report; ibid., 11 June 1958, item 10 of president's monthly report; Cliff W. Wing Jr. to Rufus C. Harris, 25 February 1959, in BOA Minutes, 11 March 1959, item 15 of president's monthly report (all quotations).

like Darwin Fenner, who gave vent to what must have been a common sentiment among Tulanians with a strong sense of loyalty to their school and region. "I am not surprised that the academic staff would prefer to draw students from all over the nation," Fenner declared in a blistering communication to Board president Joseph Jones. Fenner rejected the "staff's" alleged belief that "Louisiana students might lower the standards," and proposed instead that Tulane fulfill its "duty to Louisiana students" by offering them substantially reduced tuition.[54] Responding to Fenner's criticism in June 1957, Harris held firm to his belief that state or regional preference had no place in admissions policy. Abandoning philosophical arguments, he reminded the Board rather bluntly that "by far the greatest share of our financial support in the past few years has come from outside this region." Continued support from foundations and federal agencies, Harris predicted, would depend upon Tulane's stature as "an institution of national and international significance."[55] Returning to the theme in 1959, Harris assured the Board that local concern over excessively high academic standards at Tulane was "completely unrealistic." Support from national foundations presupposed that the university would emphasize graduate training and the "upper division of higher education" while allowing Louisiana's public colleges to assume the major burden of routine undergraduate training. With his own retirement only a few months away, Harris affirmed his conviction that "[c]hange is indicated in the function of Tulane."[56]

Understandably, perhaps, Harris and other proponents of institutional cosmopolitanism sought to emphasize the intellectual rather than the geographic consequences of selective admissions. But geography was at the heart of the "public relations" problem that Harris hoped to solve within and outside the university. As subsequent events would make clear, Louisiana loyalists like Darwin Fenner had accurately pinpointed during the spring of 1957 the one area in which selective admissions policy would have an immediate and tangible impact upon Tulane's undergraduate enrollment. At the beginning of the 1950s, no one would have hesitated to characterize Tulane as a Loui-

54. BOA Minutes, 13 March 1957, item 13 of president's monthly report (first–fourth quotations); Darwin S. Fenner to Joseph M. Jones, 4 June 1957 as quoted in Rufus C. Harris to Jones, 10 June 1957, box 8, RCH Papers (fifth–seventh quotations).

55. Harris to Jones, 10 June 1957, ibid.

56. BOA Minutes, 14 October 1959, item 17 of president's monthly report.

siana institution. During the 1949–50 academic year, only three divisions (the Schools of Medicine and Social Work, and the Department of Graduate Medicine) drew a majority of their students from out of state. By 1959–60, only four divisions besides University College had a Louisiana student majority. State and local residents comprised roughly 72 percent of engineering enrollments, 62 percent of law students, 54 percent of business administration registrants, and a bare 50.3 percent of aspiring architects. In the university as a whole, including the overwhelmingly local constituency of University College, the percentage of Louisiana students declined from 67 percent in 1949–50 to just under 60 percent in 1959–60. When University College is excluded, the number of Louisiana registrants for 1959–60 falls to 49 percent.[57]

If aggregate figures suggest a general broadening of Tulane's enrollment base, a detailed analysis of statistics for both Newcomb College and the College of Arts and Sciences reveals a pattern containing elements of both change and continuity. During the decade in question, each undergraduate college experienced a marked decline in the number and proportion of enrolled Louisiana students. The changes began during a period of shrinking enrollment in the early 1950s and continued in the expansionary cycle that was underway from 1953 onward. Calculations based upon all full-time undergraduates, including but not limited to those in Arts and Sciences and Newcomb, reveal that the proportion of Tulane's out-of-state registrants increased steadily from 26 percent in 1949–50 to 41 percent in 1954–55 and 52 percent in 1959–60. It would thus appear that the shift to university-wide selective admissions in 1957 served to reinforce and modestly accelerate a trend toward non-Louisiana enrollment that was already well under way.[58]

Chronological comparisons between the College of Arts and Sciences and Newcomb are possible only if one keeps in mind the very different external factors bearing upon male and female college attendance during the postwar era. For Arts and Sciences, 1949–50 marked the last year of peak veteran enrollments under the GI Bill, a fact re-

57. Comparative Table of Registration Excluding Summer School, 1949–50, in Vice President Scheps Files, RCH Papers. Percentages for 1959–60 have been calculated from a table in: Geographical Distribution [of Registration] Session 1959–60, in Vice President Scheps Files, RCH Papers.
58. Tulane University Financial and Statistical Profile, schedules 1–9A, Student Data—Undergraduate, schedule 6 (16 January 1961), RCH Papers.

flected in the registration of 1,714 students. By 1959–60, the college had only 1,195 students despite modest enrollment gains during the previous five years. The decade's net decline of 519 students took place at a time when Louisiana registration dropped by nearly half, from 924 to 492, a loss of 432 students. By 1960, the greatly reduced Louisiana contingent comprised less than 43 percent of the smaller Arts and Sciences student body, as compared with 54 percent of the much larger group in 1950.[59]

Few female veterans attended Newcomb, where enrollment peaked at 910 students in 1946–47 before entering a five-year decline to 627 students in 1951–52.[60] Most of the enrollment loss probably resulted from the reduced number of 18-year-olds in the general population— the so-called demographic trough caused by low birth rates during the 1930s. Indirectly, at least, the influx of male veterans and the diminished luster of women's colleges in an era of burgeoning coeducation may also have reinforced Newcomb's downward spiral. By 1952–53, however, the demographic curve had turned upward, and over the next seven years Newcomb's student body increased by nearly 50 percent, to well over 900 women by the late fifties. In a statistical sense, Newcomb's growth may be said to have occurred at the expense of Louisiana students, whose numbers declined from 435 in 1949–50 to 378 in 1959–60. At the beginning of the decade, roughly 62 percent of Newcomb students were from Louisiana. Ten years later the proportion was less than half. The central conclusion to emerge from the changing patterns of male and female enrollment is that Louisiana students accounted for most of the drop in Arts and Sciences registration and none of the growth in Newcomb's numbers.[61]

But if Louisiana students declined both in absolute numbers and as a percentage of total undergraduate enrollment, who replaced them? On this question the late fifties rhetoric about Tulane's emergence as a national institution offers a somewhat misleading impression of the undergraduate situation. At the beginning of the decade, the College of Arts and Sciences contained more nonsouthern students than any

59. Comparative Registration Table, 1949–50; Geographic Distribution Table, 1959–60. On veteran enrollments, see *Tulane Bulletin*, series 48, no. 3 (March 1947): 48; ibid., no. 13 (November 1947): 54–6; BOA Minutes, 10 October 1950; *President's Report*, 1951–52, p. 12.

60. Enrollment figures are those given in the Newcomb dean's annual reports to the president, box 32, RCH Papers.

61. Comparative Registration Table, 1949–50; Geographic Distribution Table, 1959–60.

other division of Tulane. Of the ten states furnishing the largest number of A&S students in 1949–50, five were outside the South. New York led the list with 118, while New Jersey added an additional 48. Massachusetts, Illinois, and Indiana each supplied over 20 students. By 1960 only three nonsouthern states remained in the top 10 category, and Texas now headed the list with 106 students. Although the number of A&S students who came from southern states other than Louisiana was slightly lower at the end of the decade than at the beginning, the 382 non-Louisiana southerners in 1950 represented only 22 percent of the A&S enrollment, as compared to nearly 32 percent for the 369 southern students in 1960.[62]

Although Newcomb lacked the initial geographic diversity caused by veteran enrollments in the College of Arts and Sciences, women's enrollments underwent an even more pronounced shift in their regional center of gravity. In both 1950 and 1960, eight of the ten states supplying the largest numbers of Newcomb students were located in the South, with Texas ranking first in both years. What changed was the number and proportion of students from southern states outside Louisiana. In 1950, Newcomb's 197 southern women represented 28 percent of the college's enrollment. A decade later, 379 southern students comprised nearly 41 percent of a Newcomb student body that was one-third larger.[63]

The preceding statistics leave little doubt as to the central tendency within male and female enrollment trends. If Tulane's undergraduate student body became less local during the 1950s, it also grew noticeably more southern. Regional culture may therefore deserve consideration alongside socioeconomic status, religion, intellectual attainment, and gender as an element shaping the character of undergraduate life during Tulane's metamorphosis from a commuter to a residential institution. As previously noted, the university's transformation from a collection of classrooms to a place where most students resided during the academic year began during World War II, with the provision of makeshift quarters for student-sailors in the V-12 program. A second step took place in 1946–47 with the acquisition, under federal auspices, of some 42 barracks-like buildings, which provided shelter for 296 veterans and their families as well as 216 single male students.

62. Ibid.
63. Ibid.

Although four of these structures were still housing students and faculty in the early 1960s, most had been demolished during the previous decade as the university constructed permanent dormitory facilities.[64]

Providing modern residential buildings for Tulane's increasingly non–New Orleanian student population required more than a decade of sustained construction activity. In 1949 the completion of Zemurray Hall, an athletic dormitory financed out of surplus gate receipts, inaugurated a fourteen-year sequence of increasingly ambitious projects to expand Tulane's housing capacity. Six new dormitories came on line between 1950 and 1960, including one for married students (Rosen House), four men's residences (Paterson House, Irby House, Phelps House, and Sharp Memorial Hall), and one women's residence (Johnston House). There were also major additions to two existing women's dormitories. These structures provided space for 191 married couples, 1,153 single men, and 321 women who joined a slightly larger number of women already housed in older Newcomb facilities.[65]

Although expansion would continue until 1963, it was clear by the mid-1950s that the "streetcar" phase of Tulane's existence was rapidly drawing to a close. As late as 1952 only about 600 of the 2,100 out-of-town students enrolled in all university divisions lived on campus. Newcomb women and married students vastly outnumbered the 100 or so male undergraduates in the newly opened Paterson House.[66] Three years later, in 1955, a total of 2,008 people were living on Tulane's campus. The resident population included some 900 married students, spouses, and children in the 296 wood-frame apartments originally built for veterans, and 642 undergraduate men and 466 Newcomb women who were housed almost entirely in permanent dormitory facilities. "A more extraordinary change in the style of a private university has seldom been effected in so short a time," observed the *New Orleans Times-Picayune*. If the six dormitories erected between 1949 and 1955 bore little architectural resemblance to traditional "halls of ivy," their presence seemed nonetheless to mark the university's tran-

64. *Tulane Bulletin*, series 48, no. 3 (March 1947): 7; ibid., no. 13 (November 1947): 84.
65. Tulane University Non-Statistical Profile, schedule 10 (16 January 1961): 27–8; Beatrice M. Field, "Potpourri: An Assortment of Tulane's People and Places," unpublished manuscript, Tulane University Library, pp. 82–96, provides an accurate synopsis of the construction and subsequent modification of all Tulane buildings. As of March 1955 Newcomb dormitories were filled to capacity with 380 students. See the Report on the Needs of Newcomb College for the Three Years Beginning with . . . 1955–56, p. 2.
66. BOA Minutes, 14 January 1952, item 4 of president's monthly report.

World War II barracks building. Residences for faculty and graduate students, ca. 1956.

sition from an urban commuter school to a "living community" and a "closer-bound unit."[67]

To the extent that Tulane constituted a single community in the mid-1950s, its collective identity had much to do with the university's widening separation, both fiscally and demographically, from the New Orleans environment—an irony apparently lost upon local journalistic enthusiasts. Within this framework, resident undergraduates began to exhibit a spirit of group awareness and cohesion that was most visible during episodes involving conflict between students and other groups within the academic world. One such incident took place in the autumn of 1954, when some 400–500 male occupants of the new dormitories carried out what was acknowledged to be the "first full-scale panty raid in the university's history." Touched off by the unexpected arrival of two undergraduate women outside a male dorm, the spontaneous affair involved considerable cooperation across gender lines, as Newcomb women performed exotic dances, chanted "go, go, go," and obligingly furnished a variety of undergarments to the male throng. Student solidarity was most apparent in the responses to New Orleans

67. Ibid., 12 October 1955, item 4 of president's monthly report; *New Orleans Times-Picayune*, 9 December 1955, in Tulane clipping scrapbooks.

police and campus authority figures. A typical encounter involved a psychology professor who accused the male undergraduates of behaving "like 3-year old kids" who should go back to their "lolly-pops." This plea for civic responsibility was cut short by a bucket of water cascading down from an upper story window. Earlier in the evening, other university officials had been similarly drenched after quelling a rock-throwing melee between students and police. Although no one went so far as to characterize the disturbance as a sign of institutional maturity, a distinct note of self-satisfaction crept into many undergraduate reactions. Tulane's male head cheerleader described the gathering as "perfectly respectable," a view shared by one Newcomb student, who believed the proceedings indicated growing "school spirit." Even university officials seemed to regard the event as something of a milestone, if only because it coincided with the newly imposed requirement that all out-of-town freshmen live on campus.[68]

Without exaggerating the significance of late adolescent high spirits, it is possible to recognize that the largely scripted behavior of boisterous undergraduate crowds was connected to a larger set of images and expectations concerning college life common to most white Americans of the postwar era. From the 1920s onward, as higher education became accessible to a larger and more diverse clientele, a range of alternate cultural categories developed within which students might establish individual identity and define their relationship to college faculty, administrators, and undergraduate peers. The oldest model was that of the college man (or woman), based upon a set of elitist social norms which placed heavy stress upon physical appearance, proper dress, interpersonal skills, and cultural conformity. In this model, the intellectual component of campus life was relegated to a secondary, if not a marginal, position.[69] At Tulane, the collegiate ideal found institutional embodiment in the fifteen to seventeen social fraternities and the ten sororities that comprised the Greek system of the 1950s. Both the male groups and their female counterparts perpetuated a somewhat diluted version of the traditional turn-of-the-century upper-class assumption

68. *New Orleans Times-Picayune*, 19 October 1954, in Tulane clipping scrapbooks; *New Orleans Item*, 19 October 1954.

69. Here and in the discussion of student subcultures that follows, we have borrowed heavily from the conceptualization of Helen Lefkowitz Horowitz's excellent monograph *Campus Life: Undergraduate Cultures from the End of the Eighteenth Century to the Present* (Chicago: University of Chicago Press, 1987).

that college was primarily a place to form lifelong friendships with people of acceptable breeding and social station. Instead of the informal cliques that had once developed around dormitory residences, boarding houses, or more exclusive eating clubs, Greek letter societies picked members through the highly regimented activities of rush week at the beginning of each fall semester. In essence, rush was a sequential process of human winnowing carried out through the giving or withholding of invitations to a series of social functions staged by each Greek organization. During private cut sessions, a single negative vote or blackball was usually sufficient to eliminate any candidate from further consideration. For naive or insecure freshmen the rush process could be psychologically bruising, and for all involved it ran the risk of fostering premature judgments about individuals or groups encountered under highly artificial circumstances.[70]

The Greek system loomed large at Tulane, although its influence was less pervasive than at some of the South's more legendary party schools. From a low of 963 students in 1954–55, fraternity membership rose to 1,085 in 1956–57 before falling back to 1,047 in 1959–60. During the same period, between 45 percent and 52 percent of undergraduate men joined fraternities, as compared with the approximately two-thirds of Newcomb women who pledged sororities.[71] Playing a central role in campus politics and monopolizing the leadership positions in many student organizations, the Greek system had long existed in a

70. Ibid., 39–51; Dan A. Oren, *Joining the Club: A History of Jews and Yale* (New Haven: Yale University Press, 1985), 17–24, 36–7, and esp. 80–1; David O. Levine, *The American College and the Culture of Aspiration, 1915–1940* (Ithaca: Cornell University Press, 1986), 120–2. On the mechanics of rush at Tulane, see Tulane Pan-Hellenic Council, *Guide to Fraternity Rushing at Tulane, 1958* and Newcomb College, *Rushees' Handbook, 1961–62*. Cf. "Fraternity Rushing," *Life* 41 (24 September 1956): 141–9, an illuminating blow-by-blow photojournalistic account of events at the University of Illinois, Urbana; see also, Beverly Lowry, "Blackballed," *Southern Magazine* 2 (September 1988): 19–22 for a poignant and psychologically insightful first-person account of sorority rush at the University of Mississippi in 1956.

71. Membership data compiled from annual lists of fraternity grade averages, 1946–47 to 1959–60, box 57, RCH Papers. Apparently the Newcomb College files containing detailed information on sorority membership and other facets of student life for the 1950s are no longer extant. In 1960, however, when Newcomb admitted a first-year class of 331 students, a total of 310 participated in rush (93.6 percent) and 216 (65.2 percent) pledged one of the college's nine sororities. In 1961 Newcomb's first-year class had 352 students; 308 participated in rush (87.5 percent) and 245 (69.6 percent) pledged a sorority. Newcomb Dean's Report, 1961–62, box 45, Herbert Eugene Longenecker Papers, Tulane University Archives (hereafter cited as HEL Papers); Panhellenic Evaluation Submitted by Newcomb Panhellenic Council, document accompanying letter of John H. Stibbs to Herbert Longenecker, 4 May 1966, box 61, HEL Papers.

state of tension with the university's academic and professional components. At Tulane, as elsewhere, those students who arrived at college with clearly defined vocational or professional aspirations were likely to find Greek-sponsored social activities both alluring and distracting. This was especially true in the College of Arts and Sciences, which prior to World War II had functioned mainly as an adjunct or feeder system for the Schools of Law, Medicine, Architecture, and Engineering.[72] As late as 1960, some 30 percent of premedical students and 10 percent of prelaw students spent only three years in the liberal arts division before transferring to professional school. Precisely how many of these undergraduates joined Greek organizations remains unclear, but some distanced themselves sufficiently from the collegiate syndrome to become de facto outsiders whose grimly calculating pursuit of high marks presented an ambiguous alternative to the hedonist's open disdain for academic effort. Commenting upon the phenomenon in 1959, Arts and Sciences dean William Peery reserved his sharpest censure for the college's premedical students, a group comprising one-third of the A&S enrollment. Relentless in their pursuit of the GPA necessary for admission to medical school, the young doctors-to-be struck Peery as "overcautious, ever calculating" and "too vocationally minded" to be "appreciative of the liberal-arts ideal."[73]

If utilitarian considerations led pre-professional students to take their studies seriously, the stimulus of sheer intellectual curiosity—coupled, at times, with a penchant for political and social activism—caused a small minority of students to define themselves in opposition to, rather than simply apart from, the collegiate-fraternity matrix. As will be seen in subsequent chapters, student radicals or rebels were present in small numbers at Tulane throughout the postwar era, becoming vocal during the late 1940s and considerably more muted during the silent generation of the 1950s. For present purposes it is enough

72. In 1954 Newcomb dean John R. Hubbard acknowledged that "until comparatively recently" the College of Arts and Sciences had functioned mainly as a "pre-professional [sic] school feeding its students into" the Schools of Medicine and Law. Hubbard believed, however, that since 1946 the preprofessional philosophy had been "sublimated to the true liberal arts concept." This conclusion is difficult to reconcile with A&S dean William Peery's frequent complaints about excessive and narrow vocationalism among prelaw and premedical students during the late 1950s. Newcomb Dean's Report, 1953–54, pp. 25–6; A&S Dean's Report, 1958–59, box 7, RCH Papers, 11.

73. A&S Dean's Report, 1960–61, box 45, HEL Papers, 13; A&S Dean's Report, 1958–59, p. 11 (quotations).

to acknowledge the existence of this small dissenting minority and to ask how, if at all, Tulane's 1958 shift to selective admissions may have influenced the mix of undergraduate subcultures. Evidence on the point is primarily inferential. At the beginning of the decade, Harris speculated that a combination of veteran influence and the "disquieting aftermath" of World War II had produced a more mature attitude among Tulane undergraduates, who seemed less inclined than students elsewhere to revert back to the immature behaviors of the 1920s.[74]

If the outlook of Tulane students did, in fact, depart from national norms, the difference probably had as much to do with geography and socioeconomic status as with the harsh realities of the cold war. Throughout the 1950s, Tulane's increasingly southern student body came primarily from middle-class households. Comprehensive statistical data collected by the admissions office beginning in 1958 revealed that about two-thirds of Tulane freshmen came from mid-level homes headed by parents employed in "managerial" positions. Roughly one-fourth of the students came from executive or professional families defined by the university as "upper class," while another eight percent were children of skilled or semiskilled laborers. The pattern was one likely to foster conservatism and conformity, if not maturity per se. To the extent that academic success depended upon socialization and peer group acceptance, the advantage at Tulane rested with urban, upper class students who made better grades than initially predicted on the basis of high school records and SAT scores, while rural working class students performed worse than expected. Apparently no socioeconomic assessment of fraternity and sorority membership was ever attempted, but the dues, initiation fees, and other costs of participation in Greek life must certainly have eliminated at least some of the late 1950s scholarship students, whose cumulative SAT scores no doubt exceeded their parents' monthly income.[75]

If one were to look only at the 109-point increase in aggregate standardized test scores between 1958 and 1963, it would be tempting to conclude that Tulane undergraduates had moved appreciably closer to the university's ideal of responsible young adults engaged in the coop-

74. *President's Report*, 1951–52, pp. 14–5.

75. Tulane University and Newcomb College data for 1960–61 submitted to the College Entrance Examination Board, box 10, RCH Papers (quotations); Cliff W. Wing Jr., "The Effect of Certain Cultural Background Factors on the Prediction of Student Grades in College," *Research Reports*, College Entrance Examination Board, 1960.

erative pursuit of knowledge with faculty mentors. Several factors cast doubt on the idea that higher SAT scores and secondary school class standing automatically resulted in greater maturity or a more intellectual campus environment. First, and most obviously, one must recognize that selective admissions produced no decline in the popularity of the Greek system. Indeed, dormitories opened three days early to accommodate rush, an activity that sometimes threatened to overshadow the academic program in its pre-enrollment visibility. Official publications, such as the Newcomb *Rushees' Handbook*, advised entering women that rush was a "serious business . . . not to be undertaken lightly." Men received similar admonitions, together with guidelines for dress and etiquette that were provided in considerably greater detail to Newcomb women. (At some rush parties, "cotton, church, or date dresses" might be worn; at other functions only "tea dresses," but no hats.)[76]

Tulane officials acknowledged privately that the Greek system competed with other elements of the university for the allegiance of impressionable undergraduates. In 1956, for example, Hubbard refused, despite a critical shortage of dormitory space, to abandon Newcomb's longstanding prohibition against students residing in sorority houses, all of which were located off campus. Pointing to the historic division in Newcomb's "body politic" between local students and those from out of town, Hubbard concluded that establishing "yet another distinct element" in off-campus sorority houses was "bound to be divisive."[77] Male fraternities, which did provide many of their members with rooms in off-campus chapter houses, posed an even greater challenge to the ideal of an undergraduate community imbued with institutional loyalty and academic values. Throughout the last half of the 1950s, the all-fraternity GPA hovered between 2.27 and 2.34, a low C that fell about one-tenth of a point below the all-men's average. No one seriously claimed that fraternities nurtured the life of the mind, and probably few people were surprised that between 1955 and 1960 the excuse of having "devoted too much time to fraternities" remained a

76. Mean SAT scores for freshmen rose from 1,018 in 1958 to 1,127 in 1963. *A Supplement to a Proposal to the Ford Foundation from Tulane University, September 1963,* 34; Newcomb College, *Rushees' Handbook, 1961–62,* 2, 12, 13 (quotations); Tulane Pan-Hellenic Council, *Guide to Fraternity Rushing at Tulane, 1958,* "Tips for Rushees," item 7.

77. John R. Hubbard to Rufus C. Harris, undated letter written between 4 and 10 October 1956, in BOA Minutes, 10 October 1956, item 22 of president's monthly report.

standard theme in the petitions of students seeking to avoid academic exclusion from the College of Arts and Sciences. Intellectual activity received little emphasis in the fraternity houses per se, if one may judge by the stream of complaints from neighbors protesting obscene movies, drunkenness, improper attire, rowdyism, and excessive noise running the gamut from "Texas yells" to profane screams.[78]

From 1949 onward, supervision of Tulane's fraternities rested mainly in the hands of physics professor Karlem Riess, himself a veteran of the Greek system. Riess promoted a number of worthwhile reforms, including the substitution of community service projects for pre-initiation "hell week," efforts at improved scholarship, and the reduction of fraternity influence over campus politics. Riess also had the unenviable task of personally visiting all fraternity parties to check on the presence of chaperons and the maintenance of proper decorum. Most visits were relatively uneventful, but on some occasions his arrival evoked responses that were sharply at odds with the "marked trend . . . toward considerations of scholarship and citizenship" that one local journalist discovered among Tulane fraternities. In September 1955, for example, the members of Delta Kappa Epsilon, whose alumni were conspicuous on the Board of Administrators, reacted in a most unscholarly fashion to Riess's routine inspection of an unchaperoned party by drenching the professor from behind with "a large amount of liquid smelling like a mixture of beer and punch." The incident resulted in a fifty-dollar fine and one year's probation for the politically well-connected group.[79]

Whatever Tulane's Greek system may have revealed about the strength of collegiate values among 1950s undergraduates, the university's own conduct regulations took for granted that students would be

78. Annual lists of fraternity grade averages, 1954–55 to 1959–60, box 57, RCH Papers; A&S Dean's Report, 1960–61, p. 10 (first quotation); Karlem Riess to Rufus C. Harris, 16 December 1955, box 57, RCH Papers; "Obscene Movie Seized," *New Orleans Times-Picayune*, 16 December 1955, p. 32; C. C. Kelleher to Rufus C. Harris, 25 November 1955, box 57, RCH Papers (second quotation); Kelleher to John H. Stibbs, 10 September 1956, box 57, RCH Papers. In his letter to Stibbs, an obviously exasperated Kelleher suggested that Tulane's fraternities be confined "under the Stadium or in your SLUMS . . . [with] an ex-Marine top-sergeant to keep them in line."

79. *New Orleans Item*, 3 October 1956 (first quotation); Karlem Riess to Rufus C. Harris, 15 September 1956, box 57, RCH Papers (second quotation). Following an earlier incident of alleged misconduct by the same fraternity, Board member Joseph McCloskey had advised Harris that "[a]s a loyal member of DKE I know that this cannot be true of our boys." McCloskey to Harris, 27 October 1952, box 57, RCH Papers.

likely to act in ways that adults regarded as immature. Like virtually all other universities at the time, Tulane embraced the moral and legal doctrine of in loco parentis, and assumed the role of a deputy parent responsible for the welfare and correct behavior of the student-child. It was primarily in this spirit that students, as institutional dependents, were made parties to a highly attenuated form of self-government involving the implementation of rules handed down by higher authority. Similar in loco parentis assumptions lay behind the rapid expansion of extracurricular programs and facilities for recreation and health care. As Harris expressed it, Tulane's transformation from a commuter school to a major residential campus involved an increased obligation to see that undergraduates were "fully managed and kept out of trouble." Harris made the observation in reference to the need for a university center; he did not believe that the university could, or should, seek to regulate students' conduct outside the campus. But the logic of dependency permeated the entire body of rules and procedures governing the personal lives and routine activities of resident undergraduates.[80]

Predictably, the burden of regulation fell most heavily upon lower division women in Newcomb College. All students living in Newcomb dormitories held automatic membership in the Resident Government Association, which through its various elected councils made rules and imposed penalties "with the consent of the Counselor to Women and the Faculty Committee on Student Welfare." Generally speaking, the regulatory noose became tighter as the number of nonlocal students increased and residential facilities expanded. More than three hundred Newcomb students from New Orleans lived beyond the reach of the dorm council's authority, and for a time during the mid-1950s, the same was true of the sizable contingent of out-of-town students who stayed in local "approved boarding houses" because dormitory space was unavailable. Numbering sixty students in 1955, this group swelled to more than one hundred by 1956–57. With the opening of William Preston Johnston House in 1958, however, nearly all non–New Orleans students were housed on campus and brought under effective day-to-day scrutiny.[81]

80. BOA Minutes, 12 October 1955, item 6 of president's monthly report.

81. *The Newcomber, 1959–60,* 93, pamphlet in collection of Newcomb College Center for Research on Women, Tulane University (first quotation); Newcomb Dean's Report, 1953–54, p. 1; Newcome Dean's Report, 1956–57, p. 3; Report on the Needs of Newcomb College for the Three Years Beginning with . . . 1955–56, box 30, RCH Papers, 2 (second quotation).

These changing conditions were reflected in the Resident Government Association's constitution and bylaws, which underwent six separate revisions between 1950 and 1959, primarily for the purpose of closing loopholes in earlier restrictions. By the end of the decade, Newcomb freshmen faced an intricate web of rules governing curfew hours, procedures for signing in and out, chaperon requirements, dining room etiquette, and innumerable other details, all subject to a graduated scale of punishments that began with a simple "report," escalated to a more serious "call-down," and culminated with a "campus" that prohibited the recipient from leaving the Tulane-Newcomb grounds or "having dates, social association, or communications with men." Filling seventeen closely printed pages, the conduct rules embodied social and moral premises that would have been familiar to most Newcomb students, particularly those from Louisiana and other southern states. Only the occasional concession to the festival culture of the surrounding urban environment offered a hint of New Orleans's forbidden fruit. Carnival balls, for example, merited special curfew arrangements, as did the "approved clubs in which there is dancing and a late floor show," requiring a curfew extension until 2:30 A.M.[82]

The Newcomb regulations provided an extreme example of what Arts and Sciences dean William Peery frankly described as "paternalism" toward Tulane undergraduates. Although male students suffered few of the restrictions placed upon Newcomb women, Peery was concerned about the inconsistency of trying to promote intellectual maturity among undergraduates who were surrounded by rules and policies calculated to breed dependence. In Peery's view, official procedures that relieved students of responsibility for making and correcting their own mistakes ran counter to the goal of creating an undergraduate community bound together by intellectual values and the pursuit of excellence. Paternalism, in other words, ranked alongside the fraternity system, intercollegiate athletics, urban influences, and narrow professional school loyalties as a factor contributing to the chronic "lack of unity" that plagued the Arts and Sciences student body.[83]

Peery's admittedly incomplete list of divisive cultural forces serves

82. *The Newcomber 1959–60*, 105–7 (first–fourth quotations), 99 (fifth quotation).
83. A&S Dean's Report, 1958–59, p. 11; A&S Dean's Report, 1960–61, pp. 11–3.

to highlight the difficulty of generalizing about undergraduate subcultures. How students experienced Tulane depended in part upon who they were: whether they were male or female, local or nonlocal, rich or poor, southern or nonsouthern, Jewish (like 9.5 percent of their peers in 1955) or gentile, Catholic (like 37 percent of the 1955 student body) or Protestant. Beyond a certain point, of course, the experience of each individual student was, by definition, unique. But if it is inappropriate to speak of a single Tulane experience common to all students, one may at least return to the question of predominance among cultural alternatives. At the beginning of the 1950s, Tulane was nearing the end of a postwar interlude during which the singleminded pragmatism of career-oriented male veterans had briefly overshadowed the dominance of collegiate norms. Collegiate values survived the veterans' challenge and gained ground throughout most of the decade, although their advance may have been slowed by the late fifties influx of National Merit Scholarship finalists and the appearance of honors and independent study courses in several departments in the wake of selective admissions.[84]

Substantial gains in mean SAT scores left administrators dissatisfied that Tulane, in 1961, had not yet overtaken a major regional rival like Duke. But some students were more impressed by the changes that higher admissions requirements had begun to produce. One Arts and Sciences senior, clearly a spokesman for the old order, lamented the scarcity of "leadership material" for student government, a problem he attributed to the director of admissions' perverse assumption "that a good student community can be built solely around the intellectual type student." Rejecting the premise out of hand, the writer cautioned naive administrators that student government could not "make a leader out of an intellect" in the short span of college life.[85] What may stand as the most convincing internal assessment of student responses to Tulane during the late 1950s came from John A. Mmahat, A&S student body president for 1957–58. Disturbed by the alleged influence of certain fraternities over the selection of members for one of two undergraduate leadership societies (an organization from which he as

84. BOA Minutes, 18 May 1955; A&S Dean's Report, 1960–61, p. 4. In 1960–61 a total of eighteen A&S students registered for independent study projects in seven departments.

85. A&S Dean's Report, 1960–61, pp. 1–2; President's Report, Tulane University Student Body 1958–59, box 32, RCH Papers, 18 (quotations).

well as the student body vice president had been excluded), Mmahat presented a thoughtful, if somewhat jaundiced, analysis of how sentiments of inclusion or alienation actually developed among typical undergraduates. Foreign students exhibited what Mmahat described as a "self-imposed isolationism," which was compounded by housing policies that smacked of segregation. Very few foreign students had American roommates, and "for some reason a large percentage of the foreign students always wound up in the oldest, stuffiest, and least appealing of all the dormitories." Change on all counts seemed overdue.[86]

Turning to the domestic scene, Mmahat emphasized that for most students involvement in extracurricular activities began with the Greek system. Orientation week was a confusing experience during which freshmen were "indoctrinated into university life" without coming into meaningful contact with most student groups. Upon entering the Greek system, however, students were "encouraged" to participate in extracurricular activities and easily joined groups that "no longer seem unfriendly when their frat brothers or sorority sisters personally bring them to the organization meetings."[87]

The preceding comments cast some doubt upon Newcomb's official assurance that women who remained outside sororities were not considered "different." But the central point of Mmahat's critique looked beyond the Greek system to the modern university itself, with its multiple constituencies, bureaucratic structure, research emphasis, and growing impersonality. In a passage that anticipated the arguments advanced by student activists at Berkeley and other schools during the mid-1960s, Mmahat stressed the absence of community in an environment where only fraternity and sorority members "developed a sense of 'belonging[,]' and then it is not really a sense of belonging at Tulane, but to their individual fraternities." Convinced that only a small percentage of students ever felt themselves to be "a real part of Tulane," Mmahat believed that for most undergraduates the university was "a cold empty place in a big city that has no time for individuals, only for members. No time to worry about John Smith's personal development, only time enough to schedule placement tests and stage assemblies at which no one knows if John is present or not; indeed, no one is even in-

86. John Mmahat, *Informal* [*sic*] Open Report to the President of the University by John A. Mmahat, Student Body President, 1957–58, box 32, RCH Papers, 22.

87. Ibid., 7.

terested if he is there." Coming from the elected president of the student body, these remarks can scarcely be dismissed as the grumblings of an alienated outsider. Whatever the validity of its specific details, Mmahat's critique suggested that both the university and its students were changing.[88]

88. Newcomb College, *Rushees' Handbook, 1961–62*, 7 (first quotation); Mmahat, *Informal* [*sic*] Open Report, 7–8 (all subsequent quotations).

2

THE PRICE OF THE TICKET
Academic Freedom, Cold War Anti-Communism, and the Pursuit of
National Security

Tulane's post-1945 quest for national stature coincided with one of
the most politically turbulent periods in the history of American
higher education. The onset of the cold war, with its pervasive emphasis on the political beliefs of private citizens, encouraged a spirit of national intolerance that played upon popular distrust of intellectuals
and fear of ideas that were unconventional. Because universities were
the institutions most closely identified with the life of the mind, they
soon became tempting targets for ambitious politicians and anti-
Communist zealots. Efforts to exploit popular prejudices gave rise to a
paradoxical situation in which Americans paid homage to the value of
a college degree even as they demanded that professors sign loyalty
oaths or appear before state and federal tribunals to answer questions
about their politics, personal lives, and past associations. Although
the number of college faculty members singled out for such treatment
was quite small, the entire professoriat was affected by the climate of
fear and mistrust that resulted from inquisitorial proceedings. In the
South, where white supremacists seized the Communist issue as a tool
to discredit civil rights supporters, the educational inroads of militant
anti-Communism left a permanent mark upon regional academic life.[1]

1. A comprehensive study of the impact of white supremacist anti-Communism upon southern higher education is badly needed. The best single account of academia's response to the cold
war, Ellen W. Schrecker, *No Ivory Tower: McCarthyism and the Universities* (New York:
Oxford University Press, 1986) pays little attention to the South or to regional differences.
Academic freedom at Vanderbilt during the 1950s receives thorough discussion in Conkin, *Gone
with the Ivy*, 502–14. Conkin is sensitive to the many symbolic meanings of Communism for

Paranoia about communism 40's-50's.

Tulane first became embroiled in cold war controversy during the election of 1948, when law professor Mitchell Franklin agreed to serve as the Louisiana campaign chairman for Progressive Party presidential candidate Henry A. Wallace. Franklin's decision to champion the cause of a once prominent New Dealer whom President Truman had denounced as a "parlor pink" drew Tulane into the anti-Communist debate and allowed local critics to attack the university for its supposed sympathy toward "un-American" ideas and activities. Such allegations were not entirely new. In order to place the events of 1948 at Tulane in perspective, it is necessary to look briefly at developments during the previous decade, when the university first confronted the issue of academic freedom in a context analogous to that of the postwar era.

Like other American colleges, Tulane was profoundly affected by the onset of the Great Depression. New Orleans's political and business leaders had been placed on the defensive by the demagogic tactics of Governor Huey Long, and the university came under close scrutiny during the 1930s from local watchdogs who expected Tulanians to present a solid front against challenges to the economic status quo. In

whites in the cold war South. Another aspect of McCarthyism's impact on southern universities is discussed in William A. Link, "William Friday and the North Carolina Speaker Ban Crisis: 1963–1968," *North Carolina Historical Review* 72 (April 1995): 198–228. Link's *William Friday: Power, Purpose, and American Higher Education* (Chapel Hill: University of North Carolina Press, 1995) provides additional context on academic freedom issues. A thorough assessment of southern anti-Communism must begin with the red-baiting episodes of the 1930s. See Robert P. Ingalls, "Antiradical Violence in Birmingham during the 1930s," *Journal of Southern History* 47 (November 1981): 521–44; William V. Moore, "Civil Liberties in Louisiana: The Louisiana League for the Preservation of Constitutional Rights," *Louisiana History* 31 (winter 1990): 59–81. On the cold war's general impact in the South, see Anthony P. Dunbar, *Against the Grain: Southern Radicals and Prophets, 1929–1959* (Charlottesville: University Press of Virginia, 1981), 225–58; John A. Salmond, "'The Great Southern Commie Hunt': Aubrey Williams, the Southern Conference Educational Fund, and the Internal Security Subcommittee," *South Atlantic Quarterly* 77 (autumn 1978): 433–52. The most thorough local study of southern anti-Communism is Don E. Carleton, *Red Scare! Right-Wing Hysteria, Fifties Fanaticism, and Their Legacy in Texas* (Austin: Texas Monthly Press, 1984). Also useful are Irwin Kilbaner, "The Travail of Southern Radicals: The Southern Conference Educational Fund, 1946–1976," *Journal of Southern History* 49 (May 1983): 179–202; Pamela Jean Turner, "Civil Rights and Anti-Communism in New Orleans, 1946–1965" (M.A. thesis, University of New Orleans, 1981). On the cold war's obliteration of southern support of neo-Wilsonian liberal internationalism, see Tennant S. McWilliams, *The New South Faces the World: Foreign Affairs and the Southern Sense of Self, 1877–1950* (Baton Rouge: Louisiana State University Press, 1988), chap. 6. On the upper-class anti-Communist zealotry that characterized one southern organization concerned with Latin American affairs, see Arthur E. Carpenter, "Social Origins of Anticommunism: The Information Council of the Americas," *Louisiana History* 30 (spring 1989): 117–43.

1936, amid growing labor militance on the New Orleans waterfront, several Tulane faculty members drew criticism for their off-campus political activities. The 1936 charges originated with the Louisiana Coalition of Patriotic Societies, an umbrella federation of veterans' groups and conservative genealogical societies, such as the Daughters of the American Revolution. The coalition's basic viewpoint was shared by local commercial and civic groups, including the Young Men's Business Club in New Orleans. Strongly nativist in tone, the coalition sought to "keep America American" through measures ranging from immigration restrictions in the interest of "racial and political solidarity" to attacks on those who advocated policies deemed radical or "subversive." Led in the mid-1930s by Dr. Emmett L. Irwin, a prominent local physician who would reappear as a leading segregationist in the 1950s, the coalition singled out four Tulane professors—historians Mary Allen and Mack W. Swearingen, sociologist Harlan C. Gilmore, and political scientist Herman C. Nixon—for indictment on charges of un-Americanism.[2]

Specific allegations varied from case to case, but of the four individuals named, Nixon unquestionably had the highest political profile. A scholar-activist who had broken with the backward-looking Vanderbilt "agrarians" after contributing a chapter to the 1929 antimodernist manifesto *I'll Take My Stand*, Nixon had emerged by the mid-1930s as one of the South's leading academic liberals. As early as 1931 he had declared in print that "aside from a few carpetbag reformers and native hangers-on," the South suffered from a severe shortage of both "philosophical radicals" and "intellectual liberals." In the absence of sustained internal criticism, Nixon argued, the region's gradual shift from a plantation to an industrial way of life had involved little more than "a change from one conservative outlook to another." Like his close friend William Terry Couch at the University of North Carolina Press, Nixon believed professors should take an active part in southern politics and seek to liberate their region from a laissez-faire "philosophy of progress that is not distinctly divorced from exploitation."

2. *St. Louis Post-Dispatch*, 22 November 1936, clipping in box 14, RCH Papers (all quotations); William V. Moore, "Civil Liberties in Louisiana," esp. 60–2; Objectives and Purposes of the Louisiana Coalition of Patriotic Societies, Inc., in the Harold Newton Lee Papers, Tulane University Library; Dorian Hastings, "Civil Rights Besieged: The Young Men's Business Club and the Southern Conference for Human Welfare in New Orleans, 1946–1948" (M.A. thesis, University of New Orleans, 1998), 13–4; Richard Gid Powers, *Not without Honor: The History of American Anticommunism* (New York: Free Press, 1995), 79–80.

In 1935 he chaired the liberal Southern Policy Association, a fledgling effort to mobilize political support for the New Deal and to urge federal aid for education, economic assistance for sharecroppers, legislative reapportionment, and repeal of the poll tax. Two years later Nixon helped found the much larger and more militant Southern Conference on Human Welfare, which espoused all of the preceding causes in an explicitly interracial context.[3]

At the local level Nixon and Swearingen took an active interest in labor and civil liberties conflicts in New Orleans and the surrounding parishes. Largely because of their efforts to protect the legal rights of labor organizers who faced arrest and physical abuse at the hands of local police, the two professors were portrayed as radical co-conspirators by their accusers.[4] Newcomb College historian Mary Allen, a self-professed socialist who taught a course on modern Russia, was attacked for visiting the USSR frequently and for being friendly with W. B. Binkley, the southern district organizer for the International Labor Defense and the New Orleans secretary of the Communist Party. The coalition also charged Allen with helping organize a local chapter of the League Against War and Fascism, and with promoting a series of films that depicted "Red Russia" in a favorable light while seeking to justify Soviet rulers in "murdering the bourgeoisis [*sic*]."[5]

3. H. C. Nixon, "The Changing Political Philosophy of the South," *Annals of the American Academy of Political and Social Science* 153 (January 1931): 246–50 (all quotations). For a detailed discussion of Nixon's political views and activities during his tenure at Tulane, see Sarah Newman Shouse, *Hillbilly Realist: Herman Clarence Nixon of Possum Trot* (Tuscaloosa: University of Alabama Press, 1986), chaps. 3–6. For additional context, see Daniel J. Singal, *The War Within: From Victorian to Modernist Thought in the South, 1919–1945* (Chapel Hill: University of North Carolina Press, 1982), 288–91; John M. Mathews, "Dissenters and Reformers: Some Southern Liberals between the World Wars," in *Developing Dixie: Modernization in a Traditional Society*, eds. Winfred B. Moore, Joseph F. Tripp, and Lyon G. Tyler Jr. (Westport, Conn.: Greenwood Press, 1988), 167–78, esp. 172–3.

4. *St. Louis Post-Dispatch*, 22 November 1936; Report of Special Committee [of the Board of Administrators] Appointed on 12 November 1936 to Investigate the Subject Matter of the Communication of the Louisiana Coalition of Patriotic Societies Inc., ca. 23 December 1936, box 14, RCH Papers (hereafter cited as Special Committee Report). Swearingen's bantering quip that Thomas Jefferson had favored a revolution every twenty years apparently gave rise to the allegation that Swearingen sanctioned the preaching of revolution.

5. Special Committee Report (quotations); *St. Louis Post-Dispatch*, 22 November 1936; Robin D. G. Kelley, *Hammer and Hoe: Alabama Communists in the Great Depression* (Chapel Hill: University of North Carolina Press, 1990), 129; Neil R. McMillen, *The Citizens' Council: Organized Resistance to the Second Reconstruction, 1954–1964* (Urbana: University of Illinois Press, 1971), 67, 292.

Whatever its immediate origins, the 1936 attack upon Nixon, Swearingen, Allen, and Gilmore was part of a larger national phenomenon that began with anti-Communist legislative probes the previous year at the Universities of Wisconsin and Chicago and culminated with the far more serious Rapp-Coudert committee hearings in 1940–42. The Rapp-Coudert investigation, which is often cited as a precursor of McCarthyism, resulted in the dismissal or resignation of some thirty instructors in the New York City higher education system, where Communists had gained control of American Federation of Teachers Local 537.[6] The sensational atmosphere surrounding anti-leftist investigations elsewhere in the nation, together with the ongoing reality of racial and labor unrest in New Orleans, provided the backdrop for Tulane's official inquiry into the conduct of its accused professors. Lacking any clear precedents or fixed procedures for adjudicating charges of professorial misconduct, the Board of Administrators in early November 1936 appointed a six-man committee to investigate the charges and to recommend appropriate action. There followed a month and a half of deliberations, including four closed hearings, on the charges against Swearingen and Allen. Although the committee described Mary Allen as "lacking in judgment," and believed that Swearingen had, in fact, committed "certain indiscretions" in public speeches, the lapses seemed to call for "no more than this comment" in order to insure that the mistakes "will not be repeated." In the end all charges against the two were dismissed.[7] The Board dismissed charges against Gilmore and Nixon without even requiring a formal hearing. In the case of Gilmore, whose only infraction consisted of associating with his three suspect colleagues, dismissal of the charges was a foregone conclusion. The Board's quick exoneration of Nixon, however, reflected a genuine concern for faculty rights, reinforced by an awareness that the outspoken professor had the potential to become a formidable adversary. Far from being cowed by right-wing allegations, Nixon quickly enlisted the aid of a journalistic ally at the *St. Louis Post-Dispatch* and began to mount an effective counterattack against both the Louisiana Coalition of Patriotic Societies and the New Orleans political establishment. A protracted hearing on the issues in Nixon's case raised the likelihood

6. Schrecker, *No Ivory Tower*, 69–71, 75–83.
7. Dyer, *Tulane*, 222–3; Special Committee Report, 4 (first quotation), 2 (all subsequent quotations).

of additional adverse publicity, a prospect that the Board of Administrators' investigating committee could scarcely have relished.[8]

If the Board stopped well short of endorsing militant activism on the part of Tulane faculty members, its decision helped clarify precisely what did, and did not, constitute academic freedom as the Board understood it. On March 1, 1937, only two days after being offered the Tulane presidency, Law School dean Rufus Harris received a lengthy communication from the elderly Board member Walker B. Spencer, which set forth a "concurring opinion" on the previous year's deliberations over faculty rights. Although Spencer had voted to exonerate Nixon, Swearingen, and Allen, he was anxious for the president-elect to know that concern existed about apparent excesses in faculty independence. Having concluded that Tulane's various faculties "ran a bit wild" during and immediately after President Dinwiddie's fatal illness, Spencer urged the Board of Administrators to adopt a set of eight guidelines on academic conduct as part of the official disposition of the 1936 subversion charges. Specifically he sought to prohibit faculty members from advocating any form of government that ran counter to the basic principles of the U.S. Constitution, which in his view included an unfettered "right of acquisition and disposition of private property and the sanctity thereof," as well as an absolute commitment to the "limitation of federal powers within bound[s] consistent with then [i.e., originally] existing conditions." Spencer believed the Board should recognize academic freedom "within proper bounds" while at the same time proscribing the teaching or advocacy, even in private, of Communism, fascism, or any other subversive doctrine, including "revolution" and "industrial strikes designed to overthrow or paralyze our Federal and State governments." As he advised Tulane's incoming president, "Give your professors the right of individual opinion, but I think you and the Administrators have a right to put a reasonable limitation upon their right of teaching in the University."[9]

Although death removed Spencer from the Board in 1941, elements of the viewpoint he espoused lingered into the postwar era.[10] Even be-

---

8. *St. Louis Post-Dispatch*, 22 November 1936, clipping in box 9, RCH Papers.

9. Walker B. Spencer to Rufus C. Harris, 1 March 1937 (first and sixth quotations), Spencer to Board of Administrators, ca. 22 December 1936, p. 2 (second–fifth quotations), box 14, RCH Papers.

10. Dyer, *Tulane*, 314. Dyer praised Spencer's 1936 recommendations as "statesmanlike," and ignored the restrictive implications of Spencer's position.

fore the United States entered World War II, the basic outline of the university's defensive response to cold war pressures had begun to take shape. In 1940, both President Harris and Law School dean Paul Brosman found it necessary to issue public statements after congressional candidate T. Hale Boggs, a Tulane graduate and recent secretary of the university's alumni association, was accused of being "a dyed-in-the-wool communist who loves Stalin and Red Russia." In a smear campaign that offered voters the alternative of "Americanism and [Paul] Maloney or Communism and Boggs," the latter's support of the American Student Union at Tulane during 1936–37 became the basis for wild allegations of leftist radicalism. Although Boggs categorically denied that he had belonged to the ASU or had taken the Oxford Pledge against military service, the charges inevitably reflected badly on both the candidate and his alma mater. The ASU was, quite literally, a popular front organization formed through the 1935 merger of delegates from the (Communist) National Student League and the (socialist) Student League for Industrial Democracy, a fact known on Tulane's campus in 1935. Boggs participated in events surrounding the attempted organization of a campus chapter of the ASU in 1936, apparently viewing the matter as part of his ongoing campaign for the construction of a student center. At one preliminary gathering he was one of four speakers who "explained the purposes and platform of the organization," confining his remarks to the economic benefits of student organization while other speakers discussed the group's antiwar program.[11] Aware that the charges against Boggs were groundless but undoubtedly anxious to keep Communism and the student peace movement from becoming a political issue, President Harris released a carefully worded statement that made no mention of the ASU but praised Boggs as a "campus leader" who "fought vigorously for democratic ideals" and "never engaged in anything which would approach un-American activity." Boggs's attitude, Harris noted rather pointedly, had always been one of "co-operation with university officials . . . for the improvement of the institution."[12]

11. *New Orleans Item*, 29 August 1940, p. 1 (first quotation); ibid., 28 August 1940, p. 1 for Boggs's denial; Jerry P. Sanson, "Reflections of Reform, Shadows of War, and a Portent of Things to Come: The 1940 Louisiana Congressional Elections," *Louisiana History* 33 (fall 1992): 341–61 (second quotation); Harvey Kleher, *The Heyday of American Communism: The Depression Decade* (New York: Basic Books, 1984), 309–17; Tulane *Hullabaloo*, 11 December 1936, p. 1 (third quotation) and 18 December 1936, p. 1.

12. *New Orleans Item*, 1 September 1940, p. 1 (all quotations). Several days earlier Brosman

The events of 1936–40 sent a clear message to Tulane faculty about the nature and implied limits of acceptable academic dissent. The university was clearly prepared to defend itself against external threats, including the more extreme manifestations of right-wing fanaticism. Faculty members might avail themselves of institutional protection by exercising sober judgment, avoiding "indiscretions," and generally behaving in a manner that would enhance or at least not detract from Tulane's public stature. In effect, dissenting intellectuals were being asked to place institutional welfare ahead of individual rights and to engage in what amounted to self-censorship when discussing controversial issues. There was, of course, nothing new in the idea that academic freedom required professors to divorce scholarship from propaganda and to avoid using their faculty affiliations in a reckless or irresponsible manner. In 1915 these principles had constituted part of the professional orthodoxy included in the founding document of the American Association of University Professors. Moreover, many of the prerogatives that college faculties managed to acquire during the next quarter century rested upon the willingness of individual scholars to identify their own interests with those of the administration of particular schools, as well as with the guild structure of the various academic disciplines. The resulting pattern of cooperation between scholars and academic administrators enhanced the stature of college teaching in the eyes of the general public but provided little genuine autonomy for American professors, as the heavy-handed suppression of academic dissent during World War I made abundantly clear.[13]

In pre–World War II New Orleans, Tulane faculty members and administrators had ample reason to make common cause against external critics. The interests of both groups were threatened when faculty conduct became the subject of broad-brush accusations that were rooted in intolerance for unconventional thought and antagonism toward the spirit of critical inquiry. Early in 1937 *New Orleans Item* writer Marshall Ballard provided an example of the gulf separating town from gown in an editorial that was nominally supportive of free speech and the decision to exonerate Tulane's accused professors. Believing that

---

had assured the public that Boggs's record at Tulane would "bear inspection from anyone." Ibid., 27 August 1940, p. 4.

13. Schrecker, *No Ivory Tower*, 18–23; Carol S. Gruber, *Mars and Minerva: World War One and the Uses of Higher Learning in America* (Baton Rouge: Louisiana State University Press, 1975), chap. 5.

college teachers should present "every conflicting line of thought and practice" to students in introductory classes, Ballard proceeded to caricature those professors who fell short of this ideal. Objectionable academics ostensibly sorted themselves into two distinct types. One, the "small, smart-alecky teacher," sought to gain "juvenile admiration" by being self-consciously "different" and "'peculiar.'" In the second category of academic offender, one found "the zealot type," whose obsession with a single viewpoint amounted to propaganda. A "jellybrain" of the latter variety might be expected to canonize the "most idiotic abominations of the cubists and surrealists," while equating the esthetically true and beautiful with the "scratches, scrawls, and raw colors on the walls of prehistoric Mayan temples or Egyptian pyramids." Both the smart aleck and the zealot seemed to gravitate toward disciplines such as history, economics, and sociology, as well as the field of art.[14]

Editorials that made academic freedom contingent upon adherence to cultural orthodoxy laid the groundwork for a more explicitly ideological formulation of the same argument by F. Edward Hébert, a local journalist and future U.S. Representative whose congressional district would include part of New Orleans. In an April 1940 speech to the Southern Association of Colleges and Secondary Schools, Hébert declared that the greatest offender against democracy's traditions and ideals was none other than the "sinister and dangerous . . . professor who sets himself up in his own little world as the last authority on his subject." Having attended Tulane from 1920–24 without receiving a degree, Hébert seemed unimpressed by the value of formal academic credentials. Echoing Ballard's 1937 editorial, Hébert lashed out with particular vehemence at the "smart-aleck type of professor" who was protected by "an armor of degrees a yard long" and was "drenched in the superiority of his own importance and intellect." No admirer of the modernist intellectual temperament, Hébert deplored the influence of scholarly skeptics who not only took "fiendish delight" in destroying the cherry tree legend and other patriotic myths but who also exhibited a dangerous predilection to "love the abstract and abhor the concrete." Instead of teaching "theoretical panaceas" for the solution of all governmental ills, "you professors should instruct your students in

14. "Tulane and Sedition," *New Orleans Item*, 20 January 1937, clipping in box 14, RCH Papers.

the art of good citizenship," Hébert admonished the assembled educators. In the future congressman's view, American democracy contained no serious flaws "except the liberality which permits the planting of germs of dissension and unrest" in impressionable young minds.[15]

The willingness of local politicians to seek votes through appeals to grass roots anti-intellectualism discouraged many Tulane faculty from championing unpopular causes. Although the campus remained open to free expression and provided forums for a surprisingly broad range of dissenting viewpoints during the 1930s, genuine radicalism had no more than a tiny constituency even among student orators and journalists.[16] At the faculty level, a defensive mentality rooted in the need for moderate allies became the distinguishing feature of a cautious approach to social reform, which enjoyed at least tacit sanction from university authorities. In the years between the Nixon affair and the general election of 1948, most faculty liberals channeled their energies into what was officially an off-campus organization, the Louisiana League for the Preservation of Constitutional Rights. Founded in February 1937 amid the controversy over outside attacks upon Nixon, Swearingen, Gilmore, and Allen, the league helped define the content and meaning of academic freedom without ever addressing the issue in a direct fashion.

From its inception the league was a thoroughly respectable coalition

15. F. Edward Hébert, "A Layman Looks at Your Profession," *Southern Association Quarterly* 4 (August 1940): 399–408 (first quotation p. 403, all subsequent quotations p. 404); F. Edward Hébert and John McMillen, *"Last of the Titans": The Life and Times of Congressman F. Edward Hébert of Louisiana* (Lafayette: Center for Louisiana Studies, University of Southwestern Louisiana, 1976), 33–7.

16. The most visible campus organizations representing the student Left were the Tulane chapter of the Student League for Industrial Democracy and the Veterans of Future Wars, both of which were most active between 1933 and 1935, and the International Relations Club, which hosted controversial speakers and had a membership of fifty persons in 1936 when Mack Swearingen served as faculty advisor. At one meeting in November 1936 the group heard French novelist Odette Kuen denounce the United States as "the most vicious example of a capitalist democracy that the world has ever known." Several Tulane students from the early 1930s—including Richard B. Whitten, John Blair, and Louise Jessen—were active in the cause of American socialism. After leaving Tulane Whitten served as president of Commonwealth College, a labor movement training school in Arkansas, and subsequently worked in the 1936 presidential campaign of Socialist candidate Norman Thomas. Alvin E. Johnson to Sarah Towles Reed, 17 September 1933, Sarah Towles Reed Papers, University of New Orleans; Tulane *Hullabaloo:* 2 November 1934, p. 1; 9 November 1934, p. 2; 22 February 1935, pp. 1, 5; 12 April 1935, p. 5; 26 April 1935, pp. 1, 6; 19 March 1937, pp. 1, 8.

of prudent civil libertarians, operating within the political framework of anti-Longism and appealing to the tradition of "good government" reform espoused by prominent New Orleans families. The affluent uptown area around Tulane supplied most of the league's initial members, including Social Work dean Elizabeth Wisner, physics professor and later university vice president Joseph C. Morris, Newcomb women's counselor Anna Many, and historian Mary Allen. Although Herman Nixon served as the organization's first president, philosophy professor Harold N. Lee became the guiding spirit and central figure in the league's day-to-day operations throughout its decade-long existence. Under Lee's stewardship the league adopted a "conservative liberal" stance that excluded both Communists and blacks, while placing a convenient wall of intellectual separation between civil liberties and the more politically explosive question of civil rights. Black voter registration, for example, was held to be a political issue that fell outside the scope of civil libertarian concern. Lee also took pains to avoid organizational alliances that might give the league a radical taint. The group even refused to affiliate with the American Civil Liberties Union, fearing that any national tie would revive old fears of "Yankees coming down South" to meddle in local affairs.[17]

Although some members favored a less timid approach, league policies remained firmly under the control of Lee and a small executive committee whose members were ostensibly unwilling to "rub elbows with even a mild radical." Like southern moderates of previous generations, Professor Lee and his supporters disassociated themselves from militant tactics. Neither picketing nor mass demonstrations had a place in the organization's efforts. Legalistic and educational activities lay at the heart of league attempts to curb police brutality, secure due process for criminal defendants, and guarantee rights of free speech and assembly to labor organizers, political radicals, religious groups, and ethnic minorities. Despite its tactical caution in the face of local prejudice, the league manifested a genuine concern with the legal inequities of the southern racial system. Speaking to a local radio audience in May 1940, Lee declared flatly that New Orleans "Negroes had no rights that the police felt obligated to respect," a claim borne out by the fact that blacks were involved in some two-thirds of the civil liberties violations that the league investigated. Some six years later

17. Moore, "Civil Liberties in Louisiana," passim, 78 (first quotation), 73 (second quotation).

the league quietly modified its exclusionary racial policy by appointing black civil rights lawyer A. P. Tureaud as a legal adviser to its executive committee, a group which met in private homes rather than on the Tulane campus.[18]

The gesture was a significant acknowledgment that the era of Jim Crow liberalism was drawing to a close in New Orleans, but it could scarcely alter the fact that Lee and other white civil libertarians on the Tulane faculty had spent the better part of a decade scrupulously avoiding any direct challenge to the legal edifice of segregation. Their program had been one of amelioration, of restraining the excesses of white supremacy rather than seeking to overturn an unjust racial order. If enlightened conservatives did not welcome the league's intervention in local affairs, they at least conceded that the group's activities constituted a legitimate form of political dissent. So far as is known, no Tulane Board member or academic administrator ever cautioned Professor Lee to be more discreet in his public utterances. The situation was a far cry from the inquisitorial atmosphere which had prevailed at the time of the Nixon controversy in 1936, and there can be little question that Lee's example sent a powerful message concerning the boundaries of acceptable conduct for reform-minded academics of all persuasions.

League never dealt w/ issues of segragation and the jim crow laws

II

In the end, little was settled as a result of the academic freedom debates of the 1930s. The resignations of Nixon and Swearingen in 1938 took away much of the impetus for conflict over academic freedom. If calm returned quickly to Tulane's campus, it was less because fundamental questions had been resolved than because the onset of World War II required that further arguments be postponed. At Tulane, as at most American colleges, the years between 1942 and 1945 witnessed a temporary suspension of arguments over domestic policy as the university placed itself on a wartime footing. And while there is little to indicate that militarization had a liberalizing effect upon Tulane, the

18. Ibid., 77; Charles Girelius to Harold Lee, 4 January 1937, Harold N. Lee Papers (first quotation); Moore, "Civil Liberties in Louisiana," 65 (second quotation), 67; Lee to A. P. Tureaud, 30 April 1946, Harold N. Lee Papers.

war provided a temporary breathing space for the campus's few genuinely left-leaning faculty members. Mary Allen remained at Newcomb, participating in off-campus interracial groups and teaching European and labor history from an openly socialist perspective. In 1944 Newcomb art professor Robert Durant Feild helped organize a local unit of the Communist-backed Council on American-Soviet Friendship, trying with little apparent success to interest New Orleans blacks in joining the group. Activities of this kind would become grist for the mill of McCarthy-era investigating committees, but during the war itself most New Orleanians were too preoccupied with real dangers to waste time looking for hypothetical conspiracies. At Newcomb an attitude of relative openness surrounded the wartime discussion of race and social justice. Decades later a 1944 Newcomb alumna who joined the 1960s civil rights movement would recall the role played by undergraduate sociology and history instructors in strengthening her religiously based doubts over the morality of segregation. Mary Allen, in particular, discussed "social change, human betterment, and revolutionary movements—all the things that . . . a Christian should be involved in."[19]

As important as such liberalizing encounters may have been for individual students, the war's real meaning for Tulane (and for American higher education) lay in the developments it helped set in motion. For schools throughout the nation, the war ushered in a pattern of growing institutional dependence upon federal revenue, including military funding for scientific research. New economic relationships would eventually draw Tulane and other southern universities into the national mainstream, setting in motion a prolonged struggle between Tulane's basic commitment to free thought and the ideological constraints surrounding racial segregation and postwar competition with the Soviet Union. By the late 1940s cold war pressures had begun to impose a distinctive moral framework upon American life, and political debate was gradually reconfigured around the issues of civil rights and anti-Communism. The new outlook, with its emphasis upon race rather than class and economic growth rather than wealth redistribution, would determine the shape of controversies over academic freedom at Tulane for much of the next two decades.

19. Rudolph Moses to "Fellow Citizens," 10 January 1944, box 8, A. P. Tureaud Papers, Amistad Research Center, Tulane University; Kim Lacy Rogers, *Righteous Lives: Narratives of the New Orleans Civil Rights Movement* (New York: New York University Press, 1993), 61 (quotation).

In view of the growing importance of civil rights to the Democratic Party's national agenda from the late 1940s onward, it is ironic that liberal anti-Communism became a major factor in destroying the Southern Conference on Human Welfare, the only white organization below the Potomac that was aggressively committed to integration and racial equality in the decades prior to 1960. From its inception in the late 1930s, the SCHW sought to unite academic intellectuals with labor leaders and mainstream politicians in pursuit of a program for economic and racial justice. Although outwardly unconnected to higher education, the decline and fall of the SCHW during the late 1940s had a profound impact on the political environment within which southern universities would function for the next fifteen years. Throughout the region, the publicity that surrounded the organization's demise helped cement the bond between white supremacy and militant anti-Communism. In New Orleans, where the assault on SCHW was most intense, the controversy touched Tulane directly and helped initiate what was destined to become a lengthy reexamination of academic freedom in the face of the cold war's new political and economic pressures.

From its earliest years the SCHW had paid a political price for the handful of Communist sympathizers in its ranks. But prior to the cold war the issue was never serious enough to stigmatize the group among a majority of southern liberals. As late as November 1946, when the conference moved its headquarters to New Orleans, mainstream politicians and reformers still looked upon the organization as a legitimate vehicle for promoting economic and racial change. Prominent liberal politicians, such as Florida's Claude Pepper and Georgia's Ellis Arnall, attended the first postwar convention of the SCHW, held in the Crescent City in November 1946. Liberal academics were also conspicuous at the gathering. Tulane Social Work dean Elizabeth Wisner presided at a morning session in Carpenters Hall, where speakers for the CIO political action committee urged liberal whites to assist blacks in registering to vote. At the same session, Newcomb art professor Robert Feild proposed that Negro spirituals be set aside as sentimental relics and replaced with "songs for free men, songs for victory, in whose composition we can well let Negroes take the lead." Although some local papers covered the meeting in a matter-of-fact way, the SCHW was already under attack by the Americanism Committee of the Young Men's Business Club, which had issued a report some two weeks earlier warning that many of the conference's officers possessed "definite Communistic tendencies" and were pursuing a program that would "cause mass dissension in the whole south, pitting class against class, and in their final analysis causing 'mass Revolution.'"[20]

Local reactions to the 1946 YMBC report, as well as to a sequel issued the following year, starkly revealed that the cold war had breathed new life into the Communist issue as a means of discrediting both civil rights and other liberal reforms. Initially Tulane's involvement in the controversy was limited to fending off occasional criticism over faculty participation in educational activities sponsored by the SCHW.[21] But events soon placed the university at the very center of a dispute that swirled around former U.S. Vice President and Agriculture Secretary Henry Wallace, who had emerged as the leader of a left-wing challenge to President Truman's reelection. In 1947 SCHW officials invited Wallace, who was still an unannounced candidate, to speak in New Orleans. His itinerary on November 17 included three speeches, one before a racially mixed audience of SCHW supporters, a second on the campus of predominantly black Dillard University, and a third in Tulane's McAlister Auditorium.

Wallace tailored his remarks to each audience. Speaking at Dillard in the morning, he attacked segregation and racial discrimination. His evening address to the SCHW warned against the "embryonic fascism" that lurked behind a militaristic foreign policy supported by "big business and big brass" who silenced critics "with the cry of 'Red, Red.'" At Tulane the emphasis was upon the need for U.S.-Soviet accommodation and the ostensible belief on the part of "Joe" Stalin "that peace is a worthwhile thing." Not everyone was pleased with Wallace's Tulane appearance. Some two weeks before the actual talk, a writer affiliated with the Veterans of Foreign Wars warned local newspapers,

20. *New Orleans Item*, 30 November 1946, p. 5 (first quotation); *Action: Official Publication of the Young Men's Business Club of New Orleans*, November 13, 1946, 3–4, as quoted in Numan V. Bartley, "The Southern Conference and the Shaping of Post–World War II Southern Politics," 179–97 (second–third quotations on p. 189). Bartley's essay supersedes other treatments of the subject although the following works remain useful: Thomas A. Krueger, *And Promises to Keep: The Southern Conference for Human Welfare, 1938–1948* (Nashville: Vanderbilt University Press, 1967); Charles H. Martin, "The Rise and Fall of Popular Front Liberalism in the South: The Southern Conference for Human Welfare, 1938–1948," in *Perspectives on the American South: An Annual Review of Society, Politics, and Culture*, ed. James C. Cobb and Charles Regan Wilson (New York: Gordon and Breach, 1985), 119–44.

21. See, for example, Walter M. Carter to Rufus Harris, 3 October 1947, box 29, RCH Papers.

politicians, and church groups that "Henry Wallace is going to attempt to poison the minds of our youth at Tulane University . . . in a speech sponsored by that renowned 'angelic front' . . . [the] Southern Conference on Human Welfare." Serious protest against Wallace's appearance failed to materialize, but the publicity surrounding the event prompted President Harris to issue the first of several pronouncements on academic freedom and the university's role in fostering open discussion of controversial social and political issues.[22]

In a letter addressed to the head of Tulane's alumni association but subsequently published for wide distribution, Harris defended on both pragmatic and philosophical grounds the university's sponsorship of Wallace's speech. The core of Harris's argument was taken nearly verbatim from his presidential report for the 1946–47 academic year, a document published in November 1947 but which—like his letter—was apparently written prior to Wallace's actual appearance at Tulane. Viewed collectively, Harris's two statements provide a convenient starting point from which to chart the development of Tulane's official response to the issues and pressures of the cold war. At the heart of both the presidential report and the pre-speech letter was an almost identically worded passage that aptly conveyed Harris's commitment to the core values of American academic life, as well as his conception of the university's organic relationship with society at large. "Intellectual freedom," Harris declared, "is the most cherished freedom of the student as well as the teacher. It cannot be confined to the classroom. Students do not learn only from professors. They find contacts with many persons not connected with the teaching staff of the University, including many with whose ideas the University officials do not agree. . . . Only by exposure during education to all ideas can . . . [students] become trained to appraise their validity. Any attempt to censor their minds in college would leave them easy and gullible victims for the man on the soap box."[23]

When read in isolation the above phrases contain little ambiguity.

22. Bartley, "The Southern Conference and Post–World War II Southern Politics," 192; "Big Business and Military Activities Hit by Wallace," New Orleans Times-Picayune, 18 November 1947, clipping in box 43, RCH Papers (first–fifth quotations); F. E. Finley to "Tulane University Faculty and Students," 28 October 1947, box 43, RCH Papers (sixth quotation). Additional recipients of the letter included the mayor of New Orleans, the local Knights of Columbus, the American Legion, the House Un-American Activities Committee, and the FBI.

23. Rufus C. Harris to E. Claggett Upton, as printed in Letter from Tulane 2 (November 1947), separate unpaginated leaflet, box 22, RCH Papers (hereafter cited as "Wallace Letter").

Their meaning, however, depended partly upon context, and for that reason it is useful to compare the Wallace letter with the 1946–47 presidential report that presumably inspired it. The parent document was a bold and for the most part uncompromising assertion of higher education's obligation to serve the nation through the cultivation of critical intelligence and the unfettered pursuit of objective inquiry. Harboring no illusions about the apolitical nature of academic life, Harris considered it inevitable that American universities would be "affected by and drawn into the ideological controversy" between capitalism and Communism. Higher education's role in the intellectual struggle between rival political systems would not be "a matter of indoctrination or the teaching of patriotism," Harris believed, but rather "a matter of the interpretation of values." In the view of Tulane's president, the universities of a democracy faced the contradictory tasks of "representing" their society without abandoning critical detachment or "falling into subjectivity." American colleges should enter the postwar "contest of ideas" armed with the weapons of "freedom of speech, free discussion[, and] free examination of all subjects." Where Tulane was concerned, its president was willing to be even more explicit. "The University must be a center of provocative and challenging thinking, a place where there are no 'Keep Out' signs against the inquisitive and questioning spirit." As inheritors of the classical Greek tradition, Tulane's liberal arts colleges had an obligation to encourage students to think deeply about questions of "justice and injustice, of liberty and government, of freedom and control." The university, in other words, could function only as "a place where universal truth may be sought, where any assumption may be examined, where there is freedom of research and freedom of ideas, and where responsible expression is permitted."[24]

These were sweeping assertions, and even in 1947 Harris found it necessary to temper them with the kind of ritualistic assurances that would soon become a staple feature of academia's response to cold war pressures. "As an American university Tulane asserts that the democratic form of government is the only tolerable system," Harris declared. Communism, however, would not be a taboo subject since

24. Rufus C. Harris, "Report of the President of Tulane University, Session 1946–1947," *Bulletin, The Tulane University of Louisiana* (November 1947), series 48, no. 13, pp. 5 (first, fourth–fifth quotations), 6 (second–third, sixth–ninth quotations), 6–7 (tenth quotation). The quotes do not always appear in the exact order of their appearance in the original text.

"false ideologies chiefly attract the uninformed," making it necessary for "foreign ideologies to be examined critically and objectively [at Tulane] by scholars who comprehend their falsity." Within this framework the university would function as a "faithful exponent of democracy, presenting its ideals, its aspirations, its pitfalls, and the agencies for its accomplishment."[25]

There was nothing in Harris's letter about the Wallace speech that repudiated any of these sentiments, but the tone of the shorter statement was considerably more subdued. Indeed, the letter began with a series of disclaimers that seemed to apologize in advance for the entire episode in language similar to that of an anti-Communist loyalty oath. "Tulane University did not invite Mr. Wallace to New Orleans," Harris explained. "It is not paying his expenses here. It has nothing whatever to do with his coming." Having distanced his institution from the approaching event, Harris proceeded to assure alumni that neither he nor the vast majority of Tulane students and faculty subscribed to Wallace's views. "[Y]et Tulane, like all other universities, contains scholars and students who wish to hear him." That was their "traditional privilege" since, "[a]s a matter of policy, any university worthy of the name is ever willing to permit nationally prominent persons who represent varying points of view to be heard." By allowing Wallace to appear, in other words, Tulane was simply meeting its minimal obligations.[26]

Given the somewhat anticlimactic nature of Wallace's actual speech at Tulane, Harris's 1947 policy statements might have satisfied enough faculty and alumni to preserve a rough equilibrium and shield the university from collateral damage during the political struggles of the coming year. But all hope of avoiding direct institutional involvement in the cold war's first presidential election evaporated in February 1948, when Tulane law professor Mitchell Franklin became chairman of Louisiana's newly formed Wallace for President Committee. During two decades of service on the Law School faculty Franklin had made no secret of his liberal political views, openly supporting a great many left-wing organizations and causes that would subsequently find their way onto federal lists of allegedly subversive undertakings. None of these activities attracted much notice at Tulane, except perhaps among colleagues who regarded them as proof of Franklin's naiveté and lack

25. Ibid., 5.
26. "Wallace Letter."

of practical judgment in political matters. But if dabbling in quixotic popular front alliances could be chalked up to intellectual eccentricity, taking statewide command of the Wallace campaign was quite another matter. In a single stroke, Franklin's action nullified Harris's months of tactical maneuvering, and linked Tulane not only to Henry Wallace but to the Progressive Party (with its strong contingent of American Communist supporters) and, more immediately, to the stigmatized banner of SCHW, which had given Wallace its active assistance.[27]

For many alumni, for some Board members, and eventually for Harris, the entire situation was simply too much. In a different political environment there might have been substantial sympathy among Tulane Board members for the Wallace-SCHW emphasis upon trade expansion and economic competition as an alternative to military conflict. But in the deepening tension of the late 1940s, the specter of Soviet Communism took precedence over other considerations. In addition to providing ammunition to Tulane's right-wing critics, Franklin's open partisanship inevitably created the impression that the university had, in fact, taken sides—and worse still, the "wrong" side—in an election that most Louisiana voters looked upon as a contest over segregation, states' rights, and leftist subversion. Regardless of its accuracy, this perception threatened to undermine or at least substantially weaken Harris's defense of academic freedom as a prerequisite for disinterested scholarship. The danger was apparent in mid-February, when Law School dean Paul Brosman faced the unenviable task of responding to Board member Florence Dymond's complaints about Franklin's political role. Although Brosman detested Wallace, he also recognized the potentially damaging consequences of direct intervention by the Board in the Law School's internal affairs. As long as Franklin acted "within the law," Brosman explained, there was little a dean could do to restrain him "without sacrificing other values I believe to be very important."[28]

Those other values weighed heavily upon President Harris during the next month, as he watched Robert Feild organize a Wallace forum in the Newcomb Art School while groups such as Students for Wallace and the Young Progressives began to attract a campus following. When Franklin began quoting Harris in Wallace campaign advertisements,

27. Bartley, "The Southern Conference and Post–World War II Southern Liberalism," 191–3.
28. Paul Brosman to Florence Dymond, 19 February 1948, box 29, RCH Papers.

the president's patience finally snapped. There were, in fact, substantial similarities between Harris's foreign policy views and those of Wallace. Both men desired a less confrontational approach to Russia, favored trade expansion, and opposed peacetime conscription.[29] But Harris's categorical rejection of Henry Wallace's candidacy was a matter of public record. In a letter dated March 22, Harris reiterated his opposition to Wallace and objected strongly to the use of quotations or name linkages that implied his support of the candidate. After reminding Franklin that "[y]ou and I have never discussed your chairmanship of the Wallace campaign in Louisiana," Harris voiced "serious doubts" about Franklin's unilateral acceptance of an "extra undertaking" that necessarily competed with the "first duty" which all faculty members owed to the university. The crux of Harris's letter concerned Franklin's naiveté in the no-holds-barred combat of electoral politics and the likelihood that his academic affiliation would be exploited to the detriment of Tulane. In the end there was no gentle way to state the real point. "If you are interested in avoiding any appearance of trying to 'use' Tulane University in the campaign, and thus impairing some of its value to the community, I trust you will watch such tie ups carefully," Harris advised with uncharacteristic bluntness. The coup de grace followed immediately. "No national or even state campaign has ever gone so far to involve the University previously as has the Wallace Party in Louisiana. I would not wish to be forced to publicly repudiate this activity, since I feel that would hurt you. I hope then that you will guard the University's interests as your own."[30]

Much if not all of the above advice had been implicit in Harris's statements prior to Wallace's 1947 Tulane speech. If Franklin had chosen to ignore the earlier message, this time he received it clearly. Late in April when an offer came for a temporary legal assignment in the United Nations Secretariat, he accepted it without hesitation and immediately resigned from the Wallace campaign, announcing at the

29. See various 1948 campaign flyers and leaflets, including "Pelican State Students for Wallace Conference" and "Come to the Wallace Forum . . . Newcomb Art School," box 29, RCH Papers. Apparently Harris instructed Logan Wilson to deny Feild use of Newcomb facilities for the Wallace meeting. Harris's foreign policy views were developed in several commencement addresses between March and June of 1948. See especially his May 28 address, "The Promise of Knowledge," delivered at Louisiana Polytechnic Institute and reported in the *Shreveport Times*, 29 May 1948. Full texts of this and all other Harris speeches are preserved in box 75, RCH Papers.

30. Harris to Mitchell Franklin, 22 March 1948, box 29, RCH Papers.

same time that a Guggenheim fellowship would take him to New York for a year after the UN assignment. By the time of Franklin's resignation, however, much of the damage had already been done. Tulane's right-wing critics were in full cry, with the YMBC's anti-Communist committee passing resolutions denouncing Franklin's UN appointment and alerting allies in Washington, D.C., of his impending arrival. Among those taking notice was none other than F. Edward Hébert, now a congressman and member of the House Un-American Activities Committee. In a floor speech on May 3, Hébert advised colleagues that Franklin belonged to innumerable Communist-front organizations and had been mentioned in "several recent issues" of the *Daily Worker*.[31]

Hébert's remarks did not go unanswered. In New Orleans Franklin vowed that the Wallace forces in Louisiana would "remove Congressman Hébert from American politics in the November elections and throw him into the ashcan of history." But the Canadian-born professor's technique for wooing local voters left something to be desired. In language that resonated with the doctrinaire sloganeering of the extreme left, Franklin characterized Hébert and those who attacked Progressive Party vice presidential candidate Glen Taylor as "representatives of Southern racial bigotry" and "Southern Fascists who are, after all, the prototypes of the Nazi government."[32]

Once again the Tulane-Wallace "tie up" was before the public, this time in a context that all but invited Congressman Hébert to exploit it for political gain. The opportunity to do so came two months later, when national attention was focused on HUAC's sensational investigation of the Alger Hiss espionage case. On July 31 Hébert interrupted Representative Richard Nixon's questioning of HUAC's cooperative ex-Communist witness Elizabeth Bentley to interject a few points about subversive influences in American education. After touching briefly upon the fight against Communism in New Orleans public and parochial schools, the congressman turned his attention to higher learning. "I am from Tulane," Hébert stated somewhat ambiguously. "[A]nd to my chagrin there are more Communists who infest that place than Americans." In particular there was "one man named Franklin who taught the Communist line to the students of Tulane, and who is

31. *New Orleans States*, 29 April and 4 May 1948 (quotation), in Tulane clipping scrapbooks, Tulane University Archives.
32. *New Orleans States*, 5 May 1948, Tulane clipping scrapbooks.

now on leave from that university on an appointment to the United Nations, and I cannot find out who put him there." Hébert's initial statement was an extraordinary allegation even by HUAC standards. It prompted Mississippi's ultraconservative John Rankin to observe, "When you say the university, you mean the professors." Yes, Hébert replied, "The professors."[33]

Under normal circumstances, silence might have been the most effective response to Hébert's noisy assault. In 1948, however, Rufus Harris harbored no illusions that the storm from the political right would dissipate of its own accord. Some three months prior to the Hébert episode, Harris's friend and former law student Marie Louise Snellings had alerted him to a petition being circulated among Tulane alumni in the Monroe, Louisiana, area. Alarmed by "Communist activities on the Tulane campus" allegedly involving "faculty members and particularly students who are doing apostolic work in the party line," the petitioners took issue with Harris's 1947 argument that no subject, including Communism, should be off limits for discussion. In the face of "insidious and subtle" Communist propaganda, the alumni did "not believe it possible for students to evaluate properly ideas of whose source and purpose they are unaware." Instead of free commerce in ideas, the document called for new policies requiring advance submission and approval by university authorities of "all literature" distributed to students, compulsory submission of bylaws, membership lists, and statements of origin and "program" for all campus organizations, denial of access to university facilities for any person or group with interests "antagonistic to those of the University and the American government," and finally the summary dismissal of "all faculty members who openly profess sympathy with Communism and discontent with the American form of government."[34]

The petition embodied nearly all the basic techniques that would be used to restrict academic freedom at the peak of the McCarthy era, and Harris repudiated it with considerable indignation. But in doing so he began to reveal the kind of tactical concessions that would distinguish the fight against right-wing extremism at Tulane and other south-

33. House Committee on Un-American Activities, *Hearings on Communist Espionage in the United States Government*, 80th Cong., 2nd sess., 31 July–9 September 1948, p. 552.
34. Rufus C. Harris to Mary Louise Snellings, 5 June 1948, box 29, RCH Papers (first–second quotations); unsigned petition forwarded to Harris by Snellings, late May 1948 (all subsequent quotations).

ern schools. In November 1947 Harris had placed considerable emphasis upon academic freedom and intellectual diversity as integral aspects of the university's larger commitment to democracy. Other than the affirmation that fascism and Communism should be objectively examined by "scholars who comprehend their falsity," there was no reference to the political views of faculty. The alumni petition of 1948 forced Harris to be more explicit. In two letters that he requested Snellings to share with the university's critics, the president asserted flatly that Tulane had no faculty members who professed "sympathy with Communism and discontent with the American form of government." On the contrary, Harris declared, Tulane was "one of the most conservative University [sic] campuses in the country," with "only two persons on the faculty . . . that anyone has called Communistic and they are not accused of being Communists but of following the party line. As a matter of fact I know they are not Communists." The two faculty members in question were "silly Feild" (Newcomb Art Department chairman Robert Feild), whom Harris dismissed as "a sort of Hindu Mystic," and Mitchell Franklin, who was "dumb politically and utterly harmless." "A fool possibly but not a knave," Harris concluded elsewhere.[35]

If these comments represented something less than the categorical defense of intellectual freedom that purists might have hoped for, they at least left the door open for tolerance of dissent masquerading as foolishness or mysticism. And once again Harris had avoided the hypothetical question of whether scholars had the right to sympathize with Communism if they chose to do so. The closest Tulane's president came to resurrecting the expansive tone of 1947 was in his assessment of student involvement in the Wallace campaign. There were, he reported, a total of fifty-five Tulane students in the Wallace group out of a total enrollment of seven thousand. Having talked individually with most of them, Harris summarized the students' "general position" as follows: "I fought in everything during the last war. I have little boys of my own now. I do not want any more wars and I am going to back everything that is against them. Wallace is the one chiefly against them. Therefore, I am for Wallace and if it is necessary to be called a Communist in order to fight for peace, then it will just have to be that

35. "Report of the President . . . 1946–1947," p. 5 (first quotation); Harris to Snellings, 29 May 1948, box 29, RCH Papers (second, third, and seventh quotations); Harris to Snellings, 5 June 1948 (fourth–sixth quotations).

way."[36] Perhaps recalling his own World War I combat experience that had ended with a painful convalescence to recover from exposure to poison gas, Harris added, "Personally, I understand their point of view."[37]

Harris may have understood the student outlook, but unlike the Young Progressives, he was not willing to be called a Communist or to accept the political damage that would flow from allowing Tulane to be branded a hotbed of leftist sentiment. Viewing the political landscape at the end of May, he found little cause for optimism. "I am beginning to become so wearied with hysterical people who think that everything is Communistic," Harris confided to Snellings. Hébert's May 3 "diatribe" against Franklin seemed "entirely uncalled for," and there was real danger that reckless allegations from alumni would harm Tulane in an environment where "the mere calling of names makes it so." All these concerns intensified in the wake of Hébert's July 31 HUAC performance and the correspondence between Harris and Hébert that followed. Harris did not respond to Hébert's "more Communists than Americans" assertion until late November, well after the 1948 election. In that election, a League of Women Voters straw poll indicated that over 41 percent of Tulane's faculty and students favored Republican presidential candidate Thomas E. Dewey and nearly 32 percent supported the Dixiecrat nominee Strom Thurmond, who carried the state of Louisiana. With nearly three-fourths of the Tulane community arrayed on the political right, the liberal center as embodied by Harry S Truman received only 15.5 percent support, followed by 6 percent for Henry Wallace and 5 percent for socialist candidate Norman Thomas. The overall poll results left no doubt concerning the preponderance of campus conservatism.[38]

On 24 November 1948 Harris asked Hébert to expunge his HUAC remarks about Tulane from the official record, a request that seemed reasonable enough in view of the congressman's egregious slur upon the patriotism of Tulane professors. But reason was not to prevail. Hébert did claim to have been misquoted, but instead of a retraction Tulane's president received a twelve-page single-spaced letter impugn-

36. Harris to Snellings, 5 June 1948.
37. Ibid.
38. Harris to Snellings, 29 May 1948 (first–third quotations); Harris to Snellings, 5 June 1948 (fourth quotation); "Dewey Wins in Tulane Vote," *New Orleans States*, 29 October 1948, Tulane clipping scrapbooks.

ing the loyalty not only of Mitchell Franklin but also of eight other individuals, six of whom were current or past members of the Tulane faculty. The new list of subversive professors included Robert Feild but added other names on the basis of what amounted to an openly white supremacist definition of the political left. Perhaps the most surprising name on Hébert's list was that of the self-described "conservative liberal" Harold Lee. Professor Lee, it seemed, had "appeared in public defense of the so-called Southern Conference for Human Welfare," thereby aligning himself with a notorious Communist-front group which had also been relentless in its attack on segregation. An even more implausible candidate for subversive activity was Newcomb sociologist William L. Kolb, president of the New Orleans chapter of "the leftist organization known as the Americans for Democratic Action." The ADA, Hébert explained, was "the leftist organization which disrupted the Democratic Party . . . by forcing the adoption of the so-called Civil Rights plank" in the 1948 platform, a declaration that was "almost word for word similar to Josef Stalin's 'All Races' provision of the Russian Soviet Constitution." For the congressman, support of civil rights was tantamount to subversion. Writing a few weeks after the formal disbanding of the SCHW, Hébert warned that the ADA, "while pleading anti-Communist intent," actually followed "the pattern of totalitarian government, and . . . of directives instead of law," which was the essence of Communist rule. "What is your professor Kolb doing in such company . . . [?]" Hébert asked Harris.[39]

Hébert's December allegations were the last he would make against Tulane's faculty before losing his seat on the Un-American Activities Committee, since he lacked the law degree necessary for reappointment. The congressman's disappearance as a central protagonist in university affairs occurred at a moment when higher education's response to the cold war was entering a new and more ominous phase. Throughout America, but especially in the South, an era had ended with the election of 1948. From 1949 onward, it was apparent that the range of options open to defenders of academic freedom at Tulane had begun to narrow. Both President Harris and Tulane's student journalists openly ridiculed the idea that the university was a staging area for ideological subversion. But over the next year, the emphasis of Tulane's official stance on academic freedom shifted noticeably away

39. F. Edward Hébert to Harris, 21 December 1948, box 49, RCH Papers.

from affirmation and toward denial. This path was not one that Harris followed willingly or without protest. In a speech given first before the local Rotary Club on April 20 and subsequently published after delivery at the Florida State University commencement on June 6, Harris fought valiantly to regain the offensive for the cause of intellectual freedom.

Although appearing on both occasions in his official capacity, Harris's voice was not so much that of Tulane's president as of the Yale Law School graduate, the classroom teacher, the man of ideas—and of course the politically seasoned educational leader. Drawing upon the full range of his skills in legal argumentation, Harris pled the case for tolerance before the jury of public opinion. The speech was carefully crafted, somewhat after the fashion of a defense attorney's final summation in a trial of great importance. Harris first laid out his fundamental premises in a context that took careful account of the values and beliefs of those sitting in the jury box. More than half the speech was, or seemed to be, a gloss on the conventional wisdom of southern middle-class conservatism. Beginning with a recitation of the New Deal phrases that southern traditionalists found most objectionable— "freedom from want," "social justice," "planning"—Harris reminded listeners that such aims could be realized only as "by-products of a social system in which the full energies of a people are released." But with rising levels of taxation had come "[l]arge programs employing federal funds and controls" in a manner that was potentially inconsistent with America's traditional belief in individual rights, decentralized authority, the supremacy of "established law," free speech (including the right "to criticize those in authority"), and, most important, a faith in "competitive enterprise" by people determined not to "lose their status in a super state."[40]

It was the latter possibility, and not Communist subversion, that posed the greatest potential danger to traditional American values. "The socialism to fear," in Harris's opinion, was that of the "leviathan state with business regimented, industry socialized, incomes limited,

40. Rufus C. Harris, *The Socialism to Fear: An Address by the President of Tulane University Delivered at the Commencement Exercises of Florida State University on June 6, 1949*, printed pamphlet, box 16, RCH Papers, 2 (first–fourth quotations), 3 (fifth–seventh quotations), 4 (eighth–ninth quotations). For an earlier version of the speech, see "Big Government, Little Men," typescript of Harris's speech to the New Orleans Rotary Club, 20 April 1949, box 14, RCH Papers.

thought controlled, speech forbidden, a secret police, and penalties for those who disagree."[41] For defenders of individual liberty, the political intimidation of American colleges raised the prospect of "socialized thought" in educational settings where free inquiry was discouraged or made to seem hazardous. Higher education could neither succeed in its intellectual mission nor affirm American values, Harris warned, "if it has to fight for its life and self-respect on every minor front."

It cannot make progress if it must encounter the witch hunts, and explain and apologize for every wild and malicious rumor. It has no chance if it must first and constantly overcome the clutches of those who fear that every teacher who has a view different from his own is a cheat or a crackpot if not indeed a Communist. It cannot succeed if we employ in America the totalitarian concept that disagreement is unlawful. . . . [I]f knowledge is to be advanced someone is likely to venture upon an idea that is different from that previously accepted. This must not be made dangerous. . . . Investigation of all ideas new and old must be permitted. There must be tolerated mistakes in judgment. That is not inconsistent with the American tradition is it, as long as the motive is honest and the purpose objective?[42]

"We must decide realistically whether we will really tolerate the search for truth," Harris told the assembled graduates. Otherwise, he concluded, "the only course left is to blow out the light and fight it out in the dark."[43]

By the time Harris delivered these remarks in June 1949, lamps were beginning to flicker on many American campuses as the full implications of the 1948 election became clear both to educators and to Communist-hunting politicians. In the nation's capital the House Un-American Activities Committee (now bereft of Congressman Hébert) sent letters to eighty-one colleges, including Tulane, demanding lists of textbooks used for courses in literature, economics, political science, history, and other fields. At the University of Washington an investigation by the state legislature's Fact-finding Committee on Un-American Activities resulted in the dismissal of three tenured Communist profes-

41. Harris, *Socialism to Fear*, 3.
42. Ibid., 6–7.
43. Ibid., 7.

sors in January 1949. A few months later the regents of the University of California imposed a special anti-Communist loyalty oath upon all faculty, modeling their document upon relevant portions of the Taft-Hartley Act that Congress had adopted over President Truman's veto the previous year. At first faculty resistance to the oath was strong, but eventually most professors signed under threat of dismissal. Thirty-one non-Communist liberals held out and lost their jobs as a result. In a nonbinding referendum the California professoriat voted to reject the regents' oath in favor of a less stringent one, but overwhelmingly endorsed a resolution declaring that proven Communists "are not acceptable as members of the faculty." Although four years would elapse before the Association of American Universities committed the nation's academic establishment to the sobering dictum that "present membership in the Communist Party . . . extinguishes the right to a university position," the Washington and California episodes left little doubt that the posture of higher education was becoming more defensive.[44]

This pattern was evident even in Harris's January 1949 response to Hébert's December charges against Tulane's faculty. While deploring the use of "[r]umor, hearsay, and tenuous chains of indirect evidence" to discredit liberal professors, Harris conceded that both Mitchell Franklin and Robert Feild had been "under close official scrutiny here." Despite careful investigation, the university had "been unable to find any conclusive evidence of their actual Communist Party affiliations. . . . As far as such individuals are concerned, I assure you that we have the situation well in hand. I repeat that no faculty member has ever disseminated subversive propaganda in this University." President Harris's statement probably exaggerated the degree of actual concern over Franklin and Feild, but the phraseology was itself a significant concession to the authoritarian mentality that accompanied the search for academic radicals. Any remaining hint of equivocation in Harris's own anti-Communist stance would be eliminated a few weeks later in the wake of a sensational episode that threw the Communism–civil rights nexus into sharp relief.[45]

44. David Caute, *The Great Fear: The Anti-Communist Purge under Truman and Eisenhower* (New York: Simon and Schuster, 1978), 404; Schrecker, *No Ivory Tower*, 94 (first quotation), 19 (second quotation); Rights and Responsibilities of Universities and their Faculties: A Statement by the Association of American Universities, typescript, 24 March 1953, box 24, RCH Papers, 5 (third quotation).

45. Harris to F. Edward Hébert, 11 January 1949, box 49, RCH Papers.

On the evening of 6 February 1949 approximately sixty-five people attended a party in the small New Orleans apartment of Arlene Stich, a twenty-three-year-old first-semester graduate student in the School of Social Work. The gathering was a racially mixed affair either sponsored by or held for the benefit of the Young Progressives (accounts vary), and attended by some thirty-six whites and twenty-nine blacks, nearly half of whom were students. Many had been active in the local Wallace campaign. A total of twenty-three Tulane students were present when police arrested the entire group for disturbing the peace after previously warning the men and women at the interracial gathering, "You can't do this South of the Mason-Dixon Line." Stich, an alumna of Queen's College and a former employee of the New York Welfare Department, "saw nothing wrong with having Negroes in my home," and protested when police entered her apartment without a search warrant.[46]

In the New Orleans of 1949 any interracial social gathering would have constituted a serious affront to local segregationist sensibilities. This one, however, was organized by a Yankee newcomer for the stated purpose of aiding a left-wing political group that would soon find its way onto the official HUAC list of subversive organizations. In the immediate aftermath of the episode two chastened Newcomb students, who refused to join the majority of those arrested in appealing their five-dollar fines, condemned the gathering as "definitely pink and bordering on the red side."[47] The assessment was probably more accurate than the students knew or than university officials cared to admit. At the peak of its strength in the late 1940s, the Communist Party in New Orleans claimed a following of between two and three hundred persons, perhaps a third of whom were actual Party members. Based principally in the waterfront and maritime unions, the Party also maintained a "professional branch" that included a sprinkling of medical students and physicians on university faculties. The Communists succeeded to a very limited extent in recruiting student members through the New Orleans Youth Council, the Southern Negro Youth

46. Elizabeth Wisner to Harris, 8 February 1949, box 29, RCH Papers (first quotation); *New Orleans Times-Picayune*, 8 February 1949, p. 16 (second quotation).

47. *New Orleans Times-Picayune*, 8 February 1949, p. 16 (quotation). According to the House Un-American Activities Committee's *Guide to Subversive Organizations and Publications*, 87th Cong., 2nd sess. H. Doc. 398, p. 226, the Young Progressives organization was created early in 1949 through the merger of Students for Wallace and "other Communist fronts" into a new "youth wing of the Communist-controlled (Independent) Progressive Party."

Congress, and Students for Wallace, as well as the Young Progressives.[48] One of the Newcomb students arrested at the February gathering, nineteen-year-old Gwendolyn Midlo, was an active Party member who had helped organize the New Orleans Youth Council's Conference on Racial Equality. Her father, a prominent local attorney, furnished bail money for many of those arrested. The International Longshoremen's and Warehousemen's Union provided extra seating for the party in the form of metal folding chairs bearing the ILWU initials and presumably furnished by the two white male guests who listed their occupation as "seaman."[49]

Internal investigations conducted immediately after the student arrests probably added little to what Harris already knew about the political leanings of Tulane's faculty and students. Social Work dean Elizabeth Wisner reported that with the exception of one individual "about whom we have had some question," all of the social work students at the party were "just nice young people who have a good deal of idealism and great sensitivity to what they regard as social injustice." Some had been "definitely a part of the Wallace group," while others had found themselves "drawn in but with less conviction about the Progressive Party." All of them, she emphasized, were "from out of town." In a similar vein, Dean Logan Wilson assured Harris that three of the four Newcomb students arrested had attended no prior meetings of the Young Progressives and gave no indication of "having radical ideas on racial and other questions of this sort." Cause for concern existed only in the case of Gwendolyn Midlo, who "freely admits her ideas on political and racial matters," and seemed "inclined to take a very militant attitude" toward the whole affair.[50]

Aware that the presence of even one Tulane student, much less twenty,

48. House Committee on Un-American Activities, *Investigation of Communist Activities in the New Orleans, LA, Area*, 85th Cong., 1st sess., 15 February 1957, pp. 158–60, 163–76 (hereafter cited as *Investigation of Communist Activities in New Orleans*). General information about the Party's size and structure in New Orleans is found in the testimony of New Orleans psychiatrist William Sorum, a former Communist who was among those arrested at the 1949 interracial party. *New Orleans States*, 7 February 1949, part 2, p. 1.

49. "Thursday's Child Has Far to Go: The Memoirs of Gwendolyn Midlo Hall," typescript in possession of C. L. Mohr. The authors are indebted to Professor Hall for her generosity in sharing valuable written and oral recollections of Tulane and New Orleans in the late 1940s. Also see *New Orleans Times-Picayune*, 8 February 1949, p. 16.

50. Elizabeth Wisner to Rufus C. Harris, 8 February 1949, box 29, RCH Papers (first–fifth quotations); Logan Wilson to Harris, 8 February 1949, box 29, RCH Papers (sixth–eighth quotations).

at an integrated leftist social gathering would lend plausibility to the allegations of Hébert and other right-wing extremists, President Harris moved quickly to place Tulane within the anti-Communist consensus that was rapidly emerging from the tenure and loyalty oath controversies on the West Coast. In a February 21 statement that was later printed and mailed to parents, high school principals, and all university faculty, Harris addressed both the racial and the ideological aspects of the student gathering at Stich's apartment, and explored its implications for academic freedom. He began by reaffirming the conventional wisdom that had governed efforts at black-white cooperation since the days of Booker T. Washington. While acknowledging that "some honest and sincere people" believed that social contacts between blacks and whites would promote racial understanding, Harris warned that "theoretical idealism" would be unlikely to prevail against the "facts of history and the realities of the present." More often than not, conduct that ignored "established patterns of social relationships" merely complicated the task of both black and white leaders who sought to "work patiently and quietly at the racial problem in an effort to find practicable solutions without strife or conflict." In some quarters, moreover, there were suspicions that "planted" Communist agents secretly organized interracial affairs like the one in question, a possibility Harris did not rule out. But even if Communists were involved, the president saw no possibility that Tulane could "publicly forbid its personnel upon penalty of expulsion to attend meetings of whites and blacks." The policy, he hastened to add, was no indication that the university condoned Communism. What came next was the kind of categorical pronouncement that Harris had labored to avoid during the first dozen years of his presidency. "Tulane does not and will not tolerate Communism. We appoint no Communists to the faculty. The greatest precautions are observed. There is no place for a Communist here. We do not believe there are any. . . . The acclaimed or proved Communistic affiliation of no one will be tolerated."[51]

The assurances were ones that Tulane's president would repeat with considerable regularity in the years ahead. Within a few months he had reduced the idea to a terse syllogism: "We have no Communists and will have none." Amid the firing of Communist professors in

51. Untitled typescript dated 21 February 1949, box 29, RCH Papers (all quotations). The document was subsequently published as "A Letter from the President," *Letter from Tulane* 3 (June 1949): 2.

Washington State and the imposition of loyalty oaths in California, American higher education was drawing a line in the sand. Harris intended to be sure that the 1950s would find his institution on the right side of it.[52]

[handwritten: 1950's Tulane takes a more conservative explicitly anticommunist stance.]

III

Beginning in 1949 and intermittently throughout the next four years, Tulane struggled to reconcile academic freedom with the demands of cold war politics. The task was not simplified by the presence on the Arts and Sciences faculty of John E. Kieffer, an untenured associate professor who joined the Department of Political Science in 1947 and threw himself vigorously into local crusades against leftist subversion. During 1948 he divided his energies between attacking the Henry Wallace campaign and searching for Communist propaganda in the local primary and secondary schools. A tireless and apparently rather bombastic orator, he managed during a period of roughly two years to deliver some two hundred public speeches before a wide array of educational, commercial, and civic groups, including the Young Men's Business Club. These activities gained Kieffer the dubious newspaper accolade of being a "pseudo 'Paul Revere' riding the luncheon circuit" but did little to enhance his scholarly stature. His principal publication during the period was a survey text entitled *Realities of World Power,* characterized in its own front matter as a "fighting book" that "reduces the complexities of geopolitics and the surrounding double-talk to simple, easily understood, everyday language." Kieffer's public speeches displayed a similar belligerent directness, stressing the need to stop international Communism by military force while guarding against internal subversion, reflected in Communist efforts to foment labor turmoil, "discover or create a minority problem," and attach it to an "artificially induced civil rights argument." So long as Communists—often disguised as liberals—were "boring from within" American society, local residents needed to remain on guard and recognize that there could be "no compromise between good and evil."[53]

52. "Report of the President . . . 1948–1949," 4.
53. Fred C. Cole to John Gange, 16 January 1950, box 7, RCH Papers; *New Orleans Times-Picayune,* 28 July 1948, Tulane clipping scrapbooks; *New Orleans Item,* 8 December 1949, clip-

Right wing prof challenges academic freedom

Under different circumstances Kieffer's posturing might have been seen as faintly comical, but in the tense atmosphere of 1948–50 no one in the political science department or in Tulane's administration appeared to be laughing. Relations between Kieffer and his colleagues had never been particularly good, and the situation seems to have deteriorated rapidly if one may judge by reports of stormy departmental encounters that left other faculty members "shaking with anger." Soon Kieffer was being pointedly designated in official correspondence as "visiting associate professor," and in the fall of 1949 he was informed that his appointment would not be renewed—a decision prompted in part by departmental complaints over his "growing lack of consideration" for colleagues, his "dogmatic and intemperate assertions," his alleged "snooping and spying on associates," and his "militaristic approach to political issues." Upon learning of his impending dismissal Kieffer immediately raised the issue of academic freedom, charging that he had been persecuted by a "strong leftist, ultra-liberal, ultra-progressive pinkish group" of "influential but misguided" faculty members who had made Tulane "a place where the professor who believes in American democracy finds his position untenable."[54]

As an isolated event, the Kieffer controversy would have constituted no more than a footnote—or perhaps a bizarre sidelight—to the story of academic freedom at Tulane in the formative phases of the cold war. But in conjunction with the 1948 election, the Mitchell Franklin imbroglio, the HUAC and the Hébert allegations, and the Young Progressives' 1949 interracial party, Kieffer's charges helped reinforce the idea that Tulane was a radical institution. While always a minority view, the perception was sufficiently widespread during the late 1940s and early 1950s that it created a serious fundraising problem for Newcomb College. A late 1949 survey of 147 "friends of Newcomb

ping in box 7, RCH Papers (first quotation); advertising flyer for John E. Kieffer, *Realities of World Power* (New York: David McKay, n.d.), box 7, RCH Papers (second–third quotations); John E. Kieffer, *Geopolitics and the Marshall Plan: An Address to the Members' Council, New Orleans Association of Commerce, Thursday, March 18, 1948*, separate leaflet, box 7, RCH Papers (fourth–fifth quotations); *New Orleans Times-Picayune*, 28 July 1948, Tulane clipping scrapbooks (sixth–seventh quotations).

54. William W. Shaw to Rufus C. Harris, 7 December 1949, box 7, RCH Papers (first quotation); Memorandum of a conference between Professor L. Vaughn Howard and Rufus C. Harris, 30 November 1949, box 7, RCH Papers (second–sixth quotations); *Shreveport Times*, 8 December 1949, Tulane clipping scrapbooks (seventh–eighth quotations); Tulane *Hullabaloo*, 15 December 1949, p. 2 (ninth quotation).

College"—including alumnae, husbands of Newcomb graduates (who were often Tulane alumni), parents of Newcomb students, and various "citizens" with no direct tie to the college—revealed that only 23.1 percent of those contacted approved of the school's administration and faculty. Nearly two-thirds of the responses were noncommittal, while almost 14 percent offered negative opinions. Although the latter figure represented only 20 people, "many others" joined them in condemning the Young Progressives' interracial party and in criticizing "one member of the faculty [Robert Feild] who seemed to have communistic leanings." Indeed, some of those interviewed went considerably farther, describing Newcomb as "a hot-bed of Communism" and asserting that "several girls and one teacher" had abandoned the school out of a dislike of its political atmosphere.[55]

It was thus against a background of increasingly strident local criticism, reinforced by a growing cold war conformity within the nation's higher education establishment, that Harris acted to close the door firmly against Communism, knowing even as he did so that there were some within the university who wished to see him go even further. The most outspoken advocate of stronger measures was Law School dean Paul Brosman, who cautioned against giving the faculty an overly optimistic impression of how much support for the unbridled exercise of academic freedom existed at the highest level. Like several other deans, Brosman moved in the same elite social circles as Harris, meeting and talking with Board members at Mardi Gras balls and other private events. These contacts led Brosman to question Harris's claim that the Administrators were both understanding and sympathetic concerning faculty behavior "which would embarrass the University from a public relations point of view." In a letter written six days prior to Harris's strong anti-Communist statement of February 21, 1949, Brosman explained, "What I am trying to say is that I think it would be unfortunate for all of us if some members of the board were pushed too far." Convinced that Newcomb and the College of Arts and Sciences contained the "greatest density of screwballs" within Tulane, Brosman believed "the heat should be put on" to require a more careful selection and a more thorough "initial indoctrination" of all new faculty.[56]

To his credit, Harris defended the academic selection procedures

55. Report of fundraising survey by the firm of Marts & Lundy, Inc., 25 November 1949, Newcomb College Archives, Newcomb Center for Research on Women, Tulane University.

56. Paul Brosman to Rufus C. Harris, 15 February 1949, box 29, RCH Papers.

already in place, but did agree that new faculty should be "indoctrinated" to the extent of being given a "general sense of what we regard as proper limitations upon their social action." It is difficult to imagine that after the events of the late 1940s many faculty members, whether new or old, were in much doubt about the boundaries of acceptable conduct. Those like English instructor Robert Huot, who dared to defend the Communist professors dismissed in Washington State, could anticipate harsh criticism in the local press. Huot's claim that the summary dismissal of Communists posed a threat to the security and freedom of all teachers drew a sharp rebuke from H. Mortimer Favrot, a prominent local architect whose family was represented on the Board of Administrators throughout most of the twentieth century. In an angry response to Huot's remarks, Favrot denounced "'[p]arlor pink' professors" who placed their own rights ahead of student interests and parental prerogatives. Favrot could see "no reason in the world why a private institution like Tulane, which owes its very existence to our capitalist, free enterprise system," should "harbor on its faculty professors, from other parts of the country frequently, who abuse the privilege of free speech in the classroom." There was, moreover, "no need for hair-splitting" on the issue of what to brand as un-American.[57]

The free enterprise theme would resurface with considerable regularity during the McCarthy era, expressed with varying amounts of bluntness or subtlety by wealthy alumni and potential donors. Presumably, however, no one stated the matter more clearly than a Tulane alumnus and Louisville, Kentucky, soft drink bottler who sent Harris a 1951 circular on "Socialism in Higher Education," issued by the Tennessee-based Southern States Industrial Council, an organization known to historical scholarship as "one of the most virulently anti-union and anti–New Deal groups in the South." The Louisville businessman was concerned about allegations that socialism had become a "cancerous growth" in the nation's private universities, and he sought assurances from Harris that "checks are being maintained in Tulane's colleges against the introduction of false teaching." Harris typically responded to such queries by drawing an analogy between academic

57. Harris to Brosman, 17 February 1949, box 29, RCH Papers (first quotation); H. Mortimer Favrot, "Communist Teachers and Student Rights: A Letter to the Professors," *New Orleans Times-Picayune*, 10 February 1949, p. 10 (all subsequent quotations). For Huot's original statements, see *New Orleans Times-Picayune*, 1 February 1949, p. 10.

freedom and the "freedom to invest," pointing out that Tulane, "[l]ike a private business organization," needed to operate in an atmosphere that was "free from the necessity of pleasing the government."[58]

The argument did not sit particularly well with either defenders or critics of academic freedom, and it failed to satisfy Harris's Kentucky critic, who continued to demand specifics concerning Tulane's anti-socialist program. Seizing upon Harris's free enterprise analogy, he gave vent to sentiments which other businessmen undoubtedly shared but seldom expressed in quite so literal a fashion. Higher education's clientele, the writer believed, had every right to inquire about doctrinal issues or what he preferred to call the "productive safeguards" established in colleges and universities. It was, he concluded, "only natural that sooner or later the 'buyers' (supporters) should question the 'sellers' (educational institutions)" about the nature and quality of their product line. If the academic output was found to consist of "nondescript students" with "fuzzy thoughts" and "definitely formed opinions that collectivism is better" than free enterprise, a negative market response might be anticipated.[59]

IV

In spite of pressures like those just described, Tulane never succumbed in more than a limited fashion to the repressive tendencies that swept across the nation's educational landscape during the 1950s. President Harris was in dead earnest about excluding Communists from the faculty, as events would subsequently show, but within the limits that Tulane and nearly all other research universities had set, Harris expended considerable energy and political skill in defense of the principles he deemed vital to higher learning. Once

58. Michael K. Honey, *Southern Labor and Black Civil Rights: Organizing Memphis Workers* (Urbana: University of Illinois Press, 1993), 72 (first quotation); Thurman Sensing, "Socialism in Higher Education," printed editorial circular, 1 (second quotation), enclosed with letter of Martin F. Schmidt to Rufus C. Harris, 18 October 1951, box 24, RCH Papers (third quotation); Harris to Paul F. Jahncke, 30 November 1951, box 29, RCH Papers (fourth quotation). Many examples of similar statements by Harris and other Tulane officials might be cited. Most often the argument was advanced in connection with fundraising appeals to private corporations.

59. Martin F. Schmidt to Harris, 26 November 1951, box 29, RCH Papers.

again his approach reflected a keen awareness of events taking place at the upper echelons of the university world, and a clear appreciation of the need to shape Tulane's policies in accordance with the response to McCarthyism that was evolving at Ivy League schools and other centers of power and influence. In 1951 Harris was invited to serve on the advisory committee for a three-year foundation-supported project at Columbia University that would explore the historical development and contemporary meaning of academic freedom in the American context. Endorsed by physicist J. Robert Oppenheimer as well as the presidents of Yale, Dartmouth, Vassar, and other schools, the project was partly an effort to clarify definitions, to examine vague or potentially contradictory assumptions, and to define areas of vital interest that leading universities might be called upon to defend in their sometimes uneasy relationship with government funding agencies and cold war policymakers. The Columbia Academic Freedom Project enlisted the talents of such able scholars as sociologist Robert MacIver, and historians Walter P. Metzger and Richard Hofstadter, whose book-length treatments of academic freedom in the United States connected the post–World War II era to its historical antecedents.[60]

The Columbia project bore fruit at Tulane, at least indirectly, in the form of an extensive survey of departmental attitudes concerning academic freedom undertaken by Arts and Sciences dean Fred C. Cole during the 1952–53 school year. Even without the inspiration of an Ivy League example, little argument would have been required to establish the need for clarifying, as far as possible, the diverse concepts of disciplinary autonomy and professorial prerogative that provided the language and rationale for academic freedom. These concepts, which had long been central to discussions of faculty rights, necessarily derived much of their meaning from the specific challenges posed by particular historical situations. And, as we have already noted, the challenges of the postwar era were unprecedented at the fiscal and administrative level as well as in the political realm. Indeed, the absence of any general agreement about the nature, importance, or ultimate aims of academic freedom, viewed either as a legal doctrine or as a matter of insti-

60. BOA Minutes, 19 June 1951 (president's monthly report); Richard Hofstadter and W. P. Metzger, *The Development of Academic Freedom in the United States* (New York: Columbia University Press, 1955); R. M. MacIver, *Academic Freedom in Our Time* (New York: Columbia University Press, 1955).

tutional policy, had been one of the central features of conflicts over faculty rights at Tulane from the 1930s onward.

President Harris doubtless saw the A&S survey as a tool that could help educate the Board of Administrators about academic mores and the problems unique to individual fields of study, while also laying the foundation for a genuine consensus about academic freedom among faculty members themselves. A more immediate stimulus for the survey was provided by the announced intention of Congress's three principal anti-Communist investigating bodies—HUAC, the Senate Internal Security Subcommittee, and the special McCarthy investigating committee—to focus on colleges and universities in the wake of the 1952 Republican electoral victories. If Harris did not already know of higher education's impending inquisition, it was brought to his attention on January 14, 1953, when Administrator Edgar B. Stern raised the issue and urged the Board to assist in formulating appropriate responses should action become necessary.[61]

Whatever its origins, the 1953 A&S survey provides a fascinating glimpse into the diversity of individual viewpoints and the range of disciplinary perspectives from which issues of academic freedom were interpreted at Tulane during the cold war's most militant phase. The survey asked all departments to address a series of key questions: the definition of academic freedom; its special application or meaning within a given discipline; the overall status of basic guarantees of academic freedom both at Tulane and in the larger academic world; and specific threats or dangers faced by either a particular subject field or the scholarly professions in general. Included with the survey was a copy of the Association of American Universities' March 1953 statement, "The Rights and Responsibilities of Universities and Their Faculties," a document that had already gained wide notice for its categorical denial that Communists were entitled to hold faculty positions. Every A&S department eventually responded to the survey, usually in the form of a consensus document submitted by the chair, but occasionally with separate statements prepared by each department member. Although most responses reflected considerable intellectual effort, there were a few embarrassing exceptions. The commander of U.S. Navy ROTC, for example, submitted an irrelevant two-paragraph mission statement followed by the bland disclaimer

61. Schrecker, *No Ivory Tower*, 180–1; BOA Minutes, 14 January 1953, 11 February 1953.

that as a sailor on active duty, "the Professor of Naval Science . . . does not feel free to comment on the controversial interpretations of the subject 'Academic Freedom.' "[62] At a time when faculty members who testified before state or federal investigating committees faced condemnation and possible punitive measures for invoking the Fifth Amendment, the naval science response probably did little to enhance the credibility of ROTC as a legitimate part of the Tulane curriculum. An equally disappointing, and even less defensible, response was received from the mathematics department, where the professor responding to the survey failed to get past item number one, the definition of academic freedom. "I have so far been unable to define this function in any manner," the mathematician confessed rather shamefacedly. The only course left open was that of "regretfully declining to say anything more on academic freedom at the present time."[63]

The remaining A&S departments expressed no reluctance to define academic freedom or to explore its implications. Dean Cole's summary of the departmental reports tended to stress areas of agreement, noting quite accurately that many of those responding were reluctant to separate academic freedom from other types of individual liberty. Several departments emphasized that professors enjoyed the same constitutional rights of free speech and privacy as other citizens, a point that was usually invoked in connection with objections to loyalty oaths or investigations that singled out educators as a presumptively suspect group. Psychology professor Arthur L. Irion put the matter most forcefully when he denounced such procedures as a "fundamental outrage." His anger grew out of personal experience. "Upon several occasions," he reported, "I have been called upon to testify under oath that I am not now, have never been, and have no intention of becoming a member of an un-American group. . . . All of this is true . . . but I still resent having to make a public declaration." At best the oath requirement implied that professors were untrustworthy. At worst it laid the foundation for punitive action in the event that the American Association of University Professors or the American Association for the Advancement of Science turned out to be "'Communist-front' or-

---

62. A&S Dean's Report, 1952–1953, part 2-A, Statements on Academic Freedom and Reports from the Departments, naval science department, box 7, RCH Papers (hereafter cited as Academic Freedom Reports).

63. Academic Freedom Reports, mathematics department.

ganizations as defined by the Attorney General."[64] The argument could also be taken in virtually the opposite direction, as physics professor Joseph C. Morris demonstrated. Morris spoke almost disdainfully of "so-called academic freedom," arguing that faculty members should oppose all violations of individual rights but make "no claim that the academic profession has any unique freedom." For the future Tulane vice president, a professor's institutional obligations seemed to take priority over other considerations. Although Morris could understand how "indignation" or "personal resentment" might lead innocent faculty to defy investigating committees and refuse upon principle to answer questions about Communism, he believed that "it would be far better if all innocent persons who are questioned would answer fully." And when professors chose to defend colleagues who had been maligned, they should take "great care" to make clear "beyond all possibility of misinterpretation" that their action involved "no condoning of treason or disloyalty or sympathy for subversiveness in any form."[65]

Although Morris did not address the specific issue of excluding Communists from university teaching posts, there can be little doubt as to his basic approval of the sentiments in the Association of American Universities' 1953 declaration. Other faculty members were less certain. The AAU statement had generated considerable disagreement at an earlier Arts and Sciences faculty meeting and after lengthy discussion had failed to gain endorsement. At the time of the A&S survey, astronomer Joseph F. Thompson still believed the AAU had steered a "'middle of the road' course" in the March document. "It was okay with me," he told Dean Cole, adding that he had been surprised by the faculty's failure to approve it. The viewpoint of the majority found expression in at least two survey responses. History department chairman William R. Hogan echoed former University of Chicago president Robert M. Hutchins's belief that "[a]ttempts to control the private lives and public expressions of professors" represented not only violations of academic freedom but invasions of individual liberty. Noting that the *Atlantic Monthly* had recently printed the AAU statement in an issue that also featured essays by Joseph Alsop and Howard Mumford Jones in support of Hutchins's sentiments, Hogan saw little prospect of reconciling the AAU position with those of the scholars

64. Ibid., psychology department.
65. Ibid., physics department.

just mentioned. The AAU document, Hogan concluded, came "dangerously close to arrant authoritarianism" in its restrictions upon the public conduct of professors.[66] In the political science department, where members each prepared individual statements, Professor Henry Mason tackled head-on the issue that was on nearly everyone's mind but which few seemed willing to raise directly. "Should all communists or fellow travellers be fired from their university professorships?" he asked. After reviewing arguments pro and con he posed a second and equally pointed question. "Which is the greater danger, the *known* pro-communist professor . . . or the possibility of seriously curbing academic freedom by our attempts to flush out communists and fellow travellers?" Mason then urged that faculty committees be appointed to investigate all loyalty issues that might arise, with the understanding that any recommendation for dismissal would be presented to the entire faculty for a formal vote. The key point for Mason was that each case be considered individually and on its merits, since it would be neither possible nor fair to establish a "strict code of 'crimes'" for college professors. "That is my objection to the statement of the AAU," he explained.[67]

Survey responses from the science disciplines tended to ignore the AAU pronouncements and focused instead upon the restrictive pressures that grew out of the postwar system of government funding for research. Secrecy requirements and the fear that government control would erode the autonomy of the individual scientist formed the basis of most complaints. Some scientists, particularly those with a conservative political bent, thought the problem was minimal. Joseph Morris believed that most difficulties could be attributed to the "asinine way in which restricted matter has often been classified," a process he believed to be rapidly improving and becoming more reasonable. While acknowledging that a few scientists had, on occasion, refused to participate in government programs because of "moral or practical objections to secrecy," Morris concluded that "[o]n the whole, the effect of the restrictions has not been too unfortunate," since security prohibitions applied only to those who had entered voluntarily into secrecy agreements.[68]

However, none of the other physical or social scientists seemed to share Morris's sanguine outlook. Professor Irion regarded the "prob-

---

66. Ibid., history department.
67. Ibid., political science department.
68. Ibid., physics department.

lem of national security" as having a direct and immediate bearing
upon academic freedom in the field of psychology. Both teaching and
research were affected. Laws and court rulings already prohibited
professors from disseminating restricted information to students, and
"should the security blanket spread or should the scientific findings in
certain restricted areas become more extensive," it might become all
but impossible to obey the law and still "impart honest and thorough
instruction" in the classroom. A second problem, equally serious but
more subtle, concerned the question of how far the "national interest
[should] prevail in dictating the activities of the individual scientist."
As Irion saw it, the federal government had acquired an "enormous
stake in higher education" through research grants related to national
defense. The powerful "temptation for the professor to engage in this
heavily sponsored activity" gave outside agencies what amounted to a
"degree of practical control" over the researchers, the departments,
and their home institutions. External influence might be strengthened
still further when investigators felt "ethically and patriotically obligated" to undertake defense-related projects.[69]

Chemistry professor Thomas B. Crumpler shared Irion's concerns
but was less reticent about acknowledging that scientists were, in fact,
working for the military. What saved the situation from "academic
calamity," in his opinion, was the willingness of military research offices to rely upon review panels of civilian scientists and to award contracts that fell legitimately within the realm of basic research. In the
chemistry department, Crumpler reported, military funding had supported "researches of an important and fundamental nature . . .
where emphasis on immediately useful military applications has been
secondary." Should applied research become the exclusive or principal focus of military agencies, however, the result would be intellectually stifling. In Crumpler's view, "[a] university chemistry department
where research on the organic chemistry of jet fuels or the physical
chemistry of detonations were the only phases of chemistry receiving adequate financial support would hardly be distinguishable from an industrial laboratory except for a 150% difference in salary. First class intellectuals could not be recruited and held. The freedom of inquiry which
is the consoling reward of the academic chemist would be gone."[70]

69. Ibid., psychology department.
70. Ibid., chemistry department.

Should such statements—which grew out of Crumpler's initial contention that pure and applied research were points on a single continuum of "unrestricted intellectual wanderlust" rather than separate or antagonistic activities—be read as efforts to preserve or to redefine the scope of academic freedom? As warnings against future danger or as rationalizations of changes that had already taken place? (One effect of Crumpler's argument was, after all, to depict jet fuel and explosives research as a legitimate part of a larger academic program.) Any full answer to the question of how Tulane scientists resolved the issues surrounding government sponsorship of research would require a representative sampling of opinion from medical school faculty, who received the lion's share of federal contracts from military and civilian agencies. During 1952–53, however, the medical school was grappling with the kind of academic freedom issue that left little time for surveys. Attention centered on the case of Dr. Robert Hodes, a tenured professor of neurophysiology who was being dismissed because of active involvement with the Communist Party—although neither Hodes nor the Tulane administration was willing to state the fact publicly. Deception and irony surrounded the Hodes affair from the beginning. Hodes, a pioneer in the area of clinical nerve conduction studies, was recruited from the University of Pennsylvania in 1949 by Robert G. Heath, the young and ambitious head of Tulane's psychiatry department. Hodes's interest in the physiology of sleep made him a prime candidate for the research team that Heath was assembling to undertake a bold and potentially controversial investigation into the biological basis of schizophrenia.[71]

Hodes took up his duties at Tulane in February 1949, arriving just as President Harris released his hard-line declaration that the university had no Communists and would tolerate none. According to subsequent testimony, Hodes was a Party member at the time of his appointment, a fact he neglected to reveal to the university.[72] During the next four years Hodes's leftist leanings became common knowledge, as he emphasized his dislike of local segregation practices by socializing with blacks and pressing for the inclusion of minority scientists at profes-

71. Transcript of Testimony. . . in the Matter of the Hearing Concerning the Termination of Employment of Dr. Robert Hodes at Tulane University, 3 vols., Archives of the American Association of University Professors, Washington, D.C., vol. 3, pp. 50–1 (hereafter cited as Transcript of Hodes Hearing); "Faculty Members Named," *Letter from Tulane* 3 (June 1949): 1.
72. Schrecker, *No Ivory Tower*, 242, 405 n. 1.

sional meetings. Discussions of politics and social philosophy also became staple features of social gatherings at Hodes's home, as well as a principal focus of weekday conversations between Hodes and various medical school associates. These discussions—or arguments—would eventually form the basis for the university's charge that Hodes had impaired the efficiency of his department by bringing politics into the workplace. In June 1952 Dean Maxwell Lapham met personally with Hodes and asked him to resign, a request Hodes refused. He was subsequently reappointed for the 1952–53 academic year with the understanding, at least on Dean Lapham's part, that he would use the time to secure employment elsewhere. Finally, on December 18, 1952, in the wake of a social gathering where Hodes sought to enlist the support of various graduate medical students in his conflict with Heath, Lapham, and the university, he was formally notified that his tenure at the School of Medicine would terminate on January 31, 1953.[73] The stated reason for Hodes's dismissal was that he had created undue friction and dissension among colleagues and staff members, a complaint not unlike the one leveled at militant anti-Communist John Kieffer three years earlier. Summarizing the matter for the Board of Administrators early in 1953, President Harris reported that Hodes was regarded as "arbitrary, stubborn, and egotistical to the point of being determined to have his own ideas prevail in everything." Then, with greater bluntness and candor than either Hodes or his accusers would exhibit during subsequent Board hearings on the dismissal, Harris addressed the university's central concern in the case. "In connection with these attitudes," the president explained, "it became known that Dr. Hodes was actively sympathetic with the political cause of Red China and the North Koreans—those against whom this country is presently engaged in war. Indeed, it was even stated that Dr. Hodes had attended or had held at his home meetings at which money was collected for Red China. One member of the Department later expressed the belief that Dr. Hodes was instrumental in getting money and aid to North Korea. I reported this information to the Federal Bureau of Investigation. Dr. Hodes' political activities aggravated, if they did not provoke, this dissension in the department." Having been thus briefed on the matter, the Board proceeded to impanel a committee of its own members

73. Transcript of Hodes Hearing: vol. 1, pp. 26, 42; vol. 2, p. 400; vol. 3, pp. 151, 159–60, 166–7, 181–2, 196–9, 215, 219, 247.

to conduct the dismissal hearing that Hodes and the AAUP had requested.[74]

The Hodes hearings extended from February through April 1953 and provided a scaffolding of due process—one hesitates to say impartiality—that was more than sufficient to avert further involvement on the part of the national AAUP. Presumably the lessons of 1938–39 had not been lost upon President Harris, who conducted a voluminous correspondence with AAUP secretary George Pope Shannon on various procedural issues. When examined at a distance of four decades, the three-volume, 972-page transcript of the Hodes hearing takes on an aura of staged melodrama and pervasive cynicism. On both sides the acting was poor. Aware that right-wing critics might seize upon Hodes's presence as evidence of Communist infiltration at Tulane, while academic liberals might regard Hodes's dismissal as evidence of ideological persecution, the university scrupulously avoided any allegations of disloyalty, treason, or Communist affiliation and based its dismissal of Hodes exclusively upon the charge that he had created "friction." (Hodes's counsel, the Mitchell Franklin protégé and future civil rights lawyer Benjamin E. Smith, was reduced to arguing that his client was not a "frictionable" person.)[75]

The hearing record is filled with tedious accounts of petty squabbles and incidents of actual or alleged conflict between Hodes and various doctors or laboratory technicians—scarcely the stuff that would normally result in the firing of a tenured professor. Hodes, for his part, maintained a posture of outraged innocence, remaining silent about his Communist ties and stressing his record of scientific achievement at Tulane while repeatedly protesting that he was being dismissed for political reasons. In a prepared statement he attributed his firing to "the possession . . . of unpopular political and social views at a time and place when such views of University Professors are considered grounds not only for dismissal from employment, but for incarceration as well."[76] No doubt aware that American Communists were being prosecuted under the Smith Act, this was as close as Hodes came to referring

74. BOA Minutes, 11 February 1953, item 7 of president's monthly report (quotations).
75. On the imprecise character of the "friction" charge, see Smith's post-hearing brief "In Re: Dr. Robert Hodes and Tulane University," filed with Transcript of Hodes Hearing, 4–36. On Benjamin Smith, see Sarah Hart Brown, *Standing Against Dragons: Three Southern Lawyers in an Era of Fear* (Baton Rouge: Louisiana State University Press, 1998), 49–55, 108–12, 189–93, 218–23.
76. Transcript of Hodes Hearing, vol. 3, p. 146.

even obliquely to his Party affiliation. Having previously insisted that "it was my right to think and do whatever I wished so long as these extra-curricular matters did not interfere with my work," he refused to provide details about the beliefs and activities that he alleged to be at the heart of his impending dismissal. Even when pressed during his final cross-examination, Hodes remained evasive. The following exchange was typical:

QUESTION: What do you mean by continually referring to politics? Was it State politics, City politics, or general election politics, or what type of politics?

ANSWER: I was referring to what was generally known around the department about my opinions on state, national [and] all sorts of issues—the kind of thing Dr. Heath referred to as Leftist, Progressive or whatever you want to call them.

QUESTION: Were they social politics or social theories? Is that what you mean?

ANSWER: Well, one was the race relation in the South. . . .

QUESTION: You said . . . Dr. Heath talked to you about some treasonist meeting? What meeting was that?

ANSWER: This was a gathering in my home in the Spring of 1951, sometime. I don't remember the date, at which some money was collected by a man who happened to be in the city, an old friend of mine, who came to our house . . . to collect some money to purchase books and medical supplies for China.

QUESTION: What China? "Red" China?

ANSWER: Quote, China.

QUESTION: Free China. I think you said "Red" China?

ANSWER: I was quoting Dr. Heath.

QUESTION: What was it for?

ANSWER: For collecting money for China.

QUESTION: Was it "Red" China?

ANSWER: You can call it "Red" China. It was not Chiang Kai Shek.

QUESTION: It was the same Chinamen fighting in Korea, wasn't it?

ANSWER: Right.[77]

77. Ibid., 200, 202.

This kind of dissembling, in conjunction with the fact that Hodes had kept a looseleaf diary recording the details of day-to-day conversations with Heath, Lapham, and other medical school colleagues, must only have served to reinforce the perception that his behavior had a calculated, if not a conspiratorial, dimension.

Despite the lack of candor apparent in Tulane's allegations and Hodes's responses, it is still possible to extract from the morass of conflicting testimony a sequence of revealing facts and vignettes that shed light on the evolution of medical school thinking about academic freedom during the early 1950s. The two-year period between the outbreak of the Korean conflict and the election of Dwight D. Eisenhower to the U.S. presidency—coinciding as it did with the beginning of Tulane's aggressive search for federal and private grant support to underwrite medical research—gave the administrators and researchers on the downtown campus an immediate personal stake in the ideological battles of the cold war. At the beginning of the fall semester of 1950, after fighting had begun in Korea, Heath reportedly urged Hodes to temper his public utterances because of war "hysteria." Although Hodes claimed that no further warnings were issued until May 1952, it is clear that his 1951 collection of aid for Chinese troops in North Korea caused a considerable reaction, whether or not Hodes knew it at the time. The episode prompted President Harris to contact the FBI (precisely when is unclear) and may have resulted in the bureau's recruitment of two or more medical students as informers.[78]

The 1952 presidential election seems to have brought the twin issues of Hodes and Communism to the attention of a considerable portion of the medical school faculty. Testifying some six months after the fact, Dr. Margaret Smith recalled an October cocktail party at which Dr. Ralph V. Platou, head of the pediatrics department and a member of the medical school's executive faculty, allegedly identified Hodes as a "leader of the Communist Party in New Orleans" who would be dismissed shortly "because it was not possible to keep Communists on the faculty." Dr. Hymen S. Mayerson had no doubt about his own reaction to an election eve party at Hodes's residence, a gathering Mayerson left after "being subjected to a line of thinking and discussion that horrified and alarmed me." He promptly informed the medical school

78. Ibid., 28a–28b, 150–1.

dean that "as a loyal American" he could have no further relationship with Hodes.[79]

The most revealing episodes took place after Hodes had been informed of his January dismissal. On December 15, 1952, Hodes and Heath had their last conversation on the subject of politics and departmental friction. Hodes remembered telling Heath that "dismissal for political heresy was nothing new and at the very moment, struggles were going on all over the country on this issue. I said that I was willing to fight on this issue and felt it no more than fair that the Administration should do likewise." Heath recalled the encounter somewhat differently. He remembered Hodes arguing that "those of us who were liberal even though misguided [i.e., Heath] were the ones to save freedom for those who were putting up the fight [i.e., Hodes]." Unmoved by the appeal to popular front logic, Heath reminded Hodes that his attitude was "somewhat selfish," that "his difficulties would hurt at all levels in terms of the medical students," and that he should consider "what duty we had to the University." On the specific question of Hodes's politics, Heath recalled saying, "It makes no difference if you are a Fascist or a Communist, and it makes no difference whether you are called a Fascist or a Communist, they ride on the same vehicle. This is not academic freedom."[80]

The potential for conflict between political principle and institutional obligation was, of course, endemic to the American conception of academic freedom. Conflict over the issue was neither new at Tulane nor unique to the 1950s. It is nonetheless important to keep in mind that the denouement of the Hodes affair, like the Arts and Sciences academic freedom survey on the uptown campus, took place under the shadow of actual and impending congressional investigations into academic loyalty. At the national level, the issue of how professors should respond to the potentially humiliating public spectacles staged by HUAC and its Senate counterparts created deep divisions within the academic fold, pitting liberals against liberals in disputes over the ethics of naming names, testifying only about oneself, invoking the Fifth Amendment, or refusing to appear at all. The most vociferous advocates of full cooperation with congressional investigators were ex-Communists like historian Daniel Boorstin and philosopher Sidney Hook, who blended conventional liberal viewpoints with socialist,

79. Ibid., 28a–28b (first–second quotations); vol. 1, p. 83 (third–fourth quotations).
80. Ibid., vol. 3, pp. 181 (first quotation), 235 (second–fifth quotations), 234 (sixth quotation).

Trotskyite, and other left-wing indictments of Stalinism in order to forge a powerful intellectual rationale for the exclusion of Communists from college faculties. Hook in particular played a key role in promulgating the widely accepted argument that academic Communists, by virtue of their membership in a conspiratorial, revolutionary organization that operated in secret and demanded unquestioning obedience to Party dogma, had repudiated the most fundamental tenets of intellectual life and thereby had forfeited all legitimate claim to academic guild membership. These ideas were elaborated in a series of articles appearing in the *New York Times Magazine* in February 1949, July 1950, and September 1951, with a revised text of the last two essays appearing as a 1952 pamphlet from the American Committee on Cultural Freedom entitled *Heresy, Yes—Conspiracy, No.*[81]

Some version of the latter document had come to the attention of Dr. Russell R. Monroe, also a member of the Heath research team, and on January 2, 1953, Monroe and Hodes discussed the relevance of Hook's analysis to the situation at Tulane. According to Hodes, Monroe "thought that Universities, like business corporations, had the *right* to fire people whose ideas they did not like, [but] he did not think they always acted in the best interests of themselves or society when they chose to exercise that right." In Hodes's opinion Monroe "seemed to accept" the view that a legitimate distinction existed between intellectual heretics and actual subversives, agreeing with Hook that "heretics should be protected, [but] subversives and saboteurs prosecuted." Hodes, of course, believed that his own case fell within the heretic category, although he admitted that Monroe had been "non-committal on the merits of the disputants" in the departmental controversy. In the end Hodes's dismissal was upheld and he departed from Tulane to begin a six-year expatriation in England, the Soviet Union, and the People's Republic of China. His case became part of what would later be described as a "Communist cell scandal" involving not only Tulane and Charity Hospital but also the medical school of Louisiana State University, where another alleged Communist, Dr. William Obrinsky, was forced out after refusing to sign a state-required loyalty oath.[82]

81. Schrecker, *No Ivory Tower*, 72–4, 105–9; Sidney Hook, *Heresy, Yes–Conspiracy, No* (New York: John Day, 1952).

82. Transcript of Hodes Hearing, vol. 3, p. 94 (first–fourth quotations); John Salvaggio, *New Orleans' Charity Hospital: A Story of Physicians, Politics, and Poverty* (Baton Rouge: Louisiana State University Press, 1992), 163–4 (fifth quotation).

Although the Obrinsky episode did considerable long-term damage to the LSU pediatrics program, the impact of the Hodes case at Tulane is more difficult to assess. Hodes's firing certainly demonstrated that the university was prepared to follow through on President Harris's anti-Communist pronouncements of the late 1940s. Witnesses who supported Hodes in the 1953 hearings spoke of lowered morale and concern over political dismissals among junior-level medical faculty and student trainees, but there was no mass exodus of tenured professors. On the uptown campus the local AAUP chapter was slow in responding to the Hodes hearings, a fact that no doubt reflected the medical school's physical separation and quasi-independence from the rest of the university. On April 15, 1953, immediately after the Hodes hearings had concluded, chemistry professor and AAUP chapter president Hans B. Jonassen notified President Harris that the Tulane AAUP organization, "acting on behalf of the faculty," had requested that a full transcript of the testimony and the Board's decision be placed in a central location and made available for examination by any interested faculty member. Accompanying the request was a resolution affirming the group's concern over the substantive and procedural aspects of "any case of the discharge of a faculty member possessing tenure." The resolution pointed out that members of the Tulane faculty had already been questioned about the matter by colleagues at other schools, and warned that rumors concerning the Hodes case had been "rife, and damaging to Professor Hodes, the Administration and the University."[83]

Having averted a formal investigation by the AAUP's national office, Harris moved quickly to alleviate concern and neutralize criticism from within Tulane itself. After assuring Jonassen that arrangements had already been made to deposit a copy of the hearing transcript in the library for faculty perusal, Harris went on to dispute the claim that rumors surrounding the case had proved damaging to the administration. Should that be true, Harris responded, administrative morale—"including my own"—would be seriously impaired. "Your group must know," he admonished Jonassen, "that no University tries more earnestly than Tulane to observe the best standards and practices." Harris then advised that when answering outside queries "everyone should state this, and assume that the University's

83. Hans B. Jonassen to Rufus C. Harris, 15 April 1953, box 49, RCH Papers.

actions are correct and proper." Apparently most people did. The remainder of the 1950s saw no major conflicts over the issue of academic freedom, despite the rapid intensification of segregationist pressures during the last half of the decade, as well as the turmoil surrounding two New Orleans visits from Senator James Eastland's Internal Security Subcommittee in 1954 and 1956, followed by an equally theatrical round of HUAC hearings in 1957. Tulane figured only incidentally in these proceedings and no university faculty were subpoenaed to testify.[84]

The investigations did, however, provide the impetus for creating what would eventually become the University Senate's permanent Committee on Faculty Tenure, Freedom, and Responsibility. The process began during the winter of 1953 against the backdrop of HUAC's probe into Communist influence at Harvard, and probably in anticipation of the Eastland committee's 1954 investigation of the pro-integration Southern Conference Education Fund, the New Orleans–based successor organization to the SCHW and a group in which several Tulane faculty members were actively involved. By the time Tulane began to consider the subject of outside investigations, the AAU had already released its March statement on academic rights and responsibilities. It was an avowedly "tactical and political" document that emphasized faculty obligations to act in a manner that would buttress the nation's major research universities against the onslaught of congressional inquisitors.[85] Specifically the AAU held that universities and their faculties had a positive duty to cooperate with legislative inquiries. When "called upon to answer for his convictions," a professor was obligated to "speak out" with "complete candor and perfect integrity." In the opinion of the thirty-seven college presidents who endorsed the AAU document, any professor invoking the Fifth Amendment would assume a "heavy burden of proof of his fitness to hold a teaching position." These were among the sentiments which Tulane's

84. Harris to Jonassen, 15 April 1953, box 49, RCH Papers (all quotations); Senate Committee on the Judiciary, *Southern Conference Education Fund, Inc.: Hearings before the Subcommittee to Investigate the Administration of the Internal Security Act*, 83rd Cong., 2nd sess., 18–20 March 1954; Dorothy M. Zellner, "Red Roadshow: Eastland in New Orleans, 1954," *Louisiana History* 33 (winter 1992): 31–60; Senate Committee on the Judiciary, *Scope of Soviet Activity in the United States: Hearings before the Subcommittee to Investigate the Administration of the Internal Security Act*, 84th Cong., 2nd sess., 5–6 April 1956, part 12; *Investigation of Communist Activities in New Orleans*.

85. Schrecker, *No Ivory Tower*, 187 (quotation)–205.

Arts and Sciences faculty refused to endorse, and which prompted the University Senate on May 4, 1953, to request the establishment of a joint university committee of Board members and faculty to advise any professors who were called to testify before "outside agencies" about the university's "policies and wishes . . . regarding any proposed course of action." The ad hoc body would also serve as a hearing committee in any internal disputes over "matters of academic propriety."[86] Created after the Hodes hearings had concluded, the joint committee represented an interim arrangement that was supplanted in 1955 by the University Senate Committee on Academic Freedom, Tenure, and Responsibilities (later renamed the Committee on Faculty Tenure, Freedom, and Responsibility). The senate report that outlined the functions of the new committee was, on the whole, closer to the position of the American Association of University Professors than to that of the AAU on most matters. This was particularly true with respect to the issues of membership in suspect organizations and conduct before outside committees. While recognizing the professor's obligation to cooperate in legislative investigations, the senate emphasized that the university did not require faculty members to "relinquish the freedoms and protections sanctioned by the Bill of Rights or to contravene the dictates of their own consciences." The senate also acknowledged that refusal to answer questions might lead investigating committees as well as the general public to make inferences of guilt. For Tulane, however, "neither such acts nor the admitted or proven present or past membership in any organization valid under law" would "in and of themselves" constitute justifiable cause for dismissal from the faculty.[87]

In the context of a southern city shaped by the pressures of cold war anti-Communism and the early stirrings of massive resistance to the 1954 *Brown v. Board of Education* decision, these were advanced and courageous declarations. Their adoption as official university policy set Tulane apart from more conservative schools both in and outside the South. The Hodes and Kieffer cases had, in effect, defined the lim-

86. Rights and Responsibilities of Universities and Their Faculties: A Statement by the Association of American Universities (first–fourth quotations); BOA Minutes, 12 May 1953, item 15 of president's monthly report (fifth–seventh quotations); University Senate Minutes, 4 May 1953. The 24 March 1953 AAU statement appeared as an unpaginated pamphlet in 1953 and was reprinted in 1962.

87. University Senate Minutes, 4 April 1955; Rufus C. Harris to Joseph McCloskey, 27 April 1955 and accompanying University Senate policy statement (quotations), box 9, RCH Papers; BOA Minutes, 18 May 1955, item 14 of president's monthly report.

its of academic dissent, leaving intact a broad segment of the political spectrum within which genuine freedom to espouse unpopular ideas could be said to exist. Only active Communism and the most intellectually irresponsible variety of right-wing fanaticism posed a clear and present danger to academic tenure. It would probably be an exaggeration to say that there were no repercussions for those faculty from the late 1940s who continued to work actively for left-wing causes. But the negative consequences usually were not severe. Robert Huot, who was an untenured English instructor when he attended the 1949 interracial party and defended academic Communists, remained at Tulane only one year. Instructorships were, of course, temporary appointments by definition, implying no commitment to future employment. It is clear, however that Harris regarded Huot as a political liability and did nothing to delay his departure.[88] In 1949 Harris removed Robert Feild as head of the Newcomb art department, citing lack of administrative ability as the reason for the change. Perhaps the move was an effort to distance the college from the one faculty member consistently singled out by alumni for his supposed Communist sympathies. In any case, Feild remained on the Newcomb faculty for an additional nine years, openly supporting the civil rights activities of the Southern Conference Education Fund both before and after the 1954 Eastland committee hearings that sought to discredit the group as a Communist front. In 1951 historian Mary Allen faced outside allegations of classroom subversion and was defended—or at least protected—by Harris, who assured former Governor Sam Jones that Allen was "neither a communist nor a Marxist" but simply a "Utopian socialist of the Bernard Shaw–Norman Thomas variety," the sort of person colleagues looked upon as "a completely harmless type." Newcomb dean Logan Wilson had nonetheless informed Allen "in no uncertain terms that Tulane University does not countenance propagandizing under the guise of academic freedom." Whatever the reality behind these assurances may have been, Professor Allen remained on the Newcomb faculty until her retirement later in the decade. Law professor Mitchell Franklin also returned to Tulane after his UN assignment and weathered continuing outside attacks from the YMBC and other conserva-

88. In discussing the "bad eggs we sometimes find in the nest," Harris noted the high risk involved with graduate teaching fellows and "some young instructors who are appointed for a year only, as Huot, and who generally are being tried out." Harris to Paul Brosman, 17 February 1949, box 29, RCH Papers.

tive groups for more than a decade. He would retire on schedule in 1967 amid tributes from his colleagues, and would return in 1978 to receive an honorary degree during the presidency of F. Sheldon Hackney.[89]

By and large the Harris administration's stance on academic freedom seems to have enjoyed broad faculty support throughout the 1950s. To some extent the looming presence of right-wing extremists—who were as dedicated to white supremacy as they were contemptuous of free thought—may actually have helped unify Tulane's faculty around the cause of anti-Communist liberalism. Taking their cue from Harris, professors who spoke out against McCarthyism typically combined obligatory denunciations of Communism with equally vigorous criticism of anti-Communist intolerance. During the tumult of 1948, for example, French department chair Charles I. Silin urged his colleagues and students to "dissect . . . [Communism] as a surgeon would a cancer." Five years later, in a November 1953 speech to the South Central Modern Language Association, Silin endorsed wholeheartedly the AAU position that Communists should be fired from college faculties. But he was even more outspoken in his indictment of the methods and motives of congressional anti-Communist investigators. The hearings conducted by HUAC and the McCarthy and Eastland committees, Silin charged, were not investigations but "criminal trials" in which professors appeared as defendants rather than as witnesses. Lacking even rudimentary legal safeguards, the subpoenaed professor was expected to refute anonymous allegations "that he is now, or that five, ten, fifteen, or twenty years ago he was, a member of, a contributor to, spoke before, commented favorably upon, or attended a meeting of some organization which in more recent times has become allegedly suspect and has been placed on someone's list of subversive or Communist-front organizations"—a category that already included over seven hundred groups singled out by HUAC alone. Many of the accused organizations, the Tulane professor believed, were abhorrent "only to reactionary anti-liberals" and self-seeking politicians who realized that "anti-intellectualism makes friends and influences voters." The real aim of the ongoing investigations, Silin concluded, was

89. BOA Minutes, 18 October 1949, item 11 of president's monthly report; Harris to Sam H. Jones, 5 June 1951, box 29, RCH Papers (quotations); *New Orleans Times-Picayune*, 12 July 1956, p. 31 (see YMBC resolution attacking National Lawyers Guild); BOA Minutes, 5 January 1978.

not to identify academic subversives but "to discredit liberalism in general."[90]

Two years later, in 1955, historian John Dyer voiced similar sentiments in a New Orleans speech to the Association of University Evening Colleges. As dean of Tulane's evening division, Dyer had become a front-line soldier in the struggle against anti-intellectualism and culturally sanctioned intolerance. In a book that would appear shortly after the November 1955 speech, Dyer provided a composite portrait of the mythic "James Cavendish," a prototypical part-time evening student whose painfully orthodox lifestyle and business world conformity went hand in hand with a distaste for critical inquiry. For "Jimmy," as Dyer observed in a particularly acerbic passage, thinking was often reduced to nothing more than a review of the deeply held "prejudices and . . . clichés which form the substance of his intellectual life." No doubt these images were in the back of Dyer's mind when he complained that the dishonest tactics of right-wing extremists had confused the public and caused the man in the street to become "fearful, pitifully fearful, of independent liberal thinking." Like Silin, Dyer was quick to indicate his repugnance for Communism. Intellectually the Communist was a "rather scurvy individual" who deserved to bear the brunt of cold war attacks. The problem was that anti-Communist campaigns had been "used maliciously to obscure an attack on all liberal thought." Growing "fanaticism" on subjects ranging from racial segregation to American support for UNESCO led Dyer to wonder out loud "whether America has lost the capacity for self-criticism."[91]

V

From their vantage point in New Orleans, Dyer, Silin, Harris, and other Tulanians were well situated to assess the mixed motives of

90. "Should Communism Be Taught in American Universities[?]" Tulane *Hullabaloo*, 9 December 1948, box 49, RCH Papers (first quotation); Charles I. Silin, "The Clear and Present Danger" (presidential address delivered at the tenth annual meeting of the South-Central Modern Language Association, Stillwater, Okla., 13 November 1953), box 49, RCH Papers (second–sixth quotations). By 1961 the number of "Communist-front or outright Communist" organizations listed in the House Un-American Activities Committee's *Guide to Subversive Organizations and Publications* had risen to more than eight hundred.

91. John P. Dyer, *Ivory Towers in the Marketplace: The Evening College in American Education* (Indianapolis: Bobbs-Merrill, 1956), 144–6 (first and second quotations on pp.

southern cold warriors who took the position that racial integration was a Communist plot. Such individuals did indeed have a quarrel with liberalism and the academic environment that nurtured it. Yet in the battles of the McCarthy era, most Tulane faculty were provoked not just by a simple clash of political ideologies, but also by anxiety over social status, collective esteem, and the cultural claims of academic professionalism. The generation after 1945 witnessed a dramatic growth in the size of America's professoriat, an expansion reflected at Tulane by a 45 percent increase in the number of full-time faculty between 1953 and 1963. Professors understandably felt justified in seeking recognition and tangible rewards commensurate with higher education's central place in national life. But with academia's rapid growth came sharper differentiation within the academic fold, and greater disparities between disciplines in matters of pay and influence. Federally supported scientists and traditional humanities professors came to inhabit increasingly separate places within academic institutions. They were united, if at all, by a shared commitment to the free pursuit of new knowledge and by an awareness that Americans often valued academic credentials without embracing the culture and values of those who conferred them.[92]

Thus for postwar professors, McCarthyism came to represent both a real danger to the integrity of academic life and a symbol of society's unwillingness to meet the academic world on its own terms. During the 1950s, for example, Tulane's AAUP chapter probably invested more time and effort in constructing arguments for higher faculty salaries than in any other single activity. Faculty surveys documented the young faculty member's arduous and often futile quest for home ownership, the quintessential badge of middle-class stability. Elaborate charts hammered away at the theme that the wages of skilled blue-collar workers had risen far more rapidly than professorial salaries.[93] What

145–6); *New Orleans Times-Picayune*, 16 November 1955 (third–seventh quotations), Tulane clipping scrapbooks.

92. Based upon "full-time equivalent" faculty data in "A Proposal to the Ford Foundation, Tulane University, 1963," section three, Financial and Statistical Data, table 5, pp. 22–3, Tulane University Archives. The actual number of "FTEs" grew from 355 in 1953 to 516 in 1962–63.

93. The Tulane AAUP chapter prepared three lengthy reports on faculty compensation between 1956 and 1960. The first report showed that while the real (i.e., indexed for cost of living) income of U.S. industrial workers had increased by 48 percent since 1940, faculty compensation had actually declined by 5 percent when measured in real terms. On 3 February 1956 the

was to be done? The financial problems were quite real, and for the most part impervious to quick solution, a fact which only served to increase their psychological significance. The combative tone apparent in responses to McCarthyism by professors from the chronically underpaid humanities wing of Tulane's faculty grew partly out of sheer disdain for the folly of politicians who failed to comprehend, much less appreciate, the value of intellectual activity as an end in itself. But undergirding faculty anger and contempt was the humanist's heavy psychological investment in college teaching's intangible rewards, and the corresponding realization that cold war excesses threatened to undermine societal respect for the scholarly professions. Carried to its logical extreme McCarthyism would demean all but the most utilitarian academic vocations, and in the process poison the environment for teaching and learning both on and off university campuses. As historian Arthur M. Schlesinger Jr. would note in 1956, the issues of status and respect (including self-respect) were ultimately inseparable from the defense of academic freedom. If the attack upon scholarly status was allowed to succeed, Schlesinger warned, the assault against freedom would constitute little more than a "mopping up operation."[94]

The problem went well beyond the indignities inflicted on individual scholars and scientists by federal investigators. If McCarthyism itself

---

Newcomb College faculty adopted a resolution urging that professors receive "remuneration at least roughly competitive with that of other professions." The 1958 AAUP report acknowledged some improvement but stressed that the competitive position of faculty salaries at Tulane and other universities was still "dangerously weak by comparison with other professions, and even with relatively unskilled work in business and industry." In 1960 reports of further progress were accompanied by a warning that "there are some large and hungry flies in the ointment for the teaching profession generally and for Tulane in particular." With a perceived shortage of college faculty looming on the horizon, there was now less concern about the status of teaching in comparison to other jobs and more emphasis upon the likelihood that Tulane professors would seek higher salaries at other schools. Tulane Chapter AAUP, Report of the Committee on the Economic Problems of the Profession, January 1956; ibid., January 1958; ibid., April 1960; all in box 24, RCH Papers; BOA Minutes, 21 March 1956, item 9 of president's monthly report. For earlier concerns about faculty compensation, see BOA Minutes, 8 October 1952, item 11 of president's monthly report; ibid., 11 March 1953, item 11 of president's monthly report; ibid., 8 April 1953, statement of Joseph Jones on the impossibility of equalizing salaries with peer institutions; Harold N. Lee, "Wanted: Teachers, Teachers, Teachers," *Tulanian* 27 (December 1953): 12–3. On the difficulty encountered by Tulane faculty in acquiring the down payment necessary to purchase a home, see BOA Minutes, 12 June 1957, item 14 of president's monthly report. In 1957 only 22 percent of Tulane faculty were homeowners, as compared with roughly 50 percent in the nation as a whole.

94. Arthur M. Schlesinger Jr., "Academic Freedom, A Review Essay," *Journal of Higher Education* 27 (June 1956): 338–43, 350 (quotation on p. 342).

constituted part of a painful national adjustment to America's new role of global leadership, the academic freedom struggles of the 1950s represented an effort on the part of college faculty members to adapt to unprecedented changes in the relationship between universities, the government, and society at large. McCarthyite appeals to anti-intellectualism and popular prejudice served to underscore the tenuous nature of whatever claims to authority and professional autonomy most academic disciplines had managed to establish. But more important, the deepening obsession with national security that made McCarthyism possible also cast doubt on the academic community's ability to secure official support and public sponsorship without sacrificing substantial elements of freedom and independence in the process. Implicit in the emerging government-university partnership of the 1950s was the possibility that respect, in the form of political legitimacy and public acceptance, might prove incompatible with scientific or scholarly self-determination, thereby compelling faculty members to pursue one goal at the expense of the other. This realization had been at the heart of the concerns voiced by scientists in Tulane's 1953 academic freedom survey, and their qualms about military secrecy and government influence over research provided food for thought even in departments that did not depend directly upon grant support from federal or private sources.

Whether or not they chose to acknowledge the fact, nearly all Tulane faculty in the physical and applied sciences were affected by cold war expectations that universities would serve as "instruments of national purpose" in the struggle with Communism. The principle manifested itself most directly through the proliferation of military project grants supporting faculty research in medicine, engineering, and the nonhumanities disciplines generally. At the heart of the postwar relationship between university researchers and national funding agencies was the wartime precedent set through the work of the National Defense Research Committee and the Office of Scientific Research and Development. Following the "best science" approach espoused by private foundations before the war, the NDRC negotiated open-ended research and development contracts, allowing scientists at leading universities to explore military problems without committing themselves in advance to a particular result or end product. The more direct application of scientific expertise to specific military tasks became a function of OSRD, headed by Vannevar Bush, whose 1945 report, *Science:*

The Endless Frontier, would set forth the basic principles governing postwar federal support of university research.[95]

After 1945, plans to preserve and nominally "civilianize" federal science patronage unfolded rapidly. The principal line of bureaucratic descent ran from the moribund OSRD to the embryonic Office of Naval Research, which was created in 1945 with a mandate to pursue basic research that was "pure and imaginative." Like the OSRD, the new ONR operated primarily through project grants to individual investigators on university campuses, setting a pattern for research arrangements by similar agencies within the air force and later the army. Government medical research flourished as the newly expanded National Institutes of Health absorbed much of the activity previously underwritten by National Defense Research Committee, while the ONR and its army and air force counterparts sponsored many additional biomedical projects as well as nonmedical scientific endeavors. Again the interdependence of government and academia was preserved through the project grant system. In the field of nuclear science, the legacy of the Manhattan Project fell to the Atomic Energy Commission, a civilian agency created in 1946 which oversaw extensive contract research at universities and in the private sector. By the mid-1950s the basic ground rules or "implicit contract" governing both federal and foundation-backed project research included a core of common assumptions that served to reassure all parties. Outside the engineering field, academic investigators in the natural and social sciences tended to look upon all but the most starkly utilitarian federal contracts as ethically neutral, pure research, self-initiated through a project proposal that was evaluated according to accepted standards of peer review. In theory, the central goal of each project was to expand the body of fundamental knowledge in a particular area. In reality, the situation was never so simple. Individual scientists at Tulane did conduct research at or near the frontiers of existing knowledge, but as often as not, the university's effort to secure a recognized place within the national research establishment involved a willingness to undertake practical military- or defense-related assignments.[96]

95. Adam Yarmolinsky, *The Military Establishment: Its Impacts on American Society* (New York: Harper and Row, 1971), 289–90.

96. Ibid., 291 (first quotation)–293; Harold Orlans, *The Nonprofit Research Institute* (New York: McGraw-Hill, 1972), 13–4; Carl Kaysen, "Can Universities Cooperate with the Defense

The relative mix and the likely pattern of future development were apparent almost from the outset. In 1948, for example, Tulane took understandable pride in obtaining the first Office of Naval Research contract awarded to a southern university in the field of pure mathematics. The award for work on topological algebra by Professor William L. Duren was continued throughout the 1950s. Like the esoteric theoretical advances in particle physics that had preceded the development of the atomic bomb, abstract refinements in mathematical logic and technique seemed far removed from the grisly business of actual warfare. Contemporary press releases concerning the ONR award emphasized, however, that "a formula for expressing the rate at which friction-generated heat will increase at high air speeds might be of much greater value [to national defense] than the physical process of building a larger bomb."[97] At the time of the mathematics award, ONR funds were already supporting research in the psychology and physics departments on the spatial orientation of pilots, and during the early 1950s other armed services agencies began entering the picture. At the end of the 1950–51 academic year Graduate School dean Roger McCutcheon reported that in the departments of psychology and political science Tulane was "now training a few carefully selected officers for Psychological Warfare," while also hosting an air force officer sent to Tulane for work in entomology. Although the number of military personnel was small, "their presence here is significant," the dean concluded.[98]

Events proved McCutcheon correct. In May 1951 President Harris informed the Board that the School of Engineering had been approached by the intelligence office of the New Orleans District Corps of Engineers, acting at the behest of the Engineer Research and Development Laboratories at Fort Belvoir, Virginia, to obtain clearance

Establishment?" *Annals of the American Academy of Political and Social Science* 502 (March 1989): 29–39 (second quotation on p. 32).

97. *New Orleans Item*, 20 February 1948, Tulane clipping scrapbooks (quotation). Under the terms of contract N7onr-434, Task Order 3, Duren received multiyear support for a "study of functional analysis in topological algebras having Banach spaces, and other topological vector spaces, topological lattices, and continuous groups as special cases." BOA Minutes, 19 June 1951, item 22a of president's monthly report.

98. BOA Minutes, 21 November 1950, item 16 of president's monthly report; Current Status Report, 15 March 1951, summarizing the progress of psychology professor Cecil W. Mann's work with the U.S. Naval School of Aviation Medicine and Research at Pensacola, Florida, included with BOA Minutes, 8 May 1951; Graduate School Dean's Report, 1950–1951, box 32, RCH Papers, 3 (quotations).

"for possible secret research projects to be undertaken at Tulane." A Defense Department security agreement followed in due course, and on June 14 Professor L. M. N. Bach of the medical school's physiology department signed a $20,000 contract with Fort Belvoir for "Studies and Investigations of Battlefield Illumination." Within two years the amount of the award had risen to $57,000. Other Tulane faculty became involved in the Artificial Moonlight project, which sought to aid U.S. troops in seeing targets at night while simultaneously obscuring the vision of enemy soldiers. After a February 1953 trial demonstration attended by military officials and Tulane faculty with appropriate security clearance, Harris praised the undertaking as an example of multidisciplinary problem solving through the collaborative efforts of engineers, physiologists, and psychologists. Within a year, however, praise gave way to caution as Harris and his deans weighed the pros and cons of Tulane's growing dependence upon military research contracts.[99]

In a report to the Board on February 10, 1954, Harris outlined in some detail the various "dangers and temptations" associated with Tulane's decision to embark on "a relatively large program of [federally sponsored] 'project' research" in the sciences. While acknowledging that not all outside grants bound investigators to focus narrowly upon solving practical problems within a fixed period of time, Harris harbored few illusions about the ultimate nature of federal science patronage. National defense, he advised the Board, had become the "government's chief interest" as well as the "prime political justification for most of its research contracts with universities." With defense research came secrecy requirements that restricted the "free pooling of knowledge" and allowed outsiders to dictate "on security grounds who shall and shall not participate" in research efforts. Military emphasis on "quick results which can promptly be put into production" also threatened to divert universities from their obligation to "advance fundamental knowledge irrespective of measured utilitarian values." Pursuing the latter goal would require that Tulane "improve its own resources and inner facilities for the support of its own programs in its own discretion." Although no full resolution of the basic conflicts be-

99. BOA Minutes: 8 May 1951, item 12d of president's monthly report (first quotation); 9 October 1951, item 18b of president's monthly report (second quotation); 9 December 1952, item 21a of president's monthly report; 11 February 1953, item 24a of president's monthly report.

tween military and civilian science seemed likely, Harris stressed his belief in the principle that each research contract should be integrally related to the "basic, long-term programs of scholarship which members of the faculty have carved out for themselves."[100]

Although Harris's 1954 statement did not employ the phrase "academic freedom," the issues it raised were in large part a reflection of the concerns voiced by various science department heads in the previous year's academic freedom survey. In evaluating Tulane's stance on questions of institutional and intellectual autonomy, it is important to bear in mind that neither the university's scientists nor its president sought to challenge the emerging juggernaut of government research support. By 1953–54 Tulane was receiving nearly $1.7 million in external research grants, more than half of which came from the federal government. Although the U.S. Public Health Service (i.e., the National Institutes of Health) supplied the largest single dollar amount, its contribution was roughly one-third less than the combined total of the three armed services.[101] The statistics left little doubt that the cold war had forged a permanent link between national security and academic science. Presented with a fait accompli, the task facing faculty and administrators was one of strategic adjustment to new realities. During the months following Harris's February report, the university signed additional army security agreements covering the Schools of Architecture, Business, Engineering, Law, Medicine, and Social Work, as well as the College of Arts and Sciences, Newcomb, the Graduate School, the Urban Life Research Institute, and the Biophysics Laboratory. In March 1955, Tulane's willingness to cooperate in defense research was further accentuated when the Board of Administrators unanimously adopted a resolution declaring that none of its seventeen members would be entitled to "have access to classified security information held by any of the various departments, institutes, colleges, or schools of the University."[102]

100. Ibid., 10 February 1954, item 17 of president's monthly report (quotations).

101. Gifts and Grants for Research (Classified by Types of Donors) 1945–46 through 1953–54, tabulated in Clarence Scheps to Joseph M. Jones, 15 June 1955; [Fred C. Cole], Contract and Grant-in-Aid Research at Tulane University: An Interim Report, pp. 2 and 12, figure 4. All documents in Stanhope Bayne-Jones Papers, National Library of Medicine, Bethesda, Md.

102. BOA Minutes: 10 November 1954, item 17d of president's monthly report (first quotation); 8 December 1954, item 16e of president's monthly report; 9 March 1955 (second quotation).

A final link in the chain of military-academic cooperation was forged in 1956 when Tulane became one of five founding members of the Institute for Defense Analysis, a consortium of elite research institutions organized by MIT president James R. Killian to undertake operations research and systems analysis required by the Weapons Systems Evaluation Group of the Joint Chiefs of Staff. Tulane vice president and physics department head Joseph Morris, who acted briefly as the university's representative on the IDA Board of Directors, spoke with obvious relish about the prospects for an academic-military partnership. "[W]hen this thing [IDA] gets going the majority of the work will be done at the universities," Morris told local journalists in July 1956.[103] In February 1957 General James McCormack, president of the IDA, visited Tulane's campus, and in March official recruitment brochures were distributed to faculty who had been contacted during the McCormack trip.[104] What, if any, direct results flowed from these initiatives is unclear. Many factors—including the early fiscal anemia of the National Science Foundation, the Soviet launching of Sputnik in 1958, and the long delay in establishing a civilian agency for space exploration—contributed to the growth of defense research on university campuses. Determining the impact of IDA membership on the overall volume of military research at Tulane is all but impossible, since many of the more important army and navy contracts were in force at the time of IDA's creation and were extended or replaced by related projects during the mid- and late 1950s. This would be true, for example, of the army-sponsored "Study of the Exterior Ballistics of Fin-stabilized Rockets," which spanned the second half of the decade and involved an aggregate expenditure of well over $100,000 under the direction of physicists Robert Newton and Richard Maerker.[105]

103. *Activities of the Institute for Defense Analysis, 1961–1964* (Arlington, 1964), 5; *New Orleans Times-Picayune*, 16 July 1956, Tulane clipping scrapbooks (quotation). BOA Minutes, 13 June 1956, item 18 of president's monthly report summarizes a December 1955 discussion with MIT president James R. Killian that led to Tulane's participation in the IDA.

104. BOA Minutes, 13 February 1957, item 16j of president's monthly report; R. V. Bartz to Rufus C. Harris, 21 March 1957, box 8, RCH Papers; BOA Minutes, 14 May 1958, item 18g of president's monthly report.

105. BOA Minutes, 15 June 1960, item 15e of president's monthly report. For an excellent account of the impact of post–World War II federal policies and other external factors on the engineering program of a public university in the Deep South, see Robert J. Norrell, *A Promising Field: Engineering at Alabama, 1837–1987* (Tuscaloosa: University of Alabama Press, 1990), chaps. 5–6.

Viewed strictly in monetary terms, the military component of Tulane's overall research budget was never predominant. During the second half of the 1950s, military research funding actually declined slightly in absolute terms and more dramatically in a proportional sense, from thirty-one contracts yielding over $265,000 in 1956–57 to twenty-seven awards totaling just over $222,000 in 1959–60. In the latter year military funding accounted for some 15.7 percent of the sponsored research receipts in the College of Arts and Sciences and a scant 5.6 percent of the medical school's externally funded research.[106] Whether one regards these amounts as large or small, the substantive connection between defense research and academic freedom was never a simple matter of dollars and cents. Although money was an indispensable ingredient of research, scientists in both commercial and academic settings during the cold war era made many choices that owed at least as much to prevailing patterns of professional recognition and political socialization as to purely economic considerations. The British novelist and scientific administrator C. P. Snow grasped the point clearly when creating fictional characters that embodied (among other things) the psychological and ethical gap separating scientists of the pre–World War II generation from the more utilitarian and ambitious empire builders of the nuclear age.[107] Even without the Soviet challenge, Americans of the postwar generation—obsessed with technology and progress—would undoubtedly have glorified science and its practitioners. The cold war, however, provided a nationalistic impetus and a patriotic rationale for the pursuit of experimental knowledge, elevating the archetypal "man in the white laboratory jacket" to a pinnacle of popular esteem which rivaled that of the military hero in the olive-drab tunic. When the two figures were seen in close proximity, each benefitted from the reflected luminescence of the other. For Tulane and other research universities, the working partnership between Mars and Minerva represented higher education's most effective rebuttal to the "are you now or have you ever been" variety of right-wing criticism.

At Tulane, one of the most important factors shaping the reaction to

106. Tulane University, *Financial Report*, 1956–57, schedule 4c, "Statement of Restricted Current Funds for Research," 35–45; ibid., 1959–1960, schedule 4c, "Statement of Restricted Current Funds for Research," 34–46.

107. The theme appears in several of the novels in Snow's "Strangers and Brothers" sequence. See esp. *The New Men* (New York: Charles Scribner's Sons, 1954).

McCarthyism among faculty outside the arts and humanities disciplines was the direct connection between scientific research and the balance of power in global East-West relations. At both a practical and a symbolic level, professors in the hard sciences possessed a social mandate that their colleagues in other subject areas lacked. Although both groups sought to defend and enlarge professional prerogatives, they approached the task from different angles and employed dissimilar strategies. Humanities scholars divided much of their time between telling each other why society should treat them with respect and rationalizing their tacit acquiescence when it did not. Even in their most combative moments the humanists found themselves rallying behind what were basically defensive barricades in an effort to repel the latest assault upon their patriotism and professional stature. Scientists, by contrast, were seldom on the defensive in a cultural sense, and they approached military research bureaucracies secure in the knowledge that the party could not begin without them. Reciprocity became the hallmark of collaboration between academic scientists and military sponsors—a reciprocity grounded in mutual self-interest. At Tulane no less than at other research universities, military involvement was absorbed into the professional culture of the scientific disciplines, becoming part of the reward structure and the process of legitimation that led to future advancement.

What it meant to be a Tulane scientist at the height of the cold war is best illustrated by the experiences of individual faculty members who participated in militarily funded projects throughout the 1950s. Among the dozen or so examples that might be cited, the cases of chemistry professor Hans Jonassen and neurophysiologist Robert G. Heath offer unusually clear insight into tendencies that operated, to a greater or lesser degree, across a broad scientific front. Jonassen, the son and grandson of professional chemists, immigrated to the United States from Hanover, Germany, in 1931. A decade later he entered Tulane as an adult undergraduate and studied chemistry with Professor Thomas Crumpler, receiving the bachelor of science degree in 1942 and the master's degree in 1944. Jonassen completed his Ph.D. requirements at the University of Illinois in only five semesters and joined the Tulane faculty in 1946.

Having entered graduate school at a time when American universities were deeply involved in war research, Jonassen probably saw more continuity than change in postwar patterns of military support for academic science. Although he had considerable expertise in the areas of drugs, dyestuffs, agriculture, and petroleum research, by the late 1940s Jonassen had begun to focus on a new interest—the study of solid fuel propellants for rocket motors. Throughout the next decade his work in this area was supported by contracts from the army and navy. In 1952 Jonassen became a consultant for the Frankford Arsenal and three years later he took on a similar role in naval ordnance research. He spent the 1958–59 academic year attached to the American Embassy in London, where he served as Chief Liaison Officer in Chemistry for the Office of Naval Research. As one of four American scientists working with the ONR, the Tulane professor visited some sixty European universities in order to confer with individual scientists and professional groups. At Tulane Jonassen was a genuinely popular teacher who taught large sections of general chemistry and eventually directed the work of some fifty-five graduate students. His example, in conjunction with that of several departmental colleagues, sent a clear message to younger chemists concerning the professional advantages of military sponsorship. At the time of his retirement in the mid-1970s, Jonassen stressed the importance of academic life's "fringe benefits," among which he singled out his London assignment in the late fifties and "twenty summers of research and consulting at the Naval Weapons Center, China Lake, California (in the middle of the Mojave Desert)."[108]

A somewhat different type of collaboration between scientists and the military took place in the School of Medicine, where armed services contracts supported basic research on infectious diseases and psychopharmacology, as well as less exotic studies in the fields of surgery, radiation therapy, cardiovascular problems, treatment for ocular burns, and a number of other specialties. Yet the projects sponsored by the army, navy, and air force constituted only a small fraction of the medical school's total research program. The central force behind the growth of research at Tulane and nearly every other American medical school was the dramatic rise in congressional appropriations for the National Institutes of Health, an expanding collection of "categorical" agencies devoted to seeking cures and improved treatments for specific maladies, such as heart disease, cancer, and mental

108. News releases of 1 October 1959 and 7 January 1962, Hans B. Jonassen biographical file, Tulane University Archives; "Portraits Emeriti—Perspective and Retrospective," *Tulanian* 49 (fall 1978): 8–9 (quotations).

illness. Between 1956 and 1959, for example, the total budget of NIH increased from less than $100 million to nearly $300 million. At Tulane, Public Health Service grants grew from less than $270,000 in 1952 to more than $1.15 million by 1957. The American Cancer Society was the second largest source of medical research funds in 1952 with grants of nearly $104,000, followed by the military services with expenditures of $66,000. In 1957 military funds had more than doubled to over $159,000, but were now dwarfed by NIH. Still, military support surpassed that provided by the National Foundation for Infantile Paralysis, which awarded more than $132,000, and the American Cancer Society, which now ranked fourth with grants of nearly $114,000. Private foundations, businesses and pharmaceutical companies also provided large amounts of support.[109]

Nearly all the medical research undertaken at Tulane received funding at some stage from more than one—and often from several—different sources, the majority of which were commercial, philanthropic, or civilian in nature. Military contracts typically funded one particular element of an individual scientist's larger research program and, so far as can be ascertained, no medical school faculty members relied exclusively or even primarily upon military revenues to keep the flames of their Bunsen burners glowing. This was true despite the fact that multiyear awards on the order of $15,000–$20,000 per annum were not uncommon, with some scientists receiving contract extensions that would yield totals of $100,000 to $150,000 during the decade after 1949.[110] Not surprisingly, military funding often supported research that seemed likely to expand basic knowledge in areas of potential relevance to the various armed services. At Tulane as at many other uni-

109. James A. Shannon, "The National Institutes of Health: Some Critical Years, 1955–1957," *Science* 237 (21 August 1987): 865–8; Tulane University, *Report of the Comptroller . . . June 30, 1952*, 26–32; Tulane University, *Financial Report*, 1956–57, schedule 4c, 35–45.

110. Among the larger cumulative totals for military contracts awarded to Tulane faculty in 1949–59: William Duren, nearly $195,000 in navy funds between 1948 and 1954 to study topological algebras; Cecil W. Mann, $224,200 in navy support between 1948 and 1955 for research on nonfunctional labyrinths; Morris Shaffer, over $200,000 in army support between 1949 and 1959 for research on new antibiotics for salmonella infections; John Rohrer, over $125,000 between 1951 and 1957 for the analysis and technical interpretation of psychological and psychiatric data on navy officer personnel; Robert Nieset, over $109,000 in navy support between 1954 and 1959 for research on the biological effects of microwaves. Full listings of all research grants are found in the annual printed *Treasurer's Reports*, later designated *Financial Reports*. Brief descriptions of the projects appear in the president's monthly reports to the Board of Administrators.

versities, medical researchers received military funding to develop vaccines for protection against diseases that were both potential biological weapons and naturally occurring threats to the health of human and animal populations, particularly in developing nations. The most direct example was epidemiologist John P. Fox's work on a new vaccine to immunize humans against louse-borne typhus. Supported by the army during the mid-1950s, Fox's project involved initial tests on laboratory animals followed by trial inoculations of some twenty-nine inmates of Mississippi's Parchman Penitentiary. During the period of army funding, extensive field trials of the vaccine were conducted among the Indian populations of Arequipa, Puno, and Cuzco, Peru—the latter activity being financed in part by the Pan American Sanitary Bureau.[111]

If the army's involvement in Fox's project during an era of sustained emphasis upon the development of chemical and biological weapons had no other significance, it at least served as a reminder that vaccines were a prerequisite for the use of a biological weapon in either an offensive or a defensive context. Indeed, one might plausibly argue that almost any type of military support for experimental work in virology and related fields took away some of the luster from academic medicine's humanitarian rationale. Since the basic research necessary to develop a vaccine would almost inevitably yield information that could be used to alter or intensify the effect of a given pathogen, one must wonder what thoughts passed through the minds of academic scientists as they prepared the annual work reports required by military research offices. If they looked upon basic research as ethically neutral or automatically benign in its human implications, the government itself entertained no doubts about the destructive ends to which nominally preventative measures might be directed. Meeting in executive session in 1959, the Armed Forces Epidemiological Board officially

111. BOA Minutes: 14 October 1953, item 36n of president's monthly report; 12 December 1956, item 17c of president's monthly report; 9 October 1957; 8 January 1958, item 15a of president's monthly report. See also "Progress Noted in Typhus Curbs," *New Orleans Times-Picayune*, 13 October 1954, Tulane clipping scrapbooks. During the same period Fox also tested rabies vaccine on some forty-seven inmates of the Louisiana State Penitentiary at Angola. "Convicts Test Rabies Vaccine," *New Orleans Times-Picayune*, 1 July 1954, Tulane clipping scrapbooks. It should be noted that Fox was careful to secure prior written consent from the prisoners as stipulated in a 1954 memorandum from the Office of the Surgeon General. *Final Report of the Advisory Committee on Human Radiation Experiments* (New York: Oxford University Press, 1996), 61, 72.

recognized "that offensive and defensive aspects [of biological warfare research] are inseparable. Diplomatically, the defensive aspects can be stressed as in the past." The ethos of the cold war was alive and well.[112]

The implications of military support for pure science were especially troubling in the case of psychiatrist Robert G. Heath's bold experiments into the etiology of schizophrenia. Heath joined Tulane's faculty in 1949 after participating in Columbia University's Greystone Project, a study of the use of topectomy (the removal of small portions of the brain's frontal cortex) as an alternative to the more radical procedures of prefrontal or transorbital lobotomy. At Tulane Heath and the multidisciplinary research team that worked under his direction concentrated on the region deep within the brain containing the limbic system, a group of interconnected structures including the amygdala, the hippocampus, and the septum, which generate feelings of pleasure, pain, joy, anger, sexual arousal, and other powerful emotions. Beginning in 1950 Heath and his colleagues performed surgical operations upon a number of mental patients in order to implant electrodes and small tubes into the brain's emotional core. Subsequent EEG recordings made during electrical or chemical stimulation of the selected subcortical areas provided a clearer picture of the specific circuitry and the neurochemical processes involved in schizophrenia and other psychotic conditions. The same techniques of electrical and chemical stimulation used to gather experimental data were also employed for therapeutic purposes on patients previously regarded as untreatable. Over the span of a quarter century Heath and his colleagues would operate on more than sixty patients, implanting as many as 125 electrodes in the skull of a single individual and developing methods that allowed electrodes to remain in place for years at a time Eventually technological innovations such as external push-button self-stimulators and

112. On the specious nature of distinctions between "offensive" and "defensive" biological warfare research, see Susan Wright and Stuart Ketcham, "The Problem of Interpreting the U.S. Biological Defense Research Program" in *Preventing a Biological Arms Race*, ed. Susan Wright (Cambridge: MIT Press, 1990), chap. 8; Albert E. Cowdrey, *War and Healing, Stanhope Bayne-Jones and the Maturing of American Medicine* (Baton Rouge: Louisiana State University Press, 1992), 185–6 (quotation). Barton J. Bernstein, "The Birth of the U.S. Biological-Warfare Program," *Scientific American* 256 (June 1987): 116–221 documents the participation of approximately twenty-eight American universities in secret biological warfare research during World War II. The best overall discussion of university involvement in chemical and biological warfare research remains Seymour M. Hersh, *Chemical and Biological Warfare, America's Hidden Arsenal* (Indianapolis: Bobbs-Merrill, 1968), chaps. 8 and 9.

miniature surgically implanted electrical pacemakers were employed as therapeutic devices.[113]

In the course of his long career Heath would receive both high professional acclaim and sharp criticism from his fellow physicians. A full account of either the controversy surrounding his work or the range of his scientific accomplishments falls outside the limits of this volume.[114] For present purposes, it is sufficient to note that at the beginning of the 1950s Heath and his fellow scientists were working at or very near the outer limits of existing neurophysiological knowledge—a fact that was not lost upon U.S. military and civilian intelligence agency officials, who were already engaged in highly secret efforts to develop psychochemical weapons, as well as interrogation and mind control techniques, that could be used against cold war adversaries. From the late 1940s onward, close ties existed between the army's Edgewood Arsenal, where chemical warfare research and experimentation were conducted, and the CIA and various military intelligence services. By 1951 the sometimes cooperative, sometimes competitive military-CIA nexus had given rise to a coordinated army-navy-air force-CIA endeavor called Project Artichoke. As summarized in a 1952 memorandum, the project's major objectives included, "[e]valuation and development of any method by which we can get information from a person against his will and without his knowledge. . . . Can we get control of

113. [Judith Hooper], "Interview: Robert G. Heath," *Omni* 6 (April 1984): 87–95, 112–4, 120, provides a sympathetic overview of Heath's career. Heath's research eventually resulted in more than four hundred scientific publications. Useful summaries include: Robert G. Heath, ed., *Studies in Schizophrenia: A Multidisciplinary Approach to Mind-Brain Relationships* (Cambridge: Harvard University Press, 1954); Robert G. Heath and Walter A. Mickle, "Evaluation of Seven Years' Experience with Depth Electrode Studies in Human Patients," in *Electrical Studies on the Unanesthetized Brain*, ed. E. R. Ramey and D. S. O'Doherry (New York: Paul B. Hoeber, 1960), 214–47; Robert G. Heath and Floris de Balbian Verster, "Effects of Chemical Stimulants to Discrete Brain Areas," *American Journal of Psychiatry* 117 (1961): 980–90; Robert G. Heath, ed., *Serological Fractions in Schizophrenia* (New York: Harper and Row, 1963); idem, ed., *The Role of Pleasure in Behavior* (New York: Harper and Row, 1964); idem, "Perspectives for Biological Psychiatry," *Biological Psychiatry* 2 (April 1970): 81–8; idem, "Marijuana: Effects on Deep and Surface Electroencephalograms of Humans," *Archives of General Psychiatry* 26 (1972): 577–84.

114. On the controversy surrounding Heath's work, see Elliot Valenstein, *Brain Control: A Critical Examination of Brain Stimulation and Psychosurgery* (New York: John Wiley, 1973), 60–1, 164–8; Dr. Peter Roger Breggin, "The Return of Lobotomy and Psychosurgery," reprinted from *Congressional Record*, 24 February 1972, in Senate Committee on Labor and Public Welfare, *Quality of Health Care—Human Experimentation, 1973: Hearings before the Subcommittee on Health*, 93rd Cong., 1st sess., 23 February and 6 March 1973, part 2, pp. 469–71; and Heath's own testimony, ibid., 363–8.

an individual to the point where he will do our bidding against his will and even against such fundamental laws of nature such [*sic*] as self-preservation?"[115]

The following year, in 1953, Project Artichoke grew into to a larger and more ambitious undertaking known as Project MKULTRA, the scope and nature of which remained hidden until the summer of 1977. In the wake of two congressional investigations and the reluctant disclosure of some 16,000 pages of records obtained through the Freedom of Information Act, CIA director Stansfield Turner disclosed the broad outlines of a twenty-five-year, multimillion-dollar program of research on germ warfare and on methods to alter or control human memory and behavior through the use of drugs, electricity, sensory deprivation, hypnosis, and other means. Involving 185 researchers at 88 nongovernmental institutions, including 44 colleges and universities, the project's scope and duration seemed to justify the conclusion of former State Department officer John Marks that "the intelligence community . . . changed the face of the scientific community during the 1950s and early 1960s."[116]

Certainly the Tulane experience lends support to Marks's conclusion that "[n]early every scientist on the frontiers of brain research found men from the secret agencies looking over his shoulders [and] impinging on the research."[117] Precisely when the government became interested in the Tulane schizophrenia studies remains unclear, but in March 1954 Heath was the principal speaker at a seminar conducted by the Army Chemical Corps at its Edgewood Arsenal medical laboratories. His subject was "Some Aspects of Electrical Stimulation and Recording in the Brain of Man."[118] Within a few months Tulane had

115. Harvey M. Weinstein, M.D., *Psychiatry and the CIA: Victims of Mind Control* (Washington, D.C.: American Psychiatric Press, 1990), 129 (quotation); Linda Hunt, *Secret Agenda: The United States Government, Nazi Scientists, and Project Paperclip, 1945–1990* (New York: St. Martin's Press, 1991), 162–5; John Marks, *The Search for the "Manchurian Candidate": The CIA and Mind Control* (New York: Times Books, 1979) remains the most comprehensive treatment of the subject. See esp. chaps. 2 and 4.

116. Senate Select Committee on Intelligence and Committee on Human Resources, *Project MKULTRA, The C.I.A.'s Program of Research in Behavioral Modification: Joint Hearings before the Select Committee on Intelligence and the Subcommittee on Health and Scientific Research of the Committee on Human Resources*, 95th Cong., 1st sess., 3 August 1977, 4–8; Marks, *Manchurian Candidate*, 151.

117. Marks, *Manchurian Candidate*, 151.

118. "Speakers at Seminars Chemical Corps Medical Laboratories, 1954," typescript document in authors' possession.

signed an army "facility security clearance" for the Department of Psychiatry and Neurology. In 1955 Dr. Russell R. Monroe, a psychiatrist on Heath's research team, became the principal investigator for army contract DA-18-108-CML-5596, a project listed in university records under the title, "Clinical Studies of Neurological and Psychiatric Changes during the Administration of Certain Drugs." Classified army records were somewhat more specific, listing the contract's purpose as to "[s]tudy behavior during administration, LSD-25 & mescaline."[119] In retrospect the army's interest in Heath's work is not difficult to understand. At the time Heath gave his 1954 seminar presentation at Edgewood Arsenal, behavior control of a rather primitive kind had already been achieved through electrical stimulation of the brains of lower animals. At McGill University, James Olds and Peter Milner had reported that rats with electrodes implanted in the brain's septal region would press levers at a rate of 2,000 times per hour to receive stimulation.[120] At the National Institutes of Health, Dr. John Lilly had attracted intense interest from the CIA and other agencies through his use of similar techniques on primates. After implanting multiple electrodes in the brains of monkeys, Lilly was able to identify the precise location of centers of pain, fear, anxiety, anger, and sexual arousal. In one experiment a monkey with access to a simple switch stimulated himself to produce virtually continuous orgasms, at a rate of one every three minutes for sixteen hours per day. Animal tests comprised an integral part of most academic research sponsored by military and CIA sources. In contrast, Project MKULTRA was pri-

119. BOA Minutes, 11 April 1956, item 15b of president's monthly report; Office of the Surgeon General, Department of the Army, Review of Reports on Department of the Army Grant (DA-18-CML 5596) to the Department of Psychiatry and Neurology, Tulane University, 1955–1959—Information Memorandum, dated 22 August 1975 and included with Colonel James R. Taylor and Major William N. Johnson, "Research Report Concerning the Use of Volunteers in Chemical Agent Research," 160, 165 (quotation), document in authors' possession.

120. James Olds and Peter Milner, "Positive Reinforcement Produced by Electrical Stimulation of the Septal Area and Other Regions of the Rat Brain," *Journal of Comparative and Physiological Psychology* 47 (1954): 419–28. Studies by other researchers during the 1960s established that rats would choose electrical stimulation of the brain over food and water even after lengthy periods of semistarvation. Later research demonstrated that female rats would abandon their offspring immediately after giving birth in order to obtain brain stimulation, thereby acting in opposition to what had been regarded as their most powerful natural drive. T. B. Sonderegger, "Intracranial Stimulation and Maternal Behavior," *APA Convention Proceedings*, 78th Meeting (1970): 245–6.

marily concerned with conducting drug, electrical, and other experiments involving human subjects.[121]

Army funding for the LSD and mescaline trials that Heath and his colleagues conducted brought the conflict between military and civilian science into sharp relief. The army contract ran for five years and contributed a total of roughly $60,000 to the Tulane project.[122] The few surviving army records indicate that experimental data was supplied for six subjects—exactly the number reported by Monroe, Heath, Mickle, and Llewellyn in their 1957 article, "Correlation of Rhinencephalic Electrograms with Behavior[:] A Study of Humans under the Influence of LSD and Mescaline."[123] From a scientific and medical standpoint, the experiments on institutionalized schizophrenics who had not responded to previous treatments represented an effort to develop a controlled method of correlating "behavior"—in this case temporary psychotic symptoms induced by specific drugs—with EEG recordings from deep electrodes. The research could logically be seen as a step toward the development of improved therapeutic methods. However, the army's interest in the effects of LSD and mescaline on human beings could scarcely be described as springing from therapeutic or humanitarian concerns. What was at issue in the situation was not so much the autonomy of individual investigators as the moral integrity of medical science. No one, presumably, would seek to hold scientists accountable for the use or misuse of their discoveries by outside parties with whom they were professionally uninvolved. But a $60,000 military contract represented professional involvement of more than an incidental nature. This fact became all too apparent in 1956, when CIA agents approached Heath to conduct human and animal tests of a substance called bulbocapnine that the Soviets were also testing for potential mind control applications. In 1957 Heath tested the drug on several monkeys and one human—apparently a prisoner in the state penitentiary at Angola, Louisiana—and found it to produce symptoms similar to alcohol intoxication. Some twenty-one years would elapse

121. Marks, *Manchurian Candidate*, 33–6, 61–9, 151; Weinstein, *Psychiatry and the CIA*, 129.

122. BOA Minutes, 12 November 1958, item 24d of president's monthly report.

123. *Electroencephalography and Clinical Neurophysiology, An International Journal* 9 (May 1957): 623–42. Heath and his colleagues would eventually administer a number of other psychogenic drugs to human subjects during the late 1950s and 1960s.

before the tests became public knowledge at Tulane, following disclosures in the *New York Times*.[124]

VI

Army and CIA involvement in Tulane's psychiatric program constituted an extreme example of cold war intrusion into basic research and individual academic careers. In less dramatic ways the cold war left its mark on faculty outside the physical and biological sciences, particularly in subject areas that were pertinent to the field of international affairs. In the 1950s, Tulane established or expanded programs of research and educational assistance involving several nations of Central and South America. These undertakings included a program of consultative advice for Colombia's seven medical schools begun in 1955 and based at the Universidad del Valle, a comparative law institute dating from 1949 that promoted arrangements to bring Latin American law professors and students to Tulane for periods of study and teaching, and a wide-ranging teaching and research agenda sponsored by the Carnegie and Ford Foundations and carried on through the Middle American Research Institute and the Latin American Studies Program. If one were to take literally the rhetoric of various fundraising appeals for Tulane's Latin American activities during the 1950s, it would be possible—but incorrect—to conclude that the university's entire outreach effort toward Central and South America was part of a grand strategy for vanquishing Communism in the Western Hemisphere. In 1951, for example, Harris assured Tulane Board member and United Fruit Company vice president Joseph W. Montgomery that the university's instructional program on Latin America was "geared as much as possible to practical, present-day conditions, with constant attention to the relation of Latin America to the United States." In teaching Central American history, Harris explained, Tulane's faculty

124. *New York Times*, 2 August 1977; "CIA Statement a Blunder," Tulane *Hullabaloo*, 31 March 1978. Pertinent CIA correspondence and memoranda: 14 June, 7 August, 20 and 27 September, 26 October, 1, 14, and 27 November (the latter includes contract specifications and specific research objectives), 6, 11, and 21 December 1956; 21 January, 1, 4, and 18 February, 20 May, 1 July (progress report), 31 October, 7 November (progress report) 1957; 16 September 1959. These documents are in files maintained by Professor Henry Mason as 1978 chair of the University Senate Committee on Faculty Tenure, Freedom, and Responsibility.

"emphasized how this region has been the key to the defense of the Western Hemisphere . . . and has played a major role at every important turn in United States history."[125] During the 1950s Tulane's history faculty included three specialists on Central America, Professors William J. Griffith, Mario Rodriguez, and Thomas Karnes. Whether they or other area specialists regarded Central America as "the key to the defense of the Western Hemisphere" was of little concern to cold war policymakers, whose overwhelming emphasis upon the Soviet Union and Western Europe relegated Latin American affairs to the periphery of U.S. foreign policy calculations. The major exception to this pattern of neglect was the 1954 CIA-backed coup that toppled the Communist infiltrated government of Guatemalan president Jacobo Arbenz Guzman and installed the unswervingly pro-American regime of Colonel Carlos Castillo Armas. In October 1954, while journalists were still describing Guatemala as the "first liberated Soviet satellite," Harris informed the Board of Administrators about negotiations between the university, the State Department's Foreign Operations Administration, and the Guatemalan Ministry of Education for the planning and implementation of a general program of educational reform. The goal of the project would be to remove "so far as an educational program can, those causes of dissatisfaction and unrest which have provided fertile soil for the practice of foreign ideologies."[126]

Probably few knowledgeable observers would have denied the importance of improving Guatemalan schooling, least of all Tulane's Latin American Studies director William Griffith, who from 1944–47

125. Rufus C. Harris to Joseph W. Montgomery, 1 November 1951, box 9, RCH Papers. On the relation between cold war concerns and support for international studies by the Carnegie, Ford, and Rockefeller Foundations, see Robert A. McCaughey, *International Studies and Academic Enterprise: A Chapter in the Enclosure of American Learning* (New York: Columbia University Press, 1984), chaps. 6–7; Edward H. Berman, *Ideology and Philanthropy: The Influence of the Carnegie, Ford, and Rockefeller Foundations on American Foreign Policy* (Albany: State University of New York Press, 1983), chap. 4. Daniel S. Berman, "The Middle American Research Institute: Seventy Years of Middle American Research at Tulane University" (M.A. thesis, Tulane University, 1995) offers useful insights into the evolution of Tulane's Latin American program.

126. [Ralph Lee Woodward], "The History of Central American History at Tulane," *Tulanian* 57 (summer 1986): 22–3; John Gillin and Kalman H. Silvert, "Ambiguities in Guatemala," *Foreign Affairs* 34 (April 1956): 469 (first quotation)–482; BOA Minutes, 13 October 1954, item 7a of president's monthly report (second quotation). On the coup itself, see Richard H. Immerman, *The CIA in Guatemala: The Foreign Policy of Intervention* (Austin: University of Texas Press, 1982), chaps. 6–8.

had served as a special adviser to the Guatemalan government on educational policy. Just how far Griffith or other Central American specialists might have subscribed to Harris's instrumentalist rationale for educational improvement remains open to question. Although the FOA contract never materialized, Tulane maintained an active interest and involvement in Guatemalan affairs through Griffith and through the ongoing research of political scientist Kalman H. Silvert, whose studies of national and local government in Guatemala after the revolution of 1944 appeared under Tulane's imprint in the mid-fifties. In these and other writings Silvert displayed a grasp of modernization theory and a nuanced appreciation of the interrelationships between the economic, political, and cultural components of national identity that was painfully absent from the outlook of hard-line cold warriors.[127]

In a coauthored 1956 *Foreign Affairs* article—written after an additional research stint in Guatemala the previous year—Silvert advised a generally naive and uninformed readership that the Castillo Armas government stood before its own people as well as before world opinion "in an ambiguous light." Widely regarded as a creature of the U.S. State Department, the new regime offended the nationalistic sensibilities of its neighbors, suffered from internal corruption, and lacked a clear program beyond opposition to Communism. Paradoxically, the new regime employed police state tactics through a newly created National Committee for the Defense Against Communism while at the same time embracing, at least in principle, many of the social and economic reforms of the government it had overthrown. The latter fact led Silvert to emphasize the distortion that would result from trying to understand the Guatemalan situation exclusively in terms of the cold war's ideological polarities. The "real alternatives" for Guatemala and many other Latin American nations struggling to emerge from a semifeudal past of political authoritarianism, forced labor on large agricultural estates, exploitation of indigenous peoples, and the cultural fragmentation of inwardly focused peasant communities, Silvert argued, could scarcely be reduced to a simple choice between Communism or capitalism. Since all three of Guatemala's post-1944 governments had been "in the stream of . . . what we may tritely call modern Western cul-

127. [Woodward], "Central American History at Tulane"; Kalman H. Silvert, *A Study in Government: Guatemala*, 2 vols. (New Orleans: Middle American Research Institute, Tulane University, 1954–56).

ture, whether the ideological whitewash be leftist or rightist," Silvert urged policymakers to worry less about labels and give more attention to the substantive aspects of modernization and nation building.[128]

Silvert was not the only Tulane faculty member to reject the simplistic notion that the aim of international education was to fight Communism by instilling American attitudes and viewpoints into the minds of foreign nationals. In most Latin American initiatives, there was a more or less constant element of tension between the concerns and intellectual aims of highly trained area specialists on the one hand, and the political or economic priorities of at least some outside sponsors on the other. The external or utilitarian rationale for the field of comparative law was stated bluntly by Law School dean Ray Forrester, who advised President Harris in 1953 that American companies could derive "real practical value" from sponsoring visiting professorships at Tulane for distinguished faculty from Latin American law schools. In Forrester's opinion the visiting professorships would serve "as a means of developing good will and respect for the American point of view among the members of the legal profession in Latin America, who are nearly identical with the members and prospective members of the governments of Latin America."[129]

The case for a more evenhanded approach was ably expressed by Tulane's Mitchell Franklin in a 1950 article, "On the Teaching of Advanced Foreign Civilians in American Law Schools," published in the *Journal of Legal Education*. In a pedagogical argument that was fraught with larger implications, Franklin noted the existence of "two sharply opposed conceptions of comparative law, between which a struggle possibly impends." The comparative enterprise might seek either to "achieve and justify the co-equal existence of different legal orders," or to promulgate and defend "the hegemony of a particular legal order over other legal orders." Taking the second approach would lead almost unavoidably to a quest for greater uniformity in legal systems through the "subordination of politically weak legal orders." Recognizing that America had emerged as the "dominant metropolitan state" of the postwar world, Franklin urged U.S. law schools to resist the temptation to impose Anglo-American legal norms upon other cul-

128. Gillin and Silvert, "Ambiguities in Guatemala," 469 (first quote), 481 (second and third quotes).
129. Ray Forrester to Rufus C. Harris, 5 June 1953, box 37, RCH Papers.

tures. In a passage that had clear implications for the Tulane program, Franklin warned that any attempt to blot out the advanced foreign student's Romanist or civil law traditions would inevitably fail. In reaction to such an attempt, the "national feeling in colonial states will turn in due course against the American-trained lawyer and jurist," the New Orleans professor predicted.[130]

The critical perspective displayed by Franklin, Silvert, and other Tulane faculty with Latin American interests probably had less to do with political ideology than with concern over the terms under which lawyers and social scientists might find themselves asked to participate in international endeavors. Neither the self-evident truths of militant anti-Communism nor the exuberant claims of free enterprise dogma could be easily reconciled with the complexities of politics and culture in twenty different Latin American republics. In order to make even modest contributions to the understanding of hemispheric problems, lawyers, social scientists, and other academic investigators required freedom—not only from McCarthyite red hunters but also from the more subtle tyranny of consensus viewpoints and predetermined orthodoxies. In the atmosphere of the 1950s, serious intellectuals waged a struggle on at least two distinct levels as they sought to equip themselves for purposeful accomplishment in particular fields of knowledge. The first, and by far the most difficult, challenge was to win the battle for self-liberation from the ideological and cultural constraints that were absorbed in some fashion by virtually all academic disciplines. Those who succeeded at the task of critically examining the governing assumptions of a specialized subject area faced the additional problem of weighing the personal costs of intellectual independence. Almost by definition, originality implied controversy of either a professional or a political nature. The ultimate allegiance of the committed scholar or scientist was not—indeed could not be—directed toward an academic institution, a political creed, or even a nation state. What the professor owed the university and society was not loyalty but integrity—which, in turn, implied rigor in the pursuit of new knowledge and courage in the expounding of critical insight. By their very nature both teaching and

---

130. Mitchell Franklin, "On the Teaching of Advanced Foreign Civilians in American Law Schools," *Journal of Legal Education* 2 (summer 1950): 455–65 (quotations on p. 456).

research were subversive of all orthodoxies, including those pro-pounded by super-patriots and segregationist ideologues. Doubt rather than certainty lay at the heart of all real learning, and it was this as-pect of higher education which Tulane's critics found most troubling—and most difficult to comprehend.[131]

131. Although André Schiffrin, ed., *The Cold War and the University* (New York: New Press, 1997) appeared too late to influence the writing of this chapter, the volume's many thoughtful and stimulating essays underscore the cold war's pervasive impact on individual aca-demic disciplines, educational institutions, and the scope of intellectual freedom.

3

PORTENTS OF CHANGE
Race, Intercollegiate Athletics, and the Fall of a President

By 1957 Rufus Harris had served two decades as Tulane's president, guiding the university through a cycle of unprecedented growth and change. Any of the postwar initiatives with which Harris was most closely identified—the coordination of Newcomb with Arts and Sciences, the move toward selectivity and geographical diversity in undergraduate admissions, the dramatic expansion of graduate training and sponsored research, and, most obviously, the struggle to preserve academic freedom against encroachments from without and within—any and all of these undertakings contained the seeds of controversy and placed Harris in potential opposition to groups that held a more traditional conception of the university and its mission. Recognizing that reform, to be effective, could not openly repudiate Tulane's traditions, Harris worked hard to convince alumni, Board members, and the general public that change was essential for insuring continuity of institutional purpose. On most issues and with most audiences, including his own governing board, the president eventually carried the day. With the Board of Administrators, however, gaining support for individual reform proposals was only half the battle. In order for Tulane to remake itself in the image of a modern research university, more was required than official endorsement of new academic priorities. Besides confronting the bureaucratic problems and tremendous financial burdens of advanced research, the Board was called upon to face the cultural and political implications of competing in a national arena for money, faculty members, and superior students.

Prior to World War II, Tulane had restricted its national undergraduate recruitment almost exclusively to football players, which did nothing to enhance the university's academic stature. Throughout the 1950s the deemphasis of big time athletics would constitute one of the most controversial changes that President Harris urged upon the Tulane Board as part of a basic reorientation of institutional culture. The other hotly disputed issue that Harris kept almost continuously before the Board was racial integration. Both segregation and the thirst for gridiron glory reflected cultural patterns that were deeply embedded in the history of Tulane and other southern universities. Challenging either tradition entailed great political risk, and on both fronts the president was destined to face frustration and ultimate defeat. Harris's ongoing efforts to redirect the university's racial and athletic policies complicated a relationship with the Board of Administrators that was already strained by differences in political philosophy, disagreements over proper lines of authority in university governance, and personality conflicts with Board chairman Joseph Merrick Jones. The net result would be a gradual erosion of Harris's influence over the Board during the 1950s, culminating in his early retirement and immediate departure to assume the presidency of Mercer University as the decade drew to a close.

I

Although Tulane did not admit its first black student until 1963, some three years after the end of Harris's presidency, the issue of desegregation was scarcely a new item on the university's agenda. Legal challenges to the doctrine of "separate but equal" in southern higher education had been underway since the late 1930s, and after World War II the demands of black litigants grew more insistent. Between 1948 and 1950 federal courts compelled the law schools of previously white state universities in Oklahoma, Texas, Virginia, and Louisiana to admit black students for the first time. Although not directly concerned with undergraduate education or with segregation in elementary and secondary schools, the decisions left little doubt that in institutions supported by public funds, Jim Crow's days were numbered. Judicial victories over segregation in tax-supported schools placed private universities on notice that they too should prepare for change.[1]

1. Richard Kluger, *Simple Justice: The History of Brown v Board of Education and Black America's Struggle for Equality* (New York: Alfred A. Knopf, 1975), 280–9.

From the beginning Harris sought to persuade Tulane's Board of Administrators that the university should sail with rather than against the tide of history. Looking beyond the narrow legalities of admissions policy, he called upon Board members to take a broader view of the segregation issue and to think seriously about how racial practices related to other components of the school's academic and social mission. Harris began staking out his position in the autumn of 1949, when Emil Leipziger, a prominent local rabbi, joined the president of historically black Dillard University in asking Tulane to provide integrated seating in McAlister Auditorium for a speech by U.S. State Department officer and UN delegate Ralph J. Bunche. After reminding the Board that Bunche was black, Harris went on to summarize Rabbi Leipziger's argument "that Tulane owes it to the community . . . to present an outstanding intellectual leader of the Negro race" in a setting that would "mark a step forward in race relations on a plane where there should be no discrimination—on an intellectual plane." While Harris ultimately refused the request for McAlister, he cautioned Board members against ignoring the issues that had been raised. Within the next decade, he predicted, "these matters will develop and we should be thinking and determining what position Tulane University may take in their development."[2]

The new decade had not quite arrived when, at the final Board meeting of 1949, Harris returned to the issue of segregation. Having recently prohibited Dean Wisner from using Tulane facilities to host a gathering of social workers that included representatives from Atlanta University, Fisk University, and other black schools, Harris wanted the Board to understand that the matter of black participation in professional and learned societies was becoming an "exceedingly difficult problem." He went on to introduce the key elements of several pro-desegregation arguments that he would reiterate tirelessly over the next ten years. After pointing out that both the federal government and the "learned societies in the East, the North, and the West" were growing impatient with segregation, Harris reminded the Board that navy ROTC exams originally scheduled for McAlister auditorium had been moved to an off-campus location in order to comply with nondiscrimination requirements. Without "making any recommendation or requesting any advice," the president felt a responsibility to keep the

2. BOA Minutes, 18 October 1949, item 25 of president's monthly report.

Board abreast of ongoing developments. "Some of the southern states," he noted, were "quietly providing for graduate and professional education on a rather easy going, informal, non-segregation basis." In the circumstances it seemed prudent to collect data on the experiences of institutions in the border states, where the problems accompanying desegregation had been "surprisingly few." When elaborating this line of argument over the next decade, Harris relied on three interrelated ideas as the basic rationale for change. Tulane, he reasoned, should move away from segregation because it impeded the professional and intellectual life of the university, because outside pressure from government, academia, and private philanthropy demanded it, and finally, because token integration could be implemented in a manner that would minimize adverse publicity and leave Tulane in charge of its own destiny.[3]

It seems likely that Harris genuinely believed all of these arguments and that over time he came to regard integration as an ethical obligation as well as a practical necessity. But he did not approach the segregation issue in a spirit of self-righteousness or crusading zeal. For most of Harris's life, being a liberal in the Deep South had meant spurning Yankee interference and working to ameliorate the conditions of segregation through compromises reached after civilized—if profoundly unequal—negotiation between sympathetic whites and moderate black leaders. Thus in 1943, Harris became the lone member of the State Board of Education to support higher salaries for black teachers in Louisiana's segregated public schools.[4] Five years later he praised efforts to improve Georgia's black schools, but equivocated slightly on the issue of segregation per se. "I feel that the Negro has been unfairly treated in many respects," Harris wrote, adding that if blacks were given "educational and economic opportunity, social unfairness largely will take care of itself." The same gradualist perspective caused him to look askance at the open flaunting of segregationist etiquette in episodes like the 1949 interracial party attended by Tulane students. At that time, only a few months before he began to urge token desegregation upon the Tulane Board, Harris still warned against the damage that would result from naive and idealistic gestures that aroused vio-

3. Ibid., 13 December 1949, item 17 of president's monthly report (all quotations).
4. Leon M. Wallace to A. P. Tureaud, 30 June 1943, A. P. Tureaud Papers, Amistad Research Center, Tulane University. Cf. accounts of the State Board of Education meeting in *Baton Rouge Morning Advocate*, 1 July 1943 and *New Orleans Times-Picayune*, 1 July 1943.

lent opposition and undermined the patient work of black and white moderates who sought to solve racial problems "without strife or conflict."[5]

Harris's position accurately mirrored the transitional state of southern liberal thinking during the late 1940s, at a moment when the mantle of reform leadership had passed from the politically moribund Southern Conference for Human Welfare to the more mainstream and moderate Southern Regional Council, where traditional adherence to Jim Crow paternalism was giving way to a new conviction that segregation was wrong, or at least anachronistic, and destined for elimination—preferably through the kind of voluntary local action that would preserve order, strengthen the hand of responsible leaders, and forestall federal intervention. Having witnessed the demise of SCHW at close hand, and being fully aware of the intense hostility manifested toward its successor organization, the New Orleans–based Southern Conference Education Fund, Harris took pains to avoid all appearances of overzealousness and to identify himself with the enlightened realism of the liberal center.[6]

Initially his posture struck a responsive chord with the Tulane Board, which was itself in a state of flux following the sudden death of Chairman Esmond Phelps after a heart attack in 1950 and the elevation of Joseph Jones as his successor. Despite the troubling questions raised by McCarthy-era conflicts over academic freedom, Harris enjoyed a honeymoon of sorts during the early years of Jones's chairmanship, as the Board threw itself with unprecedented vigor into the fundraising activities necessary to increase Tulane's endowment and meet the recurring deficits in annual operating budgets. For a time—from roughly the beginning of Jones's chairmanship until the year following the 1954 *Brown* decision—a majority of the Board seemed to accept the idea that token desegregation at the graduate and professional level would be an inevitable part of the university's emergence as a selective research institution. At the same time all Board members

5. Rufus C. Harris to J. W. Holley, 15 January 1948, box 99, Herbert Eugene Longenecker Papers, Tulane University (hereafter cited as HEL Papers); untitled typescript dated 21 February 1949, box 29, RCH Papers. The document was subsequently published as "A Letter from the President," *Letter from Tulane* 3 (June 1949): 2 (all quotations).

6. Anthony Lake Newberry, "Without Urgency or Ardor: The South's Middle-of-the-Road Liberals and Civil Rights, 1945–1960" (Ph.D. diss., Ohio University, 1982) provides an exceptionally dispassionate and nuanced treatment of the changing center of gravity within mainstream liberal ranks.

were aware of the provisions in the original bequests of both Paul Tulane and Josephine Louise Newcomb restricting the use of their donations to the education of whites, as well as the language in the university's 1884 state charter restricting admission to whites. Any actions that ignored or set aside racial barriers were certain to be broadly unpopular, and unpredictable as to ultimate legal implications as well. No members of the Board expressed enthusiasm over the prospect of admitting black students, and it seems likely that most who supported the idea did so reluctantly. That a consensus of any sort emerged was a tribute to Harris's skill and persistence in keeping racial policy almost constantly before the Board without seeming to press for hasty or unreasonable action.

In reality, the segregation issue would have been impossible to ignore during the early fifties even had Harris desired to do so. Loyola University, only a few yards from the Tulane campus, desegregated its law school voluntarily in 1952. The following year a survey by the Association of American Law Schools revealed that twenty-two law schools in the southern and border states did or would admit blacks, while nineteen schools still refused integration. A similar survey by the Southern Regional Council determined that by the 1954 school year, between 750 and 800 "Negro" students were enrolled in previously segregated institutions. Black enrollment was limited mainly to graduate and professional schools, particularly colleges of education, and was concentrated around a regional periphery that included Texas and the upper South. Although public institutions in the five Deep South states of Florida, Georgia, South Carolina, Alabama, and Mississippi still excluded all black students, only Mississippi had avoided at least token breaches of the color line in private church colleges and theological seminaries.[7]

The meaning of these developments was not lost upon President Harris. Neither he nor the Board of Administrators seemed particularly shocked in April 1952 when Mack J. Spears, a black public school principal in New Orleans, applied for admission to the Graduate School in Tulane's upcoming summer session. With a bachelor's degree from Dillard University and an M.A. from nearby Xavier, Spears

7. Richard Kluger, *Simple Justice*, 280–3, 289; BOA Minutes, 14 October 1953, item 23 of president's monthly report; John Robert Payne, "A Jesuit Search for Social Justice: The Public Career of Louis J. Twomey, S.J., 1947–1969" (Ph.D. diss., University of Texas, 1976), 191–5; Guy B. Johnson, "New Ways on the Campus," *New South* 10 (February 1955): 1–10.

was academically qualified for admission. His case gave substance to Harris's frequent reminders that Tulane could not avoid direct involvement in the greatest challenge facing southern universities in the postwar era. In mid-May the Board of Administrators held a "full discussion" of Spears's case and voted to refer the matter to its Law Committee with instructions that the latter group—consisting of Chairman Jones, Joseph McCloskey, J. Blanc Monroe, George A. Wilson, and Marie Louise Wilcox Snellings—prepare a letter telling Spears that "Tulane could not accept his application for entrance at this time." The phraseology seemed to imply that change was in the offing—an impression strengthened by the official notation that "[t]he Board was mindful of the present social trends and that a decision would have to be reached upon this subject."[8]

Before the May 12 meeting adjourned, Board member Clifford Favrot suggested that Harris meet with representatives of such peer institutions as Rice, Emory, Duke, and Vanderbilt to get their views on the situation facing segregated private colleges. Only a few weeks earlier, in mid-April, these same schools had joined Tulane and the state universities of North Carolina, Texas, and Virginia in creating the Council of Southern Universities, a group that would meet again at Nashville in the fall. Perhaps responding to Favrot's suggestion, Harris wrote Vanderbilt chancellor Harvie Branscomb asking if the Tennessee school would join Tulane in announcing a common policy of admitting blacks, a move that would have allowed both universities to avoid being the first to take so controversial a step. Although Branscomb favored a joint policy, the Vanderbilt trustees rejected the idea on October 10, 1952, even as they made the first tentative move toward desegregating their own School of Religion.[9]

Vanderbilt's refusal may have spared Harris personal embarrassment since, only two days earlier, Tulane's Board had directed him to make no formal commitments concerning racial policy at the upcoming meeting of the Council of Southern Universities. The preliminary agenda for the council's October session included talks aimed at achieving "a working understanding among constituent institutions, especially the private ones, with reference to the future enrollment of negroes at the graduate and professional school level." When the

8. BOA Minutes, 12 May 1952.
9. Ibid.; ibid., 17 April 1952, item 21 of president's monthly report; Conkin, *Gone with the Ivy*, 541–2, 779 n. 6.

council gathered on October 24, the group's five private schools conferred at length about current segregation requirements and the
prospects for change. Harris would later report that the talks covered
such relevant matters as "the general attitudes of the boards of trustees" and the "extent to which there were developments in the direction" of admitting blacks for graduate work. After acknowledging that
private schools would probably find it necessary to "reconsider their
positions . . . and future actions" concerning segregation, the council
discussed whether some general statement on the subject would be
helpful. In the end the schools agreed to keep each other informed but
declined to issue any joint declaration because of the "diversity of
problems" faced by individual institutions.[10]

With the South's leading private universities unable to muster even
a symbolic show of unity on the segregation issue, Harris continued to
argue that Tulane should bow gracefully to the pressures exerted by
national funding agencies and accrediting bodies. The field of law was
an area of special concern—in part, one suspects, because Harris was
a former dean of Tulane's Law School, and in part because the Tulane
Board contained a high proportion of attorneys. Throughout the
1950s Harris provided regular updates concerning the university's increasingly untenable position as one of the steadfast opponents of anti-
discrimination measures sponsored by Yale University (the president's
own alma mater) and a number of other delegations within the Association of American Law Schools. As a former president of the latter
body, Harris took no satisfaction from witnessing the University of
Texas, Louisiana State University, the University of Virginia, Emory,
Duke, and Vanderbilt vote for integrationist resolutions or policies
during the 1950s, which Tulane refused to support.[11] With sanctions

10. BOA Minutes, 8 October 1952; Agenda for the meeting of the Council of Southern
Universities in Nashville, Tennessee, at Vanderbilt University, 24 October 1952, item 3, box 7,
RCH Papers (first quotation); BOA Minutes, 12 November 1952, item 10 of president's monthly
report (second quotation); Minutes of the Council of Southern Universities, 24 October 1952,
item 7, box 7, RCH Papers (third–fourth quotations).
11. BOA Minutes: 9 January 1951, item 6 of president's monthly report; 8 May 1951, item 14
of president's monthly report; 13 November 1951, item 31 of president's monthly report; 11
December 1952, item 4 of president's monthly report; 14 January 1952, item 9 of president's
monthly report; 14 October 1952, item 23 of president's monthly report; 8 April 1953, item 12 of
president's monthly report; 13 October 1954, item 23 of president's report; 12 October 1955,
item 12 of president's monthly report; 11 December 1957, item 9 of president's monthly report;
8 January 1958, item 4 of president's monthly report; 12 November 1958, item 5 of president's
monthly report.

looming on the horizon, the university eventually fell back upon the rather transparent strategy of seeking to avoid censure by answering AALS queries with the statement that no academically qualified black applicants had been refused admission to Tulane's Law School during the previous year. This evasive response became little more than a legal technicality after 1956 when a young back attorney named Ernest N. Morial, one of LSU's first two black Law School graduates, was denied permission to audit two regular Tulane Law School courses offered to practicing lawyers as part of a larger professional study program.[12]

Tulane's quandary over the "Yale amendment" in the Association of American Law Schools grew out of the Board of Administrators' inability to resolve the legal issues surrounding black admissions for the university as a whole. From 1951 onward the Board referred all segregation questions to its Law Committee, bypassing the seemingly more appropriate Educational Affairs Committee. Although this procedure inevitably diminished the importance of faculty opinion in shaping university policy, a legalistic approach to segregation did not automatically favor either the supporters or the opponents of voluntary integration. Initially there was reason to hope that the entire matter would be quickly settled. At the time of the Spears application in 1952, the recently appointed Board member Marie Louise Snellings, an attorney and former law student of Harris, offered to make a study of the Board's legal options in light of Paul Tulane's expressed desire that his donations be used for promoting education among "the white young persons in the city of New Orleans, State of Louisiana."[13] On April 8, 1953, the Board received copies of Snellings's report, a document of just over seventeen typed pages that surveyed the gradual erosion of legal and cultural support for segregation since the late nineteenth century. After reviewing the case law that had marked the progress of the NAACP's campaign against discrimination in voting, housing, education, and public accommodations, Snellings dismissed the legal obstacles to integration at Tulane in a scant two pages—less space than

12. Ibid., 10 October 1956, item 23 of president's monthly report. Some two decades later Morial would be elected mayor of New Orleans.

13. Ibid., 8 October 1952. The phraseology is from Paul Tulane's 8 May 1882 letter to Randall Lee Gibson and the sixteen other original administrators of the Tulane Educational Fund, a document embodied in the Board's original charter dated 28 May 1882. Dyer, *Tulane*, appendices 1–3, contains the full texts of the founding documents of Tulane University and Newcomb College.

she devoted to the summary and direct quotation of Swedish economist Gunnar Myrdal's liberal manifesto, *An American Dilemma*.[14]

Whether or not most Board members agreed with Myrdal's passionate assertion that "the American nation will not have peace with its conscience until inequality is stamped out and the principle of public education is realized universally" (a passage quoted in Snellings's report), the Administrators had no choice but to think seriously about Snellings's conclusion that "[t]here appears to be no legal prohibition against the admission of negroes at Tulane, and, at the present time[,] no legal proposition to force Tulane to admit negroes." In her argument, Snellings focused upon two sets of legal facts. First, the Tulane University of Louisiana was a legal hybrid created between 1882 and 1884 when the Louisiana legislature turned over the assets and control of the old University of Louisiana to the Administrators of the recently established Tulane Educational Fund, a private body. The resulting contract between the Tulane Administrators and the state gave the university "certain public aspects," in the form of tax exemptions, revenue from state property, tuition scholarships for each legislative district, and ex officio membership on the Tulane Board for the governor of Louisiana, the state superintendent of education, and the mayor of New Orleans. In a future court test, Snellings implied, Tulane's public features might outweigh the racial restrictions of the Tulane gift. A second point, which Snellings examined only in passing, concerned the absence of the qualifying adjective "white" in the actual charter and laws establishing the Board of Administrators and the university itself. Although the intent to exclude blacks seemed clear, the language itself was ambiguous. These legal issues would preoccupy the Board for the next several years, resulting in a cycle of vacillating indecision that at times resembled administrative paralysis.[15]

The reasoning behind Snellings's position received its fullest elaboration the following year at a meeting of the Board's Law Committee that was prompted in part by pressure from the Graduate School faculty. Before discussing the specific events of April and May 1954, it is important to recall that pressures for a decision on segregation had been building steadily throughout the early fifties. In the wake of Mack Spears's application, inquiries from black students began arriving at a

14. Marie Louise Snellings, "The American Negro, Yesterday and To-Day," box 99, HEL Papers.

15. Ibid., 12–4 (quotations).

steady rate. At least twelve blacks sought admission to Tulane between 1952 and 1956, with half of the total applying during 1953 and 1954.[16] President Harris examined each application and Chairman Jones saw most of them. In reminding the Board that "well qualified Negro students" continued to seek admission, especially for graduate work, Harris made no secret of his desire to see a change in policy. "I do not wish to mention this every time [the Board meets], but neither should the Administrators conclude that there is not a continuing pressure for these admissions," he emphasized in May 1953. He then reiterated his support for token integration at the graduate level, assuring the Board that the local need was genuine, that few blacks would actually enroll, and that such a move would tend to diminish pressure for desegregation at the undergraduate level.[17]

Harris's comments came at a time when most New Orleanians were keenly aware that the United States Supreme Court would soon render a final verdict on the constitutionality of de jure segregation in public schools. Among faculty on Tulane's campus, there was a growing conviction that the university should begin opening its doors to black graduate students without further delay. This opinion was forcefully expressed on April 12, 1954, at a meeting attended by approximately two-thirds of the 155 professors who comprised Tulane's graduate faculty. At the request of philosophy department head James K. Feibleman and mathematics professor Alexander D. Wallace, the faculty took up what was officially described as "the problem of admission of Negroes to the Graduate School." After "much discussion favorable to the admission of colored students," Dean Cole moved the adoption of a pro-integration statement that a faculty group had drafted prior to the meeting. In its final version the statement read, "In view of the great need of all Southerners for opportunities to receive specialized training, the Faculty of the Graduate School recommends that steps be

16. BOA Minutes, 8 October 1952; ibid., 10 October 1956, item 23 of president's monthly report; Elijah Rhodes to Tulane School of Social Work, 20 October 1952; Forrest U. Lake to Laura R. Clark, 4 March 1953; Roger P. McCutcheon to Edna-Theresa Dandridge, 23 April 1953; R. M. Lumiansky, Memorandum of a conversation with Sibyl Haydel, 22 July 1954; Jeffery C. Bibbons to Elizabeth Wisner, 26 April 1954; Forrest U. Lake to Gloria B. Johnson, 11 May 1954; Marion P. Baker to Rufus C. Harris, 27 May 1954; Roger P. McCutcheon to Osceola Williams-Nelson, 26 May 1954; James Collins Jr. to Rufus C. Harris, 21 June 1954; Elizabeth Wisner to Herwald M. Price, 4 April 1956. All documents in box 99, HEL Papers.

17. BOA Minutes, 13 May 1953, item 27 of president's monthly report.

taken to clarify the policy of admission to the Graduate School in order that admission of Negroes may be facilitated."[18]

Passed by a nearly unanimous vote, and transmitted to President Harris without fanfare, the recommendation soon became a matter of public knowledge. On May 7 the *Hullabaloo* published an unsigned editorial entitled "Enroll the Negro," which summarized the graduate faculty proceedings and printed the text of the formal recommendation, followed by a strong editorial endorsement. Confident that most graduate students supported integration, the campus newspaper took the view that Tulane should admit blacks "freely and graciously, as early as possible, before the air is tensed by a Supreme Court order demanding that the color line be dropped." After quoting an anonymous faculty member's description of the April 12 statement as "an attempt to show the administration that we are ready to take in Negroes on absolutely the same equality basis as whites," the *Hullabaloo* paraphrased a recent campus speech by the outspoken Mississippi editor Hodding Carter, declaring that "[m]orally, there should be no objection to removing the imaginary line that brands some men as second class citizens."[19]

Public enthusiasm for racial equality was not a conspicuous feature of southern university life during the mid-fifties, and the *Hullabaloo* editorial gained instant attention. Fearing that Board members would react negatively to "a further agitative appearance of pressure" for desegregation, Harris advised Tulane's academic deans that "caution should be observed to avoid any similar resolutions by any other faculty." In response to telephone inquiries from both local and national media, Joseph Jones released a statement emphasizing the ongoing nature of the Board's deliberations over segregation. "[P]rior to the adoption of the Graduate School Faculty resolution," Jones explained, the entire matter had been referred to the "committee scheduled to consider it. . . . This is the Board's position until the Committee makes its report."[20] Jones's chronology may have been technically correct,

18. Ibid., 12 May 1954, item 3 of president's monthly report; Graduate School Faculty Minutes, 12 April 1954, box 9-D, RCH Papers; *New Orleans Item*, 7 May 1954.

19. Tulane *Hullabaloo*, 7 May 1954, p. 2.

20. Minutes of the Academic Council, 20 May 1954, box 1, RCH Papers (first–second quotations). (The authors are indebted to Ms. Melissa Kean of Rice University for calling this reference to our attention.) BOA Minutes, 12 May 1954 (third–fifth quotations).

but despite his disclaimer it seems evident that the faculty resolution and subsequent publicity brought the Board to the threshold of a decision on desegregation. On May 13, following a Board meeting the previous day and less than a week after the *Hullabaloo* editorial, the Law Committee met to consider the *"Question of Admission of Negroes,"* a subject "referred to this Committee for consideration several weeks ago." (The graduate faculty resolution had passed exactly one month earlier.)

The May 13 meeting became the occasion for a full-scale elaboration of the ideas that Snellings had presented to the Board the previous year. Confining their attention to the Administrators' 1882 charter of incorporation (which included Paul Tulane's letter referring to the "white young persons" of New Orleans) and the Louisiana constitutional amendment embodied in Legislative Act 43 of 1884 (which gave the Tulane Board the property and authority previously vested in the administrators of the state-supported University of Louisiana), the Law Committee sought to determine how far the specific language of these documents required adherence to the racial limitation in Paul Tulane's initial letter. President Harris attended the May 13 meeting, which took place in the office of Board member J. Blanc Monroe, and the resulting deliberations bore unmistakable signs of both men's skill at legal analysis. After acknowledging that Paul Tulane's letter of May 2, 1882, directed that the income from his donations be applied to "the promotion and encouragement of intellectual, moral[,] and industrial education among the white young persons in the city of New Orleans, State of Louisiana," the Law Committee noted the crucial fact that the actual instrument of donation in the Board's charter contained no such geographic or racial restrictions. On the contrary, the Administrators were designated as "absolute owners" of the donated Tulane property, a term that seemingly nullified the qualifying phrase "for the purpose already by me mentioned." More important, the Board's specific "objects and purposes," as set forth in Article III of the charter, were defined as follows: "To hold property, both real and personal, by purchase or by donation, for educational purposes, and to use and dispose of the same upon the terms and conditions upon which the said property is or may be donated or acquired."[21]

21. J. Blanc Monroe memorandum summarizing deliberations of Law Committee on 13 May 1954, box 99, HEL Papers.

The concluding phrase left no doubt that the Board of Administrators had been authorized to acquire and use property upon "terms and conditions" different from those in the original Tulane gift—a mandate they had first exercised in 1884 by assuming control of the state property previously dedicated to or used by the University of Louisiana. Under the terms of the 1884 act, moreover, the Board agreed to establish a university in New Orleans "dedicated to the intellectual, moral, and industrial education of the youth of the state." The proviso appeared twice, once in section four of the law and again in section six, where it was coupled with the phrase "under the terms of the donation of Paul Tulane." Nowhere did the adjective "white" appear in either the law or, as previously noted, in the actual legal instrument of Tulane's donation.

On the basis of these facts, the Law Committee agreed unanimously that so long as funds equal to or greater than the revenue derived from the Tulane gift were used for educating whites, there was no legal basis for claiming that the conditions of the donation would be violated by using funds from other sources to educate "persons not of the white race." The committee's second unanimous conclusion provided an even broader sanction for integration. Because Paul Tulane's actual instrument of donation had been unconditional, "the Board could utilize the income from the Tulane gift for the purpose of educating other than white persons without endangering the gift." These were the conclusions that would be reported to the full Board.[22]

Thus, on May 13, 1954, a scant four days before Chief Justice Earl Warren delivered the U.S. Supreme Court's momentous ruling in the case of *Brown v. Board of Education*, Tulane seemed poised to join the ranks of those southern private universities which had opened their doors voluntarily to black graduate and professional students. Almost immediately, however, something started to go wrong—seriously wrong, from the standpoint of those who believed the university's future hinged upon the Board's willingness to show courage in repudiating a regional legacy of racial discrimination. The first signs of trouble appeared less than a week after the May 13 meeting, when Snellings confessed to Harris that she was having second thoughts about her nominally integrationist stance. "You know I have been thinking a great deal about our race problem and I am further from a clear cut conclu-

22. Ibid.

sion in my own mind than I was a year ago," Snellings wrote on May 17, the day of the *Brown* decision. Her uncertainty would soon infect other Board members—including Joseph Jones, who at least through the May 13 meeting and probably for a short while thereafter seemed ready to make the long-anticipated announcement that Tulane was no longer an exclusive preserve of New Orleans's "young white persons." How exceedingly close Jones had come to endorsing token desegregation was revealed on June 9, when he advised the Board that after the Law Committee's May 13 meeting, "he had prepared a statement on the matter [of black admissions] which he [now] desired to refer back to the Law Committee, and that, furthermore, he is not prepared to act in the matter at this time, and suggested that the whole matter of segregation be laid over to a future date."[23]

It is impossible on the basis of surviving evidence to say with certainty how close Jones actually came to initiating desegregation in 1954 or why he failed to do so. Several factors may have come into play, including the sobering impact of the *Brown* decision itself, Jones's worsening personal relations with President Harris, the influence of new Board members Lester Lautenschlaeger and Ashton Phelps, and the likelihood that Snellings (a staunch Harris ally) would abandon her tenuous support of desegregation. Some insight into Jones's underlying intentions may be derived from the brief official summary of his remarks at the June 9 meeting. According to the Board minutes, Jones referred to the fact that in 1908 Tulane president E. B. Craighead had prepared an address to the Louisiana Legislature entitled, "As a State Institution Tulane Asks State Aid." The bid for an appropriation failed, and Jones was convinced that the legislature refused aid "on the basis that Tulane was not a state institution." The remarks almost certainly constituted the beginning of a rebuttal or counterargument aimed at neutralizing Snellings's 1953 warning that Tulane's "public aspects" might subject the university to the same desegregation requirements imposed upon state schools.[24]

Had Jones shared Snellings's initial concern, he would probably have favored token integration in the hope of avoiding a court test that could jeopardize Tulane's status as a private school—which was precisely the fate that awaited the university some seven years in the fu-

23. Marie Louise Snellings to Rufus C. Harris, 17 May 1954, Snellings Correspondence file, RCH Papers (first quotation); BOA Minutes, 9 June 1954 (second quotation).
24. BOA Minutes, 9 June 1954.

ture. It was almost as if, having been carried to the brink of action by liberal gradualist arguments envisioning a minuscule and carefully selected black presence at Tulane, Jones and his colleagues retreated in panic after realizing that the *Brown* decision placed the entire fabric of southern race relations in jeopardy. If this view is accurate, much of what transpired during the next six years can be seen as a search for reasons to avoid action—and thus to postpone the inevitable—for as long as possible. It is also possible, and perhaps likely, that Louisiana's rapid plunge into the emotionally charged politics of massive resistance to integration caused many Board members to become fearful of the institutional and personal repercussions that might flow from a decision to admit black students. This would be one plausible interpretation of what became the Board's official, and profoundly ambiguous, public stance. No doubt still other factors, including Jones's desire to have unanimous Board support for any new departure in racial policy, help explain the Administrators' failure to act. What can be said with considerable assurance is that during the month of the *Brown* decision, the outlook of the Tulane Board, president, faculty, and student body very nearly converged upon a policy of gradual, voluntary desegregation, whereas after that time the Board's policy of delay and inaction ran counter to a steadily expanding integrationist consensus that would culminate during the early 1960s.

Throughout the remainder of the decade this divergence in outlooks was often obscured by the desire of faculty liberals to believe that the Board shared their views, a perception that Jones did nothing to discourage. Behind the scenes, however, Board members reacted to the *Brown* decision with stunned apprehension and almost immediately began reassessing the potential consequences of black admissions. By the winter of 1954–55 the Law Committee's implied endorsement of voluntary graduate level desegregation had begun to seem more like a defense of the racial status quo. The change was apparent in a January 6 letter from Marie Louise Snellings to Joseph Jones, in which Snellings effectively repudiated her earlier quasi-integrationist views. Having previously argued that Tulane could legally admit or continue to exclude blacks, she now began to reformulate her position in a way that emphasized its restrictive rather than its permissive aspects. Unable to "find any legal grounds on which to base either exclusion or admission of negroes," Snellings now believed that "for the present and forseeable [*sic*] future, we should maintain a watchful policy of observation," and make no move toward black admissions. Anxious to avoid the appearance of temporizing, Snellings assured Jones that "The trend of events is in one direction and we will reach it in time. The time I refer to is a time of adjustment, a time to see how the very recent decision regarding the public schools works out. . . . It is my earnest opinion that we should try to cooperate with the Supreme Court and at the same time try to maintain our equilibrium. It may take twenty-five years for this country to work out the ways and means to carry into effect the Supreme Court decision abolishing segregation in our public schools."[25]

If attorney Snellings hoped white southerners would "try to cooperate" with the nation's highest court, she gave little indication of when or how the cooperative approach would bring black students to Tulane. "Perhaps in a year or two I may believe that we have reached the time when negroes should be admitted. Perhaps it will be five, or ten years. I do not know," she admitted in her January letter.[26] Upon receiving a copy of Snellings's letter in Shreveport on January 7, Law Committee member George A. Wilson endorsed the views of his north Louisiana colleague. Without having personally researched the matter, Wilson had come to "feel rather definitely that, as a strict legal principle, there is no basis on which persons of the negro race could force Tulane to admit them." Given the university's presumed legal impregnability, Wilson believed that "as a matter of policy" the Board should maintain its traditional posture of excluding blacks from all divisions of the university, both graduate and undergraduate. "I see no more reason for admitting them to the Graduate School than to Newcomb," Wilson told fellow Law Committee member Joseph McCloskey with an air of finality. In the end, however, Wilson, like Snellings, counseled delay rather than defiance. Within a period of "not many years," he acknowledged, the Board might take a different view of "the policy question." Until then nothing should change. "I do not think that this is the time for Tulane to be instrumental in hastening the end of segregation," Wilson declared.[27]

25. Snellings to Joseph M. Jones, 6 January 1955, box 99, HEL Papers.

26. Ibid. At one state school, Southwestern Louisiana Institute (now the University of Louisiana at Lafayette), cooperation was accompanied by action when black students were admitted without fanfare in the wake of the *Brown* decision. By September 1954 some eighty African American students were attending the previously segregated college. Clare Taylor and Michael Martin, "Justice for All," *La Louisiane* (spring 1997): 24–7.

27. George A. Wilson to Joseph McCloskey, 7 January 1955, box 99, HEL Papers.

These sentiments formed the invisible backdrop for a discussion of segregation policies when the full Board held its regular meeting on January 12, 1955. On that occasion the Board considered two Law Committee reports, the first of which concerned the Tulane Lyceum Association, a private group that sponsored evening lectures on the Tulane campus. Before deciding whether to accept black members, the Lyceum Association sought clarification of university policy concerning segregation at public events. The Law Committee concluded that the Board had legal authority to either permit or deny the use of Tulane facilities to nonsegregated audiences. Unwilling to be placed in the position of directly sanctioning integration, the Board refused to take a position on the matter. The Law Committee's second report concerned the April 1954 graduate faculty resolution that had prompted the detailed examination of the Board's charter obligations in May of the previous year. Although the committee had then agreed unanimously that accepting black graduate students would in no way jeopardize the Tulane endowment, a very different conclusion was now reported to the Board. Without completely repudiating the idea of desegregation, Law Committee chairman J. Blanc Monroe reported simply that Tulane could legally either admit or exclude black students— thus simply reiterating the ambiguous Snellings position, which had by 1955 taken on overwhelmingly conservative overtones. After further discussion the Board voted to inform the graduate faculty that the question of admitting blacks "has been under consideration for a long time and will continue to receive further serious consideration." The next month Joseph Jones elaborated the Board's position by assuring the faculty that while the Board was "presently not prepared to alter" segregation policies, the "whole matter is now, and will continue to be, until it is resolved finally, the subject of most careful study."[28]

Although an outside observer might have concluded that nothing had changed by early 1955, it is clear in retrospect that Tulane's momentum toward voluntary desegregation had been effectively halted. Within the next year it would be decisively reversed, as Louisiana's political climate worsened and new personalities made their influence felt. The Law Committee itself took on a different configuration in

28. BOA Minutes, 12 January 1955 (first quotation); Joseph Jones to Rufus C. Harris, 7 February 1955, box 99, HEL Papers (second–third quotations).

1955 with the addition of two new members, Ashton Phelps and Lester Lautenschlaeger, both of whom had been named to the Board some two years earlier. Little direct evidence exists concerning either man's attitudes toward segregation; yet it was surely no coincidence that Lautenschlaeger's law partner, Harry Gamble Jr., became actively involved in reassessing the Board's legal position with respect to the racial restrictions in the Tulane bequest. By April 1955, Board members had received Gamble's digest of relevant passages from the Board's charter and subsequent state enactments. In June, Joseph Jones announced the discovery of additional correspondence and legal documents in which Paul Tulane reiterated the requirement that his philanthropy be used only for the education of whites. Meanwhile, Gamble's father, Harry Gamble Sr., was sending mass mailings to Tulane and LSU faculty in an effort to elicit support for the Society for the Preservation of State Government and Racial Integrity, a short-lived segregationist group of which he was founder and head. Although Lautenschlaeger assured Harris that the younger Gamble's legal research had no connection with the father's "Racial Integrity" initiative, the Gambles' activities inevitably gave an ominous cast to Jones's announcement that the Law Committee would reconsider its position over the summer and report to the full Board in the fall.[29]

Supporters of desegregation would have been still more discouraged had they known about a July 1955 report to the full Board in which Snellings reviewed her previous support of desegregation and then categorically reversed her position on the basis of the documents that had come to light during the previous several months. Passing silently over the legal rationale for integration she had endorsed in May 1954, Snellings now emphasized that Paul Tulane had eventually executed three acts of donation—one in 1882, a second in 1884, and a third in 1886—all of which repeated or referred back to the "white young persons" proviso in the Board's charter. Snellings conceded that the university had ignored the restriction when admitting Chinese and Hawaiian students, but to her the point seemed irrelevant. Paul Tulane, she argued, was "deeply conscious of the negro problem in Louisiana," having made his first donation only three years after the end of the "Carpet Bag era." In using the adjective "white," Snellings explained,

29. [Harry Gamble Jr.], "Finding of Fact," April 1955, box 99, HEL Papers; Lester Lautenschlaeger to Rufus C. Harris, 10 May 1955 (quotation), box 99, HEL Papers; BOA Minutes, 8 June 1955.

the philanthropist actually "meant 'white, not negro,' and was trying to preserve an institution for white youth in an area with a huge negro population during an era when the negroes were threatening to engulf the control of Louisiana." These facts were pertinent, she continued, because Article 1527 of the Louisiana Civil Code allowed a donor to impose any conditions he pleased upon a gift so long as the provisions contained nothing contrary to "law or good morals." In Paul Tulane's case the donor's intentions were "abundantly clear," and until a court ruled that his racial stipulations ran counter to law or morality Snellings regarded the Administrators as bound to carry them out.[30]

In the closing paragraph of her report Snellings outlined what was destined to become the Board's official justification for inactivity on the race issue between 1956 and 1961. If the Administrators determined "as a matter of policy" that blacks should be admitted to Tulane, it would be necessary "for our own protection" to seek a court ruling that either invalidated the racial limitation in the original bequest or that declared Tulane to be a public school. Any other procedure, Snellings warned, might subject the Board to lawsuits from alumni or heirs of Paul Tulane "seeking a loophole to attack the donation (like Wilbur Kelley in [a] letter of May 12, 1955)." As an alternate "course of action" on segregation, Snellings proposed inaction—"to maintain our present position"—until the courts ruled that private as well as public schools must accept black students.[31]

The policy alternatives laid out in Snellings's July 1955 report constitute a useful benchmark for gauging the Board's basic priorities on the matter of race. If the Administrators desired to implement a policy of voluntary desegregation, then seeking a declaratory judgment on the racial provision of the Tulane bequest offered a simple and direct way to clarify the legal consequences of such a policy. But initiating legal proceedings toward this end made little sense unless the Board was serious about desegregation, since the entire process could lead the university into uncharted judicial territory on questions of Tulane's private versus public status and a host of other legal matters. Law School dean Ray Forrester grasped the point clearly when he cautioned President Harris against acting precipitously in the matter. "Until the Board itself decides what it wants to do on this problem of

30. Marie Louise Snellings, Report to the Board of Administrators [ca. 20 July 1955], box 99, HEL Papers, 2 (first quotation), 4 (all subsequent quotations).
31. Ibid., 5.

admitting negroes, I see little to be gained, and perhaps a great deal to be lost, by instituting litigation involving legal issues which may be resolved either way," Forrester concluded.[32]

The Board ended the decade without taking a public stand on the merits of desegregation, and no declaratory judgment on the Tulane gift was ever sought. Perhaps the Board's passivity spoke for itself. In any case the situation gave rise to a pattern of circular logic, in which attorneys counseled delay until a policy decision had been reached, while the Administrators postponed action because of the legal uncertainties. From a local standpoint, moreover, the passage of time placed ever more obstacles in the path of voluntary integration. By the spring of 1956 Louisiana's political climate had become violently hostile to even the most circumspect gestures of support for integrated education. Litigation aimed at desegregating New Orleans's public schools had been underway since 1952, and in the aftermath of the *Brown* decision white voters across the state endorsed the work of a new Joint Legislative Committee on Segregation by ratifying a constitutional amendment that authorized the full use of state police powers to maintain separate schools. Not all hard-line segregationists contented themselves with legal resistance. In July 1955, while Snellings was preparing her anti-integration report, two black graduate students were shot by an unknown gunman on the campus of Louisiana State University. At the time of the shooting episode, moreover, New Orleans was emerging as a major center of massive resistance to desegregation in south Louisiana by virtue of its support for the newly organized Greater New Orleans Citizens' Council. During the peak of its popularity the following year, the Citizens' Council packed thousands of Confederate-flag-waving spectators into New Orleans's Municipal Auditorium to hear speakers denounce integration as a Communist plot and make dire predictions of an impending race war.[33]

The chairman of the New Orleans Citizens' Council was none other than Dr. Emmett L. Irwin, past president of the Louisiana Medical Association, former head of the Department of Surgery at the LSU Medical School, and a Tulane alumnus. In 1936 Irwin had led the Louisiana

32. Ray Forrester to Rufus C. Harris, 29 September 1955, box 99, HEL Papers.

33. *Baton Rouge Morning Advocate*, 20 July 1955, clipping in possession of LSU Oral History Project; Neil R. McMillen, *The Citizens' Council: Organized Resistance to the Second Reconstruction* (Urbana: University of Illinois Press, 1971), 59–67.

Coalition of Patriotic Societies' assault on allegedly radical Tulane professors, and the ensuing twenty years had done nothing to diminish his zeal in the fight against race mixing and leftist ideology. The Tulane Board of Administrators took Irwin seriously. In a Board meeting on February 8, 1956, Joseph Jones told the Administrators that he had received a letter from Irwin, which he proceeded to read aloud, "but before so doing stated that he would request the Board to devote the next meeting entirely to the matter of segregation."[34] The letter was a resurrection of the tactics of 1936. Irwin indicted several Tulane faculty members for their involvement in pro-integration meetings. He also condemned the School of Social Work for inviting black speakers such as attorney A. P. Tureaud and "a colored man named Lawes [sic]" (local NAACP field secretary Clarence A. Laws) to present their views, while recruiting faculty members who were "prejudiced in favor of integration." Academic freedom, Irwin believed, should offer no protection to those who refused to present the segregationist side of the argument. Jones described the Irwin correspondence as "a most difficult letter to answer."[35]

In the wake of this rather pointed reminder about public opinion, the Law Committee proceeded to meet (at Jones's request) to define the Board's legal position in preparation for a conclusive vote on the segregation issue. The committee's March 9, 1956, deliberations were guided by a twenty-five page memorandum prepared by Snellings, Monroe, and McCloskey. The document reviewed all of the legal arguments developed during the previous year, quoting appropriate passages from the charters and citing relevant case and statute law at the state and federal level. After rejecting the idea that a grant of absolute ownership could free the Board to disregard the donor's restrictions, the memorandum simply ignored the rationale for desegregation advanced in 1954. Not surprisingly, the document's recommendations sounded virtually identical to those advanced by Snellings in July 1955. While acknowledging that grounds existed for a suit to compel black admissions on the basis that Tulane was a public institution under contract with the state, the memorandum warned against allowing this possibility to force the Administrators "into a position of invit-

34. BOA Minutes, 8 February 1956.
35. Emett Lee Irwin to Joseph M. Jones, 2 February 1956, box 99, HEL Papers (first–second quotations); BOA Minutes, 8 February 1956 (third quotation).

ing an attack by the Paul Tulane heirs, either in the state or the Federal courts, at this time, of such uncertainty."[36] Adhering closely to the memorandum, the Law Committee voted to advise the Board that "the admission of negroes at this time would not be free of legal complications, and it therefore recommends that there be no change in the policy on that subject at this time." What followed was largely anticlimactic. On March 14 the Board's Educational Affairs Committee went through the motions of listening to arguments on behalf of desegregation from Vice President Cole and the deans of Law, Medicine, Social Work, and the Graduate School. Before being allowed to express their views, however, the academic officers were informed of the Law Committee's meeting and the resulting vote to continue excluding blacks. A week later, the full Board ratified the Law Committee's conclusion by voting unanimously "that there be no change in the existing policies relative to the admission of Negroes to Tulane University at this time." Having wandered into the quagmire of indefinite postponement, the Board did nothing to extricate itself until lawsuits forced the issue in 1961.[37]

By the time the Board ended its flirtation with voluntary desegregation in 1956, Tulane was increasingly out of step with the South's other leading research universities. Board members frequently acknowledged that the continued exclusion of blacks could jeopardize federal research grants, tax exemptions, accreditation, and the all-important capital contributions of the Ford Foundation and other private philanthropies. Moreover, the Law Committee's own legal briefs chronicled the steady erosion of segregation's judicial underpinning in federal courts.[38] In private correspondence President Harris bluntly

36. Memorandum Relative to the Legal Position of the Administrators of the Tulane Educational Fund with Respect to the Question of Their Right to Admit or Refuse Admission to Negroes [undated document prepared after 8 February 1956 to be used at Law Committee meeting of 9 March 1956], box 99, HEL Papers (quotation on p. 23). The memorandum is signed only by Joseph McCloskey but Ashton Phelps attributed it to McCloskey, Snellings, and Monroe. See Ashton Phelps to the Administrators of the Tulane Educational Fund, 9 March 1956, box 99, HEL Papers.

37. BOA Minutes, 21 March 1956 (first quotation); Minutes of the Educational Affairs Committee, 14 March 1956, box 9, RCH Papers; BOA Minutes, 21 March 1956 (second quotation).

38. The most forthright acknowledgments of the possible negative repercussions of continued discrimination came from Snellings, who repeatedly declared her willingness to maintain segregation despite the consequences. Snellings, Report to the Board of Administrators [ca. 20 July 1955], 4; idem, To the Board of Administrators of the Tulane Education Fund, 24 January

impressed upon individual Board members the futility of embracing a defensive sectional outlook. Responding to Snellings's rather labored attempt to link modern segregation to "Carpet Bag" excesses, for example, Harris turned the historical argument back upon its author by pointing out that the "dominant sentiment of the nation—and indeed of the world—is against us in the segregation issue[,] somewhat in the same solid and determined fashion that the Abolitionists prevailed over us in the slavery issue itself nearly a hundred years ago." Harris may have been a southerner, but he had little taste for lost causes.[39]

Neither, one must assume, did the pragmatic attorneys, investors, and entrepreneurs who comprised the majority of the Tulane Board. And yet, leaving aside the invariably "unanimous" final votes on segregation and other major policy issues, no less than seven administrators—including Joseph Jones, Ashton Phelps, Joseph McCloskey, Samuel Zemurray, Joseph Montgomery, George Wilson, and Marie Louise Snellings—went on record either in writing or by proxy as opposing desegregation in 1955–56. Several other Board members shared their views. Any full explanation of the Board's posture must look beyond the stated concern over possible litigation from the Paul Tulane heirs, a subject first mentioned in July 1955—more than a year after Joseph Jones reached his eleventh-hour decision against announcing token Graduate School integration. Although Board members may indeed have come to believe that desegregation could place the Tulane gift and other donations at risk, there is no indication that such concerns prevented action in 1954. What seems far more likely is that most Board members supported legal segregation while few, if any, relished the prospect of seeing black students at Tulane, although most probably recognized that change was inevitable. Given the ambivalence of such a viewpoint, desegregation arguments rooted in the fiscal and political realities of Tulane's bid for national stature might have carried the day, provided no strong countervailing forces arose to check the momentum of events. Had the Law Committee conducted its crucial deliberations in 1953 instead of four days prior to the 1954

1961, box 24, RCH Papers. Ray Forrester to Joseph McCloskey, 7 March 1956, box 99, HEL Papers, provides a twenty-seven-page discussion of "a series of fairly recent cases which seems to establish the principle that the equal protection clause may apply to private organizations which perform certain functions of state government." See pp. 26–7 for a summary of the negative consequences of ignoring such a finding by the federal courts.

39. Rufus C. Harris to Marie Louise Snellings, 13 September 1955, box 99, HEL Papers.

Brown decision, there would probably have been support—or at least acquiescence—on the part of most Administrators when presented with what was by any standards a decidedly modest proposal. But in the fateful year of 1954, history itself intervened to shatter the fragile Law Committee consensus that Harris had labored so skillfully to create. A sense of order and control had been the linchpin of liberal gradualist logic, and after 1954 white confidence on that point all but vanished. Confronting a future that looked suddenly ominous and unpredictable, the Board's Law Committee developed new concerns over the financial consequences that might result from a course of action that had never commanded more than grudging support. The Administrators' fears would ultimately prove to be groundless, but in the emotional atmosphere of the mid- and late 1950s they gave rise to a policy stalemate.[40]

II

President Harris's inability to bring about the desegregation of graduate education formed an ironic counterpoint to his success in fostering a climate of racial tolerance within the university itself. Although Tulane was never the hotbed of militant interracialism that some local segregationists imagined, the university, under Harris's leadership, remained commendably free of the overt and subtle pressures that silenced discussion of the race issue at many southern institutions. A politically and intellectually permissive tone prevailed throughout the 1950s, and even during the orgy of sectional bombast and race baiting that followed the *Brown* decision Tulane's students and faculty routinely voiced opinions on civil rights that ran counter to segregationist orthodoxy. A 1955 poll of 528 students representing all of the university's academic divisions except University College provides some of the best insight into the distribution of liberal and conservative senti-

40. BOA Minutes, 21 March 1956; Ashton Phelps to the Administrators of the Tulane Educational Fund, 9 March 1956; Marie Louise Snellings, Report to the Board of Administrators, [ca. 20 July 1955]; Joseph McCloskey, Memorandum Relative to the Legal Position of the Administrators . . . with Respect to the Question of Their Right to Admit or Refuse Admission to Negroes; George A. Wilson to Joseph McCloskey, 7 January 1955, box 99, HEL Papers.

ment at Tulane. The poll revealed that some 64 percent of those surveyed supported desegregation in some form. Social Work students were the most liberal, with over half of those questioned favoring black admissions "as soon as possible." The majority of students in the Architecture sample were confirmed gradualists, who professed to favor desegregation provided that it took place slowly, "say over 5 to 10 years." More than 40 percent of the Engineering cohort also preferred a gradual approach, although an equal portion of the group either sought to limit integration to the Graduate School or expressed indifference to the entire issue. Newcomb College and Arts and Sciences, together with the Schools of Business Administration and Medicine, seemed more or less evenly divided between immediatists, gradualists, and defenders of the old regime. A less balanced division of sentiment existed among Law School students, with a small majority coming down on the side of desegregation while more than 40 percent sought to preserve the racial status quo—the highest figure for any part of the university.[41]

To a significant degree, the campus climate of the mid- and late fifties was a product of what had immediately preceded it. During the anti-Communist controversies of the late forties, the protection of unpopular liberal ideas had become closely intertwined with the defense of academic freedom, an issue that united faculty members across a broad political spectrum. As Harris had vowed, Tulane held firmly to the principle that intellectual "Keep Out signs" had no place in an academic institution. By the time militant resistance to integration took shape in 1955, Tulane professors felt secure enough to speak—and sometimes to act—on behalf of integration without fear of administrative reprisal. A far different situation prevailed at public institutions such as Northwestern Louisiana State College and the main campus of LSU, where sixty-six faculty members were subjected to official harassment and threatened with legislative investigation for subversive activity after signing a 1958 American Civil Liberties Union petition opposing measures that would have closed public schools faced with integration. At Tulane, by contrast, both the University Senate and the 160-member AAUP chapter passed strong resolutions defending the LSU professors and affirming that academic freedom was inseparable from the exercise of other basic rights, including the right of petition. A short time later the university made Dixon Hall available for

41. Tulane *Hullabaloo*, 29 March 1955, p. 1.

a speech by the ACLU's executive director when the group was unable to rent facilities in Baton Rouge. In another move of considerable symbolic importance, Harris agreed to serve on the federally appointed Louisiana Advisory Committee of the U.S. Civil Rights Commission, thereby giving Tulanians a relatively clear green light to champion legal equality both on and off the university campus.[42]

From the vantage point of the post–civil rights decades, the largely rhetorical nature of white liberalism at Tulane during the 1950s invites criticism which can easily degenerate into caricature. Unleavened by the actual presence of black students or faculty colleagues, most campus dialogue about "the Negro" possessed an abstract and somewhat artificial tone. Faculty members whose commitment to integration extended no further than admitting a few "qualified" minority students for graduate study often kept at least one foot in the camp of traditional segregationist paternalism, while even the most advanced integrationists gave little thought to the disparities of power and social authority that lay hidden beneath the rhetoric of individual merit. And yet, with the forces of white supremacy in full cry against the NAACP and what little remained of the southern left (primarily the New Orleans–based Southern Conference Education Fund), academic liberalism at Tulane was not entirely a milk-and-water affair.

Acting upon moral conviction, and taking their cue partly from Harris, a number of Tulane faculty members—including sociologists Forrest LaViolette, John H. Fenton, and William Lester Kolb, together with Social Work dean Elizabeth Wisner and several of her colleagues—wrote articles, gave speeches, sponsored conferences, and attended workshops on integration.[43] Some of the activities involved

42. Numan V. Bartley, *The Rise of Massive Resistance: Race and Politics in the South during the Second Reconstruction* (Baton Rouge: Louisiana State University Press, 1969), 228–9; *New Orleans Times-Picayune*, 19, 25, and 27 June 1958, clippings in box 99, HEL Papers; University Senate Minutes, 17 June 1958, University Senate Minutes and Reports, 1912–1989, box 2, Tulane University Archives; Fr. Theodore Hesburgh to Rufus C. Harris, 25 November 1958, box 45, RCH Papers; BOA Minutes, 10 December 1958, item 19 of president's monthly report; Harris to Marie Louise Snellings, 23 February 1959, box 45, RCH Papers; Harris to Robert A. Lambert, 1 April 1959, box 29, RCH Papers.

43. John H. Fenton and Forrest E. LaViolette, "Integration in the South," *Southern Patriot* (April 1957): 8; Rufus C. Harris to Robert O. Arnold, 25 April 1957, box 7, RCH Papers; Elizabeth Wisner to Harris, 4 November 1955, box 99, HEL Papers. LaViolette and art professor Robert Feild were both actively involved in the pro-integration activities of the Southern Conference Education Fund throughout the second half of the 1950s. On local interracial meetings involving sociology and social work faculty from Tulane, see the reports of a "citizens

Tulane students. In 1956, for example, the Reverend Clarence H. Snelling, who headed the Methodist off-campus Wesley Foundation, organized an interracial Bible study group that included students from Tulane and Dillard. Two years later, discussions between sociology professors at Tulane, Loyola, and Dillard resulted in the organization of an informal discussion group composed mainly of upper-level sociology majors from the three schools, as well as students from Xavier. A Tulane professor described the undertaking as "purely educational," assuring university officials that "[i]t is not an action group, although for a time some of the students wanted to make it such." Tulane students reportedly looked upon the meetings as an opportunity "to meet people of other groups of their own class and educational level, for most of them a unique experience."[44]

Although timid when compared to the activism of the following decade, the halting interracial contacts of the 1950s were the tiny stress fractures that foretold the impending collapse of segregation's vast superstructure. President Harris repeatedly tried to prepare the Board of Administrators for a process of incremental change. On two occasions, once in 1953 and again in 1957, Harris briefed the Board in considerable detail about the impracticality of maintaining a rigid color line either on or off university premises. In 1953 Harris emphasized that Tulane's International Relations Club and various student religious groups were engaging in interracial activities when they attended local conventions along with student delegates from Xavier and Dillard. Prohibitions against holding integrated meetings on Tulane's campus made it impossible for university groups to receive credit for sponsoring or hosting the events. By 1958 the list of undergraduate organizations that had at least occasional contact with black students included the ROTC Rifle Team, the Glendy Burke Debate Team, the Tulane-Newcomb Opera Workshop, and the Student Council delegates to regional and national conventions of the National Student Association (where segregation was openly discussed and debated in a

---

group" meeting at the L. E. Rabouin school and Xavier University, *New Orleans Times-Picayune*, 15 and 31 January, 5 February 1956, clippings in box 99, HEL Papers.

44. Hugh T. Murray Jr., "The Struggle for Civil Rights in New Orleans in 1960: Reflections and Recollections," *Journal of Ethnic Studies* 6 (spring 1978): 25–41, esp. 28–9; Memorandum concerning interracial discussion group, undated and unsigned but probably written by Forrest LaViolette, submitted at BOA meeting of 9 April 1958, box 99, HEL Papers (all quotations). The contents of this document were summarized in BOA Minutes, 9 April 1958, item 7 of president's monthly report.

racially mixed setting). In Harris's view, a continued policy of racial exclusion on Tulane's campus made little sense at a time when the opposite tendency was gaining momentum "everywhere in the college world."[45]

The Board was unmoved by Harris's logic, and throughout the 1950s the basic norms of racial caste hierarchy remained embedded in the routine of daily life on Tulane's campus. African Americans appeared at Tulane almost exclusively in menial or service capacities. The two races were forbidden to eat together, to use the same restroom facilities, or to drink from the same water fountains. (Where segregated fountains were unavailable, black employees were required to draw water from the "white" fountain using a personal drinking cup.)[46] Most whites simply ignored blacks or remained oblivious to their presence. It was only when blacks stepped out of their assigned roles to appear as men and women, rather than as invisible servants, that whites were forced to think about segregation's compartmentalizing effect. Public events sponsored by outside agencies but held in Tulane facilities provided one of the few campus settings conducive to seeing black people as individuals. During 1953, for example, approximately fifty black members of the New Orleans Philharmonic Symphony Society attended each of the three concerts presented in McAlister Auditorium. Smaller numbers of well-educated blacks assembled to hear Lyceum lectures in McAlister, and a substantial black audience gathered there with whites to participate in a celebration honoring New Orleans's liberal Catholic archbishop Francis J. Rummel. In addition, Harris reported that "many Negroes" attended the annual Easter Sunrise Service, a public event held on the Newcomb campus.[47]

Each of these episodes helped expose the incongruity of white supremacy and resulted in either the modification or the momentary abandonment of segregationist practice. At the Philharmonic Symphony concerts, for example, black members simply "found their own way in," while at the outdoor sunrise service blacks "seated together in the open air" were "at once considered to be segregated." A slight vari-

45. BOA Minutes, 9 December 1953, item 19 of president's monthly report; ibid., 12 March 1958, item 16 of president's monthly report (quotation). For the more detailed reports that Harris summarized to the Board, see John H. Stibbs to Harris, 3 December 1953, 10 March 1958, box 99, HEL Papers.

46. BOA Minutes, 15 June 1960, item 18 of president's monthly report.

47. Ibid., 9 December 1953, item 19 of president's monthly report (quotation); ibid., 12 March 1958, item 16 of president's monthly report.

ation on the latter theme took place when blacks sought to attend indoor events sponsored by the university. On such occasions (which were quite rare) a "competent doorman" escorted the nonwhite visitor "to a place where he is immediately understood to be segregated." But "[i]f such a person should insist on sitting where he pleases . . . the doorman is instructed to allow him to do so," Harris explained.[48] After describing Tulane's obviously inconsistent segregation policies to the Board in 1953, Harris offered what was probably his most candid statement of how far he hoped to go in an initial repudiation of southern taboos against social equality. "I would like to suggest that consideration be given . . . to a change in policy to permit Negroes to attend public meetings on the campus," the president began.

> I believe this should be done quietly and without publicity. I do not believe any incident will occur, but if it should I feel that it could be met if the Administrators would be willing to support the university administration in a statement to anyone who may complain that the University has decided to permit members of other races to attend cultural and religious meetings on the campus. . . .
> If those in attendance at such meetings (as the area conventions of student or faculty groups) are using the cafeteria, either at a banquet or as a group, the colored members of the group could be permitted to join them.

Perhaps sensing the need to make at least a token concession to the more sacrosanct areas of tradition, Harris concluded with the suggestion that "[i]n the use of toilet facilities, one booth in the rest rooms could be marked for colored."[49]

Having only begun to grapple with the larger issue of Graduate School desegregation, the Board took no formal action on Harris's request. For another ten years Tulane followed an unwritten policy of winking at the occasional presence of black scholars who attended professional meetings on campus, while simultaneously lobbying behind the scenes to discourage academic organizations from meeting in New Orleans if the "problem" of accommodating nonwhites at Tulane was likely to be raised. But in spite of the Board's obvious desire to bury the entire matter, controversy over race mixing at public events inten-

48. Ibid., 9 December 1953, item 19 of president's monthly report (first–third quotations); ibid., 10 December 1952, item 10 of president's monthly report (fourth–sixth quotations).
49. Ibid., 19 December 1953, item 19 of president's monthly report (all quotations).

sified in the mid- and late fifties, as the political leaders of resistance to integration sought to identify segregation with those aspects of southern life that were closest to the public's heart. Few activities had greater resonance with the southern electorate than college sports, and it was destined to be intercollegiate athletics rather than symphonies or Lyceum lectures that kept the issue of campus segregation on the Tulane Board's agenda.[50]

III

During the mid-1950s several southern states passed laws or took administrative action to prohibit public colleges from playing athletic opponents whose teams were racially integrated. A number of northern schools retaliated in kind by canceling or refusing to schedule games in states where black athletes and spectators faced legal discrimination. One of the most comprehensive attempts to legislate recreational segregation was a 1956 Louisiana statute forbidding "all interracial dancing, social functions, entertainments, athletic training, games, sports, or contests and other such activities," including integrated seating at sports events.[51] In addition to jeopardizing the future of the Sugar Bowl game, played annually in Tulane's stadium, the law presented a number of dilemmas over racial policy that the Board of Administrators would have preferred to avoid. During the latter part of 1954, the university had rescued the Sugar Bowl's sponsors from potential embar-

50. Joseph C. Morris to Dr. Karl Darrow, 26 May 1954, box 35, RCH Papers. After a lengthy Board discussion early in 1955, "It was the consensus of opinion that the University should permit Negro members of professional societies meeting on the campus to participate in such meetings on a non-discriminatory basis." Five years later Harris reported that "[w]e do not as a general rule have colored visitors to the campus. Very infrequently a colored person may attend some meeting." BOA Minutes, 9 February 1955 and 15 June 1960, item 18 of president's monthly report.

51. Numan V. Bartley, *The Rise of Massive Resistance*, 235–6 (quotation). For legal restrictions on interracial college sports in Louisiana, Georgia, and Mississippi, as well as reaction by nonsouthern schools, see *New York Times:* 19 January 1956, p. 22; 5 February 1956, p. 60; 17 March 1956, p. 1; 18 March 1956, section 4, p. 10; 24 March 1956, p. 15; 20 July 1956, p. 19; 22 July 1956, section 4, p. 8; 15 February 1957, pp. 1, 22; 16 February 1957, p. 10; 23 February 1957, p. 1; 17 September 1957, p. 1. Wilma Dykeman and James Stokely, *Neither Black nor White* (New York: Rinehart, 1957), chap. 13, provides an illuminating contemporary description of the importance attached to intercollegiate athletics by defenders of segregation.

rassment by making campus dormitory, cafeteria, and training facilities available to the U.S. Naval Academy's racially integrated football team. The gesture received some publicity, and may have encouraged the Yale University basketball coach to inquire about the possibility of scheduling a game with the Green Wave during the 1955–56 season. Aware that the Yale team would include "one or more Negro students," Tulane athletic director Richard O. Baumbach recommended accepting the offer, provided that Yale also played Rice and Vanderbilt during its southern tour. Early in 1955 the Athletic Advisory Committee, a group not given to social radicalism, endorsed the idea. Sensing a possible breakthrough, President Harris made it clear that he was ready to act. "I will accept the recommendation . . . to schedule the basketball game with Yale, if the matter is left to me," Harris informed Joseph Jones. The Board, however, had other ideas. Following the usual "full discussion" of the matter, the Administrators vetoed the game, noting that "piecemeal" action was inappropriate when "the whole broad problem of segregation" was still under consideration.[52]

The Yale basketball proposal was simply the first in a series of problems connected with sports segregation that the Board would seek to evade. In 1955 Tulane again made its campus facilities available to a racially integrated Sugar Bowl team, this time from the University of Pittsburgh. Football became the focus of controversy in 1956 and 1957 because of games with northern opponents that had been scheduled several years before Louisiana adopted a hard line on interracial sports. Hoping to avoid a political furor, Tulane quietly moved its 1956 Navy game to Portsmouth, Virginia, and shifted the 1957 Marquette contest to Milwaukee, Wisconsin. Neither of the changes aroused local opposition, but Tulane's luck ran out when the university attempted to proceed with the 1957 Army game in New Orleans. Integration on the field was not an issue, since the Army team had no black players and the Academy had obligingly agreed to leave its racially mixed marching corps and band at home. Tulane, for its part, hoped to circumvent laws against integrated seating by promising to admit all West Point ticket holders to a separate or "segregated" section of the east stands. Several factors conspired to undermine the plan, including northern press coverage of Louisiana's racial legislation and efforts on the part

52. Minutes of the Athletic Advisory Committee, 29 November 1955, box 19, RCH Papers; Harris to Joseph M. Jones, 21 January 1955, in BOA Minutes 9 February 1955 (all quotations).

of Republican congressman James Fulton of Pennsylvania to prevent the three service academies from acquiescing in segregation requirements at southern schools. After a full-scale public controversy erupted in the weeks preceding the game, the two schools agreed to move the contest to West Point—a change that drew howls of protest from Louisiana's most vocal segregationists. Although arch–white supremacist Leander Perez preferred to see the game played in "Hades" rather than permit race mixing in the Sugar Bowl stadium, most segregationists joined Congressman F. Edward Hébert in condemning both West Point and Tulane for becoming parties to a "propaganda trick engineered by the NAACP."[53]

The decision to move the 1957 Army game generated some of the most vitriolic protests that Harris received on any aspect of the segregation issue—a total of twenty letters and telegrams, not including various unsigned postcards filled with scurrilous accusations and vulgar racial epithets. Communications from disgruntled Law School alumni were the most polemical. "I am an avowed and unalterable opponent to integration or anything that smacks of it," wrote one attorney, who saw the Army game episode as proof that Tulane's "guiding authorities . . . were, to say the least, very broad minded on the subject" of race. Such comments seemed almost temperate when compared with those of a 1944 Law graduate who denounced "Tulane's spineless capitulation to the demands of radical negroes and their political toadies." Viewing the move to West Point as an "act of appeasement" that gave aid and comfort to Louisiana's "mortal enemies," the writer went on to resurrect the familiar claim that Communists were at the heart of the race problem. Tulane, he believed, had "in effect agreed" that Louisiana's laws "should be nullified when they are displeasing to the NAACP, the ADA, the Daily Worker [sic], and other such ornaments of the current scene." A third writer pressed cold war logic to its outer limits by elevating the Tulane-Army game to the level of a metaphorical East-West confrontation. Having allegedly compromised a basic moral principle by moving the game rather than canceling it outright, Harris was solemnly urged to consider the probable consequences for America's world position "if at the approach of every attack in the United

53. Minutes of the Athletic Advisory Committee, 29 November 1955; R. O. Baumbach to Harris, 20 September 1957, box 20, RCH Papers (first quotation); *New Orleans Item*, 17 September 1957 (second quotation), *New Orleans Times-Picayune*, 17 September 1957 (third quotation), Tulane clipping scrapbooks.

Nations . . . we just backed away and showed the free world we couldn't maintain our standards and ideals in the face of criticism by those whose thinking is not the same as ours."[54] Alumni responses to the 1957 Army controversy spoke volumes about the close psychological symbiosis that had developed around the twin issues of white supremacy and college sports. But the episode also tapped a deep vein of resentment about the direction of intercollegiate athletic policy at Tulane during the preceding five years. The events of this crucial period helped polarize campus opinion about Tulane football to such an extent that generations of loyal Green Wave fans would look back upon the 1952 season as the beginning of a fourteen-year cycle of "austerity" and "hard times," while veteran faculty members would recall the mid-fifties as an era when the university's intellectual mission was taken seriously enough to make football a secondary concern. Although partisanship has inflated both the duration and magnitude of postwar attempts at athletic deemphasis, the perception is well founded that big-time sports suffered a temporary setback under Rufus Harris's leadership.[55]

Harris had first broached the subject of reforming Tulane football in 1939, the same year that his former Yale Law School classmate Robert M. Hutchins abolished the University of Chicago's football program. Only three years earlier President Frank P. Graham had tried and failed to scale down the University of North Carolina's football regimen, and there is every reason to believe that Harris would have suffered a similar defeat at Tulane had he pressed the issue prior to World War II.[56] Wartime curtailment of athletic schedules and the reduced importance attached to football during the war raised Harris's hopes that once peace was restored, Tulane and other southern

54. Gibson Tucker Jr. to Harris, 17 September 1957, box 20, RCH Papers (first–second quotations); Allen R. Fontenot to Harris, 23 September 1957, box 20, RCH Papers (third–seventh quotations); John W. Roberts to Harris, 17 September 1957, box 20, RCH Papers (eighth quotation).

55. George Sweeney, *The Green Wave: Tulane University Football* (Huntsville, Ala.: Strode, 1980), 179 (quotations); Edward Rogge, "A Short History, and Not-So-Short Interpretation Thereof, of Tulane's 'Football Problem,'" [18 December 1991], typescript in author's possession.

56. Robin Lester, *Stagg's University: The Rise, Decline, and Fall of Big-Time Football at Chicago* (Urbana: University of Illinois Press, 1995), chap. 6; William D. Snider, *Light on the Hill: A History of the University of North Carolina at Chapel Hill* (Chapel Hill: University of North Carolina Press, 1992), 219–22; BOA Minutes, 27 November 1945, item 19 of president's monthly report.

schools could avoid a return to past excesses. In a speech to the Southeastern Conference that was subsequently published in the April 1944 issue of the *Southern Coach and Athlete*, Harris urged colleges to take advantage of diminished public pressure and seize the opportunity to reorganize intercollegiate sports upon a "sane, reasonable basis." Among the specific changes he advocated were the elimination of scouting and spring training, the restriction of fall practice sessions to one hour per day, a reduction in the number and amount of athletic scholarships, and the hiring of coaches whose vocabularies were "rich in something besides profanity" and whose literary interests extended beyond the content of "sport pages and comic strips."[57]

The best chance, and probably the only real hope, for reforming intercollegiate athletics in the South lay in regulatory measures imposed from outside the region. For a brief moment after the war such a solution seemed within reach, when nationwide concern over controlling expenses and preserving—or restoring—amateurism in college sports led the National Collegiate Athletic Association to adopt its 1948 "sanity code" limiting student athletic grants to the cost of tuition and incidental fees and requiring that awards be based upon need. Under the new regulations athletes would not receive grants covering room and board, and were expected to seek part-time employment to defray personal expenses. For the first time the NCAA seemed ready to enforce its own rules. In theory, schools that violated the code could be expelled from the national organization. Southern institutions led the way in evading or openly defying the new rules, and within three years the sanity code was effectively nullified by NCAA delegates amid "cheers and much back slapping."[58]

For Harris and other regional advocates of deemphasizing athletics (such as Vanderbilt chancellor Harvie Branscomb), the failure of reform at the national level compounded the difficulty of bringing southern football under control. Both Tulane and Vanderbilt belonged to the Southeastern Conference, where policies were shaped by major state universities and land grant schools with powerful athletic constituencies. The environment was not a congenial one for would-be re-

57. Rufus Carrollton Harris, "Post-War Intercollegiate Athletics," *Southern Coach and Athlete* (April 1944), offprint in box 20, RCH Papers (all quotations).

58. Paul R. Lawrence, *Unsportsmanlike Conduct: The National Collegiate Athletic Association and the Business of College Football* (New York: Praeger, 1987), 41–2, 49 (quotation), and appendix C (pp. 158–9).

formers, but in the absence of a southern equivalent to the Ivy League, the SEC constituted the only rule-making body to which Harris and other like-minded educators could turn in an effort to rein in college sports. At the December 1951 meeting of SEC delegates in New Orleans, Harris presented an "eight point plan for the restraint of intercollegiate athletics" which represented "largely what will be undertaken at Tulane." Specifically, Harris recommended: (1) limiting athletic scholarships to a total of 75 in football and 100 for all sports combined; (2) confining recruiting activities to the boundaries of the university campus, where "prospective students" might visit the coach in his office; (3) allowing no more than 30 calendar days for spring practice sessions and restricting participation to freshmen and sophomores; (4) setting the maximum size of football coaching staffs at one head coach and four assistants, and allowing only two out-of-state scouting trips per year; (5) limiting varsity squads, including traveling squads, to 38 players per game; (6) supporting NCAA efforts to eliminate "two platoon" football with its emphasis upon large squads of highly specialized players; (7) reducing participation in bowl games and other non-scheduled post-season events; and (8) abolishing all special degree programs for athletes or curricula in physical education except courses taken as part of normal major or minor requirements for a standard B.A. or B.S. degree.[59]

The agenda was a bold one. By the time Harris presented it to a decidedly unenthusiastic assemblage of SEC delegates in New Orleans, the major elements of a long-term football deemphasis program were already in place at Tulane. Economic necessity provided the initial justification for most of the changes Harris proposed, as he sought to distance the university from the win-at-any-cost philosophy that prevailed at other SEC institutions. During the late 1940s GI Bill stipends had given Tulane football a huge financial subsidy by providing tuition and living expenses for players who would otherwise have required university scholarships covering tuition and room and board. By 1950, however, the federal free ride had largely ended, leaving Tulane to foot the bill for a level of athletic competition that placed excessive demands upon the university's limited resources. An alarmed Athletic

59. Rufus C. Harris, An eight-point plan for the restraint of intercollegiate athletics . . . presented to the presidents of the Southeastern Conference [undated typescript, November–December 1951], box 19, RCH Papers; Forrest U. Lake to J. G. Stipe, 21 February 1952, box 19, RCH Papers.

Advisory Committee estimated that at the cost levels which had prevailed in 1949, Tulane might soon face an annual loss of $100,000 per year on football alone, to say nothing of the substantial costs of basketball and the minor sports.[60]

The news came at a particularly inopportune time. In the early 1950s Tulane faced the dual challenge of launching a major capital campaign while simultaneously coping with impending enrollment declines resulting from low Depression-era birth rates and the outbreak of the Korean War. With budget deficits looming on the horizon, Board sentiment was momentarily on the side of athletic retrenchment. Sensing that a window of opportunity had opened, Harris needed little urging to initiate the kind of fiscal measures that would make athletic deemphasis more than a subject for philosophical discussion. Football scholarships came under presidential scrutiny in March 1950, when coach Henry Frnka requested a total of 125 grants-in-aid for the coming season—some twenty-seven more awards than had been available the previous year. After Board chairman Esmond Phelps authorized reducing the number of football grants over a three-year period, Harris approved 112 awards for the 1950–51 year and advised the coach that further reductions were likely. Two months later, in May 1950, the Athletic Advisory Committee recommended that both football scholarships and coaching salaries be cut back to the levels of 1948, and Harris accordingly set targets of 90 football awards and an athletic salary budget of $50,000 for 1951–52. When Frnka attempted to evade the new quotas by awarding only 99 scholarships during the fall of 1950 but increasing the number to 123 early in the spring semester, Harris responded by imposing strict controls on all athletic expenditures and ordering a halt to all recruiting.[61]

In the autumn of 1951 Harris advised Joseph Jones that intercollegiate athletics had accumulated an annual deficit of $46,000 despite the previous year's economy measures. More drastic action was called for, and Harris stood ready to provide it in the form of his eight-point deemphasis plan. Describing the scheme as "a modified program which I think Tulane can exist on," Harris warned the Board that unless the measures were quickly adopted, the Administrators would "come face to face with the problem of giving up entirely the sport [of football] as

60. Harris to Joseph M. Jones, 18 September 1951, box 19, RCH Papers; Richard O. Baumbach, "Tulane's Athletic Policy," *Tulanian* 27 (February 1954): 16–7.

61. Harris to Horace Renegar, 7 February 1951, box 19, RCH Papers.

an intercollegiate endeavor." Harris's arguments carried the day. In the March 1952 issue of the *Tulanian*, the president announced Tulane's decision to replace "over-emphasis in university intercollegiate athletics" with a new "program of moderation" involving all the basic changes urged upon the SEC in 1951. With a reduced coaching staff, curtailed scouting activities, and a limit of 75 football scholarships for the 1952 season, Tulane could expect few victories over stronger SEC opponents. Green Wave fans were urged to show patience and console themselves with the knowledge that Tulane would surpass its athletic competitors in the pursuit of academic excellence.[62]

By the time Harris's *Tulanian* statement appeared, there was growing evidence that athletic deemphasis represented more than an effort to cope with financial stringency. In addition to its cost-cutting features, Harris's program included academic and administrative changes intended to underscore the subordinate role of athletics in the university's overall mission. Athletes, for example, were to be treated like other students and no longer housed in a special athletic dormitory. The athletic department cheerfully relinquished Zemurray Hall in exchange for a refund of the $100,000 originally contributed toward its construction, together with cancellation of additional loans advanced from the university endowment. In January 1952 the University Senate approved an Arts and Sciences recommendation to abolish the academically suspect degree of "bachelor of education in physical education." For the remainder of the decade athletes were required to pursue a standard B.A., B.S., or professional school degree, and to satisfy the graduation requirements of their college and major. State certification for high school coaching could be obtained through a physical education minor that included the mandatory eighteen hours of applied courses to be taken on a noncredit basis. In short, coaches would no longer be able to keep players from losing their academic eligibility by assigning high grades in intellectually vacuous sports methods courses. Although the coaching staff had ostensibly agreed that athletes should become "more a part of the student body," the decision to abolish the P.E. major caused anger and consternation among all who thirsted for gridiron glory.[63]

Head football coach Henry Frnka submitted his resignation almost

62. Harris to Jones, 18 September 1951, box 19, RCH Papers; BOA Minutes, 12 November 1951, item 24 of president's monthly report (all quotations).
63. BOA Minutes, 19 June 1952, item 31 of president's monthly report (last quotation); ibid., 14 January 1952, item 5 of president's monthly report (all other quotations).

as soon as the deemphasis program was announced. His successor, Raymond "Bear" Wolf, the former head coach at Florida and North Carolina, stayed only two years, and was in turn replaced by Andy Pilney, who stayed from 1954 through 1962. These were lean years in which the Green Wave continued to play major opponents but managed only two winning seasons. To many faculty members, the dismal record attested to the illogic of pursuing big time sports at a university that was unwilling to accept the monetary, academic, and ethical costs routinely incurred by major football schools. Coaches, sports-minded alumni, and eventually some Board members viewed the matter quite differently. Football enthusiasts blamed the poor seasons on recruiting and retention problems created by unrealistically high admission standards, inconvenient class schedules, and unduly burdensome curricular requirements. Complaints on the latter point nearly always centered around the fact that athletes could no longer avoid fulfilling the normal one-year mathematics requirement and taking the four to six semesters normally required to pursue a foreign language through the 300-level.

To say that faculty members and coaches approached Harris's new football program with conflicting views of the university's raison d'être would be something of an understatement. When he first announced his athletic proposals, Harris hoped to narrow the gap between classroom and playing field through the appointment of a full-time athletic director who would be "altogether objective" and have "respect and standing in academic as well as athletic circles." Richard O. Baumbach stepped into the new position in 1952, bringing credentials calculated to mollify football enthusiasts without automatically alienating those who supported the cutbacks. Having quarterbacked the Green Wave to a Southern Conference championship in 1929, Baumbach had gone on to become a successful businessman and a member of the New Orleans Port Authority. His record of ongoing involvement with Tulane included Homecoming chairmanships during the 1930s, a term as president of the Alumni Association in 1943–44, and the chairmanship of the 1948–49 Alumni Fund drive, which raised more than $107,000 for university coffers. The new athletic director possessed obvious political skills, and much would depend upon the ends toward which they were directed.[64]

64. The quotation is from paragraph five of the proof sheet of Harris's editorial "Intercollegiate Athletics at Tulane," which appeared in the March 1952 issue of the *Tulanian*. The paragraph was deleted prior to the editorial's publication.

Initially Baumbach employed the language of athletic moderation and seemed genuinely interested in working out a rapprochement with faculty critics. The dismal scholastic record compiled by Tulane football players had become an embarrassment even to the athletic department. The new athletic director promised reform, but improvement was slow in coming. During Baumbach's first four years (1952–56) only 79 out of 242 students admitted on athletic grants earned a quality point average of 1.0 or better during their first semester. The overall graduation rate for the 84 scholarship athletes admitted in 1952 and 1953 was a meager 34.5 percent. Baumbach acknowledged the serious academic difficulties that many athletes encountered and promised to place more emphasis upon intellectual ability when recruiting new prospects. Once athletes reached campus he vowed to have coaches spell out the "Tulane facts of life" (i.e., the necessity of actually attending class and studying). Tough talk would be accompanied by preventative measures, such as academic counseling and supervised study halls, in an effort to reduce the necessity for remedial work in summer school. In a May 1955 letter to Associate A&S dean Russel M. Geer, Baumbach stated flatly, "The main interest I have, in my position as Athletic Director, is to try to prove that athletes, if properly selected and indoctrinated, can do as well if not better than the average student. This was the case in my day and I have no reason to believe that it cannot be just as true today." With still greater bravado, Baumbach allegedly declared on another occasion "that if Tulane could not attract football players who were able to do reputable college work, it was time to give up Conference football."[65]

Time did bring marginal improvement in athletes' grades despite the persistent 100–130 point gap separating the average SAT scores of entering A&S freshmen from those of freshman athletes—many of whom took the SAT voluntarily after being admitted.[66] During the sec-

65. Tulane University Athletic Program, Self-Survey: Preliminary Report on Intercollegiate Athletics, 10 December 1957, box 11, RCH Papers, 20–1; Annual Report of the Athletic Division, 1957–58, box 19, RCH Papers, 5 (first quotation); Richard O. Baumbach to Russel M. Geer, 19 May 1955, box 11, RCH Papers (second quotation); Russel M. Geer to Rufus C. Harris, 28 September 1955, box 19, RCH Papers (third quotation).

66. 1954 Fall Semester Grades of Varsity Football Players, in BOA Minutes, 9 February 1955, item 14 of president's monthly report; A&S Dean's Report, 1959–1960, section D, Yards and Quality Points Gained, 3–6, box 7, RCH Papers. On the exemption of athletes from SAT tests and initial plans for voluntary testing, see Rufus C. Harris to Cliff W. Wing, 3 May 1957, box 20, RCH Papers.

ond half of the 1950s the proportion of football players receiving grades of D and F in the College of Arts and Sciences shrank from 38 percent to 27 percent, while the percentage earning A grades rose from 4.2 percent to 21.6 percent. These modest but real gains in academic performance were largely overshadowed at the time by a deepening crisis of confidence that would eventually poison the atmosphere surrounding athletic issues at all levels of university governance. One of the first clear signs of trouble appeared in the autumn of 1955 when Professor Geer resigned as associate A&S dean in protest over what he regarded as undue favoritism shown to two football players who were allowed to register in University College with a reduced academic load, after trying unsuccessfully for three semesters to bring up the low grades that had led to their exclusion from the College of Arts and Sciences. Recalling Baumbach's earlier professions of concern for academic achievement, Geer concluded that the transfer episode cast doubt on the athletic director's sincerity. There would, he predicted, be "very bitter reactions" among A&S faculty if University College were allowed to become a "refuge for football players."[67]

In the months immediately following Geer's resignation, the cloud of mutual mistrust that hovered perennially over relations between the athletic department and the A&S faculty began to grow larger. A storm was clearly brewing, and in the winter of 1956 two nasty squall lines heralded its arrival. The first one struck during a January 25 meeting of the Athletic Advisory Committee, when business school professor Paul Taylor voiced a number of pent-up frustrations about his service as academic counselor for Tulane athletes. Having earned no less than nine varsity letters during his own undergraduate days, Taylor was the former faculty chairman of athletics and unquestionably one of the university's more steadfast supporters of intercollegiate sports. As part of his counseling duties, he had devised an ambitious plan for checking on athletes' class absences via faculty reports, but the results of the scheme had proved disappointing. Taylor blamed the resulting academic problems as much on faculty who failed to report absences as on athletes who failed to attend class, and proceeded to use the ab-

67. Russel M. Geer to Rufus C. Harris, 16 (quotations) and 28 September 1955; Harris to Geer, 26 September and 3 October 1955, box 19, RCH Papers; *New Orleans Item*, 15 November 1955; *New Orleans Times-Picayune*, 16 and 20 November 1955; *New Orleans States*, 15 November 1955, clippings in box 19, RCH Papers.

sence reports as the basis for a broader indictment of A&S attitudes toward the athletic program.[68]

According to a detailed memorandum prepared by Dean of Students John H. Stibbs, Taylor insisted throughout the turbulent January 25 meeting that "the great stumbling block standing in the way of his program was the faculty." Convinced that professors were unwilling to display the "understanding and cooperation" necessary for successful tutoring of scholarship athletes, Taylor went on to imply that the faculty as a whole "actually discriminated against athletic students"—a sentiment supported by the athletic department's representatives. Disturbed by Taylor's "vague charge[,] full of unfriendly feeling," Stibbs left the meeting convinced that "we were being led into a position which would mean no good for either students, faculty, or the Athletic Department—that is to say one which would be disruptive." The potential for disruption was evident in the approach of a second athletic squall line in early 1956, this one generated by a struggle over the composition of the Athletic Advisory Committee. A few months previously, in October 1955, demands for greater faculty influence over athletic policy had resulted in a proposal from the Athletic Advisory Committee to increase faculty representation from three to five while removing the athletic director as a member. Never actually carried out, the eleventh-hour suggestions probably represented an effort to fend off more drastic changes proposed in the University Senate's newly drafted constitution, which President Harris submitted for the Board's approval later the same month.[69]

The University Senate virtually threw down the gauntlet to the Board's athletic backers in the proposed constitution's fifth article, section three of which provided that at least 75 percent of the membership on all senate committees, including the senate Committee on Athletics, would consist of full-time teaching and research faculty. The section further specified that the Committee on Athletics would report exclusively to the University Senate, which would henceforth "exercise its full power of sole jurisdiction over the athletic policy of the Uni-

68. Annual Report of the Athletic Advisory Committee, 1955–56, box 11, RCH Papers, 2; Tulane University Athletic Program, Self-Survey: Preliminary Report on Intercollegiate Athletics, 10 December 1957, p. 18.

69. John H. Stibbs to Rufus C. Harris, 26 January 1956, box 19, RCH Papers (all quotations); Annual Report of the Athletic Advisory Committee, 1955–56, p. 1.

versity." These provisions produced an immediate stalemate over approval of the larger document and, after a delay of several months, a special meeting of Board members and faculty senate representatives convened at the home of Darwin S. Fenner on the evening of March 12, 1956, to work out a compromise. In addition to Fenner, other Board members in attendance included Lester Lautenschlaeger, Clifford Favrot, and Joseph McCloskey. The senate was represented by Dean Forrester of the Law School, Dean Hubbard of Newcomb, journalism professor George Simmons, and two members of the sociology department—the outspoken Forrest LaViolette and William Kolb, who had actually written the athletic provisions of the constitution. President Harris was also present. When the meeting began at 8:00 P.M., Fenner told the professors bluntly that the Board wanted control of athletic policy to remain where it was—in the hands of the president and the Athletic Advisory Committee. The Athletic Advisory Committee then consisted of the athletic director, three faculty members, three alumni chosen by the Alumni Association, and three people selected by the Board itself—one from their own ranks and two from the faculty. What the allocation formula did not make explicit was that the Board actually had two members on the Athletic Advisory Committee (Favrot and Lautenschlaeger), one of whom was officially an alumni representative.[70]

In the ensuing three and one half hour discussion, any plan to transfer control of athletic policy directly to a senate committee was blocked by the Board's insistence upon being directly represented and the faculty's categorical refusal to allow Board members to serve on senate committees. The compromise that eventually emerged preserved the Athletic Advisory Committee with Board and alumni representation, together with several new honorary and ex officio members, and a component of five faculty members who also comprised the senate Committee on Athletics. In other words, the University Senate would now select all five of the faculty representatives on the advisory committee, instead of only three as before, and if they acted in concert the five faculty delegates would constitute a voting majority in the committee's deliberations. Although the new rules made it somewhat more likely that professors serving on the Athletic Advisory Committee would speak

70. BOA Minutes, 12 October 1955, 9 May 1956 (quotation); Report of Meeting Between Special Committee of Board of Administrators and a Committee of the University Faculty Senate on Athletic Advisory Committee, in BOA Minutes, 9 May 1956.

with a single voice, the arrangement stopped well short of giving the senate control of Tulane's football program, since the committee's function was purely an advisory one and the Board retained final jurisdiction over all athletic matters. As subsequent events would illustrate, the real significance of the March 12 meeting lay less in the specific compromise it produced than in the larger message that emerged from the face-to-face discussions between Board members and faculty.

According to the Board's official summary, nearly all the faculty members who spoke at the March gathering stressed the importance of redefining the role of the Administrators and the University Senate in a way that would place policy decisions on sports and most other matters increasingly under faculty control. Professor Kolb, for example, warned the Board not to be misled by the long history of faculty quiescence on athletics. "[F]or the past few years," he noted, the faculty had "been striving for major policy control in all University matters, including athletics." Forrest LaViolette agreed with his colleague, adding that Tulane's tenured professors "felt they were capable of controlling major policy on the $500,000 athletic business . . . as well as on all other university matters." Dean Forrester, the group's spokesman, took a larger view, emphasizing that "the trend of greater universities in the country was to turn over more and more major policy control to full time faculty members." Increasingly, he explained, university trustees simply "raised money and exercised veto power."[71]

These pointed exchanges between professors and Board members were unprecedented in both tone and substance. Even the turbulent conflicts of the mid-1930s had produced nothing comparable in the way of direct challenges to the Board's traditional sphere of authority. Having weathered the McCarthy-era's threats to professional autonomy and intellectual independence, American college professors stood poised to embark upon a fifteen-year period of prosperity and occupational mobility unequaled before or since in the history of American higher education. Stirred by a growing sense of confidence and optimism, Tulane professors were placing the Board on notice that the ground rules of university governance could no longer be taken for granted. In the end the University Senate would see its influence over college sports diminish rather than expand, but as Tulane passed

71. Report of Meeting Between Special Committee of Board of Administrators and a Committee of the University Faculty Senate on Athletic Advisory Committee, in BOA Minutes, 9 May 1956.

through the athletic squalls of the mid-fifties, the A&S faculty felt confident of its ability to survive the rough weather without trimming sail or altering course.

The athletic department, long accustomed to navigating in heavy seas, employed a variety of skillful maneuvers to regain the advantage of a prevailing wind. From the outset Baumbach stressed the competitive handicap resulting from Tulane's annual limit of 75 football scholarships at a time when several SEC schools routinely awarded 100–120 or more grants per year. After three years at the reduced level, Baumbach sought an increase to 90 awards for 1956, justifying the request partly on the grounds that freshmen were no longer eligible to play on varsity squads. He received authorization for 85 awards, to be calculated on a "general average basis" that assumed the initial signing of a still larger number, which would be gradually reduced through attrition from academic and other causes. Further increases followed, and by the 1958 season Tulane had 94 football players on scholarship, a number below that of most SEC schools but higher than the total for such major competitors as Alabama and LSU, to say nothing of Vanderbilt.[72]

Recruiting more players proved to be simpler than keeping them academically eligible for competition. By the mid-1950s, when Baumbach was still assuring doubters that properly tutored, supervised, counseled, and indoctrinated athletes could make decent grades, his long-term solution to football players' academic problems consisted of a single idea—bringing back the old P.E. major under a different guise. The genesis of the ostensibly new curricular option—which eventually came to be known as the Teacher-Coach Program—may be traced to Baumbach's February 1, 1955, "recommendation report" to the Athletic Advisory Committee. After surveying the relatively lax academic requirements faced by athletes at major southern football schools, Baumbach proposed "that a four year teacher's program be offered leading to a degree—possibly a Bachelor of Science in Education." In its original form Baumbach's proposal envisioned the restoration of academic credit for nine hours of sports methods courses and the elimination of all foreign language requirements. Concerning the

72. Annual Report of the Athletic Advisory Committee, 1955–56; Report of the University Senate Committee on Athletics, 1956–57 (quotation), box 11, RCH Papers; Tulane University Athletic Program, Self-Survey: Preliminary Report on Intercollegiate Athletics, 10 December 1957, p. 9; BOA Minutes, 10 December 1958, item 12 of president's monthly report.

latter point, the director argued that many football and basketball players came "from areas where there is no use of or appreciation for foreign languages." In the absence of any cultural predisposition toward bilingualism, the typical student-athlete viewed languages as unnecessary and lacked the motivation to study them. Baumbach clearly sympathized with the future coaches' plight. Most "prestige universities," he noted, required no foreign languages for athletes pursuing the bachelor of education degree.[73]

During the next four years Baumbach pressed his plan relentlessly through repeated meetings and conferences with the University Senate athletic committee, the president, and various deans and faculty members. Stressing the need for a degree that would fit the career interests of "rugged linemen," the athletic director argued that existing A&S requirements placed insurmountable obstacles in the path of those seeking to carry a normal load and graduate after four years with full certification for secondary school teaching and coaching. But, as Baumbach made clear to Harris in 1957, an equally important aim of the Teacher-Coach campaign was to place at least 25–30 percent of Tulane athletes in University College, where the scheduling and content of classes was "more compatible with the interests and physical requirements of the athletes," and where the "attitude toward athletes in the classrooms . . . appears much more cooperative than in the College of Arts and Sciences." If the athletic department had its way, all athletes pursuing the proposed new degree would enroll as freshmen in University College and the rules for cross registration would be greatly liberalized. By this point Baumbach had abandoned his earlier conciliatory pose, openly agreeing with his coaches that "there is nothing more we can do to keep up with the rising academic demands." Unless relief were forthcoming, he warned, "the whole football program will nosedive beyond recovery."[74]

By engaging in what amounted to a direct attack on the most jealously guarded aspect of academic prerogative, the setting of curricular requirements, Baumbach displayed what can only be described as a

73. Minutes of the Athletic Advisory Committee, 1 February 1955, box 11, RCH Papers (first–third quotations); R. O. Baumbach to Rufus C. Harris, 28 June 1956 (comprising Athletic Director's Report for the period 1 July 1952–1 July 1956), box 11, RCH Papers, 4 (fourth–fifth quotations).

74. R. O. Baumbach, Report on Academic Problems Facing the Athletic Division, in Baumbach to Harris, 6 May 1957, box 11, RCH Papers.

sublime indifference to the A&S faculty's desire for a greater say in athletic matters. Critics of the athletic program believed that more than indifference was involved. Baumbach had grown accustomed to taking counsel directly from Tulane Board members, some of whom were also his friends and occasional business partners. The knowledge of this relationship inevitably bred resentment, causing some faculty members to charge that Baumbach had become the self-appointed chairman of the university Curriculum Committee. In seeking to explain the A&S faculty's eventual distrust and suspicion of Baumbach, Harris pointed to widespread feelings that the director "was abusing the prestige of his office and [his] direct associations and relationships with powerful community forces" in order to "subvert" the faculty's efforts at holding athletes to normal academic standards. The president's personal assessment was even less charitable. From the outset, Harris believed, the coaches and the athletic director approached the new football standards with "mixed hostility and defeatism," and were supported by several Board members in an underlying belief that the new academic requirements "would or could eventually be circumvented." The result was a pervasive environment of bad faith in which Tulane's moderation program "was simply not given an adequate chance."[75]

Viewed as part of the ongoing territorial sparring between the Board and the University Senate, the Teacher-Coach initiative eventually provided an object lesson in the practical limits of faculty power. The measure's relatively brief history deserves mention primarily because of the climactic incident which brought it to a close. In March 1958, Baumbach's three-year lobbying campaign produced its first tangible result when the University Senate requested its Committee on the Preparation of Teachers to study "the state certification problems at Tulane of prospective teachers who plan to engage in athletic coaching." Three months later the committee concluded that "the preparation of teacher-coaches is a responsibility which this University should undertake," and recommended that the senate and the various concerned faculties adopt a single "feasible curriculum" to achieve the desired end. On June 12, 1958, the full senate approved the committee's report. After specifying that any curriculum adopted should be "in accordance with the usual academic standards of this University," the

75. Harris to Marie Louise Snellings, 21 March 1960, box 16, RCH Papers.

senate referred the matter to a special committee composed of representatives of the separate Curriculum Committees of the College of Arts and Sciences, Newcomb College, and the Executive Committee of University College. After a series of meetings in the summer and fall, the special committee recommended that prospective coaches pursue a standard departmental major and education minor subject to various proposed modifications, two of which—granting academic credit for nine hours of sports methods courses, and allowing a subcommittee of the senate Committee on Teacher Preparation to waive some or all of the language requirement for individual teacher-coaches—aroused substantial faculty opposition.[76]

Matters came to a head on December 5, 1958, when the A&S faculty voted to allow credit for only five rather than nine hours of sports methods classes and rejected any modification of the standard foreign language requirement. For good measure, the meeting also turned down the relatively innocuous request that prospective coaches be allowed to substitute algebra and trigonometry for finite math in order to comply with state certification rules. The Board of Administrators was not amused. At their monthly meeting on December 10, upon learning of the faculty's action the Administrators agreed unanimously that "Tulane owes an obligation to the community, which has furnished an 82,000 capacity stadium, to maintain a representative Southeastern Conference Team." Edgar B. Stern suggested that the time had perhaps arrived to create a separate School of Education "apart from the College of Arts and Sciences." The disruptive impasse which Dean Stibbs had foreseen some three years earlier seemed finally to be at hand. The following week, a hastily arranged "administrative officers–Administrators conference committee" (i.e., a meeting between Board members and the president and deans) concluded that the Administrators should take their case directly to the Arts and Sciences faculty.[77]

A meeting called especially for this purpose convened late on the afternoon of Thursday, December 18, with Board chairman Joseph

76. George E. Barton Jr. to Harris, 13 May 1958, box 11, RCH Papers (first–third quotation); BOA Minutes, 10 December 1958, item 13 of president's monthly report (fourth quotation).

77. Arts and Sciences Faculty Minutes, 5 December 1958, box 9G, RCH Papers; BOA Minutes, 10 December 1958 (first–second quotations); Arts and Sciences Faculty Minutes, special meeting, 18 December 1958, box 9G, RCH Papers (third quotation).

Jones and fellow Administrators Ashton Phelps and Isidore Newman in attendance, along with President Harris. Aware that tension was running high, Dean William Peery opened the meeting by paying tribute to the A&S faculty's "labors, loyalty, and educational idealism." He went on to stress, however, that "all who work for the University—Faculty, administrative officers, and Board alike—are seeking the same thing: a better Tulane." After urging his colleagues to consider the political pressures that Board members faced in their efforts at local fundraising, Peery turned the floor over to Joseph Jones. The flavor of what immediately followed is best conveyed through direct quotation from the faculty minutes, which on this occasion were unusually detailed:

> After expressing his pleasure at the opportunity of appearing before it, MR. JONES reminded the Faculty that for many years the Tulane Administrators have followed the policy of not intruding in what by good practice is [sic] commonly regarded as academic areas of educational administration. Though they have the authority to instruct a faculty to introduce a new curriculum, they do not intend to do so; and they certainly do not intend to do anything that might lower the academic standing of the University. The Administrators, he stated, have complete confidence in the judgment of the Faculty. . . . He did not come before the Faculty, he said, to suggest to it what ought to be done, if anything, but to put before it a problem faced by the Administrators: that the tradition of football at Tulane and the University's obligations to its community, in part growing out of its acceptance of the Stadium, seem to be an implied commitment to present creditable football teams.[78]

As Jones viewed the matter, Tulane faced a simple choice: to "give up Southeastern Conference football or go ahead." History professor John Snell and several other A&S faculty members strongly advocated the former option. Not surprisingly Jones favored the latter, although he conceded that better football was no guarantee of successful fundraising and also acknowledged that "we may find that we do not have what it takes to compete athletically." Jones closed his remarks by assuring his audience that the Board would "do what the Faculty recom-

78. Arts and Sciences Faculty Minutes, special meeting, 18 December 1958.

mends," that there would be "no attempt . . . to force a judgment," and that the "present request for a degree without language" was not the beginning of a "whittling-away process." Ashton Phelps and Isidore Newman spoke immediately after Jones, and both emphasized that Tulane should remain in the SEC. Phelps urged the faculty to weigh "all factors which go into the making of a great university," while Newman argued that "Tulane does operate in this community, and it must be interested in the interests of the people of this community." When the Board members had finished, a subdued and visibly uncomfortable President Harris spoke briefly in nominal support of the Board's position, noting that "the claim had been made" that the present curriculum hurt football recruiting and asking almost plaintively, "Is there a way to provide a program which would not require a foreign language?"[79]

Another five weeks would elapse before the reluctant A&S faculty provided an affirmative answer to Harris's query by approving the Teacher-Coach option at a meeting on January 26, 1959. In what was essentially a face-saving gesture, the faculty stopped short of abolishing the language requirement outright, voting instead to create a new faculty committee "empowered to plan the individual programs of students in the Teacher-Coach Program, in accordance with their backgrounds, needs, and interests." The committee, which included the head of the physical education department, was specifically authorized to substitute various social science and other courses in place of the odious foreign language requirement. Apart from language substitution, the new program maintained most of the standard B.A. requirements. It was a far cry from the pre-1952 bachelor of physical education degree, which required no academic major and contained a whopping fifty hours of physical education courses—presumably a staple element in the academic diet of that era's "rugged linemen." These differences allowed Harris to put the best face on what was clearly a major setback for his athletic agenda. He could, for example, state honestly that the university still provided a curriculum for prospective coaches that was "superior in content and standards to others available in a large area." Upon investigating the committee's actual operation some three decades later, historian Lawrence N.

79. Ibid. The characterization of Harris's demeanor is derived from several conversations with the late Charles Till Davis, who was present on the occasion.

Powell discovered that in the program's second year, language waivers were granted to twenty-three of the twenty-seven athletes who selected the Teacher-Coach option. The evidence convinced Powell that, whatever the faculty's intent, "the compromise soon became a victory for the proponents of big-time athletics." As the chief architect of Tulane's effort to redress the imbalance between intellectual and athletic achievement in southern higher learning, Rufus Harris was less willing to concede defeat. "Tulane's mission," he declared in his annual presidential report for 1958–59, "is too high a destiny to jeopardize for the sake of cheers in the stadium."[80]

IV

"Cheers in the stadium. . . ." Harris's strongly held belief—if not the phrase itself—was destined to form part of his valedictory. Six months before submitting his 1958–59 report, he announced his intention to retire from Tulane's presidency as soon as a successor was chosen. Although there was no acknowledged connection between Harris's athletic views and his retirement at age sixty-three, a generation of institutional folklore would perpetuate the idea that football had been the president's undoing. Football did, in fact, play a role in Harris's demise—probably a major one—but the man whose leadership stretched across twenty-two of the university's most momentous years can scarcely be written off as a single-issue president. Athletic deemphasis—like selective admissions, support for desegregation, the defense of academic freedom, and the development of graduate training and research—constituted one part of a larger agenda for change that Harris came to symbolize in a highly personal way. Few aspects of his ambitious program found equal favor with all elements of that nebulous entity known as "the Tulane community." Several parts of his agenda were all but guaranteed to generate stiff resistance from alumni and Board members, while others—like the Newcomb College

80. Arts and Sciences Faculty Minutes, 26 January 1959, box 9G, RCH Papers (first quotation); William Peery to Fred C. Cole, 31 January 1959, copy accompanying BOA Minutes, 11 February 1959, item 3 of president's monthly report; *President's Report*, 1958–59, p. 27 (second and fourth quotations); Lawrence N. Powell, Final Report, Select Committee on Intercollegiate Athletics, June 1986, box 48, EMK Papers, 71 (third quotation).

issue—had the potential to divide the faculty against itself while drawing mixed reactions from alumni and Administrators.

In post-1945 New Orleans, as in much of the South, the long-range cost of bold academic leadership was high, and Harris paid it in the coin of eroding personal influence over the Tulane Board, the body to which he was ultimately accountable. Viewed from a distance of four decades Harris's problems with the Board can be seen as part of the larger identity crisis that engulfed the white South after World War II. In an academic landscape where regional boundaries were rapidly losing importance, the entire process of becoming a research university posed challenges to Tulane's identity as a local institution. The resulting tension between old loyalties and new priorities was apparent in the outlook of many Board members, who were attracted to the idea of national prestige but reluctant to accept its cultural and intellectual implications. At times certain Administrators seemed to exhibit something akin to dual consciousness when they embraced national perspectives on graduate training and research while clinging stubbornly to a vision of Tulane's undergraduate mission that was rooted in misty recollections of their own college days. Romanticism's distorting lens impaired the Board's vision on most athletic issues, in much the same way that strong emotional attachments to the southern and New Orleans upper-class way of life colored its response to desegregation. As an apostle of change Harris repeatedly assumed the burden of asking Board members to confront issues and make choices they would have preferred to avoid.

Another complicating factor for Harris was the changing composition of the Board itself. The last dozen years of Harris's presidency brought new occupants to thirteen out of the Board's seventeen seats, resulting in a net turnover rate of 76 percent. Seven of the appointments—some 40 percent of the Board's total membership—dated from the four year period 1947–51. None of the new Administrators had prior trustee experience in higher education, and Harris expended considerable energy and political capital in educating the group about their legitimate functions in a modern university environment. Aware that the Board would be called upon to take an active part in fundraising while also wrestling with policy decisions of unparalleled scope and gravity, Harris sought to maintain a clear wall of separation between setting policy (the Board's function) and implementing it (a task he believed the president should perform).

In the decade after 1945 Harris repeatedly called the Board's attention to disputes at other universities which illustrated the damaging consequences of trustee interference in matters of internal administration.[81] At the peak of the 1948 anti-Communist excitement, Harris revealed the depth of his feelings on this point in a personal letter to future Board member Marie Louise Snellings, who had warned Harris of alumni demands that the Board intervene to curb leftist activities at Tulane. "As for the Board taking action," Harris wrote, "the Board never takes action except when I raise a matter. The Board is going to treat . . . [the Communist issue] in the way I urge them to treat it. The exact instant they do not is when I walk out with my hat on my head, and up to the present time I do not expect to be walking out. I am sure you must know how intolerable any other condition would be." Although Harris assured Snellings of the Administrators' "complete unity" in expressing a "willingness that these matters be left to me," his vow to "walk out" if the principle were violated was more than a rhetorical flourish. Two years earlier Harris had come close to accepting the chancellorship of Vanderbilt, and at the time of his letter to Snellings he had inquired confidentially about the presidencies of both Duke and Stanford. The Board was aware of the Vanderbilt overture, and no occasion arose to test Harris's resolve on the academic freedom issue during the late forties.[82]

Harris's educational effort took a different and somewhat more defensive turn in 1950, when Joseph Merrick Jones became chairman of the Tulane Board. Jones had joined the Board only three years earlier, and his elevation to the top post made Harris uneasy from the beginning. Long experience had taught the president that in the day-to-day running of Tulane, the distinction between policymaking and internal adminis-

81. The more important episodes included the outside investigations and eventual AAUP censorship of the University of Texas following the 1945 dismissal of President Homer Rainey, who had opposed the Texas Regents' attempts to censor and harass allegedly left-leaning faculty, and the December 1950 resignation of Louisiana State University president Harold W. Stoke in protest over intervention by the LSU Board of Supervisors in the school's internal administration. A few months later Harris's monthly report to the Board included the full text of a statement from the Council of Southern Universities condemning "interference by the governing board in the internal administration of a member institution." BOA Minutes: 1 January 1945, item 16 of president's monthly report; 9 January 1951, item 23 of president's monthly report; 8 May 1951, item 4 of president's monthly report.

82. Rufus C. Harris to Marie Louise Snellings, 5 June 1948, box 29, RCH Papers (all quotations); Harris to R. C. Mercier, 1 April 1948; Harris to O. C. Carmichael, 31 March 1948, box 40, RCH Papers.

tration was never a tidy one. In practice, much depended upon the personal chemistry between the president and various Administrators, particularly the Board chairman. Harris and Phelps had enjoyed a smooth and informal working alliance that made the president an indirect participant in most Board decisions.[83] With Joseph Jones the situation was destined to change dramatically. As the senior partner in New Orleans's top law firm, Jones, like Harris, had a strong personality. Accustomed to the competitive struggles of the corporate boardroom, Jones brought something of the same mentality to his chairmanship of the Tulane Administrators. He often seemed to equate leadership with the ability to command majority support among voting stockholders. Such an attitude left little room for sharing power with holders of Class-B securities—shares that gave the owner a stake in the venture but no voting privileges. This was essentially Rufus Harris's status, since Tulane's president was not a member of its Board even in an ex officio capacity.

Harris did not expect a seat at the table. However, he did seek a larger sphere of influence with the Board than Jones was willing to grant. For most purposes, Harris considered the university to be his domain and expected the Board to seek his guidance on all decisions bearing directly upon the academic enterprise, whereas Jones had a similar view of his own role with respect to the Tulane Board and expected Harris to behave somewhat in the manner of a business corporation's chief operating officer. If tempered by sufficient tact and flexibility the two outlooks might have resulted in a balanced division of labor, but they also contained the seeds of potential misunderstanding and conflict in many areas. Hoping to steer his relationship with the Board in a positive direction, Harris arranged in December 1951 to send every Administrator a copy of the winter issue of the *American Scholar* containing Wilmarth S. Lewis's essay "The Trustees of the Privately Endowed University." Delivered the previous June as the Phi Beta Kappa oration at Harvard University, the piece fit Tulane's situation and described a model of university governance that Harris personally endorsed. Lewis, moreover, was a veteran trustee who understood the outlook of Board members and had the stature to offer sage advice to newcomers in the field.

83. Years later Harris would reproach himself for being too "stunned" by Phelps's death "to out maneuver Jones['s] election." Undated manuscript fragment (ca. 1961–62) in Harris's handwriting, Katherine Davis file, RCH Papers. Dyer, *Tulane*, 242, provides a colorful description of Phelps's personal style.

Lewis's point of departure was the 1701 charter of Yale University which gave trustees the "full and compleat Right . . . to improve and encourage" the school's development. Trustees, Lewis believed, should view their role positively, employ the veto sparingly if at all, and accept annual budget deficits with equanimity. As the "nominal custodians" of their schools, his ideal trustees would scorn the "tired compromise," resist the "timid and the second rate," and give "all possible encouragement to the president to raise the standards of the university ever higher and higher." Most important, they would take their cue from the president on matters that required Board action. According to Lewis, "The sensible trustee gradually realizes that he must leave the running of the university to the president and his colleagues, that he must be content to consider the problems they bring to him[,] and be ready to carry out any specific tasks the president may ask him to perform."[84]

At least two members of the Tulane Board (Snellings and Ernest Lee Jahncke) voiced their approval of the Lewis essay, but events soon revealed that Chairman Jones took a considerably different view of how far the president should go in seeking to influence Board actions. Jones's position became clear in January 1953 when Harris, continuing a practice that had prevailed under Phelps's chairmanship, suggested the names of three people as possible nominees to fill an existing vacancy in the Board's ranks. In addition to offering names, Harris pointed out that most private universities gave the president a seat on the Board and reminded Jones of the Administrators' well-established custom of seeking presidential advice. "When I accepted this office," Harris noted, "I asked that I have an opportunity to express objection to any proposed new [Board] member." Jones responded angrily to Harris's letter, deeming the comments about Board membership and consultation gratuitous and expressing surprise that there had been "any conditions attached" to Harris's acceptance of the Tulane presidency. "It is my feeling," Jones told Harris bluntly, "that it would be in better judgment for you to assume good faith on the part of the Board as regards its self-perpetuation and thus leave yourself free to deal with the problems of running the University itself, rather than prob-

84. Wilmarth S. Lewis, "The Trustees of the Privately Endowed University," *American Scholar* 22 (winter 1952–53): 17–27, 20 (first quotation), 22 (sixth quotation), 27 (second quotation), 26–7 (third–fifth quotations).

lems connected with the inner workings of the Board of Administrators."[85]

Having been told to mind his own business, Harris hastened to assure Jones that no infringement of the Board's prerogative had been intended. "Certainly I do not wish to step on any toes," the president assured the chairman, adding that when misunderstandings arose he hoped Jones would make due allowance for the fact that "I am learning a new relationship." Harris went on to explain the assumptions behind his initial letter in language that left little doubt that he wanted the new relationship to resemble his old one with Phelps as closely as possible. "I would like for our relationship to be such that I could feel that every point of view I have would be of interest to the Board, and vice versa," he declared. "I want the Board to know the internal problems of the University, to understand them, to advise me, and to share with me the responsibility of making decisions on them. . . . In the last analysis educational policy is involved in almost every decision which I make and which the Board makes." Given the inevitable overlap between decisions reached at the Board and presidential levels, Harris believed that he had a legitimate interest in "who makes those decisions, and what their training, background, general point of view and outlook may be." The president's argument did not prevail. In 1954 Isidore Newman II, one of the three candidates Harris had proposed the previous year, became a Tulane Administrator; but taking the decade as a whole, most Board appointments reflected the chairman's preferences rather than those of the president.[86]

The 1953 dispute over the president's role in shaping the composition of the Tulane Board left a residue of ill feeling between Harris and Jones which grew deeper and more corrosive with time. Later the same year the tension manifested itself again when Harris announced to the Administrators that since the Board's previous monthly meeting he had been named Vice President of the Carnegie Foundation Board of Trustees, Vice President of the Veterans Administration's National Advisory Board, and most importantly, Chairman of the Board of Directors of the Federal Reserve Bank of Atlanta. Two days after making the announcement, which could scarcely have surprised those who

85. Rufus C. Harris to Joseph M. Jones, 7 January 1953, box 39, RCH Papers (first–second quotations); Jones to Harris, 15 January 1953, box 39, RCH Papers (third–fifth quotations).
86. Harris to Jones, 20 January 1953, box 39, RCH Papers.

knew that Harris had already spent several years as deputy chair of the Atlanta board, Harris received a letter from Jones objecting to the appointment on the grounds that it would require too much time and bring too little benefit to the university. Jones believed Harris should spend more time visiting alumni groups for fundraising purposes, and urged him to "re-examine this whole question, giving the fullest weight to your paramount responsibilities." In a paragraph that stopped just short of ordering the president to decline the Atlanta post, Jones ended with the tactless observation, "This is my message to you on this count as of now."[87]

Both the tone and the substance of Jones's comments rankled Harris, as did a subsequent letter from Board member A. B. Freeman rebuking the president for "lack of courtesy" in failing to give advance notice of the appointment and suggesting that he limit all "[c]ivic work" to New Orleans, "where Tulane gets its greatest support."[88] In a lengthy response to Jones, Harris emphasized the necessity of deciding for himself what "public endeavors" to undertake. He then proceeded to set the record straight on the matter of his devotion to Tulane in the hope "that no one may feel it necessary to urge me to give her the best I have." What followed was clearly written from the heart.

I do not work for Tulane from nine to five for five days a week. I work for her twenty-four hours a day, seven days a week, three hundred and sixty-five days a year. There is no time which I call my own. I have telephone conversations about Tulane at midnight; I hold meetings on Sundays, and this is not compensated for by golf on Wednesdays as is the case with some of our friends. I am in my office every day of the week. I do not say this in complaint. I do not wish to be anywhere else. . . .

An educational administrator undertakes some . . . public services to stimulate himself. One can get too bogged down in administration. When I spoke of being tired last year that is what I meant. . . . I had served the University a long time without extended time away from the office. I have not been too physically tired. . . . But at times I have been mentally tired—sometimes bored with the same problems which never end and somewhat

87. BOA Minutes, 9 December 1953; Jones to Harris, 11 December 1953, box 39, RCH Papers (all quotations).
88. A. B. Freeman to Jones, 23 December 1953, box 39, RCH Papers.

frustrated by the successive generations of persons who make them. . . . Sometimes one needs to get out in the great world and put his head up in the clouds again.

This, Harris explained, was the attraction of the two-year stint as chairman of the Atlanta Federal Reserve Bank. "Furthermore," he told Jones, "I will probably be named the Chairman of the Carnegie Foundation Board, and in such event, I shall try to do a good job—in the interest of Tulane and for my own peace of mind and improvement."[89]

In the end Harris accepted both the Atlanta assignment and the Carnegie chairmanship. But the quarrel over his right to set personal priorities opened a rift with Jones that would never be fully closed. The potentially damaging consequences of an ongoing feud between the two men troubled Snellings, who defended Harris and urged Jones to distinguish between supervising and dominating the president. Attempts to dominate a leader, Snellings warned, could end only in failure. "Either the leader loses his qualities of leadership or we lose the leader," she predicted as the year drew to a close. Privately Harris recognized that the alternatives confronting him were not happy ones, and he said as much after receiving a letter in which Snellings offered a "special prayer" that he and Jones would "wind up as Damon and Pythias." No doubt reluctant to assume the role assigned him in the classical allusion (that of offering to forfeit his own life as a guarantee that Pythias would return to face execution), Harris expressed hope that the prayer would succeed but added dryly that perhaps Snellings was "asking for a little too much." The following day Harris dispatched a confidential letter to Robert O. Arnold, Chairman of the Board of Regents of the University System of Georgia, inquiring about future presidential openings in the state and telling Arnold that "if ever I could leave Tulane in good conscience[,] this is about the time."[90]

Harris's departure for Georgia would not take place for another six years. In the meantime intermittent sparring between Harris and Jones continued as the Board, under Jones's leadership, turned a deaf ear to Harris's arguments for Graduate School desegregation while lis-

89. Harris to Jones, 16 December 1953, box 39, RCH Papers.
90. Marie Louise Snellings to Jones, 20 December 1953 (first quotation); Snellings to Harris, 14 January 1954 (second–third quotations); Harris to Snellings, 20 January 1954 (fourth quotation); all in Snellings Correspondence file, RCH Papers. Also, Harris to Robert O. Arnold, 21 January 1954, box 40, RCH Papers (fifth quotation).

tening sympathetically to athletic department complaints about the evils of the new football plan. Of the various policy disputes that marked the final years of Harris's presidency, only one resulted in the actual defeat of a major initiative that Jones supported. The subject at issue was a proposed study of Tulane's internal organization and administration to be conducted for the Board of Administrators by the New York management consulting firm of Cresap, McCormick, and Paget. Planned without Harris's involvement, the $34,000 survey had a wide-ranging agenda. Although the consultants did not plan to examine "curricula or teaching methods," the list of stated concerns included enrollment goals, educational objectives, the role of the University Senate, the enlargement of the medical school faculty, "academic personnel administration," the "distribution of responsibility among department heads," and a review of the responsibilities of "deans and top administrators."[91]

Harris was appalled. The proposal displayed little or no appreciation of the autonomy and self-governing procedures essential to academic life, and all but obliterated the distinction between policymaking and administration that Harris had worked to instill in the minds of Board members. Upon seeing the survey proposal on January 10, 1955, Tulane's deans and senior administrators were, if anything, more incredulous than the president. Harris conveyed their individual reactions to Jones in the form of eighteen separately written statements. To these documents the president added his own detailed assessment of the survey's objectionable features and the likely consequences of attempting to carry it out. Speaking on behalf of the deans and other members of the academic council, Harris described the proposal as "pretentious" and warned Jones that it would undermine morale, destroy faculty, staff, and administrative esprit de corps, and "serve no good end, but on the contrary . . . be misunderstood and hurtful." If a survey were undertaken at all, Harris urged that it be "carefully restricted" to business operations and conducted by "acknowledged experts whom everyone would approve."[92]

Unwilling to risk the negative repercussions that Harris described, the Board postponed action on the survey and resurrected the idea in a different and more acceptable form some two years later. The

91. Walter F. Vieh to Darwin S. Fenner, 29 November 1954, box 40, RCH Papers.
92. Harris to Jones, 10 January 1955, box 40, RCH Papers.

episode placed Jones temporarily on the defensive and caused him to assure Harris that no survey would be approved without the full support of the president and the deans. "I think you will agree that I have not ever intentionally intruded in the internal operations of the University," Jones added in a somewhat labored attempt to distance himself from the controversy. Upon reading Jones's reluctant letter of apology, Snellings was both amused and yet slightly apprehensive. "You won and he should be more gracious this time," she confided to Harris. "Joe is such a grand guy," Snellings mused, "I wonder why he can't take it."[93] The next two years witnessed an outward improvement in the tenor of relations between Harris and Jones even as the Board rejected the idea of voluntary desegregation and began to whittle away at Harris's program of football deemphasis. Privately Jones continued to snipe at the president, and events soon revealed that he hoped to avoid future policy disagreements by hastening the day when Harris would relinquish his executive duties.[94]

The year 1957 marked a turning point in the personal and political tug of war between Tulane's president and its Board chairman. At age fifty-nine, Harris anticipated another five years of presidential service before retiring on June 30, 1962. From Jones's perspective the important thing was not that Harris would be sixty-five in 1962, but that he had served twenty years as president in 1957. Once again the two men found their points of view in conflict. On the afternoon of November 13, Harris arrived at Jones's downtown office and received what was clearly an unexpected offer. After inquiring about the president's "intentions and wishes" regarding his "remaining years of service" at Tulane, Jones offered to have the Board continue Harris's salary while assigning him to a new and largely honorific position as chancellor—an

93. BOA Minutes, 9 February 1955; Jones to Harris, 18 January 1955, box 40, RCH Papers (first quotation); Snellings to Harris, 12 February 1955, box 40, RCH Papers (second–fourth quotations).

94. At its worst Jones's conduct smacked of pettiness. He alleged, in the face of considerable evidence to the contrary, that Harris was ineffective and unpopular with faculty. On one occasion, Jones telephoned his cousin Stanhope Bayne-Jones in the Surgeon General's office to take personal credit for a grant from the Commonwealth Foundation while emphasizing that "Mr. Harris really did not have anything to do with . . . [the grant] and that he (J[oseph] J[ones]) had gone to New York last week to close the arrangements." Albert E. Cowdrey, *War and Healing: Stanhope Bayne-Jones and the Maturing of American Medicine* (Baton Rouge: Louisiana State University Press, 1992), 200; Stanhope Bayne-Jones, journal entry, 19 and 22 (quotation) November 1955, Stanhope Bayne-Jones Papers, MS C155 in the History of Medicine Division, National Library of Medicine, Bethesda, Md.

office which did not then exist. Such a move, Jones suggested, would spare Harris "some of the stress, strain, and the burden that the present day university places on its president." Harris rejected the idea that his title should be changed or his authority lessened, but in the wake of Jones's offer he was forced to reassess his retirement schedule.

During the next twelve months Harris weighed the interests of the university against the realities of his own political situation, and in November 1958 he advised the Board of his willingness to retire whenever a permanent successor could be named. From that point onward Harris was essentially a lame duck president. The fact that the Board's official acceptance of Harris's offer, and thus the public announcement of his impending retirement, was delayed until April 1959 caused many campus pundits to infer a cause and effect relationship between the Arts and Sciences faculty debate over sanctioning the Teacher-Coach Program in December 1958–January 1959 and the president's decision to step aside. The assessment was a shallow one that obscured the deeper meaning of Harris's presidency. His fate had been determined not by any single conflict or episode but by all that had taken place during the preceding decade, and particularly by the struggles over integration and football deemphasis that dominated his relations with the Board under Jones's chairmanship. These issues and a host of new challenges growing out of Tulane's emergence as a major research institution would comprise Harris's legacy to the university's next president, Herbert Eugene Longenecker.[95]

95. Harris to Jones, 14 November 1957 (unrevised draft in Harris's handwriting, apparently never sent), box 40, RCH Papers. BOA Minutes: 13 May 1959, report of Executive Committee; 10 June 1959; 11 November 1959; 25 March 1960.

4

CRISIS OF THE OLD ORDER
Desegregation and the Roots of Campus Activism

On a Sunday afternoon in mid-September 1960, some two thousand students converged upon Tulane's recently completed University Center and queued up in a lengthy reception line, which at one point stretched from the second floor down the stairs and out the front door. At the head of the line stood Tulane's new president, the "smiling and personable" Herbert Eugene Longenecker. One faculty member pronounced the occasion the largest student gathering unrelated to athletic events that he could remember. President Longenecker, a native Pennsylvanian who had served in senior administrative posts at the University of Pittsburgh and the Chicago Professional Colleges of the University of Illinois before accepting the Tulane presidency, seemed genuinely impressed by the size and warmth of the student welcome. In hindsight, the cordiality of this initial meeting is ironic. At Tulane as elsewhere, the 1960s would be a decade of intense debate and conflict over the ground rules of academic life. During the decade, faculty members and administrators were often at odds over policy questions, but ultimately Tulane's students would occupy center stage in a political and cultural struggle with strong generational overtones. It was the latter conflict, intensified by a deepening fiscal crisis during the late 1960s and early 1970s, that would preoccupy the university and define the meaning of Longenecker's administration in ways that neither he nor other Tulanians could initially have anticipated.[1]

The issues that framed campus conflict in the 1960s—racial equality, civil liberties, the alleviation of poverty, and war against Com-

1. Tulane *Hullabaloo*, 23 September 1960, p. 1.

munism in southeast Asia—drew the university inexorably into a dialogue with itself, exposing some of the compromises which the cold war had exacted and calling into question many of the central premises of academic governance. Before the turbulent decade ended, there would be passionate arguments over how the university should be governed, how professors, students, and administrators should behave toward each other, and how those involved in higher education should define their obligations to society at large. Occasionally, the disputes would take the form of mass protests and public confrontations. Discontent peaked at Tulane during the 1968–69 academic year, when the antiwar activities of a militant faculty member brought campus demands for student power into momentary alignment with New Left indictments of American foreign policy. Although the radicalism of antiwar dissent among Tulane students and faculty was quite muted when compared to the protests at schools such as Columbia, the University of California, Berkeley, or the University of Wisconsin, events of the late sixties would be measured in New Orleans by a different and less permissive social yardstick. During the protest years of 1967–69 and throughout the decades that followed, individual reactions to Tulane's brief encounter with campus radicalism remained sharply divided. Some defended the student movement as an overdue moment of moral awakening while others, including many older faculty and alumni, condemned the era as a nihilistic descent into campus unrest. Few on either side of the argument sought to deny the decade's importance.

I

At the beginning of Herbert Longenecker's fifteen-year tenure as Tulane's president, there was little indication of what the future held in store with respect to campus-based social activism. What seemed clear to Longenecker, as to most realistic observers in 1960, was that a crisis over the issue of racial segregation loomed at Tulane. Coupled with ongoing difficulties over the related problems of intercollegiate athletics and budget deficits, the challenge of race was formidable. Yet when Longenecker took office a mood of confident optimism unquestionably held sway. For Tulane, as for the United States, the advent of

Herbert Eugene Longenecker,
President, 1960–75.

a new president in the autumn of 1960 signaled a change in generational leadership. With this change came a sense of heightened expectations. Affirmation rather than anxious soul searching became the hallmark of American universities in the early 1960s and on Tulane's campus even the most serious problems seemed amenable to expert solution.

Much of the optimism surrounding the early years of Longenecker's presidency grew out of the hope that Tulane would receive a major capital gift from the coffers of the Ford Foundation. In the mid-1950s, the university had benefitted handsomely from Ford largesse in the form of endowment grants for faculty salaries totaling over $2 million, as well as separate instructional support for the medical school in approximately the same amount. By the time Longenecker arrived in 1960, the campus was rife with dizzying rumors of an outright grant of $50 million, a sum slightly greater than the 1960 market value of Tulane's entire endowment. Although the fifty million figure proved to be sheer fantasy, Tulane was in fact a potential candidate for smaller but still sizable Ford grants through its Special Program in Education, which aimed to strengthen the nation's research capabilities by creating "dispersed peaks of excellence" among carefully selected private universities in all regions of the United States. The program began in 1960 and continued for eight years, making challenge grants on a 2:1 or 3:1 matching basis to a total of seventeen universities. In the South, Ford money went to Duke, Emory, Vanderbilt, and eventually Tulane.[2]

Prominent national research universities received the largest sums, including grants of $25 million apiece to Columbia, New York University, the University of Chicago, Northwestern, and Stanford, whereas no southern institution received even half that amount. Among developing institutions in the South and elsewhere, the universities that profited most from the Ford program were those like Vanderbilt, which qualified for assistance at the beginning of the decade and secured a second grant several years later. The key to Vanderbilt's success lay in the willingness of its governing board to initiate voluntary, if token, desegregation during the 1950s. For Tulane, lack of progress toward integration during the same period had now become a major obstacle to winning continued support from the nation's wealthiest and most socially conscious philanthropic organization. Tulane was invited to apply for a Ford challenge grant in the autumn of 1960, and from the beginning Ford officials made the importance of desegregation unmistakably clear. In December 1960, after meeting with Tulane's Board of Administrators in New Orleans the previous month, Ford representative James W. Armsey requested that a statement explaining "Tulane's position in the matter of segregation" be submitted to the foundation in advance of the university's formal application. Tulane's position had, of course, remained essentially unchanged since 1956; but Armsey's letter reinforced the implicit warnings contained in recent rejections of other Tulane grant applications by the Rockefeller and Ford Foundations. Concern over foundation sup-

2. Roger L. Geiger, *Research and Relevant Knowledge: American Research Universities since World War II* (New York: Oxford University Press, 1993), 111 (table 5), 113 (first quotation), 114, 115 (second quotation); BOA Minutes, 10 April 1957, item 6 of president's monthly report. The cumulative total of Ford Accomplishment Grants, ten-year endowment for faculty salaries, and instructional support in the medical school during 1956–57 was $4,591,500. This figure does not include additional Ford grants to other university programs, which totaled nearly $600,000 in the period 1956–59. Fred C. Cole to Norman Cousins, 14 May 1958, box 37, RCH Papers; BOA Minutes, 21 March 1956, 12 February and 9 April 1958, 11 February 1959; Herbert E. Longenecker, interview by C. L. Mohr, 10 November 1994, New Orleans, Louisiana.

port, together with the Board's fear of stronger anti-discrimination requirements for future federal programs, led to renewed discussions of the need to face the question of black admissions.[3]

Both Chairman Jones and President Longenecker had ample practical reason to press for an end to the policy stalemate on segregation that had developed in the wake of the *Brown* decision. Initially, however, the Board seemed no more receptive to change in the winter of 1960–61 than it had in the mid-1950s. Although very little of what the Administrators said or thought on the subject of desegregation found its way into written form, it is likely that most Board members shared the rear-guard mentality toward social change that typified the upper strata of the city's business community. For all practical purposes, the self-perpetuating Board of Administrators of the Tulane Educational Fund represented a microcosm of the Crescent City's reigning establishment. Most Board members had attended Tulane and were accustomed to regarding the university both as an educational enterprise and as an institutional component of a larger social system. Securely ensconced in a world of private clubs and exclusive preparatory schools, New Orleans's white elite—with the exception of a few reform-minded women—were instinctive guardians of tradition who had little direct stake in the outcome of desegregation except as it impinged upon Tulane or threatened to undermine peace and public order. As Tulane Board member Harry Kelleher would later concede when discussing public school integration, his friends and business associates were "probably inclined to let events take their course . . . and probably inclined to the status quo."[4]

3. BOA Minutes, 14 December 1960 (quotation) and 8 February 1961; J. G. Harrar to Herbert Longenecker, 21 December 1960, box 75, HEL Papers. At the December 14 Board meeting Jones read drafts of two alternate replies to Armsey and agreed to check with administrators McCloskey, Phelps, Lautenschlaeger, and McIlhenny before putting the letter in final form.

4. Liva Baker, *The Second Battle of New Orleans: The Hundred-Year Struggle to Integrate the Schools* (New York: HarperCollins, 1996), 339 (quotation). Pamela Tyler, *Silk Stockings and Ballot Boxes: Women and Politics in New Orleans, 1920–1963* (Athens: University of Georgia Press, 1996) provides a brilliant account of prominent women who did not accept the past as a blueprint for the future. For a glimpse of the detached and ambivalent perspective of a pro-segregation New Orleans business executive in the mid-1950s, see Robert Penn Warren, *Segregation: The Inner Conflict in the South* (1956; reprint, Athens: University of Georgia Press, 1994), 47–8, 56–7. On the composition and influence of the New Orleans elite, see Phyllis Hutton Raabe, "Status and Its Impact: New Orleans' Carnival, the Social Upper Class, and

Passivity and legal foot-dragging had appeared to serve the interests of social stability during the last half of the 1950s, when quiet diplomacy and "friendly" litigation by white moderates and middle-class black leaders secured the desegregation of city libraries and public transportation, while efforts at school integration were blunted through seemingly endless rounds of federal litigation involving school board attorneys and lawyers for the NAACP. These developments tended to foster a belief among white decision makers that basic change could be postponed almost indefinitely through a policy of delay and tokenism. Any politicians or business leaders who might have been inclined to take a more progressive view—and there is no evidence that such individuals were numerous—faced the political juggernaut of "massive resistance," with its emphasis on the use of crude racial demagoguery to drown out all exponents of compromise or moderation.[5]

Throughout the months preceding the nationally televised mob scenes that accompanied the court-ordered desegregation of New Orleans public schools in November 1960—the events that came to be known as the New Orleans "school crisis"—both the mayor and the city's leading business spokesmen remained silent and aloof. Their detachment—or paralysis—sprang from a number of causes, including racism, political calculation, fear of integration's social consequences, and a belief that court decisions rather than protest rhetoric would de-

Upper Class Power" (Ph.D. diss., Pennsylvania State University, 1973), 97–8, 113–4, 119, 193–4; Charles W. Chai, "Who Rules New Orleans? A Study of Community Power Structures: Some Preliminary Findings on Social Characteristics and Attitudes of New Orleans Leaders," *Louisiana Business Survey* (October 1971): 2–11. On the economic ties of Tulane Board members, see Arthur H. Carpenter, "Gateway to the Americas: New Orleans' Quest for Latin American Trade, 1900–1970" (Ph.D. diss., Tulane University, 1987), 138–9, 186–203.

5. Adam Fairclough, *Race and Democracy: The Civil Rights Struggle in Louisiana, 1915–1972* (Athens: University of Georgia Press, 1995), chaps. 7–8; Louisiana State Advisory Committee to the United States Commission on Civil Rights, *The New Orleans School Crisis* (Washington D.C.: GPO, 1961), 42–4. The most severe indictment of the New Orleans' business community's stance on integration, civic progress, and general public welfare is Morton Inger, *Politics and Reality in an American City: The New Orleans School Crisis of 1960* (New York: Center for Urban Education, 1969). On the massive resistance movement in Louisiana, see Numan V. Bartley, *The Rise of Massive Resistance: Race and Politics in the Deep South during the Second Reconstruction* (Baton Rouge: Louisiana State University Press, 1969), chaps. 10–12; Neil R. McMillen, *The Citizens' Council: Organized Resistance to the Second Reconstruction* (Urbana: University of Illinois Press, 1971), 59–72, 285–96. For the coarse texture of white supremacist pronouncements by Louisiana's leading demagogue, see Glen Jeansonne, *Leander Perez, Boss of the Delta* (Baton Rouge: Louisiana State University Press, 1977).

Crisis of the Old Order

termine when and how schools were integrated. Inaction by the city's leading political and civic spokesmen created a vacuum that racist demagogues were quick to fill. Some aspects of the mindset prevailing among members of the New Orleans establishment were revealed at a September 1960 meeting between Orleans Parish School Board president Lloyd Rittner and a group of prominent businessmen, including Tulane Administrators Darwin Fenner and Richard Freeman, the latter a staunch segregationist who was chairman of Delta Airlines and the owner of a local Coca-Cola plant. Talk turned quickly to the importance of maintaining segregated bathroom facilities in mixed schools and to the need for separate classes for boys and girls in schools where blacks were enrolled. Rittner's request that the group publish a newspaper advertisement calling for law and order and opposing state efforts to close integrated schools fell upon deaf ears.[6]

On November 14, 1960, four black first graders entered two previously all-white schools, prompting white supremacists to abandon all vestiges of restraint. The tone of resistance efforts was set the next day when Plaquemines Parish political boss Leander Perez urged several thousand white New Orleanians to defend their heritage. "Don't wait for your daughter to be raped by these Congolese. Don't wait until the burr-heads are forced into your schools. Do something about it now!" Perez screamed. By the time James Armsey met with the Tulane Board on November 22 to discuss the possibility of a Ford challenge grant, white mobs had already invaded the city hall and were gathering daily to threaten and intimidate anyone seeking to enter the two working-class elementary schools where desegregation was being attempted. Only a few days earlier Jones had written Dean Rusk to plead for the Rockefeller Foundation's "sympathetic understanding" as New Orleans struggled to avoid "a repetitive Little Rock situation insofar as our public schools are concerned." These events, together with the first stirrings of a new militancy among a small group of Tulane students who were attracted to the direct action program of the Congress of Racial Equality, provided the backdrop for subsequent Board delib-

---

6. Fairclough, *Race and Democracy*, 240–1. Still indispensable for a basic understanding of the events of 1960 are two works by Mary Lee Muller: "New Orleans Public School Desegregation," *Louisiana History* 17 (winter 1976): 69–88, and the same author's 1975 University of New Orleans M.A. thesis, "The Orleans Parish School Board and Negro Education, 1940–1960."

erations on desegregation. The prospect that civil rights battles would soon move out of the courts and into the streets intensified the conflict that some administrators had long felt between the pursuit of national stature for Tulane and the preservation of traditional hierarchies based upon race, wealth, and birth. In such an emotionally charged atmosphere, the Board went to considerable lengths to avoid confronting the moral aspects of segregation and to focus instead on questions of law and practical necessity. Operating within an ethically "neutral" framework that mimicked the utilitarian norms of trade and commerce, the administrators found it possible to agree that integration was necessary and economically advantageous. Just as pragmatic businessmen subordinated personal dislikes to the pursuit of profit, even the most conservative Board members came to recognize that safeguarding institutional welfare must take precedence over defending racial orthodoxy.[7]

The emotional side of the race issue was never fully eliminated from Board decisions, however, despite the systematic exclusion of moral questions from the official minutes. Inner turmoil over the prospect of encountering black people as social equals was apparent in one administrator's reaction to a 1962 request that several black college presidents be housed in campus dormitories during a proposed meeting of the Adult Education Commission of the Southern Regional Education Board the following year. "Why house the negroes?" the dissenting board member asked rhetorically. "Why impose integrated housing upon students who possibly, together with their parents, would strenuously object to such unexpected use of their established homes." No one captured the conflict between regional loyalties and national aspirations better than Marie Louise Snellings, who shared her views with other Board members in a detailed memorandum dated January 24, 1961. Snellings acknowledged that by continuing to refuse blacks admission, the university was in danger of losing federal construction loans as well as research grants from government and private sources. The Board also faced "a real pressure because we fear that we may not receive a grant of an uncertain number of millions of dollars from the Ford Foundation if we do not change our admissions policy." The eco-

7. Jack Bass, *Unlikely Heroes* (New York: Simon and Schuster, 1982), 129 (first quotation); Joseph M. Jones to Dean Rusk, 14 November 1960, box 75, HEL Papers (second–third quotations).

nomic rationale for abandoning segregation, Snellings believed, should be weighed against various countervailing factors, including the likelihood that individual donors would react to black admissions by withholding contributions and taking legal action to reclaim the Tulane and Newcomb endowments. On the latter point Snellings managed to sound both dogmatic and oddly tentative. "If we change our admissions policy at this time," she declared, "we may be prepared for a contest from the Tulane heirs as a real possibility." One sentence later, however, Snellings appeared to backtrack, admitting that "[s]uch a suit might not succeed. Also it might not be filed."[8]

The crux of Snellings's objections to desegregation had less to do with economics than with local loyalty and attachment to what has often been termed the "southern way of life." The year 1961, when Louisiana's public schools were in "a condition of upheaval and unrest," struck Snellings as an "ill advised time" to desegregate Tulane. "My loyalty to my home, my neighbors, and to the South . . . compels me to . . . vote to maintain our status quo at present," Snellings told her fellow Board members. The argument had a familiar ring. In 1955 she had held out the possibility of voting to change admissions policy within a period of from one to ten years. Now, some six years later, she no longer objected in principle to admitting "a bona fide qualified negro applicant" for graduate study, but her new timetable for actually casting an affirmative vote was "somewhere from three to ten years." This was hardly the schedule the Ford Foundation had in mind.[9]

Although Snellings believed that integrating Tulane to appease the Ford Foundation would constitute a "sell out," it is clear that most of her Board colleagues took a less jaundiced or at least a more pragmatic view of their relationship to private philanthropy. Yet even the prospect of being passed over for a major Ford grant failed initially to produce a consensus for change. The month of January 1961 came and went without any indication that Tulane's racial barriers would be

8. Lester J. Lautenschlaeger to Joseph M. Jones, 18 July 1962, box 75, HEL Papers (first–second quotations); Marie Louise Snellings to the Board of Administrators of the Tulane Education Fund, 24 January 1961, HEL Papers, box 99 (third–sixth quotations). Administrator George A. Wilson wrote Jones on August 20 in support of Lautenschlaeger's position but the Board's Executive Committee overruled the objections on 2 August 1962 and agreed to provide the requested accommodations.

9. Marie Louise Snellings to the Board of Administrators of the Tulane Education Fund, 24 January 1961, box 99, HEL Papers.

lowered. Any doubt about the consequences of keeping Tulane white vanished on February 15, 1961, when the Ford Foundation officially notified Longenecker that the university would not be included in the challenge grant program. Although the rejection could scarcely have surprised either Longenecker or Joseph Jones, it sent a powerful message to the Board as a whole about the damage caused by a prolonged refusal to face the issue of racial integration.[10] At a Board meeting on March 8, some three weeks after learning of the Ford decision and one week prior to a scheduled meeting with Ford officials in New York, Jones stressed that "recent events" made it imperative to reach a decision on desegregation. Without taking a formal vote, the Administrators concurred that it was "the sense of the meeting that the Board recognizes that it is incumbent on it, to the extent that it legally can, to change the admissions policy, [to one] which on a controlled basis, would permit the admission of any qualified student to attend any college of the University." While hardly a ringing affirmation of moral purpose, this grudging half-step toward acceptance of the inevitable represented the Board's first official departure from the posture of passivity adopted in 1956. Other actions soon followed. On April 12, 1961, a scant three days before Longenecker's formal inauguration as president, the Board released to the press a statement summarizing the racially restrictive clauses in the Tulane and Newcomb donations and announcing that "Tulane University would admit qualified students regardless of race or color if it were legally permissible." Noting that "[t]imes have changed since the University was founded," the Administrators justified their action on the ground that Tulane "must move ahead and assume its rightful place of leadership among America's outstanding universities."[11]

At first blush the April 12 statement looked like the act of a governing board that was preparing to seize the legal initiative in order to free itself from white supremacist constraints. Readers will recall that in

10. Ibid. (quotation); James W. Armsey to Herbert E. Longenecker, 15 February 1961, box 24, RCH Papers. Barely two weeks before the Armsey letter Rufus Harris had written Joseph Jones, "I deeply hope the Ford Foundation will deal generously with Tulane. I know something of your difficulty. Have you considered having Tulane publicly announce now a decision to admit qualified Negroes in September 1962, or even in 1963, to the graduate and professional schools?" Harris to Jones, 30 January 1961, box 24, RCH Papers.

11. BOA Minutes, report of President Jones, 8 March 1961 (first–second quotations); ibid., report of President Jones, 12 April 1961 (third–fifth quotations).

1955 the idea of seeking a declaratory judgment for this purpose was discussed and rejected on the ground that the ultimate ramifications of such a judicial ruling were impossible to predict. At that time, Law School dean Ray Forrester had argued that the Board should seek a court ruling only after a policy decision on integration had been reached.[12] On April 12, 1961, the policy question was effectively settled, but the Board remained unwilling to take the lead in opening Tulane to blacks. As custodians of a segregationist legacy, the Administrators chose to define their fiduciary responsibility as a negative obligation. Having announced a willingness to integrate if "legally permissible," the Board would defend Tulane's right to segregate until outside litigants secured a judicial ruling that made the racial restrictions of the endowment legally unenforceable.

No amount of fastidious legal reasoning could mask the basic ambiguity of the Board's position. The Administrators' effort to embrace the principle of integration while maintaining a policy of racial exclusion left the university open to charges of inconsistency, if not outright hypocrisy. In the summer of 1961, Jones confided to the sister of Board member Richard Freeman that he had tried to persuade the Board to seek a declaratory judgment authorizing the Administrators to disregard the racial restrictions of the Tulane gift. When pressed on his failure to do so, Jones emphatically declared, "[Y]ou just do not know my Board!" Former President Harris, who did know the Board, stated bluntly the following year that throughout the late 1950s, action to desegregate the university was blocked by "a small group of very illiberal [Board] members who wanted a court decision ordering them to integrate, which they could hide behind."[13] The Board would eventually secure a decision which authorized the admission of black students and also ruled out the possibility of lawsuits by disgruntled segregationist donors or Paul Tulane heirs—a hypothetical danger that had never advanced beyond the realm of unsupported speculation. But be-

12. Ray Forrester to Rufus C. Harris, 29 September 1955, box 99, HEL Papers.

13. Rosa Freeman Keller, Autobiography, part two, p. 40, typescript in possession of Dr. Blake Touchstone, New Orleans, Louisiana (hereafter cited as Keller Autobiography; first quotation); Rufus C. Harris to Dr. Fredrick Hard, 8 March 1963, box 40 RCH Papers (second quotation). The conversation between Jones and Keller cannot be dated precisely but it apparently occurred after the denial of admission to Barbara Guillory on 23 June 1961. Cheryl V. Cunningham, "The Desegregation of Tulane University" (M.A. thesis, University of New Orleans, 1982), 23–4.

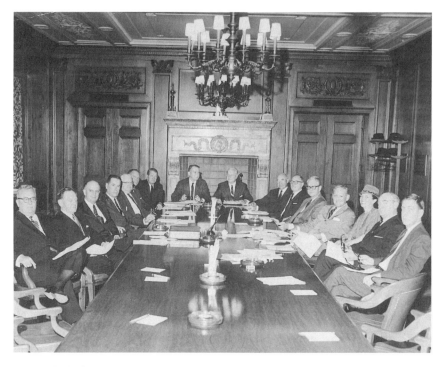

Board of Administrators and friends, 1964. Left to right: Vice President Fred R. Cagle, Sam Israel Jr. (M), Jacob S. Landry (M), Lester J. Lautenschlaeger (M), Joseph McCloskey (M), Clayton L. Nairne, Sidney Marks, President Herbert E. Longenecker, Darwin S. Fenner (M), Homer Bartee, Leon Irwin Jr. (M), Richard W. Freeman (M), Harry B. Kelleher (M), Mrs. Marie Louise Wilcox Snellings (M), Vice President Clarence Scheps, Edmund McIlhenny. (M) denotes member of the Board.

fore desegregation actually took place nearly two years would elapse, during which Tulane's position on integration would seem woefully irresolute to most outside observers.[14]

Preparations for a court test of Tulane's admission policies had been quietly underway since the fall of 1960, when three individuals— Tulane political science professor Henry Mason, Dillard University political scientist John B. Furey (a former graduate school classmate of Mason's at Columbia), and Rosa Freeman Keller, a prominent and

14. Something resembling an implied threat of anti-integration lawsuits was contained in a 21 July 1961 "equal time editorial reply" on WDSU radio and television by state Representative Welborn Jack of Caddo Parish. Jack, a Tulane Law School graduate and an uncompromising

wealthy white liberal who was the daughter of former Tulane Administrator Albert B. Freeman and the sister of Richard W. Freeman, who joined the Board in 1959—began laying the groundwork for a new round of black applications that would either prod the Board to integrate voluntarily or compel the Administrators to clarify their legal options in a court of competent jurisdiction. From his post at Dillard, Furey canvassed a number of current students and recent graduates in order to identify individuals qualified for graduate study at Tulane who were also willing to become parties to a lawsuit if their applications were rejected. Two candidates eventually emerged, Barbara Marie Guillory and Pearlie Hardin Elloie, each of whom applied for admission to Tulane in the 1961–62 academic year. Elloie sought to earn an M.A. in the School of Social Work; Guillory, who held a master's degree from LSU, applied to the Ph.D. program in sociology.[15]

Precisely when the Board first learned of the applications is unclear. As late as January 24, 1961, Snellings asserted categorically, "We have no one pressing us for admission. We have no group at this time forcing our hand." If her statement was true when written, it had ceased to be so by early March. At the March 8 Board meeting, Jones told the Administrators that one black student had applied for admission to Newcomb College. (The Newcomb applicant would later be deemed academically ineligible.) On April 12, immediately after approving the press release concerning black admissions, the Board was informed of Elloie's application to the School of Social Work and shown a letter of rejection drafted by Administrator Joseph McCloskey that would be sent out the next week over the signature of Social Work dean Walter L. Kindelsperger. Joseph Jones advised the Board that "the manner in which Mrs. Elloie's application was prepared and presented to [admissions director] Dr. Cliff Wing at his home" indi-

segregationist, objected to a 19 April 1961 WDSU editorial supporting the Tulane Board's April 15 statement on black admissions. On July 19 he called upon "the other alumni to join me and others and make the board of administrators respect the wills of Paul Tulane and Sophie Newcomb and the Constitution of Louisiana." Equal Time Reply to WDSU Editorial, box 99, HEL Papers. The Paul Tulane heirs, as represented by three Tulane sisters in St. Petersburg, Florida, seem to have learned of the Guillory suit only when they were brought in as third-party defendants in the summer of 1962. At that time they appeared quite willing to be guided by the wishes of the Tulane Board and its attorneys. Lida Tulane to "Dear Miss Susie" [Susan B. Keane], 29 June 1962, box 100, HEL Papers; Susan Keane to "Dear Miss Lida," 6 July 1962, box 100, HEL Papers; Lida Tulane to Keane, 13 December 1962, box 102, HEL Papers.

15. Keller Autobiography, part 2, pp. 37–8; Cunningham, "Desegregation of Tulane," 19–23.

cated that "a suit may result from Tulane's rejection of this application." The Board's Law Committee was duly authorized to employ outside counsel to assist in the "vigorous defense" of whatever legal challenge might be forthcoming.[16]

These facts cast considerable doubt on the oft-repeated claim that
the litigation to integrate Tulane was a "friendly" action undertaken
with the Board's tacit approval or connivance. Although the Board's
April 12 statement may have appeared to "invite" litigation, the events
that gave rise to the lawsuit filed in September 1961 had been set in motion on March 14, 1961—nearly a month prior to the Board's policy
statement—when Elloie's completed application (dated March 6) was
delivered to the Wing residence. It is true, of course, that Rosa Keller
and Henry Mason believed that speedy integration was in the university's best interest, and that they—along with John Furey—undoubtedly hoped that the Board would voluntarily abandon segregation. All
three realized, however, that change would be highly unlikely in the
absence of legal pressure. For each of them, participating in the Elloie
and Guillory case meant adopting an adversarial posture toward the
Tulane Board.[17]

Mounting a public challenge to Board policy was a step that some
took more readily than others. By 1960 Professor Mason had emerged
as a strong spokesman for increased faculty participation in university
governance. His involvement in the desegregation case grew out of personal conviction, but it was also indicative of a growing undercurrent
of impatience among professors who chafed at the Board's seeming indifference to faculty resolutions in support of integration. Rosa Keller
was impelled to action by the experience of a decade of participation in
local interracial activities, including her work with international students on the Tulane campus. Keller realized from the outset that her
role in the litigation would strain relations with her conservative
brother, while garnering little support from other members of the
Board. "The board and the administration deplored my part in the

16. Marie Louise Snellings to the Board of Administrators of the Tulane Education Fund, 24
January 1961 (first quotation); BOA Minutes, 8 March and 12 April 1961, report of President
Jones (second–fourth quotations).

17. W. L. Kindelsperger to Herbert Longenecker, 14 March 1961, with accompanying Elloie
application and transcript, box 102, HEL Papers. Kindelsperger surmised that a 28 February
1961 telephone inquiry concerning black admissions was also connected to the Elloie application.

lawsuit," Keller recalled, and in the end only Jones gave the impression of being personally sympathetic. John Furey had no professional affiliation with Tulane at the time of Elloie's application. Having witnessed firsthand the vast disparities between white and black higher education in the Deep South, the Dillard professor gave no indication that he considered himself a secret ally of those in authority. If anything, Furey threw down the gauntlet when recommending Elloie for admission by declaring that he had selected the applicant "with the same care with which the Brooklyn Dodgers selected Jackie Robinson for big league baseball." Furey hoped that instead of receiving a routine rejection, Elloie's application would "serve as the basis for a review of the admission policies of Tulane University . . . in light of its responsibilities to the New Orleans community." But he was not optimistic. "It is quite clearly my intention to put Tulane University squarely on the spot. . . . For this I make no apology," Furey declared in a personal note to admissions director Cliff Wing.[18]

On April 19, 1961, Tulane rejected Pearlie Hardin Elloie's application to the School of Social Work. On June 23, Barbara Guillory's application to the Ph.D. program in sociology suffered a similar fate. Both women were deemed academically qualified for graduate work but inadmissible on grounds of race. The rejections made a lawsuit inevitable and, with Rosa Keller paying the legal bills, efforts to secure counsel for the two black plaintiffs began immediately. After A. P. Tureaud, New Orleans's only black civil rights lawyer, declined the case because support from the NAACP's national office was unavailable, the litigants turned to John P. "Jack" Nelson, one of the few white attorneys in the city willing to identify himself with the struggle for racial equality. A Gulf Coast native who had been decorated for combat heroism in World War II, Nelson was also a devout Catholic. He had begun to question southern racial practices during the late 1940s while studying law under Father Louis J. Twomey, a Jesuit social activist who held racially integrated meetings in conjunction with a campus-based labor institute at Loyola University of New Orleans.

18. Keller Autobiography, part 2, pp. 40–1 (first quotation); Cunningham, "Desegregation of Tulane," 19–24; John B. Furey to Cliff W. Wing Jr., letter of recommendation for Pearlie Hardin Elloie, 13 March 1961, box 102, HEL Papers (second–third quotations); John B. Furey to Cliff W. Wing Jr., personal note accompanying Elloie letter of recommendation, 13 March 1961, box 102, HEL Papers (fourth quotation).

After initially specializing in labor law, Nelson was drawn increasingly into the segregation controversy, running unsuccessfully in 1958 for a seat on the Orleans Parish School Board in opposition to the outspoken segregationist Emile Wagner. Nelson subsequently participated in the Save Our Schools organization, which sought to keep public education intact during the city's 1960 integration crisis. Only a few months before taking the Guillory and Elloie case, moreover, Nelson had agreed to represent four young activists—including the local CORE chairman Rudolph Lombard and Tulane graduate student Sydney Goldfinch—following their arrest during a lunch counter sit-in at the McCrory's store in downtown New Orleans.[19]

His liberal credentials notwithstanding, Nelson hesitated before entering into a protracted courtroom battle with the city's political and economic establishment. Representing sit-in demonstrators was one thing. Leading an outright assault on Tulane's admissions policy was another matter. "The people that graduate from Tulane do not eat at McCrory's," Nelson explained to an interviewer. "They don't use drinking fountains in public places. They don't go to the local theaters. So they could care less about *that*. . . . But you don't touch their school." Having weighed the potential risk to his career, Nelson accepted the case. After preliminary discussions with the Tulane Board in early August, he indicated his intention to file suit in federal court. The Administrators had already engaged the services of Tulane Law School graduate John Pat Little of the firm of Guste, Barnett, and Little to act as the university's defense counsel (with an initial appropriation of $20,000 for legal fees and expenses). On September 1, 1961, Civil Action 11484 was initiated in Division B of the United States District Court for the Eastern District of Louisiana. The case of *Barbara Marie Guillory and Pearlie Hardin Elloie v. The Administrators of the Tulane University of Louisiana and Herbert E. Longenecker, President of Tulane University . . . and the Administrators of the Tulane Educational Fund* was underway.[20]

19. R. M. Lumiansky to Barbara Marie Guillory, 23 June 1961, box 100, HEL Papers; W. L. Kindelsperger to Pearlie Hardin Elloie, 19 April 1961, box 100, HEL Papers; Keller Autobiography, part 2, pp. 38–9; John Robert Payne, "A Jesuit Search for Social Justice: The Public Career of Louis J. Twomey, S. J., 1947–1969" (Ph.D. diss., University of Texas, 1976), 61, 191–2; Kim Lacy Rogers, *Righteous Lives: Narratives of the New Orleans Civil Rights Movement* (New York: New York University Press, 1993), 56–9, 69–70.

20. Keller Autobiography, part 2, p. 39; Rogers, *Righteous Lives*, 98 (first–second quota-

Subsequent judicial proceedings unfolded in two distinct phases. The first phase began with the filing of the suit in September and concluded with a summary judgment in favor of the plaintiffs rendered by Judge J. Skelly Wright on March 28, 1962. A second round of litigation began with Tulane's motion for a new trial on April 13, 1962, and continued until December 6, 1962, when Judge Frank B. Ellis, Wright's successor, handed down his decision in the case. Although the legal issues in the case were clearly drawn from the outset, the two sides approached the trial with very different sets of concerns. For the plaintiffs and their attorneys—including Katherine Wright, who joined Nelson as co-counsel in January 1962—the paramount issue was an ethical one. Tulane had to be integrated in order to begin rectifying the injustices of segregation. It was this overriding moral imperative, heightened by a concern for the university's national reputation, which caused Wright, a Tulane Law School graduate and the spouse of Tulane mathematics professor Fred Wright, to put aside initial misgivings about participating in a suit that might weaken the independence of her home institution.[21]

For the Tulane Board, protecting the university's private status and safeguarding its assets took precedence over other legal issues in the segregation battle. Having decided—however belatedly and reluctantly—to admit black students, the Administrators attached primary importance to keeping Tulane beyond the reach of the state legislature. The Board also wanted to ensure that any judicial act nullifying the racial stipulations of the original Tulane and Newcomb donations would leave the university in undisputed possession of the endowment funds, as well as all subsequent donations. The concerns were not new ones for the Board. In the mid-1950s, fear of an attack upon the endowment had been a significant factor in the decision not to seek a judicial ruling permitting desegregation. Although some Administrators welcomed any pretext for delaying integration, the dangers of initia-

---

tions); Memorandum of a conversation with Herbert Longenecker re. lawsuit against Tulane on behalf of Negro applicants for admission, typescript, 21 August 1961, in personal files of Beatrice M. Fields; Joseph M. Jones to Herbert E. Longenecker, 3 August 1961, box 102, HEL Papers; Request for Budget Adjustment, 1 November 1961, box 102, HEL Papers. Of the $20,000 total, half went to pay Little's fee, with an additional $350 per month allocated as the salary of attorney Wood Brown III who had joined Little as co-counsel.

21. Cunningham, "Desegregation of Tulane," 27; "Katherine Wright: Lady Lawyer Likes Work," Tulane *Hullabaloo*, 12 December 1962, p. 5; Katherine Wright to John P. Nelson, 30 June 1961, box 8, John P. Nelson Papers, Amistad Research Center, Tulane University.

ting legal action were carefully and objectively evaluated by the
Board's Law Committee in several briefs and letters prepared in the
spring of 1956. These documents, together with a separate brief on
federal case law and constitutional issues prepared by Ray Forrester,
anticipated many of the arguments that John Nelson would advance in
1961 and tacitly conceded that Tulane's position on segregation had
become legally untenable.

A primary concern of the Board of Administrators was the possibility that Tulane's private status might be undermined if university admissions policy was overturned on the basis of the Fourteenth Amendment—something that could occur only if a court ruled that the state
was substantially involved in the school's operation and governance. A
second equally troubling question had to do with the specific remedy
that might be imposed if and when a state or federal court invalidated
the racial restrictions imposed by Paul Tulane in 1882 and reaffirmed
by the state of Louisiana in its 1884 contract with the Board of Administrators of the Tulane Educational Fund. The Board's apprehension
centered around two points of law: (1) a 1909 Louisiana Supreme
Court decision holding that the recipient of a donation was bound to
execute the wishes of a donor "in the same manner and to the same extent as the debtor in any ordinary contract," and (2) Articles 1559,
1568, and 1569 of the Louisiana Civil Code, which stipulated that donations *inter vivos* (between living persons) might be "revoked or dissolved" as a penalty for "non-performance of the conditions imposed
on the donee." In such cases the donated property would be returned
to the donor or the legal heirs. If a "donee" was deemed at fault for violating a donor's wishes, moreover, the offending party could be required to return not only the original gift but all "fruits" subsequently
accumulated.[22]

Following these guidelines, a court might invalidate not only segregation but the entire set of legal arrangements that had brought the
university into being. The Board's reasoning on the problem was summarized succinctly in March 1956 by Law Committee member Esmond

22. Joseph McCloskey, "Memorandum Relative to the Legal Position of the Administrators
of the Tulane Educational Fund with Respect to the Question of Their Right to Admit or Refuse
Admission to Negroes," undated document prepared after 8 February 1956 to be used at Law
Committee meeting of 9 March 1956, box 99, HEL Papers, 19 (hereafter cited as McCloskey
Memorandum). The 1909 court decision was *Voinche v Town of Marksville*, 124 La. 712, 50
So. 662.

Phelps, who found "much force and merit" in the argument that Tulane's 1884 contract with the state to conduct a segregated university was illegal "when viewed in the light of today's jurisprudence," since the courts had made it clear that "'public' education on such a restricted basis cannot be countenanced. . . . [S]uch an interpretation would not, however . . . have the effect of requiring Tulane University, by virtue of Act 43[,] to accept other than white students. On the contrary, the charter powers being limited, it would be our conclusion that such contract would necessarily have to be set aside and the parties restored to the status quo." Tulane, in other words, might be directed to return substantial amounts of money to the Tulane and Newcomb heirs and to the state of Louisiana in order to reestablish itself on a different legal footing. This was admittedly a worst case scenario, but even a more favorable judicial outcome might leave the university and its assets in a state of legal limbo for an extended period of time.[23]

Throughout the fifteen months of litigation in 1961–62, therefore, Tulane's official defense of segregation was dictated primarily by the desire of Jones and other pragmatists to protect the university's autonomy and fiscal integrity. What Jones and Little sought was a ruling that would invalidate all charter, statutory, and state constitutional requirements for racial exclusion without jeopardizing any other facets of the school's legal status. What Nelson and Wright sought was something quite different—a class action ruling that would order Tulane to desegregate on the grounds that it was a "public" institution sufficiently tied to and influenced by the state of Louisiana to render it subject to the dictates of the Fourteenth Amendment. Nelson's argument for applying Constitutional requirements to the admissions policy of an ostensibly private school relied upon the doctrine of "state action," a line of judicial reasoning that had emerged in previous civil rights litigation involving white efforts to enforce restrictive racial covenants in real estate and to privatize state primary elections or, later, to make public schools nominally private in order to evade Constitutional safeguards for black rights. By the early 1960s the "state action" doctrine had been used to destroy the legal basis of segregation in public transportation as well as in theaters, restaurants, and other private businesses located in public facilities.

23. Esmond Phelps to the Administrators of the Tulane Educational Fund, 9 March 1956, box 99, HEL Papers.

From the standpoint of higher education law, the Tulane case was part of a series of precedents that would eventually give rise to three basic judicial criteria for determining when the actions of a private institution could be subjected to Constitutional constraints. In order to establish that the acts of a private college represented "state action," it would be necessary to show that the school acted as an agent carrying out an assignment delegated to it by the state, that it performed a function generally recognized as the responsibility of government, or that it obtained substantial financial support, encouragement, and prestige from its contacts with the state. Nelson built his case against Tulane around the "delegated power" and "government contacts" components of "state action" theory. Research into the university's history as recorded in state and municipal records, legislative proceedings, court decisions, and all 137 volumes of the Tulane Board minutes (obtained under threat of subpoena) yielded considerable evidence of a relationship with the state that had once been quite significant and had never formally ended. In an analysis that ran to nearly one hundred typed legal pages, Nelson sought to demonstrate substantial state involvement in Tulane's affairs through income derived from the property of the old University of Louisiana, tax exemptions, and the various provisions of Louisiana Act 43 of 1884.[24]

That act, which was later incorporated into the state constitution, transferred all the assets of the University of Louisiana to the enlarged Tulane Board of Administrators, which was vested with all the powers formerly exercised by the Administrators of the parent institution. The act also required that Tulane seek legislative approval for the sale of transferred state property, and stipulated that the property would revert to the state should the Board cease to use it for educational purposes. Additional provisions of the act and amendment relieved the state of any future responsibility for making appropriations to the university, while granting each member of the legislature the ongoing right to bestow free tuition upon one student "who shall comply with the requirements for admission established by said [Tulane] Board." Per-

24. William A. Kaplin, *The Law of Higher Education: Legal Implications of Administrative Decision Making* (San Francisco: Jossey-Bass, 1978), 21–8. For a more detailed summary, see "Acts of Private Institutions of Higher Education as Constituting State Action or Action under Color of Law for Purposes of the Fourteenth Amendment and 42 USCA Sec. 1983," 37 ALR Fed. 601.

haps most important, Act 43 designated "the Administrators of the Tulane Education Fund . . . with the addition of the Governor, Superintendent of Public Education[,] and Mayor of the City of New Orleans as ex-officio members thereof, the Administrators of the University of Louisiana, which shall hereafter be known as the 'Tulane University of Louisiana.'" Language of this kind, together with an 1886 court decision affirming Tulane's tax-exempt status, allowed Nelson to argue that Act 43 had preserved the old University of Louisiana and vested control of the institution in a new body comprised of the Tulane Educational Fund Administrators plus three public officials.[25]

Nelson's arguments, if accepted in their totality, pointed toward the conclusion that Tulane was a public school in the literal sense and not simply a private institution whose ties to the state were substantial enough to warrant invoking Fourteenth Amendment prohibitions against racial discrimination. Not surprisingly, attorneys for the university saw the matter in a different light. From Tulane's perspective, the University of Louisiana had ceased to exist when its property was transferred to the TEF Administrators, creating a new institution that was wholly private. If the change had not occurred with the passage of Act 43 in 1884, it had surely taken place four years later when the constitutional amendment embodying Act 43 was ratified by voters. Starting from different conceptual premises, the two sides soon found themselves engaged in an arcane theoretical argument over the identity of the university's governing board. In the end Nelson named as defendants both the Administrators of the Tulane Educational Fund and the Administrators of the Tulane University of Louisiana, a body that did not exist in the view of Tulane's lawyers.[26]

There were a number of weaknesses in Tulane's argument, which in reality was little more than a tactical ploy to counter Nelson's legal assault. For one thing, any claim that Tulane was entirely private ignored the vigorous emphasis which the university itself had placed on

25. "An Analysis of Evidence Submitted on Behalf of Plaintiffs in Their Request For Summary Judgment," John P. Nelson Papers, Amistad Research Center, Tulane University. The full text of Act 43 is reprinted in Dyer, *Tulane*, appendix 2 (quotation on p. 306).

26. Cunningham, "Desegregation of Tulane," chap. 4, and esp. 50–5. See also the defendants' motions of 1 December 1961 to dismiss, to quash service, to dismiss Herbert Longenecker as party to suit, and to quash service on Joseph Jones, and 14 February 1962 motions by Joseph Jones to quash service on himself, and defendants' motion to strike various of plaintiff's exhibits, box 102, HEL Papers.

its public status when seeking tax exemptions and when making an unsuccessful bid for legislative appropriations in the early twentieth century. A 1956 memorandum of the Tulane Board's Law Committee plainly demonstrates that the Administrators did not regard the university as bereft of a public component. The memorandum acknowledged that "[s]tate action may be involved in the Tulane situation because of the continued existence of the University of Louisiana as Tulane University of Louisiana and the contract arrangement with the state." And while refusing to recommend desegregation in 1956, the Law Committee made no effort to minimize the university's potential vulnerability in federal litigation. In a prophetic passage, the 1956 report concluded that "a suit to compel [black] admission might conceivably succeed on the theory that the Administrators of the Tulane Educational Fund is a private corporation carrying on the educational work of the Tulane University of Louisiana, a public institution, as the representative of the State or under a contract with the State, and is therefore subject to the constitutional restraints imposed upon the State itself."[27]

Thus by 1956 the Board had accurately anticipated the basic thrust of the case Nelson would present in 1961. What the Administrators could not have foreseen was the temperament of U.S. District Judge J. Skelly Wright, the jurist who presided over the initial phase of the Tulane litigation. Wright, a native New Orleanian appointed to the federal bench by President Truman, became the first district judge on the Fifth Circuit to hand down a school integration decree in the wake of the Supreme Court's 1954 ruling. On February 15, 1956, only three weeks before the Law Committee meeting that produced the memorandum quoted above, Wright invoked the *Brown* decision in requiring the Orleans Parish School Board to begin desegregation with "all deliberate speed." Over the next three years Wright would order the admission of black undergraduates to LSU, prohibit segregation on New Orleans's busses and in the city's major public park, and help overturn the state legislature's ban on interracial sports events. It was not, however, until the New Orleans school crisis of 1960 that Wright achieved heroic stature among liberals by crushing the combined efforts of the governor and state legislature to defy federal authority and

27. Dyer, *Tulane*, 42–4, 87, 120–3; McCloskey Memorandum, 19 (first quotation), 23 (second quotation).

prevent black students from entering New Orleans's schools. Judge Wright's unswerving commitment to civil rights went hand in hand with a penchant for bold judicial activism. Convinced that justice required more than the mechanical application of legal precedent, Wright sought to "press against the law in all directions" in order to expedite the process of achieving a desired outcome. Within reasonable limits Wright even thought it appropriate "to come out with a fair and just result and then look for a law to support it."[28]

Wright's judicial philosophy did not create a receptive environment in which to adjudicate the tangle of legal questions Tulane sought to resolve in 1961. Sensing that Wright would be sympathetic to the plaintiffs and impatient with Tulane, Nelson submitted a detailed evidentiary analysis and on January 20, 1962, moved for a "summary judgment," the legal term for a decision rendered by a judge in a situation where the basic facts are not in dispute. Some two months later, over Tulane's strenuous objection, Wright granted Nelson's motion and delivered an opinion in the case without proceeding to a full trial. Applying the case law relevant to the "state action" doctrine, Wright held that Tulane was indeed subject to the dictates of the Fourteenth Amendment. After declaring the segregation component of Act 43 unconstitutional and ruling that racial stipulations in the Tulane and Newcomb donations were judicially unenforceable, he granted the plaintiffs the relief originally sought, namely an injunction and restraining order forbidding Tulane officials from discriminating in admissions on the basis of race. In what was essentially an obiter dictum, Wright went on to question "whether any school or college can ever be so private as to escape the reach of the Fourteenth Amendment."[29]

Where Tulane was concerned the judge found little ground for uncertainty. Dismissing as "patent nonsense" the university's claim that an entirely private institution had been created by the constitutional amendment of 1888, Wright drew upon Nelson's research to quote liberally from the 1906 report of Tulane Board president and former state Supreme Court justice Charles E. Fenner, who had stated categorically

28. Rogers, *Righteous Lives*, 46–7; Fairclough, *Race and Democracy*, chap. 9; Jack Bass, *Unlikely Heroes: The Dramatic Story of the Southern Judges who Translated the Supreme Court's Brown Decision into a Revolution for Equality* (New York: Simon and Schuster, 1981), 115 (first quotation), 116 (second quotation). The quotations are from a 1979 interview.

29. *Guillory v Administrators of Tulane University*, 203 F. Sup. 858 (1962).

that "the Tulane University of Louisiana is nothing more nor less than the University of Louisiana established by the state in 1847, continued under a slight change of name and under control of Administrators . . . deriving their authority directly from the state." The absence of subsequent laws or court decisions ending the university's connection with the state led Wright to make an equally categorical assertion. "The complete history of Tulane University indicates that it is now, as it always was, a public institution," he concluded.[30]

Although a ruling that made Tulane subject to the Fourteenth Amendment was something which the Board's Law Committee had anticipated, the sweeping language of Wright's opinion shocked the Administrators and stiffened their resolve to continue the legal battle. If allowed to stand, Wright's ruling would open the door for direct legislative interference in the university's affairs, leaving Tulane vulnerable to the same investigating committees which were threatening academic freedom at LSU and other state schools. The ruling also raised the prospect that courts might extend the full range of Constitutional protections for civil liberties and individual rights to the Tulane campus, thereby limiting administrative options in cases of student discipline at a time when protest activity was beginning to gather momentum. These were important considerations, but for Joseph Jones and his colleagues on the Board the most serious objection to Wright's decision was its failure to settle the fiscal issues that had troubled the Administrators since the mid-1950s. In declaring the "white only" clauses of the Tulane and Newcomb gifts judicially unenforceable, Wright had specified only that such racial stipulations could not affect admissions policy. The Board's concern over protecting the endowment was relegated to a footnote in which the Loyola-trained jurist tossed the legal problem back into Tulane's lap. "Whether non-compliance with the . . . [racial restrictions] would support an action for recission of the donations is a state law question which this court need not decide," Wright observed blandly. Both the content and the generally acerbic tone of Wright's opinion angered the Administrators. Having ignored Tulane's economic concerns while ordering (rather than permitting) the university to accept black students, Wright proceeded to rub salt into the wound by implying that money rather than principle had caused the Administrators to accept integration. "The bitter fruit of the

30. Ibid., 203 F. Sup. 862 (first quotation), 863 (all subsequent quotations) (1962).

Board's segregation policy of the past should not be visited on the young men and women of the future," Wright declared in the final sentence of his ruling. Placing candor ahead of literary elegance, attorney Wood Brown III, Little's co-counsel in the case, would later declare that Judge Wright "stuck integration in Tulane's ear."[31]

II

On April 5, 1962, the Tulane Board met and unanimously authorized a press release over Joseph Jones's signature announcing that Pat Little would appeal Wright's decision to the Fifth Circuit Court of Appeals. "We believe that the district Court's summary decision, denying as it did the University an opportunity to have a trial of the case on its merits is based on incorrect assumptions of fact and misapplications of law, and we will seek a reversal of this ruling," Jones stated. Within two weeks Tulane's legal strategy changed slightly when Judge Wright accepted an appointment to the Second Circuit Court in Washington, D.C., and was replaced in New Orleans by the far more conservative Frank Burton Ellis. Instead of appealing to the Fifth Circuit, where support for Wright's ruling would undoubtedly have been strong, Tulane secured a stay of Wright's injunction and on April 19 asked Judge Ellis to vacate Wright's summary judgment and order a new trial. A month later Ellis granted the Tulane motion. After an unsuccessful appeal by Nelson, preparations began for the long-awaited "trial on the merits," scheduled to begin in August 1962.[32]

Although Tulane's actions were fully consistent with the Board's publicly announced determination not to settle for "anything less than a final court decision to determine the University's position," the Board's refusal to accept Wright's ruling cheered hard-line segregationists and did little to enhance the university's national image. Following events closely from Georgia, ex-President Harris, in private correspondence, gave vent to years of pent-up frustration by praising Skelly Wright and excoriating the Administrators for their seeming "lack of sympathy or understanding of the nature of a great university

---

31. Ibid., 203 F. Sup. 857 n. 6 (first quotation), 864 (second quotation) (1962); Cunningham, "Desegregation of Tulane," 69 (third quotation).

32. BOA Minutes, 5 April 1962.

and its raison d'être." By contesting Wright's ruling, the Administrators had assumed a public "posture of 'bitter enders,'" an outcome Harris found "almost tragic." In Louisville, Kentucky, Mark Ethridge, a prominent liberal newspaper editor and the only southern member of the Ford Foundation Board, expressed a sense of shock and betrayal after learning of the Board's "apparent turnabout" on the desegregation suit. In a confidential letter to Harris in mid-April, Ethridge provided a rare glimpse into the Ford Foundation's private deliberations over the Tulane case. "We at the Ford board were told that the suit was to protect the trustees, that the outcome was foregone[,] and that the board would not vigorously appeal," Ethridge stated. "We voted Tulane . . . $750,000 in spite of the feeling of almost all the members of the board that we were not willing to vote money to private institutions which, if not legally bound by the Supreme Court decision, were at least morally so. I must say that in my own case had I known that Tulane was doing more than to protect itself from Paul Tulane's will, I would have voted differently." To many outside observers, the Board's decision to seek a new trial in 1962 seemed inconsistent with the previously announced policy of admitting black students as soon as legally possible. In the short run, at least, protracting the court battle over desegregation damaged the Board's credibility with liberals, who began to fear that Tulane was simply resorting to the type of legal delaying tactics which had been the hallmark of segregationist resistance since 1954.[33]

Not all critics of the university's racial policies were outsiders. During the months preceding Wright's decision, Tulane faced growing pressure from both students and faculty who felt the time was ripe for the university to make a clean break with its racist past. This sentiment manifested itself most dramatically in a series of carefully planned challenges to the campus color line, carried out by interracial student groups between January and April 1962 and again during October of the same year. Known collectively as the "cafeteria sit-ins," the activities reflected the rapid growth of the New Orleans chapter of the Congress of Racial Equality (CORE), which had attracted a small but steadfast following among Tulane students. Although occasional interracial activities involving Tulane students and faculty had taken place

33. Ibid. (first quotation); Rufus C. Harris to Mark Etheridge [*sic*], 11 April 1962, box 10, RCH Papers (second–fourth quotations); Ethridge to Harris, 16 April 1962, box 10, RCH Papers (fifth–sixth quotations).

off campus during the 1950s, the origins of white student participation in the nonviolent direct action phase of the local civil rights struggle can be traced to the year 1960, when the lunch counter sit-ins conducted by black college students in Greensboro, North Carolina, inspired similar acts of civil disobedience in cities across the South. In March, black students at Southern University in Baton Rouge brought the sit-in movement to Louisiana, and in April the newly formed Consumers League of Greater New Orleans began picketing and boycotting a number of white-owned businesses on Dryades Street, where blacks shopped in large numbers but were denied employment.[34]

Among those involved in the Dryades Street demonstrations were two Tulane students, Hugh Murray, an A&S senior from New Orleans about to begin graduate study in history, and Sydney Langston "Lanny" Goldfinch Jr., a graduate student in philosophy. During the summer of 1960 they joined a number of black students—including Rudolph J. Lombard, Oretha M. Castle and several other veterans of the Dryades Street boycott—to found the New Orleans chapter of CORE. Lombard became the local CORE chairman, with Murray serving as vice chair of the fledgling organization, which contained only twenty-one active and ten associate members at the time it was chartered. By late August CORE had finalized plans for a sit-in campaign aimed at the McCrory and F. W. Woolworth stores on Canal Street in New Orleans. Initial statements of the university's policy toward students who planned to take part in the demonstrations had a decidedly conservative tone. Prospective demonstrators were cautioned not to expect help from the Dean of Students in the event of arrest, and were further advised that their continued enrollment in the Graduate School would depend in part upon the nature of any criminal charges pending against them at the time of registration. In case these hints proved too subtle, "[i]t was strongly suggested to them [the inquiring students] that, in view of the public school crisis, their wisdom in pushing another racial matter at such a time was doubtful and they were advised and counseled against doing so."[35]

Notwithstanding such admonitions, Tulane students played an ac-

34. William H. Chafe, *Civilities and Civil Rights: Greensboro, North Carolina, and the Black Struggle for Freedom* (New York: Oxford University Press, 1981); Aldon D. Morris, *The Origins of the Civil Rights Movement: Black Communities Organizing for Change* (New York: Free Press, 1984), 188–214; Fairclough, *Race and Democracy*, 267–72.

35. Fairclough, *Race and Democracy*, 272; Hugh T. Murray Jr., "The Struggle for Civil Rights in New Orleans in 1960: Reflections and Recollections," *Journal of Ethnic Studies* 6

tive role in the sit-ins which followed. On September 9 two Tulanians, Hugh Murray and William W. Harrell, a graduate student in sociology who had succeeded Murray as CORE vice chair, participated in a sit-in at the Woolworth's store at the corner of Canal and Rampart streets. Both were arrested, charged with criminal mischief, and released on $250 bail. During the same period Sydney Goldfinch, the son of a Tennessee Baptist missionary to Paraguay, flaunted segregationist custom by attending one of St. Charles Avenue's affluent white churches with a black companion. In a gesture that anticipated the cafeteria sit-ins of 1962, he also brought a black colleague to the snack bar in Tulane's University Center and objected to the presence of signs indicating that the facilities were for the exclusive use of Tulane students and faculty. On September 13 Deans Lumiansky and Stibbs met with Murray, Harrell, Goldfinch, and two other graduate students in an effort to dissuade them from further participation in civil rights demonstrations. Goldfinch, in particular, was warned that "if he aggressively attempts to introduce Negroes into the University Center he may jeopardize his status as a student."[36]

The warning had little effect. Four days later, on September 17, 1960, Goldfinch was arrested along with three black CORE members during a lunch counter sit-in at the McCrory's store at 1004 Canal Street, a location in downtown New Orleans several miles from Tulane. The arrest triggered protest meetings which did much to publicize CORE in the black community, while also focusing considerable segregationist animosity on Tulane and Goldfinch, who alone among the four defendants faced charges of "criminal anarchy"—rather than criminal mischief—and a bail figure set ten times higher than that of the black defendants. In the wake of his arrest Goldfinch was evicted from his apartment and forced to apply for a dormitory room after

(spring 1978): 25–41, esp. 25–7; New Orleans Congress of Racial Equality, Application for Affiliation, 23 September 1960, series 5, folder 44, Congress of Racial Equality Papers, microfilm collection, Amistad Research Center, Tulane University (hereafter cited as CORE Papers); Integration Problems, statement prepared for 12 October 1960 BOA meeting, box 102, HEL Papers (quotation).

36. Hugh Murray, "Righteous Lies vs. Tulane Truths," typescript in author's possession, 3; New Orleans States-Item, 9 September 1960, clipping in series 5, folder 44, CORE Papers; New Orleans Times-Picayune, 19 September 1960, clipping in series 5, folder 44, CORE Papers; University Senate Committee on Student Affairs, Subcommittee on Student Conduct, Minutes, 4 October 1960, box 102, HEL Papers, 3; Integration Problems, prepared for 12 October 1960 BOA meeting (quotation); John H. Stibbs to Herbert Longenecker, 13 September 1960, box 102, HEL Papers.

being refused accommodations by several private landlords. The involvement of Goldfinch and other Tulane students in the 1960 sit-ins forced the university to confront, if only in a reluctant and preliminary fashion, what was destined to become one of the paramount questions of the late 1960s: How should academic institutions respond when faculty members or students defied civil law or university regulations in the pursuit of what they regarded as higher moral objectives?[37]

In the short term, Tulane's public response to the sit-in phenomenon was to disclaim responsibility for the off-campus actions of adult students. Thus, even while exacting a promise from Sydney Goldfinch not to "bring his problem into the dormitory," the university tacitly acquiesced in student involvement with CORE by abandoning the longstanding policy of suspending any student accused of a crime pending completion of his trial. In September 1960, Hugh Murray and William Harrell became the first beneficiaries of the new policy when both were advised that they would not face suspension unless arrested again. Many factors—including faculty opinion, doubts about the constitutionality of state laws under which demonstrators were arrested, and the example of the crisis precipitated at Vanderbilt the previous spring by the expulsion of a leading sit-in protagonist who was also the school's first black divinity school student—contributed to Tulane's moderate stance, which was adopted only after lengthy discussions between Joseph Jones, Dean Lumiansky, and President Longenecker. Viewed from the perspective of Gibson Hall, the low-key approach was a tactic to discourage campus activism. In October, for example, Longenecker consulted closely with Vanderbilt officials on procedural matters growing out of the Nashville sit-in experience, and resolved to proceed "slowly and most deliberately" when dealing with student demonstrators in New Orleans. The meaning of the phrase became apparent later the same month, when Longenecker advised the Board of his concern over the criminal anarchy prosecution initiated against Goldfinch. The president regretted the severity of the charge not because he sympathized with Goldfinch, but because "it makes it more

---

37. Fairclough, *Race and Democracy*, 275; *State of Louisiana v Sydney Langston Goldfinch Jr. et al.*, Appeal from the Criminal District Court for the Parish of Orleans, No. 168-520, John P. Nelson Papers, Amistad Research Center, Tulane University; Integration Problems, prepared for 12 October 1960 BOA meeting; University Senate Committee on Student Affairs, Subcommittee on Student Conduct, Minutes, 4 October 1960, p. 2.

difficult for the University to take action against him . . . without appearing to persecute him."[38]

Whatever Longenecker's intent may have been, the actual effect of pursuing a cautious policy was to embolden the small minority of students at Tulane who wished to join CORE or otherwise take action against segregation. In November and December 1960, when the violence surrounding public school integration brought CORE activities to a virtual standstill, a group of some ninety-five Tulane students affixed their names to a printed pamphlet entitled *Tulanians Dissent*, which took aim at the violence and irrationality of Louisiana's resistance to court-ordered desegregation. At least fourteen of the dissenting students would subsequently participate in the 1962 cafeteria sit-ins, and several were active CORE members in 1960–61. Other activities common to many of the pamphlet's signers included membership in Tulane's recently founded Liberals Club and involvement in a writing or editorial capacity with the *Reed*, a radical student paper published as an alternative to the *Hullabaloo* and grudgingly sanctioned by university authorities between 1961 and 1963. The small band of dissidents who sustained these overlapping endeavors comprised a nucleus of politically aware social critics with whom other students could interact and, in the process, begin to examine the received wisdom of their elders. The CORE group's willingness to speak and act in opposition to palpable injustice, and to challenge duly constituted authority in both academic and civil settings when necessary, represented something new in the moral universe of cold war America—and something quite unprecedented in the personal experience of most southern college students. Here was the beginning of a generational sea change of profound significance—an incipient cultural realignment destined to be more far reaching than any force which had swept across American campuses since the depths of the Great Depression.

38. University Senate Committee on Student Affairs, Subcommittee on Student Conduct, Minutes, 4 October 1960, p. 2 (first quotation); Hugh Murray, "Righteous Lies vs. Tulane Truths," 3; Harold N. Lee to Robert M. Lumiansky, letter conveying formal statement of University Senate Committee on Faculty Tenure, Freedoms, and Responsibilities on the subject of graduate student participation in sit-in demonstrations, 24 September 1960, box 102, HEL Papers; Paul Conkin, *Gone with the Ivy: A Biography of Vanderbilt University* (Knoxville: University of Tennessee Press, 1985), 547–72; R. R. Purdy to Herbert Longenecker, 30 September 1960, box 102, HEL Papers; Longenecker to Purdy, 4 October 1960 (second quotation), box 102, HEL Papers; Integration Problems, prepared for 12 October 1960 BOA meeting (third quotation).

It was, to be sure, only the beginning. Most Tulane students remained spectators to the civil rights drama of the early 1960s, and there was no sudden influx of Tulanians into CORE until the 1961–62 academic year. By ones and twos, however, a steady trickle of Tulane recruits entered CORE ranks during the autumn of 1960 and the winter of 1961, helping insure the fledgling chapter's survival. Those who joined did not do so on a lark. The white students took their commitment seriously enough to risk arrest and personal violence in order to press for lunch counter desegregation in downtown stores. In December 1960 five Tulane and Newcomb undergraduates—Steve Blank, Allen Nathanson, Steve Chanin, Robert Heller, and Margaret Leonard—were arrested along with four black CORE members for passing out leaflets urging blacks to continue the boycott of McCrory's and Woolworth's. Leonard, whose home was in Atlanta, had been questioned by police and released on October 23, 1960, following a sit-in at Woolworth's. During the summer of 1961 she would join other CORE volunteers in Jackson, Mississippi, where she was arrested and spent sixteen days in jail.[39] Constance Bradford, a nineteen-year-old Newcomb sophomore from Birmingham, took an active part in the renewed picketing of McCrory's and Woolworth's that began after negotiations broke down in March 1961. In mid-April, while picketing on Canal Street, Bradford had an opportunity to practice nonviolence when physically attacked by a "screaming, nearly hysterical" white woman. "[A]ll I had time to think about . . . was keeping on my feet and keeping my arms down. I had no time to strike back either in anger or in self-defense," the Alabama student reported. On March 17 Bradford was arrested while taking pictures of other CORE members who were picketing on Canal and Iberville streets.[40]

The New Orleans CORE chapter came of age during the spring and

39. *Tulanians Dissent* (n.p., n.d.), leaflet, box 99, HEL Papers; Fairclough, *Race and Democracy*, 276; Rogers, *Righteous Lives*, 130; *New Orleans States-Item*, 13 December 1960; *New Orleans Times-Picayune*, 14 December 1960, in Tulane clipping scrapbooks; "Introduction to a Sit-In," *Look* 25 (3 January 1961): 40a–40b. The *Look* account was adapted from the Statement of Margaret Burr Leonard, 15 October 1960, series 5, folder 44, CORE Papers. Also see "MARGARET BURR LEONARD," typed memorandum from Newcomb College Dean's Office, 22 June 1962, box 102, HEL Papers.

40. Connie Bradford, "Report of New Orleans Action," 16 April 1961, series 5, folder 44, CORE Papers, as quoted in Fairclough, *Race and Democracy*, 279 (quotation); confidential statement made by Constance Bradford to Dean Hubbard on 21 April 1961, box 102, HEL Papers; "CONSTANCE MALONE BRADFORD," typed memorandum from Newcomb College Dean's Office, 22 June 1962, box 102, HEL Papers.

summer of 1961, when the Crescent City served as the official destination for the nationally publicized Freedom Rides. In February 1961 two Tulane students had been among the racially mixed group of local CORE members who sought and received service at restaurants in New Orleans's Greyhound and Trailways bus stations. Throughout most of the South, however, bus and train terminals remained rigidly segregated despite a U.S. Supreme Court decision declaring such practices unconstitutional. The May Freedom Rides, initiated by the national CORE organization, were aimed at forcing compliance with the law. After bus burnings and mob attacks in Alabama forced the initial Freedom Riders to abandon their journey in Birmingham, a group of New Orleans CORE volunteers traveled to Montgomery, Alabama, to continue the trip. They and other participants in the interracial challenge to Jim Crow bus terminals eventually reached Jackson, Mississippi, only to face arrest and subsequent confinement in the notoriously brutal Parchman Penitentiary. At least two Tulane students, Robert Heller and Connie Bradford, were among the more than three hundred Freedom Ride supporters eventually arrested in Jackson. By the early weeks of summer, New Orleans had become a staging area for incoming volunteers who had resolved to fill Mississippi's jails rather than abandon the crusade against interstate bus segregation. The local CORE chapter provided food, shelter, and cursory training for such individuals, as well as aid and comfort for those returning from the struggle. At the local as well as the national level, these activities gave CORE the stature and visibility it had previously lacked. Because two-thirds of the initial Freedom Riders and many of the subsequent volunteers were college students, the organization became a familiar name on campuses throughout America.[41]

During the fall semester of 1961, unprecedented numbers of white students from Tulane, LSU–New Orleans, and other local schools swelled CORE's ranks. At its peak the local chapter contained over three hundred members, at least half of whom were white. The influx of well-educated white outsiders—most of them relative neophytes in the southern struggle—destabilized the close-knit organization and

41. *Louisiana Weekly*, 25 February 1961, p. 1; Rogers, *Righteous Lives*, 128–30; Fairclough, *Race and Democracy*, 278; "Riders Receive Cool Reception," unidentified newspaper clipping, box 102, HEL Papers; Floyd H. Mann to Herbert Longenecker, 13 June 1961, box 102, HEL Papers; August Meier and Elliott Rudwick, *CORE: A Study in the Civil Rights Movement, 1942–1968* (New York: Oxford University Press, 1973), 138–45.

created a growing rift along racial lines. Educational differences—together with sexual insecurities growing out of interracial dating—lay behind the trouble, which took the form of a leadership struggle between Oretha Castle, a strong-willed black woman, and William Edwin Clark II, a white Tulane undergraduate student from Humboldt, Tennessee, who aspired to the CORE chairmanship. On February 1, 1962, events came to a head when Castle engineered a preemptive coup to prevent Clark from winning the top post. By skillfully playing upon deep historical resentments over white sexual exploitation of black women, Castle persuaded an all-black membership committee to suspend fifteen individuals deemed responsible for recent criticism in the black press of CORE's interracial social activities. A few black women were singled out, but most of those excluded were white males. All apparently were supporters of Edwin Clark, who now lacked the votes to win an election. National CORE officials later lifted the suspensions, but efforts to repair the breach proved fruitless and the entire Clark faction eventually withdrew, leaving Castle in charge of an all-black chapter.[42]

Up to the time of the white suspensions, Tulane's CORE members had been actively engaged in the desegregation battle with New Orleans's downtown merchants. As late as January 26, 1962, six Tulane students took part in a Canal Street sit-in at McCrory's, where they were doused with Tabasco sauce and squirted in the face with mustard before being arrested. Tulane's own cafeteria was, of course, still closed to blacks, but with the exception of the Goldfinch episode in 1960, there had been no demonstrations aimed at the university itself. On the night of January 23, 1962, that changed. Four black students from CORE arrived at the coffee shop in the University Center, accompanied by Edwin Clark and several other white students from Tulane and LSU–New Orleans. Employing a technique used in the downtown lunch counter sit-ins, the white students purchased food for the blacks and also served them coffee at racially mixed tables. A total of five such episodes occurred over the next two weeks, temporarily ending on February 7 in the immediate aftermath of the racial split in the local CORE chapter. In April, however, the sit-ins began again with renewed vigor and intensity. During the three-month period from

42. Rogers, *Righteous Lives*, 130–1; Fairclough, *Race and Democracy*, 295–6; Hugh Murray, "Righteous Lies vs. Tulane Truths," 3.

late January through late April, at least sixteen interracial cafeteria visits took place, involving some forty-four Tulane participants and a somewhat smaller number of black companions. Racially mixed groups also appeared at plays presented by theater department, as well as at other campus social events. Edwin Clark was present at virtually all the cafeteria sit-ins, frequently in company with John D. Bass, a graduate student in German and fellow CORE member. Other Tulane students typically limited their participation to one or two episodes in order to avoid disciplinary action by the university.[43]

Tulane officials met nonviolent direct action with their own brand of passive resistance. Campus police, under standing orders not to interfere unless violence seemed imminent, were present at all sit-ins, observing events from a distance. Cafeteria supervisors sometimes challenged the mixed groups by citing university regulations and explaining that "we are not allowed to permit negroes to use the cafeteria," but all other food service personnel had instructions not to interfere with sit-in participants and to serve black students when necessary. For the most part, the sit-ins passed off uneventfully with the exception of a tense encounter on February 7, when some two hundred students directed "a series of loud catcalls and boos" at the demonstrators, while other students approached one of the racially mixed tables in order to denounce John Bass as a "Nigger Lover." Throughout the spring demonstrations university officials seemed primarily interested in preventing violence and avoiding any incident or bureaucratic misstep which might weaken Tulane's legal position in the ongoing litigation over black admissions. The resulting policy, while nonconfrontational, was anything but sympathetic toward the young activists. Neither President Longenecker nor Dean of Students John Stibbs (who in 1957 had helped formulate plans to cope with student strikes in Pakistan) regarded civil disobedience as a legitimate form of political expression. In 1960 Stibbs had pressed unsuccessfully for the suspension of Sydney Goldfinch, and in the summer of 1961 parents of incoming freshmen received a letter from the Dean of Students warning

---

43. Joseph Willingham, "On the New Orleans Civil Rights Front," *Reed*, vol. 2, no. 5; Tulane Police Reports, 23, 28, and 30 January, 5 and 7 February, 2, 3, 5, 9 (two incidents), 10, 11, 12, 17, 24 April 1962, box 102, HEL Papers; Donald L. Brian to Herbert Longenecker, 13 May 1962, box 102, HEL Papers; Unsigned dittoed statement by students supporting Edwin Clark, 17 April 1962, accompanying a letter from William S. Woods to Herbert Longenecker, 18 April 1962, box 87, HEL Papers.

that "any participation in a group disturbance may result in disciplinary action and possible dismissal from the University."[44]
Stibbs's prediction moved a step closer to reality in January 1962.
Within hours of the first cafeteria sit-in, Clark and other participants
were called before the University Senate Subcommittee on Student
Conduct and warned to desist in their activities. Subsequent meetings
and additional warnings followed, culminating on April 9 with Clark's
suspension from the university. This was the first penalty Tulane had
imposed on any of the sit-in participants, and it provided a grievance
that protesters could use to publicize their cause among previously uninvolved students, who were now urged to support a week of additional
sit-ins in order "to confront the University administration with the
problem of conscience and principle it has artificially created by its
hypocritical rule, forcing students to connive at a policy—racial segregation—which the administration itself is ashamed to own up to publicly." Although Clark's suspension became a rallying point for student
activists, the end of the school year brought a temporary halt to protest activity.[45]

Before the spring semester drew to a close, however, it became clear
that the sit-in demonstrators were not alone in believing that Tulane
faced a crisis of conscience over campus segregation. Enough support
for Clark and other protesting students existed among faculty members in the College of Arts and Sciences to warrant a special faculty
meeting on May 11, 1962, at which the problem of continued segregation in the University Center was the principal order of business. At
the beginning of the meeting Professor Kenneth N. Vines, a political
scientist who had conducted important studies of black voter registration in Louisiana, offered a series of resolutions declaring it "unwise as
well as morally wrong" to suspend students for bringing black guests to
the University Center. While some faculty members supported Dean

44. Jesse B. Morgan, Memorandum to Dr. Scheps, 29 January 1962, box 102, HEL Papers;
Jesse B. Morgan, Memorandum to President Longenecker, 19 April 1962, box 102, HEL Papers;
Tulane Police Reports, 7 February 1962, box 102, HEL Papers (first–second quotations);
University Senate Committee on Student Affairs, Subcommittee on Student Conduct, Minutes, 4
October 1960, pp. 2–3; John H. Stibbs, "Twenty-Five Years of Student Life at Tulane University [1949–75]," unpublished typescript, John H. Stibbs Collection, Tulane University, 8;
John H. Stibbs to "Dear Parent," 10 July 1961 (third quotation), box 102, HEL Papers.
45. Undated draft of Tulane press release concerning the suspension of Edwin Clark, April
1962, box 99, HEL Papers. Unsigned dittoed statement by students supporting Edwin Clark, 17
April 1962 (quotation).

Stibbs's handling of the sit-ins, a slightly larger number were troubled by the university's inconsistency in espousing the principle of integration while continuing to practice segregation. As one exasperated professor observed, "It is the function of a University . . . to lead; and in this matter we have not led much." Amended versions of the Vines resolutions were eventually approved, along with an additional motion by English professor Richard P. Adams reaffirming the faculty's desire to accept black students "regardless of the outcome of the pending admissions suit."[46]

Because Edwin Clark was registered in the College of Arts and Sciences, that faculty's resolutions had a special relevance to his case. Clark's most vocal supporter, however, proved to be none other than the venerable Law School activist Mitchell Franklin, Tulane's principal link with the Old Left radicalism of the 1930s and a target of ongoing attacks from right-wing groups in and around New Orleans. On May 16, five days after the A&S resolutions were adopted, Franklin presented the Law School faculty with a set of scorching pronouncements deploring Clark's suspension and condemning segregation, "racist and authoritarian ideas," and "concepts of white social supremacy and anti-Negro exclusiveness" as threats to Tulane's vital interests in the realm of international legal education. Franklin's arguments, which were embellished with Hegelian references to the "world-historical" character of the Romanist legal tradition, conveyed a cosmopolitan vision that had all but vanished from conventional academic discourse. Although Franklin's colleagues killed the manifesto by refusing to second the motion for its adoption, the resolution nonetheless found its way to President Longenecker as an attachment to the official minutes. In the end, a combination of faculty support and impending legal action against the Board of Administrators determined Clark's fate. After two unsuccessful attempts to gain reinstatement to the university, Clark petitioned the Federal District Court for a temporary restraining order against the Tulane Board on the grounds that racial discrimination was illegal in a building such as the

46. Arts and Sciences Faculty Minutes, special meeting, 11 May 1962, box 87, HEL Papers. Although the quoted phrase in Adams's motion was deleted through amendment at the time of adoption, this and other passages deleted from the original Vines resolutions were restored, in brackets, to the resolutions actually presented to the Board of Administrators on 13 June 1962. For insight into Vines's views on civil rights, see John H. Fenton and Kenneth N. Vines, "Negro Registration in Louisiana," *American Political Science Review* 51 (September 1957): 714–23.

University Center, which had been financed in part by federal funds. By early June the university had relented. Clark was allowed to enroll for summer school after agreeing not to undertake further sit-in activity.[47]

III

At the time Clark's lawsuit was being settled, the Board's attention was focused on the Guillory and Elloie case, which was slowly approaching an actual trial before Judge Frank B. Ellis. Neither a reformer nor a judicial activist, Ellis was best known as a former member of the Democratic National Committee who had helped arrange financing for construction of the twenty-four-mile causeway across Lake Pontchartrain. He approached civil rights litigation with a strong concern for local white opinion and a determination to avoid drastic actions that would destabilize established educational institutions. Ellis's early years on the bench were marked by his evident desire to slow down and scale back Skelly Wright's ambitious agenda for the integration of New Orleans public schools, and he approached the Tulane case in a similar spirit of judicial retrenchment. By May 16 he had vacated Wright's summary judgment and granted the university's motion for a new trial. In setting aside the earlier decision, Ellis accepted Tulane's contention that Wright had erred in failing to recognize that significant questions of fact remained open to dispute. The most important of these factual issues, the actual degree of state involvement in Tulane's operation, Ellis declared "ripe for determination after a trial on the merits." Nelson appealed Ellis's rulings to the Fifth Circuit Court of

47. Jackson Ricau and Joseph E. Viguerie to Herbert Longenecker, 25 October 1960, box 102, HEL Papers; C. H. Lyons to Herbert Longenecker, 14 March 1961 and accompanying documents, including excerpts from "6,000 Educators," vol. 1, by Circuit Riders Inc., and undated press clipping of letter of Jack N. Rogers to editor of *Shreveport Times* [January 1961], box 7, HEL Papers; Jacqueline Nesbitt to Joseph Jones, 7 August 1961, box 7, HEL Papers; Resolution Introduced by Professor Mitchell Franklin at a Faculty Meeting of the Tulane School of Law on 16 May 1962, attachment to Law School Faculty Minutes, box 87, HEL Papers (all quotations); *William Edwin Clark, II, a minor by his next friend Edwin B. Clark v Board of Administrators, Tulane University [sic] Educational Fund*, Petition for Temporary Restraining Order, Preliminary Injunction, and Permanent Injunction, Civil Action 12193, Federal District Court, Eastern District of Louisiana; Bruce C. Waltzer to Herbert Longenecker, 16 April 1962, box 87, HEL Papers; Edmund McIlhenny to Waltzer, 8 June 1962, box 100, HEL Papers; BOA Minutes, 13 June 1962.

Appeals where he argued, in essence, that Tulane sought to dispute Wright's judicial conclusions rather than factual issues as such, and should therefore have appealed Wright's decision instead of seeking a new trial. On July 19 the three-judge appeals panel rejected Nelson's position and remanded the case to Ellis for a full and expeditious trial.[48]

On August 3, 6, 7, and 20, 1962, the long-awaited trial took place, with Board members Joseph McCloskey, Darwin Fenner, and other members of Tulane's "official family" conspicuously in attendance. Most of the issues and arguments presented at the August trial differed little from the positions previously set forth in Judge Wright's court. The most important new element in Tulane's case had appeared on May 24 in proceedings before Judge Ellis, when university attorneys added the eight living heirs of Paul Tulane and Josephine Louise Newcomb as third-party defendants to the suit, along with attorney and alumnus Harry P. Gamble Jr. as a representative of all other donors who regarded their gifts as implicitly bound by the racial restrictions of the original endowment. (Gamble, it will be recalled, had provided legal findings which helped stall President Harris's desegregation initiative in the mid-1950s.) At the trial itself the Tulane heirs, through their attorney, notified the court that they had no objection to the admission of black students. Harry Gamble deferred to Pat Little and Tulane on the matter. By this point, however, the contest before Judge Ellis had less to do with black admissions per se than with Tulane's desire to recover its legal standing as a private school. In pursuit of this aim, the university abandoned its earlier contention that state law required the exclusion of blacks—a position which now seemed to weaken the school's claim to private status.[49]

Throughout the three days of testimony and cross examination Pat Little marshaled all available evidence to establish, first, that Tulane was not a corporate body or other legal entity but rather an "activity" carried on by a private corporation, the Administrators of the Tulane Educational Fund. Little's second—and equally important—legal ob-

48. Tulane *Hullabaloo*, 2 December 1962, p. 1; Donald E. DeVore and Joseph Logsdon, *Crescent City Schools: Public Education in New Orleans, 1841–1991* (Lafayette, La.: Center for Louisiana Studies, 1991), 258–63; Cunningham, "Desegregation of Tulane," 77 (quotation)–83.

49. Cunningham, "Desegregation of Tulane," 79; Memorandum on Testimony in the Case of *Guillory and Elloie v. Tulane*, box 100, HEL Papers; Joseph Jones to Leon Irwin Jr., 10 August 1962, box 100, HEL Papers.

jective was to prove that the State of Louisiana provided negligible financial support for Tulane and played no significant role in university governance. Both points were hotly disputed. While Little stressed the absence of state officials from virtually all Tulane Board meetings in the twentieth century, Nelson countered with recent correspondence between Professor Henry Mason and State Superintendent of Education Shelby Jackson in which the latter official stressed his status as an ex officio Tulane Board member when urging Mason and other faculty members to teach their students "more about the American way of life, teaching America first in all activities, [and] recognizing the sovereignty of the respective states."[50]

On the question of state contributions to university finances, the opposing lawyers sketched pictures that were studies in the meaning of artistic perspective. As he had done before Skelly Wright the previous year, Nelson stressed that Tulane received a state tax exemption worth some $200,000 plus $160,000 in income from state property (the Shell Building in New Orleans). These figures represented, respectively, 20 percent of Tulane's endowment income and 30 percent of its income-producing property. Little saw Tulane's fiscal profile in a very different light, emphasizing that more than half the value of state tax exemptions was offset by the cost of free legislative scholarships. The combined value of tax exemptions and income from the Shell Building, moreover, comprised only 2 percent of Tulane's 1961 operating budget. And whereas Louisiana State University had received more than $185 million in state appropriations during the previous decade, Tulane had benefitted only to the extent of $2 million. Similar disagreements surrounded the meaning of the reversion clause in Act 43 of 1884.[51]

In the end Little's arguments would prevail on all major points, but before Judge Ellis rendered a decision in the case another semester elapsed during which Tulane's racial policies remained in limbo. Many students and professors had hoped the integration issue would be resolved during the summer of 1962. When it was not, both supporters and opponents of desegregation grew increasingly restive. At a special meeting of the Arts and Sciences faculty on September 14, 1962, dis-

50. Shelby Jackson to Henry L. Mason, 26 February 1962, box 102, HEL Papers (submitted as plaintiff's exhibit AA on 9 March 1962).

51. Cunningham, "Desegregation of Tulane," 89–91; Memorandum on Testimony in the Case of *Guillory and Elloie v. Tulane.*

satisfaction at the slow pace of litigation was mingled with open skepticism over the Board's motives. Discussion centered around a set of resolutions offered by Professor Richard Adams expressing concern over "what appear to be delaying tactics used by counsel for the University" in the *Guillory* case. Adams also sought an advance indication of what policy the Board would adopt if the student body was "not desegregated as a result of pending litigation." In the debate which followed, Professor John Snell of the Department of History reported on a recent meeting at which attorney John Pat Little had presented a "complete chronology of the complicated litigation" to a joint gathering of the Administration Advisory Committee and the Faculty Advisory Committee to the President. Snell had found Little's explanations convincing. He urged his colleagues to amend the resolutions and omit the paragraph in which delaying tactics were mentioned. Political scientist Henry Mason, who had helped initiate the *Guillory* suit, "was not convinced . . . that certain Administrators were not interested in delay," but in the end Snell's arguments prevailed. The resolution actually sent to Longenecker and the Board avoided allegations of bad faith, but its message—that many members of the A&S faculty were unwilling for "moral, professional, and financial reasons" to stay at Tulane if segregation continued during the next academic year—was sufficiently blunt for the purpose intended.[52]

Some two weeks later the faculty of the School of Social Work discussed the Arts and Sciences resolution at considerable length, expressing "general support of the spirit and intent of the document, [but] disagreement on the tenor." As a result the Social Work faculty drafted its own statement, closely paraphrasing key passages in the A&S resolution, with appropriate references to concern over the "individual futures" of professors at a segregated school. Echoing a theme enunciated by the A&S faculty the previous spring, the Social Work statement voiced the "firm belief . . . that the function of a university is to lead in the area of human relations." Impatience with the Board's cautious approach extended to other faculty groups, including the Newcomb art faculty, which categorically "deplore[d] the failure of this University to exercise such leadership" as the segregation issue seemed to require. As had been true during the 1950s, faculty support

52. College of Arts and Sciences Faculty Minutes, special meeting, 14 September 1962, pp. 5 (first quotation), 6 (second–third quotations), box 87, HEL Papers; Resolution of the Faculty of the College of Arts and Sciences, in BOA Minutes, 8 October 1962 (fourth quotation).

for integration tended to be least conspicuous in the professional schools. The most unqualified endorsement of the Board's actions came from the School of Engineering, which would later be a bastion of campus conservatism during the turmoil of the late 1960s. On September 25, 1962, the Engineering faculty explicitly repudiated the Arts and Sciences request for advance information on future racial policy and assured the Board "that we are willing to wait for action [on black admissions], allowing whatever time is necessary for the final, complete, valid, and dignified resolution of the matter." Seemingly untroubled by feelings of moral urgency, the engineers pledged "total cooperation in whatever the outcome" of the integration suit.[53]

Although uptown faculty members were more likely to be critical than supportive of the long delay in resolving the *Guillory* case, segregationists within and outside the university took heart from the protracted legal maneuvering. Conservative alumni had been writing Longenecker's office for more than a year to urge continued defense of the educational color line, and in 1961 the well-financed Young Conservatives organization on campus had raised a hue and cry against Sydney Goldfinch that culminated with the hanging of several effigies in front of the History Building and at other conspicuous points. Although condemnations of civil rights demonstrators were often violent in tone, they did not result in actual clashes between conservative students and the racially mixed groups visiting the cafeteria during the spring semester. But when returning CORE veterans renewed the cafeteria sit-ins in October 1962, a decidedly more menacing atmosphere soon developed. The change was partly a reaction to the tragedy unfolding some three hundred miles to the north at the University of Mississippi, where the September 29 arrival of black student James Meredith had touched off a night of fatal rioting followed by federal military occupation of the campus.[54]

Tulane students followed events in Mississippi closely via a special

53. School of Social Work Faculty Minutes, 28 September 1962, box 87, HEL Papers (first quotation); Proposal of the Faculty of the School of Social Work, 1 October 1962, box 87, HEL Papers (second–third quotations); Caecilia W. Davis et al. to Herbert Longenecker, 5 November 1962, box 102, HEL Papers (fourth quotation); Statement of the Faculty of the School of Engineering, 25 September 1962, in BOA Minutes, 8 October 1962 (fifth–sixth quotations).

54. [Kent Courtney], "Open Letter to Tulane University," leaflet accompanying Richard W. Freeman letter to Joseph M. Jones, 16 January 1961, box 7, HEL Papers; Tulane *Hullabaloo*, 9 December 1960, p. 1; M. Stanton Evans, *Revolt on the Campus* (1961; reprint, Westport, Conn.: Greenwood Press, 1979), 32, 178.

bulletin board in the University Center. Events in Oxford undoubtedly stirred the emotions of Tulane's more conservative students, who comprised roughly one-third of the 481 respondents in an October 1 poll conducted by the *Hullabaloo* measuring initial reaction to the Ole Miss crisis. The survey revealed that some 60 percent of those questioned deemed the presence of soldiers to be morally justified, while nearly 67 percent believed Mississippi governor Ross Barnett was wrong to have defied the federal courts. But a substantial minority of Tulane students, nearly 17 percent, held the federal government responsible for the riots, while over 23 percent blamed the Mississippi debacle on "racial agitator groups," a category which included the Ku Klux Klan, the Citizens' Council, the NAACP, and, by implication, CORE. It was against this backdrop that the cafeteria demonstrations were renewed.[55]

The first fall sit-in, a Wednesday evening episode lasting from 9:20–10:10 P.M., took place uneventfully on October 3, when Ed Clark, Connie Bradford, Bill Harrell, Margaret Leonard, and Chet May joined two black CORE colleagues at the University Center cafeteria. Appropriate Tulane officials—including Professor Karlem Reiss, adviser to the Greek fraternities—were duly notified. Five days later, on Monday, October 8, a second episode involving most of the same white students began unfolding at 9:10 P.M. Initially all was quiet, but after thirty minutes a *Hullabaloo* photographer arrived and began taking pictures of the racially mixed group, which included CORE chairperson Oretha Castle. At that point the atmosphere changed, becoming "tense and electric" as three students carrying small burning crosses entered the building and began to parade through the cafeteria. That display inspired other students to approach the sit-in tables with clenched fists. When the sit-in participants began to leave, a larger group gathered in the hallway, shouting, "Nigger bastards! Nigger bastards! Who the hell is going to burn the chairs the Nigger bastards sat in?" Although no physical violence occurred, campus police experienced "considerable difficulty" clearing an exit path through the hostile crowd, which continued to hurl "shouted threats and insults" at the interracial group.[56]

In the aftermath of the ugly incident, Professor Henry Mason—who

55. Tulane *Hullabaloo*, 5 October 1962, p. 1.

56. Tulane Police Report, 3 and 8 October 1962, box 102, HEL Papers (quotation from 8 October).

headed the Tulane chapter of the American Association of University Professors—wrote President Longenecker to renew the AAUP's request, initially made the previous spring, that segregation be abandoned in the University Center. Although he personally opposed the sit-ins, Mason proposed voluntary desegregation of University Center dining facilities as the best safeguard against a possible crisis which might lead to mass student suspensions. The Administrators, of course, had no intention of lowering racial barriers until the court battle was concluded, and white protest activity was beginning to lose momentum with the split in New Orleans's CORE chapter. A subsequent poll of some 650 Tulanians revealed that while most students believed the university would be integrated, a diminishing majority of freshmen, sophomores, and juniors actually opposed the change, while 51 percent of the respondents either had no opinion or were undecided about whether the sit-ins were justified. In the aggregate, 42 percent opposed integration and 48 percent favored it, with solid majority support for black admissions confined to seniors (68 percent) and graduate students (90 percent). Divided sentiment among undergraduates, together with the example of Ole Miss and the October 8 cafeteria confrontation, proved sufficient to stifle organized protest during the remainder of the fall semester. Students and faculty alike waited anxiously for the court ruling which would determine Tulane's legal status as well as its racial policy.[57]

In his summation before Judge Ellis in August, Tulane's attorney John Little had stressed that the university's sole purpose in defending the suit was to resist "allegations" of being a public institution or a school subject to the Fourteenth Amendment by virtue of the "state action" doctrine. Tulane's objective was simply to be "recognized as a private institution" with the "freedom to determine our own salvation, to reach our own conclusions on the problems we have facing us, and not to have the coercive effect of the Court." Ellis's ruling, originally expected in October, was finally handed down on December 5, 1962. Its content must have surprised even the most optimistic Board members. Conceding all of Little's major points, Ellis held Tulane to be a "private activity" of the Administrators of the Tulane Educational Fund, which was in turn a "private eleemosonary [sic] corporation."

57. Henry Mason to Herbert Longenecker, 11 October 1962, box 99, HEL Papers; Tulane *Hullabaloo*, 26 October 1962, p. 1.

State involvement in the university's affairs was "not so significant that it may be fairly said that the actions of the Tulane Board are the actions of the State of Louisiana." Tulane was thus immune to the "privileges and proscriptions of the Fourteenth Amendment to the United States Constitution." On the matter of black admissions the Board had a free hand. The Tulane heirs had already waived their right to enforce racial restrictions, and Ellis ruled the racial limitations of Act 43 unconstitutional since "a state may not compel racial discrimination in private affairs. . . . Indubitably," Judge Ellis concluded, "the Tulane Board is free to act as it wishes since neither this nor any other court may exercise its power to enforce racial restrictions in private covenants."[58]

At an informal meeting of the Law Committee on December 7, 1962, the attorneys on Tulane's Board reviewed Ellis's findings and agreed "that the decision handed down was the most favorable that could be expected, and that to continue the defense of the suit in the Court of Appeals and the Supreme Court could not possibly improve our position, but to the contrary, the courts may rule that there is sufficient State involvement to bring us under the Fourteenth Amendment." Five days later, on December 12, a meeting of the full Board concurred in the Law Committee's recommendation and voted unanimously to implement the policy decision of April 12, 1961, by admitting Barbara Guillory and Pearlie Hardin Elloie for the upcoming spring semester. The Board also approved a press release in which Joseph Jones announced that Tulane would admit black students beginning in February 1963 and went on to affirm that the Board's 1961 desegregation decision was "correct and in the best interest of the University."[59]

What followed was part victory and part anticlimax. During the long period of litigation a considerable backlog of applications from black students had begun to accumulate, and when spring semester registration was held in late January Guillory and Elloie were joined by nine other black students, including two high school teachers and seven faculty members at Southern University in New Orleans and Dillard University. By virtue of their maturity, professional orientation, and concentration in graduate-level courses, Tulane's initial contin-

58. Tulane *Hullabaloo*, 26 October 1962, p. 1 (first–third quotations); *Guillory v Administrators of Tulane University*, 212 F. Sup. 687 (fourth–ninth quotations) (1962).
59. BOA Minutes, 12 December 1962.

gent of African American students seemed well equipped to negotiate the uncertainties of a newly desegregated campus. Timely intervention by Joseph Jones, Rosa Keller, and others prevented the sort of media coverage which in itself might have triggered a racial incident during or immediately after registration. As a precautionary measure Keller had given Guillory and Elloie keys to her home near Tulane's campus for use as a "safe haven" should the need arise. Registration, however, went smoothly, and after a week both women felt comfortable enough to return the keys and proceed with their studies in a normal fashion. During the summer session seven additional black students enrolled, followed by twenty-seven more in the fall of 1963 when both Newcomb and the College of Arts and Sciences joined the list of desegregated university divisions.[60]

Although Tulane was among the last of the South's private research universities to lower racial barriers (the only peer institutions still segregated in February 1963 were Rice and Emory), no one doubted that the admission of Guillory and Elloie represented a significant turning point in the school's history. Violence of the sort seen in the 1960 New Orleans school crisis had been averted, and university officials took considerable satisfaction in having defended Tulane's private status while protecting the endowment and opening the way for a new appeal to the Ford Foundation. It was perhaps the latter prospect in particular which moved President Longenecker to "want to shout a few war whoops" upon receiving Judge Ellis's order closing the Tulane case in May 1963, after the plaintiffs abandoned their plans to appeal the decision. The mood of relief and self-congratulation which prevailed among top-level university officials in the aftermath of the Guillory case was understandable, given the fiscal concerns which hovered over the litigation. But from the standpoint of those who envisioned a genuinely multiracial campus environment, the end of formal litigation raised new questions about how rapidly and thoroughly desegregation would take place.[61]

60. Summary: Applications for Admission Received from Negroes, 1956–61, box 102, HEL Papers; Tulane *Hullabaloo*, 1 February 1963, p. 1; BOA Minutes, 13 February 1963; Keller Autobiography, part 2, pp. 41–4 (quotation); Joseph E. Gordon to Herbert Longenecker, 27 February and 14 March 1963, box 102, HEL Papers; Negro Admissions, Tulane University, February 1963–February 1964, box 102, HEL Papers.

61. Herbert Longenecker to John Pat Little, 8 May 1963, box 102, HEL Papers.

A typical classroom scene during the early years of integration.

By February 1964 Tulane had accepted a total of fifty-seven black students, over half of whom attended the School of Social Work or enrolled as part-time students in University College. All the rest were graduate students except for Deidre Ann Dumas in Newcomb and Reynold T. Decoux in the College of Arts and Sciences. Many of these early students were considerably older and more outwardly conservative than the black undergraduates who would arrive in the years ahead. Products of a transitional era in southern history, the new Tulanians were anxious to take advantage of increased educational opportunities but were still constrained by habits of deference that had prevailed during segregation. There can be little doubt that for some members of the academic community, the demeanor of African Americans at Tulane in the early 1960s helped reinforce the assumption that black students would accept the university upon whatever terms it was offered, shrugging off the inconveniences that concessions to New Orleans's conservative racial climate might entail. Even those administrators who might have preferred to accelerate the pace of internal change were often powerless to act. In December 1962, for example, A&S dean William Peery, himself a consistent advocate of desegregation, bowed to gradualist logic in denying one of the entering black students a departmental assistantship, observing simply that "[w]e take it that the University is not yet ready to put a Negro in the classroom as a teacher." Provost Robert Lumiansky, who had been instrumental in desegregating the South Central Modern Language Association during the 1950s, concurred in Peery's decision.[62]

Perceptions of the changes taking place in 1963—including judgments about whether events were moving rapidly or slowly—varied according to the racial attitudes of particular observers and the vantage point from which they viewed the desegregation process. From the perspective of those charged with implementing the practical aspects of the change from a segregated to a desegregated campus, the future seemed hazardous. On January 2, 1963, some two weeks before the arrival of the university's first black students, a fascinatingly detailed memorandum prepared for Tulane vice president and comptroller Clarence Scheps summarized the consensus view of some fourteen campus administrators regarding "problems which may occur as the result of the admission . . . of two Negro women." The memo recorded opinions expressed at a meeting that included the dean of students, the director of libraries, the director of personnel, Newcomb's counselor to women, and the director of student affairs for the School of Social Work. Everyone present realized that the changes set in motion by desegregation would involve readjustments that were fundamental in nature. The list of questions generated by the prospect of dismantling the mundane elements of campus segregation filled six typed pages and read almost like a catalog of segregation's incongruities. Issues of color and social status, once neatly collapsed into a single set of black/white polarities, now seemed to be taking a new form.[63]

Many of the questions concerned policies for university-owned housing, classes, or social functions held in segregated facilities off campus, racial exclusion in social fraternities, service in the campus barber shop, and the removal of "Colored" restroom signs and other caste symbols. In all these areas, as well as on the subject of seating

62. Negro Admissions, Tulane University, February 1963–February 1964, box 102, HEL Papers; William Peery to Herbert Longenecker, 19 December 1962, box 102, HEL Papers (quotation).

63. [Jesse B. Morgan?], Memorandum to Dr. Scheps, Vice President and Comptroller, undated but apparently submitted on 3 or 4 January 1963, box 100, HEL Papers (hereafter cited as Morgan Memorandum; quotation).

arrangements for football games (where a "colored" section had been maintained) and basketball games (from which black spectators had been excluded), Scheps's advisory group sought direction. On some decisions, particularly those involving white employees, no guidance was necessary. Supervisors of white personnel had already been directed to explain the university's position on integration and to "indicate that we will not tolerate any acts on their part which could cause embarrassment to our Negro students." The assembled deans, managers, and directors anticipated "no difficulty with the Negro students themselves," but did expect problems from student activists who previously had been involved in campus sit-ins. Several of those at the meeting predicted a "concerted campaign to test every aspect of University life to determine whether we are in fact fully integrated." The most serious anxieties, however, involved Tulane's six hundred black employees, some of whom were "known CORE members" and the majority of whom Tulane officials believed—incorrectly—to be members of the NAACP. Once the new semester began black students would be dining routinely in the University Center cafeteria. "[S]hall we permit Negro employees to make similar use of these facilities?" the memorandum asked. "Do we continue to insist that Negro employees use separate restroom facilities, while Negro students use white facilities?" (The old terminology was already problematic.) It was the consensus of the group "that we could not insist that our Negro students use Negro facilities." Apparently the sit-ins had achieved something.[64]

Given the responsibilities placed upon the administrative group that Scheps assembled, their emphasis upon desegregation's problematic aspects is perhaps understandable. Still, it seems noteworthy that the group's memorandum failed to consider the possibility that many of the difficulties accompanying desegregation might also be viewed as opportunities to initiate positive change above and beyond that required to prevent violence and avert public confrontations. In the immediate aftermath of the *Guillory* decision, as congratulatory telegrams poured in from students, faculty, and other interested groups such as the New Orleans CORE chapter, the time was ripe for conciliatory gestures from the university administration indicating that critics had been heard and that greater wisdom might result from a continued air-

64. Morgan Memorandum, 1 (second–third quotations), 2 (fifth–seventh quotations), 5 (first and fourth quotations).

ing of legitimate differences of opinion. Such reciprocity, however, was slow in coming, due to the tendency among Board members and senior university administrators to compartmentalize racial issues, supporting black admissions without entirely abandoning the idea that professors and students who joined civil rights organizations were agitators rather than potential allies. No doubt most adopted this attitude in the hope that protest would end when the admissions question was settled, allowing the university to return to its normal academic routine. This posture, advanced to Board members quite persuasively by public relations director Horace Renegar at the peak of the 1962 sit-ins, had considerable appeal as a short-term strategy for crisis management. As an approach to charting the destiny of a newly desegregated southern university in the mid- and late 1960s, it was deeply if not fatally flawed.

Tulanians at all levels were slow to recognize that genuine integration—as opposed to the mere cessation of black exclusion—would be a reciprocal process involving adjustments on the part of the university to the expectations and perceptions of a group deeply alienated from the norms of a racist society. Among the most liberal elements of the faculty there was a clear appreciation that integration, beginning with a policy of equal access to all campus facilities and activities, would succeed only to the extent that it was accompanied by a deeper change of hearts and minds. The position was most eloquently stated in November 1962 by the Newcomb art faculty, which urged the university to "make it unequivocally clear" that once admitted, black students would be entitled to the "full enjoyment of all student privileges." The faculty deemed it equally essential that Tulane adopt policies "which will support the spirit as well as the letter of the law by encouraging Negro attendance and participation in University activities such as lectures, concerts, and conferences. It should be the University's role to assist those students, faculty, and staff whose vision is not clouded by habitual prejudice in demonstrating the reality of our presumed belief in the universal values of mind and spirit. The alternative appears to us to be moral decay and an inevitable decline in quality as well as reputation."[65]

These were brave words, spoken in the springtime of the nation's civil rights odyssey, with little anticipation of the separatist impulses and demands for group autonomy that would emerge at Tulane within

65. Caecilia W. Davis et al. to Herbert Longenecker, 5 November 1962.

the next few years. Occasionally, however, even in the generally harmonious atmosphere of 1962–63, the veil of racial deference parted sufficiently to permit a glimpse of what the future held in store. In the medical school, for example, two black students had applied for the 1962–63 freshman class and had received letters stating that their academic qualifications were acceptable but that admission was impossible until pending legal questions were resolved. In the wake of Judge Ellis's decision on December 5, 1962, each applicant asked to be considered for the 1962–63 entering class, only to be informed that the November closing date had passed and that no further applications could be accepted. When a subsequent meeting with the assistant dean produced no resolution to this catch-22 predicament, one of the students lost his composure and blurted out, "I don't believe Tulane University intends to admit any Negro students. . . . I don't trust a white man." Offended by the outburst, the assistant dean declared that Tulane was "fortunate in escaping . . . [the student's] admission." For a variety of reasons, including the difficulty of arranging for the presence of black interns in the still segregated teaching hospitals, five more years would elapse before the first black student entered the School of Medicine.[66]

Open expressions of racial resentment, although rare in the early years of integration, were harbingers of the strident exchanges which would accompany the rise of student militance and black power sentiment near the end of the decade. For that reason the dissonant aspects of the civil rights struggles of 1960–63 deserve at least as much attention as the initial success of integration. On the surface desegregation represented a liberal victory at Tulane, but the consensus it produced was destined to be short-lived. The arrival of black students on Tulane's campus marked the end of an initial phase in campus racial liberalism and set the stage for an approaching era of generational conflict that would see younger and more militant leaders displace older accommodationists among students in general. Although civil rights activists comprised only a small fraction of the Tulane community during the early 1960s, their outlook pointed unmistakably toward the future. CORE and its allies introduced into campus political life a new vocabulary that pulsated with impatient moral energy. In

66. Harold Cummins to Maxwell H. Lapham, 7 January 1963, box 102, HEL Papers.

1961, for example, Tulane's Young Democrats condemned segregation as "immoral, unjust, and an affront to human dignity."[67]

The early activists made social reform a matter of individual conscience as they struggled to translate broad ethical principles into direct action against injustices close at hand. For the first time in Tulane's history, the welfare of black maids, janitors, and food service workers began to attract serious attention from faculty and students. In 1961 the *Reed* published a lengthy investigation of wages and working conditions derived from confidential interviews with black employees.[68] Professor Richard Schechner of the theater department took a more dramatic approach, urging Tulane students to reflect critically upon their place in a segregated society. "Stand in line at the University Center and look into the eyes of those who are serving you," Schechner urged in September 1962. "Doesn't it make you feel a bit strange to realize that none of these people can yet enter Tulane or Newcomb and get the same education you're getting? How do you reconcile your courses in philosophy, political science, literature, [and] anthropology with the fact that your University is going through legal contortions in order to admit/not to admit (strike out whichever you please) qualified Negro students[?] And how do you feel when you realize that even after this integration battle is won . . . the resulting integration will only be 'token'—a little pepper in with all the salt?"[69]

The rejection of timidity and compromise, acceptance of personal responsibility, and willingness to affirm truth in the face of officially sanctioned injustice defined the essence of early civil rights activism on and off the university campus. Similar moral imperatives were destined to shape student behavior a half decade later. While much would change in the space of five years, it is scarcely an exaggeration to say that the student power and antiwar protests of 1967–69 began with the lunch counter and cafeteria sit-ins of 1960–63. Discontent with the caution and pragmatism of those in authority was evident throughout the integration struggle at Tulane. Sydney Goldfinch sounded the theme

67. Tulane *Hullabaloo*, 10 March 1961, p. 2.

68. "Negro Labor at Tulane," *Reed*, vol. 2, no. 2 [ca. April 1961]; Francis C. May Jr. and Charles Chandler, Graduate Students and Delegates for *The Reed*, to Herbert Longenecker, 26 April 1961, box 102, HEL Papers; [Jesse B. Morgan], Notes on an article in the *Reed* entitled "Negro Labor at Tulane," typescript accompanying Clarence Scheps memorandum to Herbert Longenecker, 7 November 1961, box 61, HEL Papers.

69. Tulane *Hullabaloo*, 21 September 1962, p. 2.

as early as 1960 in a lengthy letter written for the *Hullabaloo* but never published. "I am not satisfied with the attitude of a majority of our 'liberals' who are willing to 'accept' integration and will merely do nothing to stop it when it comes," Goldfinch declared. "Segregation is evil," he continued. "It not only denies the rights of the Negroes but it breeds prejudice[,] bigotry[,] and hate. Segregation is America's shame."[70]

By the time of the 1962 cafeteria sit-ins, student activists voiced criticisms of Tulane that were considerably more explicit than faculty resolutions urging greater efforts toward leadership in social change. Sociology graduate student Chet May acknowledged that most professors believed the administration to be sincere in its policy. "Perhaps it is," May conceded, adding that in addition to being sincere, the administration was "also fearful, overly cautious, and inept." Virtually all the sit-in participants believed that Tulane should have integrated voluntarily, resorting to litigation only if later sued. John Bass, who was a central figure of the sit-in movement, condemned Tulane for adopting "a policy of having no policy." Jean Morrison, a graduate student in German, linked administrative inaction directly to protest activity. So long as the administration avoided its responsibility, she believed, "it was the duty of every responsible citizen to express his disagreement with the 'system.'" Both the phraseology and the ideas were new to Tulane's campus in 1962 and their significance was at best dimly grasped by the university's senior administration. Within a few years the message of the sit-in era would command sustained attention from all those concerned with Tulane's future.[71]

70. S. Langston Goldfinch to the editor, Tulane *Hullabaloo*, 25 October 1960, typescript, box 102, HEL Papers.

71. Tulane *Hullabaloo*, 12 October 1962, p. 1 (all quotations).

5

CONSENSUS AND CONTINUITY
The Liberal University at High Tide

Although the end of segregation was a crucial turning point in Tulane's history, a broad continuity of purpose marked the university's academic mission during the first half of the 1960s. President Longenecker's 1961 inaugural address, delivered only three days after the Board of Administrators' announcement that Tulane would admit black students "if legally permissible," made no mention of the race issue and focused instead upon the themes of academic excellence established during the previous decade. Tulane, Longenecker emphasized, "must continue to strive for [recognition as] a center of learning which will rank with the nation's best." In practical terms, the pursuit of national prominence involved assembling a faculty "of the very highest qualities" and a student body with the necessary talent and motivation to respond to the stimulus of a demanding intellectual regimen. National stature also required that Tulane maintain a strong undergraduate liberal arts curriculum in conjunction with "expanded opportunity for research and advanced study in the graduate and professional fields." Aware that excellence could not be purchased at a discount, Longenecker stressed that "fiscal resources . . . substantially above those presently available" would be necessary if Tulane was to offer teaching and research opportunities of "a first-rate university, as measured by national standards."[1]

The need for new physical facilities—including a science and engineering center, a humanities center, and a social sciences center—also

1. *Tulanian* 34 (July 1961): 10.

Old student center, demolished 1964.

received mention in the 1961 inaugural speech. These grand plans would not be realized during Longenecker's administration, nor would efforts to construct a new theater building come to fruition. But those seeking visible signs of progress in the form of glass, steel, bricks, and mortar were undoubtedly heartened by the construction schedule of Longenecker's first half-decade. Between 1960 and 1965 four new buildings appeared on the uptown campus, including the Bruff Commons dining and postal facility and three dormitories—the seven-story Robert Sharp Hall, the eight-story Pierce Butler House, and the imposing J. Blanc Monroe residence hall, a twelve-floor glass and steel monolith which made up in capacity what it lacked in traditional elegance. Three of the four structures opened in 1963, as did the six-million-dollar Burthe-Cottam addition to the medical school's downtown Hutchinson Building. All told, the construction of 1960–65 represented an investment of over $11 million, which was financed through a combination of private capital, university funds, and federal loans. After a brief hiatus, building activity would resume later in the decade with construction of the Howard-Tilton Library in 1968, followed in 1971 by the long-awaited science center, Percival Stern

New student center, opened 1959.

Hall, named for the donor whose $3 million pledge covered nearly half the building's cost.[2]

Additional expansion during the 1960s occurred away from the uptown and medical school campuses. In 1962 Tulane received initial funding of nearly $2.5 million from the National Institutes of Health to construct the Delta Regional Primate Research Center on a five-hundred-acre tract of land near Covington, Louisiana, approximately forty miles north of New Orleans. The Delta Primate Center, consisting of five laboratory buildings plus outdoor animal cages, opened in 1964 with an annual NIH operating budget of more than $1 million and a broad research agenda. Directed initially by Dr. Arthur J. Riopelle, who had previously headed the Yerkes Laboratory of Primate Biology in Florida, the center was administered by Tulane through the School of Medicine but was open to researchers from Louisiana State University and other schools. As one of seven such facilities funded entirely by the federal government, it represented the university's entry into the select circle of institutions hosting what were often described as freestanding federal research centers.[3]

2. For a summary of building and construction activity during the first century of Tulane's history, see Beatrice M. Field, Buildings Occupied by Academic Departments, in "Potpourri: An Assortment of Tulane's People and Places," unpublished manuscript, Tulane University Library.

3. BOA Minutes, 9 May and 8 October 1962; Tulane University, *Delta Primate Research*

Rosen House. Faculty and married student apartments, ca. 1960.

The Primate Center's official mission was to establish an "integrated program of biological research in primates that is directed toward the solution of health problems in man." During its first seven years of operation the center's greatest strength was in behavioral science research, followed by reproductive physiology, genetic and developmental disorders, and communicable diseases. In 1971 Dr. Peter J. Gerone, a microbiologist who had previously served as acting chief of the virus and rickettsia division of the U.S. Army's biological warfare research facility at Fort Detrick, Maryland, became the Primate Center's new director. With Gerone's arrival, the center's research em-

Center, undated pamphlet, ca. 1964, vertical files, Louisiana Collection, Howard-Tilton Memorial Library, Tulane University; Joseph T. Coyle, "Primates in the Service of Humanity," *Tulanian* 38 (December 1964): 1–3. Other NIH-funded primate research centers were located at the Universities of Washington and Oregon, the University of California at Davis, Emory University, the University of Wisconsin, and the Harvard Medical School. See Don L. Voss, "Silver Spring Monkeys: Archive of the Future," *Tulane Medicine* 22 (autumn 1991): 14–9.

phasis shifted to infectious disease and nutrition. In the years ahead, the center would gain recognition for its efforts in AIDS research while drawing fire from animal rights activists protesting surgical procedures used on monkeys before and after their 1986 transfer to Louisiana from Silver Spring, Maryland.

Another important off-campus location was the F. Edward Hébert Center near Belle Chase, Louisiana. Originally the site of a World War II ordnance depot, the property was acquired by Tulane in 1963. The installation's refurbished buildings became the home of the Riverside Research Laboratories, where faculty members from the School of Engineering and other scientific disciplines conducted externally funded research in aerospace engineering, physics, electrical power, environmental science, developmental biology, and other subjects. For decades much of the Hébert land would remain undeveloped.[4]

Much further away, in Cali, Colombia, the medical school opened a research center at the Universidad del Valle, where contacts had been established during the previous decade. This overseas facility was part of a larger effort funded by a 1961 NIH grant of more than $1 million to Tulane for research and training in tropical medicine. Outside the medical field, Tulane's Latin American programs continued to attract support from private foundations and other funding agencies. In the Law School, the Institute of Comparative Law continued the ambitious program of publication, teaching, and scholarly exchanges that had begun during the 1950s. The institute's initial $275,000 development grant from the Ford Foundation ran for ten years (1958–68), coinciding with a period of generous support from the Rockefeller Foundation that funded a professorship in Latin American legal studies, provided money to strengthen library holdings, and brought Latin American professors and students to Tulane for periods of study and teaching. By 1970 the institute's director, Ferdinand F. Stone, could point to an impressive record, which included publication of the *Inter-American Law Review* and an accompanying monograph series, together with an extensive program of intellectual interchange involving 28 visiting pro-

4. "Dr. Gerone Looks to the Future: Five Year Grant Submitted to NIH," in Tulane University, *Delta Primate Report* (January 1973); Voss, "Silver Spring Monkeys: Archive of the Future," 14–9. For the Riverside Research Laboratories, see [Lee H. Johnson], Annual Report, School of Engineering: 1963–64, pp. 7–8; 1964–65, pp. 7–8; 1965–66, p. 4; all in box 33, HEL Papers.

fessors from 14 Latin American countries, 35 visiting lecturers from 17 countries, 15 visiting research fellows from 10 countries, and 150 Tulane Law Fellows from 33 countries, the majority of whom remained at Tulane to take master of laws or master of civil law degrees.[5]

Tulane's Middle American Research Institute made equally important contributions to the study of the indigenous peoples of Mexico and Central America. Beginning in the late 1950s, the institute ceased to play a major role in the multidisciplinary Latin American Studies program, concentrating instead on two major academic endeavors. The first, E. Wyllys Andrews's archaeological excavations of important Mayan ruins at the ancient city of Dzibilchaltun and other sites in the Yucatán, received initial backing from the National Science Foundation and the American Philosophical Society, and was supported by the National Geographic Society throughout the 1960s and beyond. A second endeavor of major intellectual significance was the ever-expanding *Handbook of Middle American Indians*, a multivolume publication which sought to summarize the existing body of knowledge on native cultures, past and present. Edited by Robert Wauchope, the Harvard-trained anthropologist who had directed the Middle American Research Institute since 1943, the *Handbook*'s compilation was supported by a series of major grants from the National Science Foundation. The scope of the project was formidable. Eleven volumes were originally planned. By 1968 six were in print and a total of thirteen were envisioned. Four years later, in 1972, the number of published volumes had grown to eleven, with four more in preparation and plans underway for a sixteenth. In October 1976, when a campus publication described the *Handbook* as "probably the most ambitious single project of scholarly editing ever undertaken at Tulane," no one was bold enough to disagree.[6]

Throughout the 1960s the medical school remained the dominant component in Tulane's expanding research program. Of the roughly

5. BOA Minutes, 8 March 1961; John Duffy, *The Tulane Medical Center: One Hundred and Fifty Years of Medical Education* (Baton Rouge: Louisiana State University Press, 1984), 174; Ferdinand F. Stone, report on the first twenty-one years of the Institute of Comparative Law, summarized in *Tulanian* 41(June 1970): 9–11; Tulane University, *The Director's Report, 1949–1970, Institute of Comparative Law*, pamphlet in vertical file, Tulane University Archives.

6. The above paragraph is based primarily on chaps. 2 and 3 of Daniel S. Berman, "The Middle American Research Institute: Seventy Years of Middle American Research at Tulane

$10.2 million received for new projects in 1961–62, more than $9 million came from the federal government, with nearly 80 percent of the federal funds furnished by a single agency—the National Institutes of Health. Behind these figures lay a range of research efforts too diverse to permit adequate summary or even representative sampling. Over the span of the decade and beyond, Tulane physicians would conduct important clinical studies on subjects ranging from cardiac disease, profusion chemotherapy for cancer treatment, and the genetic aspects of sickle cell disease to the respiratory problems of sugar cane workers, the role of niacin deficiency in causing pellagra, and the role of yeast cells in enhancing natural defenses against various infections. Among the more controversial studies carried out during the early and mid-1960s were Dr. Robert Heath's continuing schizophrenia research involving the injection of LSD and other psychoactive drugs into deep structures of the brain, and a series of highly publicized efforts by Dr. Keith Reemtsa and his associates to transplant monkey kidneys into human patients.[7]

In fields other than medicine a number of factors influenced research activity, including the availability of external funding and the faculty culture of particular schools or departments. In the School of Engineering and the School of Business Administration, a kind of generational split divided younger research-oriented faculty from older colleagues whose principal interest was in undergraduate teaching. The very fact that some of the older professors saw research and teaching as mutually exclusive activities spoke volumes about the reorientation which had taken place after 1945, as Tulane made the transition from a local college to a research university. In reality the commitment to research had implications for teaching at all levels. Increasingly selective admissions had brought better students to the

University" (M.A. thesis, Tulane University, 1995). For an overview of all Tulane programs relating to Latin America during the early 1960s, see M. M. Kreeger, "To Serve a Hemisphere: Inter-American Activities of Tulane University" [November 1962], bound booklet accompanying president's agenda items, BOA Minutes, 12 December 1962, Board of Administrators Committee Minutes, Reports, and Correspondence, November 1961–June 1963, Tulane University Archives.

7. [Fred Cagle], Annual Report, Coordinator of Research [1961–62], box 35, HEL Papers; John Salvaggio, *New Orleans' Charity Hospital: A Story of Physicians, Politics, and Poverty* (Baton Rouge: Louisiana State University Press, 1992), 187–8, 361–2 nn. 16–8; John Salvaggio to Joseph E. Gordon, 12 December 1994, typescript memorandum in authors' possession.

Tulane campus, and better students encouraged innovative teaching strategies and intellectually demanding courses. One prominent example of the developing symbiosis between research activity and undergraduate teaching was the Scholars and Fellows (later renamed Scholars and Honors) program, begun with a $750,000 Ford Foundation grant in 1962–63, to facilitate the early identification and accelerated training of potential college teachers among Tulane undergraduates.[8]

Graduate teaching assistants constituted the most visible link between the world of advanced research and the undergraduate classroom. Whether employed as laboratory assistants, discussion group leaders, or full-fledged instructors for introductory courses—functions graduate students had routinely performed at leading American universities since the turn of the twentieth century—most TAs were young enough to share a common generational perspective with the undergraduates assigned to them. As the 1960s wore on, this generational link would become an important factor in facilitating communication over issues of student rights and institutional prerogatives. During the mid-1960s just under one-third of the freshman and sophomore sections in the College of Arts and Sciences and University College were taught by graduate teaching assistants. Graduate students taught virtually all the 100- and 200-level courses in the French and Spanish departments, as well as the great majority of introductory classes in the Departments of German, English, and Mathematics. Arts and Sciences dean William Peery regarded this as "too large a percentage in a university with tuition charges such as ours," but his concern evidently had more to do with parental expectations than with objective analysis of pedagogical skill.[9]

8. Hugh A. Thompson, interview by Joseph Gordon, 4 October 1995, audiotape in possession of authors; James Francis Fouche, "The Tulane University Graduate School of Business Administration: An Oral-Institutional History" (Ph.D. diss., University of Florida, 1978), 117–21; Tulane Scholars and Fellows Program, A Plan for the Preparation of College Teachers (Program Report from Tulane University to the Ford Foundation, 1 January 1963), typescript accompanying president's agenda items, BOA Minutes, 21 March 1963, Board of Administrators Committee Minutes, Reports, and Correspondence, November 1961–June 1963, Tulane University Archives; "Tulane Career Plan Outlined: Honors Program to Prepare College Teachers," New Orleans Times-Picayune, 11 April 1962, clipping, box 18, HEL Papers. On the early operation of the program, see Scholars and Fellows Program, folders 1–3 (1962–68), box 22, HEL Papers.

9. William W. Peery to Herbert E. Longenecker, 16 October 1962, box 29, HEL Papers; John L. Snell to chairmen of departments in the Graduate School, 7 October 1963, box 35, HEL

The TAs were, of course, apprentices in the process of learning their craft. Since the late 1950s Tulane had placed high priority upon recruiting promising undergraduates for careers in college teaching, and Graduate School policy aimed at giving all Ph.D. students the equivalent of one year of half-time classroom experience. Most graduate instructors were supervised either formally or informally by senior faculty who were presumed to be superior teachers. (Such assumptions were rarely tested.) In the Department of History, where advanced doctoral students typically taught one or two survey sections per semester for an entire academic year, beginning graduate instructors enrolled in a semester-long seminar conducted by the department chair. More than simply a methodology course, the seminar addressed the professional concerns and responsibilities of scholars in the classroom, and devoted considerable attention to the history of higher education in the United States. Each member of the seminar observed the teaching of every other member and prepared a written critique, giving each graduate instructor from five to ten evaluations by the end of the semester. These were reviewed by the department chair in individual conferences with each student. Each graduate student's major professor provided additional observation and criticism.[10]

Without the presence of graduate instructors, many introductory classes in fields such as history and English would have become the large, impersonal lecture sections common at public universities. A September 1964 survey revealed that "[a]ll but two departments indicated a strong preference for the continued use of teaching assistants rather than a change to large lecture sections, even if physical facilities permitted such a change." From a budgetary standpoint Tulane's 150 or so graduate instructors in the mid-1960s saved the university between $300,000 and $400,000, since their stipends and tuition waivers

Papers (quotation); John P. Dyer to Snell, 9 October 1963, box 35, HEL Papers. For an insightful discussion of the role of graduate teaching assistants in American universities, see Charles W. Eliot, *University Administration* (Boston: Houghton Mifflin, 1908), 184–6. Most of Eliot's observations on how graduate assistants could best be employed to produce the greatest benefit for themselves as well as for the undergraduates would have been relevant to Tulane and other universities of the post–World War II era.

10. John L. Snell to chairmen of departments in the Graduate School, 7 October 1963; Frederic W. Ness, *The Role of the College in the Recruitment of Teachers* (Washington, D.C.: Association of American Colleges, 1958), 62–3; Bernard Berelson, *Graduate Education in the United States* (New York: McGraw-Hill, 1960), 246; Dexter Perkins and John Snell, *The Education of Historians in the United States* (New York: McGraw-Hill, 1962), 192.

totaled less than half the amount ($663,320) that would have been required to replace them with 73 additional full-time faculty members. And yet, for all the significance attached to small classes and budgetary economies, the teaching assistants' most important contribution probably consisted of the example they provided for undergraduates. As students themselves, graduate instructors offered living proof to other students that the values of the academy were taken seriously by those under age thirty. Their presence in the classroom lent an aura of relevance to higher learning and provided graphic evidence that intellectual growth might begin rather than cease upon receipt of the bachelor's degree. This was perhaps the most vital message that any Tulane graduate could receive.[11]

In the applied fields, where teaching assistants were less common, the 1960s research emphasis brought important curricular changes aimed at increasing the analytic and theoretical content of undergraduate training. The shift was apparent in the School of Engineering as early as the 1959–60 academic year, when beginning engineering students first took physics rather than engineering drawing and descriptive geometry. By 1963 a new and more flexible engineering curriculum had been adopted, in which nearly half of the courses were elective. The new curriculum included an interdisciplinary major in engineering design and analysis that stressed creativity, independent problem solving, and holistic approaches to the design process. Much of the curricular and programmatic innovation in the engineering school was attributable to the tireless efforts of Assistant Dean John L. Martinez, who instituted special programs for ROTC and pre-medical students, with efforts in the latter area taking account of the growing significance of biomedical engineering in the school's overall research program.[12]

These measures helped reverse a decline in undergraduate engineering enrollment which, following national trends, had plummeted from a 1955 peak of over 500 to less than 300 by 1961. Modest but steady enrollment gains during the early and mid-sixties were accompanied by dramatic improvement in the qualitative profile of entering freshmen, as average CEEB scores in mathematics rose from 555 in 1958 to 632 in 1964. Graduate enrollment, which had been negligible

11. Graduate School Dean's Report, 1964–65, box 35, HEL Papers, 7.

12. [Lee H. Johnson], Annual Report, School of Engineering, 1959–60, box 33, HEL Papers, 2; ibid., 1964–65, p. 4.

in the mid-1950s, rose dramatically in the early 1960s with the addition of new Ph.D. programs in chemical, mechanical and civil engineering. Nearly 130 graduate students were enrolled by 1964–65, more than 50 of whom had fellowships or stipends. Support came from a number of outside sources and was closely linked to the growth of external research funding, which rose from approximately $20,000 in 1959–60 to $450,000 in 1964–65, plus an additional $23,000 in salary relief obtained through joint grants with the medical school. By the mid-sixties, 30 of the School of Engineering's 42 full-time faculty members were engaged in some form of research—an impressive, if temporary, step forward which would be eroded by university-wide budget difficulties in the coming years. By 1976, when Hugh A. Thompson succeeded Sam Hulbert as Dean of Engineering, the number of full-time graduate students in engineering had fallen to 35.[13]

In the School of Business Administration a major shift in emphasis was well underway by 1960, having begun a half decade earlier with the elevation of thirty-five-year-old Paul Grambsch to the deanship. During Grambsch's five-year tenure as dean (1955–60), the business school received a $200,000 Ford Foundation Grant for 1958–63, a period when the school expanded its graduate program and sought to liberalize the undergraduate curriculum by redirecting professional courses away from description toward problem solving and quantitative analysis. Under the new plan, undergraduate business majors would spend their first two years in the College of Arts and Sciences and take a third of their junior year coursework outside the business school in order to master the linguistic, mathematical, and other social science tools necessary for upper-level clinical courses that involved role playing in simulated business situations, as well as the use of computerized management games. (One of Grambsch's signal achievements had been the 1958 acquisition of Tulane's first computer, an IBM 7044 leased at a 60 percent discount from the IBM Corporation. The business school's computer laboratory was apparently the first in the South devoted entirely to a university's program. In 1962 the NIH funded a biomedical computer system for the medical school. Four years later, in 1966, the School of Engineering acquired a government surplus Univac Athena computer from a deactivated Titan missile base

13. Ibid.: 1959–60, pp. 2–4; 1961–62, p. 7; 1962–63, p. 2; 1964–65, pp. 1–3, 7–14; all in box 33, HEL Papers. For later enrollment figures, see Hugh A. Thompson, Report on the School of Engineering, BOA Minutes, 19 April 1990.

in California. The digital Athena was linked with the earlier analog computers to create a hybrid system.)[14]

The School of Business Administration's revised curriculum was part of a larger effort to improve the quality of the student body. Throughout the postwar era, the school had suffered from a dearth of superior talent at the undergraduate level, attracting students who scored poorly on standardized tests and who tended to equate business courses with vocational training in a narrower sense. By 1959–60, however, the school's *Bulletin* advised students to expect a "rigorous intellectual adventure" in which they would be challenged to study extensively and to think independently. As a recent historian has observed, such statements were "tantamount to a declaration that the day of easy business courses . . . was over." At Tulane and elsewhere the early 1960s were a time of declining undergraduate business enrollments, and it was an open question whether the new curriculum could attract a sufficiently large number of superior students to become viable. The entire issue became moot in December 1962, however, when the business school faculty, now led by Dean Grambsch's successor, Howard Schaller, voted to abolish the undergraduate program and concentrate exclusively on graduate training. Despite opposition from some local businesses, the Board of Administrators approved the change a few months later. By the time the undergraduate program was fully phased out in 1966, the School of Business Administration and its new dean, C. Jackson Grayson, were in the process of launching a Ph.D. program to complement the M.B.A. curriculum which enrolled approximately one hundred full-time students. The progression was a logical one, but the full development of doctoral study in business would be delayed by the larger financial crisis that overtook graduate education near the end of the decade.[15]

14. Fouche, "Tulane University Graduate School of Business Administration," 140; Tulane University, Proposal to the Ford Foundation, 1963, section 1, pp. 48–9, Tulane University Archives; [Lee H. Johnson], Annual Report, School of Engineering, 1965–66, p. 4; ibid., 1966–67, pp. 8–10. Unless otherwise stated, discussion of the business school here and in the following paragraphs is based upon chaps. 5–8 of Fouche, "The Tulane University Graduate School of Business Administration."

15. Clinton A. Phillips, *Experience with Undergraduate Business Program* (New Orleans: Tulane University, 1964), 29; Fouche, "The Tulane University Graduate School of Business Administration," 122, 136 (quotations), 158; Tulane University, Undergraduate Program in Business Administration, undated report accompanying president's agenda items, BOA minutes, 8 October 1962, box 87, HEL Papers; BOA Minutes, 18 April 1963.

In the Graduate School itself, both Dean Robert Lumiansky (1954–63) and his successor, John Snell (1963–66), emphasized enrollment growth and qualitative improvement. Although ten new doctoral programs were begun during the first half of the 1960s, bringing the number of Ph.D. fields to thirty-three, most of the expansion in graduate enrollment occurred within preexisting programs. The numerical gains of the 1960s continued a trend established in the previous decade, when the number of students pursuing advanced degrees at Tulane more than doubled after 1955 to stand at 640 in the 1959–60 academic year. Seven more years saw another increase of nearly 100 percent, as the number of graduate students peaked at 1,264 in 1966–67. Several factors lay behind this phenomenal growth rate, including the age profile of the baby boom generation, anxiety over scientific and technological competition with the Soviet Union, and the widely held belief that American graduate schools were producing too few Ph.D.'s to meet the future demand for college teachers. These concerns manifested themselves through an increasing stress on selectivity in graduate admissions, through programs aimed at reducing the time required to complete doctoral training—an idea given influential endorsement in Bernard Berelson's 1960 study *Graduate Education in the United States*—and through a dramatic increase in the type and amount of federal support for graduate study.[16]

Something of the spirit which prevailed in the Graduate School administration from the late 1950s through the mid-1960s can be seen in a statement of basic priorities laid down by historian John Snell shortly before succeeding Dean Lumiansky in 1963. As dean, Snell would be guided by a set of five interrelated objectives: "(1) get first-rate students; (2) provide them with adequate financial support for full-time or nearly full-time study; (3) inspire and require them to work very hard; (4) make them feel that teaching is important and orient them in the qualities of good teaching; and (5) turn them loose after three or four years, judging them by the quality of their work more than by its quantity and acknowledging that Ph.D. training is a beginning, not a culmination, of scholarly development."[17]

Tulane's previously mentioned Scholars and Fellows program rep-

16. All statistics are taken from the annual reports of the dean of the Graduate School, 1960–65, box 35, HEL Papers.

17. [John Snell], "Summing Up: 1962–63 through 1965–66," remarks prepared for delivery at the spring 1966 meeting of the Tulane graduate faculty, box 35, HEL Papers.

resented an initial step toward accelerating doctoral training, and shortly after taking office Snell addressed the issue more directly by offering a limited number of special University Fellowships supporting four years of uninterrupted graduate study, with financial incentives for those students who completed the Ph.D. within the allotted time. Patterned after more ambitious programs at Harvard and Washington University in St. Louis, the Tulane effort was small and short-lived but apparently not without effect. Among students receiving the Ph.D. at spring graduation who did all their graduate work at Tulane, the mean period for completion of the Ph.D. declined from 6.5 years in 1963 to 5.4 years in 1966.[18]

Increasing the overall pool of financial aid had been the principal challenge facing graduate deans throughout the postwar era, and the years from 1960 through 1967 saw unprecedented growth in aid from federal sources. In a strict bookkeeping sense, more than one million of the $2,487,510 in financial aid provided to graduate students in the peak year 1967–68 came from Tulane itself. But nearly half of the university's contribution came in the form of tuition waivers, many of which were granted in connection with fellowships and grants from federal agencies. Even the university's payment of more than $517,000 in graduate stipends tended to obscure the fact that a substantial portion of the revenue for such payments came, directly or indirectly, from overhead costs collected on research contracts and from the tuition payments or "cost of education" allowances paid to the university in connection with graduate fellowships and traineeships from the Woodrow Wilson Fellowship program (9 awards), the National Institutes of Health (15 awards), the National Aeronautics and Space Administration (26 awards), the National Science Foundation (29 awards), and the National Defense Education Act (185 awards).[19]

Departmental training grants and research contracts provided the largest single source of financial support for Tulane graduate students in the physical and social sciences—nearly $700,000 in 1967–68 alone. Next in size—and first in importance to the chronically cash-starved humanities departments—were Tulane's National Defense Education Act fellowships, with more than $500,000 spread across nearly all dis-

18. Announcement of University Fellowships (accompanying John Snell memorandum to department chairmen, 14 January 1964), box 35, HEL Papers; [Snell], "Summing Up, 1962–63 through 1965–66."

19. Graduate School Dean's Report, 1966–67, box 35, HEL Papers, 8.

ciplines in the humanities and social sciences. Established in 1958 and dramatically expanded in 1964, the NDEA program helped redress the imbalance created when students holding competitive "free choice" fellowships from the NIH, NSF, and the Woodrow Wilson National Fellowship Foundation showed a marked preference for attending Ivy League schools or the most prestigious research universities in the Middle and Far West. Like federal science traineeships, NDEA awards were granted to institutions rather than to individual students, and they allowed for a more even geographical distribution of graduate aid. During the program's first six years (1959–64) the majority of NDEA fellowships went to schools "in regions most deficient in graduate facilities." The South, which produced 9 percent of all U.S. doctorates during these years, received 22 percent of NDEA awards. With 129 fellowships to its credit during the period, Tulane ranked fourth nationally among the 23 schools to which a hundred or more awards were allocated. In the South only Vanderbilt, with 137 NDEA grants, surpassed Tulane.[20] During the second half of the 1960s the annual number of new NDEA awards available nationally quadrupled, from 1,500 to 6,000. Tulane's awards kept pace, growing from about 20 new fellowships in 1963 to 80 or more by 1966–67. Where Tulane departed from the national pattern was in the concentration of NDEA support outside the science disciplines. Nationally, NDEA funding was more or less evenly divided between science and engineering on the one hand and social science and humanities fields on the other. At Tulane 80 percent or more of all NDEA awards went to the humanities and social sciences, where they often represented the sole source of federal funding. In history, English, philosophy, and modern languages, NDEA grants became the sine qua non of expanded doctoral training in the late sixties.[21]

The steady expansion of graduate and professional training in 1960–

20. Roger L. Geiger, *Research and Relevant Knowledge: American Research Universities since World War II* (New York: Oxford University Press, 1993), 220–2; The Graduate Fellowship Program of the National Defense Education Act of 1958, section 1, Summary of the Program, 1958–64, typescript accompanying agenda for U.S. Office of Education Conference on Graduate Fellowship Program, 7 November 1964, box 35, HEL Papers (quotation).

21. [Snell], "Summing Up, 1962–63 through 1965–66"; The Graduate Fellowship Program of the National Defense Education Act of 1958, section 1, Summary of the Program, 1958–1964, p. 3; John Snell to chairmen of departments in the Graduate School, 8 October 1963, table 3, Sources of Financial Aid by Divisions, box 35, HEL Papers; John Snell to chairmen of departments in the Graduate School, 22 February 1965, box 35, HEL Papers.

67, in conjunction with unprecedented growth in the academic job market, created a spirit of optimism throughout higher education. Although faculty salaries at Tulane remained low in comparison with peer institutions, confidence in the future was high, owing in no small part to a record of accomplishment and outside recognition that seemed to justify the institutional priorities which had prevailed for more than a decade. Additional reinforcement for the wisdom of staying the course came in the form of a $6 million grant from the Ford Foundation's Special Program in Education, announced by President Longenecker in a press release on April 3, 1964. This was the program from which Tulane had been excluded in 1960–61 because of continued adherence to racial segregation, but no one at Tulane seemed to mind that the award came at a time when many of the original recipients were receiving second major grants. Discussions with the Ford Foundation, which had never entirely ceased during the three-year struggle over black admissions, resumed in earnest in December 1962, as Tulane prepared to submit current financial reports and a detailed ten-year development plan to foundation officials in New York. The resulting award provided what the university most needed—a large sum of unencumbered capital granted on the basis of demonstrated academic merit and future research potential, money that came with no strings attached and that could be used for core academic purposes. As historian Roger L. Geiger has noted, it was the kind of philanthropy which sent a powerful message about the standards to which colleges and universities at all levels should aspire.[22]

The first installment of the Ford grant—$1.5 million—was advanced to the university for immediate use on such pressing matters as faculty additions and salary increases ($400,000), faculty research and travel funds ($100,000), library acquisitions ($100,000), planning and architectural services ($300,000), development of the Riverside Research Laboratories at Belle Chase ($500,000), and renovation of uptown

22. Richard P. Adams et al., Tulane Faculty Salaries Compared with Salaries in Other Leading Schools (Tulane Chapter AAUP, Report of the Committee on the Economic Problems of the Profession), April 1960, box 24, RCH Papers; L. M. N. Bach to R. M. Lumiansky, 6 April 1960, box 24, RCH Papers; Faculty Salary Comparison, 1940–41 to 1961–62, box 10, RCH Papers; BOA Minutes, 8 January 1963; Tulanian 37 (April 1964): 2–3; Geiger, Research and Relevant Knowledge, 113–6.

campus building space recently vacated by medical school departments that had moved downtown. The initial installment, like the rest of the grant, involved a two to one matching requirement. In other words, Tulane would be required to raise a total of $12 million in private contributions in order to receive the entire $6 million Ford gift. The matching provision reflected a major underlying purpose of the Ford program, namely the encouragement of "more aggressive norms of fund raising" among private universities. Tulane responded with what became known as the Tulane Forward Fund, a three-year campaign to raise $24.4 million—more than twice the amount required to match the Ford grant. Earlier development programs had been rather sporadic in nature, and the successful Tulane Forward effort ushered in the era of organized full-time fundraising in its modern form at Tulane. Although the university's financial problems were far from over, the fiscal struggle had clearly entered a new phase.[23]

Few doubted that the Ford grant was a milestone. In an unusually perceptive editorial, the Tulane *Hullabaloo* declared that the Tulane Forward campaign was "significant as much symbolically as materially. . . . There is the immediate temptation to ask the obvious—'What good will a new library three years from now . . . be to me?' [W]hat must be understood is the intangible, and in a sense immeasurable effect such an ambitious program will have . . . in providing an additional source of pride for the present students and faculty and [in] helping to persuade more top notch people to come to Tulane. . . . Essentially the accomplishment of the goals of the fund drive will do more than build buildings. It will be . . . proof of the potential around us now." In a very real sense the Ford grant was an acknowledgment of the university's achievements over the previous ten years, as well as a vote of confidence in the faculty and administration of the mid-1960s. The resulting fund campaign was an opportunity for Board members, alumni, and supporters to embrace more fully the research university vision. Symbolically (to use the *Hullabaloo*'s phrase) the Ford Foundation was inviting the Tulane community to believe in itself.[24]

Among the ranks of Tulane supporters there had always been a core of true believers—on and off the Board of Administrators—whose deep emotional attachment to the university expressed itself through

23. *Tulanian* 37 (April 1964): 2–3.
24. Tulane *Hullabaloo*, 6 November 1964, p. 8 (all quotations).

support for intercollegiate athletics in general and for varsity football in particular. And since the deemphasis initiative of the 1950s, there had been an equally intense core of opposition to big-time athletics among faculty members on the uptown campus, particularly in the College of Arts and Sciences and Newcomb College. The gradual retreat from football deemphasis in the late 1950s, culminating with the establishment of the Teacher-Coach curriculum in 1959, set the stage for further conflict over football's place within a university seeking to distinguish itself on the basis of undergraduate selectivity and academic excellence.

President Longenecker had been in office scarcely a year when the football issue reemerged as a topic of public debate during November and December 1961. The catalyst for debate was a 62-0 loss to LSU, which prompted the resignation of head coach Andy Pilney after five consecutive losing seasons. The 1961 LSU loss was the second such humiliation at the hands of Tulane's traditional rival within a three-year period—the scores for the 1958 and 1961 LSU games were identical—and the result was more than diehard Green Wave fans could endure. Shortly before the ill-fated LSU contest, a New Orleans alumni group calling itself "Friends of Tulane" held a noisy meeting attended by some four hundred disgruntled football supporters. The widely publicized gathering adopted a set of resolutions alleging that "for the past eight years [i.e., since Harris's reforms] Tulane has let its football program deteriorate to its present deplorable state." Longing for a return to the days of bowl games, SEC championships, and national rankings, the group proposed a number of corrective measures, including the hiring of a new head coach who would be given "absolute authority over recruiting activities" and fired if he failed to produce winning teams within a specified time period. And while disavowing any desire to lower admission standards, the meeting also called upon the university to "[r]e-establish" a physical education department that would adopt "admission standards . . . in line with the requirements now effective in the majority of other Southeastern Conference schools." After meeting with the group's leaders in mid-November, Longenecker received Pilney's resignation on November 26 and issued a public statement in early December stressing the university's commitment to high academic standards. In addition to pointing out that physical education courses had never been abolished, the official press release defended the Teacher-Coach Program, and reaffirmed Tulane's intention to remain in the SEC.[25]

Behind Longenecker's public assurance of continued SEC membership, however, lay an ongoing debate over conference affiliation that dated back at least three years. The issue had first been officially broached on December 18, 1958, during the memorable meeting of the Arts and Sciences faculty at which Joseph Jones and several other Tulane Board members advocated approval of the Teacher-Coach Program. On that occasion, Jones addressed the issue of Southeastern Conference membership twice. In his prepared remarks Jones acknowledged that Tulane might "do either of two things, give up Southeastern Conference football or go ahead." He preferred the latter course, but did not rule out "the suggestion that we should perhaps get into another conference." Leaving the SEC, he cautioned, would be "a long-term thing, requiring perhaps five or six years" for the fulfillment of existing sports contracts. Later, in response to a faculty member's question, Jones went still further and stated that "[p]ersonally, he would be interested in developing another league but he had been told that that can probably not be done."[26]

By 1961 the lengthening record of losing seasons, athletic red ink, and high academic attrition rates among scholarship athletes (to say nothing of alumni protest) served to underline the deep-seated conflicts between Tulane's academic and athletic priorities. The situation was further complicated by the transitional state of the university's programs for teacher training during the early 1960s. At the beginning of the decade, three separate and largely uncoordinated curricula for teacher certification existed in Newcomb College, University College, and the College of Arts and Sciences. The lack of uniformity, including the refusal of the Arts and Sciences faculty to allow credit for physical

25. Friends of Tulane Resolution, 9 November 1961, typescript accompanying president's agenda items, BOA Minutes, 13 December 1961 (all quotations); Herbert E. Longenecker, statement to executive committee of Tulane Alumni Association on intercollegiate football, 5 December 1961, typescript accompanying president's agenda items, BOA Minutes, 13 December 1961. The statement was subsequently published as "FOOTBALL: Tulane's Position," *Tulanian* 35 (January 1962): 11–2. The Tulane *Hullabaloo*, 17 November 1961, p. 2, described the November 9 meeting as an "ill-timed and ill-mannered" protest gathering attended by alumni with "closed minds" who "lashed out violently" against both the Tulane coaches and the university administration.

26. College of Arts and Sciences Faculty Minutes, 18 December 1958, box 9-G, RCH Papers.

education courses taken by students not enrolled in the Teacher-Coach Program, led to negative outside evaluations in 1958 and 1961, and a threatened loss of state accreditation following a campus inspection visit on October 10, 1962. Tulane responded to the criticisms in the spring of 1962 by creating a Center for Teacher Education, which was comprised of a core of education professors plus additional faculty "associates" drawn from the various Tulane colleges. In December 1962, however, before the new arrangement had been fully implemented, the center's director, Professor Thomas E. Jordan, recommended the creation of a full-fledged School of Education with its own faculty and separate degree-granting authority. The proposal drew an immediate and highly negative response from uptown faculty, some 118 of whom signed a January 1963 letter to Longenecker requesting that no action be taken on the proposed School of Education until the matter had received formal consideration from the various faculties involved.[27]

Although Tulane historian and University College dean John Dyer described the liberal arts faculty of the late 1950s as harboring "an almost unreasoning fear that a school of education might be established," the evidence indicates that faculty concern was neither "unreasoning" nor groundless.[28] At the heart of the controversy was a suspicion that proponents of the education school idea were more interested in improving athletes' grades than in facilitating teacher certification. In December 1958, during the initial struggle over the Teacher-Coach curriculum, Tulane Board member Edgar B. Stern had specifically suggested that creating a separate education school might be the best way to surmount the curricular obstacles created by an uncooperative Arts and Sciences faculty. By the early 1960s, football supporters outside the university were openly backing the concept as a way to make Tulane more competitive in the SEC. These facts were widely known when the A&S faculty took up the education school proposal on January 10, 1963. Mathematics professor Alexander D. Wallace, who moved that the faculty go on record as opposing Jordan's

27. James Sylvest to Shelby M. Jackson, 27 March 1963, in BOA Minutes, 23 May 1963, president's agenda item on teacher education; BOA Minutes, 9 May 1962, 12 December 1962, and 13 February 1963; Dyer, *Tulane* 290–1. Potential problems concerning state accreditation of three separate certification programs had come to the Tulane Board's attention as early as December 1958 and had worsened during the following years. See BOA Minutes, 10 December 1958, item 10 of president's monthly report.

28. Dyer, *Tulane*, 291. Oddly, Dyer makes no mention of Jordan's 1962–63 proposal.

initiative, expressed the sentiments of many colleagues when he declared that "the establishment of a school of education would necessarily call for a Department of Physical Education. He hoped Tulane would not lower its standards." Some two months later the faculty adopted Wallace's motion and voted to approach the accreditation problem within the framework of the existing Center for Teacher Education by working with other faculties to reach agreement on standard curricular policies. In the face of strong A&S opposition the proposed education school was effectively dead, but the athletic issues surrounding the education debate remained very much alive.[29]

In a report to the Board of Administrators, President Longenecker described the controversy over teacher training as being "clouded with emotional responses," while certain senior faculty members believed that "the dissension precipitated by the proposal to establish a School of Education . . . has had no counterpart in recent Tulane History." (This in the wake of the 1962 sit-ins at the University Center.) Emotionalism, however, was not confined to the faculty side of the dispute. Important cultural subtexts lurked beneath the surface of the football versus education debates of the early 1960s, giving rise to written exchanges between Tulane Board members that revealed why athletic issues seemed immune to settlement through compromise or dispassionate cost-benefit analysis. The most forceful expression of an outlook that was shared to some degree by other pro-football Administrators came from the pen of Darwin S. Fenner, who would assume the chairmanship of the Board of Administrators in June 1963 following the tragic death of Joseph Jones in a fire the previous March.[30]

Writing to Lester J. Lautenschlaeger in February 1963, approximately a month prior to Jones's death, Fenner voiced grave doubts about Tulane's ability "under present circumstances" to compete successfully in the Southeastern Conference. "My doubts . . . stem basically from my present information as to the faculty's attitude toward athletics," Fenner explained. What followed was a bill of indictment that echoed virtually all the arguments and allegations put forward by the athletic department during the previous ten years. Fenner accepted at face value the claim that 80 percent of the most athletically

29. BOA Minutes, 10 December 1958 and 23 May 1963; College of Arts and Sciences Faculty Minutes, 10 January 1963 (quotation) and 22 March 1963, box 29, HEL Papers.

30. BOA Minutes, 13 February 1963.

promising high school prospects were unable to meet the academic requirements for freshman admission, while "a substantial percentage of the remainder are intimidated by the reports of a high percentage of failures after admission." In Fenner's view, blame for the situation rested squarely upon the shoulders of the faculty. "I am told," he continued, "that faculty antipathy in some cases reaches the point of actual discrimination against athletes at Tulane merely because they are athletes. This Freudian concept is hard for me to believe, but I would like to be reassured." Fenner also wanted reassurance about faculty attitudes toward the Teacher-Coach Program, an area in which he observed signs of "intractability and uncooperativeness completely inconsistent with the basic assumptions which have motivated the Board in its deficit financing." In the face of such attitudes, Fenner's belief in "the common concept toward the common goal . . . [had] been shattered, if not irreparably, at least substantially." Fenner prefaced these remarks with a two-page exposition of his educational philosophy, emphasizing the importance of balancing academic training with moral and physical development. Within this context he regarded the Teacher-Coach Program as important not only because it attracted football players, but also because it trained individuals who would shape the development of the rising generation. Personal experience convinced the Tulane Board member that "a great many high school and grammar school children are more influenced in their character development by their coaches and athletic directors than by their teachers." Fenner's assertion was accompanied by a footnote which read, "Remember the playing fields of Eton!"[31]

In these heartfelt (and not entirely inaccurate) declarations from a former welterweight college boxer to a former Tulane football star, one at last finds the depth of feeling and moral commitment that had been so conspicuously absent from Board deliberations over the issue of civil rights. Among Board members who tended to judge faculty behavior by the authoritarian norms of the corporate world, Fenner's comments struck a raw nerve. Administrator George A. Wilson, for example, found faculty attitudes toward athletics "completely indefensible," amounting in recent times to nothing less than "insubordination[,] which is an offense that I can neither tolerate nor excuse."

31. Darwin S. Fenner to Lester J. Lautenschlaeger, 15 February 1963, box 49, HEL Papers (all quotations).

Couched in the language of a masculine power struggle, Wilson's comments revealed how thoroughly sports had permeated the undergraduate experience of many Tulane alumni, and how closely football was intertwined with the competitive culture of the marketplace.[32]

Blaming the faculty did nothing to alter the fact that Tulane suffered a tremendous disadvantage when seeking to compete with SEC schools, where the academic expectations for football players were so lax as to be all but meaningless. One possible solution to the dilemma was to persuade other SEC members to raise their standards. Tulane had pursued this approach actively from Rufus Harris's time onward, and redoubled its efforts to elevate SEC academic requirements during the first years of Longenecker's administration. At the annual meeting of the SEC in 1961, Tulane saw its proposal to have member schools require College Board scores for all athletes rejected by a vote of eight to four. A similar attempt the following year failed by a tie vote of six to six. A Tulane proposal to limit the total number of athletic grants-in-aid was also voted down. In January 1963 the conference adopted Tulane's proposal that SAT scores (or the ACT equivalent) be made a condition for finalizing athletic grants. The action lost its significance, however, when delegates also accepted a University of Georgia motion to specify a *combined* verbal and quantitative SAT score of 750 as meeting the minimum requirement.[33]

The Board of Administrators followed these developments closely, and early in 1963 it appointed a special committee chaired by Ashton Phelps to make recommendations on future athletic policy. The central function of the committee, as Phelps defined it, was "to ascertain whether or not Tulane can continue to compete successfully in the Southeastern Conference . . . with things as they now are." More or less simultaneously the University Senate Committee on Athletics posed a similar question after reluctantly concluding that "[w]hile Tulane enrolls boys who are both fine athletes and good students, we cannot attract *enough* boys who meet both the academic standards imposed by Tulane and the general athletic (particularly football) standards required by Southeastern Conference competition." The committee rejected the idea of abandoning intercollegiate football and asked the

32. George A. Wilson to Ashton Phelps, 21 February 1963, box 49, HEL Papers.

33. University Senate Committee on Athletics, Annual Report, 1961–62, box 87, HEL Papers; Melvin Henry Gruensfelder, "A History of the Origin and Development of the Southeastern Conference" (M.S. thesis, University of Illinois, 1964), 263–5.

senate, in its advisory capacity to the Board, to choose instead between the alternatives of (1) withdrawing from the SEC and competing with "universities which have similar academic programs and aims," (2) exempting athletes from regular admissions and progress-toward-degree requirements, and (3) providing an academic program of unspecified nature that would assist in "meeting the athletic competition required by participation in the [Southeastern] Conference."[34]

On May 15 the Arts and Sciences faculty, in executive session, voted to instruct its senators to support the first alternative, withdrawal from the SEC. A week later the senate endorsed the proposal by a vote of 26-2, with only Law and Engineering delegates in opposition. By the beginning of summer local newspapers were rife with rumors that another attempt would be made to create a "southern Ivy League," composed of Tulane plus such peer schools as Vanderbilt, Duke, Virginia, North Carolina, Georgia Tech, and Rice. In mid-June the Board's special athletic committee recommended that Tulane "follow closely the rumored division in the SEC" while remaining in the conference and attempting to schedule more nonconference games against teams "with standards and objectives comparable to our own." As had been true several years earlier, nothing came of efforts to form a new league. In September 1963 the Board, while categorically ruling out the abandonment of intercollegiate football, acknowledged that a survey the previous spring had revealed a "sharp division" of opinion over whether to remain in the Southeastern Conference. The Board statement also noted rather pointedly that Tulane would honor its SEC scheduling commitments, which extended through 1965.[35]

By this point Tulane's disenchantment with the SEC involved not only the issue of academic standards but also the conference requirement that all members schedule six games per year with other member

34. Ashton Phelps to Herbert E. Longenecker, 4 March 1963, box 76, HEL Papers (first quotation); Report of University Senate Committee on Athletics, 6 May 1963, box 29, HEL Papers (all subsequent quotations).

35. College of Arts and Sciences Faculty Minutes, 15 May 1963, box 29, HEL Papers; University Senate Minutes, 23 May 1963, University Senate Minutes and Reports, 1912–1989, box 2, Tulane University Archives; "Tulane's Athletic Future," WDSU sports editorial, 15 June 1963, box 49, HEL Papers (first quotation); Report of Meeting of the Tulane Committee Appointed to Study the Athletic Situation, 18 June 1963, accompanying BOA Executive Committee Minutes, 19 June 1963, box 75, HEL Papers (second and third quotations); BOA Minutes, 19 September 1963; Statement of the Tulane Board of Administrators in Regard to Tulane Athletics, 19 September 1963, box 19, RCH Papers (fourth quotation); Athletic Advisory Committee, Survey of Intercollegiate Athletics, [undated, spring 1963], box 29, HEL Papers.

schools. The situation worsened in 1964, when efforts were made to dictate the selection of future conference opponents and even to mandate the date and location of games. Such efforts placed Tulane in the position of having to request a waiver of rules in order to schedule nonconference games, which was a step the university was unwilling to take for a number of reasons—including the loss of television revenue and the overall implication of second-class status which a waiver would entail. The prospects for academic reform also appeared bleak after January 1964, when the SEC allowed the previous year's 750 combined SAT score to stand and added an equally low equivalent of 16 on the ACT. In the same meeting Georgia Tech withdrew from the conference, ostensibly because of dissatisfaction over the limitation placed upon the total number of grants-in-aid.[36]

All these developments pointed toward an inevitable parting of ways, and by early December the decision to leave the Southeastern Conference had been reached. Actual separation from the SEC required formal action by the Tulane Board, and in a somewhat ironic twist of fate the task of initiating the Board's action fell to Darwin Fenner, who was midway through his second year as chairman. "I would like to recommend to you that we withdraw [from the SEC] in good standing," Fenner advised his fellow Administrators in a prepared statement on December 31, 1964. Although he defended the move as an effort to rebuild the athletic program, the text of his statement contained sentiments far different than those he had expressed to Lester Lautenschlaeger the previous year. Tulane, he explained, was "fast growing into a national institution. A private university today must emphasize quality and be consistent in its treatment of all students[,] rather than to attempt to educate large numbers of students. This fact causes us to have a different point of view [than other SEC members] with respect to student athletics."[37]

The official press release announcing Tulane's withdrawal from the

36. Minutes of the Executive Committee of the Southeastern Conference, 24 January 1964, accompanying president's agenda item Southeastern Conference, in BOA Minutes, 20 February 1964; Preliminary (1st) Draft of Tulane Press Release on Withdrawal from SEC, 7 December 1964, box 49, HEL Papers; Items to Consider [Concerning] Request [for] Four Year Exemption from Six Game Regulation to Schedule Maximum of Four Conference Teams, 1964–1969, eleven-point memorandum, 24 December 1964, box 49, HEL Papers; Gruensfelder, "History of the Origin and Development of the Southeastern Conference," 265.

37. [Darwin Fenner], Statement to the Board of Administrators, 31 December 1964, box 49, HEL Papers.

SEC, effective in June 1966, contained the obligatory denials of any intent to deemphasize "football, basketball, or any of the other sports." The decision was explained as simply an effort to schedule more "intersectional" games and to improve the university's competitive position. In the hope of minimizing controversy among sportswriters, all critical references to the SEC were expunged from the formal statement. Tulane's departure from the SEC did little to solve the curricular and fiscal problems associated with intercollegiate athletics, and controversies over football were destined to remain a staple feature of campus politics for the next three decades. In the mid-1960s, however, Tulane's move out of the SEC appeared to be—and in a certain sense actually was—an important element in the university's metamorphosis from a regional to a national institution. Occurring near the end of a decade and a half of sustained emphasis on research and academic selectivity, and coinciding with the $6 million Ford grant and the successful fund campaign that followed it, the abandonment of a major conference affiliation seemed to indicate a change in institutional priorities, if not an outright shift in the university's internal balance of power. In the years after 1966 such assumptions would be put to the test.[38]

38. [Statement] for Release at 7 P.M., CST, Thursday, 31 December 1964, box 49, HEL Papers; Horace Renegar to Herbert E. Longenecker, 8 December 1964, box 49, HEL Papers.

6

FAMILY QUARRELS, PART ONE
Fiscal Retrenchment and Campus Dissent

In his 1975 account of life at Tulane during the previous quarter century, veteran Dean of Students John H. Stibbs described the first half decade of the Longenecker administration as an almost idyllic period marked by generally harmonious relations between all segments of the university community. "The mid-sixties," Stibbs declared, were "great days and beautiful years." Although the turmoil of the late 1960s may have magnified the significance of Tulane's earlier tranquillity, few would deny the stark contrasts between campus conditions at the beginning and at the end of the decade. Many factors, both internal and external, contributed to the reversal of attitudes and fortunes which Tulane experienced during this eventful period. In the political realm, the combined effect of an escalated war in Southeast Asia, a truncated attack against poverty at home, and a rapid dissolution of the interracial coalition responsible for the major civil rights legislation of 1964–65 produced far-reaching changes in the way students and faculty viewed their relations both to society and to each other. The Tulane freshmen of 1969 entered a campus environment vastly different from that of 1960, whether measured by styles of dress and self-presentation, acceptance of drug usage, awareness of social injustice, or willingness to question and challenge established lines of institutional authority. Just as important, the outlook of the first-year student had undergone a significant change. Survey data collected from male and female entering freshmen at Tulane between 1966 and 1969 revealed a steadily rising predisposition to engage in protests over civil rights and the Vietnam War.[1]

1. John H. Stibbs, "Twenty-Five Years of Student Life at Tulane University [1949–75]," typescript, box 64, HEL Papers, 22 (quotation); Tulane University, Summary of Data on En-

I

No single explanation can adequately account for the dramatic reorientation of values and behavioral norms that swept American campuses in the years preceding 1970. At Tulane, economic as well as cultural and political factors played a role in dissolving the consensus that had prevailed at the outset of Longenecker's presidency. And Tulane's situation was not unique. For American research universities in general, the 1960s stand out in retrospect as a decade in which initial prosperity led almost inexorably to conditions of overexpansion and later retrenchment as university administrators struggled to meet ever-increasing costs with finite resources. Even a brief catalog of the most important economic forces at work in the field of higher learning will suggest the broad, systemic character of Tulane's fiscal problems, which differed only in degree from the difficulties faced by other institutions.

According to the Carnegie Commission on Higher Education, the core problem facing all research universities in the mid-1960s was the need—in the absence of productivity gains typical of manufacturing and other business sectors—to raise salaries to keep pace with rising U.S. living standards. Teaching simply did not lend itself to the pursuit of greater efficiency through the use of new technology or changes in bureaucratic organization. This was especially true for schools that were unwilling to accept the qualitative sacrifices associated with televised instruction and gargantuan lecture sections. Additional external pressures which bore heavily upon higher education in general during the decade after 1965 included an inflation rate at or above 5 percent, a doubling of the cost of federally-mandated fringe benefits from which colleges had once been wholly or partly exempt, a cyclical peak in the U.S. stock market that ushered in a ten-year slump in higher education fundraising after 1965, and most important, a sharp cutback in federal and foundation support for graduate fellowships, traineeships, building construction, and equipment. These subventions, which universities had expected to increase in the decade after 1967, actually shrank by some 70 percent in real terms, while levels of sponsored research remained virtually constant. Tulane, like most private research

tering Freshmen, fall 1966–fall 1969 (information submitted to Cooperative Institutional Research Program, American Council on Education, University of California at Los Angeles), material in authors' possession.

universities, had expanded graduate training more rapidly than undergraduate education, thereby increasing educational costs while limiting the amount of tuition revenue available for general purposes. The resulting pattern of heavy reliance upon outside support left the university dangerously vulnerable to the federal cutbacks of the late 1960s. The situation was exacerbated by the Ford Foundation's decision to discontinue its Special Program in Education in 1968 before Tulane could be considered for a second major capital grant.[2]

The first clear indication that the $6 million received from Ford between 1964 and 1968 had postponed rather than solved the residual problems created by more than a decade of budgetary deficits came in 1967. In that year, all but two of the eight faculty members in Tulane's Department of Theater and Speech resigned in protest over what they regarded as inadequate support from the university's central administration. A demand for new performance facilities precipitated the crisis of 1966–67, but the dispute was actually a consequence of success and a reflection of the theater department's gradual rise to a position of national prominence under the leadership of Professor Monroe Lippman, who had joined the faculty in 1937 during the first year of Rufus Harris's presidency. Initially a member of the English department, Lippman organized the Tulane University Theater and supervised its productions while struggling to cope with severe space limitations, which sometimes dictated that rehearsals be conducted in as many as six different locations on and off campus. From 1949 onward Professor Paul Hostetler directed the productions of the theater, working initially in a converted shop area that had been assigned to

2. William Bowen, *The Economics of Major Private Universities* (New York: Carnegie Commission on Higher Education, 1968), passim; Roger L. Geiger, *Research and Relevant Knowledge: American Research Universities since World War II* (New York: Oxford University Press, 1993), 202–3, 243–5. Unless otherwise indicated, my discussion of the general economic problems facing research universities relies on Geiger's analysis. The effects of these economic developments at Tulane are ably summarized in Longenecker's "Address on the State of the University" delivered at spring 1970 alumni conferences, box 125, HEL Papers. Changes in fringe benefit requirements provide a striking illustration of the overall trend in educational costs. Tulane and other universities first came under minimum wage laws on 1 February 1967 when a $1.00 per hour requirement took effect. The 1968 minimum wage increase to $1.15 added roughly $350,000 to the university's annual operating costs. By the end of the decade the cumulative effect of increased costs for minimum wages, unemployment compensation, and new regulations governing hours and working conditions were equivalent to an additional $250 per year in tuition costs for each student. Tulane *Hullabaloo*, 2 February 1968, p. 9; Longenecker, "Address on the State of the University," spring 1970, p. 5.

the theater in the 1930s but temporarily occupied by the U.S. Navy during World War II.[3]

Lippman developed a curriculum in dramatics that laid the foundation for a separate Department of Theater and Speech, which was created in the early 1940s. In 1947 the department began offering an M.A., and in 1952 added a master of fine arts degree. A critical step toward the theater program's national visibility occurred in 1957, when the university began publishing the *Tulane Drama Review*, a quarterly journal devoted to dramatic criticism, articles on the history of theater and drama, book reviews, and "important plays not otherwise readily obtainable." The launching of a doctoral program in 1958–59 constituted a second major milestone in the theater department's development. A third important change occurred in 1962 when the outspoken Richard Schechner, a former Ph.D. student of Lippman, took over as the *Tulane Drama Review*'s new editor. A fearless social activist who employed tactics of civil disobedience in support of civil rights and in opposition to the Vietnam War, Schechner was equally uncompromising in his editorial efforts to alter the professional landscape of American drama. Something of the flavor of his editorship may be gathered from a lengthy statement of principles and objectives published in the Winter 1963 issue of the *TDR*. Although initially designed to elevate the academic standing of scholarship and criticism in the drama field, the *TDR* had become increasingly committed to "the most ambitious standards and artistically perilous ventures of professional theater." The journal's main concern was not with box-office-oriented "commodity theater," but with the more boldly experimental work of resident professional theater companies scattered across the country. In formulating standards and goals for the new theaters, Schechner sought to emphasize regional decentralization, the open stage, "practical and theoretical experimentation," an "absolute commitment to professional standards," the reintroduction of the playwright into the theater's "life and craft," and a receptivity to international influences apropos of "an age which is learning to dissolve the fear of miscegenation." Among the subjects selected for thematic treatment in future issues of the *TDR* were "'Italian Theater since the War,' 'Christopher Marlowe,' 'Stanislavski in America,' 'Communist Theater Theory,'

---

3. For a useful overview of the Tulane University theater's development, see Bruce W. Eggler, "TUT—The Early Years," Tulane *Hullabaloo*, 31 March 1967, pp. 4, 9.

'New German Theater,' . . . 'Latin American Theater,' and . . . 'The Economics of American Theater.'"[4]

The seventh and final point in Schechner's 1963 manifesto, a commitment to the "redirection of educational theater into the mainstream of American theater," had clear implications for the department's relationship with Tulane. While recognizing that a complete transformation of college theater would require a "concentration of resources and policy" comparable to that of the sciences, and while acknowledging that "[o]nly a very few schools can manage full theater programs," Schechner nonetheless believed that those few should mount an effort that was ambitious and wide-ranging. "The universities must support resident professional companies, provide fully trained personnel to the professional theater, become the proving ground for new playwrights, encourage experimentation, and produce viable scholarship. The truth is that these are all interdependent and the universities had better buy the package or shop in some other store."[5]

Indirectly at least, the conception of educational theater as a comprehensive artistic and intellectual undertaking lay at the heart of the 1966–67 dispute over new physical facilities and increased levels of budgetary support. Schechner's vision was a bold one, and in 1963 his manifesto offered a blueprint for excellence that was in keeping with the optimism of the Tulane environment. From an administrative standpoint the theater department's standing had never been higher. Graduate enrollment had risen steadily, and in January 1964 Arts and Sciences dean William Peery sang the department's praises to President Longenecker. Peery accepted the view of those who praised the *Tulane Drama Review* as the finest journal of its kind in the English language, and went on to argue that at the graduate level, Tulane had "one of the most exciting Departments of Theater and Speech in the United States."[6]

All things considered, the department's hope for a larger budget

4. James E. Llamas, "and the show goes on," *Tulanian* 41 (May 1968): 2–4; *Tulane Drama Review* 2 (November 1957), statement of editorial policy facing title page (first quotation); *Tulane Drama Review* 8 (winter 1963): 9–14, 9 (second–fifth quotations), 10 (seventh quotation), 11 (sixth, eighth–ninth quotations), 13–4 (tenth quotation).

5. *Tulane Drama Review* 8 (winter 1963): 11 (fourth quotation), 12 (first–third quotations).

6. William Peery to Herbert E. Longenecker, 24 January 1964, box 29, HEL Papers (quotation). For additional accolades heaped upon the *Drama Review* by prominent theater figures and drama critics, see Quentin Ault, "The Tulane Drama Review," *Tulanian* 34 (November 1960): 3–4.

Richard Schechner, Professor of Theatre and Speech.
Editor, Tulane Drama Review. *1967.*

and better accommodations was not unreasonable. Since 1960 the theater program had been operating primarily in a renovated building
near Freret Street that had previously housed the Bruff Commons
cafeteria. Now officially designated the Theater and Speech Building,
the old Commons provided classrooms used by several departments
and also contained the Arena Theater, a facility featuring a rectangu-
lar stage surrounded on four sides by tiers of seats that accommodated
an audience of 154 persons. Other productions were staged in a separate structure known as the Phoenix Playhouse. The combined arrangements made Tulane one of only a handful of universities capable of
offering both proscenium and arena (or "theater in the round") training to aspiring actors, but the improvised theaters left much to be desired in terms of seating capacity, layout, and access to facilities for re-
hearsal, set design, and other support activities. In March 1966 a
campus radio editorial declared that pursuing graduate study in the
existing facilities was "like having a track meet on Airline Highway
during rush hour." By this point space limitations had become acute,

forcing the *Tulane Drama Review* to leave the premises and set up operations in the basement of Josephine Louise Dormitory.[7]

During the late 1950s and early 1960s there were ongoing efforts to secure Rockefeller Foundation support for a new theater building. The discussions, President Longenecker would later recall, "had gone nearly to the point of completion of a major capital grant . . . which was in the end not made for reasons related to Tulane's admissions policies." With Rockefeller as with Ford, in other words, the Board of Administrators' reluctance to confront the segregation issue cost Tulane dearly in the early 1960s. Once integration was accomplished and the Ford Foundation gift secured in 1963–64, hope for a new building and a larger budget again burned brightly in the theater department, only to grow dim when two more years elapsed without visible signs of progress.[8]

In May 1966 frustration among theater faculty and students resulted in two letters to the president, one signed by all eight professors in the department and the other by twenty-nine graduate and undergraduate students. Each document detailed the inadequacy of existing physical facilities and emphasized the need for larger production and equipment budgets. At the time these letters were drafted, the Rockefeller Foundation had shifted its focus away from large bricks-and-mortar grants to smaller awards for continuing programs, and Tulane had submitted a theater proposal in keeping with this framework. Again the decision was negative. Professor Schechner, who was personally in contact with Rockefeller officials, attributed the outcome to the university's alleged failure to spell out its long-term plans for and commitment to the department. Foundation officials later denied the accuracy of this explanation, while reaffirming the foundation's long-standing policy of giving assistance "only in terms of a university's statement of objectives" and of not "granting funds to support something a university does not wish to do."[9]

During the autumn of 1966, a series of meetings between Professors Schechner, Hostetler, and Lippman, University Development Office representatives, and the deans of the Graduate School, Arts and Sciences, and Newcomb resulted in the preparation of a report detail-

7. Richard H. Spero, WTUL Editorial, week of 20 March 1966, box 61, HEL Papers.

8. Memorandum of a Visit to Mr. Norman Lloyd of the Rockefeller Foundation, 15 February 1967 (typescript, 20 February 1967), box 29, HEL Papers.

9. Memorandum of Telephone Conversation with Mr. Norman Lloyd of the Rockefeller Foundation, 9 February 1967 (typescript, 20 February 1967), box 29, HEL Papers.

ing theater department needs, plans, and projected costs over the next several years. In its final form the report asked for a new theater building that would include "a proscenium theater to seat approximately 450, a thrust-stage theater of the same audience size, and a flexible experimental theater to seat approximately 100." The proposed facility would also include storage space, studios, classrooms, and offices for the *Tulane Drama Review* and theater faculty. In addition, the department sought a commitment from the university for four new faculty members within the next five years, and increased graduate enrollment to a total of one hundred students in the M.A., M.F.A., and Ph.D. programs. The cost of these enhancements, Lippman acknowledged, was "not inconsiderable."[10]

At a meeting in early November, the theater faculty requested a definite assurance from the university within six weeks that a new theater would be provided, and on December 22, 1966, Schechner, Hostetler, and Lippman met with Longenecker and the three deans seeking "a final decision" about the future of the theater department. The results were not encouraging. Longenecker considered the pressure for an immediate decision unreasonable, and said that if an answer concerning the new theater was required in December, "the decision would have to be a reluctant 'no.'" David R. Deener, who had succeeded John Snell as dean of the Graduate School, was more adamant than reluctant in denying the proposed expansion of graduate enrollment. The entire graduate program, he explained, would soon face "serious financial problems" caused by an impending decrease in federal aid. Under the circumstances, Deener believed that "the best interests of the University will be served by putting the major part of available funds into the 'traditional' disciplines." Here, it seemed, was a definite "no."[11]

The negative outcome was a bitter pill for Lippman, who was about to begin his thirtieth year on the Tulane faculty. In an acerbic account of the December meeting written for theater alumni, Lippman declared that Longenecker arrived without having read the report on departmental needs and proceeded to offer "a continuation of the platitudes to which the years have inured us. . . . [T]he President assured

10. Monroe Lippman, Report to Theater Majors on the Status of the Department, typescript, 6 January 1967, box 29, HEL Papers.

11. Monroe Lippman, "A Report to the Alumni," *TUT TALK: Newsletter of the Tulane University Theatre* (May 1967): 2 (first quotation); Monroe Lippman, Report to Theater Majors on the Status of the Department (all subsequent quotations).

*Monroe Lippman, George Hendrickson, Paul Hostetler,
Professors of Theatre and Speech, ca. 1960.*

us that we would get a theater as soon as possible, that we were 'high' in administrative thinking, that our efforts and accomplishments were fully appreciated, our needs recognized, our problems sympathized with. But a direct question to the President as to when we might antic- ipate having a new theatre—three years, ten years, five years, two years—was met with stony silence."[12]

By this point Lippman and other members of the theater depart- ment had become convinced that the university administration was in- different to the needs of their program, if not actually acting in bad faith. Given the downward spiral of departmental morale, only an eleventh-hour decision to provide new drama facilities could have averted what had become an impending disaster. Early in the new year Longenecker made a final attempt to retrieve the situation through Rockefeller Foundation assistance, requesting a five-year grant of $250,000 for departmental program support and renewing Tulane's

12. Monroe Lippman, "A Report to the Alumni," 2–3.

previous offer to raise $1 million if the foundation would give $500,000 toward a new theater's construction. Once again the request was turned down, with foundation officials pointing to the "uncertainty of leadership in the future from key faculty members around whom a program would need to be built" as one reason for the negative decision.[13]

By 1967 the stage was set for the final act in what some observers had come to regard as the Tulane equivalent of a Greek tragedy. On January 3, Monroe Lippman resigned as department chairman, citing as his reasons Longenecker's "demonstrated lack of genuine concern" and Deener's refusal to support expanded doctoral work in "untraditional" arts disciplines. The following week Paul Hostetler stepped down as executive director of the Tulane University Theater. Several members of the theater faculty had already begun looking openly for new academic appointments, and in the wake of the failed Rockefeller negotiations the dissolution of Tulane's drama program proceeded rapidly. By the end of the semester Professors Lippman, Hostetler, and Schechner, together with Arthur Wagner (head of the professional acting program), Associate Professor James C. Ching, and Assistant Professor Paul A. Distler, had all resigned in order to accept positions at other schools. Lippman and Schechner went to New York University, taking the *Drama Review* with them. The simultaneous departure of six key faculty members and a major national journal signaled the end of a brilliant era in the performance and study of drama at Tulane. In 1967–68 the Ph.D. program in theater was suspended and later abolished, although the M.A. and M.F.A. programs continued. The theater department survived and returned to a predominately undergraduate focus, but from the late 1960s onward it was plagued by chronic internal problems which manifested themselves through exceptionally high rates of faculty turnover.[14]

For all its unique aspects, the theater debacle of 1966–67 was not an isolated event. When the suspension of doctoral work in drama took

13. Memorandum of Telephone Conversation with Mr. Norman Lloyd of the Rockefeller Foundation, 9 February 1967.

14. Monroe Lippman to David R. Deener, 3 January 1967, box 29, HEL Papers (all quotations); Paul S. Hostetler to John H. Stibbs, 10 January 1967, ibid.; James E. Llamas, "and the show goes on," 2–4. Cf. "Theatre Chairman Resigns," Tulane *Hullabaloo*, 13 January 1967, pp. 1–2; "Five Theatre Professors Resign from Department," Tulane *Hullabaloo*, 31 March 1967, pp. 1–2; "'TDR' Moves to NYU," Tulane *Hullabaloo*, 12 May 1967, p. 1; Tulane *Hullabaloo*, 22 April 1977; Monroe Lippman to Joseph E. Gordon, 14 May 1977; James F. Davidson to Robert B. Stevens, 25 April 1977, letters in private possession.

place, Longenecker and the Board of Administrators were poised to reevaluate the entire range of existing graduate programs with a view toward concentrating resources and reducing costs. What began as an aggressive push by the Department of Theater to expand the size of its faculty and graduate program quickly took on a very different significance as the university prepared to pull back from the growth pattern of the early 1960s. Within a few months it became clear that the theater controversy of 1966–67 was, in reality, a prelude to the more general scaling back of Tulane's graduate offerings.

Although the movement to reduce the number of Tulane's Ph.D. programs had the appearance of a sudden thrust toward retrenchment, it actually represented the culmination of administrative concerns and fiscal pressures that had been building throughout the decade. Like other private research universities, Tulane had expanded graduate training sooner and at a level that was proportionately greater than the norm for public institutions. Even when measured against other private research universities in the South, Tulane's graduate program was large in proportion to the available resources. In 1967 the university had an endowment of approximately $56 million and granted the Ph.D. in a total of thirty-three separate fields. Duke, with a $300 million endowment, offered only twenty-six doctoral programs, while Vanderbilt and Emory, with endowments roughly twice the size of Tulane's, also limited themselves to substantially fewer Ph.D. subject areas. The expansion of direct and indirect federal subsidies for graduate study during the early 1960s created a growth psychology that whetted faculty appetites for still higher levels of external support and helped to disguise the underlying fiscal realities that Tulane would face when national funding priorities in higher education began to shift away from the post-Sputnik emphasis of the Kennedy era. Although administrators were not immune to the temptations of what historian Roger L. Geiger has called the "inherent inertia of expansion," those closest to the daily budgetary realities of both the Graduate School and the university as a whole had few illusions about the prospects for sustaining an endlessly upward trajectory of graduate training and research. After only a year or two in Gibson Hall, Longenecker had begun to echo the privately expressed concerns of some Board members about an "overgrowth" of the Graduate School.[15]

15. Book Funds per Doctoral Program in Seven Southern Universities, 1966–67, typescript

From a somewhat different perspective, Graduate School dean John Snell consistently emphasized the need for restraining growth and seeking qualitative improvement within existing programs. In June 1963, only a few months after taking office, Snell confronted the alternatives facing Tulane with characteristic bluntness and candor. While projecting steady growth in aggregate enrollment through the end of the decade, Snell deemed it essential to decide whether annual increases in graduate admissions and in the number of Ph.D.'s awarded should be achieved through "adding new doctoral programs or by building up some of those we already have while holding others down or even eliminating some." Snell's own view of the problem was "unambiguous and . . . based on the belief that we may have over-expanded the number of doctoral programs we now offer so that it now includes several weak programs with no prospect of becoming strong." Snell believed that Tulane could realistically hope to achieve national distinction in six to twelve fields, provided a decision was made to settle for "respectability" in twenty or so other areas where the emphasis would be upon qualitative improvement without numerical growth or additional resources. The dozen weakest doctoral programs seemed ill-suited for even the latter strategy, and Snell favored abandoning at least some of them. "I do not believe that we can hope to provide excellence in *any* field if we spread present and prospective resources equally or even roughly equally over 33 doctoral programs," the dean declared.[16]

In the expansionary environment of the mid-1960s, formidable political obstacles blocked the implementation of any scheme to limit or reduce the scope of Tulane's graduate training. In 1966, however, the graduate faculty approved a six-part resolution, submitted by the Graduate Council at Snell's urging, which called for the evaluation of any proposed new Ph.D. program by two outside consultants, as well as the reevaluation of all existing doctoral programs beginning in 1966–67. It was against this backdrop that the theater department's request for graduate level enhancement met with rejection from Snell's successor, David R. Deener, in late 1966. The theater controversy, in turn, helped to underscore the need for a general reassessment of Tu-

table, box 20, HEL Papers; Tulane *Hullabaloo*, 9 February 1968, p. 1; Geiger, *Research and Relevant Knowledge*, 246 (first quotation); David R. Deener to Herbert E. Longenecker, 5 December 1963, box 35, HEL Papers (second quotation).

16. Graduate School Dean's Report, 1962–63, box 35, HEL Papers, 18 (first–third quotations), 19 (fourth quotation).

lane's budgetary and educational priorities. On August 17 and 18, 1967, the issue was addressed at an informal summit conference in Biloxi, Mississippi, attended by Longenecker, Vice Presidents Clarence Scheps and Fred Cagle, Business Manager Jesse B. Morgan, Joseph E. Gordon (who had become dean of the College of Arts and Sciences following the death of William Peery in 1964), Charles D. Hounshell (who had assumed the deanship of Newcomb College in 1966), and David Deener (who had replaced John Snell as Graduate School dean in mid-1966 after serving as acting dean of Newcomb during the previous academic year).[17]

The agenda at the Biloxi meeting was wide-ranging and included detailed reviews of teaching loads, class size, allocation of resources among various university divisions, and the overall outlook for Tulane finances during the next ten years. Those attending agreed that preserving or enhancing educational quality would require the university to operate more efficiently and to concentrate available resources on fewer educational programs. Among major university divisions, the medical school would receive top priority within any "concentration" program, followed by the College of Arts and Sciences, Newcomb College, and the Graduate School, which were informally grouped together as the "Liberal Arts" division. The Law School was included as a third component deserving of additional support. The conference produced general agreement on the need to limit faculty size and to seek additional cost savings through reducing the number of courses and sections taught while increasing average minimum enrollment. The most important decision to emerge from the Biloxi meeting concerned the Graduate School, where existing or recently suspended Ph.D. programs in classics, German, Italian, geology, music, theater, civil engineering, business administration, social work, and "biometry" (i.e., biostatistics) were singled out for possible elimination.[18]

17. Graduate School Dean's Report, 1963–64, box 35, HEL Papers, 11; Resolution Offered by the Graduate Council for Adoption by the Graduate Faculty, 17 May 1966, typescript accompanying letter of John Snell to Clarence Scheps, 18 May 1966, box 35, HEL Papers. On 3 March 1964, the Graduate Council had approved the use of outside consultants to evaluate proposed Ph.D. programs. Also see, Suggested Agenda, Biloxi meeting of 17–8 August 1967, accompanying Clarence Scheps memorandum to Herbert E. Longenecker, Fred C. Cagle, Jesse B. Morgan, David R. Deener, Joseph E. Gordon, Charles D. Hounshell, 14 August 1967, box 20, HEL Papers.

18. Deener, Gordon, and Hounshell to Longenecker, Resume of Biloxi Meeting, 1 September 1967, box 20, HEL Papers.

The job of translating the Biloxi agreement into official policy fell to Deans Gordon, Hounshell, and Deener. Their collective recommendations for downsizing Tulane's graduate offerings were conveyed to Longenecker on a discipline-by-discipline basis in November 1967, along with reactions from department chairs and professors in the affected programs. The deans' proposals—reducing the number of engineering Ph.D.'s from three to two, while eliminating or suspending indefinitely M.A. programs in German and Slavic languages, together with doctoral programs in geology, German, music, Italian, classical languages, and theatre—followed quite closely the agenda established in August. The stated criteria for evaluating individual graduate programs included the scope of each program's involvement in both the graduate and undergraduate curriculum, its national rating or reputation, and the amount of additional resources that would be necessary to improve the program's comparative standing. Other considerations inevitably entered into what was a politically difficult and unavoidably controversial process. Professor Peter A. Firmin, an eighteen-year veteran of the Tulane faculty and future business school dean, followed the November discussions closely, and was able to deduce the policy goals that lay behind the proposed cuts from the language employed by Scheps and Deener. "Retrenchment," "survival of the successful," "preferred treatment for programs receiving considerable support from sources external to the university," and "suspension or curtailment of [the] most recently inaugurated programs" seemed to embody the informal guidelines being followed in addressing the university's fiscal problems.[19]

The graduate faculty considered the deans' recommendations in mid-November and the following month appointed a nine-member committee chaired by English professor Richard P. Adams to act jointly with a six-member ad hoc subcommittee of the Graduate Council in formulating a response. Working under a presidential deadline of January 20, 1968, the joint committee submitted a memorandum to Longenecker on January 19, noting the lack of prior consultation with

19. Recommendations to suspend or terminate M.A. programs in German and Slavic Languages, together with doctoral programs in geology, German, music, Italian, classical languages, and theater, were contained in letters to Longenecker and Clarence Scheps bearing the signatures of Gordon, Hounshell, and Deener. Five of the letters were dated 8 November and two 15 November 1967. Originals in box 35, HEL Papers. Also see Peter A. Firmin to Herbert E. Longenecker, 1 December 1967, box 35, HEL Papers (all quotations).

the graduate faculty about the proposed cuts and expressing doubt about the "academic soundness" of the deans' recommendations. The committee endorsed a balanced budget but questioned the need to achieve it through reductions that would involve a "heavy cost to Faculty morale." Seeing little evidence that the value of doctoral programs had been adequately weighed against other university activities, the committee believed that "a much better impression would have been made if non-academic programs [a euphemism for intercollegiate athletics] had been cut back as much as possible" before changes in the graduate program were proposed. With no alternate plan to offer, the committee sought a one-year delay in implementing the deans' proposals to allow time for new recommendations to be drafted jointly by the faculty and administration on the basis of a comprehensive academic plan.[20]

The proposal was dead on arrival in the president's office. Fiscal pressures simply did not permit a year's delay. Longenecker had convened the Biloxi summit in an effort to cope with the serious budgetary shortfalls that had plagued the university throughout most of the decade. These shortfalls subsided temporarily in the wake of the 1964 Ford Foundation grant, only to return with even greater severity once the Tulane Forward capital campaign was concluded in 1967. Facing the prospect of an annual operating deficit in excess of $2 million for the 1967–68 academic year, Longenecker was determined to move swiftly to hold down instructional costs and to freeze the Graduate School budget at least temporarily. On January 26, 1968, he sought and received Board approval to implement the deans' recommendations as originally planned. During the next few months Dean Deener proceeded to reallocate vacant faculty positions, student stipends, library funds, and other available resources from the discontinued graduate programs to those which remained intact. As a temporary holding measure the strategy worked, and the Graduate School operated in 1968–69 with a total of twenty-seven Ph.D. programs and a budget that was some $35,000 less than that of the previous year.[21]

20. Richard P. Adams, Frank L. Keller et al. to Herbert E. Longenecker, 19 January 1968, box 35, HEL Papers. The full text of the joint letter was subsequently published in the Tulane *Hullabaloo*, 2 February 1968, p. 9.

21. Tulane University, *Financial Report*, 1967–68, p. 7; Herbert E. Longenecker to David R. Deener, 29 January 1968, box 35, HEL Papers; Graduate School Dean's Report, 1967–68, box 35, HEL Papers, 9.

Occurring at a time of rapidly intensifying student activism at Tulane, the Graduate School retrenchment of 1967–68 was fraught with larger political significance. Several years earlier, in an article on faculty participation in university governance, Richard Adams had described the graduate faculty as "the most fully representative body of the whole University," and had gone on to declare that in matters of curricular change, faculty committees exercised "what amounts to final authority, within the limits of budgetary possibility." Lack of initial faculty involvement in drafting recommendations for cuts in the graduate program, together with Longenecker's summary rejection of the joint graduate faculty/Graduate Council moratorium proposal, appeared to cast doubt on the finality of faculty authority in curricular matters. And as Tulane's fiscal situation worsened over the next few years, the seemingly innocuous reference to the "limits of budgetary possibility" in Adams's earlier essay took on decidedly Malthusian overtones. At the height of the theater controversy in 1967, political scientist Henry Mason offered a succinct formulation of an operating principle that faculty in many academic disciplines would soon come to share. "[I]t's a zero-sum game today, where one department's gain is another department's loss," Mason observed in an interview some six months prior to the Biloxi summit.[22]

The events of 1966–68 marked the beginning of an institutional crisis of confidence for Tulane that was reflected in a pattern of declining morale and growing alienation among faculty on the uptown campus. Initial reactions to retrenchment were often shaped by calculations of departmental interest or concern over the changing balance of power in relations between the faculty and central administration. But larger issues were also at stake. In the minds of many faculty members, the fundamental question posed by the fiscal crisis of the late 1960s was whether Tulane could or would continue to measure itself against the exacting standards of its more affluent peers in the ranks of American research universities. Public speculation about the university's future began during the theater controversy, when Professors Henry Mason, Richard Adams, Paul Hostetler, and L. Matthew N. Bach (who taught in the physiology department) appeared before the Liberals Club in March 1967 to discuss the topic, "Is Tulane in academic and financial

22. Richard P. Adams, "Tulane University: Faculty Participation in the Government of the University," *AAUP Bulletin* 49 (September 1963): 221–5, 223 (first–third quotations); Tulane *Hullabaloo*, 10 February 1967, p. 2 (fourth quotation).

decline?" The professors' answers ranged from "[a] cautious 'yes'" to the somewhat ambiguous assurance that Tulane was not yet "in ashes." Writing privately a few months later, Graduate School dean (and newly appointed provost) Deener told President Longenecker that the "vision of Tulane as an institution striving for scholarly excellence is not dead although it may be fading." Deener urged the president to launch a long-term campaign to raise $50 million in additional endowment for the support of graduate programs. "Otherwise," he predicted, "we will find our faculty being ground to bits, as the press of outside offers, internal frustration and insecurities, and the increasing amount of time and effort that has to be devoted to obtaining bits and pieces of money from this source, that source, and the other take their inevitable toll."[23]

II

There can be little doubt that a sudden doubling of Tulane's endowment in the late 1960s would have bolstered the morale of faculty and administrators alike. But without the stimulus of another multimillion-dollar challenge grant from a major philanthropy, the prospects for such a development were remote at best. A large Ford Foundation grant was no longer a possibility. Instead of a major capital campaign for graduate education, the 1968–69 academic year brought a new round of controversy over the festering problem of intercollegiate athletics. Played out against the backdrop of Board willingness to write off major cash deficits for athletics in the midst of Ph.D. cutbacks, the conflict was triggered by a heavy-handed move to reinstitute an undergraduate major in physical education over the objections of the Arts and Sciences and Newcomb faculties.[24]

Pressure for a relaxation of academic requirements in the interest of athletic recruitment and retention was hardly a new development at

23. Henry Kline, "Four Professors Discuss 'Decline' of the University," Tulane *Hullabaloo*, 17 March 1967, pp. 4 (first–third quotations), 16; David R. Deener to Herbert E. Longenecker, 10 January 1968, box 35, HEL Papers (fourth–sixth quotations).

24. Geiger, *Research and Relevant Knowledge*, 115. As Geiger notes, "The decision not to renew the [Ford] Challenge Grants Program was one increment in the gradual withdrawal of Foundation patronage from the specific commitment of strengthening private research universities."

Tulane. Football supporters on and off the Board of Administrators had hoped the Teacher-Coach option of 1959–67 would provide an escape hatch for academically marginal athletes, and had blamed the uptown faculty for obstructing the proper working of the system. The push for an outright return to the P.E. major (which had been eliminated under President Harris in the mid-1950s) seems to have begun in 1966 following the resignation of head football coach Tommy O'Boyle and the arrival of his successor Jim Pittman. To some extent the P.E. initiative may have been viewed as a gesture necessary to offset negative alumni response following Tulane's withdrawal from the SEC. By 1968 the university was beginning its second year without conference affiliation, and alumni who participated in a campuswide self-study for reaccreditation purposes that year recommended a reevaluation of admissions and curricular policies affecting athletes. Events soon revealed that significant support for a new P.E. major existed in the ranks of the President's Athletic Advisory Committee, as well as among football supporters on the Board.

In October 1968 specific proposals materialized when athletic director Rix N. Yard sent Longenecker a report entitled, "An Assessment of the Athletic Program *As Requested by the Board of Administrators*" (emphasis in original). Yard argued that Tulane should "take the steps necessary to provide the climate in which a successful team may operate," a climate distinguished by "an academic program that would enable the marginal student to have a fair chance to succeed." The program began with the creation of a physical education major in which the foreign language requirement was waived, a practice already followed in the Teacher-Coach Program and in the bachelor of business studies degree offered by University College. The P.E. major might be established in either the Center for Teacher Education or in University College. Yard believed that the Arts and Sciences faculty "would not be as upset" if University College housed the program, and he proposed a rules change that would allow athletes to be admitted directly to the evening division as full-time students. In early November a set of three proposals from the Athletic Advisory Committee came before various faculty committees, with an admonition from the University Senate that "decisions on such sensitive subjects as academic programs for athletes must involve not only the Senate and its Committee on Educational Policy, but also the faculties of all undergraduate schools and other affected schools," because "curricular matters . . .

anywhere in the University are primarily the responsibility of the faculty." Although the proposals did not specifically mention a P.E. major, they embodied the substance of Yard's October proposals and also called for his appointment as a tenured professor of physical education in the College of Arts and Sciences, from which he would serve as University Chairman of Physical Education and head a proposed Department of Physical Education to be established in either the Center for Teacher Education or University College. (The creation of a department obviously implied the creation of a major.)[25]

The de facto floor leader on behalf of the proposals was Professor Hugh F. Rankin, a member of the Athletic Advisory Committee and a prolific scholar in American colonial history who had played semiprofessional football before attending graduate school at the University of North Carolina. In separate presentations to the University Senate on November 12 and to the faculty of Arts and Sciences on November 19, Rankin employed identical language to defend proposals that he knew many of his colleagues would oppose. Having previously believed the Teacher-Coach Program could produce athletic success, Rankin had "now grown weary of losing money and football games." His assessment of the inherent conflict between maintaining high academic standards and achieving a winning football record was candid. "Under the present system," Rankin noted, "we have some good, even excellent, football players, but we do not have enough. Those we need are usually referred to as the 'blue chips' or 'studs.' These athletes are not attracted to Tulane when we have only liberal arts and engineering to offer them. At one time it was said of a school some ninety miles up the river (which shall remain nameless), that the best recruiting aid they had was the Tulane catalogue. The players recruited under a proper program are those who can win games."[26]

With equal candor Rankin went on to argue that, "from a practical standpoint," physical education belonged in University College, where flexible admission standards would allow acceptance of athletes whose high school grades and test scores indicated that they would achieve a college average of 1.6 (i.e., a D average)—the minimum requirement

25. Rix N. Yard to Herbert E. Longenecker, 28 October 1968, box 50, HEL Papers (first–fourth quotations); Resolution Adopted by the Athletic Advisory Committee, 4 November 1968, box 50, HEL Papers; Resolution Adopted by the University Senate, 4 November 1968, box 50, HEL Papers (fifth–sixth quotations).

26. College of Arts and Sciences Faculty Minutes, 19 November 1968, box 29, HEL Papers.

imposed by the NCAA. If a physical education department facilitated the admission of athletic "studs," the proposal to admit full-time students to the bachelor of business studies program in University College would "open the door a bit wider" by compensating for the absence of an undergraduate curriculum in Tulane's business school. Although the B.B.S. program lacked accreditation, the issue could be dismissed as irrelevant to the career plans of those who were likely to enroll. Rankin was convinced that, despite competition from New Orleans' professional Saints franchise, Tulane's football attendance and the accompanying revenue would increase significantly if the university produced winning teams. He asked the faculty to give the program a five-year trial, with the understanding that lack of success would constitute grounds for seriously considering the abandonment of football.[27]

Despite Rankin's high standing among his academic colleagues, the A&S faculty rejected the Athletic Advisory Committee's proposals by a lopsided vote of 69-26, and instead adopted a motion by historian William Griffith declaring "that an order of priority that places football ahead of academic programs would not be acceptable." But the gesture was a futile one. A week later the University Senate met in special session to consider the establishment of a physical education major in University College. The senate's own Committee on Educational Policy opposed the plan, as did the delegates from Arts and Sciences and from Newcomb College, which had rejected the previous week's proposals by a vote of 29-23. Representatives from the School of Engineering and University College (which had no permanent full-time faculty) reported overwhelming support for the P.E. major in their schools. After heated debate and several counterproposals from angry A&S and Newcomb delegates, the University Senate approved the new degree program by a vote of 29-3. On the following day the senate's action was ratified at a special meeting of the Executive Committee of the Tulane Board.[28]

For those who had supported the vigorous assertion of academic over athletic values during the previous decade—a judgment seemingly reaffirmed by Tulane's withdrawal from the SEC—the 1968 decision to

27. Ibid.

28. Ibid. (quotation); University Senate Minutes, 26 November 1968, box 73, HEL Papers; Minutes of the Executive Committee of the Administrators of the Tulane Educational Fund, 27 November 1968, box 50, HEL Papers; Tulane *Hullabaloo*, 22 November 1968, p. 1; ibid., 6 December 1968, p. 1.

restore the P.E. major looked like a serious step backward. Philosophy professor Edward G. Ballard spoke for many disgruntled colleagues when he condemned both the cultural and academic implications of what he interpreted as an effort to restore "semi-professional football . . . to something like the place it held before 1951." For Ballard, the combination of a shrinking graduate program and an expanding football squad conjured up visions of a "Joe-college, rah-rah atmosphere" that was at odds with the "greater seriousness and maturity . . . displayed in recent years by our student body." In a similar, if less temperate, vein, the student newspaper saw the whirlwind campaign for a P.E. major as evidence that "a crepe paper and chicken wire mentality" had triumphed through a process in which faculty opinion was "arbitrarily ignored" and student sentiment "humiliatingly overlooked." Those responsible for the outcome were the Board of Administrators ("a group of willful and provincial old men") who together with "their lackey deans and University Senators" had "opted for a winning team and a losing education."[29]

Such comments suggest how the academic and budgetary decisions of the post-1965 period polarized campus politics in a manner that aligned alienated professors with dissident students in common opposition to the central administration. It was significant, for example, that some forty student and faculty demonstrators gathered outside the Norman Mayer Building to protest the P.E. major, which the University Senate was discussing inside. The rally had been called by the Tulane chapter of Students for a Democratic Society and was attended by mathematics professor Edward Dubinsky, the SDS faculty adviser, together with several colleagues, including an assistant professor of anthropology who dismissed intercollegiate football as the outgrowth of a Victorian "saltpeter complex" that prescribed "a hardy game of football, a cold shower, and a dose of saltpeter . . . to take the emphasis away from sexual impulses." By national standards Tulane in 1968 was, and would remain, a relatively conservative school. Within the context of its own past, however, the university had entered upon a decidedly radical phase unlike anything it had experienced since the early 1930s. From roughly 1967–70, both the bureaucratic mechanisms of university governance and the moral assumptions un-

29. Edward G. Ballard, "An Athletic Reinstitution," Tulane *Hullabaloo*, 6 December 1968, clipping, box 50, HEL Papers (first–third quotations); "P.E.—A Condemnation," Tulane *Hullabaloo*, 6 December 1968, clipping, box 50, HEL Papers (fourth–ninth quotations).

dergirding the basic pattern of Tulane's postwar development were destined to receive a series of short, sharp, shocks that would subside as quickly as they had begun, leaving the university outwardly untouched but inwardly altered for a generation to come.[30]

III

If history were a simple matter of social seismology, the rumblings of dissent at Tulane in the late 1960s might be dismissed as aftershocks, or secondary tremors, produced by more violent upheavals at elite universities in California, Wisconsin, and the East Coast. But while early and widely publicized episodes of student protest unquestionably set precedents for subsequent occurrences elsewhere, the student movement of the late 1960s was always a local as well as a national phenomenon, shaped by the unique histories and social characteristics of particular schools and locales. At Tulane the emergence of student dissent was a gradual process, which began with the sit-in activities conducted by New Orleans CORE members during the desegregation lawsuit of 1961–62 and continued through a series of less dramatic skirmishes with bureaucratic authority over the next several years before culminating in what the beleaguered Dean of Students John Stibbs would later characterize as the university's "Time of Troubles" between 1967 and 1970. Understandably, perhaps, the battle-scarred dean tended to stress the influence of external events and the role played by individual students and faculty members in undermining Tulane's devotion to traditional collegiate norms. What Stibbs refused to concede was the likelihood that challenges to institutional authority in the late 1960s built upon, and in many ways grew out of, what preceded them during the outwardly tranquil times at the beginning of the decade.[31]

Although the integration of Tulane and the ouster of whites from the

30. Tulane *Hullabaloo*, 6 December 1968 (all quotations). A smaller SDS demonstration had also taken place outside the A&S faculty meeting which rejected the Rankin proposals.

31. Stibbs, "Twenty-Five Years of Student Life at Tulane University [1949–75]," 37 (quotation). For an excellent discussion of the importance of institutional differences in shaping the character of antiwar protest at public universities in Michigan, Pennsylvania, Ohio, and New York, see Kenneth J. Heineman, *Campus Wars: The Peace Movement at American State Universities in the Viet Nam Era* (New York: New York University Press, 1993).

local CORE organization checked the development of civil rights activism among students of the early 1960s, the theater department's Richard Schechner continued to lead marches and demonstrations against segregation in New Orleans during the year or so after Tulane had ended its racial restrictions. In 1963, civil rights activity in the city focused on the issues of jobs for blacks and the desegregation of City Hall, where the cafeteria still refused to serve black customers. Prolonged and largely fruitless negotiations between a group of business leaders—including Darwin Fenner and a citizens' committee representing all major civil rights organizations—eventually prompted a renewal of demonstrations in the fall. In October, Schechner led a group of some thirty Tulane students and several faculty spouses to join a larger protest march at Shakespeare Park. The next month Schechner was one of five Tulanians arrested for taking part in sit-in activities at the mayor's office and the city hall cafeteria.[32]

The incidents were minor footnotes to the history of local desegregation efforts, but they had a symbolic meaning that would not have been lost upon politically perceptive faculty and graduate students. Although Tulane played no official role in the 1963 negotiations, the city's gradualist strategy of incremental concession owed much to the influence of what young activists in the South had already come to call the "white power structure," the New Orleans version of which included such men as Richard Freeman, Ashton Phelps, Clifford Favrot, and Darwin Fenner—leading business figures to whom the pragmatic Mayor Victor Schiro looked for guidance in matters of racial policy. The four Tulane Board members were acutely conscious of the economic and public relations damage to the city that would accompany any renewal of segregationist violence or civil disorder. Fenner, in particular, remained adamantly opposed to mass demonstrations and threatened to withdraw from behind-the-scenes negotiations if the tactic was employed. By participating in the marches and sit-ins of late 1963 and encouraging other Tulanians to do likewise, Schechner thus placed himself in tacit opposition to several of the university's most influential Administrators. His acts were not so much a challenge as a testing of limits. By elevating civil liberty and moral conviction above

32. *New Orleans Times-Picayune*, 6 November 1963, clipping, box 7, HEL Papers; Tulane *Hullabaloo*, 4 October 1963, p. 1; ibid., 28 February 1964, p. 10; Arthur J. Chapital to Herbert E. Longenecker 7 October 1963, box 7, HEL Papers; Lolis E. Elie et al., Petition to the Greater New Orleans Community, box 7, HEL Papers.

the ideal of faculty cooperation that Board members often invoked, the young *Drama Review* editor's actions helped enlarge the scope of legitimate protest for campus activists in the years ahead.[33]

Apart from sporadic concern with continued segregation in business establishments near the university, the mid-1960s witnessed relatively little civil rights activity involving Tulane students and faculty. Episodes such as the picketing of Phillips Pizza restaurant after the proprietor refused to serve a racially mixed group in 1964 were noteworthy primarily because of the involvement of Liberals Club members Bruce Krueger and Cathy Cade, a future SDS leader, whose presence served to connect civil rights activism to other emerging campus issues such as free speech and the regulation of student conduct. From the standpoint of its impact on later protest activity, the civil rights struggle was a catalyst that helped initiate a more complex set of changes by drawing attention to issues of civil liberty, moral authority, individual responsibility, and the distribution of power within established institutions. Although few Tulane students actually joined the CORE activists of 1961–62, the group's actions in distributing unauthorized literature on campus, staging demonstrations in the University Center cafeteria, and inviting black guests to dormitory rooms had clear relevance to contemporary disputes over campus newspaper censorship, the right to hear controversial speakers, and the regulation of visiting practices in residence halls. In the idiom of the time, these issues formed part of a larger internal dialogue—or mild tug of war—over the university's traditional mandate to act in loco parentis (in the place of a parent) when establishing rules of conduct for students who were not yet legally adults.[34]

Long before the phrase "student power" was employed or its meaning defined at Tulane, the preconditions for a challenge to bureau-

---

33. Adam Fairclough, *Race and Democracy: The Civil Rights Struggle in Louisiana, 1915–1972* (Athens: University of Georgia Press, 1995), 281–2, 336–8.

34. Tulane *Hullabaloo*, 10 December 1964, pp. 1, 3; ibid., 17 December 1964, p. 1. Earlier in the year the University Senate Committee on Student Affairs asked Dean Stibbs to contact businesses near the campus concerning their attitude toward "the admission of negro [*sic*] students to their establishments." Stibbs reported that "[t]hey could not accept the idea that negroes [*sic*] must have the things they offer in their establishments." He felt, however, that "nothing more should be done at this time." During the 1965–66 academic year the Student Senate pressed for integration of restaurants and stores near the campus. By this point, of course, discrimination in public accommodations had been prohibited by the Civil Rights Act of 1964. University Senate Committee on Student Affairs, Report to the University Senate, 1963–64, box 99, HEL Papers; Stibbs, "Twenty-Five Years of Student Life at Tulane University [1949–75],"

cratic authority were established through the in loco parentis skir-mishes of the first half of the 1960s. In some cases the cause and effect relationship was quite direct. Issues of newspaper regulation and cen-sorship, which touched off the first large-scale demonstrations of uni-versity students in 1968, had their roots in unresolved controversies earlier in the decade. Conservative editorial control of the *Hullabaloo* at the beginning of Longenecker's presidency led to the creation of the *Reed*, a politically left of center mimeographed publication by grad-uate students and faculty that appeared irregularly between 1961 and 1964 (after being initially suspended while its backers secured official university sanction). Negative community reaction to the *Hullabaloo*'s publication of a 1961 column on "Sex in College" and a 1962 editorial critical of the medical profession resulted the next year in the creation of a formal editorial board, plus a separate editorial advisory commit-tee that allowed the paper's faculty adviser to veto objectionable mate-rial. A step toward professional supervision occurred in 1962 when Tulane secured the part-time services of Pulitzer Prize–winning jour-nalist Hodding Carter to act as writer-in-residence and publications adviser for the paper, a relationship that would end some five years later in renewed disputes over student editorial freedom.[35]

Debates over the role and authority of student government consti-tuted a second area of direct linkage between campus issues of the early and late 1960s. In October 1962 the *Hullabaloo* carried an un-usually assertive editorial entitled, "Student Council Policy: Rights for Students or 'In Loco Parentis'?" Aimed partly at Dean Stibbs, the editorial focused on the lack of substance beneath the external forms of student government. It pointed out that as an advisory body deriv-ing its power from the University Senate, the Student Council did not so much govern students as provide a kind of grievance committee for bringing student concerns to the attention of the dean. "When students want to do something," the *Hullabaloo* complained, "Dean Stibbs says[,] 'There isn't a thing you can't talk about.' The implication is that you had better not do anything about what you discuss." The campus editor found little merit in Stibbs's definition of student gov-

35. BOA Minutes, 10 May 1961; Tulane *Hullabaloo*, 27 October and 10 November 1961, 21 September 1962; BOA Minutes, 13 December 1961, 13 February and 23 May 1963; R. Gordon Holcombe to Herbert E. Longenecker, 22 January 1963, box 61, HEL Papers; Longenecker to Holcombe, 8 February 1963, box 61, HEL Papers; Hodding Carter to Joseph E. Gordon, 13 May 1966, box 61, HEL Papers.

ernment as a "training ground for citizenship," a view which seemed to imply that "you need your parent, the University, to protect you from the cruel world and teach you to govern yourself." In retrospect, the 1962 editorial can be read both as a call for increased undergraduate autonomy and as an early formulation of the argument that normal bureaucratic mechanisms of self-government served the ends of administrators rather than those of students.[36]

Although the early controversies surrounding student government and control of campus journalism were not overtly political in nature, quite the opposite was true of contemporary conflicts over university sanction of outside speakers. In the early 1960s a militantly conservative local women's group known as "Discussions Unlimited" arranged through the Young Conservatives Club, a campus organization, to use McAlister Auditorium on two separate occasions for speeches by William F. Buckley Jr. and U.S. Senator J. Strom Thurmond. Both events provoked disorder in the building, and Thurmond's speech was accompanied by minor physical altercations. In the wake of these episodes the university revised its policies on the use of campus facilities by student-sponsored speakers. More or less simultaneously, in February 1962 the University Senate Committee on Student Affairs denied the Young Conservatives' request to hold a debate between political scientist Herbert Jacob and conservative commentator Fulton Lewis III on the subject of the House Un-American Activities Committee. The decision prompted Professor Richard Adams, a political liberal, to offer a senate resolution declaring that "intellectual debate at this university should not be stifled, rationed, or censored." In the end the matter was referred back to the student affairs committee, where it remained until October 2, 1962, when the Liberals Club tried unsuccessfully to gain permission from the senate's major events subcommittee to cosponsor a campus appearance by folk singer Pete Seeger. Undeterred by the refusal, the students returned on November 13 to seek permission to invite socialist Michael Harrington and historian Herbert Aptheker, a longtime member of the American Communist Party, to speak at Tulane. The committee approved Harrington (although his proposed talk in the University Center did not constitute a "major event") but vetoed the request for Aptheker to speak in McAlister Auditorium "because of the delicate position in which the

36. Tulane *Hullabaloo*, 5 October 1962, p. 2.

University finds itself in the community at the present time." The decision drew an immediate protest from Liberals Club members who had been leaders in the cafeteria sit-ins a few months earlier, thereby revealing the link between civil rights activism and other campus issues. Editorializing early in 1963, the *Hullabaloo* reduced the issue to a single key question: "[S]hould students control student activities or should the control rest in the hands of the faculty and the administration?"[37]

A subtheme emerging from disputes over in loco parentis doctrine during the first half of the 1960s was the idea that being liberal was tantamount to being pro-student. But as the university's response to pressures for less restrictive housing policies revealed, the time had not yet arrived when being pro-student automatically meant being anti-administration. In the debate over in loco parentis, parietals became a subject of particular concern for both college students and their parents. And the contradictory pressures exerted by each group placed university officials in the middle of a contest that pitted adolescent hormones against the anxieties of checkbook-wielding adults. In the end, hormones and the sheer force of unrelenting pressure close at hand helped tip the scales in the students' favor. During the 1963–64 academic year, requests from the university's various dormitory House Councils and the Newcomb and A&S student government organizations led the University Senate Committee on Student Affairs to authorize open house periods, including visits to individual student rooms, in men's and women's residences on Sunday afternoons between 2:00 and 6:00 P.M. The concession was a relatively modest one that might have gone largely unnoticed by outsiders, had not a *Newsweek* article announcing "The Morals Revolution on the U.S. Campus" appeared shortly after the policy took effect. The alarmist piece sent shock waves through the Newcomb Alumnae Association and prompted an organized letter writing campaign by the ad hoc group "Citizens for Student Welfare," whose supporters deluged the Board of Administrators with protests from alumni and concerned parents. Virtually all those writing drew explicit analogies between the college dormitory

37. Ibid., 1 December 1961, p. 2; Rufus C. Harris to Henry Mason, 11 May 1961, box 24, RCH Papers; John H. Stibbs to Leonard Oppenheim, 3 January 1962, box 99, HEL Papers; Oppenheim to Stibbs, 20 February 1962, box 99, HEL Papers; BOA Minutes, 13 June 1962 and 23 May 1963; Policies and Procedures in the Use of University Meeting Facilities, 14 February 1963, box 99, HEL Papers; University Senate Minutes, 5 February 1962, box 87, HEL Papers (first quotation); Tulane *Hullabaloo*, 11 January 1963, p. 2 (second–third quotations); ibid., 18 January 1963.

and the family home, and insisted that Tulane prohibit opposite sex visitations to "bedrooms."[38]

Although the number of protest letters—at least 116 within roughly a one-month period—vastly exceeded the response to any single episode in the desegregation struggle, university officials refused to assume the mantle of surrogate parent. Staunchly defending the new policy in an April 1964 speech to the Louisiana Academy of Religion and Mental Health, Stibbs called for "increased freedom with [an] accent on responsibility," and assured doubters that "the high seriousness of our students today implies that they are capable of assuming greater responsibilities for their own conduct, sexual or otherwise."[39] Momentarily, at least, students and administrators occupied common ground, but the rhetoric was somewhat misleading. At colleges throughout America, a gradual retreat from arbitrary moral supervision took place during the early and mid-1960s. But rather than reflecting a groundswell of confidence in student maturity, liberalized policies tended to mirror the changing legal climate created by the extension of due process rights to students as a result of court cases arising from the sit-in movement, together with an ongoing legal and philosophical assault on in loco parentis doctrines by groups such as the United States National Student Association (NSA) and the ACLU.[40]

It was the underlying connection between housing regulations and

38. University Senate Committee on Student Affairs, Report to the University Senate, 1963–64, box 99, HEL Papers; Harriet Bobo and Tucker Couvillon, "Tulane–Newcomb Open Houses," [undated, 1964], box 61, HEL Papers; "The Morals Revolution on the U.S. Campus," *Newsweek*, 6 April 1964, pp. 52–9; Stibbs, "Twenty-Five Years of Student Life at Tulane University [1949–75]," 28.

39. John H. Stibbs, "Address before the Louisiana Academy of Religion and Mental Health," 28 April 1964, box 61, HEL Papers (first–second quotations); Alan Katz, "Enforced Morality Held Unwise," *New Orleans States-Item*, 29 April 1964, clipping, box 61, HEL Papers. The 116 figure refers to the number of letters and communications in "Protests" folder, box 61, HEL Papers.

40. Neal Johnston, "An Examination of the Theory of In Loco Parentis," introductory working papers, conference no. 5, session no. 2, 14th National Student Congress, United States National Student Association, box 99, HEL Papers; "In Loco Parentis": Statement of Fact, Principle, and Declaration adopted by 14th National Student Congress, United States National Student Association, box 99, HEL Papers; Dorothy Dunbar Bromley and Susan McCabe, "Impact of the Sit-In Movement on Academic Freedom," box 99, HEL Papers; Martin Levine, "Private Government on the Campus—Judicial Review of University Expulsions," *Yale Law Journal* 72 (June 1963): 1362–96; William T. McCay Jr., "Student Protest and Discipline at Private Institutions" (paper delivered at conference on Student Protest and the Law, University of Georgia Institute of Higher Education, 24 June 1970), box 67a, HEL Papers; Edmund McIlhenny to John H. Stibbs, 15 November 1963, box 99, HEL Papers.

other aspects of student protest that gave significance to what was otherwise little more than an expedient institutional withdrawal from the enforcement of legally problematic and culturally outmoded restrictions on personal conduct. An early demonstration of the manner in which disputes over housing rules could be politicized and linked to larger external issues took place during the 1965–66 academic year, when three Newcomb freshmen attacked the existing House Council system in a mimeographed flyer entitled, "Women Strike for Rights." The proto-feminist vocabulary of the document, with its emphasis on the "Lie of Custodianism" and the "Lie of Immaturity," breathed the spirit of the emerging student Left. And while the authors' allegations that House Council officers exercised power illegally were easily brushed aside, other issues raised by the freshmen critics—including the double standard surrounding curfews and conduct rules for women and men, as well as the requirement of self-accusation in disciplinary proceedings—struck at the weaknesses of a social policing system that would soon find itself under siege. As on prior occasions, moreover, civil rights became linked to the attack on in loco parentis when Susan Jennings, one of the dissenting freshmen, received a racist postcard after participating in the initial stage of sorority rush in company with two black students from New Orleans. Occurring several years before the advent of feminist consciousness-raising groups, these episodes nevertheless suggested that problems traditionally regarded as strictly personal in nature might also have a political dimension.[41]

There were other indications in 1965–66 that the tenor of student attitudes was beginning to change. The previous year had seen an initially minor dispute over free speech at the Berkeley campus of the University of California expand into a widely publicized student revolt against the bureaucratic, impersonal "multiversity" or "knowledge factory" that former Berkeley chancellor Clark Kerr had described in his 1963 volume, *The Uses of the University.* In the fall of 1965, as the College of Arts and Sciences was experimenting with its first tentative system of student course evaluation, *Hullabaloo* editorials questioned the quality of the undergraduate learning experience at Tulane and wondered out loud whether problems of curricular rigidity and bureaucratic stasis would be addressed "before the Berkeley boiling point is reached." At its first meeting of the year, the Liberals Club

41. Tulane *Hullabaloo*, 13 January 1966, p. 1 (quotations), 5; ibid., 9 December 1965, p. 1.

treated prospective members to a rancorous internecine debate over whether the group should remain "campus oriented" or focus on issues outside the university. Sociology graduate student and future SDS leader Cathy Cade pressed for the latter option, while the chairman insisted that the club's members were "not a bunch of radicals, nor were they 'fighting' the administration." Within a year the organization would be moribund.[42]

Black enrollment at Tulane had been slowly increasing, and with more nonwhite undergraduates on campus, initial patterns of minority deference began to recede. Sophomore sociology major Edwin Lombard, the younger brother of former national CORE vice chairman Rudolph J. "Rudy" Lombard, helped usher in a new era of assertiveness by arguing that black students as a group should be allowed to cancel meal contracts at Bruff Commons since they were excluded from Tulane's all-white social fraternities, the only groups with special permission to take meals off campus. Lombard also helped found the "Deacons-on-Campus," a bureaucratically unsanctioned black student group whose name was apparently inspired by the militant Deacons for Defense and Justice, a paramilitary organization created by blacks in Jonesboro, Louisiana, in 1964 to counter the threat of armed attacks by the Ku Klux Klan. By the time Lombard's campus group adopted the name in late 1965 or early 1966, the Bogalusa chapter of the Deacons had gained national attention for its armed protection of CORE workers seeking to desegregate local businesses. Tulane's more physically secure Deacons ran a mock ticket in the spring 1966 Student Council elections with a facetious platform calling for "free love," a "4-man world dictatorship," the abolition of student government, and "the burning of Bruff Commons."[43]

The Bruff plank was an indirect slap at the campus Greek system, which had proved less than hospitable to black students. In November 1965, following a front-page *Hullabaloo* story documenting the disillusioning experiences of six black students who had attempted to participate in fraternity rush, the University Senate Committee on Student Affairs directed the Tulane and Newcomb Pan-Hellenic Councils to conduct self-studies describing their purposes and functions and ex-

42. Ibid., 14 January 1965, pp. 1, 3; 22 April 1965, p. 8; 30 September 1965, pp. 8 ("boiling point" quotation), 13 (all subsequent quotations).

43. Fairclough, *Race and Democracy*, 342–3, 357–60; Tulane *Hullabaloo*, 11 November 1965, p. 1; ibid., 21 April 1966, p. 15 (quotations).

plaining "their value to the University, to the students not in fraternities, and . . . to the fraternity members themselves." Eliminating discriminatory clauses in fraternity charters seems to have been the principal result of the committee's directive, which incorporated Professor Henry Mason's admonition that fraternities "make up their minds whether they should be a part of Tulane University or not." In the spring of 1966 the men's Pan-Hellenic Council announced that "written restrictive clauses have been either abolished or waived," and submitted a policy statement endorsing the principle of selection on the basis of individual merit, but also declaring that "social discrimination is not subject to legislation" and defending each fraternity's right to "[s]elf-determination in the selection of members." Not surprisingly, most black students seemed unimpressed. Deploring "country-club divisions" within the Tulane community, the *Hullabaloo* printed a "segregated" issue that was divided into separate Negro, white, and Jewish sections.[44]

United States military involvement in Vietnam was the last major item added to the agenda of student concerns at Tulane in 1965–66. The 1964 Presidential election had seen Lyndon Johnson win a landslide victory over Barry Goldwater by running as something close to a peace candidate, an incumbent commander in chief who assured voters, "We don't want our American boys to do the fighting for Asian boys." Military escalation began a few months after the election, with extensive bombing of North Vietnam in Operation Rolling Thunder and the arrival of the first officially acknowledged U.S. combat troops in Vietnam in March 1965. By April, U.S. ground troops had begun offensive operations. At the end of 1964 just over 23,000 American military personnel were in Vietnam; one year later, troop strength had surpassed 184,000 and continued to rise. More than six hundred U.S. soldiers had already been killed in action. These developments gave the Vietnam situation—now a de facto American war—a new importance on college campuses throughout America. Antiwar sentiment found expression through the first "teach-in" at the University of Michigan in March 1965, followed by a series of similar campus forums

44. "Tulane Fraternities Fail Integration Test," Tulane *Hullabaloo*, 21 October 1965, p. 1; Minutes of the University Senate Committee on Student Affairs, 3 November 1965, box 61, HEL Papers (first–second quotations); Tulane Pan-Hellenic Council, A Study of Tulane Fraternities, 16 March 1966, box 61, HEL Papers (third–fifth quotations); Tulane *Hullabaloo*, 21 April 1966, pp. 1, 4 (sixth quotation).

staged nationally in May. Between these dates the national SDS organization held its first antiwar rally in Washington, D.C.[45]

In the American South, pro-military sentiment was initially strong on most campuses and Tulane was no exception. In November 1965 political science professors Henry Mason and Warren Roberts sponsored a petition supporting American involvement in Vietnam, which garnered some 3,500 signatures from Tulane students, faculty, and staff over a four-day period. Besides offering a general endorsement of U.S. policy, the petition made specific acknowledgment of "the invaluable services being rendered by the United States military in the Vietnam area." The Mason and Roberts petition was symptomatic of the rapid hardening of political lines that accompanied the Americanization of the Vietnam conflict. A perceptive student columnist in the *Hullabaloo* grasped the point clearly in late December when he warned that the upsurge of patriotic support for American troops threatened to render antiwar dissent politically illegitimate and thus create an atmosphere in which polemics would replace reasoned argument. Perhaps hoping to stave off such a development, the Liberals Club, with Mason's support, sponsored an all-night debate on Vietnam (originally characterized as a "Teach-in") featuring four separate panels of supporters and critics of U.S. actions. Among those defending American policy at the February 1966 event were John Piercy of the U.S. State Department, Edward Butler of the Information Council of the Americas (a local anti-Communist group), attorney David Treen (a future Republican governor of Louisiana), and Mason himself. Opponents of the war included local CORE leader Oretha Castle, Cornell political scientist George Kahin, Nancy Gitlin of the national SDS, David McReynolds of the War Resisters League, and Richard Schechner of Tulane.[46]

Beginning in McAlister Auditorium and continuing in several rooms

45. Allen J. Matusow, *The Unraveling of America: A History of Liberalism in the 1960s* (New York: Harper and Row, 1984), 150 (quotation)–151. Unless otherwise indicated all general factual references to political and military aspects of the Vietnam conflict are based upon James S. Olson and Randy Roberts, *Where the Domino Fell: America and Vietnam, 1945–1990* (New York: St. Martin's Press, 1991), an admirably succinct and balanced account. For knowledge of the antiwar movement we have relied upon Charles DeBenedetti, *An American Ordeal: The Antiwar Movement of the Vietnam Era* (Syracuse: Syracuse University Press, 1990).

46. Tulane *Hullabaloo*, 11 November 1965, pp. 1 (quotation), 12; Paul Schulman, "Disunity Threatens," Tulane *Hullabaloo*, 9 December 1965, p. 9; Minutes of the Subcommittee on Speakers, University Senate Committee on Student Affairs, 13 January 1966, box 61, HEL Papers; Tulane *Hullabaloo*, 3 February 1966, p. 1.

of the University Center, the oftentimes heated discussions drew a large audience, including the Stibbs and Longenecker families, who remained until 2:30 A.M. The program was educational at several levels, exposing spectators to the anti-establishment ideas and demeanor of the New Left. McReynolds, for example, had burned his draft card during a November 1965 antiwar rally at Union Square in New York City, an event held only four days after radical pacifist Norman Morrison had died by self-immolation within sight of the Pentagon. The very intensity with which local conservatives denounced the antiwar contingent (a "mighty sorry bunch" of "dirty, ragged beatnicks [sic]" with "beads and dirty feet") attested to the polarizing effect that the war would produce on college campuses and in society at large. A week after the debate Tulane's first antiwar demonstration took place. Some thirty-five student protesters carrying signs reading "Love Not War" and "Strategic Hamlets Equal Concentration Camps" assembled in front of the library "amid jeers and catcalls" to begin a march down Freret Street to an off-campus rally staged by former CORE activists in the New Orleans Coordinating Committee to End the War in Vietnam. Conservative publicist Kent Courtney, a nemesis of pro-integration students several years earlier, appeared in a mask of Fidel Castro and taunted the antiwar group with shouts of "All right comrades, let's get the march underway." Passing motorists were less subtle, resorting to shouts of "Go Burn Yourselves." Strictly speaking, Tulane was not a target of the February demonstration, but the event left little doubt that the war, even more than civil rights, threatened to polarize political sentiment in a manner that would divide the university against itself.[47]

The advent of serious debate over America's role in Vietnam helped strengthen the connection between campus concerns and external political and moral issues that had first emerged during the civil rights struggles of the early 1960s. In part, at least, the rise of social and political consciousness among Tulane students of the late 1960s represented a turning outward to engage human problems that the academic world had traditionally kept at arm's length. Many factors contributed to the new worldliness, including the cosmopolitanism of the uni-

47. DeBenedetti, *An American Ordeal*, 128–30, photo insert following p. 138; "Ethel" to Hale Boggs, 18 February 1966, Hale Boggs Papers, Tulane University (first–third quotations); Stibbs, "Twenty-Five Years of Student Life at Tulane University [1949–75]," 25; *New Orleans States-Item*, 12 February 1966, clipping, box 7, HEL Papers (all subsequent quotations).

versity itself. By the mid-sixties the Junior Year Abroad Program, which had been in operation for a decade, enrolled some seventy students each year, with participation split more or less equally between Newcomb College and the College of Arts and Sciences. In 1964–65, sixty of the seventy-one students participating in JYA came from the southern states, including thirty from the lower South states of Mississippi, Alabama, and Louisiana. Most had never traveled abroad before, and while their exposure to third world students was limited to incidental contacts at the forty British and European universities where the program operated, the experience had a broadening effect that was often quite dramatic. Arts and Sciences dean Joseph Gordon reported "an almost 100 percent change in outlook" among male students returning as seniors after a year abroad. Many expressed interest in international service careers. Gordon estimated that 75–80 percent of the former JYA students went on to graduate school, compared to about 50 percent of other A&S students. Newcomb dean John Hubbard found returning female JYA students to be considerably more mature than other seniors and increasingly impatient with "the spoon-fed system of American education."[48]

Students who remained in New Orleans encountered a liberal sprinkling of foreign students in classes and dormitories. Of the 320 non-U.S. students enrolled at Tulane in 1964–65, approximately half were from various Latin American countries. European students comprised the next largest group, followed by small but growing contingents from Taiwan and India. Campus contact with international students and with returning Peace Corps volunteers helped foster awareness of the gulf between American affluence and conditions in developing nations. By the spring of 1966 Tulane students were rubbing elbows with youthful Peace Corps veterans newly back from two-year assignments among the ordinary people of Honduras, Costa Rica, the Dominican Republic, Malaysia, Nigeria, and other third world countries struggling to throw off the legacy of European colonialism. The idealistic, but no longer naive, volunteers exemplified a concept of national service that

48. *The University Looks Abroad: Approaches to World Affairs at Six American Universities* (New York: Walker, 1965), 108, 109 (first quotation), 110 (second quotation). In 1965–66 a sample of 134 respondents out of the 264 Arts and Sciences graduates revealed that 72 percent planned some type of formal post-baccalaureate education, including graduate school (33 percent), medical school (21 percent), or law school (18 percent). Nineteen percent faced stints of military service and only 8 percent anticipated immediate entry into the civilian work force. A&S Dean's Report, 1965–66, pp. 6–7, box 29, HEL Papers.

had direct relevance to the battle against poverty and prejudice in America. "It's time we climbed out of our cardboard box," the *Hullabaloo* announced in a 1966 editorial, which described Tulane as "a unique and privileged society not at all like much of the rest of New Orleans."[49]

Desegregation had been the focus of campus activism during the first half of the 1960s but by 1966, in the wake of major legislative victories in the areas of education, employment, voting rights, and public accommodations, the movement's heroic phase was drawing to a close. As black power slogans began to drown out the interracial optimism of "We Shall Overcome," urban riots focused national attention on the blighting effect of ghetto poverty. Those seeking to bridge the gap between black and white society singled out "cultural deprivation" as the central cause of poor academic performance by minority children, and offered "compensatory education" as a proposed solution. Efforts to broaden the experiences of disadvantaged youth brought a small but significant number of Tulane undergraduates into direct contact with the reality of life in poor inner city neighborhoods. At the institutional level Tulane was forging new relationships with local black colleges and public schools. Efforts underway by the mid-sixties included two cooperative programs involving Tulane and Dillard. One sought to improve engineering education; the other was a five-year project supported by the Ford Foundation to develop curriculum materials and provide in-service training for teachers in two predominantly black public schools.[50]

By far the most ambitious program of direct student involvement with the black community was conducted by the Community Action Council of Tulane University Students (CACTUS). The seeds for CACTUS had been planted in 1963–64 with Tulane's initial participation in Project Opportunity, a long-term program directed at "potentially superior students from disadvantaged backgrounds" and sponsored by

49. *The University Looks Abroad*, 110; Tulane *Hullabaloo*, 9 December 1965, p. 9; ibid., 14 October 1966, p. 8 (quotation) The Peace Corps veterans, all of whom were enrolled Tulane students, made themselves available for speaking engagements and worked actively to encourage interest in the Corps and its ideals. They also decided "with a degree of reluctance" to establish an organization of former volunteers. On 22 November 1966 the group, Volunteers International, which included veterans of both the Peace Corps and VISTA, was recognized by the Student Senate.

50. Herbert E. Longenecker to Diane Palmer, 8 September 1966, box 18, HEL Papers. During the summer of 1965 Tulane students held weekly evening seminars intended to encourage a group of twenty black high school students to continue their education.

the Ford and Danforth Foundations in conjunction with the Southern Association of Colleges and Secondary Schools. In New Orleans, successive groups of seventh-grade students from all-black Priestly Junior High School were selected for an intensified academic program that continued through high school, augmented by a variety of enrichment activities provided by Tulane students. Typically the Tulane volunteers spent afternoons, Saturdays, or evenings tutoring students, familiarizing them with college, bringing them to the Tulane campus, and holding special classes in drama, science, music, literature, and art. Initially the Project Opportunity program involved some 15–20 undergraduates recruited by admissions director Edward Rogge, but in 1966 the level of student participation tripled when Tulane law student Donald Mintz became project coordinator. In the fall of 1966 Mintz and other Project Opportunity tutors organized CACTUS, which gained official recognition as a student organization the following year. By 1967 some 150 Tulane students were involved in four CACTUS projects, and the scope of overall university interest in educational outreach efforts was continuing to grow under the stimulus of grants from the U.S. Office of Education that were related to Project Head Start. In 1968 William Hill, a black undergraduate, assumed the leadership of CACTUS and maneuvered skillfully to maintain the involvement of white students without subjecting the program to charges of condescension or paternalism. "There is no longer a need for confused, frustrated, neurotic, guilty people," Hill announced in the *CACTUS Newsletter*. "If you are uncertain about your ability to justify your involvement to your parents, your fraternity brothers, your sorority sisters, your roommate, your best friend, or whatever, then you had better 'Get Your Thing Together.'"[51]

IV

By the time Hill's comments appeared in print, many Tulane students were well on the way toward reorienting their personal priorities. It has become fashionable to speak of the late 1960s as an era of conflict in higher education, and Tulane's history provides ample evidence of

51. John Egerton, "Cactus Is the Word," *Southern Education Report* 4 (September 1968): 27–9; "Tulane Engages in Concerted Efforts to Equalize Educational Opportunity," *Tulane Report*, no. 2 (fall 1968–69); Tulane University Affirmative Action Compliance Program, January

the disunity and political polarization common to American universities at the time. But the cycle of protest which unfolded at Tulane between 1967 and 1970 would have been impossible in the absence of certain unifying forces at work on the uptown campus. If the boundary separating the university from its external environment had grown indistinct by the late 1960s, a similar eroding of barriers was evident among the students themselves, as conventional peer group distinctions dissolved in the face of shared lifestyles and galvanizing campus issues. Through a slow process of cultural osmosis, older concerns about newspaper censorship, dormitory rules, and other in loco parentis constraints began to merge with new issues such as antiwar protest, participatory democracy, and countercultural styles of dress and demeanor. The result was a gradual melding of previously incompatible student subcultures. The old antagonisms—rooted as they often were in cultural and class differences—did not disappear, but over time their relevance to student life was diminished. And as the lines between fraternity and sorority members, professional students, and intellectual rebels became increasingly blurred, the stage was set for a temporary alteration in the shape and texture of campus politics.

If cultural changes did not cause student radicalism, they constituted a basic precondition for the development of a new politics. Prior to the late 1960s, neither the rise of dissatisfaction over in loco parentis regulations nor the emotional appeal of defying established authority could offset the fact that those undergraduates with the talent and inclination to become student leaders were drawn almost inexorably into what Dean Stibbs described as "the old and honorable areas of student interest—fraternities, football, and student government"— activities which were far and away the most tradition-bound segments of undergraduate life. When President Longenecker took office in 1960, the three pillars of collegiate orthodoxy seemed secure and the Greek system loomed larger than ever, its organic relationship to student government being a matter of considerable pride for those involved. In a self-evaluation during the mid-1960s the Newcomb Panhellenic Council stressed that "sororities encourage their members to run for office, to attend student body meetings, [and] to vote in campus elections." This claim was supported by statistics showing that all

---

1969, typescript, boxes 27–8, HEL Papers, 11–2; Bill Hill, "Concerning CACTUS: Past and Future," *The CACTUS Newsletter* (March 1970) (quotation); "Project Opportunity," ibid.

thirteen members of the Newcomb Inter-House Council were sorority members, as were all four cheerleaders, ten of eleven Mortar Board members, and thirteen of fourteen members of the *Jambalaya* staff.[52]

In the wake of desegregation, however, Tulane's Greek system came under growing criticism for policies of ethnic exclusion. Sometime around the middle of the decade Tulane sororities abandoned the long-standing practice of holding what were, in effect, two separate rushes—one for Jewish girls and the other for gentiles. The old practice, which had involved assigning high pledge quotas to the two Jewish sororities and sending out forms during the summer asking female freshmen to return photographs and select Jewish or non-Jewish rush, may have been abandoned as unnecessary in light of the universal requirement that female pledges have letters of recommendation from sorority alumnae. Black students, however, posed difficulties that were less easily resolved. The rebuffs experienced by black rushees in 1965 were repeated two years later, causing widespread negative reaction. In 1967 no black women participated in sorority rush. One fraternity went out of existence in 1967 because of falling membership, and although the number of male freshmen who pledged one of Tulane's eighteen fraternities remained constant between 1967 and 1968, hovering near 460 students or 60 percent of the entering class, there were clear signs of impending trouble. In 1968 an informal consensus existed among blacks to discourage participation in rush, and even Tulane's Jewish fraternities, by far the most liberal in their racial views, failed to attract a single black rushee. In a strong anti-fraternity editorial, the *Hullabaloo* warned incoming students that "discrimination, in general, is an inherent and obvious part of the fraternity system." The paper went on to note that personal relationships formed through dorm life, classes, and extracurricular activities could be just as plentiful "and just as satisfying as the friendships made through a fraternity." By the end of the decade the number of male students who joined fraternities declined by some 40 percent, from a peak of nearly five hundred to approximately three hundred a year.[53]

52. Stibbs, "Twenty-Five Years of Student Life at Tulane University [1949–75]," 24 (first quotation); Newcomb Panhellenic Council, Panhellenic Evaluation, box 61, HEL Papers (second quotation).

53. Eli N. Evans, *The Provincials: A Personal History of Jews in the South* (New York: Atheneum, 1973), 244–5; Tulane *Hullabaloo*, 22 September 1967, pp. 1–2; ibid., 10 November 1967, p. 1; ibid., 20 September 1968, p. 8 (quotations); ibid., 27 September 1968, p. 1; Tulane

The loss of the Greek system's monopoly on campus politics opened the way for a new style of leadership more in tune with the currents of idealism and alienation that were evident in student life. With the old administration–student government–fraternity/sorority nexus temporarily weakened, it became possible to secure recognition from fellow students by challenging the "establishment" and making demands upon it, instead of joining it and seeking concessions. For a brief period near the end of the decade, confrontation and rhetorical radicalism entered the political mainstream, producing a culture of opposition that drew in a substantial segment of the student body. The unity that students forged through collective dissent was flexible enough to withstand strong centrifugal forces. In the fall of 1966, for example, Tulane's black students began challenging the assimilationist assumptions of white liberals through the newly established, and as yet officially unrecognized, Afro-American Congress of Tulane (ACT). If ACT reflected the growing conviction among younger blacks that group solidarity was the only practical alternative to dependency, it also signaled that minority enrollment at Tulane had reached a critical mass. The number of black students had been rising since 1964, when the university received a five-year grant from the Rockefeller Foundation to provide generous scholarships for disadvantaged undergraduates. A total of 54 black students (or 18 per year) were admitted during the program's first three years, at least 42 of whom returned for the 1966–67 school year. This group, together with other full- and part-time students, brought Tulane's black enrollment to a reported total of 57 by the fall of 1966. Approximately 30 of this number comprised the original membership of ACT.[54]

Having rejected the idea of including whites in favor of a black united front, ACT struck many white liberals as a step backward toward self-segregation. But while the chauvinistic rhetoric of racial pride employed by some ACT members offended integrationist sensibilities, the organization's real significance lay in the underlying willingness of black students to assert their claim to a place within the university. ACT cochairman Steven Barbre, who would later be described

---

Student Senate Minutes, 18 November 1969, ASB, 1954–92; Stibbs, "Twenty-Five Years of Student Life at Tulane University [1949–75]," 24.

54. Tulane *Hullabaloo*, 10 October 1966, p. 8; ibid., 4 November 1966, pp. 1, 8; [Edward Rogge], Admission and Academic Performance of Negro Undergraduates at Tulane University (report to the Rockefeller Foundation), 8 November 1967, box 18, HEL Papers, 1 and table 1, "Negro Students 1964–65–66."

*Intramural activity was one of many ways in which black students
participated in university life.*

as "probably the most militant black student at Tulane," declared in
October 1966 that "[w]e are willing to work with any groups on campus . . . what we want to show is that the Negro on campus is not just a
non-entity; that he is concerned with what goes on here." The meaning
of Barbre's words became clear a month later, when ACT boycotted
the Tulane homecoming dance held on the often segregated riverboat
SS *President.* Instead, ACT joined the Liberals Club and the Graduate Student Association in picketing the University Center in an effort to reverse the Student Senate's decision to "consider practicality
[amended from economy] primarily and the issue of segregation secon-
darily" in making contracts for student organizations. The "practicality" resolution had been adopted by a vote of 24-22. In a subsequent
senate meeting attended by several ACT members, the group's spokes-
person disavowed any desire to disrupt campus activities but reiterated that black students were "a part of the University." Most black
students cared little about attending the dance but regarded the insen-
sitive resolution as "a slap in the face."[55]

55. Tulane *Hullabaloo:* 10 May 1968, p. 11 (first quotation); 10 October 1966, p. 8; 28

Over the next two years ACT rhetoric grew more strident, as the group demanded and eventually received separate physical facilities in a home formerly used as a faculty residence. But even in 1968–69, when the national vogue for black pride and other forms of cultural nationalism was approaching its zenith, ACT's chief demand upon the Tulane administration was for the continuance of minority scholarships that were threatened by the expiration of the four-year Rockefeller grant. By this point the group had received formal recognition as a student organization and was behaving more like a special interest bloc than an alien element in the undergraduate body politic. During the era of student demonstrations ACT's militant posture earned it an autonomous place beside SDS on the student Left, while black demands became a routine component of the larger quest for "student power."[56]

In addition to the emergence of ACT, several other developments—including the first arrests of Tulane students for using marijuana in campus residences—marked out 1966–67 as a transitional year in which the liberal consensus of the early sixties began to crumble. Threaded through the year-long controversy over the theater department were visible strands of approaching conflict over Vietnam, race, and student rights. Administrators in close contact with undergraduate affairs understood that the times were, indeed, in flux. As early as the summer of 1966, Arts and Sciences dean Joseph Gordon reported his "growing awareness of a crystallizing demand of the students for a voice (or at least representation) on some of the major policy committees of the college," including the Curriculum Committee and the Executive Committee. At the time no faculty committees had considered including undergraduates in their deliberations, but candidates for student offices had raised the issue in a manner that left little doubt as to its future importance. "I am sympathetic to some of the students' requests," Gordon noted in his annual report to President Longenecker. He favored a small, nonvoting representation for students on key A&S committees, but anticipated faculty resistance to the idea. Gordon's reading of student and faculty sentiment would be validated in May

October 1966, p. 8 (second quotation); 4 November 1966, pp. 1, 8. Minutes of the Tulane Student Senate, 18 October 1966, ASB, 1954–92 (third quotation); ibid., 25 October 1966 (fourth–sixth quotations). The old Student Council had been renamed the Student Senate in the new Constitution of the Associated Student Body, approved by the Board of Administrators in September 1966.

56. These points receive further discussion in the following chapter.

1967, when the A&S faculty voted by a ratio of roughly two to one against allowing student representation in the University Senate.[57]

Although lacking an official voice in the University Senate, students made themselves heard during the spring semester in a variety of ways, including organized protest against ROTC. On March 23, March 30, and April 6, 1967, the Tulane campus experienced its first Vietnam-era antiwar demonstrations when Richard Schechner, who was preparing to leave the university at the end of the semester, led small bands of students and faculty members to the University Center quadrangle during the scheduled drill period for air force ROTC cadets. Covering their heads with black hoods of the type once worn by public executioners, the protesters bore symbolic witness against the university's role in military training but made no effort to interfere with drill during their first two appearances. On April 6, however, the squad of fourteen hooded (and therefore anonymous) demonstrators moved onto the field while drill was in progress, chanting, "hup-one-two-three-kill," and marching between the ranks of cadets in an effort to ridicule the military exercises. In the aftermath of the brief episode, which ended when campus security chief Robert Scruton ordered the group to leave, Professor Schechner explained that the demonstration was not a picket but rather a "staged event" intended to underscore the "absurdity and brutality of militarism" by parodying the drill maneuvers that ROTC students were required to perform. The demonstration also had a larger message, which Schechner summarized for the local press. "We protest the increasing militarism in the country at large, on college campuses, and specifically at Tulane," he told a reporter from the *New Orleans Times-Picayune*. Colonel Scruton had claimed the "parade" interfered with "what amounts to an academic function" of the university, but Schechner and his followers disagreed. "We don't believe that ROTC is an academic function," the *Drama Review* editor explained. Convinced that military training had "no place at a university," Schechner voiced his group's concern that students were "spending so much of their time involved in military matters, particularly in the face of the Vietnam war, which seems . . . to be morally unjustifiable."[58]

From April 1967 through May 1970, the related issues of Vietnam

57. A&S Dean's Report, 1965–66, box 29, HEL Papers, 6 (first quotation), 7 (second quotation).

58. Tulane *Hullabaloo*, 14 April 1967, p. 1 (first quotation); *New Orleans Times-Picayune*, 7 April 1967 (all subsequent quotations).

and ROTC would cause recurring conflict at Tulane, serving as one of several flash points in a spreading pattern of confrontation and protest. During the spring of 1967 anti-ROTC actions included the use of balloons with peace slogans and a display of paper flowers arranged to spell "LOVE" on the quadrangle where drill was conducted, as well as the hooded marches already described. These activities were intermingled with other demonstrations, including one staged by some thirty students who picketed Nicaraguan president Anastasio Somoza when the dictator visited Tulane's campus. While the number of students who actively participated in public protests remained extremely small—perhaps fifty in all—their actions were beginning to seem less exotic and no longer altogether alien to the fabric of student life.[59]

In reality, the protests were part of a gradual but ongoing metamorphosis in the political atmosphere on Tulane's campus. The leaven of change often worked quietly in the minds of individual undergraduates. As late as October 1966, *Hullabaloo* coverage of the ACT and Liberals Club efforts to move the homecoming dance had focused not on the protesters but on a counterdemonstration staged by fraternity members, who ridiculed the integrationists with signs reading "Ban the Bomb" and "Prepare to Meet thy God." One of the counterdemonstrators, Dallas, Texas, sophomore and Delta Tau Delta member Lawrence Wright, began to rethink his position only a week later, when he served as a one-man welcoming committee for the glamorous Dionne Warwick, who was scheduled to perform at homecoming on the temporarily desegregated SS *President*. Arriving with Warwick at a downtown hotel, Wright was humiliated and enraged when the desk clerk at the illegally segregated establishment attempted to deny the black singer accommodations. "I suddenly felt sick about my idiocy of the week before," Wright recalled. "I had made fun of something which I clearly hadn't understood. That was the force of the repression for which I, being white, was responsible." Within eighteen months Wright would be among the hundreds of students marching on President Longenecker's residence to protest campus censorship.[60]

In the realm of student government, signs of a leftward shift in the

---

59. Tulane *Hullabaloo*, 7, 21, and 28 April 1967. The balloon incident took place on April 13 and the "LOVE" episode occurred on April 20. Students picketed Somoza on April 3.

60. Ibid., 4 November 1966, p. 1 (sign captions quoted from photograph); Lawrence Wright, *In the New World: Growing Up with America from the Sixties to the Eighties* (New York: Random House, 1987), 84, 89–91 (quotations on p. 91).

political center of gravity appeared in February 1967, when the Student Senate endorsed a "Proposed List of Reforms" prepared by the Academic Affairs Committee. The document, which was candidly described as a "list of grievances drawn up by the various student interest groups," took the Longenecker administration to task for being "inadequately aware of the high level of general dissatisfaction among the students." Specific sources of complaint ranged from high bookstore prices to the need for a full-time academic provost to act as an "unequivocal spokesman for the academic point of view in university planning." The need for someone to monitor Tulane's "intellectual health" was suggested by the "awkward and inadequate manner" in which the theater department problems had been handled, leaving students convinced that further measures—including a "Keep the Theater" drive—should be undertaken to preserve the drama program. The document concluded with a passage that left little doubt as to the shape of future conflicts over the distribution of power within the university. "Underlying these grievances is an inadequate provision for participation by students in the formulation of the significant policy decisions of this university. . . . Therefore the students request that they be given representation on all policy making committees where such participation is feasible. . . . As a demonstration of good faith the university should provide for immediate participation of student representatives in the university senate."[61]

The reform proposal was really the opening gambit in the spring 1967 elections for Student Senate officers, a contest that would emerge in retrospect as a crucial turning point in the evolution of late-sixties campus politics. Bringing together issues of race, fraternity influence, student rights, and social activism, the contest began in a time-honored fashion with backstage maneuvering among Tulane's largest fraternities—a Jewish/gentile bloc comprised of Sigma Alpha Epsilon, Sigma Alpha Mu, Zeta Beta Tau, and Alpha Epsilon Pi. By the time nominations closed, two tickets had emerged. One, backed by Sigma Alpha Mu and Alpha Epsilon Pi, took the name "Mandate" and was headed by Pi Kappa Alpha member Bud Brown, who had agreed to leave his studies as a JYA student in Germany long enough to fly back to New Orleans for some quick electioneering. The other ticket, calling itself "Strike," was headed by Sigma Alpha Epsilon member Henry H.

61. Tulane Student Senate Minutes, 14 February 1967, ASB, 1954–92; Student Senate Academic Affairs Committee, Proposed List of Reforms, typescript, box 62, HEL Papers (all quotations); Tulane *Hullabaloo*, 17 February 1967, pp. 1, 3.

"Hank" Harnage, and had the support of Zeta Beta Tau as well as the backing of Harnage's fraternity. Both the Strike and Mandate slates contained the traditional mix of three men and one woman (the candidate for secretary), and on each ticket the female nominee was a member of a large and prestigious campus sorority.[62]

Despite the fact that a total of six fraternities and two sororities were represented on the two tickets with no independent candidates in the field, the 1967 election represented considerably more than a routine factional struggle among otherwise indistinguishable components of the campus Greek system. At bottom, the election involved a dispute over the nature of the Greek system and its relevance to the changing values of Tulane students. The contest's larger meaning became clear when supporters of the Mandate ticket sent letters to all Tulane fraternities deploring the "rising tide of anti-fraternity feeling" that had emerged over the preceding two years, and warning that "[a] vote for Hank Harnage is a vote for the ultimate destruction of the fraternity system." In support of this implausible claim, the letter quoted statements made by Harnage several weeks earlier after the University Senate Committee on Student Affairs had narrowly defeated a motion by Professor Henry Mason that would have granted only "minimal recognition" to fraternities which continued to practice racial discrimination. Although Harnage had voted against the motion, initially exclaiming, "How can I face the boys at the house after voting for *that*," he subsequently agreed that "a problem definitely exists . . . you can't close your eyes to it. . . . All students are not welcome at all times and I think they should be." Harnage supported the creation of a special committee to "explain exactly to the fraternities that if all students are not welcome in the future, fraternities will no longer be recognized." In words that would be seized upon by his political opponents, he went on to declare, "I don't want fraternities to exist if they are going to be discriminatory."[63]

The Brown ticket's letter drew condemnation from the *Hullabaloo* for its "racist tone" and led the paper to endorse Harnage as "the more progressive candidate, willing to back, in a time of ethical crisis, his student body before his fraternity." Additional support came from Newcomb's student body president, who sent a letter to all women under-

62. Tulane *Hullabaloo*, 17 February 1967, p. 1.

63. Ibid., 10 March 1967, p. 8 (first–second quotations); ibid., 3 March 1967, pp. 1 (third quotation), 2 (fifth–seventh quotations); Hans A. Schmidt to editor, *Southern Patriot* 26 (May 1968), 6 (fourth quotation).

Henry H. "Hank" Harnage,
President of the Associated Student
Body, 1967–68.

graduates endorsing the Strike ticket. For its part, the Harnage coalition issued a series of "Crisis" newsletters calling for increased support of Project Opportunity and other CACTUS programs, and presenting a detailed platform that reiterated many of the key provisions of the Student Senate reform document adopted a few weeks earlier, including demands for student representation on policy-making committees and the appointment of an academic provost. Harnage won the election handily, carrying every polling place except the School of Engineering and receiving particularly strong support from Newcomb College. The outcome was not so much a repudiation of fraternities as an indication that the Greek system was in a state of transition, with the most energetic leadership poised to align itself with an activist agenda that had previously been looked upon as the exclusive domain of a radical fringe.[64]

Although the full significance of the Student Senate's reform proposals and the Harnage election victory would not become apparent until the next academic year, the University Senate began to reevaluate its policies on student participation after the Committee on Student Affairs (which already had student members) recommended adding

64. Tulane *Hullabaloo*, 6 March 1967, p. 2 (second quotation); ibid., 10 March 1967, pp. 1, 8 (first quotation); undated "Crisis" flyers and "STRIKE Student Demands in Policy and Planning," separate leaflets, box 67, HEL Papers.

students to a total of eight senate committees and amending the constitution to permit the seating of the student body president as a voting
member of the University Senate. The senate received the proposals in
May and agreed to place students on a total of five additional standing
committees the next fall. President Longenecker was by no means
oblivious to these developments, and in a series of speeches and interviews during the first two weeks of March he sought to address the
many causes of dissatisfaction among students and faculty. In addition
to the overarching problem of university finances (which the theater
department controversy had served to underscore), Longenecker also
stressed the need for students to become more familiar with university
affairs by participating in the self-study that was about to begin. In response to questions about the Student Senate's resolution calling for
student participation on policy-making committees, the president deferred to the authority of the University Senate, while agreeing that
"[w]e need this engagement of students in committees." In terms of his
future relations with students, Longenecker's most revealing comments came during a portion of his speech to the Newcomb student
body that was devoted to the importance of academic freedom. Beginning with the premise that "the University does not take a position
on political or social issues," he went on to explain that modern history
illustrated the danger of straying from the principle of institutional
neutrality. "One can argue that a University should be an active social
agency. . . . But this was the tragedy of German universities in the
1930s," Longenecker told his Newcomb listeners.[65]

The allusion spoke volumes about the gap in perception and experience that separated Tulane's president from the students of the late
1960s. Like most Americans who had been adults at the time of World
War II, Longenecker was appalled by the manner in which totalitarian
regimes had manipulated public sentiment in order to trample on civil
liberties and sanction mass murder. In 1937, while completing his doctorate in chemistry, Longenecker had spent a semester in Cologne,
Germany, working in the laboratory of a distinguished German scientist
who greeted his subalterns each morning with the phrase "Heil Hitler,"
accompanied by a Nazi hand salute. During this period Longenecker
and his wife Jane lived in a private home where one son served in the

65. University Senate Minutes, 8 and 22 May 1967, University Senate Minutes and Reports,
1912–89, box 2, Tulane University Archives; College of Arts and Sciences Faculty Minutes, 9
May 1967, box 29, HEL Papers; Tulane *Hullabaloo*, 10 March 1967, p. 2 (all quotations).

Luftwaffe while the other headed the local Hitler Youth organization. Once, on a visit to Düsseldorf, the Longeneckers stood within "easy gunshot range" of Hitler and his entourage. On a later trip to Nuremberg the young couple came upon the horrifying spectacle of thousands of ardent Nazis assembled for a mass rally. In the postwar era such experiences were "indelibly fixed" in Longenecker's mind, and both before and after coming to Tulane he stressed the dangers of conformity and importance of individualism and intellectual independence.[66]

In a 1962 University of Florida commencement address that was subsequently printed in the *Tulanian*, Longenecker set forth the basic tenets of a liberal academic credo that would guide his actions during the conflicts of the late 1960s. Contrasting American universities with those of Nazi Germany and the contemporary Soviet Union, he acknowledged that within a "conforming cultural climate" shaped by "opinion polls, mass media, advertising techniques, [and] mass demonstrations," higher education could be "manipulated to produce a generation of persons who tend to look alike, think alike, and act alike." In order to avoid such a result, and to safeguard individualism while preventing indoctrination and ensuring maximum freedom to faculty and students, universities should neither "take a position in public issues" nor "act repressively" against members of the academic community whose views or actions were unpopular. Aware that the path of tolerance and restraint was not an easy one, Tulane's president confessed to occasional moments of exasperation with rebellious youth. "As I observe a student in sloppy, even smelly clothes, and sometimes with several days growth of beard on his chin, I am inclined to take forceful steps in a direct fashion," he admitted. But inevitably, a mental "reminder bell" sounded to chase away repressive impulses and substitute in their place a conviction that "we had better be prepared for the occasional individualist in dress, speech, act, or thought."[67]

Longenecker's perspective, which echoed the critique of "mass society" advanced by Hannah Arendt and other émigré intellectuals who had fled the Nazi regime, was thoroughly in tune with the prevailing academic liberalism of the 1950s and early 1960s. For obvious reasons it was less well suited to the political climate of the late 1960s, when the challenge posed by hundreds of protesting students would require

66. Herbert E. Longenecker, interview by C. L. Mohr, 20 April 1994, New Orleans, Louisiana (all quotations). Audiotape in the authors' possession.

67. Herbert E. Longenecker, "Concern for the Individual," *Tulanian* 35 (July 1962): 1–2.

President Longenecker at ROTC exercises, 1962.

more than a benign tolerance for the "occasional individualist" who
strayed from the norms of middle-class life. Beginning with the 1964
Berkeley demonstrations, Longenecker paid close attention to the development of student activism on campuses throughout America, accu-
mulating extensive files on the subject of "student unrest." In a tactical
if not a philosophical sense, he was well prepared for the onslaught of
mass demonstrations that would commence at Tulane in 1968. Once
student protests had begun, he would display surprising flexibility in
adapting to the fluid leadership and rapidly changing agenda of the
student power and antiwar movements. But for all his agility and cool-
ness under pressure, Longenecker remained incapable of empathizing
with student militants or of understanding their cultural perspective.

Nor was he unique in his inability to transcend the decade's legendary generation gap. During the late 1960s Longenecker and Tulane's student activists could agree on little beyond the need for "improved communication," a term which vied with "relevance" to become

the period's leading cliché. And while communication of a sort did take place in the era of mass demonstrations, there was little to indicate that either Tulane's president or the students who opposed him ever understood each other in more than a superficial way. For Longenecker the sight of marching students always evoked unsettling recollections of prewar Germany and the tyranny of the "Hitler mob." He did not, of course, equate Tulane students with Nazis; yet in the mass demonstrations Longenecker saw not simply a threat to the orderly operation of the university but an abdication of individual judgment that struck at the very core of intellectual freedom. A basic antipathy toward civil disobedience had caused Longenecker to look unfavorably upon the cafeteria sit-ins of 1962. During the demonstrations of the late sixties, his continued adherence to the totalitarian versus individualist dichotomy would prove both an asset and a liability, sharpening his ability to offer an intelligent critique of student activism even as it limited his insight into the worldview of the students themselves.

Tulane students of the late sixties approached campus politics with generational blinders of their own. At the broadest level they shared a confidence that was rooted in postwar prosperity, a time perspective that was compressed through the immediacy of television, and a psychological posture that was buoyed by the optimism and brashness of young adulthood. But more important than any of these factors in creating a generational bond was the cultural and intellectual impact of the cold war. Whether they were participants or onlookers during the era of mass demonstrations, Tulane students of the mid- and late 1960s shared common moral reference points that were linked to race and anti-Communism. America in the 1950s and early '60s had been a nation of dichotomies: North and South, black and white, free world and Soviet bloc. In such an environment, youthful idealism had absorbed much of the rhetoric and moral urgency generated by global struggles over racial, economic, and political hegemony.

Schooled from an early age in the curriculum of American exceptionalism, college students of the mid- and late sixties developed a hair-trigger capacity for indignation at society's moral failings. Their outlook was often naive and impatient. Having awakened to the reality of injustice much in the manner that a beginning theological student might stumble across the problem of evil, students learned to question the workings of power as they called upon the nation and the university to fulfill the perfectionist ideals which the cold war had inspired or reinforced. But behind even the most shrill student utterances it was usually possible to detect a mindset that was more liberal than radical, provided that the cold war's influence upon liberal rhetoric is taken into account. For a generation whose political consciousness began with a youthful chief executive's vow that America would "pay any price" and "bear any burden" in defense of freedom, a degree of moral absolutism seemed fully consistent with liberal thought. And however real the specter of totalitarianism or mass psychology may have appeared to those who recalled the rise of fascism in Europe, many students in the late 1960s came to regard collective protest as an act of intellectual rebellion and a declaration of personal independence. To challenge the "establishment" was to affirm individuality and freedom, whereas acquiescence to the dictates of established institutions bespoke conservatism, indifference, or conformity—a quality which student activists despised even more passionately than Tulane's president. Such differences in generational vocabulary and outlook paved the way for conflict over a host of campus issues.[68]

68. Jeffrey Turner, "Conscience and Conflict: Patterns in the History of Student Activism on Southern College Campuses, 1960–1970" (Ph.D. diss., Tulane University, 2000) draws upon extensive archival research to treat a complex subject with skill and originality. Other useful studies about campus dissent below the Potomac include Charles U. Smith, ed., *Student Unrest on Historically Black Campuses* (Silver Spring, Md.: Beckham House, 1994); William C. Hine, "Civil Rights and Campus Wrongs: South Carolina State College Students Protest, 1955–1968," *South Carolina Historical Magazine* 97 (October 1996): 310–31; Martin Khulman, "Direct Action at the University of Texas during the Civil Rights Movement, 1960–1965," *Southwestern Historical Quarterly* 98 (April 1995): 551–66; Doug Rossinow, "'The Breakthrough to New Life': Christianity and the Emergence of the New Left in Austin, Texas, 1956–1964," *American Quarterly* 46 (September 1994): 309–40; William A. Link, "William Friday and the North Carolina Speaker Ban Crisis: 1963–1968," *North Carolina Historical Review* 72 (April 1995): 198–228; Fayette County Project Volunteers, *Step by Step: Evolution and Operation of the Cornell Students' Civil-Rights Project in Tennessee, Summer 1964* (New York: W. W. Norton, 1965); David Andrew Briggs, "The First One Hundred" (honors essay, Department of History, University of North Carolina at Chapel Hill, 1992); John P. Scherer, "A Code of Civility: Antiwar Dissent at Davidson College during the Vietnam Era" (honors thesis, Davidson College, 1989); John Hennen, "Struggle for Recognition: The Marshall University Students for a Democratic Society and the Red Scare in Huntington, 1965–1969," *West Virginia History* 52 (1993): 127–47; Jeffrey A. Drobney, "A Generation in Revolt: Student Dissent and Political Repression at West Virginia University," *West Virginia History* 54 (1995): 105–22; Mitchell K. Hall, "A Crack in Time: The Response of Students at the University of Kentucky to the Tragedy at Kent State," *Register of the Kentucky Historical Society* 83 (1985): 36–63; Thomas M. Bello, "The Student Strike at the University of North Carolina at Chapel Hill (May 1970): An Eyewitness Historical Memoir" (honors essay, Department of History, University of North Carolina at Chapel Hill, 1971); Anthony W. James, "A Demand for Racial Equality: The 1970 Black Student Protest at the University of Mississippi," *Journal of Mississippi History* 62 (summer 1995): 97–120.

7

FAMILY QUARRELS, PART TWO
Days of Decision

Real issues were at stake in the protests of the late sixties, and any serious analysis of student dissent must take account of the ideas and organizations behind the student power and antiwar movements. At Tulane, as on most southern campuses, the taproot of student activism ran to the civil rights struggle of the early sixties. But a more immediate inspiration for the initial phase of campus mobilization in 1967–68 came from the United States National Student Association (NSA), a federation representing the student governments of some three hundred colleges and universities. Founded in 1947, the association was known for its early adoption of a student bill of rights and its consistent support of racial desegregation. Unknown to most NSA members, the Central Intelligence Agency provided a large financial subsidy to the NSA from 1953 onward in return for cooperation in foreign intelligence gathering. Tulane had joined the NSA in the 1950s but withdrew several years later, when the organization's political liberalism and civil rights activity made it unpopular in the South. In 1965 the university renewed its NSA affiliation by action of the student government, only to withdraw again after an April 1966 campus referendum in which Tulane students voted 1,606-620 against NSA membership on the grounds that the organization was "too politically oriented [and] too liberal in its social and political standards." In February 1967, public revelations of the longstanding CIA-NSA connection shocked both liberals and conservatives, bringing an abrupt end to the secret relationship. Replacing CIA funds with grants from the Department of Education, the Stern Family Fund, and the Office of Economic Opportunity, the NSA recovered quickly and lost little if any credibility among member schools.[1]

In August 1967, Tulane's newly elected Student Senate president Hank Harnage and vice president Larry Rosenblum attended the NSA's twentieth annual convention at the University of Maryland, where some 1,200 delegates severed the group's last CIA tie. Under pressure from more radical black members and a counterconvention of SDS representatives, the delegates stiffened the group's opposition to the Vietnam War and the draft, launched a drive to prevent the reelection of Lyndon Johnson, and endorsed a controversial resolution in support of black power. After heated debate over both Vietnam and racial politics, the convention closed ranks through the virtually unanimous passage of sweeping student power resolutions that demanded increased student government control of disciplinary proceedings, dormitory hours, social and housing rules, the chartering of student organizations, and the financing of student activities. Expanding student government functions in these areas had been a major NSA objective for several years, but the delegates broke new ground by calling for students to assume joint authority with administrators and faculty over course requirements, admissions policies, grading systems, and the hiring and dismissal of professors.[2]

The convention's commitment to student power was reaffirmed when Oberlin College alumnus Edward Schwartz narrowly defeated antiwar activist Sam Brown for the NSA presidency. During the previous year Schwartz had traveled to more than fifty campuses, urging students to take more control of their education and to assert themselves in support of free speech and in opposition to the draft. A liberal who shared the reformist outlook that had initially characterized SDS, Schwartz favored cooperation among all elements of the student Left, and believed students would constitute a crucial element in any political coalition that might emerge to lead the fight for progressive social

1. Philip G. Altbach, *Student Politics in America: A Historical Analysis* (1974; reprint, New Brunswick, N.J.: Transaction, 1997), 122–32; Angus Johnston, "A Brief History of NSA and USSA," document on United States Student Association Internet web page; Tulane *Hullabaloo*, 30 September 1965, p. 8; ibid., 15 December 1967, p. 1 (quotation); Sol Stern, "NSA: CIA," *Ramparts* 5 (February 1967): 29–39; *New York Times*, 20 August 1967, p. 38.

2. Tulane *Hullabaloo*, 8 December 1967, p. 1. For national coverage of the NSA, see *New York Times:* 12 August 1967, pp. 1, 5; 14 August 1967, pp. 1, 15; 21 August 1967, pp. 1, 17; 22 August 1967, pp. 1, 25.

change. For the immediate future Schwartz planned to press for the creation of experimental colleges without traditional grading systems, where students might "develop new models for curricula" that would include academic credit for "organizing the poor in urban ghettos." Building institutional mechanisms for the sustained expression of student influence became the central thrust of the twentieth National Student Congress, which Schwartz would later credit with bringing the phrase "student power" to national prominence.[3]

The 1967 NSA convention was the first in a series of events that transformed the nature of student activism at Tulane. Harnage returned from the meeting excited about the possibilities of student power and determined to renew the university's NSA affiliation, which had survived only through the Tulane Graduate Student Association's ongoing status as a non-dues-paying member of the national group. By the time the fall semester began, there were signs of a new political temper on the uptown campus. Returning students found that the *Hullabaloo*, under the editorship of third-year law student Charles J. "Jeff" Howie, had moved beyond the conventional boundaries of college journalism to publish serious review essays on the intellectual ferment at work in higher education. In the first of several special supplements entitled "The Tulane Review of Books," Professor William R. Hogan of the Arts and Sciences history faculty discussed Henry Steele Commager's *The Search for a Usable Past*, while admissions director, speech professor, and ACT adviser Edward Rogge provided lengthy reviews of Nathan Wright's *Black Power and Urban Unrest* and Fred Powledge's *Black Power, White Resistance: Notes on the New Civil War.* Rogge commended both works "to whites particularly, and most particularly to whites who have not kept up with developments in the equality movement." A few weeks later alumni who attended the Green Wave homecoming game in search of nostalgia were greeted as well by the *Hullabaloo*'s pronouncement that "this seems to be the year of 'student power.' "[4]

In a speech to incoming freshmen on September 12, 1967, Harnage

---

3. *New York Times*, 21 August 1967, pp. 1, 17; ibid., 23 August 1967, p. 27 (all quotations); Edward Schwartz, ed., *Student Power—A Collection of Readings*, rev. ed. (Washington, D.C.: United States National Student Association, 1969), 2.

4. Tulane Student Senate Minutes, 8 November 1966, ASB, 1954–92; "Tulane Review of Books," supplement to Tulane *Hullabaloo*, 6 October 1967 (first quotation); ibid., 27 October 1967, p. 8 (second quotation).

made a skillful appeal for the kind of generational self-assertion that would use radical tactics to create or strengthen the institutional mechanisms for student empowerment. Noting the mid-1960s "surge of student demonstrations and striving for a greater part in decision making processes," Harnage urged the freshmen to "[a]rgue, protest, demonstrate, strike—whatever you will. Only make use of the opportunities available. Talk to professors, pressure your senators, come to see us. Nothing is outside our inspection and involvement—academic affairs, community relations, civil rights. . . . We are willing to . . . assume the responsibilities that previous young people were afraid to touch."[5]

Shortly after his freshman address, Harnage arranged for the use of a University Center meeting room by some seventy-five Tulane students (described initially as "liberal activists") who organized what would become the campus chapter of Students for a Democratic Society. Leadership of the new group fell to Eric Gordon, a second-year M.A. student in Latin American Studies who had become politically active as a Yale undergraduate by working for a local peace candidate in New Haven, Connecticut.[6] If Gordon gave SDS a link to the antiwar movement, Catherine E. "Cathy" Cade, a doctoral student in sociology who succeeded Gordon as head of the SDS chapter in 1968, provided an equally important connection with the civil rights struggles of the early and mid-1960s. After graduating from high school in Memphis, Tennessee, Cade attended Carleton College in Minnesota until the spring of 1962, when she enrolled as a junior year exchange student at Spelman College, a black women's school in Atlanta, Georgia, that was alive with protest activity. Her arrival coincided with a sit-in at the Georgia legislature organized by radical historian Howard Zinn, a white member of the Spelman faculty. Cade joined the demonstration—her first—and went on to work in the protracted campaign for desegregation in Albany and surrounding areas of southwest Georgia. After entering Tulane she took part in the famous Mississippi Freedom Summer of 1964, participated in CORE-sponsored "free schools" and local Community Action projects, and helped launch the Southern

5. Tulane *Hullabaloo*, 15 September 1967, pp. 1–2.

6. Ibid., 6 October 1967, p. 2; Herbert E. Longenecker, Memorandum Concerning Students for a Democratic Society, 29 September 1967, box 62, HEL Papers; Eric Gordon, "Personal Statement," [March 1972], Tulane University Latin American Studies Program Biographical Files, examined with the permission of Dr. Eugene Yeager.

Student Organizing Committee, a group that initially saw itself as a regional analogue to SDS and sought to increase the involvement of young white southerners in movements for social change. Cade's presence gave Tulane's fledgling SDS chapter a genuine "movement" pedigree.[7]

In the wake of their first meeting, the Tulane SDS group announced a list of concerns that ran the gamut from opposition to Selective Service to concern over high bookstore prices and dormitory visitation rules. Also on the SDS agenda were the issues of student freedom to invite speakers without administrative "interference," and what was vaguely described as "the harassment policy of the University administration concerning the student body." The seemingly incongruous mixture of mundane student problems and larger political issues reflected the SDS axiom that "all issues are interrelated." In a 1966 paper entitled, "Toward a Student Syndicalist Movement or University Reform Revisited"—a document that President Longenecker distributed to all Tulane deans—national SDS vice president and theoretician Carl Davidson had argued that college dormitory rules were related to Vietnam as aspects of "corporate liberalism—a dehumanizing and oppressive system" sustained by university graduates who had been conditioned on the curricular assembly lines of American "knowledge factories" to serve as "a new kind of scab" for exploitative bureaucracies. Within this framework, numerous "secondary issues" of immediate concern to students might serve as useful beginning points for organizing a movement aimed at the radical transformation of higher education's basic function and at the radicalization of student political consciousness.[8]

Davidson's emphasis upon the transformation of individual con-

7. Gregg Michel, "Building an Organization: The Founding of SSOC" (chap. from Ph.D. diss. in progress, University of Virginia); Sara Evans, *Personal Politics: The Roots of Women's Liberation in the Civil Rights Movement and the New Left* (New York: Vintage Books, 1980), 35, 38, 183; Tulane *Hullabaloo*, 17 December 1964, p. 1; *Southern Patriot* 24 (March 1966): 1, 3; Catherine Elise Cade, "Orientations toward Social Change in the Negro Community of a Southern Town" (Ph.D. diss., Tulane University, 1969); Christina Greene, "'We'll Take Our Stand': Race, Class, and Gender in the Southern Student Organizing Committee, 1964–1969," in *Hidden Histories of Women in the New South*, ed. Virginia Bernhard et al. (Columbia: University of Missouri Press, 1994), 191, 202.

8. Tulane *Hullabaloo*, 6 October 1967, p. 2 (first–second quotations); Carl Davidson, "Toward a Student Syndicalist Movement or University Reform Revisited," working paper, National Convention of Students for a Democratic Society, Clear Lake, Iowa, August 1966, box 62, HEL Papers (third–sixth quotations).

sciousness through struggles for student power reflected a basic shift in SDS's strategy. From 1966 onward, the organization's national leadership abandoned efforts to build coalitions with liberals and the left wing of the Democratic Party, and concentrated instead upon radicalizing a "new working class" of college-trained teachers, engineers, and salaried professionals—the group that according to neo-Marxist doctrine constituted the nearest equivalent in the late-twentieth century to Marx's nineteenth-century conception of the alienated factory laborer. The intellectual underpinning for SDS's new strategy was taken partly from the American sociologist C. Wright Mills, partly from André Gorz and other French radicals, and partly from the German-born political philosopher Herbert Marcuse, whose books *Eros and Civilization* (1955) and *One Dimensional Man* (1964) enjoyed considerable cachet in academic circles. Collectively the new ideas helped redirect SDS attention to American college campuses, where it was hoped that the student component of a redefined white-collar proletariat might come to understand and reject its own enslavement to the values of a corporate, bureaucratic system. Not all SDS members accepted this logic, but for those who did the goal of campus activism shifted from protest to "resistance"—the involvement of students in a Marcusean "Great Refusal" that would prepare them for continued struggle after graduation.[9]

Although the fluid orthodoxies of the youthful Left furnished a new vocabulary and a loose intellectual framework for the articulation of student protest, there is little to suggest that either "new working class" theory or other fine points of New Left philosophy held any particular fascination for the majority of those who attended the organizational meeting of Tulane's SDS chapter. What most college students at Tulane and elsewhere knew about student activism in the fall of 1967 was derived from media coverage of civil rights marches, the 1964 Berkeley demonstrations, and the still infrequent antiwar protests on a few high-profile college campuses. In October, however, as student

---

9. Irwin Unger with the assistance of Debi Unger, *The Movement: A History of the American New Left, 1959–1972* (New York: Harper and Row, 1974), 94–101; Allen J. Matusow, *The Unraveling of America* (New York: Harper and Row, 1984), 321–5; Carl Davidson, "Multiversity: Crucible of the New Working Class," in *Thought from the Educational Reform Movement (Mainly Catching Up): A Collection of Essays with Editorial Interventions Gathered by Rick Kean* (Washington, D.C.: United States National Student Association, 1968), 122–56. Cf. John P. Diggins, *The Rise and Fall of the American Left* (New York: W. W. Norton, 1992), 268–76.

By the late 1960s, men's dormitories had proliferated along McAlister Drive.

radicals, hippies, rock groups, poets, writers, and prominent intellectuals joined antiwar liberals and pacifists to stage a highly publicized march on the Pentagon—an event brilliantly portrayed in Norman Mailer's contemporary account, *The Armies of the Night*—the *Hullabaloo* carried a detailed summary of the student power resolutions adopted by NSA delegates in Maryland a few weeks earlier. The *Hullabaloo* also printed in parallel columns articles by Edward Schwartz and Carl Davidson, which outlined respectively the reformist NSA and the radical SDS views of what student power should represent. The NSA position, to which Harnage generally subscribed, employed the language of Deweyan progressivism to argue that student power was an educational principle rather than a legal doctrine. According to this view, demands for student power were grounded in the conviction that "people learn through living, through the process of integrating their thoughts with their actions, through testing their values against those of a community, through the capacity to act." Student power thus implied "the ability to make decisions, . . . the creation of a new process for the enactment of rules, . . . [and] the development of a democratic standard of authority." In more concrete terms, it meant that students should make all rules concerning their personal, residential, social, and recreational life, and that students and faculty members should "co-decide" curricular policy. Decisions affecting the university as a whole should likewise be jointly agreed upon by professors, administrators, and students. Properly understood and implemented, student power would redefine relationships within the "university community" while reducing the influence of external groups such as trustees or alumni who might seek to impose authoritarian standards.[10]

The NSA view of student power had much in common with the ideal of "a democracy of individual participation" inspired by radical sociologist C. Wright Mills and embraced in the 1962 Port Huron Statement, the founding document of SDS.[11] By 1968, however, the reformist optimism that had inspired early SDS members to see the transformed university as an ally in the struggle for social change had given way to a radical critique that was sharply at odds with liberal assumptions. In his essay, "Student Power: Radical View," Carl Davidson dismissed as "Bullshit" the idea that students were oppressed. On the contrary, students were "being trained to be oppressors" in a system of higher education that was merely a "service station and job-training factory adjunct to corporate capitalism." Under such conditions, university reform could only be achieved through transforming the larger society of which the university was a part. From the radical perspective, student power hinged upon acceptance of a few key syllogisms. "Administrators are the enemy." Trust people rather than programs. "Refuse to be 'responsible.'" Reject the on-campus versus off-campus dichotomy. Demand "seriousness by dealing with serious issues—getting the U.S. out of Vietnam, getting the military off campus. . . . In short, make a revolution."[12]

Despite differences in philosophy and approach, the programs of SDS and the NSA were far from being mutually exclusive in practice. Both groups espoused the cause of university reform and favored an agenda of institutional change that was broadly similar in its emphasis upon student decision making and power sharing with administration

10. Tulane *Hullabaloo*, 27 October 1967, p. 9.

11. James Miller, *"Democracy is in the Streets": From Port Huron to the Siege of Chicago* (New York: Simon and Schuster, 1987), 333, appendix.

12. Tulane *Hullabaloo*, 27 October 1967, p. 9.

and faculty. On the matter of organized student government, however, the two groups seemed hopelessly at odds. The NSA (and Harnage) viewed student government as a potential vehicle for student empowerment, while SDS (and Eric Gordon) dismissed campus electoral politics as an empty ritual leading to a kind of sham representation in powerless deliberative bodies that were easily "co-opted" by administrators. Convinced that "[t]he Student Senate doesn't do anything; it means nothing and discusses only meaningless issues," Gordon summarized his own conception of student government by quoting the SDS motto: "Let the people decide."[13]

In one of the many ironies surrounding the initial phase of student activism at Tulane, it would be Hank Harnage, the liberal fraternity man turned student power advocate, who would come closest to bringing about the actual repudiation of student government. In the 1967 fall semester, while SDS pursued antiwar activity through demonstrations against ROTC and protests against campus recruiting by the CIA, the armed services, and the Dow Chemical Company (manufacturer of napalm), Harnage worked diligently to build a consensus for student power among the Student Senate's various constituencies. The previous fall, as a member of the senate's Human Relations Committee, he had helped black students rescind the senate's October 18, 1966, decision to place "practicality" ahead of racial integration when arranging student social events. In place of the controversial measure, the senate had pledged its unequivocal support for the "rights, equality[,] and dignity of every individual," and had declared racial integration to be a "primary consideration" in making contracts with off-campus businesses. Now, a year later, in November 1967, the senate invoked the spirit of the 1966 rescinding resolution and urged Tulane students to support an economic boycott of local restaurants where segregation was still practiced. In early December the senate unanimously approved the application of the Afro-American Congress of Tulane for provisional recognition as an official campus organization, leaving the University Senate Committee on Student Affairs to resolve

13. Ibid., 6 October 1967, p. 2 (quotations); ibid., 27 October 1967, p. 9. In the essay that the *Hullabaloo* reprinted, Carl Davidson conceded that student government might be "a good place for initiating on the campus the movement for human liberation already in progress off the campus." What he did not make explicit was that the kind of liberation SDS envisioned involved the elimination of existing student assemblies and their replacement by "Free Student Unions" or other syndicalist "counter-institutions" embracing the mass of students and dedicated to the "abolition of the grade system."

By 1972, black students no longer faced the degree of isolation that their predecessors had encountered.

ambiguities in the group's constitution that combined a seemingly nondiscriminatory membership policy with a preamble that began, "We, the Black students of Tulane University. . . ."[14]

Another group seeking official university recognition in the fall of 1967 was SDS. Less than a week before the senate took up the matter, Eric Gordon announced that the group's constitution would be left intentionally vague in order to avoid rejection by "some phony Student Senate or Executive Committee." Throwing down the gauntlet to conservatives, he went on to note that the organization would not alter or abandon any of its radical aims "because a bunch of stupid frat rats say so." Two rancorous senate meetings and the active support of Harnage were required to gain endorsement for SDS, with its constitution-

14. Tulane *Hullabaloo*, 27 October 1967, p. 1; ibid., 3 November 1967, p.1; ibid., 15 December 1967, p. 4; Tulane Student Senate Minutes, 18 October 1966 (first quotation); ibid., special meeting, 3 November 1966 (second quotation); ibid., 7 November 1967; ibid., 5 December 1967 (third quotation), ASB, 1954–92; Tulane *Hullabaloo*, 8 December 1967, p. 2.

ally stated intention to "support and engage in such programs of research and action [as] will make of students and the University agents for responsible change." Opposition to SDS came from several sources, including career-minded University College students who hoped to "get through Tulane without a lot of bayonets and clubs" and were apprehensive that SDS might transform the university into "a Berkeley, a Wisconsin or a Chicago." Ideological hostility to student radicalism was centered in the School of Engineering, where an informal poll revealed that only two out of sixty-four students looked favorably on SDS. After one Engineering senator was ruled out of order for posing the question "Are you a Communist?" to Eric Gordon, the SDS constitution was approved by a vote of 25-14.[15]

Like virtually all Student Senate actions in 1967, the approval of new campus organizations was subject to veto by higher authority. Before decisions reached in the student legislature took effect, they faced review by the University Senate Committee on Student Affairs (a faculty body in which students were represented) and ultimately by the University Senate itself (a body comprised of senior administrators and faculty representatives from Tulane's various colleges). The cumbersome process involved lengthy delays in the approval and implementation of even the most routine measures, and served to underscore the Student Senate's lack of real control over most matters upon which it sought to legislate. Expanding the Student Senate's autonomy and giving students a more direct role in the existing mechanisms of university governance became a central goal of Harnage's campaign for student power. This campaign began dramatically on November 14, 1967, when the senate's entire Executive Cabinet—including all major senate officers, the chairman of CACTUS, and the president of the University Center Board—offered their "provisional resignations," together with a recommendation that the senate vote to abolish Tulane's student government. Before announcing the cabinet's action to the assembled senate—thirteen of whose members had run without opposition in the fall elections and few, if any, of whom maintained meaningful contacts with actual constituencies—Harnage read aloud lengthy excerpts from Edward Schwartz's essay, "Student Power, As It Hap-

15. Tulane *Hullabaloo*, 6 October 1967, p. 2 (first–second quotations); SDS Constitution, accompanying Tulane Student Senate Minutes, 10 October 1967, ASB, 1954–92 (third quotation); Tulane *Hullabaloo*, 27 October 1967, p. 1 (fourth–sixth quotations); Tulane Student Senate Minutes, 24 October 1967, ASB, 1954–92.

pens," a document in which the national NSA president applauded recent advances in student rights and urged students to press for further gains. Harnage criticized both faculty and administrators for their lack of response to previous student initiatives at Tulane, and announced that the resignations would take effect at the beginning of the spring semester unless the powers of student government were increased and its "effectiveness" demonstrated by the members themselves.[16]

When the floor was opened for discussion in the wake of Harnage's remarks, the senate meeting became "a virtual anti-administration 'bitch-in,'" with various students calling for better academic fundraising, the disclosure of secret military research by university faculty, the "non-recognition" of fraternities, the creation of a bookstore cooperative, and the election of student delegates to the University Senate who would be instructed to "attend the meeting until they are thrown out." Other speakers urged the Student Senate to schedule an open meeting with the administration and "demand that the deans and President Longenecker come to it." The overall tone of the discussion was best captured by the president of the University Center Board, who declared at one point, "I am sick of listening to what the administration likes or doesn't like. In fact I am sick of listening to the administration, which thoroughly revolts me most of the time."[17]

At a special meeting the following week, the Student Senate overwhelmingly approved an Executive Cabinet report affirming support for the NSA definition of student power "as a movement designed to gain for students their full rights as citizens and their right to democratically control their non-academic lives and participate to the fullest in the administrative and educational decision-making process of the university." As a road map for future action, the report outlined five basic objectives, including: the implementation of a student judiciary system endorsed by the senate the previous spring; the creation of a "Joint Board for University Planning" composed of students, faculty, and administrators; new arrangements to provide a "meaningful and effective voice" in curricular decisions for students in all Tulane divisions; student control of dormitory regulations and visitation policies; and, finally, a guarantee of greater faculty and administrative responsiveness toward student government through prompt action on all

16. Tulane Student Senate Minutes, 14 November 1967, ASB, 1954–92; Tulane *Hullabaloo*, 17 November 1967, p. 1 (quotation); ibid., 16 February 1968, p. 8.

17. Tulane *Hullabaloo*, 17 November 1967, p. 2.

Student Senate recommendations. The last point generated a follow-up resolution declaring that Student Senate measures not acted upon by the University Senate within thirty-five class days should be considered as passed. In the event Student Senate actions were rejected after efforts at compromise with the University Senate, students would be encouraged to ignore the rejection and abide by the Student Senate's decision. On December 12 the resolutions came before the University Senate Committee on Student Affairs, where they touched off a heated debate over student power. In a meeting that saw the committee vote 9-4 in favor of granting provisional recognition to SDS, political scientist Henry Mason, who had previously labeled SDS members as "fascists of the left," denounced the Student Senate resolutions as a "move toward a coup d'état." Even sympathetic University Senate members like business school professor Stephen Zeff regarded the proposals as extreme and cautioned the students against alienating their faculty support.[18]

In both syntax and substance the Student Senate's agenda for change reflected the influence of the National Student Association. To no one's surprise, Harnage made rejoining the NSA a major component of his campaign for student power. At a special meeting on December 12, 1967, the Student Senate, at Harnage's urging, voted 32-2 with two abstentions in favor of reaffiliating with the NSA, provided that students approved the action in a campuswide referendum early the next semester. During the December 12 meeting and in the weeks that followed, supporters of the NSA enumerated the practical benefits of membership, such as participation in the national organization's Office of Economic Opportunity grant for teacher and course evaluation. But the real meaning of NSA membership was to be found at the symbolic level. Besides keeping Tulane in touch with student rights advances at peer schools across the nation, reaffiliation would constitute a tacit declaration that the university was part of the emerging student movement. Only in this manner, supporters believed, could the student body "break out of a possible slump into provincialism." Those

18. Tulane Student Senate Minutes, 20 November 1967, ASB, 1954–92 (first–fourth quotations); Tulane *Hullabaloo*, 15 December 1967, pp. 1 (fifth quotation), 5 (sixth quotation). The Student Senate definition of student power was taken verbatim from a resolution on the same subject adopted by the National Student Association at its August 1967 convention. Tulane *Hullabaloo*, 15 March 1968, p. 10.

who opposed reaffiliation, such as the vice president of the Arts and Sciences freshman class, launched a vigorous counterattack that smeared the NSA with broad brush anti-Communist rhetoric borrowed from publications of the conservative Young Americans for Freedom. Ignoring the NSA's twenty-year connection with the CIA, opponents unblushingly reprinted decade-old statements by a former investigator for the House Un-American Activities Committee who had charged that NSA policies and programs embraced elements of the Communist Party's official line.[19]

Conducted under the threat of resignation en masse by the established student leadership, the NSA referendum campaign evolved quickly into an effort at raising the political consciousness of the still quiescent majority of Tulane undergraduates. Dramatic gestures became the order of the day, beginning with the December resignation of *Hullabaloo* editor Jeff Howie following a reprimand by the Publications Board for printing a news report containing a one-sentence excerpt of indecent language from an antiwar pamphlet that SDS members had distributed in Tulane's University Center until stopped by campus police. The reprimand had been supported by two student members of the Publications Board and opposed by three others, including Harnage and Newcomb student body president Sylvia Dreyfus. If the split reflected political divisions within the undergraduate population, it also suggested that freedom of the press was the kind of issue that students took seriously enough to defend—both as a prerequisite of civil liberty and as a symbol for the entire range of issues embraced by the student movement. Howie's resignation elevated the *Hullabaloo* to a level of new symbolic importance, which was underscored by the fact that the former editor refused to reconsider his decision so long as the student body remained "apathetic" and oblivious to "any realization of what we are trying to do." Before the controversy surrounding Howie had fully abated, a second name was added to the resignation list in January 1968, when CACTUS chairman Gary Barker stepped down from his post. In a widely quoted resignation letter to Harnage, Barker echoed Howie's complaint, charging that neither the faculty, the Tulane administration, the Student Senate, nor the student body as a whole possessed the "conviction, courage, de-

---

19. Tulane Student Senate Minutes, 12 December 1967, ASB, 1954–92; Tulane *Hullabaloo*, 15 December 1967, p. 1 (quotation); ibid., 9 February 1968, p. 1.

sire, or ability to effectuate . . . changes fundamental to the creation of a progressive university."[20]

The state of campus political sentiment received its first direct test some two weeks later, when students voted against joining the NSA by a margin of roughly three to two (970-615) in a contest that attracted less than 20 percent of the eligible electorate. Although this was a better showing than the two to one rejection of the NSA in 1966, the outcome was a keen disappointment to Harnage, who resigned as president of the Student Senate on February 6, 1968. Describing the response to his student empowerment initiatives as "hardly better than pitifully weak," Harnage explained that he had attempted to foster a "more mature approach for the students to their own daily living here," but had discovered that "the student body is not back there behind me, let alone the Student Senate." As in the cases of Howie and Barker, Harnage's resignation—for all its seeming pessimism—was carried out in a climate of anticipation rather than despair. In a parting editorial Jeff Howie praised Harnage as "a man before his time," who had tried with some success "to awaken the student body to its own potentiality." The *Hullabaloo* agreed that "[p]robably most students do want 'student power' even if they don't understand exactly what the term means." Student Senate vice president Larry Rosenblum, who together with the remainder of the Executive Cabinet postponed resigning in order to gauge the response of the student body, offered what may have been the most perceptive comment on the prospects for student mobilization in the spring of 1968. "Students here are not apathetic," Rosenblum declared. "[T]here just has not been an issue in the four years I've been at this school which has had sufficient impact to arouse them."[21]

Arousal would not be long in coming. By the time Rosenblum's remarks appeared in print in February 1968, the issue that would become a rallying point for the decade's first mass protest by Tulane students was already taking shape in the editorial offices of the *Hullabaloo*, where a special literary supplement entitled "Sophia" was in the final stages of preparation. The theme for the issue was "Pornography and Art," a topic the paper planned to illustrate with two pho-

20. Tulane *Hullabaloo*: 8 December 1967, pp. 1, 3; 15 December 1967, pp. 1, 2; 2 February 1968, p. 1 (first–second quotations); 12 January 1968, p. 2 (third quotation).

21. Ibid.: 9 February 1968, pp. 1 (first–third quotations), 2, 8 (fourth–fifth quotations); 16 February 1968, p. 8 (sixth quotation), p. 2 (seventh–eighth quotations).

tographs. One showed a piece of sculpture that the New Orleans police had confiscated as obscene. The second and more controversial illustration was a photograph of the sculpture "Adam and Eve," consisting of stylized male and female figures executed vaguely after the fashion of primitive art, with a pronounced emphasis upon female breasts and male genitalia. The work was the creation of Newcomb art professor Gabor Gergo, who was shown seated naked next to his creation. On March 1, 1968, the day set for the literary supplement's appearance, a heated debate within the Publications Board resulted in a 4-3 vote in favor of publishing the photographs. At this point Dean of Students John Stibbs intervened. "Knowing very well that the pictures were pornographic in the extreme," Stibbs "picked up" the photographs and according to his later recollection, "quietly declared that they would not be published at Tulane University." With the angry protests of students on the Publications Board ringing in his ears, Stibbs locked the photographs in his desk and departed for Chicago after getting President Longenecker's approval for his actions. During the next few days, again to borrow Stibbs's phraseology, "all hell broke loose."[22]

From the standpoint of those who were urging students to work through the system, the timing of Stibbs's actions could scarcely have been worse. The events of 1967 had resulted in increased student participation in the mechanisms of academic governance. By the fall of 1967 a total of nineteen students were serving on seven standing committees of the University Senate, and in November the latter body voted to allow the president of the Student Senate to attend University Senate meetings in a nonvoting capacity. Several college faculties were moving toward the inclusion of students on important committees, and in the College of Arts and Sciences, students were already serving on and chairing the newly revamped Honor Board. Radical students had long argued that such concessions were little more than window dressing, and Stibbs's heavy-handed assertion of the "implied powers" of college administrators seemed to underscore their point. If college officials could summarily overturn decisions of a duly constituted admin-

22. James E. Llamas, "Winds of Discontent," *Tulanian* 41 (March 1968): 1–2; *New Orleans States-Item*, 6 March 1968, vertical file, Howard-Tilton Memorial Library; Lou Jeansonne, "The *Hullabaloo* Censorship Controversy of 1968," Tulane *Hullabaloo*, 10 February 1995, p. 6 (for title of sculpture and publication of the Gergo photograph); John H. Stibbs, "Twenty-Five Years of Student Life at Tulane University [1949–1975]," typescript, box 64, HEL Papers, 29 (all quotations).

istrative, faculty, and student committee, the notion of real power sharing within the existing bureaucracy became a transparent fiction. By brushing aside the decision of the Publications Board (on which the Dean of Students served as a voting member), Stibbs gave student power advocates the one thing they had previously lacked—a galvanizing issue.[23]

Organized opposition to Stibbs's action began on Sunday evening, March 3, with a meeting in the *Hullabaloo* office attended by the paper's editor Carol Sowell, the literary supplement editor William Rushton, and a cross-section of Tulane's elected student leaders, including acting Student Senate president Larry Rosenblum, retiring Newcomb student body president Sylvia Dreyfus, and former Architecture student body president William Harlan. Also in attendance were Michael Kliks, a student senator representing the medical school, and Cathy Cade, the newly elected chairperson of SDS. Calling themselves the "Ad Hoc Committee of Concerned Students," the group wasted little time in calling for a demonstration outside the Norman Mayer Building, where the University Senate would be holding a regularly scheduled meeting on Monday afternoon. Despite the short notice, some 125–150 students appeared at the appointed time to hear speeches by Dreyfus and Rushton, who had prepared mimeographed leaflets urging students to "show the University that we will not continue to 'go through channels' until integrity is restored to administration-student relationships." The demonstration, which was covered by two local television stations, marked the beginning of a week of mass meetings and protest marches that grew steadily in size and public visibility.[24]

By the end of the day on Monday the Ad Hoc Committee had absorbed several new members, including Eliot Levin (a 1966 A&S graduate), Ernest McCormick (an A&S junior), Hank Harnage, and student senator Jim Porter, a recent associate editor of the *Hullabaloo*. The expanded group decided to call a joint meeting of the Student Senate and the student body in the University Center the next evening. What the *Hullabaloo* described as "one of the strangest [Student

23. University Senate Minutes, 3 April, 8 and 22 May, 2 October, 6 November 1967, box 72, HEL Papers; Minutes of the Faculty of H. Sophie Newcomb Memorial College, 15 March 1968, box 45, HEL Papers (hereafter Newcomb Faculty Minutes); A&S Dean's Report, 1966–67, box 29, HEL Papers, 6.

24. Tulane *Hullabaloo*, 8 March 1968, pp. 1 (first quotation), 2 (second quotation).

Senate] meetings in recent years" began at approximately 7:00 P.M. on Tuesday, March 5, with about four hundred students present but only a "bare quorum" of the senate in attendance. The censorship dispute was the only item of business. Senators eventually passed two resolutions. One was a vote of formal censure against Stibbs for his "arbitrary and unconstitutional usurpation of power" in overriding the Publications Board; the other was a motion to "support the opinions and actions of the Ad Hoc Committee of Concerned Students in their effort to rectify the arbitrary policies of the administration." Once the senate had concluded its formal session, the gathering continued in the form of "a general student body mass meeting" given over to several hours of wide-ranging discussion about the disputed photographs, "the administration's alleged lack of concern for students," and various related topics. In the course of the proceedings, President Longenecker agreed by telephone to meet the next day with members of the Ad Hoc Committee and to address the student body in the near future.[25]

Hundreds of students still crowded the University Center at 11:00 P.M., the normal closing time, raising the prospect of an illegal occupation and a possible confrontation with campus police. Around 11:15 John P. McDowell, Associate Dean of the College of Arts and Sciences, urged the students to adjourn the meeting until after the Ad Hoc Committee had met with Longenecker the next day. Initially Larry Rosenblum, Carol Sowell, and other committee leaders agreed and "warned the students against pushing too hard." Sensing a weakening of collective resolve, SDS leader Cathy Cade, whose tactical skills had been honed through years of civil rights activism, vigorously opposed any hiatus in student pressure. Longenecker, she argued, should be forced to set a definite date for his address to the students and should agree in advance to publication of the *Hullabaloo* photographs. Cade's remarks struck a responsive chord with Rosenblum, who abandoned his conciliatory posture and vowed to remain in the UC all night. Other students began to contemplate still bolder action. With attention refocused on Longenecker, and with concrete objectives now defined, the group responded enthusiastically to proposals for a march on the president's home. Leaving the UC around 12:30 A.M., some three hundred students—roughly twice the number involved in the previous

25. Ibid., 2.

day's demonstration—made their way to 2 Audubon Place, where they stood outside and chanted, "Censorship, Censorship," "Abide by the Rules," and "We Want the Photos." Longenecker eventually addressed the group from his veranda and met with a small delegation inside the residence, but conceded nothing of significance. Around 1:30 A.M. the students departed, leaving behind an effigy of Stibbs hanging from a tree.[26]

At 10:00 the next morning (Wednesday, March 6) Longenecker, flanked by Provost David Deener and Vice President Clarence Scheps, met in his Gibson Hall office with approximately a dozen representatives of the Ad Hoc Committee, including Harlan, Harnage, Rushton, Porter, Levin, Sowell, Dreyfus, and Cade. Outside, a crowd had begun to gather and students were distributing flyers proclaiming, "STUDENT POWER BECAME A REALITY LAST NIGHT." Issued in the name of "The Ad Hoc Committee, Bill Rushton, Chairman," the leaflets made six demands on the Tulane administration and called for a student strike of class attendance until the "integrity crisis" was resolved. Little noticed at the time was a brief clash between two mathematics professors over what was destined to become the burning issue of the next academic year—the use of civil disobedience as a tactic to compel change.[27]

The conflict involved mathematician Edward Dubinsky, SDS faculty adviser, and Bruce Treybig, a departmental colleague whose office on an upper floor of Gibson Hall overlooked the student demonstrators gathering on the Freret Street side of the building. Annoyed by the crowd's noise, Treybig put aside his work after 10:30 A.M. and soon admitted a small group of math students to his office to watch the events taking place outside. Upon hearing around 10:50 A.M. that students favoring a strike would attempt to block the building exits, Treybig grew irate and went to investigate. As he would later recall, "I looked out the window and to my amazement, there was Ed Dubinsky directing the seating of students so as to block the steps. . . . I then went down . . . and told Dubinsky he had damn well better not keep my students from coming to class." Most of Treybig's students appeared for the

26. Ibid., pp. 2 (all quotations), 3.
27. Ad Hoc Committee flyer, typescript in records of the Edward Dubinsky case maintained by the Tulane University chapter of the American Association of University Professors (hereafter cited as Tulane AAUP Files; all quotations). This material was used through the courtesy of Professor Henry Mason. See also Tulane *Hullabaloo*, 8 March 1968, p. 3.

11:00 course, but later in the day he again "jumped Dubinsky about blocking the steps" and was told that "they were not really blocking the stairs but were just making it difficult for students to attend class." The explanation was not to Treybig's liking. Quoting once more from his own version of the incident, "I then told Dubinsky that he had no right to interfere with my classes, and he said that it was too bad but sometimes people's rights conflicted. Meaning I had a right to teach my class but he also had a right to interfere with it. . . . I then told him that if that was his attitude, he had no business being in this mathematics department." For the time being, the clash of moral imperatives remained unresolved.[28]

Shortly after noon Longenecker and the Ad Hoc Committee representatives emerged to face television cameras and to advise a restive crowd of some 150 students of the meeting's inconclusive results. Longenecker had set March 25 (later changed to March 13) as the date for addressing the student body, and he had agreed that the role, function, and composition of the Publications Board would receive consideration through normal university channels. There would be no reprisals against the previous night's marchers or against other students who might engage in "future peaceful demonstrations." Deans would be authorized to allow free class cuts throughout the day on Wednesday, and the question of whether or not to publish the photographs would be referred to the Board of Administrators—the body that, in any case, possessed final authority in disputed policy matters. With considerable aplomb Longenecker described the meeting as "a very fine exchange of views, the kind we would welcome having much more frequently." Titters of laughter followed the remark.[29]

The most immediate result of the morning's discussions was an afternoon meeting between Harry B. Kelleher, chairman of the Board of Administrators' Committee on Student Affairs, and several members of the Ad Hoc Committee. On this occasion Harlan, Rushton, and Dreyfus were joined by a new colleague, Charles Lewis "Chip" Lord Jr., the president of the School of Architecture student body. The meeting did not go well. The Administrators had already indicated their full support for the decision to ban the disputed photographs and

28. Bruce Treybig to Frank Birtel and other mathematics department faculty, 12 March 1968, Tulane AAUP Files. No contemporary account of the episode by Professor Dubinsky has come to light.

29. Tulane *Hullabaloo*, 8 March 1968, p. 3.

Kelleher reaffirmed the Board's position. Students who had assembled in the UC for a second mass meeting early Wednesday evening received a firsthand report of the frustrating conference couched in language that was calculated to arouse indignation. Participants described an intimidating atmosphere that had hovered over the afternoon discussion, and expressed anger at Kelleher's perceived aloofness and imperious demeanor. "I felt that I was a box of corn flakes to him, and when he was through with it he would throw it away," one member of the Ad Hoc Committee declared. Earlier in the day, literary supplement editor William Rushton had assured a local reporter that "[w]e're going to get what we want or damn it, we'll close this university down!" By 7:30 P.M. the UC gathering had decided to stage another march on Longenecker's home. After an hour of recruiting in the dormitories, between six and seven hundred marchers—again more than double the previous night's number—were on their way to Audubon Place.[30]

Upon reaching their destination around 8:30 P.M. the students found the president's house darkened, although Longenecker and various guests were actually inside proceeding with a previously scheduled social event. When some thirty minutes of chanting failed to elicit another front steps dialogue with the president, there was brief talk of a sit-down demonstration on the sidewalk. But as uniformed New Orleans policemen began to gather at the scene, plans for further action were quickly abandoned. By 9:05 P.M. students had begun moving back to the University Center, where they dispersed after discussing plans for a boycott of the Tulane cafeteria and bookstore. The swift pendulum swing from drama to anticlimax anticipated the overall trajectory of the student protest movement. Developments over the next few days made it clear that the Wednesday evening march constituted both the high point and the beginning of the end for the university's first serious encounter with mass demonstrations. No cafeteria or bookstore boycotts ever materialized. While on Friday, March 8, some 1,200 students (attracted by the weekly free movies in McAlister Auditorium) voted overwhelmingly to endorse the protest leaders' actions, attempts to stage a student

30. Ibid. (first quotation); *New Orleans States-Item*, 6 March 1968, vertical file, Tulane University Library (second quotation).

demonstration outside Longenecker's office the next week (on the eve of his scheduled address to the student body) attracted only forty to fifty participants. Temporarily, at least, the bloom was off the rose of student rebellion.[31]

Explaining the rise and decline of the 1968 protests to alumni, Longenecker would later conclude that "on Wednesday evening [March 6] . . . the basic student leadership . . . lost control of the situation," allowing "other elements" to exploit student frustration for their own purposes. The statement was correct as far as it went. Rapid growth over a four-day period, with a quadrupling of the number of campus demonstrators in forty-eight hours, inevitably introduced new elements into the protest movement's leadership cadre. Internal lines of stress became evident on Thursday morning, March 7, when Rosenblum and several supporters withdrew after arguing unsuccessfully for a moratorium on further demonstrations until after Longenecker's March 13 speech. In the wake of the split the Ad Hoc Committee formally disbanded and was replaced by a new coalition composed of Harlan, Lord, and McCormick, together with history graduate students Alton Bryant, Newton Gingrich, and David Kramer, the last of whom had been a leader of the Wednesday night march. Showing little concern for euphonic nomenclature, the new group called itself MORTS—an acronym for Mobilization of Responsible Tulane Students.[32]

Although MORTS quickly reabsorbed most of the key participants in the Ad Hoc Committee, including Rosenblum, Rushton, and Dreyfus, the protest impulse lost momentum rapidly. The very diversity of the enlarged and reconstituted group made unified action more difficult. Protest leaders could agree on the value of "student power," but understandings of the term's meaning varied widely. For Harnage and Rosenblum, student power was a kind of active university citizenship best achieved through a more vigorous Student Senate and expanded student membership on academic and administrative committees. SDS members such as Cade and Gordon (who prepared a pamphlet for MORTS listing the business affiliations of some Tulane Board members) hoped to link the campus demonstrations and the student power

31. Ibid.; ibid., 15 March 1968, pp. 1, 15, 19.
32. Longenecker's alumni address is quoted in Llamas, "Winds of Discontent," 2–6 (quotation on p. 6); Tulane *Hullabaloo*, 8 March 1968, p. 3.

slogan to larger political concerns, including the Vietnam War and the putative evils of "corporate liberalism."[33]

Another bloc of protest leaders stressed the importance of defending civil liberties, together with all forms of artistic, esthetic, and intellectual freedom. This viewpoint was primarily associated with the *Hullabaloo* staff and with students enrolled in the School of Architecture. Not surprisingly, the group's emphasis on freedom of creative expression went hand in hand with pronounced differences in personality and style among individual members. Charles Lord, the president of the Architecture student body, struck one fellow student as a "quiet mind" who "like Madame Defarge . . . sat and knitted and thought." He stood in marked contrast to William Harlan, whose wire-rim glasses, goatee, mustache, and flowing red hair bespoke a "wonderful disregard for convention," which caused some to proclaim him "the first hippie of Tulane and everybody's archetypal notion of a hippie." William Rushton, who was both an architecture student and the editor of the censored literary supplement, was less flamboyant than Harlan in personal appearance but equally dedicated to shattering cultural restraints. Rushton came from a background in high school journalism and subsequent newspaper work in his hometown of Lake Charles. Tulane classmates would later recall that Rushton arrived in New Orleans "with no need for deprogramming," and he quickly emerged as a vocal critic of all barriers to individualism or creativity. Categorically opposed to censorship, he took the position that society as a whole would benefit if people were allowed "to say and do exactly what they wanted." Here was a somewhat different conception of student power, which, for all its youthful naivete, tapped an important and deep vein in the dissenting campus culture of the late 1960s.[34]

What held the student movement together was not so much a program as an outlook—a basic orientation that was youth centered, antiauthoritarian, and quasi-existentialist in its emphasis upon individual autonomy and free choice. This shared consciousness, refracted through

33. Transcript of Meeting of Student Leaders with President Longenecker, 11 March 1968, box 62, HEL Papers. Graduate students Bryant, Gingrich, and Kramer failed to articulate an original program, although Kramer was clearly an imposing figure with considerable dramatic presence, while Gingrich, who spoke incessantly during student meetings with Longenecker, seemed to compensate through sheer volubility for his lack of innate charisma.

34. Bernard Lemann, Malcolm Heard Jr., and John P. Klingman, eds., *Talk about Architecture: A Century of Architecture Education at Tulane* (New Orleans: Tulane University School of Architecture, 1993), 175 (first–fifth quotes), 176 (sixth quote).

the lens of distinctive personal experience, lent a coherence to the events of March 1968 that transcended the student movement's many internal divisions. Permeating the language and sensibility of student activists, it was the animating spirit of the protest rally, the aura surrounding the dissident speechmaker, and the solvent that ate through traditional boundaries separating fraternity members from independents and graduate or professional students from undergraduates. It ran like a bright thread through the mottled fabric of shifting leadership coalitions. And President Longenecker, having witnessed the new spirit at close quarters, was quick to grasp its importance, if not its larger meaning.[35]

In his March 13 State of the University address, delivered in McAlister Auditorium to an audience of some two thousand students and faculty, Longenecker took the measure of the student power movement as it appeared to members of the pre–World War II generation. Stressing the pervasiveness and national scope of conflicts over the "general structure of authority" on college campuses, Tulane's president acknowledged that students and administrators often saw the world through different eyes. "In my view," he told the assembled students, "your generation is developing a moral perspective that mine has some difficulty understanding." Paraphrasing a contemporary analysis of student activism by a professor at Antioch College, Longenecker concluded that for the generation of the late 1960s, the enlargement of human well-being and the fullest development of one's human capacities had become the basic moral category against which all types of educational activity—and all forms of campus authority—would be measured. Believing that higher learning should represent more than simply "trained intelligence," students had embraced a "new morality" that encompassed the concept of "freedom as a search for per-

35. The multilayered complexity of student activism in the late 1960s has defied easy synthesis. Few writers have come closer to establishing underlying commonalities of outlook and moral assumption among youthful activists than James A. Farrell. In *The Spirit of the Sixties: The Making of Postwar Radicalism* (New York: Routledge, 1997), Farrell argues for the centrality of a political "personalism" combining elements of Catholic social thought, communitarian anarchism, radical pacifism, and humanistic psychology. To these elements the student movement added "dissident sociology and psychology, existentialism, and civic republicanism." See pp. 6–19, 137 (quotation). Doug Rossinow, *The Politics of Authenticity: Liberalism, Christianity, and the New Left in America* (New York: Columbia University Press, 1998), which appeared too late to influence the present work, stresses the importance of Christian existentialism and populist liberalism among 1960s student activists at the University of Texas.

sonal identity." Up to this point Longenecker had said little with which student activists could disagree, but in his next breath he undercut their position by asserting that "most importantly [the new student morality] recognizes that freedom has never been achieved in the absence of restraints."[36]

The emphasis upon limits was less an objective description of student attitudes than an effort to place protest marches and other militant tactics outside the boundaries of legitimate dissent. In a passage that was clearly aimed at student power advocates, Longenecker offered what was essentially a caricature of the campus dissenters who had gained prominence during the preceding ten days. Without specifying the exact target of his remarks, he singled out for criticism those students who professed to accept the new morality but remained "wholly amenable to the suggestion that freedom should be equated with the rejection of constraints. [T]hey seem to be saying[,] 'Don't impose any requirements on me.' They ask the question of their faculty advisers, 'Who are you to tell me what courses to take?' In noncurricular areas the familiar form of the question relates to dormitory visitation rules or expected standards of personal conduct."[37]

The remainder of Longenecker's speech took a conciliatory line, focusing on the increased presence of students on university committees, the possibility of publishing the *Hullabaloo* under independent auspices, the need for more presidential attention to student concerns, and the importance of providing students with freer access to deans and other university officials. Such access, Longenecker was quick to emphasize, must occur through established channels. Throughout the preceding week he had worked to restore the influence of the elected student leaders who had "lost control" of events on the sixth of March. On Monday, March 11, for example, a scheduled meeting with the student affairs committee of the Tulane Board was limited to the *Hullabaloo* staff and the president of the Student Senate, ignoring the newer MORTS emissaries. On March 12 Longenecker gave an interview to local reporters in which he stressed that "student government should play the main role" in airing student complaints, because MORTS and the demonstrations were controlled by elements that were "not as fully representative as student government would be." Now, in his State of

36. Herbert E. Longenecker, Address to Students, 13 March 1968, typescript, box 125, HEL Papers.

37. Ibid.

the University address, he reiterated that university officials deemed it "impractical" to deal with "the many and varied groups of students who have presented themselves in this trying period, each professing to represent major components of the University's students. Student government must function effectively, particularly when there are differences to be resolved," the president concluded.[38]

For those who recalled the role of Student Senate president Hank Harnage in initiating the drive for student power, Longenecker's post-demonstration emphasis on the role of student government must have seemed ironic. Harnage, of course, had resigned his office largely out of frustration over the failure to transform the senate into an effective vehicle of student empowerment. In a *Hullabaloo* column published two days after Longenecker's speech, Harnage reviewed at length the official declarations of the NSA and the AAUP concerning the right of students to participate in formulating and applying institutional policies. Unless students were allowed to make real decisions and take responsibility for them, Harnage argued, democracy would be only a game, something "exercised through illegitimate student governments which have no power, or which use the forms of power without its substance." Tulane's recent marches and protest meetings, Harnage wrote, were "not demonstrations of 'student power' but rather manifestations of student powerlessness and examples of the tactics which the powerless often must use in our society to change things."[39]

Underscoring the gulf between student activists and Longenecker on questions of university governance, the Harnage column offered a more accurate barometer of Tulane's political climate than did the lackluster Student Senate elections held the next month. What the *Hullabaloo* described as "one of the most typical of all campaigns in one of the most atypical of years" featured two slates of candidates backed, as usual, by rival Greek system factions. Although MORTS, which ran no candidates, published a detailed student rights yardstick by which to measure those seeking campus office, the effort had little apparent effect. The platforms of both candidates called for course and teacher evaluations, student representation in the University Senate, and improved communication between student senators and their constituents. The losing contender for the senate presidency felt that

38. Tulane *Hullabaloo*, 15 March 1968, pp. 15, 20 (first–second quotations); Herbert E. Longenecker, Address to Students, 13 March 1968 (third–fourth quotations).

39. Tulane *Hullabaloo*, 15 March 1968, p. 10.

the senate should concern itself with student representation rather than student power, while the victorious candidate, Gary Ferris, stressed the need to publish bills in proper form before the senate discussed them. In a scathing assessment of the 1968 contest the *Hullabaloo* concluded that "[t]he tickets are manned by the usual Gant-shirted fraternity members who have been in the student government game since junior high school, students whose looks and reputations will hardly frighten deans or alumni into fear of a radical take-over."[40]

Taken together, the March protests and the April elections accurately mirrored the divided state of campus sentiment after the first year of direct exposure to the ideas and methods of the student movement. It would be an exaggeration to say that the events of March 1968 radicalized the Tulane student body. The long list of conservative, indifferent, or conventionally minded nonparticipants was at least as significant as the shorter roster of active dissidents. Apart from the School of Architecture, the university's professional students played little role in the protests. In fact, a group of 62 law students, together with some 286 other conservatives (including a large contingent of fraternity members), signed petitions in support of Stibbs's decision to suppress the *Hullabaloo* photographs. Even among undergraduates, actual protesters never comprised more than 20 percent of the combined Newcomb and A&S enrollment even by a generous estimate. The real significance of the March demonstrations lay in their precedent-setting nature. At Tulane, as on other southern campuses, student willingness to challenge institutional authority had developed almost imperceptibly, through slow accretions, over the span of a decade. As part of a line of progression that began with the cafeteria sit-ins of 1962 and included the mid-sixties skirmishes over in loco parentis, the protests of March 1968 represented the emergence of mass demonstrations as a badge of generational identity. During the next academic year and the one that followed, protest activity would enter the mainstream of campus life.[41]

40. Ibid.: 5 April 1968, pp. 1, 2, 8 (quotation), 9; 19 April 1968, pp. 1, 2; 26 April 1968, p. 1.

41. The 20 percent estimate is based upon a combined Newcomb and A&S enrollment of 3,188 for 1967–68 and makes the assumption that 650 of the estimated 700 marchers on 6 March 1968 matriculated in the two colleges. In reality graduate students probably comprised a considerably larger portion of the marchers. The 650 undergraduate estimate allows for the possibility that many Newcomb and A&S students supported the protest without participating in the Wednesday evening march.

II

Although the spring elections promised to remove student government as an arena for campus dissent in 1968–69, there were few if any members of the Tulane administration who anticipated smooth sailing in the next academic year. A clear indication of President Longenecker's attitude toward the March demonstrations, and a preview of the hard-line attitude he would adopt for the remainder of the decade, came in his "Charge: To the Class of 1968," delivered at the Tulane commencement ceremony on May 27. On that occasion Longenecker stressed the "paramount importance" of preserving "the integrity of teaching and research against the irrational and almost fanatical attempts in some quarters to curb it. When dissent becomes indistinguishable from civil disobedience and joins hands with insurrection," he continued, "the purposes of a university are no longer being served. Those who desire the preservation of the university cannot countenance the intransigence and emotional eccentricities of those few members whose tactics are akin to revolution and destruction." Uttered only a few weeks after the highly publicized April occupation of classroom and administration buildings at Columbia University by SDS followers and militant blacks (a six-day episode that ended in an orgy of police violence), Longenecker's words reflected the prevailing mood of apprehension among educators, who feared that the next academic year would see fulfillment of the radical exhortation, "Two, three, many Columbia's" on campuses throughout the United States.[42]

Events of the summer did little to allay the concerns of college administrators, who worried about what was increasingly being branded as campus rebellion rather than student unrest. The effect of the Columbia crisis and the March demonstrations at Tulane can be fully appreciated only when placed within the context of a spiraling pattern of conflict along racial and generational lines that seemed to spin out of control during the spring and summer of 1968. Within the space of less than six months Americans witnessed, in rapid sequence, a series of violent episodes that included nationwide rioting touched off by the murder of Martin Luther King Jr. in April, the shocking and tragic assassination of Senator Robert F. Kennedy in June, and the nationally

42. Herbert E. Longenecker, "Charge: To the Class of 1968," commencement address, 27 May 1968, box 125, HEL Papers.

televised battle between police and college-age yippies and antiwar activists at the Chicago Democratic National Convention in August. These events were played out against the backdrop of transatlantic social ferment, including student demonstrations and strikes in France that nearly toppled the de Gaulle government. Adding to the already anxious public mood were the official findings of the Kerner Commission, which cited racial discrimination as the chief cause of urban rioting in black ghettos and warned that the United States was in danger of becoming two nations divided by skin color.

In addition to paving the way for the election of Richard Nixon to the American presidency, the conflicts of 1968 helped set in motion a law-and-order, anti-liberal backlash that would have far-reaching implications for the future of higher education. The increasingly negative public reaction to civil disorder placed university officials in a delicate position, as they sought to preserve intellectual freedom and the right of dissent while also persuading skeptics that academic institutions were being run in a responsible manner. At times the balancing act was all but impossible, forcing college presidents to choose between the alternatives of talking tough and acting forcefully or being regarded as weak. More than a few university leaders, including President Longenecker, sought to preserve the internal stability of their schools by adopting strong, no-nonsense policy declarations in anticipation of troubled periods. During the summer of 1968 Longenecker prepared a lengthy statement on Tulane's policy toward demonstrations and dissent. Bearing the title "Official Notice to New and Returning Students From the President of the University," the document received blanket distribution among students and was published for a wider audience in the November 1968 issue of the *Tulanian*. As the single most important administrative statement on campus protest, the notice merits consideration both for its tone and for the elements of change and continuity it embodied.

In reality the 1968 document was less of a new departure than many readers imagined. Six years earlier, in an atmosphere colored by the 1962 cafeteria sit-ins, the University Senate Committee on Student Affairs had addressed the matter of collective protest when adopting the university's first code of rules and procedures for the supervision of student conduct. The resulting document pointed out that "[s]tudent demonstrations, often harmless, can become aggravated into mob action. Each student should understand that any participation, even as an on-looker, in a group disturbance may subject him to immediate disciplinary action." In following years, Dean Stibbs—who had played a major role in drafting the conduct code—employed similar language in an annual informational letter sent to the parents of A&S freshmen. In 1966, before the emergence of student power on Tulane's campus, Stibbs took note of the risk to life and property caused by "student demonstrations and mob actions" at various American schools. He gave freshmen and their parents to understand that "any participation in a group disturbance may result in disciplinary action and possible dismissal from the University."[43]

In the relatively tranquil atmosphere which still prevailed at Tulane in 1966, Stibbs's euphemistic reference "group disturbances" could have applied as easily to panty raids or the drunken escapades of fraternity members as to organized protest movements. By the summer of 1968, there was no longer any uncertainty about the type of activity that Tulane officials hoped to prevent. Prompted by concern over the "disorderly, disruptive, and dangerous demonstrations on university campuses during the last year," Longenecker's statement on campus dissent reflected the wish "to preclude any diversion of resources of time, energy, finances, or enthusiasm for the accomplishment of our basic purposes for having and being a university." After reiterating Tulane's recognition of the right to dissent as well as its commitment to freedom of inquiry and expression, and after affirming the school's desire for "responsible student participation in University affairs," Longenecker introduced the central theme of his message. "At Tulane we respect the constitutional rights of individuals," he wrote, "and we believe these rights are sustained by acceptance of the responsibilities that make them possible."

Civil disobedience is not accepted as a right. Tulane permits expression of views by peaceful picketing and demonstrations on campus under specific rules. . . . However, we will not tolerate interruption of the normal processes of the University, such as academic functions, administrative functions, business functions, and recreational activities on campus. We intend to safe-

43. Supervision of Student Conduct at Tulane University, president's agenda item accompanying BOA Minutes, 13 June 1962 (first quotation); John H. Stibbs to "Dear Parent," 15 July 1966, box 62, HEL Papers (second–third quotations). The 1962 conduct code was approved by the University Senate on 7 May 1962 after several months of work by members of the Student Affairs Committee.

guard the right of each student to partake of any University program or service, especially the attendance of classes. No individual or group can be given the right by demonstration, picketing,
sit-in, or other device to impede regularly scheduled University
functions. . . . Tulane does not condone illegal or extra-legal actions on its campus. Nor will it yield to threats of violence and disorder. . . . All parties should be on notice that any demonstrations of a violent nature will be dealt with promptly and
decisively. . . . [P]enalties imposed [for violating the code of stu-
dent conduct] may include monetary fines, loss of academic
credit, suspension from the University or expulsion.[44]

This stern warning drew praise from local businessmen, civic
groups, alumni, and other interested parties outside the university,
who sent Longenecker some sixty letters of congratulation at the beginning of the fall semester. Longenecker's firm stand elicited a formal
resolution of praise from the New Orleans Area Chamber of Commerce, and his message was quoted in the *Wall Street Journal* and the
Chicago Tribune. An indication of the political coloring that tinged
many supportive utterances may be gleaned from the actions of Congressman F. Edward Hébert, the old nemesis of Tulane liberals, who
pronounced Longenecker's statement "magnificent and refreshing"
when inserting the full text into the *Congressional Record*. Although
campus reactions were mixed, only SDS went so far as to issue a formal
rebuttal. In a two-page document entitled "An Unofficial Letter to New
and Returning Students From Students for a Democratic Society,"
Tulane SDS members chided Longenecker for employing threatening
language when affirming that the university would not yield to threats.
While taking issue with the president on a number of factual points,
the main thrust of the SDS response was to dispute Longenecker's
major premises concerning the March 1968 demonstrations and to call
for fundamental change in the university's underlying aims. From the
SDS perspective, the previous year's demonstrations had been altogether positive in nature, marked by restraint, "very little disruption," and goals "of the very highest order." Instead of violent confrontations there had been only "large numbers of students, picking

44. Herbert E. Longenecker, Official Notice to New and Returning Students from the President of the University, box 63, HEL Papers (all quotations). Cf. First Draft, University Position
on Student Unrest, box 63, HEL Papers.

their issues, their leaders[,] and their actions as they saw fit." In the absence of more tangible accomplishments, the demonstrations had succeeded in "uniting for a time elements of the University community which had not previously spoken to each other."[45]

According to SDS, the basic disagreement between student dissenters and the Longenecker administration concerned the question of whether Tulane should prepare students to "function in society as it is" or equip them to "fight the struggle for human survival in the Twentieth Century." The latter goal would require an educational experience that challenged the status quo within the university itself. "We are not talking about violent overthrow or chaos," the SDS letter explained. "We are talking about building a community of the University in which the Faculty and Students and Administration, and yes even the working staff[,] have an equal say over what happens at Tulane[,] with each group having major authority in the area in which it is most concerned." Where Longenecker's "Official Notice" had stressed order as a precondition of freedom, the SDS document, with its idealized vision of a university governed through an egalitarian social compact, stressed freedom as a prerequisite for order. The point became clear near the end of the statement in a passage declaring that when the combined forces of "business, bureaucracy, and militarism" prevented the realization of humane values, "then maybe a little disruption is not the worst thing."[46]

The generally moderate tone and the overall civility of the public exchange between SDS and Longenecker belied the distrust and hostility with which the two sides had come to view each other. By the time SDS drafted its response to the president, members of the Board of Administrators had already supplied Longenecker with a number of press and magazine accounts purporting to show the existence of a "student underground" stretching from New York to Cuba and "linking the ivy halls of Columbia . . . with the crowded Communist universities of Belgrade, Warsaw, Cracow, and Prague." More important, Board members had secured copies of Tulane SDS membership and mailing lists,

45. "Extensions of Remarks," *Congressional Record*, 10 September 1968, pp. E-7798–9, off-print, box 63, HEL Papers (first quotation); An Unofficial Letter to New and Returning Students from Students for a Democratic Society, undated mimeographed typescript, box 63, HEL Papers (all subsequent quotations). Responses to the Longenecker statement are collected in the folder labeled "Student Life—President's Message to New and Returning Students and Comments," box 63, HEL Papers.

46. An Unofficial Letter to New and Returning Students from Students for a Democratic Society.

the contents of which—some sixty-six names in all—were sent to Washington, D.C., to be checked for evidence of subversive affiliation as defined in the carefully indexed dossiers of the House Committee on Un-American Activities. En route the material passed through the hands of Congressman Hébert, who personally requested a search of the committee's files.[47]

The covert investigation produced no damaging information about any of the SDS members or their associates. It did, however, attest to the Board's underlying suspicion that sinister forces were at work in episodes of campus dissent. Suspicion of SDS was based partly upon the group's national reputation for disruptive activity and partly upon the Board's willingness to accept conspiratorial arguments linking the student Left to international communism. In retrospect it is difficult to avoid the conclusion that SDS was singled out for reasons that had relatively little to do with the group's small role in the previous spring's student power activities and censorship protests. Clashes between SDS and the Tulane administration during the 1967–68 academic year had centered around the student group's antiwar activities, which ranged from the distribution of literature to protests against Department of Defense recruiting, opposition to selective service, and picketing of ROTC drill. Although administration hostility to such activities was a matter of record, neither SDS members nor the professors who taught them were aware of the Board's contacts with HUAC in the summer. Strong objections would certainly have greeted any disclosure of the secret HUAC inquiries, but in the absence of such information, antiwar activity languished in the fall of 1968 as other issues captured center stage. Not until the spring semester, with the renewal of a direct attack on ROTC, would the depth of presidential and Board sentiment against SDS become fully apparent.

To the surprise of some and to the relief of others, the fall semester of 1968 witnessed a temporary lull in campus struggles over the issues of student power and the Vietnam War. Longenecker's warning message undoubtedly played a role in inhibiting a quick return to student

47. Alice Widener, "Subcellar Student Subversion," USA 15 (1 March 1968): 1–4; Drew Pearson, "Conspiracy Links Revolt of Students," newspaper column, undated (all quotations); offprints accompanying letter of Clifford F. Favrot to Herbert E. Longenecker, 18 June 1968, box 67a, HEL Papers; Chester D. Smith to F. Edward Hébert, 28 August 1968, box 67a, HEL Papers; Ashton Phelps to Darwin Fenner, 3 September 1968, and photocopied enclosures, box 67a, HEL Papers.

activism, as did the absence of a spokesman for student power at the helm of student government. For SDS, an additional check upon tactical militance grew out of the need to present a responsible image in order to win University Senate approval as a permanently recognized student organization. During discussions in the Committee on Student Affairs in November 1968 and in debates before the full faculty senate in January 1969, Professor Edward Dubinsky, the SDS faculty adviser, defended the provision in the SDS constitution that affirmed the group's intention to pursue programs of "research and action" that would make the university an agent of change. "[O]ur society really needs great changes and a university is probably a good place to conduct experiments on this," Dubinsky declared.[48]

Somewhat earlier, on November 14, 1968, Dubinsky and two student members of SDS had appeared before the Committee on Student Affairs to present the Tulane chapter's case for permanent recognition. At that time, in response to questions about their reaction to Longenecker's "Official Notice," the group produced a copy of the SDS message to new and returning students, which was read aloud to the committee. Prior to the reading an exchange took place that was recorded as follows in the official minutes: "Professor Dubinsky said that SDS did not like [the portion of] the President's letter pertaining to interruption of normal activities of the University. Miss [Gail] Shaw [an SDS student representative] said that the regular processes of a university were subject to change. Professor Dubinsky said that there may be a time to disrupt the processes of a university. Mr. McIntosh [the other SDS student representative] asked if justice comes before law and order." Dubinsky's comments, together with a student's explanation that SDS actions in any given set of circumstances would depend upon the "magnitude of the atrocity" involved, provided fuel for considerable debate in the full senate. In the end SDS won recognition by a vote of 16-10, over the strong opposition of civil engineering professor Frank Dalia and University College dean Robert C. Whittemore, a philosophy professor who had read widely in the literature of student radicalism and the American Left.[49]

In the course of the senate deliberations, unexpected support for

48. Tulane *Hullabaloo*, 10 January 1969, pp. 1, 2 (all quotations).

49. Minutes of the University Senate Committee on Student Affairs, 14 November 1968, unprocessed archival records, Howard-Tilton Library, Tulane University (first quotation); Tulane *Hullabaloo*, 22 November 1968, p. 1 (second quotation); ibid., 10 January 1969, pp. 1, 2. In a

SDS came from Henry Mason, who only a year earlier had condemned the group's adherents as "fascists of the left." Mason explained his change of heart by noting that SDS members had abided by university regulations during the previous year. More important to Mason, SDS had succeeded in opening lines of communication with Tulane's black students, whose concerns occupied center stage throughout much of the fall semester as various segments of the campus community reacted to the new assertiveness of students who now rejected the traditional term "Negro" in favor of "black" or "Afro-American." A crisis over the relationship of black students to the university community had been in the making for several years. Incubated by the struggles over fraternity segregation in 1966 and 1967, the emergence of a politically charged sense of collective identity among black Tulanians received a major stimulus in February 1968 when James Farmer, the former national director of CORE, delivered a major campus address. While stopping short of endorsing the black power movement, Farmer spoke at length about the importance of affirming the dignity of blackness as an act of psychic liberation from the negative self-images fostered by life in a racist society. Two months later, in the wake of Martin Luther King Jr.'s murder, the campus radio station WTUL produced a major broadcast on "The Negro at Tulane" in which black and white students, fraternity spokesmen, faculty members, and administrators gave their views on all aspects of campus race relations.[50]

When the *Hullabaloo*, with commendable far-sightedness, printed extended excerpts from the broadcast interviews, it became clear that blacks and whites evaluated the campus racial climate on the basis of substantially different assumptions and experiences. White students reported little meaningful contact with blacks at Tulane and tended to assume that integration operated as a process of black assimilation into the behavioral patterns and governing conventions of (white) middle-class society. Black students were divided on the meaning of integration and spoke of a significant generational split between those who had entered Tulane in 1964 or 1965 at the beginning of desegregation and those who arrived later, when the number of blacks had in-

---

rather careless report on the November 14 meeting, the *Hullabaloo* transformed McIntosh's rhetorical question into a categorical assertion that "justice comes before order," attributing the remark to the entire SDS group. Tulane *Hullabaloo*, 22 November 1968, p. 1.

50. Minutes of the University Senate Committee on Student Affairs, 14 November 1968; Tulane *Hullabaloo*, 23 February 1968, p. 4.

Harold Sylvester, early black athlete, 1968.

creased and the interracial consensus of the civil rights movement had
given way to demands for black power. The older students often distanced themselves from ACT and stressed individualism over racial
identity. Several held important positions in mainstream campus organizations, and they acknowledged that younger blacks often regarded
them as "Uncle Toms." Blacks who entered Tulane in the late 1960s
were attracted both emotionally and intellectually by the rhetoric of
black nationalism. As admissions director Edward Rogge observed,
many believed that only economic and political power could give substance to legal and Constitutional guarantees of equality. At times their
desire to assert their independence from the dominant culture approached the threshold of racial separatism. Steven Barbre, who in
1966 had stated that ACT was willing to work with any group on campus,

refused to be interviewed in 1968. "I think the white community needs an education, but I don't know if it's my obligation to give it to them," he said, adding that "what the white community considers militancy, I consider honest."[51]

What may have been the single most discerning assessment of black attitudes at Tulane during the 1960s came from A&S senior Nelson Brown, an ACT member who was also the assistant general manager of the campus radio station. In a passage that would remain relevant to the university's racial situation a generation later, Brown sought to explain the ambivalence with which many blacks viewed their presence in a predominantly white institution. "[I]ntegration the way white America calls it isn't quite the way it should be," Brown began.

> [B]ecause white Americans, when they think of integration, think of the Negro being processed and changed from his original self, so [that] he comes out stamped and approved and can integrate into society as acceptable. But then the Negroes on campus realize that this just won't happen. Maybe some of us go through the "whitewashing process," as James Farmer put it, but we just can't be expected to change completely like that. So ACT was an effort to gain and retain this black consciousness as needed. . . . [O]ne day when America progresses far enough, the white man and the black man will be able to confront each other as they are, will accept each other as they are. That's the way it should be.[52]

After the spring of 1968, moderate voices among Tulane's black undergraduates became increasingly rare. But if public rhetoric grew more combative, private dialogue continued to center around goals that were ultimately compatible with the integrationist ideal. In July and August, ACT representatives met on several occasions with Vice President Clarence Scheps, Provost David Deener, A&S dean Joseph Gordon, and Newcomb dean Charles D. Hounshell. The agenda that emerged from the discussions was contained in an "Order of Discourse," typed on ACT letterhead and dated August 23, 1968. The document made a number of demands upon Tulane, including improved conditions for black workers (particularly the hiring or promotion of blacks into white-collar, nonmenial jobs), a substantial in-

51. Tulane *Hullabaloo*, 10 May 1968, pp. 11 (all quotations)–12.
52. Ibid., 11.

crease in the number of black students admitted each year, the inauguration of an Afro-American Studies program, and the hiring of black
faculty. The students' first point represented more than a simple desire to enhance the career prospects of Tulane's black staff, as important as better job prospects were to those involved. In raising the issue,
the students were calling attention to the systemic nature of racism as
it existed at most white colleges and more generally in American society. In a subsequent memorandum ACT argued that both black and
white students would benefit once blacks were adequately represented
across the entire range of Tulane's occupational and status hierarchy.
Black freshmen would feel less alienated in an atmosphere where skin
color was not a badge of menial status, while white students would be
forced to reexamine the logic of a belief system that automatically dismissed talented blacks as exceptions to a general rule of racial inferi-
ority. In a campus environment where many white students "falsely
but perhaps sincerely believe that blacks are inferior," ACT argued,
"[s]eeing a few 'exceptional' blacks in nonmenial positions on campus" tended to perpetuate rather than undermine racist attitudes.[53]

Unhappily, ACT's demands for black faculty and a program of
Afro-American studies, legitimate enough in their own right, were justified on grounds that even the most sympathetic white faculty member
was likely to reject. Reasoning that "[t]he lies that have been perpe-
trated under the guise of 'scholarship' must be confronted and erradi-
cated [sic]," section E of the "Order of Discourse" took the position
that "[u]nder certain conditions, only a Black instructor is qualified to
'tell it like it was.' We do not trust our history in the hands of a white
instructor." Admissions director Edward Rogge, who had accompanied black students on an April 1968 bus trip to Washington, D.C., in
the aftermath of the King assassination, and who took pains to maintain a close rapport with black undergraduates, understood the students' frustration. Rogge hoped, through quiet effort, to bring about
internal changes that would dispel anger and alienation while addressing the genuine problem of institutional insensitivity toward the
African American experience. Other faculty members, no less well dis-
posed toward black students, chose to attack head-on what they re-

53. Ralph W. Edwards to Herbert Longenecker (dated from internal evidence prior to 11
July 1968), accompanying Clarence Scheps memorandum to David R. Deener, Joseph Gordon,
and Charles D. Hounshell, 15 August 1968, box 62, HEL Papers; ACT memorandum, 6 September 1968, apparent recipient Clarence Scheps, box 62, HEL Papers (all quotations).

garded as the dangerous drift toward ethnocentrism on campus. In September 1968 Professors Henry Mason and Richard P. Adams challenged the right of ACT to hold closed meetings at Tulane—that is, gatherings from which whites were excluded. The challenge took the form of a reverse sit-in, which saw the two professors along with some twenty other whites refuse to leave an otherwise segregated orientation meeting that ACT was conducting for black freshmen in the University Center. The episode ended inconclusively when ACT adjourned the gathering, leaving the professors to argue with Dean Stibbs about whether or not such closed events had official sanction. Professor Dubinsky, who served as faculty adviser to ACT as well as SDS, would subsequently offer the tongue-in-cheek observation that the white sit-in constituted precisely the type of disruptive activity that Longenecker's official message had forbidden.[54]

Faced with younger and increasingly strident black spokesmen, white students and faculty expressed growing concern over racial polarization. In a radio interview shortly after the September clash with ACT—a program boycotted by black representatives—Mason conceded that "[w]e are facing a generation of black students who will make little attempt to fit in." A majority of the students polled by the *Hullabaloo* in early October believed that black students should be allowed to hold at least some meetings from which whites were excluded, while the paper itself, reasoning that African American identity was in a "new and formative stage," refused to equate "black consciousness" with racism and agreed with ACT "that there might be some things best said to black freshmen in private." It was at this juncture—as the university scrambled to put together a menu of history, English, sociology, and anthropology courses with African American content (twenty-two in all) and prepared to offer a black literature class, an anthropology seminar on African cultures, and a special political science colloquium on black power for the spring semester of 1969—that Tulane SDS members arranged to meet jointly with ACT to discuss problems in racial relations at Tulane.[55]

54. [Afro-American Congress of Tulane], Order of Discourse, 23 August 1968 (quotation), accompanying Clarence Scheps memorandum to Herbert E. Longenecker, 23 August 1968, box 62, HEL Papers (first–second quotations); Tulane *Hullabaloo*, 20 September 1968, pp. 1, 2.

55. Tulane *Hullabaloo*, 20 September 1968, p. 1 (second quotation); ibid., 4 October 1968, pp. 1 (first quotation), 2; Leonard Reissman to David R. Deener, 8 July 1968; Charles P. Roland to David R. Deener, 9 July 1968; J. L. Fischer to David R. Deener, 28 June 1968; Tulane *Hullabaloo*, 18 December 1968, p. 1. All letters in box 18, HEL Papers.

By 1973–74, Tulane had begun to take on the appearance of a genuinely integrated university.

Although ACT spokesmen ruled out any direct collaboration between the two groups and emphasized that "assistance from SDS or any other white student organization is neither needed nor desired," the joint meeting came off as planned, and was judged a considerable accomplishment. The gathering allowed ACT to appear on an equal footing with SDS and to publicize its concern over the potential threat to minority enrollment posed by the expiration of the special Rockefeller grant in 1968–69. In the weeks that followed, the admissions question rose quickly to the top of the ACT agenda. In February 1969 the group delivered an "Ultimatum" to Rogge and other university officials demanding that Tulane "recruit and admit 100 Black students for the fall semester of . . . [1969] and subsequently provide whatever means necessary for their continued studies here." Six weeks before receiving the ultimatum, Rogge had met with the chairman of the ACT Admissions Committee, who stressed that increasing the number of black freshmen was the organization's "priority issue." Shortly after that meeting Rogge advised the provost that in light of persistent inquiries about minority admissions from both ACT and the *Hulla-*

baloo, "we will very soon have to come up with some specific answers either as to what we . . . are doing to obtain supplementary funds or [else acknowledge] that we are not going to be able to obtain such funds."[56]

ACT's February ultimatum confirmed Rogge's prediction, making it necessary that the university take a public stand on the matter of minority enrollment. At the urging of Tulane AAUP president Richard Adams and upon the advice of the University Senate Committee on Admissions, Longenecker announced the creation of a special Educational Opportunity Grant Fund to replace and enlarge the financial aid previously supplied by the Rockefeller grant. In addition, the president authorized the formation of a Committee on Expanding Educational Opportunity under the direction of Provost Deener to begin seeking long-term solutions to the problem of recruiting and retaining black students. Although the university nearly doubled the number of black freshmen receiving full financial aid from seventeen in 1968–69 to thirty-three in 1969–70, the transition to a genuinely integrated university had scarcely begun. Efforts to address the specific cultural, occupational, curricular, and recruitment concerns of ACT would continue, with varying degrees of intensity or neglect, for the next generation. Where admissions and hiring were concerned, Tulane had begun a process of change that would unfold with glacial slowness, yielding results measurable over the span of three decades but scarcely visible within the boundaries of a four-year undergraduate career. During the spring semester of 1969, moreover, the issues raised by ACT would be temporarily eclipsed by a new phase of antiwar activity directed against campus ROTC programs and their place in the university curriculum.[57]

56. Tulane *Hullabaloo*, 11 October 1968, p. 2 (first quotation); "Ultimatum" [17 February 1969] accompanying statement of Henry L. Mason, 19 February 1969, box 62, HEL Papers (second–third quotations); Charles Hounshell to Herbert Longenecker, 21 February 1969, box 62, HEL Papers; Edward Rogge, Memorandum to the Provost, 12 February 1969, box 62, HEL Papers (fourth–fifth quotations). Copies of the ACT demands were also given to Newcomb Dean Charles Hounshell, to the *Hullabaloo*, and to radio station WTUL.

57. Tulane *Hullabaloo*, 28 February 1969, p. 1; O. W. Wagner to Edward Rogge, 16 January 1969, box 62, HEL Papers; Richard P. Adams to Herbert E. Longenecker, 19 and 24 February 1969, box 62, HEL Papers; Statement on minority admissions and related issues by the President of the University, 26 February 1969, typescript, Longenecker biographical files; University Senate Minutes, 11 November 1968; Financial Aid Awards to Black Students by Class for 1967–68, 1968–69, 1969–70, tabular information accompanying C[ommittee on] E[xpanding] E[ducational] O[pportunity], Some Data on Financial Support for Disadvantaged Students (Undergraduate), 11 November 1969, box 18, HEL Papers.

III

A discussion of the 1969 ROTC controversy must begin with a clear appreciation of the important place occupied by military programs in the overall life of the university. Throughout the 1950s, both before and after Tulane's affiliation with the Institute for Defense Analysis in 1956, research in the medical sciences, mathematics, chemistry, engineering, physics, and psychology received substantial support from the armed services. By the early 1960s, the National Institutes of Health, the National Science Foundation, and the National Aeronautics and Space Administration had displaced the Department of Defense as a principal source of research funding. Stipends from these and other civilian agencies, together with fellowships granted under the National Defense Education Act, provided much of the direct support for students pursuing advanced degrees in the core scientific and humanities disciplines.

On a more limited scale the armed services also subsidized graduate training at Tulane through several similar but bureaucratically distinct programs. The oldest of these, the Army Career Development Program, operated throughout the 1950s and 1960s, sending an average of five graduate students per year, typically majors or colonels, to pursue advanced degrees in political science and psychology before returning to assignments in international relations, psychological warfare, or teaching at West Point. By the early 1970s, the Department of Political Science had awarded over thirty M.A. degrees and two Ph.D.'s to army students. For some programs army support was of critical importance. Beginning in 1960, when the Department of Physics lacked the strength and reputation to qualify for either NDEA awards or NSF traineeships, graduate work depended to an unhealthy degree upon military revenue. During the sixties, approximately ninety graduate students studied physics at army expense. "As matters now stand," the physics department chair wrote in 1965, "we find ourselves in the position of keeping the number of army students (terminal M.S. students) large and even needing to increase the number simply because they bring their own support. This is to keep the total number of graduate students in the department large enough to justify classes and the physics program." Army students were equally vital to the Graduate School of Business Administration, where by the end of the 1960s, a total of seventy-seven career military officers had earned

M.B.A. degrees in a specially tailored operations research program. Comprising 25–30 percent of the total enrollment, the highly motivated and academically well-qualified army officers "often dominated both curricular and extracurricular affairs" in the business school, which remained largely untouched by the winds of student dissent. In addition to these programs, Tulane also conducted summer seminars in the late 1960s in which as many as 120 reserve officers received graduate credit for classes on the developmental problems facing Latin America.[58]

Thus the antiwar conflicts of 1969 did not take place in a vacuum. Although the programs described above were easily overlooked in the larger mosaic of externally funded Graduate School endeavors, their importance to the professors and departments involved was far from inconsequential at a time when many programs were threatened with severe retrenchment. And while army subsidies did not restrict institutional autonomy or impinge directly upon matters of personal conscience, the existence of a larger pattern of research and teaching relationships with the armed services helped define the context within which academic doves as well as hawks debated Tulane's most conspicuous military undertaking, the Reserve Officer Training programs offered to medical students and male undergraduates. By almost any standards, the scope and duration of Tulane's involvement with ROTC was impressive. From a naval unit enrolling 76 freshmen in 1938, the university's ROTC offerings had grown to include all four service branches by the early 1950s. In the mid-fifties over 1,100 students enrolled annually in ROTC, a figure that represented 37.1–40.6 percent of all male undergraduates. By the time President Longenecker took office in the 1960–61 academic year, Tulane ranked second in the nation in the percentage of students voluntarily enrolled in ROTC. Throughout the next seven years (i.e., through 1967–68), the proportion of undergraduate men in the army, air force, and navy/marine programs hovered between 31 and 36.5 percent. During the same

---

58. Herbert E. Longenecker, "Tulane University's Role in Officer Education Programs," speech, 2 December 1971, box 125, HEL Papers, 10–2; C. L. Peacock to John Snell, 8 March 1965 (first–second quotations), box 35, HEL Papers; Snell to Peacock, 10 March 1965, box 35, HEL Papers; James Francis Fouche, "The Tulane University Graduate School of Business Administration: An Oral-Institutional History" (Ph.D. diss., University of Florida, 1978), 157, 184 (third quotation). Both Tulane and Georgia Tech had similar contracts to train career army officers. Tulane specialized in management and operations research while Georgia Tech focused on computer science.

eight-year period, the university graduated nearly six hundred commissioned officers. Individual motives for participating in ROTC ran the gamut of influences that shaped other life choices among Vietnam-era college students. Family pressures, financial benefits, occupational considerations, and simple patriotism all played a role in bringing Tulane students into the ROTC fold. But if enlistment was voluntary in the sense that the university did not require students to participate, there were few male undergraduates who evaluated ROTC outside the context of the military draft. As U.S. troop strength in Vietnam approached and then surpassed the half million mark in 1967–68, the Selective Service System and the war in Southeast Asia became omnipresent realities on the Tulane campus.[59]

With its high campus profile and direct bearing upon the future plans of many students, ROTC was a natural lightning rod for antiwar protest. During the initial phase of antiwar activism in 1966–67, Richard Schechner had taken the lead in mounting organized opposition to university-sponsored military training. After 1967, leadership of the campus antiwar forces eventually devolved upon Associate Professor of Mathematics Edward Dubinsky. A native of Philadelphia, Dubinsky had taken an active interest in politics since his teenage years, when he rang doorbells for a reform mayoral candidate in his home city. As an undergraduate at Temple University from 1952 to 1956, he had been among the liberal citizen-activists who rallied to the cause of Democratic presidential candidate Adlai E. Stevenson. While pursuing the Ph.D. in mathematics at the University of Michigan between 1959 and 1962, Dubinsky worked in the presidential campaign of John F. Kennedy. Before joining Tulane's faculty in 1964, Dubinsky spent two years in Africa teaching at the University College of Sierra Leone and the University of Ghana. In addition to providing an external perspective from which to evaluate American policy toward the developing world, such experiences presumably invited comparisons of the racial attitudes and practices prevailing in Africa and the United States.[60]

59. ROTC Programs at Tulane, president's agenda item, BOA Minutes, October 11, 1961; Summary of ROTC Enrollments by Military Service, 1955–56 to 1969–70, Institutional Research Report, 29 September 1969, box 60, HEL Papers; Tulane Graduates Commissioned Through ROTC and World War II Programs, 1941–42 to Present, Institutional Survey, 6 December 1971, accompanying Endicott A. Batchelder Memorandum to Deans and Directors, 9 December 1971, box 60, HEL Papers.

60. Curriculum Vitae of Edward L. Dubinsky (undated), Biographical Files, Tulane University Archives; Excerpts from oral interviews with Edward Dubinsky by Clarence Doucet

Dubinsky's arrival in New Orleans coincided with a flurry of demonstrations aimed at compelling local businesses to obey the public accommodations provisions of the 1964 Civil Rights Act. During the next two years the young mathematics professor became involved with local CORE veterans and other civil rights activists who organized a tutoring program for inner city black youth. When interviewed in 1966, Dubinsky had no illusions about the magnitude of the task facing those who wanted to bring about meaningful change. Aware that tutoring programs could not compensate for the deficiencies of the schools that black children attended, he saw the project's real goal as creating grass-roots pressure to improve the school system by helping local residents realize that "education really can be more than what the schools are giving them." The tutoring program and related activities brought Dubinsky into contact with college students interested in community organizing, and paved the way for his subsequent role as adviser to both ACT and SDS. By the late 1960s, if not sooner, he had abandoned mainstream liberalism in favor of the radical critique of American institutions espoused by the New Left. The year 1969 found Dubinsky strategically positioned to influence the direction of student protest at Tulane, but he seems to have played little part in initiating the events that led to the renewal of campus demonstrations against ROTC.[61]

The immediate impulse for renewed debate over ROTC came from a series of three investigative reports examining complaints against the officer training regimen at Tulane. Appearing in the *Hullabaloo* during February and March 1969, the articles raised serious questions about the quality and content of ROTC courses and about the amount of academic credit awarded for military study. Readers learned, among other things, that the amount of ROTC credit accepted toward graduation varied from college to college, that the ROTC curriculum consisted of military, technical, and "indoctrination" courses taught by active duty personnel, that military field manuals were written at a sixth-grade level, and that only five of the fifteen officers teaching in

in Clarence Doucet, *Shapes of Protest* (New Orleans: Times-Picayune Publishing Co., 1969). This is an unpaginated pamphlet reprinting a series of articles which appeared originally in the *Times-Picayune* between 23 May and 1 June 1969. The Doucet articles are interesting today as artifacts of the less sophisticated variety of conspiratorially-minded anti-Communist exposé journalism which flourished at the peak of the cold war. Doucet did, however, conduct three interviews with Dubinsky, two of which were tape recorded. Use of the pamphlet is confined to personal background material quoted or closely paraphrased from these interviews.

61. *Southern Patriot* 24 (March 1966): 1, 3 (quotation).

the program possessed master's degrees, while none held the Ph.D. If the specific revelations were surprising to many Tulanians in 1969, concern over the academic status of ROTC was not an entirely new phenomenon. A decade earlier President Harris had advised the Board of Administrators that spokesmen for engineering and science disciplines, as well as outside accrediting agencies, were increasingly reluctant to sanction curricula in which ROTC courses comprised the usual 24 out of 120–130 semester hours required for graduation. Harris saw an approaching conflict between military and academic priorities at Tulane, and warned that "calm and wise counsel" would be required to achieve an "adjustment between two very opposite points of view."[62]

These warnings were uttered in 1959, a year before Harris's departure, but the issue was not resurrected by Longenecker until outside events forced ROTC onto the university's policy agenda in the late 1960s. The relative absence before 1967 of critical discussion about campus military training cannot be attributed solely to the vagaries of domestic politics. If Harris had been a supporter of ROTC, Longenecker became its unswerving advocate, and his public utterances during the early 1960s were studded with expressions of support for the role of higher learning in national defense. In September 1960 he encouraged "each Tulane freshman to consider carefully the individual programs offered by each service and to enroll in the ROTC of your choice." After describing the university classroom as a "strategic weapon" in the cold war in June 1961, Longenecker went still further the following November in declaring that "every aspect" of higher education was related to national defense. Within this framework, military training comprised a "valuable part of liberal education" because it emphasized "the importance of responsibility and obligations." Liberty, Longenecker cautioned, "does not imply an absence of obligations and cannot survive if responsibilities are neglected."[63]

62. "ROTC Academic Credits, Discrepancies Examined," Tulane *Hullabaloo*, 28 February 1969, p. 4; "New Navy Curriculum and Indoctrination Examined," ibid., 7 March 1969, p. 15; "Curriculum Control for ROTC by Watch-Dog Committee Suggested," ibid., 14 March 1969, p. 4. All of the articles were authored by Bill King. BOA Minutes, 13 May 1959, item 8 of president's monthly report (all quotations).

63. Herbert E. Longenecker, "To the Students Entering Tulane University," 1 September 1960, box 125, HEL Papers (first quotation); News release, 3 June 1961, on Herbert Longenecker commencement speech at Auburn University, biographical files, Tulane University Archives (second quotation); News release on Herbert Longenecker speech to Tulane University Army ROTC Fall Banquet, 16 November 1961, biographical files, Tulane University Archives (all subsequent quotations).

President Longenecker presents ROTC award, 1968.

In August 1961 Longenecker accepted an invitation to serve on the Department of Defense's Advisory Panel on ROTC Affairs, a group comprised of administrators, faculty, and staff from schools with officer training programs. According to the chairman of the Reserve Forces Policy Board, the invitation was prompted by Longenecker's position as president of a school with major ROTC programs, his experience at the University of Illinois, and his "long service to the Department of Defense, as an advisor in the fields of chemical and biological warfare, and of research and development applied to military problems." As the latter comments indicate, Longenecker had established a number of re-lationships with the military that predated his arrival at Tulane. Unlike Harris, who had suffered a painful convalescence following exposure to poison gas during World War I, Longenecker did not view the military through the eyes of a combat veteran. He had come of age scientifically and professionally during World War II, when the foundations were being laid for an extensive pattern of peacetime science patronage under federal government auspices. As a chemist specializing in the study of fats and oils, he had chaired the National Research Council Committee on Fats from 1943–49 while serving simultaneously as a consultant on fats and oils for the Office of the Quartermaster General (1943–47) and the Army Medical Nutrition Laboratory in the Office of the Surgeon General (1944–46). As a result of these and other assignments, he received certificates of appreciation from both the army and the navy for his contributions to the war effort in the field of scientific research and development. Beginning in 1948 and continuing through the 1950s, Longenecker served on the Technical Advisory Panel on Biological and Chemical Warfare in the Office of the Assistant Secretary of Defense for Research and Development. During the same period he was also a member of the Advisory Council to the Chief Chemical Officer, Department of the Army. For a number of years he chaired the Medical Committee of the latter body, and from 1951–54 he served on the Committee on Biological Warfare in the Office of Naval Research.[64]

Longenecker's support for ROTC programs should thus be understood, at least in part, as an extension of the larger pattern of postwar relationships that tied American higher education to national defense and federal sponsorship of science. His longstanding ties to the military, together with his prolonged service on the Department of Defense's Advisory Panel on ROTC Affairs, helped explain the absence of ROTC from the otherwise exhaustive list of subjects considered in Tulane's 1967–68 self-study prepared in conjunction with the university's reaccreditation by the Southern Association of Colleges and Secondary Schools. At the national level, however, ROTC had become impossible to ignore. In 1967, as the antiwar movement began to gain momentum at Tulane, the Planning Committee of the College of Arts and Sciences recommended that the amount of academic credit allowed for ROTC courses be reduced. Beginning in the fall of 1968, a special committee representing Cornell, Dartmouth, Yale, Stanford, and the Department of Defense held a series of eighteen meetings to evaluate ROTC. The committee's findings, known popularly as the Cornell Report, criticized "indoctrination" courses as incompatible with the aims of higher learning, and recommended that courses in

64. John Slezack to Herbert E. Longenecker, 16 August 1961, box 60, HEL Papers (quotation); All information concerning military consultant and advisory service is based on the 1 September 1960 version of Longenecker's curriculum vitae, biographical files, Tulane University Archives.

military etiquette, weapons assembly, and drill be limited to summer encampments or naval cruises. The Cornell Report provided much of the inspiration for the *Hullabaloo* articles on ROTC at Tulane and gave intellectual ammunition to faculty and students who felt that military training in general and drill exercises in particular had no legitimate place on a university campus.[65]

Reacting to the *Hullabaloo* articles and to the national climate of academic concern over ROTC, the Curriculum Committee of the College of Arts and Sciences decided to initiate its own review of the officer training program at Tulane. In mid-April the Curriculum Committee issued a formal position paper supporting the retention of ROTC at Tulane, but urging a number of modifications that supporters of the program were sure to find unpalatable. In language that echoed Harris's cautionary words to the Board a decade earlier, the committee warned of problems in ROTC instruction that threatened to generate "considerable friction between various campus elements." Unless problems in the system were quickly addressed, the committee envisioned a loss of student and faculty support for the programs, which could lead to the withdrawal of ROTC from the Tulane campus. The committee's recommendations for curricular change conformed rather closely to the proposals advanced by the Cornell Report. The military services should, in general, make greater use of regular university faculty for instruction in modern languages, computer science, and the physical, biological, social, and behavioral sciences. Courses with "substantive political or policy content" should be offered only in the appropriate academic departments, and should never be taught by instructors who were active duty military officers. Finally, "all drill, indoctrination[,] and training in military skills should be non-credit activities . . . confined to summer camps and cruises, or made totally extracurricular. Under no circumstance should they be scheduled during 'prime time'" or included on grade reports sent to the College of Arts and Sciences.[66]

65. Hearing before the Tulane University Senate Committee on Academic Freedom, Tenure, and Responsibility, with Reference to Charges Against Dr. Edward L. Dubinsky, Held at Tulane University, Norman Mayer Building, Morton A. Aldrich Conference Room, 29–31 May 1969, 3 vols., box 67b, HEL Papers, vol. 2, p. 446 (hereafter Dubinsky Hearing); Tulane *Hullabaloo*, 7 March 1969, p. 15 (quotations).

66. Curriculum Committee, College of Arts and Sciences, Position Statement on ROTC, 18 April 1969, box 60, HEL Papers.

The release of the Arts and Sciences Curriculum Committee report on April 18 coincided with the *Hullabaloo*'s publication of a strong anti-ROTC editorial that appeared simultaneously in twenty-five other college newspapers throughout the nation. The editorial, "On ROTC Credits," summarized the arguments being advanced at a number of leading research universities in support of the position that "ROTC is not only antithetical to the ultimate purposes of higher education, but contrary to basic pedagogical principles as well." Alleged pedagogical deficiencies ranged from the "rigidly hierarchical structure of military education" to the use of course materials that were "conjectural, non-analytical, cheaply moralistic, and often blatantly propagandistic." Noting that ROTC had been spawned by the "simplistic 'my country right or wrong' patriotism" of World War I, the editorial went on to decry academic involvement in the military phase of "an expansionist foreign policy opposed by a sizable segment of the population." Concluding with the blunt assertion that "training soldiers whose ultimate aim is to kill is totally hostile to the principles of academia," the politically charged language of the April 18 statement injected a new level of emotional intensity into the ROTC debate at Tulane and helped set the stage for what was to follow.[67]

The spring semester's first demonstration against ROTC took place on Tuesday, April 22, when a group of approximately twenty-five "Tulane and Newcomb students" sat on the side of the University Center quadrangle chanting and shouting slogans during the drill exercises officially designated as the naval ROTC "military leadership laboratory." The incident involved no physical disruption of drill activities. A spokesman for the demonstrators, after denying that SDS was involved in the incident, said that the protest had been planned the previous evening by "a group of concerned students" who opposed giving academic credit for ROTC but who were "not against having ROTC on campus." Nonetheless, the stated goal of the demonstration was "to make ROTC look like the farce it is." Two days later, at 11:00 A.M. on Thursday, April 24, most of the original protesters reappeared to provide verbal harassment aimed at air force ROTC cadets. As onlookers joined their ranks, the demonstrators soon numbered over a hundred students who marched around the quadrangle chant-

---

67. Tulane *Hullabaloo*, 18 April 1969, pp. 8 (first–second quotations), 9 (all subsequent quotations).

Protest group against ROTC, 1969.
Foreground: Edward Dubinsky,
Associate Professor of Mathematics.

ing, "Kill, Kill," and shouting antiwar slogans. Again, there was no physical interference until the end of the drill period, when the Drum and Bugle Corps was surrounded and prevented from marching. Attempting to follow the other cadets off the field, the band walked into the group of students surrounding it, momentarily catching two of the demonstrators in the front rank. Pro-ROTC students unexpectedly intervened to remove the two demonstrators, and the band left the scene without further incident.[68]

The demonstrations attracted wide attention, and by the end of the week it was clear that ROTC had moved onto center stage as a campus issue. Shortly after Thursday's demonstration, anti-ROTC students issued a call for a rally outside Gibson Hall at noon on Friday and a group calling itself the Student Coalition Supporting ROTC began circulating petitions for a campuswide referendum on the question of academic credit for military science. Later on Thursday, in what was

68. Ibid., 2 May 1969, p. 1.

generally regarded as a show of patriotic muscle flexing, approximately eighty Tulane athletes met, with official blessing, "to discuss their role as a group, if any, in future demonstration[s]." Finally, the April 25 *Hullabaloo* featured an extremely able column by Major Robert Ainsworth of the Tulane air force ROTC program, writing in rebuttal to the previous week's anti-ROTC editorial. Drawing upon the writings of civilian sociologist Morris Janowitz, a specialist in military subjects, Ainsworth conceded the need for reform in many ROTC practices, including the possible elimination of "hardware courses" and campus drill, but chided the *Hullabaloo* for resorting to emotional and ideological arguments and for succumbing to popular stereotypes about soldiers and military life. Ainsworth concluded his rebuttal with an eloquent passage affirming that officers commissioned out of ROTC were not "expected to exchange . . . respect for human life and the concept of the brotherhood of man for a set of fatigues and a gold bar." It was possible, Ainsworth believed, "to serve humanity with compassion and love; yes, even in places like Vietnam."[69]

As these events rapidly unfolded President Longenecker convened a late afternoon meeting of his official Faculty Advisory Committee and expressed "deep concern" over the prospect of an "ugly situation" in connection with the ongoing ROTC protests "unless some relief could be felt to the pressures that had been mounting throughout the early afternoon" on Thursday. Longenecker saw the intervention of ROTC supporters at the 11:00 A.M. air force drill as a bad omen, and he feared that both student athletes and ROTC cadets, as well as conservative groups off campus, might attend the Friday rally. In such a situation, the inevitable "release of pent-up emotions" could produce a "chaotic and possibly unmanageable situation." All present at the meeting agreed that the university faced a potentially serious conflict, and all four faculty members promised to be present at the Friday rally to help keep order. The group also planned to make informal contact with the opposing parties and counsel restraint, or, in the idiom of the day, to urge both sides to cool it.[70]

Apparently such efforts had the desired effect. The Friday rally attracted some five hundred students who listened or occasionally heckled and applauded while pro- and anti-ROTC spokesmen traded allegations

69. Ibid. (first quotation); ibid., 25 April 1969, p. 8 (all subsequent quotations).

70. Memorandum of a Meeting of the President's Faculty Advisory Committee, 24 April 1969, typescript, box 62, HEL Papers.

and aired their views. The meeting was moderated by law student Collins Vallee, an ROTC opponent who read a statement from "The Concerned Students of Tulane" supporting the recommendations of the A&S Curriculum Committee. Architecture student and former *Hullabaloo* associate editor William Rushton, now a student senator, threatened legal action against the university's athletic director if Tulane players sought to disrupt future anti-ROTC demonstrations. Two students, including the chairman of the conservative Young Americans for Freedom, spoke on behalf of ROTC, while the newly elected Student Senate president Walter Blessey, himself an ROTC cadet, opposed blanket judgments about ROTC classes and argued that decisions about academic credit should be decided by the faculty on a course-by-course basis. After an hour and a half the meeting ended uneventfully.[71]

The next three days were a time of preparation and reassessment. Up to this point most anti-ROTC demonstrations had been noisy but nondisruptive actions falling well within the university's established guidelines for peaceful picketing and assembly. A change of direction now seemed to be in the offing. On the evening of Monday, April 28, members of SDS and other students opposed to the existing system of ROTC academic credit met to plan strategy for the next day's demonstration at the drill field and to discuss long-range tactical issues. Hardly a clandestine gathering, the meeting was attended by reporters for WTUL and by Neil Campbell and Paul Schulman, who were respectively editor and associate editor of the *Hullabaloo*. In a verbal account of the meeting given to Longenecker the next day, Campbell and Schulman assigned Professor Dubinsky the key role in persuading the student group to move from conventional protest to a posture of civil disobedience. In a memorandum prepared shortly after talking with Campbell and Schulman, Longenecker summarized the student editors' comments:

> They told me in some detail of the discussion held by the SDS group. . . . There was a strong disposition within the group to continue the demonstrations against ROTC Programs. Those who proposed non-disruptive programs suggested a continuation of speeches, meetings, signs, etc. When it appeared that the group proposing non-disruptive tactics was in the majority and

71. Tulane *Hullabaloo*, 2 May 1969, pp. 2, 6.

would prevail, Dr. Dubinsky, seated on a table at the front of the room, made two statements: (1) that such proposals had characterized the groups earlier in the year and it was now time to change tactics; (2) it was important to consider . . . (a) [that] the University administration was out to get him and he could now predict that he would not long be at Tulane because of the repressive attitudes being expressed by the University administration, and (b) [that] no confidence could be placed in the faculty groups considering ROTC at this time because, as usual, they would take forever and eventually fail to deal with ROTC questions in set situations. . . . Following the presentation of these views, the whole attitude of the group changed markedly. There was an immediate proposal for disruptive action which was overwhelmingly adopted and this was followed by specific and more detailed planning after the regular meeting was discontinued.[72]

When questioned about the meeting several weeks later, Dubinsky recalled that there had been a long discussion, "some of it about tactics," but primarily concerned with "the political position that was going to be put forward the next day." The principal question, as Professor Dubinsky recalled it, was whether the group should limit itself to opposing academic credit for ROTC or issue a broader statement on "the relationships between ROTC on Tulane's campus and other political situations that exist." Asked about his own role in the proceedings, he denied having "particularly espoused any position as to what the students ought to do or ought not to do." Elaborating on the point, he explained that he had simply advised the students "not to take any action in a light way, but to consider very seriously what reasons they may have for doing this or doing that, that in fact whatever they did the next day was indeed going to be a political act, and that they should attempt to develop a political basis for that political act, and that was it." However one may evaluate the two versions of the meetings in question, at least one point seems indisputable. Whether the students were manipulated (as Longenecker appeared to believe) or simply persuaded by the logic and moral force of Dubinsky's argument, the psychological groundwork was laid on the evening of April

72. Memorandum of Conference with Neil Campbell and Paul Schulman, 29 April 1969, box 62, HEL Papers.

Anti-ROTC protest, 1969. Foreground: Colonel Robert Scruton, Director of Security.

28 for an escalation of the ROTC demonstrations to a more self-consciously political level that was fully compatible with a resort to tactics of civil disobedience. The protesters, including Professor Dubinsky, were now on a collision course with Tulane administration.[73]

At 11:00 A.M. on Tuesday, April 29, the date and time previously fixed for a tri-service review, a crowd of approximately 250 people gathered at the UC quad. Some were spectators; others carried signs supporting or opposing ROTC. Even the most cursory glance at surviving photographs reveals a story told in slogans: "WE SUPPORT ROTC"; "ROTC IS WRONG"; "STOP SDS"; "THOU SHALT NOT KILL"; "LIBERATE THE WORLD . . . SMASH U.S. IMPERIALISM." Both pro- and anti-ROTC students displayed American flags, as did the ROTC cadets. An outside observer might readily have concluded that the various factions were contending not so much over the fate of campus military training as over the meaning of patriotism and the content of American values. As the time for drill exercises drew near, campus security director Robert Scruton announced through a bullhorn,

73. Dubinsky Hearing, vol. 3, pp. 678–9 (first–second quotations), 680 (third quotation), 682 (all subsequent quotations).

ROTC support group, 1969.
(Participants not identified.)

"Today from 11:00 o'clock this drill field is a classroom. This tree line and this lamp line is [sic] the limits of that class. I request that no person get on this drill field beyond this tree line." Scruton's edict was promptly challenged by law student Collins Vallee, who claimed the actual drill area was a smaller portion of the quad designated by red marker flags that had been placed at least twenty yards from the tree line mentioned by Scruton. "This quad belongs to the students and not the Defense Department," Vallee declared, adding, "I think our rights go out to the red flags." Carrying an American flag on a standard, Vallee then led a group of some fifty protesters onto the field, proceeding as far as the markers and ignoring Scruton's requests to move back. When it became clear that the demonstrators had no intention of leaving, Scruton signaled with a wave of his hat to summon ten additional campus policemen, armed with nightsticks but not guns, to the scene of the confrontation. The patrolmen immediately began arresting protesters and handcuffing them to a fire hydrant on Newcomb Place. As the ROTC cadets stood in tight formation, those sit-in demonstrators

*Associate Professor Edward Dubinsky forcibly removed from drill field
after protest demonstration, April 1969.*

who would walk were led off the field in custody, while others were
physically dragged from the scene. Among the latter group was Professor Dubinsky, who assumed a semiprone position and was hauled off
the field from behind by three patrolmen, two of whom grasped the
mathematician's left arm while a third officer pulled from the right.
These events took approximately half an hour, at the end of which it became apparent that conditions suitable for completing the scheduled
drill could not be achieved within the time remaining. Shortly after
11:30, the ROTC units marched off the field. By this point a total of thirteen people—twelve students plus Dubinsky—had been detained by the
campus police. As soon as the last ROTC units had departed, all those
arrested were released to face future disciplinary action.[74]

74. Tulane *Hullabaloo*, 2 May 1969, p. 6 (all quotations except poster slogans, which are
taken from press photographs of the April 29 demonstration preserved in the Tulane University
archives. Many are readable in the photographic section of the 2 May 1969 issue of the Tulane
Hullabaloo.); James E. Llamas, "Governance in Academe," *Tulanian* 42 (September 1969):
3–10, p. 4; Tulane University Security Division, Police Report 8130, 29 April 1969, Tulane
AAUP Files.

ROTC protests throw the conflict of generational values into sharp relief, April 1969. (Participants not identified.)

The climax of the antiwar movement at Tulane occurred a week later on Tuesday, May 6, when a packed audience of supporters and critics of ROTC assembled in McAlister Auditorium for the annual awards ceremony for all campus military units. On the previous day more than 70 percent of the 1,710 students voting in a campus referendum had favored the reevaluation (50 percent) or outright elimination (21 percent) of academic credit for ROTC classes. Those who opposed campus military training as part of a larger protest against American policy in Vietnam came prepared to make their presence known at the awards program. Occupying most of McAlister's upstairs balcony, the protesters began boisterous chants of "Stop the War!" as the ROTC cadets filed into the lower floor and seated themselves. When a trumpet blast announced the arrival of President Longenecker and the platform guests, the chants changed to "Sieg heil!"—a phrase that must have confirmed Longenecker's worst suspicions about the dangers of mass crowd behavior. As the ceremony proceeded, shouting contests between supporters and foes of ROTC developed, and chants were increasingly laced with obscenity. According to a firsthand report filed by the director of campus security, "Mother Fucker . . . Mother

Protesters in McAlister Auditorium during ROTC awards ceremony, May 1969.

Fucker . . . Mother Fucker was the theme of the [anti-ROTC] chants,"
which were often sufficiently loud to drown out the platform speeches
for various awards. When at length Longenecker rose to speak, he was
greeted by chants of "IDA Must Go"—a reference to his membership
on the Board of Trustees of the Institute for Defense Analysis.[75]

Not surprisingly, Longenecker abbreviated his remarks. After apol-
ogizing to guests for the disruption, he assured the demonstrators, including Professor Dubinsky, that "having asked for it, I'm sure they
will be subjected to the critical review of their colleagues in this University for appropriate action." All told some twenty-two people—
twenty-one students plus Dubinsky—received sanctions for their part
in the ROTC protests of April 24–May 6. Student penalties ranged
from cautionary warnings to "indefinite suspension," a euphemism
for expulsion. The most severe disciplinary action was reserved for Dubinsky, who was accused of willfully disrupting "regularly scheduled

75. Tulane *Hullabaloo,* 9 May 1969, p. 4 (first, second, and fourth quotations); Tulane
University Security Division, Police Report 8179, 6 May 1969, Tulane AAUP Files (third quotation).

classes and academic activities" during the April 24 and 29 ROTC drills and the May 6 awards ceremony. On May 13 Dubinsky was officially notified of the charges against him and cautioned that the offenses, if proven, were deemed "serious and substantial" enough to constitute "possible grounds for dismissal." He was further advised of his right to propose a settlement of the case or to request a formal hearing before the University Senate Committee on Academic Freedom, Tenure, and Responsibility, a body composed of nine faculty members representing each school and college within Tulane.[76]

Dubinsky chose the latter alternative. With anthropology professor Munro Edmonson acting as his academic counsel, Dubinsky presented his case in a hearing that took place on May 29, 30, and 31. On June 4, after two days of post-hearing deliberation and before sufficient time had elapsed to prepare or review the 778-page transcript of the testimony, the Hearing Committee, as the senate panel was officially designated, delivered its finding of fact and its accompanying recommendations to Longenecker. At the factual level the committee found that on April 24 and 29 Dubinsky had indeed "interfered" with ROTC drill as the university alleged. But with respect to the more specific claims that Dubinsky had "physically entered into the ROTC formations, which action, coupled with similar actions by others, caused a cancellation of the drill" on April 24, and the related charge that Dubinsky had placed himself "on the drill field in such a position as to impede or render impractical the continuation of the drill" on April 29, the committee found insufficient evidence and declared both charges to be "not proved." Consideration of the third charge against Dubinsky—that he had shouted, booed, and otherwise vocally disturbed the May 6 award ceremonies in McAlister Auditorium—resulted in another verdict of "not proved." Having thus limited their definition of the nature and scope of Dubinsky's alleged transgressions, the committee agreed that his actions constituted "a serious violation of University policy," but also concluded that the offenses "were not sufficient to warrant dismissal at this time." With Engineering professor Walter E. Blessey strongly dissenting in favor of dismissal, the committee recommended that Dubinsky be issued a letter of reprimand, that he be forbidden to

76. Llamas, "Governance in Academe," 4 (first quotation), 5 (second quotation); Joseph E. Gordon, David R. Deener, and Herbert E. Longenecker to Edward L. Dubinsky, 13 May 1969, Tulane AAUP Files (third–fifth quotations). This document and virtually all other material on the Dubinsky case may be found in box 67b, HEL Papers.

interfere with scheduled university activities, and that he be notified that future violations of university policy could result in additional, more severe penalties.[77]

Longenecker accepted the committee's finding of guilt but rejected the suggested sanctions as too mild. On June 5, the day after receiving the committee's recommendations, he submitted a report to the Board of Administrators asking for Dubinsky's immediate dismissal from the faculty with a grant of one year's salary from the date of termination. Like the Hearing Committee, Longenecker made his recommendation without consulting the transcript of testimony. Under established university procedures, a presidential recommendation at variance with that of the faculty Hearing Committee entitled the accused party to appeal the decision directly to the Board. In early July Dubinsky submitted a written request for an appeal, in which he questioned Longenecker's motives for overruling the Hearing Committee, observing pointedly that "[w]hen I confronted [m]y accusers in 'open court,' I won my case!" Passing over the testimony in the case, a transcript of which was now available to the Board, Dubinsky called the Administrators' attention to a range of activities outside the classroom that bore upon his fitness for continued faculty membership. Among the latter were a "large number of public talks . . . at various churches, youth groups, fraternities, and sororities," in which the Tulane professor had managed to ignite a "spark of communication which lit the darkness of misunderstanding and dispelled the fear and hatred on many of those occasions." When interacting with Tulane students, Dubinsky explained, "I have tried to help them be productive according to their lights." On August 14 Dubinsky appeared in person to present his appeal to the Administrators, who then voted unanimously to approve Longenecker's recommendation for immediate termination. A formal decision of twenty-four typed pages was drafted by the Board's Law Committee and approved by the Executive Committee on behalf of the full Board on August 21, 1969. The decision rejected the faculty Hearing Committee's interpretation of the evidence concerning

77. Leonard Oppenheim, Report to the University Senate on the Case of Edward L. Dubinsky, 6 October 1969, Tulane AAUP Files, 1–3 (hereafter cited as Oppenheim Report); Leonard Oppenheim to Herbert E. Longenecker, 4 June 1969, attachment 6 of Oppenheim Report (all quotations), Tulane AAUP Files. The Oppenheim Report provides a thorough chronology of the proceedings against Dubinsky. Nearly all items of important correspondence and internal memoranda are appended to it.

two of the three charges against Dubinsky, and gave the Hearing Committee members until September 3 to offer written comments. On September 4, 1969, the Board's decision took effect and Dubinsky was officially dismissed from the Tulane faculty.[78]

Dubinsky's dismissal marked the beginning of a three-year procedural dispute that was the culmination of a pattern of steadily rising tension between the faculty and the Tulane administration as represented by President Longenecker and the Board of Administrators. Given impetus by Dubinsky's decision to appeal his dismissal to the national office of the American Association of University Professors—an organization best known to university presidents for its power to place rogue institutions on a widely publicized list of censured administrations—the Dubinsky controversy took on the visceral quality of a dispute among aggrieved family members. Like quarreling in-laws, members of the faculty and administration found themselves linked together in a legal relationship that had become clouded by resentment, mistrust, and mutual recrimination. The point immediately at issue was the unwillingness of either Longenecker or the Board to follow the recommended AAUP policy of returning the Dubinsky matter to the Hearing Committee for reconsideration before reaching a final decision on whether or not to overrule the faculty tribunal. A complex and increasingly arcane debate developed around this seemingly minor procedural point. The Hearing Committee and many faculty members insisted that the AAUP's procedural standards should have been followed, while Longenecker and Tulane Board members maintained that the University Senate "Statement on Faculty Membership, Tenure, Retirement, Freedoms, and Responsibilities" adopted in July 1967 took precedence over the nonbinding AAUP guidelines, which the senate had never formally adopted.

Behind the procedural dispute lay more fundamental concerns about academic freedom and what the AAUP described in 1968 as the college faculty's "first-hand concern with its own membership" in matters of appointment, promotion, and dismissal. At a still deeper level

78. Report of the President of the University to the Executive Committee of the Tulane University Board of Administrators, Re: Edward L. Dubinsky, Associate Professor of Mathematics, 5 June 1969 (attachment 8 of Oppenheim Report), Tulane AAUP Files; Edward L. Dubinsky to the Administrators of the Tulane Educational Fund, undated memorandum (attachment 14 of Oppenheim Report; all quotations); Oppenheim Report, 11–2; Decision of the Board of Administrators of the Tulane Educational Fund in the Matter of the Appeal of Dr. Edward L. Dubinsky, Associate Professor of Mathematics (attachment 24 of Oppenheim Report).

the controversy may be regarded as an airing of several years of pent-up frustration over such issues as the restoration of the physical education major, the loss of the *Tulane Drama Review* along with key members of the theater faculty, and the graduate program reductions of 1968. All of these changes had sparked feelings of resentment and marginalization among faculty members, who believed they had been excluded from the decision-making process in situations that touched their vital interests. Political and ideological disagreements also entered the equation, and made the Dubinsky affair an emotional symbol of what some Tulanians had come to regard as a moral struggle over the balance of power within the university.[79]

During the 1969–70 academic year the Dubinsky case became a cause célèbre and a rallying point for critics of the Tulane administration. Before classes ended in May, students marched on the president's home to demand blanket amnesty for those accused in the ROTC protests. Throughout the summer, members of the Dubinsky Hearing Committee—as well as national AAUP representatives—urged the Board to modify its stand and return the case for faculty reconsideration, or at least to allow additional time for the Hearing Committee to prepare written comments. On September 10, sociologist Leonard Reissman, a member of the Hearing Committee, wrote Board chairman Harry Kelleher to express "considerable dismay" at the procedures employed and the penalty imposed in the Dubinsky case. Having learned of the Administrators' action through stories in the local press, Reissman felt that Dubinsky "was being dismissed without the Board's customary courtesy." He was equally troubled by the Board's willingness to impose a penalty that seemed "extremely severe" when Dubinsky's brief, nonviolent protest was viewed in conjunction with the violence and forcible takeover of academic buildings that had occurred on many American campuses during the 1968–69 academic year. In a hastily arranged meeting in Reissman's office the following week, Board members A. J. Waechter and Ashton Phelps restated the Administrators' position and explained that they "were distressed at the attitude of some people . . . who felt that they could read into the Board's action restrictive motives."[80]

---

79. "Statement on Procedural Standards in Faculty Dismissal Proceedings," *AAUP Bulletin* 54 (winter 1968): 439 (quotation)–41.

80. Tulane *Hullabaloo*, 1 August 1969, p. 1; Leonard Oppenheim to Percy A. Generes, 12 June 1969 (attachment 10 of Oppenheim Report), Tulane AAUP Files; Jordan E. Kurland to Harry B. Kelleher and Herbert E. Longenecker, 20 June 1969 (attachment 12 of Oppenheim

If the Administrators were displeased by faculty attitudes at the beginning of the fall semester, developments in the following weeks and
months could only have intensified their concern. Professor Reissman
went public on the Dubinsky case by releasing his September 10 letter
to the press and allowing its publication in the *Notices* of the American
Mathematical Society, a scholarly body that had passed a resolution in
late August deploring Dubinsky's impending dismissal. Further resolutions were soon forthcoming. On September 16 the faculties of the
College of Arts and Sciences and Newcomb College, meeting separately, considered identical resolutions to "deplore the decision of the
Board of Administrators to go against the advice of its faculty committee" in the Dubinsky case. Critics of the Board employed blunt language in urging their proposal upon the A&S faculty. University mathematics chairman Paul Mostert, whose department had submitted the
resolution, declared that Dubinsky was the first Tulane professor
"since the McCarthy era to be dismissed for political reasons." English
professor and campus AAUP leader Richard Adams, who had opposed the Vietnam War since 1965, warned that "if one man can be
dismissed contrary to the findings of the faculty," then all were vulnerable to a similar fate. "Do we have tenure?" Adams asked his colleagues. The A&S faculty adopted the resolution by a vote of 74-43,
while Newcomb College agreed to continue discussing the matter at its
next meeting. On October 16 the Newcomb faculty passed a more
lengthy substitute motion expressing the group's "sincere desire . . . to
resolve the misunderstandings and apprehensions that exist both
within the Tulane family and between Tulane and the national academic community." Toward this end, the faculty unanimously requested the Board to "reconsider the Dubinsky case from the point at
which the Hearing Committee presented its decision to the President,
and that this be done by requesting the hearing committee to formulate
the reasons for its decision." The faculty further resolved that "the
final decision taken in the case" should be reached using the much-
discussed AAUP procedures.[81]

Report), Tulane AAUP Files; Leonard Reissman to Harry B. Kelleher, 29 August 1969 (attachment 22 of Oppenheim Report), Tulane AAUP Files; Leonard Reissman to Harry B. Kelleher,
10 September 1969 (attachment 28 of Oppenheim Report), Tulane AAUP Files (first–third quotations); Ashton Phelps to Leonard Reissman, 19 September 1969 (attachment 29 of Oppenheim
Report), Tulane AAUP Files (fourth quotation).

81. "Dismissal of Dr. Dubinsky," American Mathematical Society *Notices* 16 (November
1969): 1027–31; Richard P. Adams to Hale Boggs, 16 March 1965, letter in authors' possession;

Apart from a September resolution of the School of Engineering faculty commending the president and the Board for their "forthright action" in the Dubinsky matter, and an even stronger Homecoming Day endorsement of Dubinsky's firing by the Executive Committee of the Tulane Alumni Association, the fall semester saw little in the way of positive reaction to the university's handling of the ROTC dispute. Early in October the national headquarters of the AAUP appointed an ad hoc committee to report on Dubinsky's dismissal. On December 10, the day the AAUP investigating committee arrived on campus, a meeting of the Tulane graduate faculty voted 62-34 to express the faculty's "lack of confidence in the President, Provost, and Board of Administrators to cooperate . . . in the joint efforts essential for conducting the affairs of this University." In less than a week, a newly formed student-faculty group calling itself the Committee for the Defense of Academic Freedom had collected over a thousand signatures in support of the graduate faculty resolution. In the medical school, however, support for the administration was overwhelming. Approximately two hundred faculty members endorsed a December statement approving the action of the president and the Board in firing Dubinsky.[82]

As the Christmas holiday approached, Newcomb dean James Davidson, who was completing his first semester at Tulane, offered a frank assessment of the political situation he had encountered on the uptown campus. "Increasingly," Davidson wrote, "I am impressed by the extent of the gulf in understanding and sympathy which large numbers of the students and faculty here apparently have felt between themselves and [the] 'administration,' particularly as it is symbolized by the Board. This is not limited to those who can be designated as radical, dissident, or even political; and the activities of such groups or persons do not account sufficiently for the general feeling. . . . There is

---

Tulane *Hullabaloo*, 26 September 1969, pp. 1 (first quotation), 2 (second–fourth quotations); College of Arts and Sciences Faculty Minutes, 16 September 1969, box 30, HEL Papers; Newcomb Faculty Minutes, 16 September 1969, 16 October 1969 (fifth–seventh quotations), box 45, HEL Papers.

82. Tulane *Hullabaloo*, 7 November 1969, p. 1; James E. Llamas, "L'Université / Return to Governance," *Tulanian* 43 (December 1969): 2–6, esp. 3–4 (all quotations); John P. Dawson, Samuel H. Baron, and Carl M. Stevens, "Academic Freedom and Tenure: Tulane University," *AAUP Bulletin* 56 (December 1970): 424–35, esp. 425; Herbert E. Longenecker, Memorandum to Administrators of the Tulane Educational Fund . . . [on] Faculty Resolutions and Dean's Comment on the Dubinsky Case, 29 December 1969, Tulane AAUP Files.

no doubt that some members of the University faculties hope for [AAUP] censure. . . . Some . . . want their roles in the [Dubinsky] case vindicated; others see the possibility of censure as a whip with which someone will punish administrators for unrelated decisions on budget, athletics, etc."[83]

In the university as a whole, faculty opinion on the Dubinsky case was deeply divided—a fact made apparent in January 1970 when the graduate faculty rescinded its earlier no-confidence motion by a vote of 141-82 in a meeting heavily attended by professors from the professional schools. But the anti-administration sentiments that Dean Davidson described were quite real, especially in Newcomb and the College of Arts and Sciences. The full extent of such feeling was displayed in excruciating detail during two unprecedented meetings attended jointly by the faculties of Newcomb College, the College of Arts and Sciences, and the senior Tulane administration, including President Longenecker, Provost and Graduate dean David Deener, A&S dean Joseph Gordon, and Board of Administrators chairman Harry Kelleher. Convened on March 20 and April 22 in response to a petition signed by 106 Newcomb and A&S professors, the extraordinary gatherings sought to elicit unambiguous answers about the role of the two faculties in (1) questions of dismissal, promotion, and tenure, (2) decisions on the selection, function, and retention of university administrators, and (3) the weight given academic versus nonacademic priorities in overall university planning.[84]

All three subjects plus a myriad of tangential issues received extensive discussion, which is preserved in a verbatim transcript of some fifty single-spaced typed pages. The meetings highlighted areas of disagreement but produced little in the way of genuine consensus. Faculty members aired grievances on matters ranging from the creation of the P.E. major and the appointment of deans to the proper role of the University Senate and the president's Faculty Advisory Committee. At times the discussion sank to the level of complaint about departmental salaries and budgets, while at other times it engaged serious philosoph-

83. James Davidson, Memorandum to President Longenecker . . . [on] Compelling Reasons, 8 December 1969, Tulane AAUP Files.

84. Tulane *Hullabaloo*, 6 February 1970, p. 1; Resolution Adopted by the Faculty of the Graduate School at the Meeting of 21 January 1970, accompanying BOA Minutes, 22 January 1970; Special Joint Meeting of the Faculties of the College of Arts and Sciences and Newcomb College, 20 March 1970, box 30, HEL Papers. The agenda appears on p. 4 of the typescript.

ical issues. In the end, however, even the most high-minded efforts tended to take on a combative edge. On one occasion Kelleher was asked to comment on whether the issue of the P.E. major could be re-submitted to the A&S and Newcomb faculties. After speaking a single sentence he was cut off by shouts from the floor of "Yes or No!" (Kelleher responded in the negative.) At another time the mathematics department chair offered the observation that just as the faculty did not enjoy the confidence of the Board, "at this time there are administrators who do not have the confidence of this faculty." What may have been the least conciliatory sentiment came from an English department spokesman, who told the assembled dignitaries that "if I wanted to be terribly crude, and I guess I do, [I would say that] the faculty and the students can do without you, or the Board should I say, more than the Board can do without us."[85]

The crisis of confidence on the uptown campus overlapped with the final stages of the student power and antiwar movements in the spring of 1970. Early the previous fall, the Student Senate had designated October 15, 1969, as an official Day of Peace, during which Tulane students placed crosses on the UC quad, arranged for antiwar speakers, films, prayer services, and singing activities. The next month a number of Tulane students participated in the citywide marches, rallies, and seminars held in conjunction with the Vietnam War Moratorium Committee's November 15 March Against Death. As antiwar sentiment deepened, Tulane and Loyola professors led informal seminars on topics such as "The Moral Conscience of the War," "The History of U.S. Involvement in Vietnam," and "The Myth of the Free Academy." Campus radicalism may be said to have peaked in April 1970 with the occupation of the University Center by a short-lived coalition known as the Tulane Liberation Front. Involving a number of individuals who had been active in the Dubinsky conflict of the preceding year, the TLF was born during an all-night encampment of students on the UC quad in the aftermath of a campus speech by antiwar activist and Chicago Seven defendant Rene Davis. Davis's April 7 appearance, together with a subsequent free speech rally in the University Center, touched

85. Special Joint Meeting of the Faculties of the College of Arts and Sciences and Newcomb College, 20 March 1970, p. 19 (first quotation); Special Joint Meeting of the Faculties of the College of Arts and Sciences and Newcomb College, 22 April 1970, box 30, HEL Papers, 13 (second–third quotations).

Protest demonstration, 1969. Note effigy of President Nixon and mock graves.

off demonstrations in front of the Longenecker residence that were followed by the burning of an unused ROTC barracks.[86]

Coming in the wake of major peace marches in New Orleans the previous fall, and a series of controversial speakers such as Strom Thurmond and Dr. Benjamin Spock earlier in the spring, Davis's appearance and its immediate aftermath generated sufficient momentum to
bring about a momentary convergence of radical forces on April 8,
when some five hundred students "liberated" the University Center
following a debate between rival slates of candidates for Student
Senate offices. During the next six days the occupying students engaged in noisy confrontations with Longenecker and several Board
members and disrupted a meeting of the Board of Visitors. The TLF
leadership, claiming to act in lieu of student government, took posi-

86. Tulane *Hullabaloo*, 17 October 1969, pp. 1, 3, 7, 14; ibid., 15 November 1974, pp. 16–9.
All quotations are from the *Hullabaloo* of 31 July 1970, which contains a useful summary of the
fall 1969 antiwar activities, while the 15 November 1974 issue assembles 1970 press accounts of
the TLF in a useful retrospective.

tions on virtually every topic that had generated controversy at Tulane since 1967. The movement's agenda for change included demands for student evaluation of instructors, "self-rule" for the faculty, creation of a viable atmosphere for black students "as defined by blacks themselves," the liberalization of visiting and curfew rules, an end to "censorship" in the choice of campus speakers, abolition of all ROTC courses not taught by regular civilian faculty, the reinstatement of Professor Dubinsky and all students suspended after the 1969 demonstrations, and the implementation of a student bill of rights.[87] None of the demands found acceptance in the form presented. The Longenecker administration, however, exercised considerable restraint during extended negotiations between the TLF leaders and representatives of the University Senate, and eventually a settlement materialized. The occupation ended peacefully on April 14 after the Student Senate refused to endorse the TLF's actions and a much-discussed strike of classes failed to materialize. In what was essentially a face-saving gesture, the TLF leadership announced that the focus of the movement was shifting from political to cultural issues, but the declaration was premature.[88]

Politics reasserted itself in early May, when campuses across the nation erupted in protest against the Nixon administration's decision to send American troops into Cambodia. The most serious clashes occurred at Kent State University in northeastern Ohio, where National Guardsmen shot thirteen unarmed students, killing four outright and wounding nine others. In Ohio, the National Guard's actions enjoyed wide support from local residents, who had long been deeply resentful over the political views, lifestyle, and physical appearance of radical students; for Americans in general, Kent State became a symbol of the larger clash of generations and values in the late 1960s. At Tulane, as on most campuses, the episode had a polarizing effect. A May 5 memorial service was overshadowed by a violent clash between three to five hundred antiwar students (including many TLF supporters) and a

87. Ibid., 10 April 1970, pp. 1, 3, 6, 8, 10, 13; ibid., 14 April 1970, pp. 1–4.

88. University Senate Minutes, special meeting, 11 April 1970, adjourned special meeting, 12 April 1970, box 73, HEL Papers; Student Senate Minutes, 12 April 1970, ASB, 1954–92; Tulane *Hullabaloo*, 17 April 1970, pp. 1–7. For a view of these events written from the perspective of a leader of the TLF who later served as ASB president and student representative to the Board of Administrators, see Ralph Wafer, "The Mid Sixties Were Glorious If One Wore Blinders," *New Orleans Magazine* (September 1971): 32–3, 58–60, 62, offprint in box 65, HEL Papers.

group of Tulane athletes and members of the right-wing Young Americans for Freedom, who engaged in fistfights on the Newcomb quad in the course of a dispute over the lowering of the American flag to half mast in memory of slain students.[89] Somewhat later mock graves were dug on the uptown campus, Richard Nixon was burned in effigy, President Longenecker canceled an ROTC awards ceremony, and the air force ROTC barracks was seriously damaged by a fire bomb of unknown origin. Concerned over the possibility of further violence, and aware that some students planned to leave for Washington, D.C., where larger antiwar protests were scheduled, the faculties of Newcomb, Arts and Sciences, Engineering, and Architecture voted to allow students to waive final exams, take grades of incomplete or pass-fail, and leave school before the semester officially ended. In this indirect sense, at least, the TLF could claim to have succeeded in shutting down the university.[90]

In ways that only gradually became apparent, Kent State marked the end of a distinct era at Tulane that coincided with the coming of age of the post–World War II college generation. Beginning with the civil rights struggles of the early 1960s, the tide of campus activism had crested near the end of the decade. For a period of some three years in the late 1960s, faculty and student discontent had reinforced each other in ways that challenged all Tulanians to reexamine conventional assumptions about university governance and the ultimate aims of higher learning. After 1970 the political conditions which had fueled academic activism dissipated rapidly, as the Vietnam War wound down and the student Left descended into factional anarchy. At Tulane the Dubinsky case lost much of its symbolic importance in April 1971, when the AAUP voted at its national convention to continue monitoring events at the university but not to recommend censure at that time. A major factor in the decision against imposing sanctions was the university's revision of its own procedures in dismissal cases to conform

89. *New Orleans Times-Picayune*, 6 May 1970; *New Orleans States*, 7 May 1970, Tulane clipping scrapbooks. What may stand as the most reliable firsthand account of the flag pole dispute is contained in Law School professor Wayne S. Woody's letter to the editor of the *Times-Picayune*, printed in the paper's 12 May 1970 issue. Woody was also chairman of the University Senate's Committee on Student Affairs.

90. Tulane *Hullabaloo*, 8 May 1970, pp. 1, 2, 4, 5, 11; College of Arts and Sciences Faculty Minutes, 7 and 19 May 1970, box 30, HEL Papers; Newcomb Faculty Minutes, 7 May 1970, box 45, HEL Papers; *New Orleans Times-Picayune*, 7 and 9 May 1970, Tulane clipping scrapbooks.

with all AAUP guidelines.[91] During the next twelve months a series of
meetings took place at Tulane between an ad hoc committee of the
Board, the newly renamed University Senate Committee on Faculty
Tenure, Freedom, and Responsibility, the remaining members of the
original Dubinsky Hearing Committee, and President Longenecker.
Although these meetings did not fully eliminate disagreements about
the Dubinsky case, they helped restore an air of comity and cooperation between faculty and administration representatives. On April 10,
1972, the University Senate Committee on Faculty Tenure, Freedom,
and Responsibility, after acknowledging that the Board had acted in
good faith, concluded its final report on the Dubinsky case with the affirmation that academic freedom at Tulane was "safe and secure." At
its annual meeting in May 1972 the national AAUP, in an act of con-
summate ambiguity, officially closed the Dubinsky case by first agreeing with the original Dubinsky Hearing Committee that a penalty less
severe than dismissal would have served the interests of all concerned,
but then going on to conclude "in the light of the discussions described
above" (i.e., the Board-faculty consultations of 1971–72) that "Committee A cannot say that the Board of Administrators by its action departed from its responsibility to protect the freedom of the entire
Tulane University community." By the time the final AAUP action occurred, the pressure of a rapidly worsening fiscal situation at Tulane
had begun to consume the energy and attention of former Dubinsky
antagonists. Inadequate financial resources had been at the heart of
much of the conflict between administrators and faculty members
throughout the late 1960s, and the looming economic crisis of the mid-
1970s would test the collegiality and good will of all those directly concerned with Tulane's future.[92]

91. *AAUP Bulletin* 57 (June 1971): 195; University Senate, Statement on Academic Freedom,
Tenure, and Responsibilities, 1 March 1971, accompanying BOA Minutes, 2 March 1971. See es-
pecially article 6 (Dismissal Procedure), and article 7 (Action by the Board of Administrators of
Tulane University), 6–9.

92. [Francis G. James], Summary of the Consultations Between the Ad Hoc Committee of the
Tulane Board of Administrators and Members of the Original Dubinsky Hearing Committee, 27
March 1972, box 67b, HEL Papers; Herbert E. Longenecker, Report to the American
Association of University Professors, 14 April 1972, box 67b, HEL Papers; Tulane *Hullabaloo*,
14 April 1972, p. 8 (first quotation); *AAUP Bulletin* 58 (June 1972): 151 (all subsequent quota-
tions)–152.

8

CREATIVE TENSION
1975–1980

On January 3, 1974, some eighteen months after the AAUP's closure of the Dubinsky affair and nearly four years after the university's last major bout of campus demonstrations, the Board of Administrators met in executive session to consider President Longenecker's request to retire no later than July 1, 1975, at the end of his fifteenth year as Tulane's chief executive. In an earlier letter to Board chairman Edmund McIlhenny, Longenecker had noted the Board's willingness to extend his tenure to age sixty-eight but concluded that such an extension "would not be in the best interest of the University." The president, who would turn sixty-three in May 1975, indicated that "he and Mrs. Longenecker had given long and thoughtful consideration to this matter and felt that they would like to have time while they still enjoyed good health to travel and write and do many things that they had not previously had time to do." After discussing the matter at length, the Board approved Longenecker's request with "profound regret."[1]

An important consideration in Longenecker's decision to step down two years before the usual retirement age of sixty-five was the realization that Tulane urgently needed a major capital campaign. Aware that the fundraising effort would be a long-range task, he believed the project should be entrusted to an incoming rather than an outgoing president. The search for Longenecker's successor began almost at once, and proceeded in a manner that reflected both the internal power struggles of the late 1960s and the deepening fiscal crisis of the early 1970s. At the time of President Harris's departure in 1959, the Board itself had conducted the search for a successor, ascertaining

1. BOA Minutes, 3 January 1974, pp. 64–5.

faculty views through letters from individual professors and from meetings with a special University Senate committee that had formulated a set of qualifications deemed important for a new president to possess. By 1974, more than half a decade of conflict with an increasingly alienated faculty and student body had made the Board anxious to avoid the appearance of unilateral action. Thus, when naming a ten-person search committee, the Administrators included three faculty representatives and two students, as well as two alumni representatives, two Board members (including Chairman McIlhenny), and one member of the administration. Board vice chairman Gerald L. Andrus chaired the search committee, and Clarence Scheps, Executive Vice President of Tulane, acted as secretary. Even more striking than the inclusion of students and faculty on the search committee was the Board's decision to seek the "advice and consent" of the University Senate concerning a group of between three and ten acceptable candidates to be presented to the Board no later than October 30, 1974. Although the senate spoke for both the faculty and the university's senior administration, its role in the search represented something approaching an academic veto over Board actions. This unprecedented concession on the part of the Administrators undoubtedly owed much to the criticism Tulane had received from the national AAUP over the issue of faculty consultation in the Dubinsky case.[2]

If the campus conflicts of the late 1960s formed an important backdrop for the presidential selection process of the mid-1970s, the university's monetary problems stood at the forefront of the 1974 search, which was conducted in the shadow of a deepening fiscal crisis. Potential candidates were alerted to the gravity of the situation in a section of the published job announcement, which explained that "Tulane, like all privately endowed educational institutions, is faced

2. Herbert E. Longenecker, interview by C. L. Mohr, 20 April 1995, New Orleans, Louisiana, tape recording in authors' possession; Charles I. Silin et al., Report of the Faculty Advisory Committee on the Selection of a President, April 1960, box 24, RCH Papers; Clarence Scheps, The Presidential Search for a Successor to Dr. Herbert E. Longenecker, personal memorandum to the Board of Administrators, 27 August 1976, box 9, F. Sheldon Hackney Papers, Tulane University Archives, 3, 9 (hereafter cited as FSH Papers; quotation on p. 9). Search committee members included: Gerald Andrus, Chair of the committee and Vice President, BOA; Frank Birtel, faculty representative; Gayle Dalferis, alumni representative; Bruce Feingerts, student representative; George Ann Hayne, student representative; Edmund McIlhenny, Chairman, BOA; C. Murphy Moss, alumni representative; Edward B. Partridge, faculty representative; Bernard Saltzberg, faculty representative; Clarence Scheps, Administrative Officer.

with the necessity of developing additional financial resources from external sources. Thus, the new president of Tulane University should be able to represent the University's case to the public and possess the experience, aptitude, and interest in order to develop new and additional resources for the institution."[3]

The brief statement put the best face on what had become a sobering encounter with harsh budgetary reality. Tulane's fiscal crisis was rooted in an unbroken cycle of deficit financing that had begun in the late 1950s as a temporary expedient to cover shortfalls in annual operating revenue resulting from the rapid growth and qualitative enhancement of research and teaching activities across a broad front. Over time the costs of this strategy had begun to outweigh the potential benefits, as Tulane's fungible assets, known as "funds functioning as endowment," shrank at an average rate of more than $1 million per year between 1958 and 1974. Aware that the pattern could not be allowed to continue, the Board had resolved in 1969 "that a balanced budget must be achieved within the next 3–5 years," and had directed "each of the academic and operating units" to draft plans toward that end. This policy, known euphemistically as the philosophy of "each tub on its own bottom," made individual schools and colleges responsible, after a three-year grace period, for generating income equal to their pro rata share of university operating costs.[4]

Although never fully implemented, the system raised the prospect of additional curtailment of academic programs and placed future salary raises in jeopardy for faculty in less affluent divisions of Tulane. It also caused the University Senate to take a keen interest in the deficit issue as it related to campuswide academic planning in the face of steadily dwindling cash reserves. Early in 1970 the senate created a special Budget Review Committee to monitor fiscal priorities and report on instances of budgetary noncompliance, including any allocations that might be considered "not in the best interests of the University." Near the end of the year, the importance of close budgetary scrutiny was highlighted by a report from the Carnegie Commission on Higher Edu-

3. Scheps, Presidential Search for a Successor to Dr. Herbert E. Longenecker, 4–5.

4. Tulane *Hullabaloo*, 5 April 1974, p. 1; Budget Review Committee Report to University Senate, 22 March 1973, item 2, accompanying University Senate Minutes, 2 April 1973, box 73, HEL Papers; BOA Minutes, 4 September 1968; Joseph E. Gordon et al., *Tulane University, The Liberal Arts and Sciences: Toward a Balance of Academic and Budgetary Priorities*, 22 September 1969 (rev. 1 October 1969), box 30, HEL Papers; Annual Report of the Budget Review Committee, 1971–72, box 73, HEL Papers, 1 (quotations).

cation that listed Tulane among some 540 academic institutions considered to be in "financial difficulty."[5]

Much of the Budget Review Committee's attention during the next two years focused on the large annual deficits in medicine and intercollegiate athletics. Although the medical school deficit was larger, the athletic deficit threatened to explode once the Superdome was completed and the temporary infusion of revenue from the New Orleans Saints' rental of the Tulane stadium came to an end. In 1972 the Budget Review Committee negotiated an agreement establishing an allowable deficit for athletics equal to the value of all athletic grants-in-aid, the number of which stood at 180 in 1972–73 with planned reductions to 140 in 1975–76. In theory at least, cash shortfalls over and above this amount were to be charged against the next year's allowable deficit, while surpluses would be credited against future shortfalls. For a short time the system appeared to work. By April 1973, however, in the face of burgeoning deficits in the Schools of Medicine and Public Health caused by the Nixon administration's cuts in federal education funds, the Budget Review Committee had concluded that "the present magnitude of the University's financial difficulties forecloses relief through accounting practices." The committee went on to note ominously that "[f]unds available to meet annual operating deficits are limited and will be consumed in the foreseeable future." In response to the approaching crisis, the senate proceeded to set up a Special Recommendations Committee charged with reviewing Tulane's financial position and making any recommendations deemed appropriate.[6]

In April 1974, as the search for a new president was getting underway, the Special Recommendations Committee returned to the University Senate with a set of proposals that even the most optimistic delegates must have found chilling. As of July 1, 1974, the committee reported, approximately $4.4 million would remain in the university's

5. University Senate Minutes, 16 February (first quotation) and 9 March 1970, box 73, HEL Papers; Tulane *Hullabaloo*, 18 January 1971, p. 1 (second quotation).

6. Annual Report of the Budget Review Committee for the Year 1971–72, separate typescript accompanying University Senate Minutes, 1 May 1972, box 73, HEL Papers, 9–11; Lawrence N. Powell, "Final Report [of the] Select Committee on Intercollegiate Athletics, Position Papers, Analytical Memos, Reports, and Statistical Material, June 1986," typescript in authors' possession, p. 72; Budget Review Committee Report to University Senate, 22 March 1973, item 2-A (Recommendation for Immediate Action: Creation of a Special Recommendation Committee), accompanying University Senate Minutes, 2 April 1973, box 73, HEL Papers (quotations); Wayne S. Woody to Harry B. Kelleher, 2 May 1973, box 75, HEL Papers.

cash reserves, nearly half of which was sequestered as collateral for an outstanding loan. Thus, with a budgeted deficit of $2 million for the next fiscal year, the university would face the prospect of attempting to operate without even a minimum fiscal safety net after July 1, 1975. The Tulane administration had reacted to the situation by submitting a revised budget with a deficit of only $1 million, but the reduction merely postponed the crisis until the following year. The Special Recommendations Committee endorsed the scaled down budget but went on to propose "a declaration by Tulane University of financial exigency to allow the termination of tenured faculty members so that the budget for the University can be brought into balance in the 1975–76 school year." The senate accepted the committee's analysis as accurate but looked for a less damaging remedy than the one proposed. Amid warnings that a declaration of financial exigency would harm student recruitment, cause "great damage to faculty morale," and impair the university's ability to secure a first-rate president, the senate decided to postpone action until the next academic year, while the deans of various colleges sought ways to bring their budgets into balance.[7]

This was essentially the situation confronting Tulane as the 1974 presidential search entered its concluding phase. While all the finalists for the Tulane presidency were made aware in a general way of the university's precarious fiscal position, the true meaning of the school's money problems could scarcely be conveyed to presidential candidates who viewed events from a distance. In retrospect, it is clear that the university's protracted financial troubles had taken a heavy toll in morale among the professors, deans, and other university officials who had participated in the retrenchment agonies of the previous five years. At some point between the Ford Foundation capital grant of 1964 and the Ph.D. cutbacks of 1968, internal perceptions of Tulane's finances had shifted from a positive to a negative frame of reference. What had begun optimistically in the late 1950s and early 1960s as a determined effort to surmount the challenge of a modest endowment had degenerated by the early 1970s into a grim twilight struggle against impending financial disaster. Any new president would thus face a dual challenge upon taking office. During the second half of the 1970s the test of leadership would involve not simply the ability to raise

7. University Senate Minutes, 1 April 1974 (first quotation) and 8 April 1973 (second quotation), box 73, HEL Papers.

money, but also the more difficult task of renewing confidence in Tulane's future and in the shared vision that had brought the university to the threshold of national academic distinction.

By June 11, 1974, the Presidential Search Committee had considered the names of some 265 applicants, a dozen of whom were selected for personal visits by a delegation comprised of Board members Edmund McIlhenny and Gerald Andrus, together with the search committee's three faculty representatives. In mid-August, after receiving reports of the visits, the search committee voted to submit to the senate the names of seven external candidates and one internal nominee. Five candidates were approved by the senate, and the committee agreed to submit to its secretary its preferential ordering of these five. This procedure allowed the search committee chairman the discretionary use of this information in contemplation of the October 3 meeting of the Board. The five candidates invited to campus for two-day visits were: E. Howard Brooks, Provost, Claremont Colleges; William A. Clebsch, Chair of the Department of Religious Studies, Stanford University; F. Sheldon Hackney, Provost, Princeton University; Kenneth M. Hoffman, Chair of the Department of Mathematics, Massachusetts Institute of Technology; and Lowell J. Paige, Assistant Director for Education, National Science Foundation. All except Clebsch visited the campus. On December 5, 1974, the Executive Committee of the Board unanimously decided to invite Francis Sheldon Hackney to become president of Tulane University. After a visit by McIlhenny and Andrus at his home on December 13, Hackney reported on January 2 that he was pleased to accept the offer. His decision was announced in the local press on January 3, 1975.[8]

Thus the forty-one-year-old F. Sheldon Hackney became the twelfth president of Tulane. A native of Birmingham, Alabama, Hackney had attended Vanderbilt on a navy ROTC scholarship during the Korean War. Upon graduation in 1955 he began a three-year tour of sea duty as gunnery officer aboard the destroyer USS *James C. Owens*, followed by a two-year stint (1959–61) on the faculty of the United States Naval Academy, where his desire to teach history was thwarted by an instructional assignment in the field of naval weapons systems. Shortly after leaving Annapolis, Hackney began doctoral work in American history at Yale University, where he studied with C. Vann Woodward,

8. Scheps, Presidential Search for a Successor to Dr. Herbert E. Longenecker, 10.

Francis Sheldon Hackney,
President, 1975–80.

the nation's preeminent authority on the post-Reconstruction South. In 1966 Hackney received the Ph.D. after completing a brilliant and methodologically sophisticated study of political reform in Alabama at the turn of the twentieth century. Published in 1969 to wide acclaim, the prizewinning book secured Hackney's place as a major interpreter of the southern past and added luster to his career at Princeton, where he had risen from the rank of instructor in 1965 to professor of history and provost in 1972.[9]

As provost at Princeton, Hackney was responsible both for long-term financial planning and annual decisions on the allocation of institutional resources. This experience had obvious relevance to the requirements of the Tulane presidency, and together with his intellectual stature and Ivy League affiliations, it marked him out as a figure

9. F. Sheldon Hackney, interview by C. L. Mohr, 8 November 1995, New Orleans, Louisiana, tape recording in authors' possession; F. Sheldon Hackney curriculum vitae, Tulane biographical files. F. Sheldon Hackney, *Populism to Progressivism in Alabama* (Princeton: Princeton University Press, 1969) won the American Historical Association's Albert J. Beveridge Prize for the best book in American history published in 1969. It also received the Southern Historical Association's Charles S. Sydnor prize for the best work on the history of the South published in 1968 and 1969.

equipped to lead the university at a critical juncture in its history. Many in New Orleans pointed to Hackney's Alabama roots and his regional academic focus as evidence of an underlying concern with the future of southern higher learning, a perception the new president mildly encouraged in early interviews and press conferences. What may have been his most powerful claim to legitimacy in the eyes of southern liberals existed by virtue of his marriage to the personable and talented Lucy Durr Hackney. A native of Montgomery, Alabama, Lucy Hackney was the niece of U.S. Supreme Court Justice Hugo Black and the daughter of Clifford and Virginia Durr, a couple whose steadfast liberalism and unswerving support for racial justice in the postwar South provided inspiration to beleaguered reformers across the region. Like many young women in the 1950s who had interrupted their education upon marriage, Lucy Durr Hackney returned to school in the next decade and completed her B.A. at Princeton. During her years in New Orleans she would earn a law degree from Tulane and press for reforms in the field of mental health. These activities were, of course, undertaken in addition to the many social obligations that devolved upon her as the wife of a university president. It is probably fair to say that, as a modern academic couple, Sheldon and Lucy Hackney broke new ground in the conservative milieu of uptown New Orleans society. Approaching their official duties with enthusiasm and refreshing informality, the Hackneys and their three children— Virginia (sixteen), Sheldon (fourteen), and Elizabeth (ten)—added zest and new life to the presidential residence at 2 Audubon Place.[10]

10. Lucy Durr Hackney was no stranger to activism in social and political affairs. Her father, Clifford Durr, a staunch New Dealer, championed civil liberties and the elevation of public interests over private gain in a number of federal agencies, including the Reconstruction Finance Corporation and the Federal Communications Commission. As president of the National Lawyers Guild in the late 1940s, Durr vigorously protested the conduct of the FBI in loyalty investigations. Driven from public life at the beginning of the McCarthy era, he returned to Montgomery, Alabama, in 1951 to practice law. One of his more celebrated clients was Rosa Parks, the courageous black woman who defied bus segregation in the cradle of the Confederacy. Virginia Durr, Lucy's mother, was a leader of the Southern Conference for Human Welfare, the first interracial civil rights organization founded in the South in the twentieth century. It was branded as a subversive organization by the House Committee on Un-American Activities, although HUAC found no violation of the law by the conference. Virginia Durr worked actively to enfranchise black Americans in the South and served as vice chair of the National Committee to Abolish the Poll Tax, an offshoot of the SCHW. See John A. Salmond, *The Conscience of a Lawyer: Clifford J. Durr and American Civil Liberties, 1899–1975* (Tuscaloosa: University of Alabama Press, 1990); Hollinger F. Barnard, ed., *Outside the Magic Circle: The Autobiography of Virginia Foster Durr* (Tuscaloosa: University of Alabama Press, 1986); *New York Times,* 9

In the words of the *Tulanian*, the date chosen for Hackney's installation, October 23, 1975, was the type of day the youthful new president wanted, "one long on open simplicity and short on pomposity." In
an outdoor setting on the Newcomb Quadrangle, Hackney was officially installed as the president of Tulane by Board chairman Edmund
McIlhenny in a ceremony that lasted less than an hour. A sizable crowd
attended the installation, but less than two hundred turned out that
evening to hear six distinguished educational leaders, including Hackney's mentor C. Vann Woodward, discuss "American Higher Education: The Challenges of An Uncertain Future." Hackney's inaugural
address, preceding the thinly-attended symposium, was upbeat but
laced with realism. Stressing the need for flexibility and resilience if
American society was to escape a "secular Armageddon," the new president advised his listeners that "all our institutions will have to adapt . . .
[and] learn to perform old functions under new conditions." The core
of his message was contained in a sentence suggesting an analogy between the crisis of Tulane in the mid-1970s and the crisis of the nation
in 1933. Employing language with clear Rooseveltian overtones,
Hackney counseled Tulanians, "We must learn to face the future with
confidence, even with joy, or we will surely create the doom we fear."[11]

The inaugural speech left little doubt that Hackney had entered
upon the presidency with his eyes wide open. From the time of his first
meeting with the search committee in July 1974, he had sought and received detailed information on budgetary matters, and he was beginning his tenure armed with full knowledge of the university's fiscal
plight. But his diagnosis of Tulane's problems extended beyond financial matters to include concern over the university's public image and
the precarious state of alumni, faculty, and student morale. As Hackney saw it, Tulane suffered from a severe crisis of confidence that was
compounded by the lack of a unifying vision or a well-developed sense
of community. Fiscal problems may have been at the heart of the uni-

July 1975; *New Orleans Courier*, 4–10 September 1975, p. 9; Tulane *Hullabaloo*, "Interview
with Lucy Hackney," 22 October 1976, pp. 4, 10; Marshall Ledger, "A President at Ease,"
Pennsylvania Gazette (December 1980): 16–27, esp. 26.

11. *Tulanian* 47 (January 1976): 2 (first–second quotations), 6 (third–fourth quotations), 7
(fifth quotation). Symposium participants included: David Matthews, Secretary, Department of
Health, Education, and Welfare; Mary I. Bunting, Emeritus President of Radcliffe; C. Vann
Woodward, Sterling Professor of History, Yale University; David E. Rogers, President, Robert
Wood Johnson Foundation; Norman Francis, President, Xavier University, New Orleans;
Logan Wilson, Emeritus President, American Council of Education.

versity's collective malaise but money alone could not set matters right. In his overall assessment of Tulane's situation, Hackney unknowingly echoed the views of Rufus Harris, who had cautioned the 1974 search committee against allowing economic issues to dominate the process of presidential selection. What was needed above all else, Hackney believed, was a renewal of institutional pride and a reaffirmation of a shared commitment to excellence in all areas of university life, from research and teaching to fundraising and intercollegiate athletics. It was toward this larger end that his policies were shaped and his energies directed over the next five years.[12]

Most new college presidents have the advantage of beginning their duties with a clean slate, unencumbered by the factional squabbles and personal or political feuds that accompany the exercise of power within an academic setting. Hackney was no exception to this rule, and at the start of his presidency he enjoyed wide support among both professors and students. The faculty, particularly in the liberal arts and sciences, accurately regarded him as one of their own, a scholar-teacher who by some quirk of fate had found his way into academic administration. Initially these perceptions were reinforced by tangible signs that the young president intended to break decisively with the past. The existence of numerous vacancies at the senior administrative level provided an opportunity to clear the air of old quarrels and tensions by installing fresh faces in key positions. As previously planned, Provost and Graduate School dean David R. Deener announced his resignation (to return to the faculty) effective June 30, 1976; Sam Hulbert, dean of the School of Engineering, left to assume the presidency of Rose-Hultman Institute of Terre Haute, effective the same date; and searches were already underway for the dean of the Business School and the dean of Student Affairs. Edward Rogge, Director of Admissions, also planned to return to a teaching position on June 30.

New appointments were soon forthcoming. In December 1975 Hackney announced that Professor of Mathematics Frank Birtel would become Special Assistant to the President, charged with drafting a mis-

12. Frank T. Birtel, Report of the Visiting Search Team on Francis Sheldon Hackney, Records of Presidential Search, 1974–75, Tulane University Archives; F. Sheldon Hackney, interview by C. L. Mohr, 8 November 1995; Rufus C. Harris to Gerald L. Andrus, 22 April 1974, Records of Presidential Search, 1974–75, Tulane University Archives.

sion statement for the university and identifying the resources needed to fulfill it. In March and April several appointments to become effective July 1, 1976, were announced. Robert Stevens, a native of England and a professor of law at Yale, was named Provost; Special Assistant to the President Frank Birtel was appointed Deputy Provost. Acting Dean of Students, Donald R. Moore, was elevated to Vice President for Student Services, and Annette Ten Elshof came from Wichita State University to fill the Dean of Students post. The Graduate School's new dean would be biology professor Richard D. Lumsden, and Hugh A. Thompson, Professor of Mechanical Engineering, was chosen as Dean of the School of Engineering. Clarence Scheps, in addition to his position as Executive Vice President, was named Secretary to the Board of Administrators. John Martinez, Associate Dean of the School of Engineering, was made Dean of Admissions. Announced after the March-April comprehensive listing of new appointments but also effective in the coming fiscal year were those of the new athletic director, Hindman Wall, succeeding Rix N. Yard, who resigned, and the transfer of Albert J. Wetzel, Director of Development, to the post of Vice President of University and Alumni Affairs, succeeding Bea Field, who would retire on December 31, 1976. Rarely if ever in Tulane's past had there been so many administrative personnel changes effective on a single date.[13]

Many additional administrative changes would take place during Hackney's presidency, the most notable of which occurred in 1978–79 with the departure of Provost Robert Stevens and business school dean Harper Boyd, both on board barely two years, along with the retirement of Vice President for Business Jesse B. Morgan after a tenure of thirty-two years at Tulane. Morgan had labored mightily in the business affairs of the university, through good times and bad, earning the respect and friendship of fellow administrators and faculty members alike. A major addition to Hackney's administrative team came with the appointment of S. Frederick Starr as Vice President for Academic Affairs (as of January 1980), the chief academic officer of the uptown campus. Starr was a product of Yale and King's College, Cambridge, with a doctorate in history from Princeton. He came to Tulane from his position as director of the Kennan Institute for Russian Studies,

13. *Tulanian* 47 (April 1976): 1–2.

which he had helped found. Starr's appointment added further academic distinction to the Hackney administration, even as it required a reconfiguration of duties and responsibilities that critics regarded as duplicative and potentially divisive. Frank Birtel retained his position as Provost and Dean of the Graduate School but was made responsible to Starr. Francis Lawrence served as Assistant Academic Vice President and Deputy Provost. The combined administrative talents of Provost Birtel and Vice President Starr had the potential to operate as a powerful force for change, provided that a satisfactory division of authority and responsibility could be agreed upon. Before the problems inherent in the arrangement could be satisfactorily resolved, however, Hackney's presidency had come to an end.[14]

Another senior appointment that proved to be of major importance became effective on July 1, when Eamon Michael Kelly became Executive Vice President. Clarence Scheps, formerly the Executive Vice President, agreed to be Acting Vice President of Business after Jesse Morgan's departure, to assist Kelly in his first transitional year, and to continue his part-time service as secretary to the Board of Administrators. An economist by training, Kelly had served in the Department of Commerce, the U.S. Small Business Administration, and the Department of Labor before joining the Ford Foundation in 1969 to supervise economic development programs related to civil rights and other social issues. At the time of his Tulane appointment Kelly was in charge of a $50 million portfolio of Ford Foundation program-related investments. Although his appointment occasioned little fanfare, Hackney gave him immediate responsibility for "coaxing the necessary economies out of an already tight budget." In 1980, as Tulane began its second consecutive year of balanced budget operations, Hackney advised the Board that Kelly had "performed superbly."[15]

In contrast to his largely unheralded appointment of Kelly, who was destined to become Tulane's next chief executive, Hackney made one administrative change that caused a greater campus stir than all his other appointments combined. It was made public in a letter to the Newcomb College faculty on May 7, 1976, when Dean James F. Davidson dropped a bombshell with the announcement, "In response to the expressed desire of President Hackney to effect a change in the admin-

14. F. Sheldon Hackney to the Board of Administrators, 29 March 1979, box 33, FSH Papers.

15. *President's Report*, 1975–80, box 26, FSH Papers, 9 (all quotations).

istration of Newcomb College during the coming year, I have requested to be relieved as Dean of Newcomb College, effective June 30, 1977." Davidson had served Newcomb since 1969 and his seemingly abrupt termination raised old concerns about faculty rights and presidential prerogative. In language reminiscent of the Dubinsky dispute, the Newcomb faculty passed a unanimous resolution requesting Hackney to "consult" with its members and explain the reasons underlying his action. The *Times-Picayune*, in a front-page story with Davidson's picture, quoted Tulane's president in a partial explanation of his action that conceded little to the cause of faculty influence. "I had been talking with him [Davidson] about this for months, and I made it known to him that I felt Newcomb would be better off with another leader," Hackney stated.[16]

On May 11, the president wrote a lengthy letter to the Newcomb faculty in which he sought to provide context for the change in leadership while reassuring all interested parties of his commitment to the college. "[Y]ou should all know that I have in mind no plans to change Newcomb or alter its role in the University or its relationship to the rest of the University," Hackney assured the faculty. "Improvement and greater cooperation are always desirable but I harbor no particular ideas or fantasies about Newcomb's future. I do think that, as a coordinate college with a strong separate identity, Newcomb offers a unique opportunity in the education of young women, especially so at this time in our society's history, and that it is not being exploited or developed as fully as I hope it might be in the future." In the wake of this statement, public expressions of faculty concern diminished rather quickly, and Davidson took up his tenured position as a professor of political science on July 1, 1976—not 1977 as he had originally requested. In consultation with the Newcomb faculty Executive Committee, Hackney appointed Francis L. Lawrence, Professor of French in Newcomb, to serve as acting dean of the college.[17]

Hackney's decision on the Newcomb deanship reflected a larger concern with women's issues that was beginning to manifest itself at major universities during the second half of the 1970s. Stimulated in

16. James F. Davidson, Memo to the Faculty of Newcomb College, 7 May 1976, box 23, FSH Papers, 1 (first quotation); Newcomb Faculty Minutes, 7 May 1976, box 23, FSH Papers (second quotation); *New Orleans Times-Picayune/States-Item*, 9 May 1976, p. A1 (third quotation).

17. F. Sheldon Hackney, Memo to the Newcomb College Faculty, 11 May 1976, box 23, FSH Papers, 1 (all quotations).

no small degree by the dialectic of empowerment and frustration that accompanied female participation in civil rights struggles and subsequent phases of campus activism, organized feminism made its campus debut at Tulane in 1969 with the creation of a short-lived group called "Tulane Women's Liberation." Feminist consciousness received an additional boost the next year with the organization of the New Orleans chapter of the National Organization for Women, and in 1971 the University Senate gave official recognition to Tulane Women for Change, apparently the successor organization to the 1969 Women's Liberation group. According to Margaret Katz, one of the founders of Tulane Women for Change, the group aimed to provide a forum in which women might "come to grips with the socialization that impedes their progress." In what may have been a bureaucratic coincidence, 1971 was also the year when, as part of a revised affirmative action plan, Tulane began to address the issue of salary inequities involving female faculty members. Although male students at Tulane remained overwhelmingly traditional in their attitudes toward women (a scientifically selected sample of 119 male undergraduates in 1975 found only 9.3 percent who were "positively willing" to marry a feminist), dissent over sex stereotyping became more vocal among men and women. In 1972, for example, unsuccessful efforts to make individual accomplishment rather than beauty the basis for selection to the homecoming court drew strong support from the *Hullabaloo*, which editorialized against the "sexist beauty court" and urged alumni to end the practice of "treating women as prize cattle to be paraded and inspected and evaluated on appearance."[18]

The early 1970s also witnessed a renewed debate over the role of an

18. The Place of Women, flyer announcing meeting of Tulane Women's Liberation, 13 November 1969, box 27–8, HEL Papers; University Senate Minutes, 1 November 1971; Tulane *Hullabaloo*, 12 November 1971, p. 4 (first quotation); Celeste M. Newbrough to "Dear Friend," undated form letter announcing formation of New Orleans affiliate of the National Organization for Women, box 27–8, HEL Papers; J. Valenti memorandum to Herbert E. Longenecker, Subject: Discrimination Against Women, 15 January 1971, box 27–8, HEL Papers; Jane N. Kohlmann, "The Male Perception of Females' Changing Roles: A Study of Tulane Male Undergraduates" (senior honors thesis, Tulane University, 1975), 63 (second quotation); Tulane *Hullabaloo*, 29 September 1972, p. 10 (third–fourth quotations). On the history of women's consciousness-raising experiences in New Orleans and their relation to prefeminist involvement in social activism, see Cathy Cade, *A Lesbian Photo Album: The Lives of Seven Lesbian Feminists* (Oakland, Calif.: Waterwomen Books, 1987), 85. Cf. Sara Evans, *Personal Politics: The Roots of Women's Liberation in the Civil Rights Movement and the New Left* (New York: Vintage Books, 1980), 35, 38, 183.

undergraduate women's college at Tulane, a matter that had received periodic discussion since the 1950s when the matter of coordinating Newcomb with the College of Arts and Sciences first emerged. Over time, concern had arisen among Newcomb loyalists that the college's separate status, if not its very existence, might be jeopardized by pressures to avoid academic duplication in the interest of efficiency. During the mid-1960s the efficiency argument was combined with the egalitarian logic of coeducation in a manner that did not augur well for Newcomb's autonomy. The 1964 supplement to Tulane's application for the all-important $6 million capital grant from the Ford Foundation faced the issue squarely when arguing that the presence of separately administered male and female undergraduate units had "limited the total development of the University." Tulane's Ford application found "little reason for continuing two distinct colleges" and concluded that a Newcomb–A&S merger could be accomplished "without affecting the traditions and life of either college."[19]

By the early 1970s concern over duplication of effort still loomed large, but the women's movement had added a new dimension to discussions of Newcomb's future. The decade witnessed a steady national decline in the popularity (and number) of women's colleges, as a smaller group of female freshmen faced a larger array of educational choices. In an effort to enlarge its entering classes, Newcomb at times all but abandoned selectivity, accepting 87 percent of its applicants in 1970 and 94 percent the following year (916 of 979 applicants) to obtain an enrolled class of 418 in 1971. From 1970 to 1980 the combined freshman SAT scores at Newcomb lagged behind those of Arts and Sciences, Engineering, and Architecture. Although Newcomb retained a strong sense of community throughout the period, disillusioned feminists within the Newcomb student body warned that "a revolution in the minds and hearts of those who run the Newcomb system" would be necessary if the college were to justify its existence in a new era of women's activism. In a 1971 valedictory to the school, a graduating Newcomb senior summarized a line of criticism that was steadily gathering momentum. "[S]ororities and the Newcomb Student Senate together form a reactionary block which discourages independence, free thinking, feminine aggressiveness, intellectuality, self-expression, and

19. Supplement to a Proposal Submitted to the Ford Foundation from Tulane University, September 1963 [January 1964], bound volume in authors' possession.

creativity within the college—all the things that any women's college should stand for. The emphasis should be on encouraging every effort at self-sufficiency [that] any student puts forth—especially since Newcomb is in the South, a region not noted for its hordes of liberated women. . . . We defenders-to-the-death of Newcomb autonomy are fighting what presently seems to be a losing battle against creeping co-education, state university style," the writer concluded.[20]

Debate over Newcomb's future continued in the years prior to President Hackney's arrival, and it is clear that he was not alone in wishing to see the college reorient its outlook in the face of new realities. Although gender-related questions were never at the forefront of his administration, Hackney was more receptive to the importance of feminism and the changing expectations of academic and professional women than any previous Tulane president. From 1976–79 Hackney served on the American Council on Education's Commission on Women in Higher Education. During the first year of his presidency, in addition to hiring the university's first woman dean of students, Tulane adopted a comprehensive report urging greater equity in women's athletics as required under Title IX of the 1972 amendments to the Higher Education Act of 1965. In March 1976 anthropologist Margaret Mead spoke at the official dedication of the Newcomb Women's Center, and the following month the *Tulanian* published a thematic issue entitled, "Spotlight on Women." The spotlight section opened with the observation that "[e]very time we liberate a woman we liberate a man"—a phrase quoted from Mead's Women's Center address.[21] While there is little evidence that Hackney directly admonished deans or academic

20. Barbara M. Solomon, *In the Company of Educated Women: A History of Women and Higher Education in America* (New Haven: Yale University Press, 1985), 44, 203; Francis L. Lawrence, Tulane Freshmen Enrollment, 1958–80, box 2, Eamon M. Kelly Papers, Tulane University Archives (hereafter cited as EMK Papers); Francis L. Lawrence, Twenty Years of Challenge, 1980–2000, box 2, EMK Papers, 24; Margaret Blain, "Toward Co-Education," Tulane *Hullabaloo*, 7 May 1971, p. 8 (all quotations). During the early 1970s venerable male bastions such as Yale, Princeton, and the University of Virginia admitted women undergraduates, while equally prominent women's colleges such as Vassar admitted men. By 1976 only 5 percent of American colleges and universities restricted their enrollment to women. Two decades earlier the figure had been 13 percent.

21. For a representative sampling of the ongoing debate, see Judy Mofitt, "Forum Discusses Newcomb's Autonomy and Visitation," Tulane *Hullabaloo*, 26 March 1971; Alan Loeb, "Newcomb: Can It Keep Its Identity?" ibid., 17 March 1972, p. 9; Kay Kahler, "Unliberated Newcomb," ibid., 9 February 1973, p. 10; Louisa Rogers, "Slipping Newcomb Noose," ibid., 9 February 1973, p. 14; *Tulanian* 47 (April 1976): 3 (quotation), 5, 8.

By the 1980s, the digital age was beginning to dawn at Tulane.

departments to appoint more women, it is clear that those participating in the two-year search for a new dean of Newcomb College attached considerable importance to identifying strong female candidates. Their efforts resulted in the appointment of Susan Wittig, Associate Professor of English and Associate Dean of the Graduate School at the University of Texas, who took office on July 1, 1979.[22]

If women became more visible at Tulane during the second half of the 1970s, the same was true of African Americans. Although the university did not undertake an aggressive campaign of minority recruitment—at least when compared to the 1980s and 1990s—Hackney was aware of the need to increase the presence of blacks as students and in

22. Newcomb Dean Search Committee to Members of the Faculties of Newcomb College and the College of Arts and Sciences, 17 September 1976; Raymond A. Esthus to F. Sheldon Hackney and Robert Stevens, 11 May 1976; Hackney to Esthus, 20 December 1976; M. Y. Darensbourg to Hackney and Stevens, 2 March 1977; Weber D. Donaldson Jr. to Hackney and Stevens, 4 March 1977; John William Corrington to Hackney, 20 April 1977; Hackney to Corrington, 29 April 1976; Stuart S. Bamforth to Michael Mislove, 11 September 1978; Mislove to Hackney, 17 December 1978; all correspondence in box 23, FSH Papers. Also see *President's Report*, 1978–79, box 10, FSH Papers; BOA Minutes, 5 July 1979.

positions of influence. In 1978, after several years of internal discussion, the Board elected its first black member, Dr. Henry E. Braden III, a local physician. With Braden's arrival the university was at last fully desegregated. In the same year Andrew Young, the Georgia civil rights leader who served as U.S. Ambassador to the United Nations during the Carter administration, received an honorary degree at the Tulane commencement. The choice was important for its symbolism, and it was accompanied by substantive action when the Board and the University Senate adopted a revised affirmative action program expanding upon earlier reports submitted to HEW and other federal agencies beginning in 1969.[23]

Upon assuming his duties at Tulane's president, Hackney took the pulse of the student body and quickly concluded that the patient was unwell. Echoing a concern that Dean Gordon had expressed at the beginning of 1974, Hackney pointed to the high rate of undergraduate attrition as evidence that students were transferring out of the university in unusually large numbers. The phenomenon, Hackney believed, had little or nothing to do with educational quality, which remained on balance quite high. Taking Princeton as a reference point, the president attributed the student outflow to a poorly developed sense of community among Tulane undergraduates and a corresponding lack of confidence in the university's long-term prospects of maintaining its stature as a prestigious private institution. Throughout his presidency Hackney worked to bolster student morale on campus and to cultivate the sense of participation, belonging, and esprit de corps that would translate into an Ivy League sense of institutional loyalty and lifelong commitment to Tulane among future alumni and alumnae. In contrast to

23. Gerald L. Andrus to F. Sheldon Hackney, 14 May 1976, box 10, FSH Papers; Bill Monroe to Andrus, 28 May 1976, box 10, FSH Papers; BOA Minutes, 5 January 1978. One Board member, A. Jung, asked to be recorded as a "no" vote on approving the honorary degree for Ambassador Young. The Administrators had committed themselves to a policy of nondiscrimination at a Board meeting on 17 September 1964. Between January 1969 and May 1970 the U.S. Office of Civil Rights conducted three contract compliance reviews of Tulane's Equal Employment Program. The evolution of affirmative action policies in response to the reviews may be traced in the following documents: S. E. Shomer, Progress Report, Civil Rights Contract Compliance, 30 January 1969, box 98, HEL Papers; Tulane University Affirmative Action Compliance Program, January 1969, box 98, HEL Papers; J. L. Thomas to Herbert E. Longenecker, 27 May 1970, box 98, HEL Papers; Longenecker to Thomas, 28 May 1970, box 98, HEL Papers; Tulane University Affirmative Action Compliance Program, rev. May 1970, box 27–8, HEL Papers.

his immediate predecessor, whom students had regarded as remote and aloof even prior to the conflicts of the late 1960s, Hackney mingled freely with undergraduates, granting frequent interviews to *Hullabaloo* journalists, meeting regularly with the leaders of student government, participating in campus festivals and entertainments, and appearing unannounced at Friday afternoon beer busts. Students came frequently to the Hackney residence as invited guests, and the president appeared so trimly athletic and youthful that he might almost have been mistaken for a student as he jogged or played football in Audubon Park. In the beginning Hackney's preference for an informal collegiate mode of attire was a subject of frequent comment among Tulane watchers, one of whom went so far as to assert that new chief executive dressed "less like a college president than [like] a less-than-stylish undergraduate invited to a faculty tea."[24]

Ultimately, of course, the president's popularity with students rested upon much more than personal style. Hackney was in many ways a product of the late 1960s environment at Princeton, where he had openly opposed the Vietnam War and sympathized with student protesters on issues of minority rights and student decision making. During his early years on the Princeton faculty he had directed a university-sponsored Upward Bound program for disadvantaged youth, and had later helped organize the school's first Afro-American Studies program, which he subsequently chaired. Prior to becoming provost Hackney's most direct involvement with campus governance occurred in 1968–69, when he served on a committee that pressed successfully for the creation of a 57-member "Council of the Princeton University Community," comprised of alumni, administrators, trustees, junior and senior faculty, graduate and undergraduate students, and staff members. The council, which operated as a consensus-building mechanism in making recommendations to the president and trustees, was widely credited with securing the triumph of moderate over extremist proposals during the May 1970 antiwar protests touched off by the invasion of Cambodia. For Hackney, in other words, the late sixties had been a period of oppor-

24. Joseph Gordon, Comments to the [A&S] Faculty, 29 January 1974, box 30, HEL Papers; F. Sheldon Hackney, interview by C. L. Mohr, 8 November 1995; *New Orleans Courier*, 4–10 September 1975, p. 7 (quotation); Marshall Ledger, "A President at Ease," *Pennsylvania Gazette* (December 1980): 16–27.

tunity, moral engagement, and satisfying accomplishment that had marked the beginning of his rapid ascent into the ranks of senior academic administration.[25]

At Tulane, Hackney sought to preserve and extend the opportunities—first gained in the late sixties—for students to influence campus decision making. Yet the Tulane that Hackney encountered in 1975 was a profoundly different institution from the one which had greeted Longenecker fifteen years earlier. Although student power demands gradually subsided after the 1970–71 academic year, when Student Senate president and former TLF leader Ralph Wafer led another unsuccessful campaign to renew Tulane's membership in the National Student Association, many of the changes set in motion by student activists of the late sixties survived and became firmly incorporated into university life.[26] For several years prior to his retirement, Longenecker had held weekly forums to answer student questions face-to-face. Although attendance was usually thin, the sessions set a precedent for greater presidential openness. In 1973 an official "Statement of Student Academic Rights, Freedoms[,] and Responsibilities of the Associated Student Body of Tulane University" (the elusive "student bill of rights" first proposed in 1967) finally gained approval from the University Senate and the Board of Administrators, thereby giving official sanction to many of the civil liberties and participatory devices that students of the late 1960s had championed. By the early 1970s,

25. Paul Sigmund, "Princeton in Crisis and Change," *Change* 5 (March 1973): 34–41, is an excellent overview of Princeton's response to student and faculty activism in the 1967–70 period. See also Dotson Rader, "Princeton Weekend with SDS," *New Republic* 157 (9 December 1967): 14–6; *New York Times*, 3 May 1968, p. 53; ibid., 4 March 1969, p. 29; ibid., 12 March 1969, p. 30; ibid., 19 April 1969, p. 17; ibid., 22 April 1969, p. 34; ibid., 24 April 1969, p. 35; Stanley Kelley Jr. et al., *A Proposal to Establish the Council of the Princeton University Community: A Report of the Special Committee on the Structure of the University, May 1969,* printed pamphlet, box 67a, HEL Papers; Stanley Kelley Jr. to Gerald L. Andrus, 9 September 1974, Records of Presidential Search, 1974–75, Tulane University Archives; Lawrence Stone to Gerald L. Andrus, 10 September 1974, Records of Presidential Search, 1974–75, Tulane University Archives; F. Sheldon Hackney, interview by C. L. Mohr, 8 November 1995.

26. For good summaries of changes initiated in the early 1970s and of generally positive student reactions, see the entire September 1971 issue of *New Orleans* magazine. In addition to the Ralph Wafer article previously cited, the issue contains illuminating pieces by Pat Schuster (1971–72 editor of the *Hullabaloo*), Bruce Feingerts (1971–72 ASB president), antiwar activist Sheperd Samuels, and Jimmy Mashburn, one of the students expelled from Tulane after the 1969 ROTC demonstrations. See also the extensive commentary on the changed campus climate in the 1971 *Jambalaya*, the Tulane yearbook. On the 1970 NSA ratification campaign, see Tulane *Hullabaloo*, 16 October 1970, p. 1; ibid., 23 October 1970, p. 1.

moreover, the abolition of student curfews and dramatic loosening of other conduct regulations, together with the advent of coed housing arrangements, sounded the death knell for the in loco parentis system. By that point few could be found to mourn the passing of the old order.[27]

A particularly important set of changes resulting from the activism of 1967–70 was preserved in the arrangements that most Tulane faculties had made to give students a direct, if limited, voice in academic decision making. As Hackney sought to instill a sense of participation and belonging among Tulane undergraduates, he was able to take advantage of a committee structure which already accorded students a presence and a voice. With the exceptions of Law and Engineering, all faculties by the mid-1970s gave students representation and voting rights on at least one or two faculty committees—the inclusion of Newcomb College students on the Curriculum Committee, the Student-Faculty Welfare Committee, and the Junior Year Abroad Committee being a typical example. In the School of Social Work and the Graduate School, students attended faculty meetings as nonvoting participants. Social Work students also served on all committees "excepting those which involve personnel folders or confidential information." From 1970 onward students attended meetings of the university's elected Graduate Council, leaving only when executive sessions were convened. The greatest strides in student representation had occurred in the University Senate, which included four students as voting members of the senate itself and provided for student membership on a total of ten senate committees, including Educational Policy, Financial Aid, and Admissions, as well as Student Affairs and Student Housing. These arrangements went well beyond tokenism and generally reflected Hackney's own views concerning the areas of university life where student participation was most valuable and legitimate.[28]

27. Ralph Wafer, "The Mid Sixties Were Glorious If One Wore Blinders," *New Orleans Magazine* (September 1971): 32–3, 58–60, 62, offprint in box 65, HEL Papers; Tulane *Hullabaloo*, 7 May 1971, p. 8; ibid., 21 February 1975, p. 14; University Senate Minutes, 16 April 1973, box 73, HEL Papers; BOA Minutes, 7 June 1973. A somewhat different version of the student rights declaration had previously been approved by the Student Senate, ratified in a campuswide student referendum, and approved by the University Senate Committee on Student Affairs. Tulane *Hullabaloo*: 14 February 1969, p. 1; 14 March 1969, p. 2; 21 March 1969, pp. 1, 5.

28. Newcomb Faculty Minutes, 16 September and 26 May 1970, box 45, HEL Papers; Social Work Faculty Minutes, 25 April, 16 May, and 27 November 1968 (quotation), 21 April and 24 October 1969, all in box 46, HEL Papers; Draft of proposed amendment to the constitution of

Because of the advances already achieved, it was unnecessary for Hackney to seek broad structural reforms in order to give students a role in university governance. His emphasis, therefore, was upon personal consultation and the solicitation of student assistance and advice rather than upon creating new bureaucratic mechanisms for power sharing. In at least one university division directly affecting students, the Office of Admissions and Financial Aid, Hackney did make basic changes in official policy. Since the adoption of SAT requirements in the late 1950s, Tulane had followed other selective institutions in basing financial aid decisions on a calculation that took account of need as well as academic merit. Under the traditional formula, even the brightest student would receive only a token financial award if he or she came from a family of substantial wealth. During the period of peak demand for college admissions the policy worked well and allowed the university to raise standards without entering into bidding wars with more affluent schools. By the 1970s, however, circumstances had changed. In the major undergraduate divisions, grades began to rise even as SAT scores declined. Concerned about these tendencies, as well as the high acceptance rate of some 80–85 percent of all freshman applicants in some years, Hackney pushed for measures that would reverse the trends and increase the number of academically superior students in entering classes. With strong faculty support and despite opposition from the dean of Arts and Sciences, Hackney obtained University Senate approval in 1976–77 for a program of non-need-based scholarships. Initially twenty awards of $10,000 each were designated for superior students. The program proved to be highly successful in attracting top-flight applicants and was expanded steadily over the next fifteen years. By 1991–92, when the nation's academic institutions were engaged in what amounted to a marketing competition, Tulane would distribute a total of 120 of the merit-based

---

the graduate faculty, 5 February 1969, filed with Graduate School Minutes, 1968–69, box 35, HEL Papers; Graduate Faculty Minutes, 21 January 1970, box 35, HEL Papers; Graduate Council Minutes, 16 December 1970, box 36, HEL Papers; University Senate Minutes, 3 April, 22 May, 19 September, 2 October, 6 November 1967, 5 and 12 May, 3 November 1969, all in box 72, HEL Papers; ibid., 9 March and 5 October 1970, box 73, HEL Papers; Joseph Gordon to Hank Harnage, 19 September 1967, box 72, HEL Papers. The Newcomb faculty committees on Admissions and Advanced Standing and Examinations were also authorized to invite representatives of the Newcomb student government to meet and advise with faculty on matters of general interest to students.

awards, which were now officially designated as Dean's Honor Scholarships.[29]

In addition to recruiting superior students, Hackney sought to strengthen the undergraduate experience in ways that would foster greater bonds of community and long-term institutional loyalty. Early in Hackney's presidency, Provost Robert Stevens commissioned a lengthy and excellent study on "the quality of the first year at Tulane University." The study was carried out by a joint committee of faculty, students, and staff members under the chairmanship of anthropology professor Harvey Bricker. The report assessed quite thoroughly such critical issues as student attrition, quality of teaching, curriculum, residential and extracurricular life, faculty academic advising, and food services. Unlike many official documents that gather dust after their initial release, the group's research and analysis circulated widely on campus, eventually finding its way to the University Senate, the academic officers and the faculties, and the Tulane Board's Committee on Faculty and Student Affairs. In all quarters the freshman year study received praise as a valuable project that had been ably executed.[30]

Another indication of Hackney's concern with the undergraduate experience became evident in 1976, when the University Senate approved the addition of a third and fourth year undergraduate program in the Graduate School of Business Administration, with students to come primarily from the College of Arts and Science and Newcomb College through transfer. Since the abolition of the undergraduate business degree in the mid-1960s, there had been a surge of demand from students—and their parents—for some type of business degree below the master's level. As a consequence many students gravitated toward courses taught in University College, which had offered the only available route to an undergraduate business degree for almost a decade. This in turn posed a special problem with the accrediting agency for business schools, the American Association of Schools of Business Administration, which demanded that all academic programs

29. A&S Dean's Report, 1970–71, box 29, HEL Papers, 1–3; University Senate Minutes, 19 January 1976, Report of Committee on Student Financial Aid, "Merit Scholarships" folder, box 2, FSH Papers.

30. Final Report to the Provost of Tulane University by the Committee on the First Year, Harvey Bricker, Chair, 18 March 1978, box 10, FSH Papers.

in business education be under the control of the principal academic division for business—in Tulane's case, the Graduate School of Business Administration.[31]

This problem was not a new one. Objections to an unaccredited program had been raised but brushed aside in 1968 at the time of the restoration of the P.E. major. The University College program had always aspired to be more than an escape valve for academically weak athletes, but by the late 1970s a new spirit of utilitarianism among A&S and Newcomb students created a compelling rationale to take business education out of Tulane's evening division. Besides solving the accreditation dilemma and meeting student demand, the new program, strongly promoted by Hackney, provided reasonable guarantees that business majors would receive a solid exposure to the core liberal arts curriculum before embarking on the technical courses required for degrees in accounting, marketing, and management. Immediately popular with its intended constituency, the undergraduate business major has remained a rigorous and intellectually challenging program throughout the two decades that have elapsed since its creation.[32]

Although Hackney acquired a reputation as a "students' president," there is no indication that he gave their opinions undue weight. When students sought to infringe upon areas of traditional administrative authority, the president showed no hesitation in affirming his independence. A clear demonstration of the subordinate role of student opinion under Hackney was furnished in November 1977, when the *Hullabaloo* published a letter to the ASB Executive Cabinet, allegedly authored by the ASB president, urging in the strongest terms that Dean of Students Annette Ten Elshof should be replaced. The document raised a number of issues that caused concern for President Hackney and his Vice President for Student Affairs Donald Moore, but the call for Ten Elshof's ouster went unheeded. The episode indicated the practical limits of student power under Hackney and belied the allegation that he had established a cult of youth on St. Charles Avenue.[33]

31. University Senate Minutes: 9 January 1976, pp. 5–7; 8 March 1976, pp. 2–5; 5 April 1976, pp. 2–4.
32. Chap. 6 of the present work discusses the 1968 controversy over the P.E. major and its relation to an unaccredited business program in University College.
33. Tulane *Hullabaloo*, 18 November 1977, p. 1. At the time of Hackney's departure for the University of Pennsylvania in 1981, Tulane political scientist Henry Mason, a self-described

Professor Frank Monachino, Department of Music,
rehearses the cast for Yeomen of the Guard, *ca. 1974.*

On balance, Hackney's willingness to interact with students and to take their views into account seems to have gone far toward bringing about the revival of undergraduate morale that the president sought. Only four months after the Ten Elshof episode, Hackney received an effusive letter from the ASB vice president that read in part, "I don't know how hard it is for you to judge your own image on campus, but comparing it to that which existed before your arrival, your image, in the eyes of the students[,] is an extremely positive one. We all know that, given your leadership, Tulane has the potential to exceed even our most outlandish dreams. I truly believe that student self-esteem has risen remarkably in the last two years. . . . On behalf of the student body, I am very proud to thank you for, almost single-handedly, making it possible for us to be proud of Tulane and hopeful in its future."[34]

By the time these remarks reached Hackney's desk in the spring of

member of the president's "loyal opposition," told a visiting reporter that Hackney had "followed a youth cult" at Tulane. Robin Davis, "An 'Accidental' Leader," unidentified clipping, Hackney biographical files.

34. Randolph Wykoff to Sheldon Hackney, 22 April 1978, box 29, FSH Papers.

1978, the honeymoon phase of his presidency had long since come to an end. The scope of Tulane's problems was broad, encompassing an array of issues that extended from medical education to intercollegiate athletics, and involving constituencies as diverse as the Green Wave Club and the Arts and Sciences faculty. Inevitably, Hackney's efforts to achieve progress on one front triggered reactions of skepticism, resentment, or outright opposition in other university divisions. There was little in Hackney's Princeton experience to prepare him for the competitive and contentious atmosphere at Tulane. Whereas Princeton had relied upon wealth, small size, and an exceptionally strong sense of community to produce consensus with a minimum of bureaucratic formality, Tulane, with its eight separate faculties and historic traditions of quasi-autonomy for the more affluent professional schools, was too large and decentralized—and too painfully short of ready cash—to settle its internal differences in genteel fashion. As Hackney soon discovered, the task of university governance in New Orleans depended more upon balance-of-power diplomacy than upon appeals to the spirit of an academic *Gemeinschaft*.

One obvious difference between Princeton and Tulane was the absence of a medical school at the New Jersey institution. From the beginning of his Tulane administration, Hackney had to grapple with the place of medical education in the larger scheme of university operations. The not altogether happy experience was soon reflected in a piece of bittersweet luncheon humor that Hackney used repeatedly before audiences of all varieties. The story's protagonist was a college president who died and went promptly to hell—only to be told upon arrival that as a special punishment he was to be returned to earth to be a university president. When the deceased president protested that he had just come from such a situation, the devil replied, "Oh, yes, but this new institution has a medical school." The witticism, with its hint of nostalgia for Princeton, aptly conveyed the tenor of Hackney's involvement with the Tulane Medical Center complex.

In the years preceding Hackney's arrival, the School of Medicine had accounted for the largest single portion of Tulane's annual operating deficit. During the late 1960s and early 1970s, a combination of rising costs and shrinking levels of federal support made it imperative that the school find new sources of revenue or face the prospect of serious decline. The fiscal crisis, along with other factors, resulted in a decision to construct a $32 million teaching hospital and clinic to be operated in conjunction with a faculty practice plan. The decision had been a gamble, or at the very least a calculated risk, in which the Board (with President Longenecker's concurrence) had pledged nearly all the university's liquid assets as security for an initial construction loan in 1973, at the very moment when the uptown campus was feeling the full impact of academic retrenchment. Fortunately, subsequent bond sales by a state authority financed the project on a long-term basis, and the hospital and clinic were dedicated during the first year of Hackney's administration. Hackney thus inherited a medical center complex with the potential to solve or at least alleviate the medical school's chronic deficits, provided its somewhat ambiguous relationship to the rest of the university could be adequately clarified.

From an administrative standpoint the problem was one of confused and potentially conflicting lines of authority arising from the fact that the Medical Center had a separate Board of Governors to whom the Board of Administrators had delegated "operational responsibility" in 1970 amid worsening economic conditions.[35] The arrangement had come under sharp questioning from persons experienced in corporate administration who sat on the Tulane Board of Visitors, the university's chief advisory body. In August 1975, Hackney received a preliminary oral report from representatives of the Booz, Allen, and Hamilton consulting firm on their findings relative to management systems and reporting procedures in the medical school, as well as the new hospital faculty practice plan. In a memorandum for his files, Hackney noted that "there were many and serious problems to solve," although none seemed insurmountable. The greatest need singled out by the consultants was for better management procedures in the university as a whole. The report urged the adoption of uniform and objective methods for reaching decisions in all key areas of university operations, accompanied by data gathering and reporting systems designed to fit the procedures.[36]

At the political level Hackney was concerned about the ill-defined scope of the Board of Governors' jurisdiction, where it began and ended, and what effect it had on the ultimate power of the Board of

35. John Duffy, *The Tulane University Medical Center: One Hundred and Fifty Years of Medical Education* (Baton Rouge: Louisiana State University Press, 1984), 192 (quotation)–197.

36. F. Sheldon Hackney, Memo for the Files on Tulane Medical Center, 2 September 1975, box 21, FSH Papers, 1–2.

Administrators. In a personal letter to Medical Center chancellor John Walsh in April 1976, Hackney expressed dismay at several of the recent actions by the Board of Governors that suggested a lack of proper regard for higher authority. He cited the governors' consideration of leaves of absence for principal administrators (including Joseph Beasley, who had resigned as dean of the School of Public Health following a 1974 conviction for misuse of federal funds), their unilateral action in the naming of the pavilion at the Medical Center in honor of Jack Aron (who chaired the Board of Governors), their presumption that their action was "definitive," and the formation and functioning of search committees in the medical complex which bypassed the central administration. According to Hackney, it was "the old problem that we faced before about how the Board of Governors is going to operate without crushing you (Walsh), bypassing me, and infuriating the Administrators. . . . We need to talk further about these things." No clear-cut division of authority over medical school affairs was achieved under Hackney, but the problem receded as the hospital and clinic began returning a profit in the late 1970s. The School of Medicine also became a source of increased prestige and scientific stature for the university on October 13, 1977, when the news media announced that Dr. Andrew Schally, a professor in the medical school and a senior medical investigator at the Veterans Administration Hospital, had been awarded the Nobel Prize in Medicine. His teamwork with Dr. Robert Guillemin of San Diego, involving discoveries on peptide hormone production of the brain, had brought him—and Tulane—this international distinction.[37]

On at least a superficial level, one can see a philosophical equivalence between President Hackney's complaints about the independence of the Medical Center Board of Governors and President Harris's efforts during the 1950s to rein in Tulane coaches and other athletic department personnel who bypassed him and dealt directly with sympathetic Board members on matters of recruitment and football grants-in-aid. The situations were similar in that both men placed a premium on establishing the supremacy of presidential authority over the university's internal operations. But on the subject of intercollegiate athletics, Hackney held views that bore little resemblance to those of his predecessor. From the time of his earliest meetings with the

37. F. Sheldon Hackney, Memo for John Walsh, 12 April 1976, box 20, FSH Papers, 1 (quotation); Tulane *Hullabaloo*, 14 October 1977, p. 1.

Tulane search committee, Hackney had stressed his commitment to maintaining Division I football at Tulane and had underscored his belief that the university should make a serious effort to field winning teams. These were neither halfhearted assurances nor the grudging concessions of a scholar-president who supported football out of political necessity. A close student of regional values, Hackney looked upon intercollegiate athletics as a basic component of institutional prestige for a southern school. He believed moreover that winning teams offered the best, if not the only, hope for making Tulane's sports program economically self-sustaining.

The first clear demonstration of Hackney's sports allegiances came in the wake of a disastrous 1975 football season when, after extensive consultation with Tulane's athletic backers, the president decided to buy out the long-term contract of football coach Bennie Ellender. In a lengthy justification of his decision written for the *Tulanian*, Hackney explained that while "everyone has a high opinion of Bennie Ellender as a person and coach . . . there was a consensus that some change was necessary for the program to progress from its present plateau. . . . The dilemma was easily apparent to me. If no changes were made in the current situation, the financial impact on Tulane would be devastating. Season ticket sales would fall precipitately . . . and the University would lose almost all the contributions, currently about $225,000 per year, which come in through the Green Wave Club. . . . On the other hand we had contractual obligations to the current staff which amounted [to] more than $400,000 over the life of the contracts. . . . There was no way to win financially."[38]

Assistant coach Larry Smith, at the University of Arizona for the three preceding years, was chosen to succeed Ellender. And the albatross of chronic crisis in intercollegiate athletics began to drape itself around the neck of the new president, as it had his two immediate predecessors. At the time Hackney announced his decision to change coaches, Professor Eric Vetter, chair of the University Senate Committee on Athletics, had prepared a study predicting serious deficits in athletics through 1978. The gloomy forecast was aggravated by a report to the senate on January 9, 1976, from Professor Wayne Woody, chair of the University Senate Committee on Budget Review, warning

38. "A Statement by the President on Intercollegiate Athletics," *Tulanian* 47 (January 1976): 24–5.

that the earlier presumed athletic deficit of $462,000 was now esti-
mated to be $995,000 for 1975. In the intensive debate that followed,
the senate reaffirmed its unwavering support for the "allowable
deficit" limit on intercollegiate athletics adopted in 1971–72 and twice
accepted by the Board of Administrators. In a separate resolution the
senate instructed the budget review committee and the athletic department to report by April 5, 1976, on the steps that would be taken to
bring the deficit within the limits set in 1971–72.[39]

Those attending the January 9 senate meeting received advance
copies of Hackney's *Tulanian* statement, which went well beyond financial arguments in its defense of intercollegiate athletics. Aware that
many faculty members would interpret any dramatic move to improve
football as "a symbol of misplaced values," Hackney argued that "a
well-run intercollegiate athletic program, in addition to an extramural
program and opportunities for recreational sports, can help a high-
quality university achieve its academic goals." The assertion was followed by a defense of intercollegiate athletics as a key source of
institutional cohesion. In Hackney's view, football and basketball
provided the "chief point of contact between the University and its
alumni," while also giving the campus community a common experience that helped offset the "diffusion of attention and psychic energy"
among Tulane faculty and students. The resulting "sense of identity"
made sports "good for the University." As a scholar and an intellectual, Hackney knew that there were many on the faculty who entertained fundamental objections to athletics, and he did not hesitate to
address their arguments directly. "Some believe that sports have little
place in the house of intellect, or decry the overemphasis on sports in
college as an unhealthy distraction from the real purpose of the University," he acknowledged. For such individuals, the president had a
pointed observation. "Perhaps because I have integrated intellectual
and athletic activity in my own life, I have never thought that there
was an inherent conflict between the two in a university."[40]

Whether or not Hackney intended to impugn the manhood of those
who opposed college sports—one suspects he did not—his implied endorsement of the "sound mind/sound body" axiom opened the door for
what might have been a productive intellectual exchange concerning

39. BOA Minutes, 8 January 1976; University Senate Minutes, 9 January 1976, pp. 2–11.
40. *Tulanian* 47 (January 1976): 24–5.

the place of athletics within the house of learning. A partial rebuttal to Hackney's position had been drafted a quarter century earlier at Columbia University by the intellectual historian Richard Hofstadter, who argued that American universities had acquiesced in what was essentially an entrepreneurial program of semiprofessional sports. The vitiating effect of intercollegiate games upon the intellectual climate of schools that stressed athletics seemed obvious to Hofstadter, who approached the question from the standpoint of social psychology. Taking note of the alcohol-induced revels common among spectators at weekend football games, he pointed out that the prestige traditionally accorded athletic stars inhibited the development of a vigorous intellectual culture among undergraduates and exerted a blighting influence on alumni who were, in effect, encouraged to live vicariously through the team while deriving fulfillment as adults from a constant replication of the violent play activities of childhood. Before Hackney left Tulane, Hofstadter's position would be reinforced from a new angle by the cultural historian Christopher Lasch, whose 1979 book *The Culture of Narcissism* contained an incisive analysis of the role of intercollegiate athletics in what Lasch termed "The Degradation of Sport." There were, of course, potential rejoinders to the arguments advanced by opponents of college sports, and Hackney's defense of Tulane football invited not so much a faculty rebuttal as a serious internal discussion of the meaning and character of intercollegiate athletics as practiced in the 1970s. But no member of the Tulane community stepped forward to initiate the dialogue. It was evident where Tulane's new president stood on the question, and his position would not waver despite ongoing conflict over athletics in the years ahead.[41]

41. Richard Hofstadter and C. DeWitt Hardy, *The Development and Scope of American Higher Education* (New York: Columbia University Press, 1952), 112–4. Repudiating conventional lines of sports criticism, Lasch argued that games satisfied human psychic needs to the degree that they preserved ancient qualities of ritual and public festival in which participants and spectators suspended disbelief, accepted arbitrary rules and standards, and invested "play" with serious intent, thereby allowing it to become a metaphor for the basic values of a society to which it was organically connected. From this standpoint the degradation of sport consisted not in its being taken too seriously, but in its trivialization and secularization—a process which began in America in the 1890s when games were pressed into the service of patriotism and character building, and which culminated in the mid-twentieth century transformation of sport into "an object of mass consumption." As Lasch read the evidence, colleges and universities had played a key role in the degradation of games from authentic rituals into empty spectacles. "The first stage in this process [of degradation] was the establishment of big-time athletics in the university and their spread from the Ivy League to the large public and private schools, thence

In February 1977, roughly a year after Hackney's initial statement on Tulane football, the University Senate received an update on athletic finances. Expenses were $89,000 over budget; revenues fell short of expectations by $268,000. The final deficit was expected to exceed $1 million. Naturally, this produced a storm of criticism from senators, whose vehemence was not ameliorated by events of the May meeting when the Committee on Budget Review reported. Departing from customary procedure, the committee proposed not to carry forward the previous year's athletic deficit (as provided under the "allowable deficit" formula of 1972). Alternatively, it recommended increasing the allowable deficit to $568,000. The proposal evoked much debate, centering on the question of whether to support Hackney in the modified budget or to recommend the termination of football. A motion to support the Committee on Budget Review passed by a large majority. The outcome, however, probably used up a sizable part of Hackney's personal and political capital among faculty members, and it set the stage for more serious conflict over football in the next academic year.[42]

The climax of Tulane's tug-of-war over athletic policy would occur late in 1977 against a background of deepening faculty frustration over university finances. President Hackney had inherited a tenuously balanced budget for 1975–76, the year that Louisiana governor Edwin Edwards signed a bill providing capitation grants of $125 per semester for Louisiana residents attending private institutions. The legislation came at an opportune moment but litigation delayed actual payments until July 1977, when a court decision cleared the way for Tulane to receive $481,000 in capitation grants that had been held in escrow. By that point the funds were badly needed. The 1975–76 academic year

---

downward into the high schools. The bureaucratization of the business career stimulated the growth of sports in another way. It made the acquisition of educational credentials essential . . . and thus created in large numbers a new kind of student, utterly indifferent to higher learning but forced to undergo it for economic reasons. Large scale athletic programs helped colleges to attract such students, in competitive bidding for enrollments, and to entertain them once they enrolled." The result, according to Lasch, was a degeneration of college sports into entertainment spectacles aimed at "a clientele for whom the classroom had no real meaning" and accompanied by a flourishing "alumni culture" that centered around "clubs, fraternities, alumni offices, money drives, homecoming ceremonies and football." Christopher Lasch, *The Culture of Narcissism: American Life in an Age of Diminishing Expectations* (New York: W. W. Norton, 1979), 181–219 (quotations on 195, 211–2).

42. University Senate Minutes, 7 February 1977, University Senate Minutes and Reports, 1912–89, box 2, Tulane University Archives, 4–6.

had been grim from a fiscal standpoint. In an August memo to the Board of Administrators, Executive Vice President Scheps gave a succinct picture of Tulane's balance sheet. A deficit in intercollegiate athletics of $1,089,068 combined with a *surplus* of $47,463 in the university's academic divisions had resulted in an overall deficit of $1,041,605. Even more appalling was the diminution of the reserve known as "funds functioning as endowment" to its lowest ebb of $1,726,723 as of June 30, 1976. With cash reserves virtually exhausted in a period of continued budgetary shortfalls, the university was in a precarious position.[43]

In addressing the worsening financial status of the university, Hackney announced the creation of a special support group known as the President's Council. This body, consisting of various distinguished persons who upon invitation agreed to help represent the university (and raise funds), held its first meeting during the 1976 homecoming. In a State of the University address on January 26, 1977, Hackney expressed optimism concerning the likelihood that admissions and annual giving would provide a measure of financial relief. The opening of the new Tulane Hospital and Clinic in October 1976 also promised long-term therapy for the total university budget, as well as for the Medical Center itself. The Board of Administrators, moreover, was committed to doubling its previous level of giving. Finally, after a long search, Hackney was able to announce to the Board in February 1977 the July appointment of Gary Bayer as Vice President for Development and University Relations. Bayer had just directed a successful fundraising endeavor at Stanford University Law School, and his appointment raised expectations that the long-awaited major capital campaign would soon be underway. A concurrent announcement named Lawrence Peterson as Vice President for Finance, a new position with a deputy in the Tulane Medical Center, and Jesse B. Morgan as Vice President for Business, also with a TMC deputy.[44]

Despite these hopeful signs, the corrosive effects of protracted fiscal stringency were taking a heavy toll in key sectors of university life. In February 1977 the University Senate Committee on Libraries reported a set of depressing statistics. In a peer group of 94 academic institu-

43. BOA Minutes, 7 July 1977; Clarence Scheps, Memo to the Administrators of the Tulane Educational Fund, 24 August 1976, box 10, FSH Papers, 1–3.

44. University Senate Minutes, 1 November 1976, University Senate Minutes and Reports, 1912–89, box 2, Tulane University Archives, 6–7; BOA Minutes, 3 March 1977.

tions, Tulane ranked 92 out of 94 in number of volumes added during the previous year, 90 out of 94 in serials subscriptions, and 89 out of 93 in total salary and wage expenditures. Despite its lack of resources, however, Tulane was making a strong effort for the library. University library expenditures constituted 3.78 percent of total expenditures, compared with the national median of 3.5 percent. Of at least equal concern to most faculty members was the erosion of individual purchasing power and economic well-being that had begun early in the 1970s, as constricted salary budgets failed to provide annual raises that kept pace with the rising cost of living. From the beginning, disgruntled professors saw a link between parsimonious academic pay scales and large athletic deficits. In 1972 the Arts and Sciences faculty made the point explicit in a resolution, declaring it "contrary to the principles of equity for the Administrators of Tulane University to provide annual salary budgets below the rise in cost-of-living for faculty and staff members engaged in valid academic programs as long as the Athletic Program is allowed to operate with continuing huge deficits." In succeeding years inflation worsened and faculty purchasing power shrank, while athletic deficits continued and academic job mobility all but disappeared. The combination of circumstances was not a happy one, and it compounded the sense of frustration that had begun with the academic retrenchment of the late 1960s. In attempting to create a faculty consensus in support of improved athletics, President Hackney, the historian, was in a sense struggling to throw off the weight of Tulane's own history.[45]

The full magnitude of the latter task became evident in a meeting of the faculty of the College of Arts and Sciences on November 8, 1977, when Professor Henry Mason proposed a motion to remove Tulane from "big time sports." The Newcomb College faculty followed suit with a similar resolution, as did the graduate faculty, and all passed with strong majorities. Obviously, responses from President Hackney and the chairman of the Board of Administrators were called for. Hackney reiterated the theme that he had advanced consistently: Tulane was making progress toward resolving the problem of athletics'

45. University Senate Minutes, 7 February 1977, University Senate Minutes and Reports, 1912–89, box 2, Tulane University Archives, 2–3; A&S Faculty Minutes, 18 January 1972, box 30, HEL Papers (quotation). A second resolution adopted at the same meeting declared it "contrary to the academic policy of Tulane University" to reduce library support or eliminate academic programs "as long as the Athletic Program is allowed to operate as usual despite deficits."

financial loss, but additional time would be required—perhaps five years. Edmund McIlhenny, speaking for the Board, stated that his group was willing to give football two more years before considering the question. In a student poll conducted in December, 72 percent of 331 respondents supported McIlhenny's two-year extension. The University Senate, however, took a less sanguine view in December when it directed that a new watchdog body, the Special Committee on Intercollegiate Finances, be created. This action was implemented in February 1978.[46]

As the preceding paragraphs suggest, the overall tenor of relations between Hackney and the faculty deteriorated over time. In retrospect Hackney would attribute many of his difficulties to a deeply entrenched "habit of opposition" among faculty leaders who exhibited what at times seemed like a "trade union mentality" concerning faculty interests. Although Hackney's relations with the faculty were no worse, and possibly somewhat better, than those of his immediate predecessor, there can be no doubt that the president's unswerving support for athletics in the face of tight academic budgets served to alienate many professors who might otherwise have supported the administration. Evidence of the gulf between presidential and faculty perceptions of athletics—and proof of Hackney's very real desire to narrow differences through reasoned dialogue—may be found in a December 1977 exchange of correspondence with biology professor Stuart Bamforth. In a balanced assessment of faculty attitudes, Bamforth acknowledged the academic improvements that had occurred during Hackney's first two years at Tulane, but then went on to sketch the recent history of athletic disputes from a faculty perspective. His letter concluded with a brief paragraph that vividly captured the emotional tenor of faculty sentiment. "How can one part of the Unversity community 'put its shoulder to the wheel,' and how can the Administration encourage it to do so, when another part [the athletic program] has not shown the same responsibility? A credibility gap has arisen that must be quickly eliminated to achieve the unified community we all desire."[47]

46. Tulane *Hullabaloo*, 18 November 1977, p. 1 (quotation); ibid., 2 December 1977, p. 1; ibid., 9 December 1977, p. 1; University Senate Minutes, 13 February 1978, University Senate Minutes and Reports, 1912–89, box 2, Tulane University Archives, 2.

47. F. Sheldon Hackney, interview by C. L. Mohr, 8 November 1995 (first–second quotations); Stuart S. Bamforth to F. Sheldon Hackney, 19 December 1977, box 5, FSH Papers (third quotation).

Hackney's response to Bamforth might have surprised those critics who had forgotten that despite the burdens of academic administration, the president remained a scholar and an intellectual. "Thank God for your letter!" Hackney exclaimed.

> It is only the second letter from a faculty member about my response on intercollegiate athletics, and I was beginning to feel a little paranoid. Even if you don't agree with me it is good to argue about it in rational terms. . . . I recognize that most of the faculty comes at this problem from a different basis in experience than mine and perhaps also with a slightly different perspective on what it takes to get something so complex as a university moving together in the right direction. . . . I do admit to being mystified about why the faculty proceeded as it did with these votes. . . . I suppose I am trained to prefer a more deliberate conversation to this sort of public drama.[48]

Other factors contributed to a pattern of worsening faculty relations, including the untimely death of Professor Richard P. Adams on March 25, 1977. A distinguished scholar of American literature, Adams had played an active role in campus affairs throughout his twenty-five-year career at Tulane, concerning himself with nearly every issue that touched upon the faculty's role in university governance. The absence of his rational and customarily calm voice created a void in senate debates precisely when serious tensions were developing. From 1977 onward the monthly meeting of the University Senate became an arena of conflict where political science professors Henry Mason and William Gwyn, law professor Wayne S. Woody, history professor Charles Davis, and English professor Edward Partridge took the lead in calling Hackney to account. If the thrust of faculty argument across a broad range of issues were summarized, most disputes would be found to partake in some degree of Professor Mason's oft-repeated contention that the senate had a responsibility to verify that Tulane made no expenditures which ran counter to academic policies agreed on by the senate.

Not all of Hackney's problems emanated from the faculty. In November 1977, just as the legal problems and negative news coverage related to the Family Health Foundation and Joseph Beasley affair seemed to be fading into the past, Tulane received a new jolt of bad

48. Hackney to Bamforth, 22 December 1977, box 5, FSH Papers.

press due to the criminal investigation of a member of the Board of Administrators, Frederic B. "Fritz" Ingram. Although the Tulane community and the public had been made aware of the court proceedings involving Ingram, his brother, Bronson Ingram, in Nashville, and others in Chicago who were charged in a bribe conspiracy trial, the announcement of the verdict of guilty came as a distinct shock. On November 14, 1977, U.S. District Judge John F. Grady ordered Fritz Ingram to begin serving a four-year sentence on January 2, 1978. Bronson Ingram was acquitted. On January 5, Chairman McIlhenny reported to the Board that Fritz Ingram's resignations from the Medical Center Board of Governors and the Board of Administrators had been received.[49]

In the early months of 1978 President Hackney decided to address a matter that had caused him concern since his arrival at Tulane: the size, composition, and role of the Board of Administrators. In a long and thoughtful February letter to Edmund McIlhenny, Hackney reiterated his earlier misgivings over the anomalous role of the Board of Governors of the Medical Center. Turning to the Board of Administrators itself, he went on to argue that the group's small size limited its ability to bring individuals with the capacity for leadership in fundraising into the highest level of university deliberations. The same factor, Hackney believed, made it difficult to include persons with all the skills that a modern university required to plan intelligently for the future. Since the size of the Board (seventeen) was set by the 1884 Act 43 of the Louisiana Legislature, the president proposed that an amendment to the act be sought to enable an increase in size. As for the Board of Governors, Hackney's plan was more complex. Basically, it involved adding to the Board of Administrators those governors who had been most active and most helpful in supervising the Medical Center, and secondly, creating a committee of the Board of Administrators whose task it would be to oversee the operations of the Medical Center. To accommodate a larger Board, with a larger proportion living outside Louisiana, Hackney envisioned a revised committee structure and a more active Executive Committee that would allow the Board to operate efficiently with fewer meetings per year.[50]

Hackney provided Darwin S. Fenner, former Board chairman and

49. *New Orleans Times-Picayune/States-Item*, 9 November 1977, p. A1; ibid., 15 November 1977, p. 15; BOA Minutes, 5 January 1978.

50. F. Sheldon Hackney to Edmund McIlhenny, 6 February 1978, box 10, FSH Papers.

now an associate member, with a courtesy copy of his letter to Chairman McIlhenny. In a response that reflected the Board's traditional aversion to seeking changes in state legislation, Fenner cited the risk that enemies of Tulane, known and unknown, might come out of the shadows if given an opening during consideration of a charter amendment. Reacting to Hackney's proposal for changes in the governance of the Medical Center, Fenner agreed that "something must be done about the Board of Governors of the Medical Center. There is an anomaly in our system of government and John Walsh doesn't know whether to turn to you as President or accept his orders from the Board. . . . It might simplify matters if we merged the two [Boards]." This was a surprising display of flexibility from the individual who had long been regarded as the Medical Center's chief advocate on the Tulane Board.[51]

John Phillips succeeded Edmund McIlhenny as chairman of the Board of Administrators in the fall of 1978 and pursued Hackney's proposals by appointing an Ad Hoc Committee on the Structure and Organization of the Board, with Robert Boh as chairman. In April 1979 the administrators approved the wording of a resolution to amend Act 43 to permit enlargement of the Board, without specification of actual size. The amendment was taken up and passed without any threats to Tulane in a subsequent session of the state legislature. In March 1980 the Board increased its allowable membership from seventeen to nineteen, and at its May session it enlarged the number to twenty-two. Other amendments to the Board's by-laws would follow, allowing changes in the geographic origins of its members. The Board of Governors of the Tulane Medical Center seems to have been unaffected by this progression of events, but Hackney's sustained effort to effect changes in the Board of Administrators had borne substantial fruit.[52]

In 1977 and 1978 several other presidential initiatives moved forward with Board approval. During the postwar era Tulane's campus had been transformed by ongoing construction projects, but few observers would have argued that the growth was shaped by any unified vision of land use or architectural design. In a lengthy memorandum to the Board's Ad Hoc Committee on Campus Planning in June 1977,

51. Darwin S. Fenner to F. Sheldon Hackney, 12 April 1978, box 10, FSH Papers.
52. BOA Minutes, 5 April 1979; ibid., 26 March and 1 May 1980.

Hackney set forth in detail the rationale for securing someone from outside the university to create a master plan for the campus. The response of key administrators was prompt and positive. In its July meeting the Board set aside $40,000 from the dwindling "funds functioning as endowment" to employ consultants to prepare a long-range site-use study of the uptown campus. Sasaki and Associates, a Boston consulting firm, subsequently took on the assignment of producing a master plan. An additional $100,000 was approved at the July 1977 Board meeting to provide for the demolition of the north, east, and west steel stands of the Tulane stadium. The action represented the outcome of what had been a long and often acrimonious argument over whether the Green Wave would continue to play on campus or move to the New Orleans Superdome, as eventually occurred. In April 1978 the Board approved construction of the Monk Simons Memorial Center for housing intercollegiate athletic activities, with financing of $350,000 supplied by the Simons Memorial Foundation.[53]

Other significant achievements reflecting credit on the new administration included the 1977 announcement that the Sloan Foundation had provided an initial grant of $250,000 to launch an interdepartmental program of Public Policy Studies in the liberal arts and science divisions. Of still greater long-term importance was the negotiation in January 1978 of an "Affiliation Agreement" between the Tulane University School of Medicine and the Alton Ochsner Medical Foundation. This three-year agreement created a formal basis for a working relationship between the two institutions in areas of mutual interest, including patient care, education, and research.[54]

Despite these developments Tulane's overall fiscal health remained poor. The annual report of the University Senate Committee on Budget Review revealed that faculty salary raises for 1978–79 were expected to average 6 percent, a figure that once again failed to match the rising cost of living index. In the wake of this news, the senate called a special meeting for April 21, 1978, to consider what course the university should take. The meeting approved a set of resolutions authored

53. F. Sheldon Hackney, Memo on Campus Planning, 13 June 1977, box 12, FSH Papers, 1–5; BOA Minutes, 7 July 1977 and 5 January 1978.

54. BOA Minutes, 7 July 1977 and 5 January 1978. The School of Law also secured a permanent dean in 1978 when Paul Verkuil, Professor of Law at the University of North Carolina at Chapel Hill, was appointed to begin July 1. Two years had elapsed since the resignation of Dean Joseph M. Sweeney.

by business school professor Irving LaValle calling on the administration "to formulate and commit themselves to achieving a long-range strategic plan for Tulane University." The plan should provide the means for carrying out its various provisions and should also include "a timetable and concrete goals" by which results could be measured. Finally "and, most specifically," the senate urged the president and Board to undertake a major fundraising drive "to achieve the long-range financial stability of the University." At the time of the resolution, Tulane's endowment had a market value of approximately $44 million.[55]

Just prior to the strongly-worded senate resolution, the Executive Committee of the Board held a special meeting to consider the university's financial condition, which had worsened significantly after initially optimistic projections. Both the chairman and the president made lengthy presentations linking current conditions to specific aspects of Tulane's financial history. At a subsequent meeting of the full Board on May 4, 1978, the Budget Committee reported a probable deficit of $1.2 million for 1978–79, with small likelihood of it being reduced. The budget was approved at the deficit level indicated, but Hackney was requested by the Budget Committee to appoint a task force to plan and execute guidelines for a balanced budget for 1979–80. How this might be achieved without damaging the academic core of the university remained unclear.[56]

The precariousness of the financial situation could not be kept secret, of course, and it served to exacerbate existing tensions between the president and the faculty. In a lengthy personal letter to Hackney, a normally moderate senior faculty member wrote in part as follows:

I'm sure you're aware—so I won't belabor the point—that the Administration's reaction to the football resolutions, and the low average salary increase projected for next year, have both quite naturally tended to hurt faculty morale. But I think that there are other serious, if less obvious, sources of discontent. One of these is a seemingly widespread belief that the Administration has little respect for the faculty in general—that the faculty is regarded as being, on the whole, lazy and/or mediocre. Whether accurate or not, this faculty perception of Administration attitude has considerable currency on the "grapevine." It has, I think,

55. University Senate Minutes, 21 April 1978, p. 9.
56. BOA Minutes, 4 May 1978.

been reinforced by a general sense that the Administration is more concerned to communicate and establish rapport with the students than with the faculty.[57]

The nearest approach to an open clash between the president and the faculty came the following year, when Hackney vetoed a recommendation from the College of Arts and Sciences to promote and grant tenure to an assistant professor in the Department of Germanic and Slavic Languages. A favorable recommendation from the candidate's department was approved at all levels through the provost, but in a move reminiscent of President Harris's actions in the 1950s, Hackney chose to apply higher and more rigorous intellectual standards. Throughout his presidency at Tulane, Hackney stressed the importance of seeking not simply competence but exceptional ability and talent in all faculty ranks. Despite budgetary constraints the president held fast to the principle of "finding the best person available" to fill any opening, and his action in the tenure case was intended to place departments on notice that he would make personal judgments about the scholarly credentials of Tulane faculty, buttressed by outside opinions solicited in addition to those obtained by individual departments and the Committee on Promotions and Tenure.[58]

Reaction to Hackney's veto was not long in coming. At the December 1979 meeting of the University Senate, Professor Henry Mason, chairman of the senate's Committee on Academic Freedom, Tenure, and Responsibility, presented a special report on the disputed case—stressing issues of primary faculty jurisdiction and the necessity for continuing dialogue between the opposing sides. In due course Hackney placed before the Tulane Board relevant correspondence from Mason's committee and from the local chapter of the American Association of University Professors. Then and later it was apparent that the president would stand his ground. On a motion by the faculty of the College of Arts and Sciences, a three-person arbitration committee was established to review the case and "evaluate any issues of exceptional circumstances." The committee ruled in favor of Hackney's decision, effectively ending the dispute.[59]

57. John Glenn to Sheldon Hackney, 11 April 1978, box 23, FSH Papers.

58. University Senate Minutes, 3 December 1979, pp. 7–16.

59. Ibid., 4 February 1980, pp. 2–4 (quotation); F. Sheldon Hackney, Policy Memo on Tenure Distributed to Academic Council of Tulane University, October 1979, box 12, FSH Papers.

Throughout the tenure controversy, Tulane's fiscal problems continued to preoccupy both Hackney and his adversaries. The Task Force on Financial Planning, appointed by the president, had reported that a balanced budget for 1979–80 could be achieved, and in a letter to Edmund McIlhenny in mid-August 1978, Hackney stated that he "had begun to see in clearer and more realistic detail than ever before the shape and scope of a healthy financial future for Tulane." By this point both Hackney and McIlhenny agreed that the chief problems lay on the revenue-producing side of the ledger—not on the expenditure side. In line with that concern, the Board's Executive Committee met on October 5, 1978, to discuss the preparation and staffing of a capital campaign of three to five years, to be led by Gary Bayer, Vice President for Development. The campaign and the closely related subject of athletics were slated for additional discussion at the Board of Administrators' retreat in mid-November.[60]

Economic problems and the internal conflict they generated tended to dominate campus politics during the 1978–79 academic year, overshadowing even the sensational press accounts of Andy P. Antippas, Associate Professor of English in the College of Arts and Sciences, who had been apprehended and had pled guilty to a charge of stealing valuable maps from the Yale University Library and the Newberry Library in Chicago. Some fifty-two maps were involved, valued at over $20,000. Prior to a conclusive action in federal court, the Grievance Committee of the College of Arts and Sciences voted four to one to recommend that dismissal proceedings be instituted against Professor Antippas. On January 11, 1979, Antippas resigned from the faculty, and subsequently was sentenced by U.S. District Judge Ellen B. Burns to one year in prison. The Board had been restless with what some Administrators regarded as the slow pace of internal procedures related to Antippas's faculty status, but there was no attempt at intervention. Years had been required to heal the wounds from the Dubinsky case, and no one was anxious to risk a new struggle over the division of authority in matters of faculty discipline. In the University Senate Professor Mason reserved his strongest criticism for the *Hullabaloo*, which had maintained a discreet silence on the entire matter. Antippas had been faculty adviser for the Tulane paper.[61]

60. F. Sheldon Hackney to Edmund McIlhenny, 15 August 1978, box 10, FSH Papers (quotation); BOA Minutes, 5 October 1978.
61. *New Orleans Times-Picayune/States-Item*, 9 January 1979; Joseph E. Gordon to

Notwithstanding such episodes, the principal challenge facing the university throughout Hackney's presidency was the all-too-familiar one of spreading limited resources across a broad spectrum of programs and activities that mirrored the diverse and often conflicting interests of faculty, alumni, administrators, and students. In September 1978, several months prior to the Antippas affair, *Hullabaloo* editor Brad Steitz sorted out the priorities of various Tulane constituencies as they appeared from a student perspective. The faculty, Steitz believed, wanted higher salaries and an end to intercollegiate athletics; students sought an end to the faculty exodus and relief from tuition increases; alumni pressed for more football victories and additional money for intercollegiate athletics; nonacademic personnel needed salary hikes to keep up with inflation; and the Board of Administrators was intent on balanced budgets, financial progress, and a few Green Wave victories. In a closing paragraph about the expected deficit for 1978–79, Steitz noted that "[t]he Board is not going to like it. The pressure is on and nobody knows it more than the man in the hot-seat himself, Sheldon Hackney. This is the beginning of his crucial year ahead."[62]

The potential for conflict over budgetary issues became evident in February 1979, when the senate's Committee on Budget Review brought forward a number of resolutions concerning financial matters. In response to the committee's proposals, the senate endorsed the proposed balanced budget for 1979–80 and urged that the portion of the athletic deficit in excess of the allowable level established in 1971–72 should be offset by "funds functioning as endowment" (as opposed to budget cuts in academic programs). The senate also called upon Hackney to place the compensation issue before the Board, and to urge administrators to make more strenuous efforts to improve faculty salaries. The senate resolutions were a foretaste of things to come. In April 1979, after hearing a report from the senate Committee on Development, several senate members voiced their impatience with the delay in starting a major capital campaign. Vice President Gary Bayer explained that time was needed to build relationships with major donors, but his explanation failed to satisfy most critics. Later in April the chairman of the budget review committee, Professor William Gwyn, reported that

F. Sheldon Hackney, 9 January 1979, box 3, FSH Papers; University Senate Minutes, 5 February 1979, p. 7.

62. Tulane *Hullabaloo*, 8 September 1979, pp. 7, 9 (quotation).

the $605,000 contingency fund set up in the forthcoming 1979–80 budget had been exhausted before the fiscal year even began—and that the Board was insisting that it be reconstituted from other budgeted sources. Hackney stated that it had been used for (1) a $200,000 increase in utilities costs, (2) appointments in senior administrative positions, and (3) to make up for the budgetary oversight of not including a 7 percent raise for the Medical Center faculty and staff. The senate promptly passed a resolution demanding that the shortfall be made up from sources other than the 7 percent salary raises and the 8 percent allocation for the library already promised for 1979–80.[63]

In his annual report for the academic year 1978–79, Hackney noted several key objectives that had been identified at the beginning of the year and subsequently achieved. These included making suitable appointments for important administrative positions (e.g., Starr, Kelly, Wittig, and Walter Spencer, dean of the business school), constructing a balanced budget for 1979–80, beginning the process of long-range strategic planning with a five-year financial plan developed by a task force under Clarence Scheps, and finally, completing a curriculum self-study as part of the reaccreditation process required by the Southern Association of Colleges and Schools. The visiting reaccreditation team had responded with a generally favorable report. On several fronts, moreover, developments augured well for Tulane's future. Legislation to expand Board membership passed both houses of the state legislature and was signed without incident. The state capitation grant for Louisiana students at Tulane increased from $125 to $150, and Tulane received major grants of $750,000 from the National Endowment for the Humanities and $600,000 from the Mellon Foundation.[64]

Before the contents of Hackney's upbeat report could be widely disseminated, the *Times-Picayune* of October 20, 1979, published a lengthy feature story entitled, "Tulane: At the Financial Crossroads," which aired for public view a sympathetic but far from sanguine analysis of the university's fiscal problems, present and anticipated. The following month President Hackney received a letter from the Tulane chap-

63. University Senate Minutes: 5 February 1979, pp. 8–9; 5 March 1979, pp. 3–4; 2 April 1979, pp. 5–7; 30 April 1979, pp. 3–4.
64. F. Sheldon Hackney, Annual Report for 1978–1 October 1979, box 10, FSH Papers, 1–3. Hackney also called attention to an extension of the History Building made possible by a grant from the F. Edward Hébert Foundation and other donors.

ter of the AAUP declaring that "because of disappointments of the past two years and the extent of erosion in faculty salaries, the Executive Committee is compelled to conclude that it will almost certainly be necessary for the faculty to move toward formal collective bargaining." Although there was no indication that the university administration ever considered faculty unions a real likelihood, the AAUP action undoubtedly helped confirm Hackney in the belief that his critics placed too much emphasis on adversarial negotiations and spent too little time cultivating the sense of intellectual community that should prevail at a top caliber university.[65]

The fall semester of 1979 also brought Hackney a letter of resignation from Vice President Gary Bayer, who acknowledged the existence of "irreconcilable differences" between himself and the Board of Administrators. Hackney had been aware of Bayer's difficulties with the Board, not all of which related to the timing of the capital campaign. In a letter of acknowledgment to Bayer, the president expressed his understanding of the reasons for the latter's departure. Warren Johnson, whom Bayer had hired from the University of Chicago to direct a special gifts program at Tulane, was named Director of Development in the wake of Bayer's resignation. Bayer may have been justified in believing that more time was needed to establish an infrastructure, cultivate relationships with potential donors, and generate the momentum needed for a major campaign. But time had run out for him by the fall of 1979. If one may credit the *Hullabaloo*'s campus sources, "the Board lowered the boom." It was the newspaper's judgment that the Board's action "claimed one victim and seriously wounded another," the "other" being President Hackney himself.[66]

Whether or not Bayer's departure reflected a lowering of confidence in Hackney, there can be no doubt that the president's relationship

65. Christopher Drew, "Tulane at the Financial Crossroads," *New Orleans Times-Picayune/States-Item*, 20 October 1979, p. A2; Executive Committee of the Tulane Chapter of the AAUP, An Open Letter to the President of the University, 26 November 1979, box 3, FSH Papers (quotation).

66. Gary Bayer to Sheldon Hackney, 17 September 1979, box 13, FSH Papers; Hackney to Bayer, 18 September 1979, box 13, FSH Papers; Brad Steitz, "The Board Lowers the Boom," Tulane *Hullabaloo*, 21 September 1979 (quotations). It should be noted that 1979 also brought to the university great loss in the deaths of two persons: Darwin S. Fenner, former board chairman and indefatigable supporter of Tulane's welfare for decades; and Professor Robert Wauchope, Emeritus Director of the Middle American Research Institute and internationally reputed scholar in archaeology.

with Board chairman John Phillips had grown increasingly tense and strained. An open breach was averted in 1979, and the beginning of 1980 brought better news when the football team netted some $250,000 for its losing effort against Pennsylvania State University in the Liberty Bowl at Memphis. In addition, the budget success of 1979–80 led to the presentation to the Board in March of another balanced budget for 1980–81. In July Hackney was able to report that Tulane had not only achieved its first black ink budget since 1955, but had ended the year with a surprising surplus of approximately $400,000. The return on the administrators' investment portfolio was 28.9 percent, and freshmen enrollments during the past year had exceeded targets in every division. Remaining problem areas, as Hackney saw them, were faculty salaries, library resources, renovation and upgrading of the physical plant, and planning for the use of the stadium area.[67]

Beneath these optimistic comments, however, lay the less appealing reality of a poisoned relationship between Tulane's president and the chairman of its Board. The two men had found themselves at odds over the pace of fundraising and the type and amount of cuts in academic programs that could be tolerated in pursuit of a balanced budget. Serious friction also resulted from the clash between academic and corporate-managerial styles of governance. In short, the stage was set for an eventual parting of ways, although few besides the parties immediately involved were aware of the conflicts that had developed. Most Tulanians were thus taken by surprise when, on September 28, the local press reported that Hackney had accepted the presidency of the University of Pennsylvania and would move to that position on January 1, 1981, in the middle of the academic year.

In comparison to the presidents who preceded and followed him, Sheldon Hackney served a relatively short term. He took office shouldering many of the same heavy burdens that had worn down Presidents Longenecker and Harris before him: enormous financial problems, conflict over intercollegiate athletics, and an insular, if not parochial, Board of Administrators. In addition he inherited a legacy of adversarial relations with a faculty that felt resentment over inadequate salaries and suspicion of power wielded by the central administration. By any standards, the Tulane presidency offered Hackney a "full plate."

67. F. Sheldon Hackney, interview by C. L. Mohr, 8 November 1995; BOA Minutes, 3 January, 6 March, and 10 July 1980.

In most students' eyes, Sheldon and Lucy Hackney came and left as winners. Much of the president's success with students was a natural result of the couple's youth and their open and engaging personal style. They made the president's house a focal point for mixing students with faculty, Board members, and other students. Students responded enthusiastically to Hackney's willingness to preserve and build upon the new politics of inclusion that had taken shape in the 1960s. If the emphasis on youth had a political cost, it was found in the resentment that occasionally cropped up among faculty and other groups who felt that their access to and influence upon the president had been diminished.

Hackney did not solve the institution's financial woes, but it was during his tenure that balanced budgets became the order of the day. It was regrettable that his initial rapport with the liberal arts and science faculties faded noticeably in the face of unpalatable salary economies and pressures for higher qualitative standards in matters of recruitment and promotion. Alone among modern presidents of Tulane, Hackney found himself briefly in a position to gain Board support for abandoning college football, had such a move been deemed essential for the university's economic survival. He elected instead to support a continued football emphasis in the hope of fostering alumni loyalty and enhancing athletic revenue. The first aim was realized to some degree. The second goal proved elusive. Among Hackney's most enduring accomplishments must be counted the enlargement and reconstitution of the Tulane Board of Administrators, a change that was in accord with the demographics of the student body and the university's continued pursuit of national stature. During his first few weeks at Tulane in 1975, the president predicted in a press interview that he and the faculty would work together harmoniously despite occasional periods of "creative tension." Both creativity and tension were destined to become hallmarks of the Hackney era. Like the cosmopolitan Edwin A. Alderman at the beginning of the twentieth century, Hackney came to Tulane at a critical juncture in the school's history and remained long enough to invigorate the university for the task of surmounting new challenges in the decades ahead.[68]

68. F. Sheldon Hackney, interview by C. L. Mohr, 8 November 1995; John G. Phillips to G. Shelby Friedrichs, 31 January 1979, box 9, FSH Papers.

9

EPILOGUE
The 1980s and Beyond

Sheldon Hackney's resignation in the fall of 1980 was followed almost immediately by the appointment of Eamon M. Kelly to serve as acting president. In April 1981, after a national search involving 245 candidates, Kelly became Tulane's thirteenth chief executive and embarked upon a seventeen-year tenure that would end with his retirement in the 1997–98 academic year. Kelly began his presidency with several unique assets, not the least of which was his ten-year association with the Ford Foundation (1969–79) where he initially directed a $15 million program in the Office of Social Development, encompassing grants related to civil rights and racial equality, community development, women's rights, and conflict resolution. During the five years before his arrival at Tulane in 1979, he had managed the Ford Foundation's $50 million portfolio of Program Related Investments, which had included grants in the field of higher education. Thanks largely to the breadth of Ford programs, Kelly had amassed firsthand knowledge about matters as diverse as black poverty in the rural South and the creation of a domestic communications satellite network for the Public Broadcasting System. During periods of temporary leave from the Ford Foundation, Kelly had accumulated a valuable fund of Washington experience. He had personal contacts in the Economic Development Administration, the Small Business Administration, and the Department of Labor, where he had brokered a settlement to the vexed problem of the $1.4 billion Central States Teamsters Union Pension Fund.

A little-noted aspect of Kelly's background was his "real world" experience in local politics as city council president and councilman at large in the city of the Englewood, New Jersey, from 1974–77, during the tenure of the community's first black mayor. Tulane's new president would later single out his stint in municipal government as particularly useful preparation for the political and logistical challenge of managing a complex academic institution. With a Ph.D. in economics from Columbia and several years of university teaching experience in the early 1960s, Kelly understood the culture of the academic world, although he remained apart from it to a considerable degree. Less conspicuously identified with higher education than any of his immediate predecessors, he brought to the Tulane presidency a combination of fiscal and managerial expertise, social awareness, receptivity to technological innovation, and demonstrated political acumen—qualities highly relevant to the demands placed upon academic leadership in the 1980s.

Since it is too soon to draft a full and judicious account of Tulane's development in the closing decades of the twentieth century, what follows should be regarded as a selective summary of certain developments after 1980 which illuminate ongoing themes in Tulane's modern history. In designating these pages as an epilogue rather than a conclusion, the authors seek to underscore the need for continuing analysis and to acknowledge the tentative and conditional nature of judgments about a past so recent that it has yet to sever its active connection with the present.[1]

I

If the presidency of Sheldon Hackney comprised the closing episode in a drama that had begun in the 1960s, the Kelly era may be regarded as the opening phase of a new epoch defined by fundamentally different political, economic, and demographic realities. The first dozen years of Kelly's presidency coincided with a period of conservative resurgence in American politics, accompanied by increased competition among colleges for a shrinking pool of talented students and a relatively static fund of federal research and education dollars. Tulane's

1. Because of the selective and summary character of the account that follows, there has been no effort at exhaustive documentation. Footnotes are employed primarily to identify quotations and to call attention to important secondary works.

Eamon Michael Kelly,
President, 1980–98.

new president understood that a sea change was underway in the world
of private higher education, and in his October 1981 inaugural address he sought to indicate the shape of things to come. Delivered on a
sunlit Saturday morning to a large outdoor assembly of Board members, alumni, and distinguished guests (including former Tulane presidents Rufus Harris and Herbert Longenecker), together with faculty
from all university divisions attired in full academic regalia, Kelly's
speech stressed the themes of diversity and pluralism in describing the
unique contribution of private universities to higher learning in the
United States.

Mindful of his mixed audience and of the conservative upsurge that
had helped propel Ronald Reagan into power, Kelly attacked coercion
in all its forms. McCarthyism and intrusive federal regulations, Water-
gate abuses of power, and the "general rebellion against any authority" that "swept our nation's campuses" during the era of antiwar protest came in for equal criticism. His sharpest barbs were reserved for
the rigid intolerance of the Moral Majority, whose supporters would
"place a bell jar over the land and in that stifling hothouse legislate
their own narrow values and rigid beliefs, denying the rest of us a
breath of fresh air or a fresh idea." It was possible to hear in the new
president's remarks either a reaffirmation of liberal academic ideals
or an endorsement of the entrepreneurial values of the free market.
The two viewpoints had never been mutually exclusive, and Kelly's

Goldring/Woldenberg Hall. A. B. Freeman School of Business, 1987.

speech represented a skillful effort to find common ground among the university's multiple constituencies. The inaugural address anticipated Kelly's leadership style in the years ahead as he sought to pursue both excellence and democratic access while balancing the competing claims of the classroom and the athletic field, the research laboratory and the corporate sponsor—to say nothing of Newcomb College and the rest of Tulane.[2]

The first economist to lead the university, Kelly assumed the presidency armed with a detailed knowledge of Tulane's finances that he had gained in his two-year stint as executive vice president and interim president. His budgetary skill had been a principal consideration in the presidential selection process, and those who looked to him for relief from the seemingly endless fiscal problems of the previous decade were not to be disappointed. By any objective standard, Tulane's economic and academic revival in the 1980s was dazzling. At the start of the decade faculty salaries at Tulane lagged 20–40 percentage points behind the compensation level of professors at wealthier peer institutions such as Duke and Vanderbilt. Beginning in 1981, a succession of

2. See Eamon Kelly, "Pluralism and the Private University," *Tulanian* 52 (fall 1981): 38–9, for the full text of Kelly's installation address. All quotations appear on p. 39.

double-digit pay increases—a phenomenon with no precedent in the university's modern history— boosted faculty purchasing power as well as Kelly's popularity. Other morale-enhancing achievements included a substantial increase in the library's acquisition budget, a revitalization of the financially troubled School of Social Work, a rapid expansion in undergraduate financial aid with an emphasis on merit-based awards to top students, the beginning of a sustained 150-point rise in freshman SAT scores (from 1060 in 1981 to 1210 in 1996), and the rapid completion of deferred maintenance on campus buildings (at the expense of a whopping $17 million). In all of these accomplishments Kelly was most ably assisted by Provost and Graduate School dean Francis L. Lawrence, who had assumed office following the resignation of Frank Birtel in 1981.

The quickening academic pulse of the early and mid-1980s manifested itself in many ways: through the awarding of prestigious Guggenheim Fellowships to faculty members in the Departments of Anthropology and History, in the growth of sponsored research from $22.4 million in 1981 to $48.47 million in 1988, and in the development of new academic programs and intellectual resources. On the uptown campus the Murphy Institute of Political Economy, newly set apart from the Department of Economics, broadened its focus after 1984 under the leadership of historian Richard Teichgraeber, who inaugurated an ambitious series of seminars, colloquia, and publications, and implemented a new interdisciplinary curriculum for a growing number of undergraduate majors. In 1986 the Murphy Institute was joined in Tilton Hall by the Amistad Research Center, an independent archival repository renowned for its collections in the field of nineteenth- and twentieth-century African American history. The Amistad Center complemented faculty strengths in the fields of law and history, and almost immediately began to stimulate research and teaching activities that would facilitate the development of a program in African Diaspora Studies by the early 1990s.

Additional academic enhancement came in the form of new endowed chairs in the business school, the Newcomb art department, the history department, the theater department, and the Schools of Engineering, Public Health, and Medicine. Tulane students of the early 1980s compiled an impressive record in competition for coveted postgraduate awards. During the single academic year 1981–82, graduating seniors won a Watson Fellowship, a Marshall Scholarship, a Luce

*J. Bennett Johnston Building. Health and Environmental Research,
Medical Center, 1994.*

Scholarship, and a Truman Scholarship, all nationally competitive
and highly prestigious awards. Two seniors in the School of Medicine
each received one of fifty national Kaiser Merit Awards for top minority students, and a Newcomb College alumna, Shelly Errington, won a
much-sought-after MacArthur Foundation grant for exceptionally
talented individuals. Between 1983 and 1988 a total of five Tulane and
Newcomb students were named Rhodes Scholars, while many others
were selected as finalists in the Rhodes competition.

The progress of the 1980s becomes even more noteworthy when
placed within the context of Tulane's relatively small endowment (only
$73 million in 1980–81) and the lack of a major capital campaign in the
decade preceding Kelly's presidency. Enlarging the endowment became a key priority, and in 1983 a $150 million fund drive was
launched under the leadership of Board member Charles Murphy and
the newly appointed Vice President for Development and Alumni
Affairs, Warren Johnson. By the end of the 1984–85 academic year,
the Major Funds Campaign had produced a total in excess of $160 mil-

lion. The endowment had grown to $132 million, while "funds functioning as endowment," the assets most accessible for annual budgetary purposes, had risen from $4 million to $39 million. By 1989 the endowment's book value was approaching $200 million despite the 1987 stock market crash, and "funds functioning as endowment" stood at $63 million.

Many additional factors contributed to the economic revival of the 1980s, including revenues from the Tulane Medical Center Hospital and Clinic, which soon surpassed the expectations of even its most ardent supporters. The clinic and 285-bed hospital produced a substantial surplus for much of the decade. New programs—such as the Kidney Transplant Center, the Hemophilia Center, and Sudden Infant Death Syndrome Center—expanded the Medical Center's constituencies and enhanced its recognized role as a tertiary care institution. The Faculty Practice Plan was described in a 1981 report by Chancellor John Walsh as being "eminently successful," having brought $7.5 million to the medical school in faculty salaries and bonuses in the previous fiscal year. Plan members, in Walsh's opinion, were among Tulane's largest donors and were truly subsidizing medical education.[3]

Additional fiscal help came from University College, where enrollment expanded vigorously under the able leadership of Dean Louis E. Barrilleaux, a veteran administrator who had helped build Tulane's education department to a position of strength in the previous decade. Fully alive to the growing educational importance of foreign travel and part-time study by adult students, Barrilleaux launched a number of curricular initiatives that broadened the University College clientele. Particularly notable was the Tulane Summer Abroad Program begun in 1983 and the master of liberal arts program inaugurated the next year in order to bring graduate study within reach of many able adults who would not otherwise have pursued advanced degrees. Legislative and legal actions also produced significant economic benefit. Before the economic slump triggered by falling oil prices in the mid- and late 1980s, Louisiana's political climate was a congenial one for those laboring to shore up university finances. In 1984, following the election of Democrat Edwin Edwards as governor of Louisiana and the appointment of Judge Edmund Reggie of Crowley, Louisiana, to a seat on the Tulane Board of Administrators, State Attorney General William

3. President's Council Minutes, 21 October 1981, box 8, EMK Papers, p. 10.

Lindy Claiborne Boggs Center for Energy and Biotechnology, 1988.

J. Guste Jr. rendered an advisory opinion that Tulane was "exempt from the payment of sales and use taxes levied by the State, parochial, and municipal authorities." Guste's opinion was based on the provision of Act 43 of the Louisiana Legislature of 1884 that established Tulane as a private institution. The ruling meant a significant financial gain for the university, and in its session of February 1984, the Board expressed appreciation to Judge Reggie for his help in presenting the matter—and for the concurrent increase in capitation grants from the state. President Kelly estimated that the annual saving would be upward of $3 million.[4]

All of the financial strategies pursued in the 1980s would have counted for little if Tulane's undergraduate enrollment had seriously declined. Despite impressive growth in the endowment and other revenue sources, the university continued to wear the hair shirt of tuition dependency throughout the decade. Indeed, during the last half of the

4. Robert G. Sherer, *University College: A History of Access to Opportunity, 1942–1992* (New Orleans: Tulane University Office of University Relations, 1992), 11; BOA Minutes, 16 February 1984.

1980s, the portion of annual operating revenues derived from tuition actually rose from 74 percent to 83 percent. By the end of the decade, unrestricted endowment income accounted for only 2 percent of the annual operating budget. These figures take on added meaning when viewed against the background of profound changes in the distribution of wealth and income occurring at the national level. Beginning late in the 1970s and continuing at an accelerated rate throughout the next decade, the upper 10 percent of American families (as ranked by income) grew substantially wealthier while the economic position of the bottom 60 percent—including much of the nation's broad postwar middle class—steadily eroded. By the mid-1980s the rising expectations of the baby boom generation were being replaced by deepening anxiety about income, lifestyles, and job security.[5]

The new pattern of accumulation had important implications for private higher education. Throughout the 1980s the upward redistribution of wealth and income went hand in hand with a widening gap between the earnings of college graduates and Americans who lacked the baccalaureate degree. But as the wage premium associated with higher education climbed ever higher, college grew steadily more expensive. By 1985 the average cost of keeping one child in a four-year private college or university had risen to a staggering 40 percent of the median family income for U.S. households. To a greater extent than ever before, students and their families began to weigh the merits of individual schools in terms of academic quality and institutional prestige. As had long been true, the diplomas most sought after were those conferred by highly selective research universities where the financial cost of attendance was typically quite substantial, even after the allocation of need-based financial aid.[6]

Tulane had long emphasized quality and selectivity, a fact which

5. Kevin Phillips, *The Politics of Rich and Poor: Wealth and the American Electorate in the Reagan Aftermath* (New York: Random House, 1990), chap. 1, contains an excellent summary of the upward redistribution of wealth in the 1980s.

6. Yolanda K. Kodrzycki, "Labor Markets and Earnings Inequality: A Status Report," *New England Economic Review*, Special Issue: Earnings Inequality (May–June 1996); David A. Brauer, *Using Regional Variation to Explain Widening Earnings Differentials by Educational Attainment*, Federal Reserve Bank of New York Research Paper 9521 (October 1995); Phillips, *Politics of Rich and Poor*, 22. Professor Paul K. Conkin of Vanderbilt University has written incisively about the impact of 1980s developments on higher learning in *The Mature but Anxious University: Hungry, Captive, Politicized, and Deconstructed* [Louise McBee Lecture, 1992] (Athens: University of Georgia Institute of Higher Education, 1993).

Brandt V. B. Dixon Performing Arts Center, 1984.

helped the university compete successfully for a finite supply of wealthy and talented students during the 1980s, despite a steady decline in the nation's 18-to-24-year-old population. In the decades prior to Kelly's arrival, an economist might have argued that the university's undergraduate tuition did not fully reflect the "cash value" of the education it provided. (Certainly tuition and fees defrayed only a portion of the actual cost of providing instruction.) As SAT scores began to climb in the 1980s, undergraduate tuition rose even more dramatically, from $4,400 in 1980–81 to $6,650 in 1989–90, which was an increase of more than 50 percent over the span of nine years. In the absence of mitigating factors, the 1980s combination of rising costs and increased academic selectivity could scarcely have failed to narrow the university's socioeconomic base, as students were drawn in increasing numbers from the nation's wealthiest income groups. Such an outcome would have flown in the face of Kelly's avowed commitment to the goals of diversity and pluralism.

Fortunately, the socioeconomic impact of rising tuition was offset by a prodigious increase in the university's own financial aid budget,

Law School, John Giffen Weinmann Hall under construction. Completed 1995.

which ballooned from less than $6 million in 1980–81 to $32.5 million in 1988–89, or more than a fivefold increase in eight years. Some of the money was devoted to a major expansion of the Dean's Honor Scholarship program for superior students in 1983, but need-based aid became an increasingly important consideration for freshman students who chose Tulane over other institutions. In 1978–79, only 18 percent of Tulane freshmen received financial aid directly from university sources. Four years later, in 1982–83, that number stood at 30 percent and would continue to rise over the decade until more than half of all freshmen received financial assistance. Although few would have described the financial burden of undergraduate tuition as a light one, Tulane emerged from the 1980s with a student body that was more geographically, economically, and ethnically diverse than that of many private universities. By 1988, when African Americans comprised 6.5 percent of the student body, the university ranked ninth in black enrollment among peer institutions. Overall, minorities accounted for some 13.1 percent of Tulane students. The mid-1990s would find undergraduate minority enrollment at an all-time high of 21.6 percent. By that point more than 10 percent of Tulane's nonforeign undergraduate students were black, while Hispanic American and Asian American students comprised respectively 5.3 percent and 5.1 percent of the undergraduate population. Professional schools such as Law and Medicine counted record numbers of African Americans and women in their entering classes. These results constituted a point of justifiable pride for all who believed that diversity and pluralism were essential to the vitality of higher learning. In the face of significant countervailing pressures, Tulane had continued to elevate academic standards while opening the doors of opportunity in an unprecedented fashion.

It is customary to describe the 1980s as a time of diminished idealism, renewed cultural conformity, and burgeoning vocational interest among American college students. Portions of the Tulane experience lend credence to such a view, although long-term trends present a picture that is decidedly more complex. The Greek system offers a case in point. In the fall semester of 1985, a total of 558 Newcomb women—some 95 percent of the entering class—registered for rush activities. Of this group, nearly 300 subsequently pledged one of the college's eight sororities. By the spring of 1986, approximately 40 percent of Tulane's male undergraduates and 55 percent of all undergraduate women belonged to Greek-letter social organizations. Such statistics indicate that by the 1980s fraternities and sororities no longer suffered from the crisis of legitimacy that had afflicted them in the late 1960s and early 1970s. In broader perspective, however, the Greek system's popularity had declined substantially since the late 1950s. During the 1980s this gradual downward trend was reinforced by rising educational costs and the desire of many students to place academic and professional goals ahead of purely social activities. By the mid-1990s, aggregate fraternity and sorority membership hovered around the 40 percent level, amid indications that the Greek system had assumed a permanent minority status.[7]

If statistics on fraternity and sorority membership suggest something about broad cultural tendencies, the results of a survey completed by some 1,200 Tulane freshmen in the 1981–82 academic year both support and contradict the conventional view of eighties students as apolitical, career-minded pragmatists. Among those freshmen who would comprise the senior class of 1984–85 the most popular major was engineering, followed closely by business and pre-medicine. Only

7. Annual Report of the [Newcomb] Program Coordinator, 1986, p. 3, records of the assistant dean for Newcomb life, Newcomb Center for Research on Women; Tulane *Hullabaloo*, 9 April 1986, p. 7.

2.2 percent expressed an initial preference for history, and even fewer favored English as an area of concentration. Many factors, especially ROTC scholarships, job prospects, and parental pressure help explain the tilt toward scientific, professional, and applied fields. Still, it is note-worthy that the two "life objectives" cited most frequently by Tulane freshmen were "being an authority in my field" (77.2 percent) and "be[ing] very well off financially" (71.7 percent). Politically the fresh-men of 1981–82 were slightly more centrist and slightly less conservative than students in the nation as a whole. Just over one fourth (26.5 per-cent) described themselves as liberals, while a nearly identical number embraced the conservative label. By far the largest proportion—some 45 percent—preferred to stay in the "middle-of-the-road."[8]

Academic and political preferences notwithstanding, it would be misleading to characterize students of the 1980s as latter-day counter-parts of the 1950s legendary Silent Generation. If anything, Tulane's Reagan-era undergraduates exhibited attitudes that grew out of Ameri-can society's effort to reconcile traditional middle-class values with the cultural upheavals of the decades immediately past. The result could be seen in questions regarding social issues, where responses blended liberal and conservative positions in a seemingly incongruous fashion. By large majorities, freshmen agreed that criminals had too many rights, that inflation was the nation's greatest domestic problem, and that government should do much more to control pollution and protect consumers. Consumerism, in various guises, was a common thread in responses to questions about social issues. Within the framework of consumer consciousness, many of the radical proposals of the late 1960s had undergone a subtle metamorphosis. Some 70 percent of the 1981 freshmen, for example, believed that they should evaluate fac-ulty members. Student power advocates had voiced similar demands in the 1960s, usually as part of a larger program to democratize the structure of learning and academic decision making. Indeed, for many student activists of those years, university reform had been rooted in the idea of education as an act of self-liberation. The 1980s students, by contrast, seemed conditioned to view education as a commodity or consumer item that might be purchased with money and weighed in the balance scales of customer satisfaction.[9]

8. "Tulane's Class of 1985: A Survey," *Tulanian* 53 (spring 1982): 26–7.

9. Ibid.; Paul Rogat Loeb, *Generation at the Crossroads: Apathy and Action on the*

Although organized feminism scarcely existed on Tulane's campus in the 1980s, the women's movement and the sexual revolution had left their mark on undergraduate youth culture. Once again careerism and idealism managed to find common ground. Of all questions asked in the 1981 survey, the item evoking the highest degree of consensus (95.3 percent) was the statement that "[w]omen should have the same salaries and opportunities for advancement as men in comparable positions." Tulanians who could recall the agonized parental outcry that had accompanied the cautious liberalization of Sunday afternoon visiting hours in campus dormitories in the early 1960s had much to ponder in the brave new world of 1980s sexual freedom. Nearly half the class of 1985 believed that divorce laws should be liberalized and large families discouraged. A majority considered it acceptable to live together before marriage, and 63 percent agreed that sex was "O.K. if the people like each other."[10]

Although the 1980s witnessed nothing comparable to the campus activism of the previous generation, the steady growth of minority enrollments insured that racial equality would remain a live issue. The early years of Kelly's tenure saw few public ripples on the surface of campus race relations. Tulane's black students now numbered several hundred rather than a few score as in the late 1960s, and for most of them, the epic struggle against legal segregation was an artifact of history. Yet only the most naive observer would have supposed that racial distinctions no longer mattered on the uptown campus. Any doubts on this score vanished in April 1987 when the Delta Kappa Epsilon fraternity, already under sanction by the university for previous violations, paraded down McAlister Drive in a display that constituted a provocative gesture of racism. Some members wore blackface and were clad in T-shirts bearing the ACT insignia of the Afro-American Congress of Tulane; others carried lighted flambeaux. During the course of the parade, several Tulane students, including some black students, were intimidated by the marchers, insulted with obscene gestures, or had lighted torches thrust at them. It was the university's

---

American Campus (New Brunswick, N.J.: Rutgers University Press, 1994) does an excellent job of conveying the complexity of college student attitudes and behavior in the 1980s and early 1990s.

10. Alexander W. Astin et al., *The American Freshman: National Norms for Fall 1982* (Los Angeles: Cooperative Institutional Research Program of the University of California at Los Angeles and the American Council on Education, 1982), 139 (first quotation); "Tulane's Class of 1985: A Survey," 26–7 (second quotation).

ugliest racial episode since the early 1960s, when hostile students had surrounded CORE demonstrators during the cafeteria sit-ins.

Kelly responded immediately with an open letter to the Tulane community condemning the "Dekes" in the strongest terms. He promised to prosecute the participants to the fullest extent possible under the Code of Student Conduct, to seek revocation of the New Orleans chapter's national charter, and to advise incoming freshmen and their parents that the DKE fraternity was "an aberrant and outcast organization with a dismal history of irresponsible behavior." After the parade, black students met with Kelly to discuss a variety of concerns raised by the episode. The meeting was cordial and low-key, but important. As summarized for the Administrative Council in late April, the black students' concerns bore a striking resemblance to the issues raised by their predecessors two decades earlier. Tulane's African American students of the late 1980s pointed to the lack of black faculty members and senior staff appointments, together with high attrition among black students and continuing segregation in social fraternities and sororities as problems requiring attention.[11]

In the early 1990s efforts to speed progress toward racial and gender diversity would provoke bitter resistance on the part of a small but vocal minority of Tulane faculty. But in 1987–88 concern over racial policy focused on the issue of university investment in corporations doing business in South Africa. Nationwide pressure for an economic assault on apartheid had been building for several years, and a number of educational institutions had purged their investment portfolios of morally tainted securities in response to student and faculty campaigns. The topic had received intermittent attention at Tulane during the first half of the 1980s, and on September 19, 1985, in a move to forestall heightened student and faculty criticism, Tulane's Board approved a statement opposing the "violation of human rights wherever such violations exist." The Board directed its investment subcommittee to make an annual review of the "quality of corporate citizenship" for companies in the university's portfolio and to "[t]ake appropriate action with respect to both investment decisions and execution of shareholder voting rights provided such action is not inconsistent with the Board of Administrators' fiduciary duties."[12]

11. Eamon M. Kelly, open letter to the Tulane community, 24 April 1987, box 55, EMK Papers, 1 (quotation).
12. BOA Minutes, 19 December 1985.

The statement committed the Board to very little in the way of financial sacrifice, and throughout most of 1987 the *Hullabaloo* kept up a steady divestiture campaign, urging students to protest for a change in university policy. External events soon brought the campaign to a climax. Early in the spring of 1988 Archbishop Desmond Tutu of South Africa agreed to visit New Orleans for a major speech to be sponsored by the city and Tulane. Before departing, he would also accept an honorary doctorate at the commencement exercises of the College of Arts and Sciences. With the divestment issue still unresolved, the *Hullabaloo* published an editorial calling the forthcoming honorary degree a "sham." Student protesters planned a sit-in for the Board meeting of April 21, 1988, and together with several sympathetic faculty members they lined the hallway through which the president and Board members would pass en route to their afternoon session. Shortly thereafter Kelly invited the students to attend the Board meeting as guests, but despite their presence, the Board reaffirmed its 1985 policy of reviewing investments annually with no promise of selling profitable assets.[13]

In the wake of the meeting, symbolic shanties were nailed together near McAlister Auditorium, the site of an April 19 speech by Maki Mandela, the eldest daughter of Nelson Mandela. The series of events culminated in Archbishop Tutu's decision to decline the honorary degree offered by Tulane and to forgo a visit to New Orleans at that time. In an Associated Press story of May 9, Tutu stated in part, "I regret that the University did not share fully with me its position on South Africa at an earlier stage. . . . I am willing to accept the degree in a year's time should Tulane review its decision not to divest." Hardly a triumph of university public relations, the divestment controversy would soon be rendered moot by the demise of South Africa's white regime.[14]

In retrospect, the anti-apartheid campaign stands out as a harbinger of the renewed undergraduate concern with educational policy that would manifest itself somewhat ambiguously in the next decade, when mid-1990s budget cuts prompted the first student march on the president's office in more than a quarter century. For many Tulane administrators, however, the racial disputes of the mid- and late 1980s

13. Tulane *Hullabaloo:* 2 October 1987, p. 4; 23 October 1987, pp. 3–4, 10; 13 November 1987, p. 13; 4 December 1987, p. 14; 20 January 1988, p. 17.

14. *New Orleans Times-Picayune/States-Item*, 10 May 1988, p. 1.

were overshadowed by the reemergence of two familiar problems from Tulane's past. One centered around women's education and the status of Newcomb College; the other involved the perennial issue of deficit budgets in intercollegiate athletics and more immediately, the exposure of corruption in Green Wave basketball. Neither the depressing sports scandal nor the protracted internal maneuvering over collegiate realignment can be adequately explored in a brief epilogue. For present purposes a précis of each episode must suffice. First, the Newcomb story.

For a period of some eighteen months beginning in July 1986, a newly formed organization called the Friends for Newcomb's Future—led by various pre-1960 Newcomb alumnae and their supporters—carried on an intensive lobbying and personal pressure campaign with Kelly and the Board of Administrators in opposition to various physical and administrative changes which had been undertaken in the recent—and not-so-recent—past. Alarmed by what they regarded as a diminution of Newcomb's separate identity and a loss of many distinctive elements in an older Newcomb experience, the Friends coalition objected to a number of otherwise routine actions, such as elimination of the music department's role in scheduling space in Dixon Hall, the relocation of certain academic departments (including women's physical education) to sites outside Newcomb Hall, the shift from some all-female to coed dormitories, and the high turnover rate in Newcomb deans since the late 1970s. Discontent over some of these issues had simmered since the latter part of the Hackney administration, but it was not until the mid-1980s that two loosely related developments provided a catalyst for organized opposition.

In 1985 the University Senate, over strong objections from Newcomb delegates, adopted a single Code of Conduct for male and female undergraduates. Somewhat later, in 1986, the previously separate Tulane and Newcomb admissions staffs were consolidated into a single centralized organization, located in Gibson Hall. The unified conduct code was perceived by its opponents as a blow to the Newcomb system of student self-government, while the consolidated admissions office assumed the character of a symbolic threat to the autonomy or identity of Newcomb College. For traditionalists, both actions seemed to chip away at important boundaries between Newcomb and the all-male College of Arts and Sciences. By contrast, those favoring the changes tended to regard the new conduct code as a long overdue step toward the elimination of an outmoded sexual double standard, and to look upon centralized admissions as a more rational and cost-effective approach to undergraduate recruiting for both Newcomb and the College of Arts and Sciences. The decision to consolidate admissions had, in fact, been prompted by a 1983 shortfall of some one hundred students in the Newcomb freshman class.

The controversy that grew out of these and various ancillary issues prompted a general reexamination of the Newcomb–Arts and Sciences relationship. Before the matter was resolved, both the Board and the University Senate found it necessary to appoint special committees on collegiate organization. First the Newcomb Friends organization and then the university administration engaged legal counsel, and the inevitable team of outside consultants weighed in with independent recommendations. Eventually, the University Senate and the Board were asked to choose between three alternate models of collegiate organization. Plans A and B, advanced by the University Senate's Special Committee on the Future of Collegial Education at Tulane, offered the choice of making Newcomb a more "separate college" and allowing the College of Arts and Sciences to admit women as well as men (the "Barnard model"), or of following the Harvard/Radcliffe example by merging the two college faculties into a single body with one dean. Under the latter arrangement, students would continue to enroll in Newcomb or Arts and Sciences as before, and each college (but not the united faculty) would be administered by a separate dean. Academic requirements would be identical, and there would be one Honor Board, one Committee on Promotions and Tenure, one Curriculum Committee, and one admissions operation. Plan B was widely perceived to be favored by President Kelly, Provost Lawrence, Arts and Sciences dean James F. Kilroy, and other members of the Tulane administration. The Newcomb faculty, the Newcomb Alumnae Association Board, and the Friends for Newcomb's Future endorsed Plan C, which would have reestablished the collegiate structures as they existed prior to 1979. Newcomb would have a separate director of admissions, and its curriculum would be allowed to differ from that of Arts and Sciences. The Newcomb endowment would be separated from that of the university as a whole, and the faculty would be allowed to grow to the size of the College of Arts and Sciences.

Deliberations over the three plans began in November 1986 and consumed a considerable part of two academic years. What is remarkable in the surviving record of committee proceedings is the seeming preoccupation of all parties with bureaucratic and organizational matters (or what might be called turf disputes) and the corresponding neglect of underlying questions concerning the relative merits of single sex versus coeducational learning environments. Several factors help explain the focus on organizational issues. In part it reflected the exasperation of Kelly and more than a few uptown deans and faculty members who had wearied of the bureaucratic duplication inherent in dual committee structures for promotion and tenure decisions, honor code enforcement, and a host of other mundane but time-consuming matters. By the 1980s there was also a growing conviction among younger faculty that appointments to separate colleges within the same academic department served little purpose beyond the perpetuation of petty internecine feuds, the origins of which often lay in events beyond the memory of even the oldest faculty colleagues. Thus, while the University Senate's Special Committee on the Future of Collegial Education had been charged to find "new and positive ways for the Colleges of Arts and Sciences and Newcomb College to carry out their traditional missions of providing support to men and to women for their special needs," the group's actual meetings produced little serious discussion of the intellectual arguments surrounding women's education. Attention focused instead on that part of the committee's mandate that stressed the need to "identify the structure and levels at which unified action by the colleges is necessary and those at which separate procedures and services may be effective."[15]

It was apparent from an early date that the Newcomb issue would inspire no carefully crafted position papers, no collection of published essays similar to the volume *Trends in Liberal Arts Education for Women* that had marked the retirement of Anna Many and the arrival of Newcomb dean John Hubbard in 1954. What resulted instead was a classic political compromise. In November 1987 the Board of Administrators adopted a lengthy policy statement ratifying Plan B, which the outside consultants and the University Senate had previously endorsed. Henceforth Newcomb College and the College of Arts and Sciences (later renamed Paul Tulane College) would have a single faculty of Liberal Arts and Sciences, common academic and honor code

---

15. Jefferson L. Sulzer, Memo on Appointment of Special Committee in Collegiate Education, 14 November 1986, box 42, EMK Papers, 3.

requirements, and a single promotion and tenure process presided over by a single dean. The campus area bounded by Broadway, Zimple Street, Newcomb Place, and Plum Street was officially designated the Newcomb College campus, and the Board declared that the university Departments of Art and Music would henceforth be known officially as the Newcomb Department of Art and the Newcomb Department of Music. Finally, $2 million of university funds were dedicated to a Newcomb Foundation to demonstrate the Board's commitment to the special goals of Newcomb College and to encourage their support by other constituencies. More than thirty years after Rufus Harris had started down the rocky road of collegiate coordination, the journey seemed to have reached an end.

If the Newcomb issue comprised a piece of unfinished business from Tulane's past, much the same can be said of the athletic crisis, which exploded on March 27, 1985, when the *New Orleans Times-Picayune* reported that "Tulane's All-Metro Conference basketball player John 'Hot Rod' Williams and another student were arrested Tuesday night on charges of shaving points in two Tulane basketball games this season." A total of eight people were indicted in the ensuing scandal, including Tulane players John Williams, David Dominique, and Bobby Thompson, together with nonplaying students Gary Kranz, Mark Olensky, and David Rothenberg. Nonstudents indicted were Roland Ruiz, a forty-eight-year-old convicted gambler, and Craig Bourgeois, aged twenty-three. Two players, Clyde Eads and Jon Johnson, under a grant of immunity, implicated themselves and the three other players in the point-shaving scheme. Prosecutors were told that the five basketball players divided about $18,000 for shaving points in games with the University of Southern Mississippi on February 2, 1985, and with Memphis State on February 20. The Kranz indictment also included nine counts of cocaine distribution and one count of possession of cocaine.

On April 4, Kelly announced that he had accepted the resignation of head basketball coach Ned Fowler and assistant coaches Max Pfeifer and Mike Richardson after Fowler admitted that he had paid money to at least one of the players, a serious violation of the rules of the National Collegiate Athletics Association. Tulane had no monopoly on either scandals or coaching resignations in the big money world of 1980s college sports, and the president made it clear that he regarded the nationwide problem of corruption in intercollegiate athletics as too serious to be solved through personnel changes. "The only way I know to demonstrate unambiguously this academic community's intolerance of the violations and actions we have uncovered," Kelly declared, "is to discontinue the program in which they originated. . . . The principal role of a university is learning. That is our strength and it will continue to be our strength."[16]

With strong support from the University Senate, and with only modest opposition from a minority of hard-core basketball fans and "streetcar alumni," Kelly gained Board approval to discontinue basketball and to appoint a special committee "to determine whether continued participation in 'big time' athletics was compatible with our central mission as a teaching and research university; and, if that determination was affirmative, to discover ways that Tulane could do a better job of harmonizing its sports program with its essential educational purposes." Buoyed by these developments, together with Kelly's continued emphasis on the primacy of academics during a three-month period of intense media coverage at the local and national level (including an appearance on the network interview program *Meet the Press*), a few faculty members on the uptown campus dared hope that the chronic financial burden imposed by involvement in Division I-A sports might at last be lifted through a decision to abandon "big time" play in favor of a more modest level of competition. At one point the *Hullabaloo* advocated going even further and "making the entire Tulane sports program truly amateur." But it was not to be.[17]

After nearly a year of meetings, consultation trips to other schools, and intensive archival research and data analysis, the Select Committee on Intercollegiate Athletics—chaired by historian Lawrence N. Powell and composed of students, alumni, faculty members, deans, and athletic department representatives—delivered its formal report to the University Senate and the Board in April 1986. Although the report and its thick appendices contained a sobering thirty-year chroni-

---

16. *New Orleans Times-Picayune*, 5 April 1985, pp. 1, 6. The basic problems afflicting Tulane athletics were similar in most fundamental respects to those identified for American colleges in general in a series of penetrating reports issued by the Knight Foundation Commission on Intercollegiate Athletics between 1991 and 1993. See especially *Keeping Faith with the Student Athlete: A New Model for Intercollegiate Athletics* (March 1991). The authors are grateful to William Friday for making copies of the Knight Foundation reports available.

17. Report of the Select Committee on Intercollegiate Athletics, March 1986, p. 2 (first quotation), box 48, EMK Papers (hereafter cited as Powell Report); Tulane *Hullabaloo*, 12 April 1985, p. 31 (second quotation).

Reily Student Recreation Center, 1987.

cle of red ink athletic budgets, large structural deficits, and weak academic performance by scholarship athletes, the conclusion wrung from such evidence was "that continued participation in Division I-A athletics can make a positive contribution to our primary mission as an educational institution." In an illuminating passage that echoed many of the arguments Sheldon Hackney had voiced a decade earlier, the committee explained the rationale for their I-A recommendation:[18]

> We recommend a Division I-A profile for Tulane because we feel it is a vital link between the institution and our increasingly national alumni, and because it can be a force for bringing together the diverse constituencies that comprise a large and complex university like Tulane. Whether we individually approve or not, nothing enhances the national visibility of an educational institution more than a major athletic program and nothing seems to unite an educational community as much as a winning team. This appears to be an unalterable fact of American life and culture. When the football or basketball team does well a contagious eu-

18. Powell Report, 23.

phoria sweeps the campus and the city, affecting the community at every level. It is a positive spirit, inseparable from the college experience itself.[19]

The committee's endorsement of continued involvement in top-level sports competition came at a price, namely the elimination of the intellectually suspect physical education major, which had been reinstituted in 1968 over the bitter objection of the Arts and Sciences faculty. In what would prove to be the most far-reaching change to emerge from the basketball imbroglio, the committee secured Board approval for the enrollment of all athletes in regular B.A., B.S., or bachelor of general studies degree programs in Tulane's various undergraduate colleges. In addition, the Board agreed to a system of serious faculty scrutiny of athletic admissions, supplemented by new programs of remedial assistance and monitoring of individual academic performance. Although the admissions standards for football and basketball players remained far below the requirements applied to most entering freshmen, the select committee's internal reforms provided reasonable guarantees that the worst abuses would be checked. Thoughtful supporters of the Green Wave tradition found grounds to hope that the term "student athlete" would acquire added legitimacy in the years ahead.

The committee's least successful proposals concerned the raising of a stabilization fund large enough to offset past and future revenue losses in college sports. By the early 1990s basketball had returned to the Tulane campus and was enjoying considerable popularity and fan support. But "surprise" deficits on the million-dollar level and above continued to mar the athletic picture. As the decade progressed it became increasingly evident that the financial demands of intercollegiate sports, while serious in themselves, merely compounded a larger economic problem that was rooted in the university's inability to increase income rapidly enough to keep pace with rising educational costs. At the national level, college operating expenses were increasing by an annual average of 6 percent while revenues grew by only 3 percent. Tulane was no exception to the national trend. The problem had been recognized as early as December 1988, when a consultant's study indicated that without cost reductions and revenue increases Tulane could experience a negative annual cash flow of $5 million within two to three

19. Ibid., 24.

James W. Wilson Jr. Center for Intercollegiate Athletics, 1988.

years. To an even greater extent than many of its wealthier peer institutions, Tulane faced a narrowed range of economic options in the 1990s. As cold war justifications for federal support of higher education began to recede, the university encountered growing pressure to turn its intellectual resources and research apparatus into profit-making channels. The decade would be one of rising tension and strain in which initial debates over multiculturalism and affirmative action were played out against a background of institutional restructuring, temporarily frozen salary levels, and increasingly stark choices about the relative importance of various university functions.

The full magnitude of the fiscal problem became evident in 1996, when financial pressures led to the downsizing of most Tulane graduate programs, the abolition of financial support for terminal master's degrees, and the elimination of all graduate student stipends in several fields—an act tantamount to cancellation of graduate work in those disciplines. Although the action seemed sudden, it marked the culmination of a process that had been underway since 1992, when an internal academic base study recommended outside evaluation of the quality of all graduate programs "with a view toward reallocating resources so as to build on strength." In October 1995, a few months before the graduate program cuts were announced, Graduate School dean Susan Allen distributed an analysis of the National Research

Council's 1993 reputational ratings of graduate programs across the nation. A number of Tulane departments ranked extremely well when compared with schools of approximately the same size. Just as important, the university had made significant progress in several fields since the beginning of the decade, changes that were too recent to be fully reflected in reputational surveys. The challenge, as Dean Allen saw it, was not only to "maintain that level of excellence in the face of impending drastic budget cuts but also to continue to improve quality." In the faculty of Liberal Arts and Sciences, which bore the brunt of the graduate program cuts, reaction was sharply negative. Angered by the university's willingness to spend over $1 million of endowment capital to cover athletic deficits at a time when academic programs were being reduced, a heavily attended meeting of the LAS faculty in the spring semester of 1996 gave nearly unanimous support to a resolution expressing lack of confidence in the Board of Administrators. Unlike the no-confidence motion passed by the graduate faculty during the Longenecker era, the LAS vote was neither repealed nor expunged.[20]

In the wake of the 1996 reductions, the situation facing Tulane seemed paradoxical. Standard measures of student quality, research productivity, and stature among peer institutions at the graduate and undergraduate level placed Tulane in the strongest position it had occupied for a generation. The gains, however, were primarily a reflection of initiatives taken during the previous decade, many of which seemed threatened as the size of the faculty and the budget of the Graduate School began to shrink while the size of the student body and the level of athletic funding moved upward. For all concerned, the task of setting institutional priorities had never seemed more urgent or more daunting. President Kelly himself identified the true meaning of involuntary retrenchment in his 1981 inaugural speech when he declared that "[i]f our private universities and colleges are forced to curtail or eliminate established programs—or raise tuition dramatically to help offset projected decreases in revenues—we shall be impoverished for it." By the mid-1990s, that passage had acquired a prophetic ring. Although restructuring policies, including the sale of a controlling interest in the Tulane Hospital and Clinic to health care giant

20. Tulane Academic Base Study, 20 August 1992, p. 11, typescript in authors' possession (first quotation); Susan Allen, memorandum to deans, directors, and department chairs, 13 October 1995, Graduate School Files, Gibson Hall, Tulane University (second quotation).

Columbia/HCA, led financial analysts to upgrade Tulane's bond rating from A to A+ in the summer of 1997, the academic and intellectual impact of the decade's budgetary economies had yet to be fully measured. As the university prepared to grapple with yet another episode in the ongoing cycle of postwar monetary struggles, all that could be said with certainty was that the future would pose challenges that were no less formidable that those of the recent past. Would the Tulane community summon the necessary unity, creativity, and breadth of vision to sustain recent advances and continue on an upward trajectory? This was the question for a new century.[21]

21. Kelly, "Pluralism and the Private University," 39.

TABLE 1

Total University Budgets, 1950–90

(as estimated and approved for fiscal years indicated)

Fiscal Year	Total Revenue	Total Expenditures	Surplus* (or Deficit)
1950–51	$4,045,658.05	$4,135,001.16	-$89,343.11
1955–56	8,846,070.50	8,665,962.38	180,108.12
1960–61	14,972,330.80	16,791,462.92	-1,819,132.12
1965–66	31,626,639.00	32,788,981.00	-1,162,342.00
1970–71	40,872,481.00	42,359,692.00	-1,487,211.00
1975–76	58,143,365.00	58,143,365.00	0.00
1980–81	93,587,000.00	93,082,000.00	505,000.00
1985–86	204,396,000.00	203,467,000.00	929,000.00
1990–91	207,681,000.00	202,712,000.00	4,969,000.00

*As "booked" at beginning of fiscal year. The "end-of-year" figure could—and often did—vary significantly.

TABLE 2

Unrestricted Educational and General Resources (1) as related to Unrestricted
Endowment Income (2) and Tuition and Fee Income (4)

Year	(1) Unrestricted Educational and General Revenues	(2) Unrestricted Endowment	(3) Ratio of (2) to (1)	(4) Tuition and Fee Income	(5) Ratio of (4) to (1)
1950	$4,428,472	$1,025,103	.23	$2,300,940	.52
1960	12,907,963	1,778,529	.14	4,678,170	.36
1970	19,738,043	1,986,981	.10	12,679,821	.64
1975	27,457,410	1,902,630	.07	23,200,000	.84
1980	49,868,524	2,530,364	.05	42,600,000	.85
1985	101,105,000	4,241,000	.04	75,161,000	.74
1990	170,140,000	3,959,000	.02	140,714,000	.83

TABLE 3

Geographic Origins of Freshmen, 1950–90

Region or State	1950* No. (%)	1960 No. (%)	1970 No. (%)	1980 No. (%)	1990 No. (%)
Northeast	78 (1)	23 (2)	36 (3)	512 (32)	107 (8)
Mid-Atlantic	380 (5)	102 (10)	156 (12)	**	281 (21)
Mid-South (includes Tex.)	248 (4)	74 (7)	79 (6)	60 (4)	58 (4)
Southeast (excludes La. and Fla.)	697 (10)	117 (12)	162 (13)	114 (8)	177 (13)
Midwest	272 (5)	119 (12)	159 (13)	162 (11)	147 (11)
West	98 (1)	26 (3)	26 (2)	55 (4)	73 (6)
Territories and Foreign	162 (2)	15 (1)	50 (4)	57 (4)	38 (3)
Florida	226 (3)	82 (8)	128 (10)	174 (12)	105 (8)
Louisiana	4,524 (65)	342 (34)	325 (26)	284 (19)	241 (18)
Texas	302 (4)	112 (11)	137 (11)	68 (5)	102 (8)
Totals	6,987* (100)	1,012 (100)	1,258 (100)	1,486 (100)	1,329 (100)

*Figures for 1950 depict entire student body, including Medicine. Separate data for freshmen not available.
**Northeast and Mid-Atlantic combined for 1980.

TABLE 4
Presidents and Principal Academic Administrative Officers, July 1, 1950 to Date

Presidents
Rufus Carrollton Harris 1937–1960
Maxwell Edward Lapham (Acting) 1960
Herbert Eugene Longenecker 1960–1975
Francis Sheldon Hackney 1975–1980
Eamon Michael Kelly (Acting) 1980–1981
Eamon Michael Kelly 1981–1998

Executive Vice Presidents and Academic Vice Presidents
Fred Carrington Cole (Acad.) 1954–1959
Clarence Scheps (Exec.) 1957–1978
Eamon Michael Kelly (Exec.) 1978–1980
Stephen Frederick Starr (Acad.) 1980–1981
Charles B. Knapp (Exec.) 1982–1987
Francis Leo Lawrence (Acad.) 1982–1990
Paul Nelson (Exec.) 1987–1990

Chancellors
John Joseph Walsh Jr., M.D. Medical Center 1973–1989
Neal A. Vanselow, M.D. Medical Center 1989–1994
Paul B. Firstenberg, Resource Planning & Development 1989–1991
John C. LaRosa, M.D. Medical Center 1994–1999

Provosts
Robert Mayer Lumiansky 1960–1963
Maxwell Edward Lapham, M.D. 1963–1965
David Russell Deener 1967–1976
Robert Bocking Stevens 1976–1978
Frank Thomas Birtel (Acting) 1978–1979
Frank Thomas Birtel 1979–1981
Francis Leo Lawrence (Acting) 1981–1982
Francis Leo Lawrence 1982–1990
James F. Kilroy (Acting) 1990–1991
James F. Kilroy 1991–1996
Eamon M. Kelly (Acting) 1996–1997
Martha W. Gilliland 1997–2000

Deans of the Faculty of Liberal Arts and Sciences
James F. Kilroy 1988–1990
William E. Cooper (Acting) 1990–1991
William E. Cooper 1991–1996
Teresa Soufas (Acting) 1996–

Deans of the School of Architecture
Buford Lindsey Pickens (Director) 1950–1953
John E. Dinwiddie 1953–1959
John W. Lawrence (Acting) 1959–1960
John W. Lawrence 1960–1971
William K. Turner 1972–1980
Ronald Coulter Filson 1980–1992
Donna Virginia Robertson 1992–1996
Donald F. Gatzke (Acting) 1996–1997
Donald F. Gatzke 1997–

Deans of the College of Arts and Sciences (renamed Tulane College in 1993)
Fred Carrington Cole 1947–1955
William Wallace Peery 1955–1964
Joseph E. Gordon 1964–1984
James F. Kilroy 1984–1989
William E. Cooper 1989–1990
Alan J. Avery-Peck (Acting) 1990–1992
Anthony M. Cummings 1992–

Deans of the School of Business Administration
Robert Warren French 1949–1955
Paul Victor Grambsch (Acting) 1955–1956
Paul Victor Grambsch 1956–1960
Howard Graham Schaller 1960–1963
Charles Jackson Grayson Jr. 1963–1968
Clinton Adam Phillips (Acting) 1963–1964
Peter Arthur Firmin 1968–1974
James Murphy (Acting) 1974–1976
Harper Boyd 1976–1978
James Murphy (Acting) 1978–1979
Walter Oscar Spencer 1979–1980
James Murphy (Acting) 1980–1981
Mayer Feldberg 1981–1986

Walter Burnett (Acting) 1986–1988
James W. McFarland 1988–

Deans of the School of Engineering
Lee Harnie Johnson 1950–1972
Frank McDonald (Acting) 1972–1973
Samuel Foster Hulbert 1973–1976
Hugh Allison Thompson 1976–1991
William C. Van Buskirk 1991–1998

Deans of the Graduate School
Roger Philip McCutcheon 1937–1954
Robert Mayer Lumiansky 1954–1963
John Leslie Snell 1963–1966
David Russell Deener 1966–1976
Richard D. Lumsden 1976–1978
Frank Thomas Birtel (Acting) 1978–1979
Frank Thomas Birtel 1979–1981
Francis Leo Lawrence (Acting) 1981–1982
Francis Leo Lawrence 1982–1990
James F. Kilroy (Acting) 1990–1992
Susan Davis Allen 1992–1996

Deans of the School of Law
Paul William Brosman 1945–1951
Clarence James Morrow (Acting) 1951–1952
William Ray Forrester 1952–1963
Cecil Morgan 1963–1968
Joseph Modeste Sweeney 1968–1978
Robert Force (Acting) 1978
Paul R. Verkuil 1978–1986
John Kramer 1986–1996
Edward F. Sherman 1996–

Deans of the School of Medicine
Maxwell Edward Lapham 1945–1963
Charles Cameron Sprague 1963–1967
Oscar Creech 1967
Robert D. Sparks (Acting) 1967–1968
John Joseph Walsh 1968–1969
Robert D. Sparks 1969–1972
John Joseph Walsh (Acting) 1972–1973
William Gentry Thurman 1973–1975
James Turner Hamlin III 1975–1987
Blackwell B. Evans (Acting) 1987–1989
Vincent A. Fulginitti 1989–1993

James J. Corrigan Jr. (Interim) 1993–1994
James J. Corrigan Jr. 1994–

Deans of Newcomb College
Logan Wilson 1944–1951
Anna Estelle Many (Acting) 1951–1953
John Randolph Hubbard 1953–1965
David Russell Deener (Acting) 1965–1966
Charles David Hounshell 1966–1969
James Francis Davidson 1969–1976
Francis Leo Lawrence (Acting) 1976–1978
William G. Smither (Acting) 1978–1979
Susan Wittig 1979–1981
Raymond Esthus (Acting) 1981–1983
Sara Chapman 1983–1985
Mary Ann Maguire (Acting) 1985–1987
Emily H. Vokes (Acting) 1987–1988
Ann H. Die 1988–1992
Beth A. Willinger (Acting) 1992–1993
Jeanie Watson 1993–1997
Valerie D. Greenberg (Acting) 1997–

Deans of the School of Public Health and Tropical Medicine (established as a separate school in 1967)
Grace Arabell Goldsmith 1967–1973
Joseph Diehl Beasley 1973–1974
Frank I. Moore 1974–1975
James E. Banta 1975–1987
J. Thomas Hamrick (Acting) 1987–1991
Harrison C. Spencer 1991–1996
Ann M. Anderson (Acting) 1996
Paul Whelton 1997–

Deans of the School of Social Work
Elizabeth Wisner 1939–1958
Walter Lewis Kindelsperger 1958–1973
Fred Morris Southerland 1973–1980
Helen Cassidy (Acting) 1980–1982
Margaret M. Campbell 1982–1994
Suzanne England 1994–

Deans of University College
John P. Dyer (Director) 1948–1952
John P. Dyer 1952–1968
Robert Clifton Whittemore 1968–1978

Appendix

Wayne Shaffer Woody (Acting) 1978–1980
Wayne Shaffer Woody 1980–1981
Louis Barrilleaux 1981–1996
Richard A. Marksbury 1996–

Deans/Directors of Admissions
Forrest Unna Lake (Dean) 1945–1956
Cliff Waldron Wing (Director) 1956–1965
Edward Alexander Rogge (Director)
1965–1976

John L. Martinez (Dean) 1976–1979
Fred Zucker (Director) 1979–1981
Jillinda Jonker (Director) 1981–1986
Lois Conrad (Dean) 1986–1992
Nancy G. McDuff (Acting) (Director)
1992–1993
Richard Whiteside (Dean) 1993–

TABLE 5
Administrators of the Tulane Educational Fund, 1882–Present

Randall Lee Gibson* 1882–1892
Charles E. Fenner 1882–1906
James McConnell 1882–1914
Tobias G. Richardson 1882–1892
Edward Douglass White 1882–1897
Edgar Howard Farrar 1882–1922
Pascal Neilson Strong 1882–1892
Benjamin Morgan Palmer 1882–1902
Hugh Miller Thompson 1882–1884
Charles Augustus Whitney 1882–1893
Samuel Horton Kennedy 1882–1893
Walter Robinson Stauffer 1882–1932
Cartwright Eustis 1882–1900
Henry Ginder 1882–1920
John Timmons Hardie 1882–1895
Robert Miller Walmsley 1882–1919
William Oscar Rogers 1882–1884
William Forrest Halsey 1883–1887
John Nicholas Galleher 1885–1891
Joseph Chandler Morris 1885–1903
Charles Morgan Whitney 1889–1892
George Quintard Whitney 1892–1903
Leonard Matthews Finley* 1892–1894
John Baptist Levert 1892–1930
Charles Jasper Brickham 1893–1896
Walter Chew Flower 1893–1900
Charles Janvier 1894–1927
Ashton Phelps 1894–1909
Walker Brainerd Spencer* 1895–1941
Beverly Ellison Warner 1898–1905
Walter Denis Denegre 1898–1908
John Dymond Jr.* 1901–1932
Daniel C. Scarborough* 1903–1912
John Westley Castles 1903–1904
Gustaf R. Westfeldt 1903–1910
Charles Rosen* 1904–1954
Ernest B. Kruttschnitt 1904–1906
Beverly Ellison Warner 1905–1910
Fredrick William Parham* 1906–1914
Alfred Raymond* 1908–1920
James Hardy Dillard 1908–1913
William R. Irby 1910–1926

Abraham Brittin 1910–1932
John Callan 1911–1923
Ernest Lee Jahncke* 1914–1960
Joseph Arsenne Breaux* 1914–1926
Marcus Johns Magruder* 1914–1946
Esmond Phelps* 1915–1950
Paul Hill Saunders 1920–1936
Samuel Zemurray 1920–1961
Arthur Devereaux Parker 1920–1922
Florence Dymond* 1922–1951
Chauncey French 1922–1938
Fredrick William Parham* 1925–1927
Jules Blanc Monroe* 1926–1960
James Pierce Butler* 1926–1940
John Barnwell Elliot 1927–1935
George Elliot Williams* 1927–1947
S. Walter Stern* 1932–1943
Charles Allen Favrot 1932–1939
Joseph Wheadon Carroll 1933–1947
Charles L. Eshleman* 1936–1959
Charles S. Williams 1936–1946
Joseph Woodruff George* 1936–1951
Albert Barnett Paterson 1938–1952
Bernard Henry Grehen* 1940–1952
Samuel A. LeBlanc* 1941–1955
Alfred Bird Freeman 1944–1955
Edgar B. Stern* 1944–1959
Joseph W. Montgomery* 1947–1967
Joseph Merrick Jones* 1947–1963
George A. Wilson* 1948–1968
Joseph McCloskey* 1951–1968
Clifford F. Favrot* 1951–1968
Mrs. George Snellings Jr.* 1951–1961
George S. Farnsworth* 1951–1958
Darwin S. Fenner* 1953–1973
Lester J. Lautenschlaeger* 1953–1973
Isidore Newman II* 1954–1971
Leon Irwin Jr.* 1955–1968
Ashton Phelps* 1955–1972
Richard West Freeman* 1959–1972
Gerald L. Andrus* 1960–1975
Jacob Segura Landry* 1960–1968

Edgar B. Stern Jr. 1960–1977
Arthur Louis Jung Jr.* 1961–1982
Sam Israel Jr.* 1968–1979
Harry B. Kelleher* 1963–1975
Charles G. Smither* 1967–1976
Edmund McIlhenny* 1968–1979
Clayton L. Nairne* 1968–1973
John W. Deming* 1968–1983
G. Shelby Friedrichs* 1968–1982
Arthur J. Waechter Jr.* 1968–1983
William B. Monroe Jr.* 1971–1982
Lanier A. Simmons* 1971–1986
Fredric B. Ingram 1972–1977
Charles H. Murphy Jr. 1972–1988
Ford M. Graham 1973–1976
Alden J. Laborde 1973–1982
Floyd W. Lewis* 1973–1988
Erik F. Johnsen* 1975–1990
W. Boatner Reily III* 1975–1991
Robert H. Boh* 1976–1994
John G. Phillips 1977–1991
Louis M. Freeman* 1977–1992
Henry H. Braden 1978–1990
Brooke H. Duncan* 1979–1994
Robert E. Flowerree* 1979–1991
George Denegre* 1980–1993
Harry J. Blumenthal* 1980–1988
Peter A. Aron* 1980–1995
John F. Bookout 1980–1986
Sybil M. Favrot* 1981–1996
W. Kennon McWilliams Jr.* 1981–1991
John G. Weinmann* 1981–1991
Avron B. Fogelman* 1982–1984
Louis L. Frierson* 1982–
John J. Phelan Jr. 1983–1987
Edmund M. Reggie* 1983–1992
Donald J. Nalty 1984–
Charles R. Sitter (resigned 9/93) 1985–1993
Samuel Z. Stone 1985–1995
Margaret P. Wilson* 1985–1990
H. Mortimer Favrot Jr.* 1986–
William Goldring* 1986–
Robert L. Turchin* 1987–1993
Virginia N. Roddy* 1988–
James W. Wilson Jr.* 1988–
Sandra L. Robinson* 1988–

Sidney W. Lassen* 1990–
Edwin A. Lupberger 1990–1995
William E. Mayer 1990–
Robert E. Young* 1991–
William A. Slatten* 1991–
H. Leighton Steward 1991–
Martin D. Payson 1991–
Milton H. Ward 1992–1992
Mortimer L. Curran* 1992–
Joyce F. Menschel* 1992–
Frank B. Stewart* 1992–
John G. Weinmann* 1993–
Charles C. Teamer* 1993–
John E. Koerner III* 1994–
Philip J. Carroll* 1994–
Carol D. Cudd* 1994–
Lawrence J. Israel 1995–
Richard W. Freeman Jr. 1995–
Catherine D. Pierson* 1995–
Robert B. Acomb Jr.* 1996–
James M. Lapeyre Jr.* 1996

EMERITUS ADMINISTRATORS
George S. Farnsworth* 1958–1976
Charles L. Eshleman* 1959–1976
Joseph W. Montgomery* 1967–1977
Clifford F. Favrot* 1968–1989
Leon Irwin Jr.* 1968–1989
Jacob S. Landry* 1968–
Joseph McCloskey* 1968–1982
George A. Wilson* 1968–1987
Isidore Newman II* 1971–1981
Mrs. George Snellings Jr.* 1971–1978
Richard W. Freeman* 1972–1985
Ashton Phelps* 1972–1983
Darwin S. Fenner* 1973–1979
Lester J. Lautenschlaeger* 1973–1986
Clayton L. Nairne* 1973–1989
Gerald L. Andrus* 1975–
Harry B. Kelleher* 1975–
Ford M. Graham 1976–
Edgar B. Stern Jr. 1977–
Edmund McIlhenny* 1979–1991
G. Shelby Friedrichs* 1982–1991
Arthur Louis Jung Jr.* 1982–
William B. Monroe Jr.* 1982–

John W. Deming* 1983–1996
A. J. Waechter Jr.* 1983–
Lanier A. Simmons* 1986–1990
John F. Bookout* 1986–
John J. Phelan Jr. 1987–
Charles H. Murphy Jr. 1988–
Floyd W. Lewis* 1988–
Henry E. Braden 1990–1994
Erik F. Johnsen* 1990–
Margaret P. Willson* 1990–
W. Boatner Reily III* 1991–
Robert E. Flowerree* 1991–
W. Kennon McWilliams Jr.* 1991–

John G. Phillips 1991–
John G. Weinmann* (reelected 2/18/93) 1992–1993
Louis M. Freeman* 1992–
Robert L. Turchin* 1992–
Charles R. Sitter 1993–
George Denegre* 1993–
Robert H. Boh* 1994–
Brooke H. Duncan* 1994–
Edwin A. Lupberger 1995–
Samuel Z. Stone 1995–
Peter A. Aron* 1995–
Robert E. Young* 1996–
Sybil M. Favrot* 1996–

TABLE 6

Distribution of Religious Preferences in Students, 1950–90

Academic Year	% Catholic	% Jewish	% Protestant	% Other/None
1950–51* (all students)	36.2	8.4	49.9	5.5**
1955–56 (all students)	37.5	10.4	37.8	14.3
1960–61 (all students)	28.4	19.2	47.5	4.9
1965–66 (freshmen only)	26.1	22.1	48.1	3.7
1970–71 (freshmen only)	25.8	21.1	43.7	10.3
1975–76 (freshmen only)	28.2	26.9	25.1	0.7/19.1
1980–81 (freshmen only)	25.7	28.9	21.7	6.5/17.2
1985–86 (freshmen only)	29.4	24.8	22.4	15/8.4
1990–91 (freshmen only)	28.2	25.3	23.9	4.4/18.2

*University records did not reveal statistics for freshmen only until 1965. Average participation in questionnaire by students each year was 69 percent.

**The nature of early records did not permit accurate distinction between "other" and "none."

TABLE 7
Periodic Comparisons of University Enrollments, 1950–51 to 1990–91

School	1950–51	1960–61	1970–71	1980–81	1990–91
Arts and Sciences	1,490	1,228	2,032	2,280	1,875
Newcomb	680	926	1,319	1,623	2,168
Architecture	179	140	207	340	357
Bus. Admin.	530	345	***	220	344
Engineering	430	337	465	914	648
Totals (undergrad.)	3,309	2,976	4,023	5,377	5,392
Graduate	383	765	1,145	1,020	972
GR—Bus. Admin.	—	39	294	408	444
GR—Medicine	359	190	324	439	451
Law	271	305	427	758	1,026
Medicine	520	500	538	615	592
Social Work	191	127	268	222	262
SPHTM	*	30	176	330	369
Totals (grad. and prof.)	1,724	1,956	3,172	3,792	4,116
University College	1,955**	1,902**	1,258**	871**	1,977**
Totals (all)	6,988	6,834	8,453	10,040	11,485

*School of Public Health and Tropical Medicine not a separate academic division at that time.
**Includes full-time and part-time students.
***Undergraduate programs (at junior and senior level) not reinstituted until 1976–77.

Geer, Russel M., 169, 170
Geiger, Roger L., 258, 279
General Education Board (GEB), 6, 6n9
Georgia Tech, 266, 267, 362n58
Gergo, Gabor, 335
Germany, 315–6, 318
Gerone, Peter J., 246–7
GI Bill, 7, 26, 27, 35–6, 165
Gibson, Randall Lee, 138n13
Gibson Hall, xxiv, 279, 338, 370, 454
Gilmore, Harlan C., 53, 55, 60
Gingrich, Newton, 341, 342n33
Gitlin, Nancy, 300
Glendy Burke Debate Team, 157
Goldfinch, Sydney Langston "Lanny,"
    Jr., 206, 217–20, 223, 224, 231, 241–2
Goldring/Woldenberg Hall, *441*
Goldwater, Barry, 299
Gordon, Eric, 323, 328, 329, 330, 341–2,
    408
Gordon, Joseph E., 30, 281–2, 302, 309,
    367, 385
Gorz, André, 325
Government-funded research. *See*
    Research
Graduate education: in 1940s, 2, 10,
    10n13; foundation funding for, 6, 6n9,
    10, 11n14; and Harris presidency,
    8–15; in 1950s, 8–15, 10n13; in 1960s,
    10, 10n13, 255–6, 270–1, 273, 279–80;
    at Newcomb College, 20–1; women
    enrolled in, 21–3; integration of, 135;
    Berelson on, 255; for students from
    Arts and Sciences College, 302,
    302n48. *See also* Graduate School
Graduate Record Exam (GRE), 26
Graduate School: in 1940s, 4; doctoral
    programs in, 6, 9–10, 10n13, 13, 251,
    255–6, 278–84; in 1950s, 8–15, 21,
    255; enrollments in, during 1950s, 10,
    21, 255; foundation funding for,
    11n14; controversies in, 13–4; women
    enrolled in, 21–3; admissions policy
    of, 26; and defense research, 112;
    black applications denied for admis-
    sion to, 135–6, 139–42, 146, 147, 152,

153, 155, 156, 200n10, 203, 205; black
    students in, 234–7; and teaching expe-
    rience for Ph.D. students, 251; enroll-
    ments in, during 1960s, 255; goals of,
    255; in 1960s, 255–6, 270–1, 279–82;
    fellowships for, 256–7; retrenchment
    of, during 1967–68, pp. 279–84, 382;
    budget of, in 1968–69, p. 283; military
    students in, 361–2; and Dubinsky
    case, 384; student representation in,
    411; program cuts in 1990s, 461–2;
    deans of, 469. *See also* Graduate edu-
    cation; and specific professional
    schools, such as Medicine, School of
Graduate Student Association, 308, 322
Grady, John F., 427
Graham, Frank P., 163
Grambsch, Paul, 253
Grayson, C. Jackson, 254
GRE, 26
Great Depression, 52–6
Green Wave Club, 419
Greystone Project, 119
Griffith, William J., 125–6, 288
Guatemala, 125–7
Guggenheim Fellowships, 442
Guillemin, Robert, 418
Guillory, Barbara Marie, 201n13,
    203–6, 203n14, 234–5
Guillory case, 202–15, 227–31, 233–4, 235
Guste, William J., Jr., 444–5
Guste, Barnett, and Little, 206
Gwyn, William, 426, 433–4

Hackney, F. Sheldon: honorary degrees
    during presidency of, 104, 408; educa-
    tional background of, 396–7; selection
    of, as Tulane president, 396; photo-
    graph of, *397*; at Princeton, 397, 409,
    416; marriage and children of, 398;
    and fiscal problems of Tulane,
    399–400, 422–5, 429–35; inaugural
    address of, 399; installation of, as
    president, 399; and academic excel-
    lence and institutional pride, 400; ad-
    ministrative appointments by, 400–3,

Art" issue, 336–7; 1968 elections for, 345–6; and antiwar movement, 386. *See also* Student Council

Students: change from commuter to residential population, xxiv, 38–9, 46; in 1950s, xxiv; women students, 21–3, 402–7, 449; loans for, 32; Louisiana versus out-of-state students, 33–7, 467; boisterous behavior of male undergraduates in 1950s, 39–40; and panty raids, 39; cultural categories of, 40–1; radical students, in 1940s–1950s, 42–3; socioeconomic characteristics of, in 1950s, 43; conduct regulations for, 45–7, 295–7, 348–9, 411, 454–5; paternalism toward, in 1950s, 46–7; leaders among, 48, 305–7; subcultures of, 48, 305; foreign students, 49, 302; radical students in 1930s, 60, 60n16; and Wallace campaign, 69, 73–4; and interracial social gathering in 1949, pp. 79, 80–1, 83, 84, 133; black students, 131, 234–7, 240, 307, 354–60, 407–8, 448–9, 451–2; pro-integration activities and attitudes of, 154–5, 157–8, 216–25, 232, 233; athletes' academic problems, 169–71, 174–5; drug usage by, 269, 309, 457; due process rights of, 296; and Hackney presidency, 400, 407–15, 414–5n33, 437; in 1980s, 445–52; Asian American students, 449; Hispanic American students, 449; 1981 survey of freshmen, 449–51; geographic origins of, 467; religious preferences of, 474. *See also* Admissions policy; Enrollments; Financial aid; Fraternities and sororities; Recruitment; Student power movement; Tuition and fees; and specific students

Students for a Democratic Society. *See* SDS

Students for Wallace, 79n47, 80

Sudden Infant Death Syndrome Center, 444

Sugar Bowl, 1, 160–3
Summer Abroad Program, 444
Superdome, 394, 429
Swearingen, Mack W., 53–6, 54n4, 60, 60n16, 62
Sweeney, Joseph M., 429n54
Sylvester, Harold, *355*

Taft-Hartley Act, 78
Taylor, Glen, 71
Taylor, Paul, 170–1
TDR. See *Tulane Drama Review* (TDR)
Teacher-Coach Program, 174–80, 190, 260, 261–2, 264, 286, 287
Teacher Education Center, 262, 263, 286, 287
Teacher training, 261–3, 262n27, 303
Teaching assistants, 14, 14n20, 250–2
Teamsters Union Pension Fund, 438
Teichgraeber, Richard, 442
Ten Elshof, Annette, 401, 414, 415
Theater and Speech Building, 274
Theater and Speech Department, 271–9, 284, 312, 315, 382, 442
Theater building, 271–2, 274–8, *447*
Thomas, Norman, 60n16
Thompson, Bobby, 457
Thompson, Hugh A., 253, 401
Thompson, Joseph F., 90
Thurmond, J. Strom, 294, 387
Tilton Hall, 442
Title IX of 1972 amendments to Higher Education Act (1965), 406
TLF. *See* Tulane Liberation Front (TLF)
Treen, David, 300
Treybig, Bruce, 338–9
Truman, Harry, 7, 52, 65, 78, 212
Tuition and fees, 5, 446, 447, 466
Tulane, Paul, xxi, 13, 135, 138–9, 138n13, 142–3, 148–9, 207, 208, 213, 214, 216, 228; heirs of, 152, 153, 200–1, 203n14, 209, 228, 234
Tulane College. *See* Arts and Sciences, College of (A&S)